STUDENT DEVELOPMENT IN COLLEGE

STUDENT DEVELOPMENT IN COLLEGE

Theory, Research, and Practice

THIRD EDITION

Lori D. Patton
Kristen A. Renn
Florence M. Guido
Stephen John Quaye

A Wiley Brand

Published by Jossey-Bass
A Wiley Brand
One Montgomery Street, Suite 1000, San Francisco, CA 94104-4594-www.josseybass.com

Jossey-Bass books and products are available through most bookstores. To contact Jossey-Bass directly call our Customer Care Department within the U.S. at 800-956-7739, outside the U.S. at 317-572-3986, or fax 317-572-4002.

Wiley publishes in a variety of print and electronic formats and by print-on-demand. Some material included with standard print versions of this book may not be included in e-books or in print-on-demand. If this book refers to media such as a CD or DVD that is not included in the version you purchased, you may download this material at http://booksupport.wiley.com. For more information about Wiley products, visit www.wiley.com.

Library of Congress Cataloging-in-Publication Data

Names: Patton, Lori D., author. | Renn, Kristen A., author. | Guido-DiBrito,
   Florence, 1952- author. | Quaye, Stephen John, 1980- author.
Title: Student development in college : theory, research, and practice / Lori
   D. Patton, Kristen A. Renn, Florence M. Guido, and Stephen John Quaye.
Description: Third edition. | San Francisco, CA : Jossey-Bass & Pfeiffer,
   2016. | Includes bibliographical references and index.
Identifiers: LCCN 2015041426 (print) | LCCN 2015046247 (ebook) | ISBN
   9781118821817 (cloth) | ISBN 9781118821862 (pdf) | ISBN 9781118821794 (epub)
Subjects: LCSH: College student development programs—United States. |
   College students—United States—Psychology.
Classification: LCC LB2343.4 .P38 2016 (print) | LCC LB2343.4 (ebook) | DDC
   378.1/98—dc23
LC record available at http://lccn.loc.gov/2015041426

Cover design by: Wiley
Cover image: © Florence M. Guido

Printed in the United States of America

THIRD EDITION

PB Printing   V10003681_082118

We dedicate this book to higher education and student affairs professionals who give of themselves daily to enhance the development of college students.

CONTENTS

10 Disability Identities and Identity Development   230

11 Social Class and Identity   243

12 Emerging Theoretical Perspectives on Student Experiences and
    Identities   265

Part Three: Psychosocial, Cognitive-Structural, and Integrative
                  Development   281

13 Psychosocial Identity Development   287

14 Epistemological and Intellectual Development   314

15 Moral Development   336

16 Development of Self-Authorship   355

Part Four: Reflecting on Theory to Practice   379

17 Student Affairs Educators as Partners in Using Student Development
    Theory   383

18 Implications and Future Directions for Practice, Research, and
    Theory Development   397

    Afterword   409

    Appendix: Case Study Scenario: Introducing Prescott University's
    Selected SAHE Graduate Students   411

    References   433

    Index   505

FIGURES AND EXHIBITS

Figures

Exhibit

ABOUT THE AUTHORS

Lori D. Patton is an associate professor in the Higher Education and Student Affairs program at Indiana University. She has been recognized nationally for research examining issues of identity, equity, and racial injustice affecting diverse populations in postsecondary institutions. Her scholarship on critical race theory, black culture centers, LGBT students of color, and African American undergraduate women has been published in top peer-reviewed journals such as the *Journal of College Student Development, Journal of Higher Education*, and *Journal of Negro Education*. She is a coauthor of the Second Edition of *Student Development in College* and a contributor to several other Jossey Bass publications including *Student Services: A Handbook for the Profession*, 5th ed., and *The Handbook of Student Affairs Administration* (3rd ed.). She is the editor of *Campus Culture Centers in Higher Education: Perspectives on Identity, Theory and Practice* (Stylus, 2010), coeditor (with Shaun R. Harper) of the *New Directions for Student Services Monograph, Responding to the Realities of Race* (2009), and co-editor (with Natasha N. Croom) of *Critical Perspectives on Black Women and College Success* (Routledge). She is actively involved in and has been recognized for her scholarly and service contributions to ACPA, NASPA, ASHE, and AERA. She earned her Ph.D. in higher education at Indiana University, her master's degree in college student personnel at Bowling Green State University, and her bachelor's degree in speech communication at Southern Illinois University at Edwardsville.

Kristen A. Renn is a professor of Higher, Adult, and Lifelong Education and Associate Dean for Undergraduate Studies/Director for Student Success

Initiatives at Michigan State University. She is a coauthor of the Second Edition of *Student Development in College*, coauthor of *College Students in the United States: Characteristics, Experiences, and Outcomes* (Jossey-Bass, 2013), and author of *Mixed Race Students in College: The Ecology of Race, Identity, and Community on Campus* (SUNY, 2004) and *Women's Higher Education Worldwide* (Johns Hopkins University Press, 2014). She has published extensively on student identity in higher education, student leadership, new professionals in student affairs, LGBTQ education research, and women's higher education institutions. She was associate editor for international research and scholarship for the *Journal of College Student Development* and serves or has served on the editorial boards of other leading journals in the field (*Review of Higher Education, Journal of Higher Education, Journal of Diversity in Higher Education, Educational Researcher, American Educational Research Journal*). In 2015 she received the Contribution to Knowledge Award from ACPA. She earned her bachelor's degree in music at Mount Holyoke College, her master's degree in educational leadership at Boston University, and her Ph.D. in higher education from Boston College.

Florence M. Guido is a professor of Higher Education and Student Affairs Leadership at the University of Northern Colorado. Her scholarship and contributions to the profession have been recognized numerous times by ACPA and NASPA. She served as the first scholar-in-residence for ACPA's Standing Committee for Women. She also served on the editorial boards of the *Journal of College Student Development* and the *NASPA Journal*. She is an original author of *Student Development in College* and a major contributor to the second edition. Her idea also sparked the eventual publication of the first edition of *Student Development in College*. In addition to her numerous publications including quality journal articles and books chapters, her photographs grace the cover of three books in student affairs including *Student Development in College, 2nd edition* (2010), *Identity and Leadership* (2013), and *Empowering Women in Higher Education and Student Affairs* (2011). Her research interests include student development of ethnic groups, students and social class, paradigms of qualitative research, photoethnography as method, and autoethnography as culture. She earned a Ph.D. in Educational Administration (with an emphasis in higher education) from Texas A&M University, a master's degree in college student personnel administration in Higher Education from Ball State University, and a bachelor's degree in art history from Briarcliff College, Briarcliff Manor, NY.

Stephen John Quaye is an associate professor in the Student Affairs in Higher Education Program at Miami University. He is a believer in the power of personal storytelling and strongly believes that hearing and sharing our stories with others can foster connections and learning across differences. He values dialogue as a vehicle to promote change in society, and specifically studies how facilitators can navigate shame and guilt in dialogue spaces and the strategies facilitators can use to engage students in dialogues about privilege, power, and oppression. He is coeditor (with Shaun R. Harper) of *Student Engagement in Higher Education: Theoretical Perspectives and Practical Approaches for Diverse Populations* (Routledge, 2014). His work is published in different venues, including *The Review of Higher Education, Teachers College Record, Journal of College Student Development,* and *Equity & Excellence in Education.* In addition, he is the recipient of the 2009 NASPA Melvene D. Hardee Dissertation of the Year Award. His Ph.D. in higher education is from Penn State University, his master's degree in student affairs is from Miami University, and his bachelor's degree in psychology is from James Madison University.

ACKNOWLEDGMENTS

Many people have contributed to this work in very significant ways. First, we would like to thank our colleagues at Jossey-Bass, especially Shauna Robinson, for all of their support, encouragement, and understanding during the process of completing this book. Thanks to Erin Null, who was instrumental in the early stages of this project. We also appreciate our student affairs colleagues, who offered helpful suggestions for approaching the content of this book. Furthermore, several colleagues reviewed chapters in this book and offered excellent feedback for revision, including Marylu McEwen, Bill Cross, Joan Ostrove, Susan Jones, Chris Linder, Alyssa Bryant Rockenbach, Jane Fried, Leilani Kupo, and Alicia Chávez. David Nguyen, a doctoral candidate at Michigan State University, deserves particular thanks for his contributions to this volume, which included wrangling the entire reference list and four authors. We are extremely thankful to Nancy Evans and Dea Forney for their excellent leadership on the first and second editions of this book, as well as reviewing various chapters in the current edition. Nancy, thank you for constructing a solid and thoughtful Preface for the book. Dea, thank you for contributing the Afterword and for your continued support.

In addition to our collective acknowledgments, we each wish to share a few personal acknowledgments.

Lori D. Patton is thankful to her partner, Tobias Davis, and her children, Preston and Parker, for their amazing love and support. I could not have completed this project without you. Thanks to my St. Louis family for all of the prayers and encouragement. I truly appreciate the support of my friends and colleagues, particularly Chayla Haynes Davison, Shaun Harper, and Sha'Kema Blackmon for always lending an ear and offering encouraging words. Mary Howard-Hamilton, thanks for nurturing my initial and continued interest in student development theory. Special thanks to my Indiana University colleagues and to the many graduate students, particularly those in my student development theory courses, who offered critiques and honest feedback to enhance this book. Jessica Harris and Samantha Ivery, thank you for not only offering your perspectives but also gathering important research and data for inclusion in the book. Steve Mobley, Jr., thanks for the excellent resources during my time crunch. Last but not least, thank you Kris, Flo, and Stephen for embarking on this journey with me. I'm thrilled that, despite the many personal and professional priorities in our lives, we were able to collaborate and produce an excellent book.

Kristen A. Renn thanks her coauthors for the opportunity to work together on this project, with special thanks to Nancy Evans and Dea Forney for trusting us with this new edition. I appreciate the intellectual contributions of countless colleagues who have moved the field of student development forward and allowed me to participate in this community of scholarship and practice. At Michigan State University I appreciate the support of colleagues and students in my academic department. Shortly after we embarked on this edition, I agreed to lead a campuswide student success initiative at MSU, a role that reminds me of the important work that student affairs educators do every day to support students' personal, academic, and social development. I thank the professionals with whom I currently do this work for their patience, guidance, insight, and inspiration as I relearned to apply theory to practice in contemporary higher education.

Florence M. Guido would like to thank the hundreds of students enrolled in the student development classes I have taught since 1992. Your stories keep me grounded in theory to practice. A special thanks to spring 2015 Advanced Student Development Theory students Gia Lemonedes, Larry Loften, Courtney Matsumoto, Katie McCue, and Christine Smith; you remind me why I teach. Lainey Brottem, your editing was just in time. Gabriel Serna, Chayla Haynes Davison, Tamara Yakaboski, and Matt Birnbaum, colleagues at UNC, your generosity in giving me space and support to focus on my part of the manuscript did not go unnoticed. Lori, Kris, and Stephen, thanks for slipping into Nancy Evans and Dea Forney's shoes with aplomb. Kris Renn, thank you for your feedback on my writing for this third edition. Finally, thanks to friends and family, particularly my dad, Cosmo F. Guido—how blessed I am that you encourage me to laugh at myself and live my life, while being a part of yours. Not to be remiss, thanks Jack for taking Bella swimming so I could write.

Stephen John Quaye offers gratitude to his son, Sebastian, for helping him learn how to blend his life as a parent with his work. Your inquisitive mind, curious spirit, and kind heart help me remember of my two roles—parent and faculty member—which one matters most, and I appreciate the ways you enable me to pay attention and see the world anew through your eyes. Thank you to my colleagues at Miami University—Elisa Abes, Marcia Baxter Magolda, Kathy Goodman, Peter Magolda, David Perez II, Judy Rogers, and Mahauganee Shaw—for creating an environment where I feel mattered and validated and can thus do my best work. Chris Linder, thank you for talking through ideas with me, reading my work, and most importantly, encouraging my voice and validating who I am. Finally, I extend my gratitude to Jessica Gunzburger for reminding me, when I felt stressed or overwhelmed, why I do what I do. Your listening ear was exactly what I needed in those moments.

PREFACE

As the lead author of the first two editions of *Student Development in College,* I read the chapters included in the third edition with feelings that are both bittersweet and joyful; bittersweet as I have had only a minor role in this edition, and joyful about the fine job my colleagues, Lori Patton, Kristen Renn, Flo Guido, and Stephen Quaye, have done in carrying on the tradition of producing a high-quality and insightful work that will ensure that student affairs graduate students are grounded in student development theory and can use it effectively in their work with students now and in the future. These authors know the field of student affairs very well, are effective teachers, and understand the nuances of using theory in student affairs settings.

The overall purpose of this book remains the same as in earlier editions: to provide a general overview and introduction to student development theory in a book that will continue to serve as the go-to resource for those most committed to conscious and intentional student affairs practice. However, the organization and focus of this edition of *Student Development in College* are quite different than they were in the first two editions and may surprise readers who have used one or both of those editions.

First, the authors expanded and revised the content of the introductory and closing sections. The introduction includes a greatly expanded review of the philosophical underpinnings of student development research and practice and a revised discussion of the use of theory in student affairs settings. Of particular importance, in Chapter Two the authors included an expanded discussion of worldviews and paradigms that undergird student development research. Researchers within the fields of education, sociology, and psychology, as well as other fields that contribute to an understanding of student development, now use more varied methodologies grounded in a variety of paradigms, including constructionist and critical approaches, along with the more widely recognized positivist paradigm. Students and users of student development theory must understand these newer approaches and how they shape theoretical propositions and ways of thinking about theory and its use in practice. In the final introductory chapter on the use of theory, Patton and her colleagues offered discussion of the developmental process, including streamlined reviews of ecological and transition theories, each of which previously had its own chapter. The authors have correctly pointed out that these theories focus on the manner in which development occurs rather than on development itself. Patton and her coauthors also introduced a recently published theory-to-practice model that should be of great utility to those who are new to the topic. The focus on ways of using theory in various settings, found in the closing section, has also been shifted. Rather than presenting scenarios, as found in the second edition of *Student Development in College,* the authors of the third edition have addressed theory-to-practice applications by exploring how to engage others in discussions of various theories, discussing ways in which theory can be taught in graduate student affairs classes, examining how theory can be used in difficult dialogues, and exploring ways of using theory in self-analysis both to better learn the theory and also to share it more effectively with others. This new approach to exploring use of theory in practice is very practical for students, faculty, and student affairs professionals.

After the introductory section, the authors open the discussion of theories in the third edition with a greatly expanded section focused on social identity theories rather than using the more traditional chronological approach, starting with psychosocial and cognitive developmental theories, that the second edition authors used. The third edition authors also included several chapters on social identities that had not previously been examined in the book (for example, disability and social class identity as well as emergent digital and national identities). In some of the social identity chapters, Patton and her colleagues deleted previously included theories in favor of newer theories that appear to have more potential for broader and more inclusive student affairs applications than older theories did (for example, a new theory of sexual identity development, which applies to heterosexual identity development as well as non-heterosexual identity development, replaces the theories included in the second edition that apply only to gay, lesbian, and bisexual identity development). Appropriately, given the attention that these topics are receiving in the student development literature, Patton and her coauthors have also expanded their discussion of multiple dimensions of identity and the intersectionality of social identities. These authors still addressed the more familiar psychosocial and cognitive-structural theories, but later in the book and in a more condensed version.

Readers may be wondering why these somewhat radical changes in organization and content were made. If readers are familiar with student development research conducted since 2010, when the second edition of *Student Development in College* appeared, the answer will be apparent. During this time period, almost all the research related to student development has centered on social identity and foundational knowledge related to privilege, oppression, multiple identities, and intersectionality. With the exception of new work examining the sources and outcomes of self-authorship, which was again given its own chapter in the third edition, only minimal work has centered on psychosocial and cognitive structural development. Another advantage of starting the examination of theory by discussing social identities is that this approach is more likely to engage diverse students whose background may relate to one or more of these theories. Getting all students involved in class discussions early in the process may help to create a richer and more critical analysis of theories.

Another change that will be readily apparent to readers of earlier editions is the omission of student profiles at the start of each chapter. Rather than offering short scenarios that might seem rather stereotypical, the authors have developed a complex scenario along with expanded life stories of students about to start their journey within a student affairs graduate program, which can be found in an appendix. As they review each chapter, readers are encouraged to consider how the various theories might help to explain how the profiled students might respond to situations within the ongoing scenarios and how the situations might affect development of these profiled students. In addition, at the end of each chapter, the authors have provided a number of thoughtful questions and activities to assist readers in recalling and retaining the most important points about each theory and other content included. The questions can also be used to spark discussion in and out of class.

While the changes in *Student Development in College* may seem overwhelming at first glance, a more thorough study of the book will convince most readers that the changes that Patton, Renn, Guido, and Quaye have brought to the book are meaningful, based on current directions in the student affairs literature, and intended to strengthen readers' learning of the most important literature base in the student affairs profession: student development theory and its uses in the practice of student affairs. I encourage readers to approach this new edition with an open mind. I know that they will be rewarded with a much broader knowledge of student development theory and application than readers gained from the earlier two editions.

The opening section of the book, *Part One*, provides an overview of student development theory, particularly the process of understanding, using, and translating theory to practice. The three chapters in this section trace the historical context and evolution of student development (*Chapter One*), situate student development theory within the context of diverse worldviews and paradigms (*Chapter Two*), and provide recommendations and strategies for approaching theory and its use from a holistic and integrative framework (*Chapter Three*). Collectively, these chapters provide readers with a solid foundation for gaining a nuanced comprehension of theory.

Part Two places significant emphasis on social identity development processes in college. Patton and her colleagues have expanded this section of the book, which closely mirrors the trajectory of the research conducted in the field. In *Chapter Four*, they introduce concepts related to social identity development, especially privilege and oppression. They also describe multiple identity models and the interconnections between diverse identities. *Chapter Five* includes content on racial identity development models and theories. The chapter is framed through a critical race lens before presenting the general model of Derald W. Sue and David Sue, the Black identity model of William Cross and Peony Fhagen-Smith, the White racial identity models of Janet Helms and Wayne Rowe and his colleagues, Jean Kim's model of Asian American identity development, Bernardo Ferdman and Plácida Gallego's model of Latino identity development, Perry Horse's examination of how race is viewed in American Indian communities, and Kristen Renn's ecological approach to multiracial identity.

In *Chapter Six*, the authors examine concepts such as ethnic identity and acculturation through various models, including Jean Phinney's model of ethnic identity, Vasti Torres's Latino identity model, and acculturation models that explain the experiences of Asian American, Indigenous, African American and Afro-Caribbean, and European American identity groups. *Chapter Seven* includes an examination of sexual identity development that centers the experiences of not only lesbian, gay, and bisexual students, but also those identifying as heterosexual. Rather than presenting the models of Vivienne Cass, Ruth Fassinger, and Anthony D'Augelli found in the second edition, in this chapter, Patton and her coauthors introduce Frank Dillon, Roger Worthington, and Bonnie Moradi's unifying model of sexual identity development, which presents sexual identity development as a universal process. The focus of *Chapter Eight* is on gender and gender identity. The authors again take a more inclusive approach and add more information to disentangle the confusion some readers may have with understanding gender identity. They explain in detail Kay Bussey's social-cognitive theory of identity development, which is similar to other ecological processes examined earlier in the book.

In *Chapter Nine*, the authors introduce significantly expanded content on theories of faith and spirituality. Theories offered by James Fowler and Sharon Daloz Parks are still featured, but this chapter is expanded to include Alexander Astin, Helen Astin, and Jennifer Lindholm's spiritual and religious constructs as well as Lori Peek's Muslim identity model and Jesse Smith's atheist identity development model. *Chapters Ten, Eleven,* and *Twelve* are new and extremely relevant additions to the book. In *Chapter Ten*, the focus is on disability identities and models. The emphasis in *Chapter Eleven* is on social class identities and theories of social reproduction and capital. In *Chapter Twelve* the authors provide a description of diverse student identities that are increasingly emergent in the literature. They focus on national, digital, feminist, veteran, and athletic identities.

In *Part Three*, Patton and her colleagues present psychosocial, cognitive structural, moral, and integrative theories. In *Chapter Thirteen*, they introduce Erik Erikson's psychosocial identity theory and the theories of two individuals who built on his work, James Marcia and Ruthellen Josselson. The chapter also includes an overview of Arthur Chickering's theory of psychosocial development, focusing particularly on his revised theory, developed in collaboration with Linda Reisser. *Chapter Fourteen* focuses on William Perry's cognitive structural approach, which examines the intellectual and ethical development of college students, and theories influenced by his work including Mary Belenky and her colleagues' study of women's intellectual development and the reflective judgment model of Patricia King and Karen Kitchener.

Chapter Fifteen focuses on moral development, a specific component of cognitive structural development that deals with how people make decisions that affect their lives and the lives of others. The pioneering work of Lawrence Kohlberg is featured, followed by an examination of James Rest's neo-Kohlbergian theory and Carol Gilligan's alternative explanation of moral development. In *Chapter Sixteen* the authors present theories of self-authorship, reviewing Robert Kegan's theory of self-evolution, Marcia Baxter Magolda's original research on epistemological development of men and women, and Baxter Magolda's breakthrough work on self-authorship that builds on Kegan's work.

Part Four concludes the book with a focus on student affairs educators as advocates and partners in the learning process and future directions in theory. *Chapter Seventeen*, a newly added chapter, provides recommendations for promoting the use and translation of theory to practice and offers an example of how intergroup dialogues can be used in student affairs related settings to tackle difficult conversations that often emerge in discussions of theory. Finally, to close the book, Patton and her coauthors examine the current state of student development in *Chapter Eighteen* and provide recommendations for future research, practice, and application. As with previous editions, the authors continue the tradition of providing a user-friendly book that prompts further exploration of theory and provides an update to readers who want to learn about updated and recently introduced theories. This book will certainly make a meaningful contribution to the student affairs knowledge base.

Nancy J. Evans
Professor (on permanent medical leave)
Student Affairs Program
School of Education
Iowa State University
Ames, Iowa

PART ONE

UNDERSTANDING, USING, AND TRANSLATING STUDENT DEVELOPMENT THEORY

Regina is about to begin her masters program in student affairs adminis-tration. In addition to maintaining a 3.5 GPA, Regina was active as an undergraduate in student government and the Association for Multicultural Understanding (AMU). When she decided early in her senior year that a career in business was not for her, the advisor to AMU suggested she think about stu-dent affairs administration. Regina had never heard of this profession, but she enjoyed the college environment and thought that the work her advisor did was important and interesting. She wanted to have the same kind of impact on others as he had on her. So she investigated various graduate programs and ended up with an offer from one of the best programs in the country along with an assistantship in Multicultural Student Affairs. Needless to say, she is excited but also a little anxious.

Regina is hoping the course in student development theory for which she is registered will give her some clues about how to approach the students with whom she will be working. After her orientation to the Multicultural Student Affairs office, all she knows is how the phone system works, what her email address is, and who the other people in her division are. Aside from a brief meeting with her assistantship supervisor, no one has provided much infor-mation about the issues students are facing on campus or how to go about addressing them. At this point all she has to go on is her own experience as an undergraduate, and she is perceptive enough to know that students at this large research university might have different concerns from hers and those of her peers who attended a historically Black college.

In preparation for her first class, Regina pages through her student development theory text. There are so many theories! How will she ever learn them all? Surely she won't be expected to memorize them all? Will she be able to use all of these concepts meaningfully in her work? Regina is feeling overwhelmed.

◆ ◆ ◆

As Regina has intuited, understanding student development is crucial in order to be an effective student affairs educator. The growth and development of students is a central goal of higher education, and student affairs professionals play an integral role in its achievement. To accomplish this goal, educators must be familiar with an extensive literature base focusing on student development and be able to use relevant concepts and ideas effectively in their daily interactions with students. In addition, program planning and policy development are enhanced when student development concepts are used as a guide. Becoming knowledgeable about student development requires serious study, including critical analysis and evaluation of theory and research.

◆ ◆ ◆

In Part One, "Understanding, Using, and Translating Student Development Theory," we set the stage for examining student development. We introduce a number of concepts to provide a context for the study of specific student development theories presented later in the book. While some of this material may initially seem abstract, we encourage readers to refer back to the text of Part One when exploring later chapters that describe specific student development theories. In Part Four, we will revisit many of these ideas by examining the use of theory in practice, the role of student affairs educators as learning partners, and the current state of the student development knowledge base.

In Chapter One, "An Introduction to Student Development Theory," we present definitions of the term student development and clarify the various ways in which the concept has been applied. To provide historical background and a sense of how and why student development became the foundation of the student affairs profession, we trace the evolution of the student development approach, provide an overview and trajectory of the theories examined later in the book, and connect student development to student learning.

In Chapter Two, "Foundations for Understanding Student Development Theory," we introduce a diverse array of worldviews and paradigms to illustrate the complexities that undergird the creation of theory. We discuss their influence on student development theory and research related to college students. We also describe content and process models and theories, which focus more on the context of development and the influence of the environment. These models and theories are helpful for understanding, analyzing, and critiquing theory.

The content in Chapter Three, "Using Student Development Theory," details recommendations and strategies for using and applying student development theory. We explain the critical role of theory in student affairs practice, provide suggestions for evaluating the potential utility of theories, and offer both cautions and challenges associated with using student development theory. We present a theory-to-practice model and offer examples of integrative approaches for using theory. The chapter concludes with a brief case scenario to help readers begin the practice of considering theoretical application from a holistic perspective.

Though the study of student development can be overwhelming at first, the present wealth of knowledge about what happens to students in college is also gratifying and exciting. In an effort to promote learning and theory application throughout this book, we have provided a larger case study scenario in the appendix. The case ushers readers into an introductory, graduate-level student development theory course at Prescott University. We then provide individual portraits of students in the course and focus on their individual developmental journeys. We also offer thought-provoking questions about each student's portrait, to foster the application of various theories to their stories. While readers may review the case and portraits at any point, we recommend visiting the case study in the appendix before proceeding to Chapter Five, which begins our full discussion of specific theories.

CHAPTER ONE

AN INTRODUCTION TO STUDENT DEVELOPMENT THEORY

College student development theory is a body of scholarship that guides student affairs and higher education practice. "College students" are individuals engaged in postsecondary learning experiences, typically those taking place in formal settings such as colleges, universities, and other higher education institutions; college students are also engaged in learning outside of institutions, when they are at work, doing service, studying abroad, or living in the community. "Development," simply defined, is the process of becoming increasingly complex. In this chapter, we describe development in depth and then elaborate on developmental theories and processes throughout the book.

In social science research, where many student development theories originated, "theory is a unified, systematic causal *explanation* of a diverse range of social phenomena" (Schwandt, 2007, p. 292, emphasis in the original). It is a set of ideas that attempt to explain something in the social world. Theory may be relatively informal or simple, as in concepts that guide analysis or understanding, or it may be formal and have broad application to explain complex social phenomena (for example, cognitive development or racial identity development). Theory in student affairs practice is a useful tool that answers the question "Why?" (Jones & Abes, 2011) and is beneficial when it "helps explain a piece of the world to us" (Brookfield, 2005, p. 4). From this perspective, "theorizing is a form of meaning making, born of a desire to create explanations that impose conceptual order on reality" (p. 5). Some social scientists see theory as a guide for "ways to make decisions and think about how to interpret individuals, environments, and organizations" (Jones & Abes, 2011, p. 163), not to dictate a single explanation.

Most scientific traditions define theory as a tested and testable hypothesis proven often and over time. Over 20 years ago student development scholars Moore and Upcraft (1990) defined theory as a "[set] of definitions and statements specifying a relationship between concepts" (p. 179). They considered theory as definitive, highly structured, and based on deductive reasoning, causal connections, unitary understandings of truth, and separation between the researchers and researched.

Contemporary theorists frame theory as a way to "describe, explain, predict, influence outcomes, assess practice, and generate new knowledge and research" (Jones & Abes, 2011, p. 151). In short, theory framed from any worldview or paradigm can be a tool to enrich practitioners' and scholars' work with students. In Chapter Two, we discuss worldviews and paradigms and their relevance for student development theory and practice.

Early student development theorists Knefelkamp, Widick, and Parker (1978) grouped student development theories by "theory clusters" or "families" of theories (p. xi). Adding to their developmental nature, these theories include those that "focus on the individual, including social identities; those that examine students in the collegiate context such as student success and engagement, and learning; theories that explain the relationship of the campus environments to student development and success; and those focused on organizations and institutions of higher education" (Jones & Abes, 2011, p. 152). Renn and Reason (2013) pointed out that some student development theories derive from research on college students, while others have been adopted from academic fields including psychology, sociology, and human ecology. Regardless of their origin, all student development theories can influence practices and opportunities designed to promote student learning and growth (Renn & Reason).

Taking these multiple concepts into account, we define *student development theory* as a collection of theories related to college students that explain how they grow and develop holistically, with increased complexity, while enrolled in a postsecondary educational environment. In this book, we present and describe the growing number of student development theories and perspectives applied in higher education and student affairs. We highlight theories and perspectives that focus primarily on the individual student in a variety of collegiate contexts, and those we believe are most useful to and used by higher education and student affairs researchers and educators. Given the impracticality of creating one book with all of the theories that might possibly be of use to student affairs educators, we included what we believe is most applicable to the college student experience.

Defining Student Development Theory

This chapter provides an overview of the definitions of college student development and examines the origins and evolution of major student development theories created since the second half of the twentieth century. We begin with a discussion of definitions of student development and their historical roots and end with the ways in which student development theory is linked to student learning. Overall, we outline the underpinnings of this broad concept.

Definitions of Student Development

Student development is a term used extensively in student affairs practice and research, yet it evokes many meanings even within the student affairs professional community. Professionals talk about "facilitating student development," offices are titled "Student Development," and graduate students study "student development theories." Student development is almost universally viewed as a good thing, despite Parker's (1974) critique of student affairs professionals for attaching vague and nonspecific meanings to this term. Parker suggested that for many, student development had become a catchphrase with no direct application to their work. What, then, does the term "student development" mean exactly?

In 1967, Sanford defined *development* as "the organization of increasing complexity" (p. 47). Sanford distinguished development from *change* (which refers only to an altered condition that may be positive or negative, progressive or regressive) and from *growth* (which refers to expansion but may be either favorable or unfavorable to overall functioning). He saw this positive growth process as one in which the individual becomes increasingly able to integrate and act on many different experiences and influences. Rodgers (1990) defined student development as "the ways that a student grows, progresses, or increases his or her developmental capabilities as a result of enrollment in an institution of higher education" (p. 27). More recently, Jones and Abes (2011) defined student development as "some kind of positive change [that] occurs in the student (e.g., cognitive complexity, self-awareness, racial identity, or engagement)" (p. 153).

Student development is also a philosophy that has guided student affairs practice and serves as the rationale for specific programs and services since the profession's inception (Rodgers, 1990). Rodgers summed up this philosophy as "concern for the development of the whole person" (p. 27). A related application of the term *student development* is programmatic in nature and is based on what student affairs professionals do to encourage learning and student growth (Rodgers, 1990). In a frequently quoted definition reflecting this perspective, researchers suggested that student development is "the application of human development concepts in postsecondary settings so that everyone involved can master increasingly complex developmental tasks, achieve self-direction, and become interdependent" (Miller & Prince, 1976, p. 3).

The student development literature we discuss in this book includes social identity, psychosocial, cognitive-structural, and integrative perspectives. These theories expand Sanford's (1967) definition of *development* by identifying specific aspects of development and examining factors that influence its occurrence. Seeking parameters to identifying developmental theory, early researchers requested responses to four questions (Knelfelkamp et al., 1978) that are still useful to frame this dynamic process:

1. What interpersonal and intrapersonal changes occur while the student is in college?
2. What factors lead to this development?
3. What aspects of the college environment encourage or retard growth?
4. What developmental outcomes should we strive to achieve in college?

Student development theory provides the basis for higher education and student affairs practice designed to stimulate positive growth in students. Knowledge of student development theory enables higher education and student affairs professionals to identify and address student needs, design programs, develop policies, and create healthy college environments that encourage positive growth in students. While student development theories focus on intellectual growth and self-authorship as well as affective and behavioral changes among college students, they also encourage partnerships between student affairs educators and faculty. These partnerships have the potential to enhance student learning and maximize positive student outcomes in and out of the classroom.

A Brief History of the Student Development Movement

In this section we describe how the student development concept evolved and how institutions, researchers, and organizations responded to the need for more intentional efforts to support students in college. We begin by discussing the vocational guidance movement of the 1920s and describe the trajectory of student development and its relevance to the student affairs field through the 1950s.

Historical Roots of Student Development Theory

Early in the twentieth century, the relevance to the collegiate environment of the newly organized disciplines of psychology and sociology became apparent. Whereas theologians had previously espoused fostering Christian moral character as a goal for eighteenth- and nineteenth-century educators, psychological theorists such as Freud, Jung, and later Skinner examined human behavior through a different lens (Upcraft & Moore, 1990). As the scientific study of human development evolved, the academy responded by hiring student personnel workers who were viewed as human development specialists (Nuss, 2003). Focus on vocational guidance came first; however, the tumultuous events of the mid-twentieth century prompted significant changes in the student personnel profession and how the profession viewed student development. Events that influenced and contributed to a renewed focus on students included an embryonic student affairs field, the psychology of individual differences, and the need for institutions, particularly during the Great Depression of the 1930s, to place students in the world of work (Nuss, 2003; Rhatigan, 2000).

The 1920s Guidance Movement

In the 1920s, the vocational guidance movement began in earnest as colleges and universities graduated students who increasingly sought occupational security in business and industry. Credited with initiating the vocational guidance movement (Rhatigan, 2000), Frank Parsons (1909) was the first to articulate a "match" between personal characteristics and particular occupations to determine the "best fit" for individuals in the work environment. For the next forty years, vocational guidance in higher education (and elsewhere) rested on this premise. Students in the early 1920s took more interest in vocational preparation than in developing themselves in a holistic way (Arbuckle, 1953). They sought practical knowledge to propel them into the world of work. At the same time, higher education and industry joined to create new knowledge and train new workers. In reaction to student demand for work preparation and industry demand for applied research, critics who believed economic ties between industry and higher education had to be severed in order to preserve academic freedom and integrity sounded an alarm (Veblen, 1918/1946). Pragmatic philosophers, who asserted that optimal learning occurs when students' rational and emotional selves are integrated (see Carpenter, 1996; Rhatigan, 2000), alerted educators to the need to make education more than just vocational preparation. Combined, the critics and philosophers created a moral imperative for higher education to address students' multidimensional needs rather than focusing exclusively on vocational preparation.

The Student Personnel Point of View: 1937 and 1949

In 1925, representatives from fourteen higher education institutions met to discuss vocational guidance problems. World War I was over, and increased enrollments left educators scrambling for ways to evaluate students and their needs. Educators and researchers developed several specialized assessment tools, such as personality rating scales, to examine students' ability and performance (American Council on Education, 1937/1994a). The culmination of these efforts was the American Council on Education's 1937 statement, the "Student Personnel Point of View" (SPPV). This landmark report recognized that educators must guide the "whole student" to reach their potential and contribute to society's betterment. In short, the statement was a reminder to the higher education community that the personal and professional development of students was (and remains) a worthy and noble goal. In 1949, the American Council on Education (1949/1994b) revised the 1937 SPPV statement to include an expanded delineation of the objectives and goals of student affairs administration. Returning to the late nineteenth–century focus on the psychology of individual differences, the document called for faculty, administrators, and student personnel workers to encourage the development of students, recognize their "individual differences in backgrounds, abilities, interests and goals" (p. 110), and give more attention to democratic processes and socially responsible graduates.

Formal Statements about Student Development

In the late 1960s and 1970s, professional associations, such as the Council of Student Personnel Associations (COSPA) and the American College Personnel Association (ACPA), and private groups, such as the Hazen Foundation, began to reconceptualize the role and mission of student affairs (see Evans, 2001). The Hazen Foundation created the Committee on the Student in Higher Education (1968), which encouraged colleges and universities to "assume responsibility for the human development of [their] students" (p. 5). At the same time, Tomorrow's Higher Education Project (T.H.E.), initiated by ACPA, explored the viability of student development as a philosophy of the profession (Brown, 1972) and specifically examined the student affairs professional "commitment to student development—the theories of human development applied to the postsecondary education setting—as a guiding theory, and the continued attempt to ensure that the development of the whole student was an institutional priority" (Garland & Grace, 1993, p. 6).

In his influential monograph *Student Development in Tomorrow's Higher Education (The T.H.E. project)—A Return to the Academy,* Brown (1972) challenged college administrators and student affairs professionals to "hold up the mirror" to each other in order to confront the incongruities between the stated goals of higher education and what was happening to students. The project questioned whether student affairs professionals should be the only ones on campus concerned about student development and, more important, whether student development can be nurtured without the support and influence of those in the academic domain. A forerunner of the Student Learning Imperative (ACPA, 1996) and *Learning Reconsidered* (Keeling, 2004), the T.H.E. project recommended that student affairs educators increasingly emphasize academic outcomes and teaching-learning experiences, reorganize student affairs offices and functions, be accountable by conducting outcomes assessments, and develop new sets of competencies.

Soon after the publication of *Tomorrow's Higher Education,* the Council of Student Personnel Associations (1975/1994) sought to define the role of the student development specialist and close the gap between theory and practice in the field. Miller and Prince (1976) carried the concept one step closer to implementation by highlighting the developmental tasks of college students and suggesting program options to help students reach their developmental goals. In later efforts to seek empirical evidence of the student development concept, researchers created instruments that focused on measuring student development outcomes (Winston, Miller, & Prince, 1979) and assessing the effect of the institutional environment on students (Pace, 1984). These statements of philosophy, along with the early research, provided impetus for the student affairs field to redefine itself in ways that helped professionals meet the challenges of intentional and holistic growth for increasingly diverse student populations.

The Evolution of Student Development Theory

In this section we describe the evolution of student development theory as a body of knowledge. We map its contours as it emerged as an area of inquiry and practice, from the 1960s through the early twenty-first century. It is important to note that while this presentation follows chronological introduction of theories, we avoid designating any set of theories as "foundational"—a term that implies other theories may be derivative or less essential to good student affairs educational practice. That said, we do believe that it is important for professionals to understand the intellectual history of a field and therefore it is wise to know how the contemporary body of student development theory evolved from its beginning.

Early College Student Development Theories: Through the 1970s

The 1960s saw the beginning of significant changes in student affairs and higher education as the country faced nearly a decade of social turmoil brought on by the Vietnam War and the civil rights and women's movements. The student population no longer consisted primarily of upper- and upper-middle-class men. Women, veterans, and students of color from all social class backgrounds enrolled in college in increasing numbers. Student affairs administrators sought information about the needs and perspectives of these diverse college students and turned first to psychologists (for example, Erikson, 1950, 1968; Piaget, 1952) for information about human development that would help them understand the students with whom they were working. Social psychologists and sociologists, such as Kurt Lewin (1936), contributed knowledge about group dynamics and the effect of the environment on human interaction.

In time, theorists began focusing specifically on the experiences of students in college. Nevitt Sanford's (1967) insights about the process of development (see Chapter Two) provided an enduring perspective on student development as a function of cycles of differentiation and integration and of the need to balance adequate challenge with adequate support for student development. Douglas Heath (1968) and Roy Heath (1964) each focused on maturation in college students. Sociologists Kenneth Feldman and Theodore Newcomb (1969) delineated the impact of peer group influence on individual students, including helping students accomplish family independence, facilitating the institution's intellectual goals, offering emotional support and meeting needs not met by faculty, and so on. Their book, *The Impact of College on Students,* marked a watershed in the emergence of scholarship on college students, their environments, and their development.

In the mid-twentieth century, Erik Erikson (1959/1980) conducted groundbreaking research on adolescent identity. Because the vast majority of college students in that era were in their late adolescent years, the application of this work to a college student population was sensible. Building on Erikson's

(1959/1980) ideas about identity development, Arthur Chickering focused specifically on developmental issues facing college students. Chickering's book *Education and Identity* (1969) quickly became a mainstay for professionals interested in student development and in psychosocial development in particular. Around the same time and also working within the psychosocial tradition, Marcia (1966) used Erikson's (1959/1980) ideas as a foundation for his research to investigate identity development in adolescence. In 1968, William Perry introduced a cognitive-structural theory of intellectual and ethical development of college students, one of the first to take hold extensively in student affairs practice. Lawrence Kohlberg's (1969, 1976) theory of moral reasoning, built on Piaget's (1932/1977) study of moral development in children, also gained popularity in student affairs. For some time, student development professionals based their practice largely on these theories (of Marcia, Chickering, Perry, Kohlberg). We discuss and critique these theories, which are still frequently used in student affairs, in Chapters Thirteen, Fourteen, and Fifteen.

In the 1970s, student affairs educators began to recognize and acknowledge the vast limitations of the early theories in addressing diverse experiences of gender, race, and ethnicity in higher education. Basing their conclusions on homogenous populations (comprising predominantly white men at private colleges), Chickering, Marcia, Perry, and Kohlberg made important contributions to the nascent understanding of college student development, but their theories failed to account adequately for the experiences of students of color and of women students of all backgrounds. Scholars and practitioners turned to psychological and sociological models of racial identity development such as Atkinson, Morten, and Sue's (1979) *Minority Identity Development* model and Cross's (1971) explanation of Black identity development.

Recognizing that development does not happen in a vacuum, counseling psychologists James Banning and Leland Kaiser (1974) introduced a campus ecology model that Banning (1978) later expanded into a monograph. This approach was popularized by work and publications of the Western Interstate Commission on Higher Education (WICHE) and its associates (see Aulepp & Delworth, 1976). Campus ecology focused on the interaction of the student and the campus setting (Banning, 1978), the principles of person-environment interaction that undergird applications of theory to practice.

While not developmental in that they do not describe progression from less to more complex ways of being, a number of typology theories with implications for student learning and career development gained popularity in the 1970s. Building on the work of Carl Jung (1923/1971), Myers (1980) explored differences in personality type. Student affairs educators, particularly those who worked in the area of career development, also found helpful Holland's (1966, 1973) theory of vocational choice (see Chapter Two).

Building on Psychosocial and Cognitive-Structural Theories: 1980s–1990s

The 1980s and 1990s saw the introduction of a number of theories that built on earlier psychosocial and cognitive-structural theories, with a continuing emphasis on addressing the experiences and development of increasingly diverse populations of college students. Ruth Ellen Josselson (1987a, 1996) extended Marcia's work specifically to women to understand their identity development. In 1993, to incorporate new research findings related to the order and sequence of student identity development, Chickering collaborated with Linda Reisser to revise his book *Education and Identity*. In Chapter Thirteen we highlight the research of Erikson, Marcia, Josselson, and Chickering and his later revisions with Reisser.

Basing their work on twenty-five years of research, James Rest and his colleagues introduced a neo-Kohlbergian theory of moral development (Rest, Narvaez, Thoma, & Bebeau, 2000) that is less rigid and more concrete than Kohlberg's (1976). Carol Gilligan (1982/1993) identified care-based rationales for moral decision making that also illuminated the processes of moral development. We discuss these moral development theories and subsequent elaborations of them in Chapter Fifteen.

Several theorists sought to expand Perry's cognitive structural theory. Suggesting that Perry had confused intellectual and psychosocial development in his final stages, King and Kitchener (1994) examined cognitive development beyond relativism, a process they labeled reflective judgment. Also building on Perry's theory, Belenky, Clinchy, Goldberger, and Tarule (1986) were the first researchers to investigate the intellectual development of women apart from men. Marcia Baxter Magolda extended the work of Perry (1968) and Belenky and her colleagues (1986) by including both men and women in a longitudinal study of the epistemological development of individuals whom she originally interviewed when they were students at Miami University (Baxter Magolda, 1992). These theories of intellectual development have each, in their own way, made a significant contribution to understanding student development, and we discuss them in more detail in Chapter Fourteen.

Social Identity Theories: 1990s to Present

As the United States becomes more diverse and students from different backgrounds enter higher education, understanding them is increasingly important, and theories focusing on social identities have become a mainstay in the student development literature. These theories are grounded in the socio-historical context of the United States, in which some groups have privilege and some groups are oppressed. Collectively, social identity theories examine the development of both dominant and nondominant identities (McEwen, 2003a). While these identity models focus on the process of self-definition, many of them also examine how individuals move through stages of increasing cognitive complexity with regard to their self-identification (Torres, Jones, & Renn, 2009). In addition to bringing in theories from outside higher education, student development researchers draw on psychology, sociology, social psychology, and human ecology, among other disciplines, to create models for college student identity development. In Chapter Four we provide an overview of the context and processes of social identity development.

Psychosocial identity development models address, among others, identities related to race (e.g., Cross, 1991; Gallegos & Ferdman, 2012; Hardiman & Keehn, 2012; Jackson, 2001; Kim, 2012), ethnicity (Choney, Berryhill-Paapke, & Robbins, 1995; Phinney, 1990), sexual orientation (Dillon, Worthington, & Moradi, 2011; Fassinger, 1998; Worthington, Savoy, Dillon, & Vernaglia, 2002), and gender (Bilodeau, 2005; Bussey, 2011). Models may be stage-based, describing development "through progressive, linear stages or statuses that lead to an end point in which identities are internalized, synthesized, and permanent" (Torres et al., 2009, p. 582). Or they may describe a nonlinear array of identity patterns, statuses, or stopping points, focusing on the influences of local features and systemic structures that privilege some identities over others. In Chapters Four through Twelve we present models that describe several areas of social identity in college students.

Integrative Approaches to Psychosocial, Cognitive, and Affective Development

Although early student development proponents wrote that attempting to design one "comprehensive model of student development" (Knefelkamp, Widick, & Parker, 1978, p. xi) was futile, contemporary theorists have nevertheless made great strides in that direction. They argue that it is not possible to separate cognitive and affective aspects of development, and they explore both cognitive and psychosocial dimensions of identity and how these factors are interwoven throughout life. They examine how components of social identity (for example, ethnicity, race, gender, sexual, religious, and so on) integrate to create a whole. For example, student development theorists have adapted the work of Robert Kegan (1982, 1994), who introduced a life span model of development that takes into account affective, interpersonal, and cognitive processes. Kegan (1982) focused on the evolution of the self and how individuals make sense of their world, particularly their relationships with others. An important outcome of development that Kegan identified is self-authorship—"the internal capacity to define one's beliefs, identity, and social relations" (Baxter Magolda, 2008, p. 269). Following her former students into their adult lives, Baxter Magolda (1999a, 2001, 2007) used Kegan's concept of self-authorship to explain the shift she identified in young adulthood from an identity shaped by external forces and others' viewpoints to an internal identity created by individuals themselves. We discuss self-authorship in Chapter Sixteen.

Connecting Student Development and Learning Theory

Student affairs educators do not work in isolation from the core missions of higher education, and there is important work under way that links student development to learning. For example, situated cognition, also called contextual learning (Merriam & Bierema, 2014), transformational learning (Fried & Associates, 2012; Mezirow, 2000), critical and postmodern perspectives (Merriam, 2008; Merriam, Caffarella, & Baumgartner, 2007), disciplinary perspectives (Donald, 2002), and cultural frames (Chávez & Longerbeam, in press) are relevant, as they provide a wide range of views to examine how students learn, their frame of reference, and what they gain through new knowledge both in and out of the classroom. Additionally, most of these theories and perspectives on learning advocate for new ways of teaching to achieve optimal student learning for all students. Approaches such as the Learning Partnerships Model (Baxter Magolda, 2004b) make explicit links between student development theories (in this case, self-authorship) and applications in curricular and co-curricular settings.

Conclusion

It should be clear by now that the development of the whole student is more complex than one theory or even a cluster of theories can explain. The establishment in a relatively short period of time of a robust literature on student development underscores this point. The sheer volume of theoretical literature currently being produced is daunting even for scholars in the field. New approaches and the complexity of perspectives in use provide a strong foundation for understanding and working with today's diverse college-going population. Learning student development theory and learning to apply it are challenging but worthwhile goals for postsecondary educators. It is incumbent upon higher education and student affairs educators to use theory to inform not only practice but also larger public discourse on the uses and purposes of higher education in the twenty-first century. Development of the whole person is a critical outcome even as collegiate students change at such a rapid pace.

Student development theory now incorporates a half-century of research and professional practice with college students. Just as Knefelkamp and colleagues (1978) parsed the field into clusters or families, we do so in this book. Student development includes theories of social identities (for example, race, ethnicity, sexual identity, gender, religion, ability, social class), psychosocial identity development, cognitive/epistemological development, moral development, and holistic self-authorship. The categories are not mutually exclusive; they overlap in the lived experience of college students, as for example in the ways that increased complexity in ways of thinking (cognitive) leads to increased complexity in ways of understanding moral dilemmas. As we discuss in Chapter Two, student development theories are informed by worldviews and supported by models that help explain the processes through which development occurs.

In this chapter we have presented a brief history and a more or less chronological elaboration of the emergence and consolidation of the body of student development theories. We noted at the outset of the overview that we are cautious about presenting some theories as foundational and later ones as derivative; we believe that doing so risks establishing a fixed canon of theory, or creating the perception that the first theories—often those based on homogenous populations of students from privileged groups—are unquestionable and everything else is secondary, less important, "extra," or optional. We therefore organized this volume to include—after this introduction and the next chapter on paradigms or worldviews—first theories of social identities, then Eriksonian psychosocial theories, and then cognitive/ epistemological models. Self-authorship theory brings the pieces together at the end of the book, before we discuss applying theory to practice. Locating students' social identities early reminds readers that students—and student affairs educators—bring their identities with them into every campus context. Of course it is possible to use the book in a different order from the one we present, and we encourage readers to undertake topics in the order they choose after reading about paradigms and worldviews that shape student development theory and student affairs practice.

Discussion Questions

1. Describe what theory is and create one or two metaphors you would use to help you and others understand the concept.
2. What is student development theory?
3. Name some of the early scholars of the student development idea. What concepts did they contribute to the literature?
4. What are the four questions that frame student development theory, and how are they useful today?
5. Give a brief summary of the student development movement and the evolution of developmental theory. Identify significant events in each era that may have shaped how educators thought about student development.
6. Identify and outline the major contributions of the early documents related to college students.
7. Draw representations or metaphors of social identity and integrative student development theories. How do these representations and metaphors help you better understand their relation to student development?
8. How are student development and student learning connected? How do they differ? Give examples.
9. What about student development theory do you most want to learn? What approaches will you use to facilitate your learning?

CHAPTER TWO

FOUNDATIONS FOR UNDERSTANDING STUDENT DEVELOPMENT THEORY

Student development theory as a concept emerged from mid-twentieth-century research in psychology and sociology. Today, student development theory connects to a number of additional disciplines and multidisciplinary fields including anthropology, social psychology, biology, humanities, and higher education. These areas represent a variety of worldviews, or ways in which individuals make sense of their relationship to the world (Jones, Torres, & Arminio, 2014). Some academic traditions favor one worldview over the many available (Guba, 1990; Guido, Chávez, & Lincoln, 2010). For example, logical positivism, as enacted through the scientific method, predominates in many physical sciences. But some other fields incorporate—albeit not without controversy—multiple perspectives. Social sciences, humanities, and education are examples of the latter, in which a host of perspectives inform research, teaching, and institutional systems. As we describe throughout the book, student development theories incorporate a wide range of approaches and worldviews.

Theory and practice in higher education reflect the worldviews of people who enact them. For the purposes of this book, we consider worldviews—or paradigms—as the underlying philosophical systems that guide thought and action. These underlying systems include how individuals understand the nature of being (ontology) and the nature of knowledge (epistemology). For example, do people construct identities? Or do identities construct the self? Is knowledge absolute, fixed, and discoverable? Or is it contextual, fluid, and constructed? In this chapter, we describe several worldviews that influence student development theory. We outline the paradigmatic contours of the field from one that was largely based in a positivist worldview of orderly, linear developmental progression, to one that embraces constructivist theories describing contextual, nonlinear, fluid processes of student development.

It is important to note that newcomers to the study and practice of student development may encounter competing, even contradictory, worldviews in the literature. We contend that the diversity of paradigms in use in higher education and student affairs scholarship benefits the field, but we also acknowledge that it can be daunting to student affairs educators beginning their journey. For example, there are overlapping and interconnecting elements across paradigms, and sometimes the same language is used in different ways in different contexts. At the leading edge of scholarship, theorists combine paradigmatic perspectives, some in additive ways (for example, Jones, 2009) and others in intersecting ways (for example, Abes, 2012). Scholars are also conducting inquiry accentuating multiple theoretical shifts across paradigms (Guido et al., 2010; Lincoln & Guba, 2013). It is worth the effort to map and explore the complexity of multiple worldviews. Student affairs educators who understand multiple underlying philosophical tenets are in a better position to use, critique, and create theories, as well as to work across campus units with educators—faculty and administrators—whose worldviews differ from their own.

We cannot introduce and explain all of the worldviews and processes used in the field; instead we present a group that highlights the underlying assumptions and beliefs of positivist/post-positivist, critical/cultural, and constructivist/interpretivist literature in student affairs and higher education. This chapter lays the groundwork for understanding student development theory and the paradigms and theoretical frameworks of research related to it. First, we describe paradigmatic perspectives and theoretical worldviews and models. We then illuminate how several processes and theories may be related to student development theory or its application in practice. Although some of the process/content theories and models do not describe development of particular aspects of a college student, the ones we outline here are in common use across student affairs and higher education settings.

Before proceeding, it is important to note one transition in our language. Throughout this chapter and the remainder of the book, we use the terms "minoritized" and "majoritized." Minoritized is a more appropriate term than minority "to signify the social construction of underrepresentation and subordination in U.S. social institutions, including colleges and universities. Persons are not born into a minority status nor are they minoritized in every social context (for example, their families, social fraternities, and churches). Instead, they are rendered minorities in particular situations and institutional environments that sustain an overrepresentation of whiteness [or another oppressive system]" (Patton, Harper, & Harris, 2015, p. 212). We use the term "majoritized" to emphasize the power that dominant groups exercise over nondominant groups, creating both minoritized and majoritized groups.

Paradigmatic Perspectives and Theoretical Worldviews

Formal student development theories derive from research and systematic observation. Researchers' worldviews and paradigmatic perspectives shape what questions they ask, how they ask them, and what theories emerge from their work. Scholars do not agree on consistent definitions or uses of paradigms in social science inquiry and theory (Anfara & Mertz, 2015), but there are concepts from educational research that guide an understanding of student development theories. In his foundational writing about qualitative educational research, Guba (1990) described a paradigm as a framework, a "basic set of beliefs that guides action" (p. 17). Denzin and Lincoln (2005), also qualitative researchers, later defined a paradigm as "overarching philosophical systems" (p. 230). Based upon these ideas, we define a paradigm as a system that guides action in research, practice, and theorizing. Paradigms feature three main philosophical components, addressing questions of ontology, epistemology, and methodology. Ontology explores the nature of reality. Does the researcher believe there is a singular, universally true voice and reality for everyone, or is reality socially constructed through many voices? Epistemology examines how the inquirer comes to understand the world. In studying a phenomenon, is the researcher at a distance from research participants or do researcher and participants authentically connect in meaningful ways? In a research context, methodology focuses on the process of how information is obtained "and involves analysis of the assumptions, principles and procedures" (Schwandt, 2007, p. 193) of inquiry. Methodology covers a range of research activity including study design and the processes of data interpretation and analysis. Methodology answers questions such as the following: How will the researcher conduct the research? What are the best ways to plan, handle, and treat the data throughout the research, from planning through analysis? Methodology is thus broader than "methods," which are the specific data collection techniques employed in any study.

Together, these philosophical components and corresponding questions create a structure for understanding paradigms and worldviews and their use in research and theory-building. The answers to the philosophical questions ideally play out in a more or less consistent, parallel manner within each paradigm. For example, an ontology that holds reality as a shared social construction aligns with an epistemology that embraces multiple sources of knowledge, which in turn supports a research methodology that incorporates diverse perspectives and methods such as open-ended interviews that allow multiple voices to contribute. A paradigm enacted in research in this way might lead to a theory that acknowledges socially constructed identities or ways of learning. Not all research and theories reflect a solitary worldview or paradigm; researchers may combine elements of different worldviews, or they may begin a line of research in one paradigm and, over the course of their careers, shift to new ways of understanding the nature of student development. Regardless of paradigm, a hallmark of high-quality research and the theories derived from it lies in theorists' ability to explain their paradigmatic assumptions and demonstrate alignment of ontology, epistemology, methodology, and resulting knowledge claims.

Paradigms represent basic beliefs, and as such cannot be proven (Guba & Lincoln, 1994); paradigms are human constructions, subject to human error. Guba and Lincoln cautioned that "no construction is or can be incontrovertibly right; advocates of any particular construction must rely on *persuasiveness* and *utility* rather than *proof* in arguing their position" (p. 108). Theory development occurs in part as a result of shifting (McEwen, 2003a) and multiple (combined) paradigms (Guido et al., 2010; Lincoln & Guba, 1985, 2003). Paradigms guide thought about theory, research, and practice. Student affairs educators have the opportunity—even the obligation—to examine their own paradigmatic beliefs and explore how these beliefs influence which theories seem most sensible, what research they most value, what developmental outcomes they deem most important for students, and what educational practices they embrace as most likely to lead to those outcomes.

In higher education and student affairs, including student development, the predominant paradigm in research and practice in the twentieth century was grounded in positivism and post-positivism (Guido et al., 2010). In the last 30 years, a number of academic disciplines and multidisciplinary fields such as higher education have come to embrace other worldviews, including critical and cultural paradigms and constructivism. The theoretical worldviews we describe here, though not a comprehensive list, represent three paradigmatic perspectives important in contemporary higher education and student development scholarship and practice: positivism and post-positivism, constructivism, and critical and cultural paradigms.

Positivism and Post-postivism

Positivism was the guiding paradigm for theory and research in science and social science from the nineteenth century forward (Crotty, 1998; Guba & Lincoln, 1994; Kerlinger, 1964). Rooted in Enlightenment ideals of human reason and science over religion (see Anchor, 1967), a positivist elucidation of the world assumes a strictly objective reality that is time- and context-free and stated in the form of cause-and-effect laws. Assuming themselves to be independent of the object investigated, positivist researchers study a phenomenon purportedly without influencing the outcome or being influenced by the object of study. Post-positivists believe that an objective reality exists, but research and theory reflect the limitations of human knowledge as conjecture (Creswell, 2013). By controlling for researcher biases and other potential influences on the outcomes, scholars can study the effects of, for example, particular activities (for example, undergraduate research, sports participation, fraternity membership) on students. Education research in these worldviews has largely followed the post-positivist approach.

In the post-positivist paradigm, the methodology used to study phenomena is often experimental or quasi-experimental. Formulating hypotheses and subjecting them to empirical testing for verification, researchers control conditions potentially interfering with the results. This paradigm in educational research, for example, places a high value on randomized control trials, sometimes in laboratory-based intervention studies, in which researchers assign individuals randomly to treatment (intervention) or control groups (Yin, Hackett, & Chubin, 2008). Some research on stereotype threat uses this methodology (see Steele & Aronson, 1995), as do some studies of resilience, grit, and mindset (see Yeager & Walton, 2011). The benefits of this paradigm include the ability to test existing theories and to experiment with interventions that may promote student development, learning, and success.

The field of student development theory began in post-positivism, and a number of theories we present in this book align with this paradigm. For example, many of the cognitive development theories come from an educational psychology perspective, which in the twentieth century privileged a post-positivist position. As we discuss in Chapter Fourteen, King and Kitchener (1994) presented stages of cognitive development that they believe are apparent in the thinking of individuals regardless of the situation in which individuals find themselves. King and Kitchener studied cognitive development using a standardized set of interview questions and trained interviewers to present these questions in a similar manner to all research participants.

These scholars outlined a program of research based on explicitly stated hypotheses, which they then tested in a predetermined manner, using the scientific method to verify the concepts associated with their theory. Others who created and tested student development theory predominantly from a post-positivist perspective include Perry (1968), Kohlberg (1976), Cross (1971), Helms (1993a), and Baxter Magolda in her early research. These studies demonstrate the utility of a post-positivist frame in defining and describing development in models with clear stages or phases.

Like all research, that based in post-positivism is limited by its paradigmatic assumptions. Though one advantage of carefully conducted post-positivist studies with diverse samples is the ability to make some generalizable claims, the increasing diversity of undergraduate institutions and students—and the complex social systems in which higher education operates—presents challenges to making "universal" claims that apply to every student. Still, the ability to use, for example, large longitudinal data sets such as the Cooperative Institutional Research Program (CIRP, pronounced "serp") (see http://www.heri.ucla.edu/cirpoverview.php) to understand broad trends is an important contribution of contemporary post-positivist work. The field of student development as a whole benefits from encompassing multiple paradigms. Most studies are located in only one paradigm, but taken together as a body of literature, student development theory benefits from the ways that multiple perspectives allow the advantages of each to counterbalance the disadvantages. We turn now to constructivist, critical, and cultural paradigms, which can address some limitations of positivism and post-positivism.

Constructivism

Constructivism grew from an interpretivist framework (Lather, 2007), both of which declare that "multiple realities exist, differing in context, and knowledge is co-constructed between researcher and researched" (Abes, 2009, p. 144). As a paradigm, constructivism is "emergent, contextual, personal, socially constructed and interactive" (Guido et al., 2010, p. 15). A constructivist worldview defines "reality" by specific individual and group experiences, and thus it changes over time. The variable and personal nature of social constructions can be identified through dialogue between those who want to know (researchers) and those who do know (study participants) as they co-construct knowledge (Jones & Abes, 2011).

Constructivist studies are common in contemporary research on college student experiences, attitudes, and development. For example, scholars have used this approach to understand transformative learning in a short-term immersion program (Jones, Rowan-Kenyon, Ireland, Niehaus, & Skendall, 2012), student veterans' transition to college (Rumann & Hamrick, 2010), the influence of racial identity on involvement in African American student organizations (Jones, 2014), and the need for skilled educators to facilitate student discussions about race (Quaye, 2014). Although the topics are disparate, the studies share underlying commitments to the idea that dialogue—often but not always in the form of interviews—is the route to understanding student experiences, sense-making, and development. This paradigm was so compelling to Baxter Magolda (1999a, 2001, 2009) as she conducted a longitudinal study of how students thought about their worlds that she shifted her study from a cognitive-structural approach to a constructivist one (Baxter Magolda, 2004a). Her well-known model of self-authorship (see Chapter Sixteen) emerged from the constructivist perspective as she co-constructed meaning with her participants over the first 16 years of her study.

Critical and Cultural Paradigms

Critical paradigms reflect "theoretical foundations promoting the deconstruction and critique of institutions, laws, organizations, definitions and practices to screen for power inequities" (Guido et al., 2010, p. 9). In contrast to post-positivist assumptions that there is a "truth" to discover and the best way to do so is to control as much as possible for extraneous variables, adherents of a critical perspective contend that the beliefs of the inquirer inevitably influence research findings and that these influences do not inherently pose problems or threaten the quality of the study. For these proponents, inquiry is transactional, typically enacted as a dialogue between the researcher(s) and researched. One purpose of inquiry is to promote fundamental social change by raising consciousness and correcting injustices. The work of many contemporary identity scholars in student development falls within the critical paradigm.

The underlying theoretical foundation of *cultural paradigms* holds that truth is socially constructed, based on "unacknowledged gender, culture, sexuality, class, language, and even personality preferences" (Guido et al., 2010, p. 10), among others. Looking at the world in congruence with a cultural eye, these parallel paradigms reflect a descriptive/interpretive goal. Examining phenomena from an anthropological/sociological lens, cultural paradigms focus on the norms, values, assumptions, beliefs, and meanings undergirding an artifact, population, policy, or organization. Magolda's ethnographies of campus rituals (for example, 2000, 2002) and religious student organizations (Magolda, 2007; Magolda & Ebben, 2006) originated from a cultural paradigm.

One of the most widely utilized paradigms to emerge in recent decades combines aspects of both critical and cultural paradigms (Guido et al., 2010). The knowledge resulting from this dual paradigm is subjective, experiential, and transactional. Tenets of this broad and complex paradigm include emancipation of minoritized groups to alter their oppression, intersections of multiple critical/cultural views (for example, class, race, ethnicity, gender, sexuality, and ability), and the high priority of ethical considerations. The infusion of racial, ethnic, border, liminal, and postcolonial epistemologies (Delgado & Stefancic, 2012; Denzin, Lincoln, & Smith, 2008; Sandoval, 2000; Shahjahan & Kezar, 2013; Smith, 1999), and the proliferation of feminist, gender, and queer theories (Abes & Kasch, 2007; Ahmed, 2006; Nicholson & Pasque, 2011; Renn, 2010), as well as embodied perspectives (Butler, 1993, 1999; Denzin et al., 2008; Freiler, 2008; Nguyen & Larson, 2015) create new ways to understand students' intersecting social identities. For example, Rhoads, Saenz, and Carducci (2005) studied students engaged in social reform, Chávez (2009) conducted an autoethnography of leadership, and Chávez, Ke, and Herrera (2012) used narratives of culture and student learning, which offer both cultural description and critical analysis.

Innovative paradigmatic thinking leaves an imprint on all fields, including student affairs (Fried & Associates, 1995, 2012; Guido et al., 2010; Kuh, Whitt, & Shedd, 1987). Scholars—for example, Jones and Abes (2013)—are reconceptualizing student development within these new frameworks. Understanding the paradigmatic assumptions underlying a theory is crucial to using theory appropriately. Throughout this book we discuss the background of relevant theories and the contexts in which they were created, to give the reader a sense of the ontological, epistemological, and methodological bases of research on college student development. Understanding research design, such as data collection and analysis/interpretation, enhances understanding of student development theory creation, refinement, and application. In providing this research background to the theories, we hope to cultivate interest in readers to expand and deepen the student development literature. The following theoretical perspectives—critical race theory, Black feminist thought, feminist theory, intersectionality, postcolonialism, poststructuralism, and queer theory—are linked to a critical/cultural paradigm promoting social justice and equity for marginalized groups. They are not student development theories per se, but like positivism and post-positivism offer worldviews through which to consider college student development.

Critical Race Theory. Critical race theory (CRT) is a perspective that emphasizes the centrality of race and racism and challenges white supremacy in the law, education, politics and other social systems. CRT evolved from the 1960s civil rights movement as legal scholars of the 1970s observed that legal strategies had become ineffective for promoting social change. In addition, legal scholars of color became concerned about the failure of critical legal studies to acknowledge the inherent nature of racism in the law. Drawing inspiration from the writings of icons such as Martin Luther King, Jr., César Chávez, and Malcolm X (Delgado & Stefancic, 2013), Black, Latino, Native American, and Asian legal scholars advocated a deeper understanding of the relationships between race, racism, and the law. In response, their scholarship and advocacy served as the impetus for CRT. Over the past 30 years, CRT has become an important perspective in social science research, including studies of higher education and student development (Patton, McEwen, Rendón, & Howard-Hamilton, 2007).

CRT includes an explicit goal to challenge and disrupt normative structures that fuel racism and racial oppression (Crenshaw, Gotanda, Peller, & Thomas, 1995; Delgado & Stefancic, 2013; Dixson & Rousseau, 2005; Ladson-Billings, 1998; Lynn & Dixson, 2013; Solórzano, 1998). Tenets of CRT include a belief that current understandings of race privilege White identities, behaviors, and thought processes, while simultaneously marginalizing people of color. Additionally, CRT scholars assert that racism is so ingrained in U.S. culture that it is unrecognizable to most people, particularly those who have the power and influence to dismantle racial hierarchies. In order to address inequities experienced by racially minoritized people, critical race theorists advocate the centering of their voices through counternarratives and counterstorytelling; for example, students of color are recognized as creators and holders of the knowledge they communicate through their counterstories (Delgado Bernal, 2002). CRT advocates assert an activist agenda for social justice and encourage researchers to use their findings to create a more racially just society (Ladson-Billings & Donnor, 2005).

CRT scholars also challenge notions of colorblindness and race neutrality. Delgado and Stefancic (2013) explained, "rules and laws that insist on treating blacks and whites alike (i.e., colorblindness), remedy only the more extreme and shocking forms of injustice that do stand out" (p. 2). Although colleges and universities are no longer racially segregated by law and discrimination based on race and ethnicity is illegal in educational settings, racial microaggressions—everyday, accumulative acts of hostility, ignorance, and discrimination—have a substantial negative impact on campus climate and the experiences of students of color (Solórzano, Ceja, & Yosso, 2000). To address ongoing, systemic racism, critical race theorists use counternarratives, critiques, and policy analyses to provide evidence of ongoing injustices and inequities (Harper, 2009; Harper, Patton, & Wooden, 2009; Patton & Catching, 2009).

Higher education scholars using CRT illuminate how people of color have been ignored or made invisible in research that guides the field. Patton et al. (2007) used CRT to analyze the dearth of racial diversity in samples that measure or examine commonly applied student development theories. Moving racially minoritized groups to the center of theory creation and application creates space in the literature, research, and on campus for validation of diverse perspectives. Another study in which CRT was used highlighted focus group data from African American students at three U.S. universities to reveal how these students experienced racial microaggressions and a negative campus racial climate (Solórzano et al., 2000). This type of research is crucial especially when educators apply these findings to practice, which might yield the creation and maintenance of spaces for students of color to counteract subtle and overt forms of racism. These findings might also influence campuswide efforts to educate campus members about their complicity in racial injustices on campus. Patton et al. (2007) encouraged serious scrutiny of traditional student development theory with an eye toward "critical examinations that provide an accurate context of the theorists' backgrounds, identities, and assumptions; the population on which the theory was based; how sociopolitical and historical contexts, privilege, and power may have shaped the theory; and the applicability of the theory to various student populations" (p. 49).

A CRT perspective requires that student development researchers consider their own race and its intersections with other social identities (for example, gender, social class, ability), as well as the social identities of research participants. For a long time, many writers and users of student development theory ignored the saliency of race in the most widely applied theories (Patton et al., 2007). Recently, more scholars and student affairs educators have become aware of the need to be more intentional and cognizant of the role of race and racism in student development research, theory, and practice.

Black Feminism. Black feminism, sometimes expressed as the plural Black feminisms or in Alice Walker's (1983) term *womanism*, is a perspective that links sexism, racism, and classism as central forces in society. Black women's activism has a long history in the United States. Black women abolitionists in the nineteenth century and Black women suffragists of the twentieth century are the predecessors of Black feminist groups such as the Combahee River Collective that emerged during the late 1960s and early 1970s. Defying racism and sexism in the gay movement, homophobia in the Black community, sexism in Black civil rights organizations, and racism in white feminist organizations. Black feminists were among the first activists and scholars to articulate connections across multiple identities and the intersections of these identities—particularly race, class, and gender—which, decades later, still result in their experience of multiple oppressions (Nicholson & Pasque, 2011). Patricia Hill Collins' scholarship on Black feminist thought is among the most well known perspectives for succinctly describing distinguishing features that illuminate the unique experiences of Black women, individually and collectively (Collins 1991, 1993, 1996, 2009).

Wheeler (2002) defined a Black feminist as "a person, historically an African American woman academic, who believes that female descendants of American slavery share a unique set of life experiences distinct from those of black men and white women" (p. 118). Black feminist research on U.S. higher education focuses on the experiences of Black women scholars and students. Recent studies include examinations of identity development in Black women undergraduates (Porter, 2013) and graduate student experiences (Patton, 2009; Patton, Njoku, & Rogers, 2015; Robinson, 2013). Outside the United States, Black feminists have defended the equality of Black women and men; connected theory, practice, and politics; and consciously engaged in feminist praxis. These scholars research topics such as equity and diversity in the academy (Wane, 2009), the Black female research experience (Maylor, 2009), pedagogies and politics in higher education (Ali, 2009), and problems and paradoxes for Black feminists (Ahmed, 2009). Black feminist scholars have brought forward a perspective long ignored, undervalued, and rejected in higher education and are demonstrating how their voices influence research and practice in substantial, generative ways.

Feminist Perspectives. There is no consensus on the definition of feminist theory and research in education, although scholars generally agree that it exposes the obvious and obscure gender power relations that influence the content and structure of knowledge production (Ramazanoğlu, 2002). Feminist theorists aim to center women in their scholarship and highlight their diverse experiences, and the institutions that shape their circumstances, thereby creating more equitable circumstances for all genders. Feminist inquiry often takes the form of women's narratives in which different perspectives merge in a "new synthesis that in turn becomes the grounds for further research, praxis, and policy" (Olesen, 2000, p. 216). Reflecting an epistemology in which the researcher and researched are closely connected, "feminist theory researchers question the utility, morality and truthfulness of drawing distinct, impermeable lines" between investigator and participant

(Broido & Manning, 2002, p. 442). Focusing on subjectivity, multiple truths and voices, and ethics in research, feminist scholars, along with critical race, queer, and other identity theorists, are opening more avenues for understanding a broader perspective of the human experience.

Feminist theory derives from the history of feminism in the United States, which emerged in three historical waves spanning the late nineteenth and early twentieth centuries (first wave), the 1960s through 1990s (second wave), and the 1990s to present (third wave) (Krolokke & Sorensen, 2005). Middle class White women led the transformation in the first wave and largely excluded women of color from the movement. Out of the second wave grew separate movements that yielded uneven results for Black, Chicana/Latina, and White feminists (Roth, 2004), with White women again reaping most of the benefit (Nicholson & Pasque, 2011). Women of color, lesbian women, and women with disabilities became more radicalized during this time. Significant events that resulted from the U.S. women's movement during the second wave included legislative approval of Title VII of the Civil Rights Act of 1964 and Title IX of the Educational Amendments of 1972, as well as the *Roe v. Wade* Supreme Court decision and creation of the National Organization for Women (NOW) (Taylor, 1998).

The third wave of feminism from the 1990s to the present breaks gender boundaries and, sometimes filtered through postcolonialism and postmodernism, stirs up "disagreement around identity politics between feminists" (Nicholson & Pasque, 2011, p. 5). Feminist theories evolving from the three waves were numerous, including liberal feminism, radical feminism, Black feminism, womanism, and Marxist and socialist feminism (Nicholson & Pasque, 2011). Student affairs educators use theories that emerged from some of this work, including models of moral development (see Gilligan in Chapter Fifteen), cognitive development (see Belenky, Clinchy, Goldberger, and Tarule in Chapter Fourteen), and social identity development (see Chapter Four).

Intersectionality. A framework steeped in critical underpinnings, intersectionality (Bowleg, 2008; Crenshaw, 1991; Dill & Zambrana, 2009) highlights the complexities of lived experience while discovering relationships "between identity and intersecting systems of inequality" (Abes, 2012, p. 189). It recognizes that all people possess multiple, intersecting identities; these identities influence and constitute one another; and as a result individuals experience the paradox of simultaneous marginalization and privilege. Emerging from critical race theory and critical race feminism, intersectionality began as a strategy to focus on the marginalization of women of color and their experience of marginality at the intersection of their multiple identities in the legal context

(Crenshaw, 1989; 1991). Intersectionality has gained traction in education research and provides "a non-reductionist framework for the complicated and complicating ways that different differences interact and shift across various contingencies to shape all aspects of our lives" (Lather, 2006, p. 50).

Some scholars frame intersectionality as "a perspective on theory that may be useful in examining student development theories" (Renn & Reason, 2013, p. 167) from the viewpoint of identifying who benefits and does not in the construction and application of complex, intersecting identities. Intersectionality is not a student development theory, but it can be used to understand the contexts in which individuals develop. It embraces praxis—an orientation of consistent reflection on the interchange between theory and practice (Freire, 1970/1997)—and embraces a commitment to social justice (Jones & Abes, 2013).

Cutting-edge student development theorists (see Jones & Abes, 2013; Patton, 2011; Stewart, 2009) push boundaries "to build upon linear models to examine the complexity of students' experiences with power, privilege, and oppression" (Linder, 2015). For instance, Jones and Abes (2013) offered a significant contribution to the identity literature by demonstrating how different theoretical viewpoints, often at the borderlands or margins, can explain students' identity development. They pointed to intersections of context, personal characteristics, and social identities. Jones and Abes also incorporated autoethnographic details to reveal their stance intertwined with student voices and to make clear the epistemological underpinnings and theoretical backbone of their study.

Postcolonialism. Postcolonial theory accounts for the global history of imperialism and its lasting effects on shaping contemporary societies. It spotlights "the worldwide oppression against the 'other' and the ability of dominant groups to define the terms of being and nonbeing, of civilized and uncivilized, of developed and undeveloped, of human and non-human" (Ladson-Billings & Donnor, 2005, p. 67). Postcolonial theory is helpful specifically for thinking about the influence of European colonialism and Euro-American imperialism on societies around the world, as well as who within those societies has been minoritized as a result of this domination (Hickling-Hudson, 1998). As noted earlier, we use the terms "minoritized" and "majoritized" here and throughout the remainder of this book, rather than "minority" and "majority," because the former makes clear that dominant groups enforce minority status on nondominant groups, creating minoritized groups and, by extension, majoritized groups. Postcolonial studies demand a denunciation of white privilege and centering of the dominant, nonindigenous culture.

For student development theory, postcolonialism urges a move away from a unitary view of identity, to an "understanding of self and identities as mutating formations, not absolute states of existence" (Zaytoun, 2006, p. 56). Student affairs educators in the United States and other colonized territories can use postcolonial thinking to examine how theory and practice reinforce dominant norms. All higher education professionals considering the use of student development theories to inform their work should be cautious about how modern-day colonization of student services and practices can occur despite the best intentions. Educators should be aware that the theories highlighted in this book were based on research in the United States, with U.S. student populations; hence U.S.-based thought and tradition would likely inform the application of these theories in practice.

Poststructuralism. Poststructuralist theory interrupts the linear, structured, causal relationships of traditional science and instead offers "nuanced understandings of subjects' positionings in relation to social and institutional discourses" (Talburt, 2010, pp. 111–112). Defying stable categories or positions, poststructural theory enlarges the notion of what is considered "normal" (Renn, 2012). Classifying identity as a social construction, poststructural theorists deconstruct and reconstruct identity, believing that "all knowledge and meaning are historically and culturally bound" (Renn, 2012, p. 22). Rooted in the humanities, specifically literary studies, and subsequently fused into the social sciences, poststructuralism stands in contrast to the linearity, absolute certainty, and structured hierarchy of modernism and its research counterparts.

Poststructuralism "seeks to encourage ambivalence and multiplicity, exceed the boundaries of what can be imagined, expose dichotomies and illusions, and advocate for resistance to subjugation" (Jones, Torres, & Arminio, 2006, p. 21). The ephemeral nature of poststructuralism makes "truth" difficult to capture and generalizability temporal at best. Assuming many options for how society can be structured (Rhoads & Black, 1995), poststructuralism often attaches to other critical lenses: for example, queer theory (Abes, 2009; Abes & Kasch, 2007; Narui, 2011; Renn, 2010; Torres et al., 2009), critical race theory (Cabrera, 2014; Ledesma & Calderón, 2015; Solórzano et al., 2000; Villalpando, 2003), revolutionary Black feminism (Neville & Hamer, 2001), and feminism (Hoffman, Iverson, Allan, & Ropers-Huilman, 2010; St. Pierre, 2000).

Queer Theory. Queer theory exposes the differential power structures that exist among socially constructed groups and identities. Queer theory also illuminates the manner in which power structures unfold and reinforce ideas of normativity to maintain dominant and marginalized groups. A poststructural perspective, queer theory emerged from philosophy (for example, Derrida, 1967/1978; Foucault, 1978; Lyotard, 1984). In higher education research, queer theory is useful in asking and answering questions related to sexual orientation and gender identities (i.e., asexual, bisexual, gay, heterosexual, lesbian, queer, cisgender, genderqueer, transgender) and to the ways heterosexual and cisgender identities are framed as normative (Abes & Kasch, 2012). Queer theorists assert that sexual and gender identities are constantly constructed, and they prioritize attention to processes of deconstructing categories assigned to gender and sexuality rather than concentrating on any one group (Gamson, 2000).

A key tenet of queer theory is the deconstruction of the idea of false dichotomies such as heterosexual/LGBTQ, cisgender/transgender, and masculine/feminine (Ahmed, 2006; Broido & Manning, 2002). Placing an emphasis on identities that have not always been considered "normal," queer theory opens avenues for recognition, acceptance, and affirmation of fluid sexual and gender identities (Britzman, 1997; see Chapters Seven and Eight for a discussion of these identities).

There is a small but growing body of research using queer theory in higher education and student affairs scholarship (Patton, 2011; Renn, 2010). One study on lesbian identity development (Abes, 2009)—which uses paradigms of queer theory and constructivism, as well as multiple identities—is an excellent example of the way in which challenging dominant epistemological and ontological structures in student development theory places the researcher in "theoretical borderlands." In this analysis, Abes (2009) unveils new ways to conduct research through multiple paradigms and multiple identities; she reconciles these differences while avoiding comparisons of heteronormativity and queer. Abes's scholarship opens up contemporary ways to deal with "policies, programs, and curriculum that might best support student learning and development" (Renn, 2010, p. 135).

Content and Process Theories and Models

We turn now from worldviews or paradigms to content and process theories and models that help student affairs and other postsecondary educators address the needs of college students. Although not all are constructed from a developmental lens, they offer insight into aspects of development and developmental processes not highlighted elsewhere. Indeed some give a temporal snapshot of influences on students' characteristics, environments, and experiences that influence developmental opportunities and processes. Unlike the majority of theories and models detailed in this book, which focus on individual development, content and process theories deepen an understanding of student development by focusing primarily on person-environment interaction—not *what* is being developed, but *where* and *how* development takes place.

We do not intend readers to consider the theories we present here as absolute and universal, yet there are some general concepts that appear to be durable and adaptable to multiple, diverse students and higher education contexts. A substantial research base indicates that college students who are involved in meaningful activity (Astin, 1984), who experience appropriate challenge and support (Sanford, 1966), who believe they matter (Schlossberg, 1989a), and who are validated by faculty, staff, and peers (Rendón, 1994) are likely to experience increased development as well as success in college. Additionally, helping students identify who they are and how they interact with career choice opportunities (Holland, 1966) and college environments (Bronfenbrenner, 1993) assists them in participating actively in their own holistic development. Finally, lifespan development models, which are grounded in psychology and sociology, offer a brief introduction to the growth patterns of adult learners—including graduate students—as well as the path of traditional-age students long after they graduate (Elder, Johnson, & Crosnoe, 2003).

Involvement (Alexander Astin)

Student involvement theory (Astin, 1984) has overwhelming support in the literature as a key underlying concept in college student development. This theory proposes that meaningful educational engagement in college stimulates increasing cognitive complexity, leading to learning and development (Renn & Reason, 2013). Defining involvement as "the amount of physical and psychological energy that the student devotes to the academic experience" (Astin, 1984, p. 297), the theory refers to behavior—what the student actually does—rather than the student's feelings or thoughts. Astin included five postulates to ground his theory:

1. "Involvement refers to the investment of physical and psychological energy in various objects." An object is anything from the student experience as a whole to a specific activity, such as an intramural volleyball game.

2. "Regardless of the object, involvement occurs along a continuum." Some students invest more energy than other students, and any particular student may be more involved in certain activities than others.

3. "Involvement has both quantitative and qualitative features." A quantitative aspect of involvement centers on the amount of time devoted to an activity, while a qualitative component is the seriousness with which the object was approached and the attention given to it.

4. "The amount of student learning and personal development associated with any educational program is directly proportional to the quality and quantity of student involvement in that program." Basically, the more energy students put into an activity, the more benefits they accumulate.

5. "The effectiveness of any educational policy or practice is directly related to the capacity of that policy or practice to increase student involvement." (Astin, 1984, p. 298)

Rather than examining developmental growth, Astin's involvement theory focuses on factors facilitating development. Engaging actively in the environment is a prerequisite for student learning and growth. College and university educators play a significant role in creating opportunities for students to be involved in meaningful and transformational educational experiences outside and inside the classroom, setting the foundation for students to make developmental strides.

Challenge and Support (Nevitt Sanford)

Sanford, a psychologist, was one of the first scholars to address the relationship between college environments and students' transition from late adolescence to young adulthood (Strange, 1994). He brought forth two insights about the process of development—cycles of differentiation and integration, and balancing support and challenge—that are foundational concepts when considering student development (Evans, 2003; King & Kitchener, 1994; Moore & Upcraft, 1990). Differentiation and integration occur as students understand themselves as unique (differentiated) and as members of groups (integrated). These processes are evident when students learn about their own personality characteristics and understand how these characteristics shape their individual identities (Sanford, 1962). Challenges occur in situations for which the individual does not have the skills, knowledge, or attitude to cope (for example, academic, social, psychological). Supports are buffers in the environment that help the student meet challenges to be successful (Sanford, 1967).

Sanford (1966) proposed three developmental conditions: readiness, challenge, and support. One of the first developmental theorists to focus on the idea of student development as a function of person-environment interaction, he contended that individuals cannot exhibit certain behaviors until they are ready to do so. Readiness results because of either the internal processes associated with maturation or beneficial environmental factors.

The amount of challenge a student can tolerate is a function of the amount of support available. Depending on the quality of the challenge and support provided by the environment as well as a student's characteristics, the range of optimal dissonance for any particular student varies. If the environment presents too much challenge, students may do the following: regress to earlier, less adaptive modes of behavior; solidify current modes of behavior; escape the challenge; or ignore the challenge if escape is impossible. If there is too little challenge in the environment, students feel safe and satisfied but their development is limited (Sanford, 1966).

All students face challenges in college and need support to succeed in their educational endeavors. Challenges may be different for traditional age students and returning adult learners, students from majoritized identity groups and those from minoritized groups, domestic and international students, and students who differ in any number of characteristics. If the university environment fails to provide the kind of support this diverse student population needs, or if students do not experience the supports available, then the challenges posed by coursework, family, peers, work, and so forth may be too great, leading to a host of negative outcomes including, at the extreme, leaving higher education.

Mattering and Marginality (Nancy Schlossberg)

Schlossberg (1989a), an adult development theorist, pointed to the importance of considering the concepts of marginality and mattering when examining the impact of the college experience on student development. Feelings of marginality often occur when individuals take on new roles, especially when they are uncertain about what the new role entails. Schlossberg described marginality as a sense of not fitting in that can lead to self-consciousness, irritability, and depression. For members of minoritized groups, marginality is often a permanent condition; others, such as first-year students from dominant populations, may experience these feelings temporarily.

When individuals feel marginalized, they worry if they matter to anyone (Schlossberg, 1989a). Mattering is "our belief, whether right or wrong, that we matter to someone else" (Schlossberg, 1989a, p. 9). Drawing on the work of Rosenberg and his colleagues (cited in Schlossberg, 1989a), Schlossberg investigated four aspects of mattering: *attention,* the feeling an individual is noticed; *importance,* a belief the individual is cared about; *ego-extension,* the feeling that someone else will be proud of what an individual does or will sympathize with their failures; and *dependence,* a feeling of being needed. Based on her own research, Schlossberg added a fifth dimension: *appreciation,* the feeling that others appreciate an individual's efforts. As a precursor to students' involvement in activities and academic programs that facilitate development and learning, higher education institutions should help students feel like they matter (Schlossberg, 1989a).

Transition Theory (Schlossberg)

Grounded in the adult development literature, Schlossberg's theory of transitions includes an examination of what constitutes a transition, different forms of transitions, the transition process, and factors that influence transitions. A transition is "any event, or non-event, [which] results in changed relationships, routines, assumptions, and roles" (Goodman, Schlossberg, & Anderson, 2006, p. 33). Self-perception plays a role in Schlossberg's theory because a transition exists only if defined as such by the individuals experiencing it (Goodman et al., 2006). Changes may occur without individuals attaching much significance to them, in which case these changes would not be considered transitions in this model.

The type, context, and impact of the transition are important to understanding the meaning a transition has for individuals (Goodman et al., 2006). There are three nondiscrete types of transitions: (a) *anticipated transitions,* which occur predictably; (b) *unanticipated transitions,* which are not predictable or scheduled; and (c) *non-events,* transitions that are expected but do not occur. Non-events can be classified as *personal* (related to individual aspirations), *ripple* (felt due to a non-event in the life of someone close), *resultant* (caused by an event), and *delayed* (anticipating an event that may still happen). Non-events are associated more with probability than possibility (Schlossberg & Robinson, 1996). Only when an event is likely to occur but fails to do so does it qualify as a non-event. The meaning attached to transitions by different individuals is relative, as is the way in which the transition is categorized by type.

Context refers to an individual's relationship to the transition (one's own or someone else's) and to the setting in which the transition occurs (work, personal relationships, and so forth). *Impact* is determined by the degree to which a transition alters daily life. Both positive and negative transitions, as perceived by the individual, produce stress. The presence of multiple transitions can compound the stress, which also depends on the ratio of the individual's assets to liabilities at the time the transition occurs.

The Transition Process.   While a transition may be precipitated by a single event or non-event, dealing with a transition is a process that extends over time. Essentially, individuals move from a preoccupation with the transition to an integration of the transition. The time needed to achieve successful integration varies with the person and the transition. Transitions may lead to growth, but decline is also a possible outcome, and individuals experiencing transition may view them with ambivalence. Goodman et al. (2006) endorsed the concept of transitions consisting of a series of phases, which they termed "moving in," "moving through," and "moving out," using the language that Schlossberg (1989b) initially introduced.

The 4 S's of Transition.   Four major sets of factors influence an individual's ability to cope with a transition: situation, self, support, and strategies, known as the "4 S's" (Goodman et al., 2006). The individual's effectiveness in coping with transition depends on the resources in these four areas—in other words, the assets and liabilities individuals possess at that time. The ratio of assets to liabilities helps to explain "why different individuals react differently to the same type of transition and why the same person reacts differently at different times" (Schlossberg, Waters, & Goodman, 1995, p. 57). An individual's appraisal of the transition is an important determinant of the coping process (Goodman et al., 2006). In each instance, people in transition conduct primary and secondary appraisals, which in turn determine their ability to cope. Primary appraisal is an individual's view of the transition itself as positive, negative, or irrelevant. Secondary appraisal is a self-assessment of access to resources for coping with the transition. Both types of appraisal are subject to change as individuals proceed through the transition process. The 4 S's provide a framework for the appraisal process.

Situation.   In examining a situation, the following factors are important:
Trigger—What precipitated the transition?
Timing—Is the transition considered "on time" or "off time" in terms of one's social clock, and is the transition viewed as happening at a "good" or "bad" time?
Control—What does the individual perceive as being within his or her control (for example, the transition itself; one's reaction to it)?
Role change—Is a role change involved and, if so, is it viewed as a gain or a loss?
Duration—Is the transition seen as permanent, temporary, or uncertain?
Previous experience with a similar transition—How effectively did one cope, and what are implications for the current transition?

Concurrent stress—Are multiple sources of stress present?

Assessment—Who or what is seen as responsible for the transition, and how is the individual's behavior affected by this perception?

Self. Factors considered important in relation to the self are classified into two categories: (1) personal and demographic characteristics and (2) psychological resources. *Personal and demographic characteristics* affect how an individual views life. This category includes socioeconomic status, gender, age (emphasizing psychological, social, and functional age over chronological) and stage of life, state of health, and ethnicity/culture. *Psychological resources*, or aids to coping, include the following: ego development; outlook, in particular optimism and self-efficacy; commitment and values; and spirituality and resiliency.

Support. Support comprises three facets: types, functions, and measurement. "Support" in this model refers to social support, and transition theory identifies four types: intimate relationships, family units, networks of friends, and institutions/communities. Affect, affirmation, aid, and honest feedback serve as the functions of support. Incorporating the work of Kahn and Antonucci (1980), Goodman et al. (2006) suggested that social support can be measured by identifying the individual's stable supports, supports that are to some degree role dependent, and supports that are most likely to change.

Strategies. In discussing the fourth "*S*," strategies, descriptions of coping responses fall into three categories (Pearlin & Schooler, 1978): those that modify the situation, those that control the meaning of the problem, and those that aid in managing the stress in the aftermath. In relation to the differing goals reflected by these categories, individuals may also employ four coping modes: information seeking, direct action, inhibition of action, and intrapsychic behavior. Individuals who cope effectively demonstrate flexibility and use multiple methods (Goodman et al.). (Exhibit 2.1 provides a summary of the transition model.)

Validation (Laura Rendón)

In a study examining the experiences of students in college (Rendón, 1994), "traditional students" expressed few concerns about their academic success, while "nontraditional students" (whom Rendón defined as those from diverse racial/ethnic and cultural backgrounds) often doubted their academic ability. Active intervention in the form of validation was needed to encourage nontraditional students to become involved in campus life and enhance their self-esteem. Validation is "an enabling, confirming and supportive process initiated by in- and out-of-class agents that foster academic and interpersonal

Exhibit 2.1. Schlossberg's Transition Model

Transitions: Events or non-events resulting in changed relationships, routines, assumptions, and/or roles.

Meaning for the individual based on:
    <u>type</u>: anticipated, unanticipated, non-event

    <u>context</u>: relationship to transition and the setting

    <u>impact</u>: alterations in daily life

The Transition Process
    reactions over time

    moving in, moving through, and moving out

Coping with Transitions
    Influenced by ratio of assets and liabilities in regard to four sets of factors:

Situation
    trigger, timing, control, role change, duration, previous experience, concurrent stress, assessment

Self
    <u>personal and demographic characteristics</u>: socioeconomic status, gender, age, health, ethnicity/culture

    <u>psychological resources</u>: ego development, outlook, commitment, values, spirituality and resilience

Support
    <u>types</u>: intimate, family, friends, institutional

    <u>functions</u>: affect, affirmation, aid, honest feedback

    <u>measurement</u>: stable and changing supports

Strategies
    <u>3 categories</u>: modify situation, control meaning, manage stress in aftermath

    <u>4 coping modes</u>: information seeking, direct action, inhibition of action, intrapsychic behavior

Source: Compiled from information in Goodman, Schlossberg, and Anderson (2006).

development" (Rendón, 1994, p. 46). Students who were validated developed confidence in their ability to learn, experienced enhanced feelings of self-worth, and believed they had something to offer the academic community. Validation can occur in a variety of settings, including the classroom, student organizations, or the community. Validating agents can be instructors, classmates, student affairs staff, relatives, friends, or other people who are significant to the student in some way.

Validation reflects a process rather than an end goal because "the more students get validated, the richer the academic and interpersonal experience" (Rendón, 1994, p. 44). Validation is most powerful when offered during the early stages of the student's academic experience, preferably during the first few weeks of classes. Validation is necessary for every student but is particularly critical for students who may doubt their ability to succeed. The students in this category vary by institution but may include adult learners, first-generation college students, part-time students, international students, students who discover that their pre-college preparation was different from that of their peers, and minoritized students (see Acevedo-Gil, Santos, Alonso, & Solórzano, 2015; Barnett, 2011; Linares & Muñoz, 2011; Maramba & Palmer, 2014; Tang, Kim, & Haviland, 2015). Evidence is clear that validation promotes student success.

Developmental Ecology (Urie Bronfenbrennner)

Ecology models explain the processes—but not the outcomes—of human development. In higher education they provide a way to understand how students interact with campus environments to promote or inhibit development (Renn & Arnold, 2003). An ecological approach accounts for individual differences and multifaceted contexts in holistic student development. Student affairs educators can use ecological models to understand how student development may occur and to consider how to shape campus environments to promote optimal growth and development for diverse student populations. Developmental psychologist Bronfenbrenner (1979, 1993, 2005) introduced a four-component person-environment theory of development that higher education scholars have adopted. The four components are process, person, context, and time (PPCT). Interactions among these components create an individual student's developmental ecology or environment.

Process. *Process* is at the core of the model and "encompasses particular forms of interaction between organism and environment, called *proximal processes* that operate over time and are posited as the primary mechanisms producing human development" (Bronfenbrenner & Morris, 2006, p. 795). To achieve optimal development, proximal processes should be progressively more complex and be buffered appropriately so as not to overwhelm the developing individual. Student affairs educators recognize these functions as Astin's (1984) theory of involvement and Sanford's (1966) idea of challenge and support.

Person. Bronfenbrenner (1993) proposed that the "attributes of the person most likely to shape the course of development, for better or for worse, are those that induce or inhibit dynamic dispositions toward the immediate environment" (p. 11). He called these attributes *developmentally instigative characteristics* and identified four types. Renn and Arnold (2003) summarized them and offered examples for college students. First are those that act to either invite or inhibit responses from the environment; different students elicit different responses from administrators, peers, and faculty. Second are those of "selective responsivity" that describe how individuals explore and react to surroundings, including such activities as joining student organizations or preferring solitary pursuits. "Structuring proclivities" are third; these relate to how individuals engage or persist in the increasingly complex activities that are keys to development—for example, students who consciously seek more difficult courses or leadership positions exhibit stronger structuring proclivities than those who limit new challenges. "Directive beliefs" are fourth; these describe how individuals experience agency in relation to environments; high-achieving students who believe that their accomplishments are the result of hard work directed at appropriate academic targets demonstrate these characteristics.

Developmentally instigative characteristics influence how individuals experience environments and how environments respond to them. In these person-environment interactions, "developmentally instigative characteristics do not *determine* the course of development; rather, they may be thought of as 'putting a spin' on a body in motion. The effect of that spin depends on other forces, and resources, in the total ecological system" (Bronfenbrenner, 1993, p. 14). The "force-resource" approach echoes Sanford's (1966) principles of challenge and support.

Context. Bronfenbrenner (1979, 1993) proposed a nested series of four levels of *context.* The person is in the center, surrounded by the *microsystem, mesosystem, exosystem,* and *macrosystem.* The micro-, meso-, exo- and macrosystems are where the work of development occurs, as an individual's developmentally instigative characteristics inhibit or provoke reactions—forces and resources—from the environment in the course of proximal processes. Renn and Arnold (2003) represented the context component of the PPCT model as nested circles Figure 2.1.

FIGURE 2.1. AN EXAMPLE OF THE CONTEXT OF COLLEGE STUDENT DEVELOPMENT

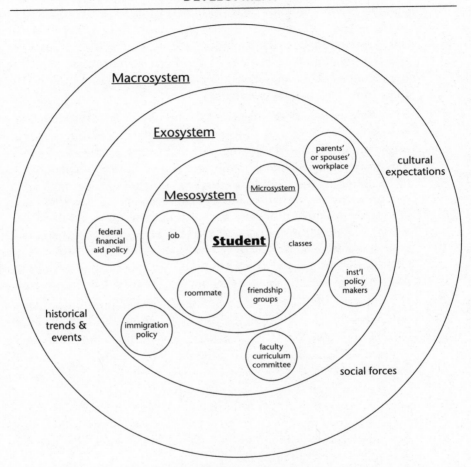

Source: From Renn and Arnold (2003). Copyright: The Ohio State University Press.

Microsystems. "A microsystem is a pattern of activities, roles, and interpersonal relations experienced by the developing persons in a given face-to-face setting with particular physical, social, and symbolic features that invite, permit, or inhibit engagement in sustained, progressively more complex interaction with, and activity in, the immediate environment" (Bronfenbrenner, 1993, p. 15). We extend this definition by including digitally mediated spaces in which contemporary students learn and construct identities. Renn and Arnold (2003) suggested that roommates, friendship groups, work settings, athletic teams, families, and faculty relationships represented potential microsystems for students. Higher education researchers often study one microsystem at a time (for example, student-faculty relationships, peer groups, sports teams), but an ecological approach requires examining important interactions *between and among* microsystems. Bronfenbrenner accounted for these interactions in the mesosytem.

Mesosystems. As defined by Bronfenbrenner (1993), a mesosystem "comprises linkages and processes taking place between two or more settings containing the developing person. Special attention is focused on the synergistic effects created by the interaction of developmentally instigative or inhibitory features and processes present in each setting" (p. 22). The synergy across microsystems and webs of mesosystems create additional possibilities for proximal processes that promote development. Renn and Arnold (2003) noted that institutions with highly consonant mesosystems—military academies, for example—create ecosystems that favor certain developmentally instigative characteristics. Students with these characteristics will thrive, while their peers with equal ability but unfavorable characteristics may not.

Exosystems. Exosystems do not contain developing individuals but exert influences on their environments through interactions with the microsystems (Bronfenbrenner, 1993). Exosystems that may affect students include parents' or partners' workplaces, institutional decision makers who make tuition and financial aid policies, faculty curriculum committees, federal financial aid policies, and immigration and visa agencies (Renn & Arnold, 2003). The exosystem provides a mechanism to examine factors outside the institution that influence students' environments. They also provide a way to address a diversity of student experiences—adult students with full-time jobs and families, for example—in student development discussions.

Macrosystems. The broadest level of context in the developmental ecology model is the macrosystem. The macrosystem "consists of the overarching pattern of micro- meso- and exosystems characteristic of a given culture, subculture, or other extended social structure, with particular reference to the developmentally instigative belief systems, resources, hazards, lifestyles, opportunity structures, life course options and patterns of social interchange that are embedded in such overarching systems" (Bronfenbrenner, 1993, p. 25). Renn and Arnold (2003) claimed that macrosystems encompass "meritocratic notions derived from democratic values and capitalist ideology," as well as "cultural understandings of gender, race, and ethnicity" (p. 273).

Macrosystems shape college-going (that is, who goes to college and who goes to what college), as do sociohistoric influences related to economics, the workforce, and societal values.

Time. Developmental ecology is concerned with time in individual lives and across the lifespan (Bronfenbrenner & Morris, 2006). Bronfenbrenner and Morris described *time* at three levels: "*Microtime* refers to continuity versus discontinuity in ongoing episodes of proximal process. *Mesotime* is the periodicity of these episodes across broader time intervals, such as days and weeks. Finally, *Macrotime* focuses on the changing expectations and events in the larger society, both within and across generations, as they affect and are affected by, processes and outcomes of human development over the life course" (p. 796, italics in original). Renn and Arnold (2003) provided examples of time operating in the developmental ecologies of college students: (1) the timing of family events (birth of a sibling, parents' divorce, family move) in a young person's life and (2) the timing of college attendance (for example, immediately after high school, returning after working for a time).

Taken together, the process, person, context, and time create a useful heuristic for understanding student development. They can provide a snapshot of one moment of a student's development-in-progress, or they can serve as a terrain on which to map the locations of development across a number of domains. Student development scholars have used ecological models to study student identities such as race and ethnicity (Guardia & Evans, 2008; Hoffman & Peña, 2013; Renn, 2003, 2004) and campus contexts such as academic advising (Stebleton, 2011), residential colleges (Jessup-Anger, 2012), and White students at Historically Black Colleges and Universities (HBCUs) (Peterson, 2014).

Person-Environment Theory (Holland)

Holland (1997) explored satisfaction, achievement, persistence, and degree of "fit" between persons and the environments in which they find themselves. Seeking to explain vocational behavior, Holland introduced concepts that are also useful in explaining behavior in social and educational settings. Like the other theories in this section, Holland (1997) does not describe a developmental trajectory. He explains person-environment fit and begins with three major assumptions. First, to varying degrees, people resemble each of six personality types. Second, there are also six model environments that parallel qualities and attributes of each personality type. Third, people seek out environments that provide them with opportunities to use their talents and express their values and attitudes—that is, people seek out environments made up of individuals similar to themselves.

Specific interests, behaviors, attitudes, and belief systems comprise Holland's (1997) six personality types. These personality types fit differently into diverse environments. They resemble ecological approaches in that different environments favor different characteristics, behaviors, and so forth. Here we review the six personality types:

Realistic people tend to be interested in and prefer activities that involve working with objects, tools, machines, and animals. They are persistent, thrifty, no-nonsense, and practical.

Investigative types prefer activities that call for systematic investigation designed to understand physical, biological, or cultural phenomena and to solve problems. They can be described as inquisitive, analytical, intellectual, precise, and cautious.

Artistic people prefer spontaneous, creative, unregulated activities that lead to the creation of various art forms. They value aesthetic qualities such as self-expression and tend to be emotional, expressive, imaginative, and impulsive.

Social individuals prefer activities that involve working with others in ways that educate, inform, cure, or enlighten. They value helping others and engaging in social activities. Social types can be described as helpful, friendly, and empathetic.

Enterprising types prefer working with other people to achieve organizational goals or material outcomes. They value political and economic achievement and tend to be optimistic, extroverted, self-confident, resourceful, and adventurous.

Conventional types like activities that involve working with data in systematic, orderly, and explicit ways. They value business and administration, and can be described as careful, conscientious, efficient, orderly, and practical.

These types combine to form personality profiles consisting of two to six types, but most typically three. The dominant type is listed first, the second most dominant appears second, and so forth. The environment is the situation or atmosphere created by those who dominate the context and reflects the typical characteristics of its members. So an individual who is Enterprising, Social, and Investigative might fit well in a professional environment, such as student affairs administration, that values leadership, empathy, and evidence-based decision making.

Four secondary assumptions apply to both personality types and environments. These assumptions help explain how people and environments interact and how types influence behavior.

Consistency refers to the degree to which pairs of types are related. Holland (1997) hypothesized that some types are more similar to each other than they are to other types.

Differentiation refers to the degree to which a person or an environment is well defined. A differentiated person has interests that are characteristic of mainly one type (for example, interests that are associated only with the Realistic type), while an undifferentiated person has a variety of interests characteristic of many different types (for example, Realistic, Social, and Enterprising). Environments that are differentiated include a predominance of people of one type.

Identity refers to the "clarity and stability" (Holland, 1997, p. 5) of the person's goals, interests, and abilities or, in an environment, the degree to which goals, tasks, and rewards are stable over time.

Congruence, the most influential of these factors, refers to the degree of "match" between a person and an environment. Perfect congruence occurs, for example, when a Social person is in a Social environment. Congruent environments provide opportunities for individuals to use their skills and interests and reward them for doing so. Incongruent environments, however, may present challenges and promote feelings of discomfort.

Student development scholars use the Holland Types, as this theory is known colloquially, to study a range of topics, many of which relate to careers, academic majors, and students' fit with them. For example, Holland Types framed the study of low-income prospective first-generation college students (Garriott, Flores, & Martens, 2013), high-impact learning experiences and graduate school plans (Rocconi, Ribera, & Laird, 2014), and major changes and academic outcomes (Pozzebon, Ashton, & Visser, 2014). There have been extensions to the theory as well (see Pike, Smart, & Ethington, 2012; Tracey, Wille, Durr, & De Fruyt, 2014), and the theory is in common use especially in vocational and career development contexts. The cross-cultural applicability of the Holland Types—including their applicability across genders, races, ethnicities, and nationalities—is a matter of inquiry (see Fouad

& Kantamneni, 2011). It is important to understand the areas of agreement and disagreement in the research literature in relation to its use with diverse college students. Finally, behavior results from the interaction of the person and the environment.

Life Span Approaches

In the middle of the twentieth century, lifespan descriptions based on "facts and concepts" (Chickering & Havighurst, 1990, p. 17) allowed social scientists to expound on individual personal and social development over decades of life. Scholars identified patterns, some clearly age-linked (Buehler, 1962). Erikson's (1950, 1959/1980) psychosocial theory of development was a big step in examining development across the lifespan (see Chapter Thirteen) and has inspired a wide scope of venues for investigation. Psychosocial theorists who followed Erikson in the study of adult development adhere mainly to psychological or sociological perspectives. Life stage, life events and transition, and life course approaches move from an internal focus (highlighting psychology) to an external focus (with an emphasis on sociology and environments) (Evans, 2011). Adding to the diversity of perspectives, integrative models that incorporate biological, sociological, and psychological facets of development (for example Bronfenbrenner, 2005; Magnusson, 1995) contribute to the literature.

Life Stage Perspectives. Life stage perspectives posit that most individuals experience change that appears dictated by an internal clock, as influenced by environmental factors. In this life stage approach, individuals become unique and complex as they grow older. Always linear, life stage developmental tasks are predictable and build on each other so that one is finished before the next begins. Generally, these theories either are tied explicitly to age (Levinson, 1978, 1996) or are not tied to age but still occur in a sequential order (Howell & Beth, 2002).

Life Events and Transition Perspectives. This approach explores how individuals deal with life transitions and the significant events that often determine life change and course. Evans (2011) framed these cultural life events around "timing, duration, spacing, and ordering" (p. 173). Different from the previous lifespan approach, life events and transitions perspectives are not ruled by predictable patterns. Instead, this approach highlights the meaning individuals give to critical life events and how they manage the spin-off of these periods of change. Examples of critical life events might include entering or ending a committed partnership or marriage, becoming a parent, losing a job, or starting graduate school. When these events occur, how long they last, how far apart one is from the next one, and the order in which they occur all determine how individuals experience life's transitions. These elements are similar to other models such as transition (Schlossberg) and ecology (Bronfenbrenner).

Life Course Perspectives. More than the preceding two perspectives, life course perspectives stress the unpredictability of human growth and development and the importance of the environment in individual change. Three foci form the basis for life course perspectives: what roles individuals take over a lifetime (Ferraro, 2001), when life events occur (Bengtson, 1996), and how individuals build and respond to their environment (Elder, 1994). Life course perspectives are socially constructed, which means that society influences what individuals believe about the roles they undertake such as parent, friend, and partner (Hughes & Graham, 1990). As a theoretical view across the lifespan, life course perspectives also consider the individual's impact on modifying, redefining, or losing important roles in life. Timing of events (Neugarten, 1979), linking of significant others' individual lives, and how they unfold in the context of current and historical time (Elder, 1994) all affect life course perspectives.

What's Next?

Offering an array of perspectives, the paradigms, worldviews, theories, and processes presented in this chapter highlight the complexity of assumptions and knowledges underlying student development research and practice. The expansion of worldviews is likely to continue as minoritized experiences, viewpoints, and identities become the focus of theorizing and research. The interconnection of academic fields, scholars, and ideas through digital media facilitates the spread of new perspectives, even as it reinforces the dominance of the status quo. Student affairs educators are positioned to carry forward the elements of older paradigms that guide practice in equitable and socially just ways and to embrace new paradigms that create space for the holistic development of all students, regardless of backgrounds and identities. Student development scholars are also positioned to contribute new theories and new ways of understanding college student development. We encourage readers to explore the worldviews and frameworks discussed here and use them to analyze, understand, and critique the theories we present in the remainder of the book.

Discussion Questions

1. What are paradigms and worldviews, and why are they important to understand when studying student development theory?
2. Define epistemology, ontology, and methodology and describe how these research terms relate to paradigms/worldviews.
3. What are the defining characteristics of positivist/post-positivist, constructivist, and critical/cultural paradigms?
4. Name three of the critical or cultural paradigms and discuss how they relate to one another. What are the connections and differences across them?
5. Choose a topic about college students that interests you. Now frame this topic (i.e., epistemology, ontology, and methodology) within each of the three paradigms (i.e. positivist/post-positivist, constructivist, and critical/cultural paradigms). How would you study that topic based upon your selected paradigm? What questions would you ask? How would you go about collecting data?
6. How do content and process models promote more in-depth understanding of college student development? What are some strengths and weaknesses of these models?
7. Identify and briefly describe two of the content and process models. Provide an example of how the model could shape student affairs practice.
8. How do lifespan models contribute to a more complex understanding of college student development?

CHAPTER THREE

USING STUDENT DEVELOPMENT THEORY

In the previous two chapters, we described student development theory, provided the historical roots of theory, and discussed theoretical worldviews and processes for understanding student development theory. In this chapter, we offer recommendations for using student development theory. As faculty members in higher education and student affairs programs, we are aware of how common it is for graduate students and new professionals to express frustration about how best to apply the plethora of student development theories to diverse student experiences and how to use them to inform intentional and thoughtful practice. How can student affairs educators possibly choose among so many theories? What theories are the most useful in making sense of college students' development? Similarly, we see student affairs educators make decisions in their practice either through implicit, informal theories or no theories at all. Although using intuition, hunches, or informal theories to guide practice works in some cases, being more intentional when using theory in practice results in better professional practice (Evans & Guido, 2012). In this chapter, we support the use of formal theory in practice and provide examples of how to apply theory when working with college students.

This chapter begins with explaining the role of theory and ideas for evaluating theory. We then discuss cautionary considerations when using student development theories followed by several challenges of using student development theories. The final portion focuses on adopting an integrative perspective to using student development theory. Given the large number of theories, we recommend using them holistically and provide examples of what such an integrative framework might entail.

The Role of Theory

As explained in Chapter One, theory results from the need people have to engage in sensemaking of their lives and experiences. Theory enables the organization and interpretation of enormous amounts of information existing in the world. All people have a set of organizing principles, or "informal theories," that they use to make sense of experiences. Early in the evolution of student development theory, Parker (1977) defined *informal theory* as "the body of common knowledge that allows us to make implicit connections among events and persons in our environment and upon which we act in everyday life" (p. 420). This definition holds true today.

McEwen (2003a) asserted that each student affairs educator has informal theories about students, environments, and human development. Unfortunately, informal theory is not self-correcting (Parker, 1977). People have no basis upon which to determine if their interpretations are accurate or not. The professional field of student affairs needs formal theories, validated by research, to ascertain whether individuals' perceptions hold for the students with whom they work and the situations in which they find themselves. Rodgers (1980) defined formal theory in student development as "a set of propositions regarding the interrelationship of two or more conceptual variables relevant to some realm of phenomena" (p. 81). Theory helps to explain how variables interact and provides a framework for the study of these relationships.

We shared in Chapter One that student development theory is useful to "describe, explain, predict, influence outcomes, assess practice, and generate new knowledge and research" (Jones & Abes, 2011, p. 151). At the first level, description, theory provides a conceptualization of what is happening. For example, Chickering and Reisser (1993) identified a series of developmental issues, such as developing competence and managing emotions, to describe college student experiences (see Chapter Thirteen). At the explanatory level, theory can be used to explain the causes of behavior. For example, Perry's (1968) theory of cognitive development suggests that some students exhibit dualistic, either/or thinking, which might explain why a student is having trouble in a course that involves a great deal of analysis and evaluation of arguments (see Chapter Fourteen). Prediction is the goal at the third level. A powerful theory might enable individuals to predict the developmental outcome of mixing students with different levels of moral development in a class discussion setting. Kohlberg's (1969) theory suggests that exposure to students who reason at "plus one" stage above will prompt students in earlier developmental stages to develop more complex ways of moral reasoning (see Chapter Fifteen).

At the level of influencing outcomes, theory might guide student affairs educators to design learning communities that promote cross-cultural dialogue, which contributes to intercultural development (Pascarella & Terenzini, 2005). Theory is also useful in assessing practice. Any number of theories in this book could provide useful outcomes for program and curricular assessment. Finally, theories are useful for generating research and new knowledge. For example, many theories in this book are interconnected and inform the development of one another. Baxter Magolda's work on self-authorship (see Chapter Sixteen) emerged from her understanding of Perry's cognitive development schema (Chapter Fourteen) and Belenky and colleagues' "women's ways of knowing" (Chapter Fourteen). Student development theories are individually and collectively useful in student affairs practice, assessment, and scholarship.

Evaluating Theory

The number of student development theories has increased significantly since 1965. Not all theories are of equal value to educators. In the 1970s, two student development scholars provided guidance that remains relevant today. Walsh (1973) noted that to be useful, theories must exhibit the following qualities: (a) *comprehensiveness*—a theory should make predictions that account for a wide range of behavior; (b) *clarity and explicitness*—concepts and relationships should be defined precisely; (c) *consistency*—a theory should allow for inclusion of findings within a logical framework; (d) *parsimony*—explanations should be concise, simple, and easy to follow; and (e) *heurism*—a theory should generate ideas for research (Walsh).

Lee Knefelkamp (1978) suggested a number of questions for evaluating the utility of theory that also remain helpful today:

1. *Upon what population is the theory based?* It is important to determine the population upon which the theory was based and whether the theory has been tested with people who have different characteristics. Some aspects of the theory may be specific to the original population, while other concepts may apply to people more generally.
2. *How was the theory developed?* The assessment instruments or techniques that were used in the original study should be clearly described.
3. *Is the theory descriptive?* Does the theory provide a comprehensive view of individuals' development and specific aspects of the developmental process?

4. *Is the theory explanatory?* Does the theory outline how development occurs?
5. *Is the theory prescriptive?* Does the theory discuss ways in which specific outcomes can be produced and lead to the prediction of events or relationships that can be verified through observation or experimentation?
6. *Is the theory heuristic?* Theory should generate research ideas.
7. *Is the theory useful in practice?* Student development theory should help in understanding students, in developing programs to serve them, and in evaluating the effectiveness of services provided.

Most theories fall short on one or more of these criteria. For example, most student development theories are largely descriptive rather than explanatory or predictive. It is also important to remember that no theory is absolutely objective (McEwen, 2003a). Each theory reflects the perspective of its author. However, existing theories are sources of awareness that serve as a means for helping educators to organize, think, and guide the choices they make while working with students.

Cautions and Challenges in Using Student Development Theories

In this book, we introduce a number of student development theories, and there are likely other theories that could guide educational practice. It can be challenging for professionals at any level to learn theories well enough to use them in practice, especially when the theories are new to readers. Initially identifying a few theories that make sense and seem to explain development in a helpful, useful way is a good strategy for determining which theories to study in depth and use in practice. However, it is important to be aware of the limitations of theories when used in practice and to consider the context in which theory application occurs. As an example, given different institutional contexts, student affairs educators might apply racial or ethnic identity development theories differently to Black students' experiences at historically Black colleges or universities (HBCUs) than to those at predominantly White institutions (PWIs). This example illustrates how theories can rarely be applied in "whole chunks," without regard to context. Specific concepts and ideas associated with a particular theory can be useful in certain cases, while other concepts from the same theory may not apply in practice. The ability to identify theoretical concepts applicable in professional contexts is an important skill worth developing.

Cautions in Using Student Development Theory. We offer three cautions in using student development theory. First, individuals must understand the undergirding assumptions of theories. Since the contexts in which people use theories are diverse, it is necessary to scan the environment to see what challenges students face. For example, an educator might see that first-generation students struggle with understanding certain institutional norms and unspoken expectations that continuing generation college students take for granted. A theory of college transition specifically focused on a particular level of students' integration into the academic and social milieu of campus might miss key aspects of first-generation students' experiences and identity. Thinking theoretically means paying attention to assumptions, sensing how theories are limited, and determining how else to understand students' development.

Second, we caution against the use of shorthand terms as broad descriptors for students. When applying theories to practice, it is easy to use labels to describe students. For example, some educators might label students as "dualist" (i.e., a term used by cognitive development researchers to describe yes or no, all or nothing thinking). Carefully explaining the meaning of terms and presenting evidence to support their use is a wise strategy for practice. For example, rather than saying students are "dualist," it would be preferable to say their behaviors reflect thinking from a dualistic perspective. This change in language leaves room for alternative explanations but also helps describe and assess student behaviors and propose ways to prompt changes in those behaviors when change would be desirable.

A third caution in using student development theory is that theories are descriptive and do not indicate what behaviors or changes are best for students. Given the Westernized, Eurocentric value system on which most of these theories are based, this caution is especially important. Also, students are unique individuals. Theoretical concepts need to be evaluated in light of individual differences, meaning that the student must always take precedence over theory. Educators must also avoid the tendency to view students as inert substances that can be manipulated in desired directions. The role of educators is to provide scaffolding opportunities that empower students, rather than to make decisions for them. Since student development theory does not explain all behavior, it is critical to acknowledge both its benefits and shortcomings. Keeping these caveats at the forefront will help in using various theories to make sense of students' experiences and guide professional practice.

Challenges in Using Student Development Theory. Despite the helpful suggestions in Robert Reason and Ezekiel Kimball's (2012) theory-to-practice model (described in depth shortly), challenges still exist when using theory to guide daily professional practice. Student affairs educators are often asked to do more with fewer resources; thus, time is often a challenge. In addition, student affairs educators often face competing priorities, such as assessing the needs of a student in crisis while also maintaining quality supervision of multiple student staff members, which presents challenges for determining which priorities are most important at any given time. Some professionals hold the false belief that using theory in practice takes more time than practice alone. We maintain that thoughtful practice informed by theory takes no more time than practice based on no theory at all. Engaging in intentional, theory-based practice does take effort, which can develop into a professional habit that flows expediently regardless of the situation or priority. Still, we acknowledge that learning to use theory in practice takes time.

Another obstacle in using theory is educators' lack of knowledge or inability to remember theories they previously learned. Student affairs educators need access to literature that discusses existing and newly introduced theories, as well as ongoing research and innovative uses of theory. Examination of literature should be a regular component of staff training programs, as well as an individually initiated activity.

Educators may also encounter "theoretical resistance" among colleagues and students who dismiss the knowledge base of theories (Patton & Harper, 2009). These attitudes may arise from a lack of understanding the value of theories or a desire to avoid having to stay current with literature and learn new information. Colleagues who did not have the benefit of a student affairs education may not be aware that there is a rich theoretical base to guide the field, or they may worry that they will seem unprepared when others openly discuss theory in practice. Demonstrating the effective use of theory may help to convince others of its value (Reason & Kimball, 2012). Moreover, making it accessible to colleagues who did not complete a graduate program in student affairs, or may have finished their graduate work years ago is equally important.

In some instances, student affairs educators perceive developmental activities as too expensive, perhaps due to their belief that implementing developmental theory requires costly instruments or expensive labor to analyze data. However, most theories do not cost anything to implement, and informal assessments can be substituted where assessment is needed. The question of whether trial-and-error is likely to be less expensive in the long run deserves to be raised, especially if programs are ineffective or result in students who, for example, decide to leave the institution due to insufficient scaffolding for their developmental challenges. Overall, using theory to better understand students' experiences and as a basis for programming and policy decisions is inexpensive and can be helpful.

Student affairs educators can employ different strategies for dealing with the challenges we describe. These strategies include providing solid rationales, avoiding jargon, using language and approaches appropriate to the audience (for example, using theory, research, and data to promote ideas with faculty), building alliances, persuading staff members one at a time, being unobtrusive, identifying and using windows of opportunity, using pilot programs, demonstrating perseverance, and recognizing and celebrating successes in using theory in practice. Helping others—such as professional staff, faculty, and graduate students—become familiar with the content of theory and its potential uses in a straightforward manner can render theories more user-friendly. Helping potential users see connections between theory and their own experiences and demonstrating (as opposed to telling) how theory has been used successfully facilitates openness to theory among those who are unfamiliar with the content and its value.

Integrative Approaches to Using Student Development Theory

Student development theories fall into several categories, or families, depending on the domain of development or object of the theory. We organized this book by families, with social identity development followed by psychosocial identity, cognitive/epistemological, moral, and self-authorship, which integrates interpersonal, intrapersonal, and cognitive dimensions. In fact, we believe that it is impossible to isolate one aspect of a student's experience, identity, or development for the purposes of singular focus. Students bring their whole selves into every encounter, and those selves are likely to be complex and varied across domains. A student with sophisticated ways of thinking about gender identity may express less complexity in moral reasoning, and demonstrate expertise in some kinetic-cognitive development such as elite-level athletics or musical performance.

Given the importance of focusing on students' whole selves, we advocate for an integrative approach when using and applying student development theories. In this section, we offer three ideas for what an integrative approach might entail. We begin with Reason and Kimball's (2012) theory-to-practice model. Then we discuss what a theoretical borderlands

(Abes, 2009) approach can offer, before closing this section by highlighting the importance of listening to students' stories (Coles, 1989).

Theory-to-Practice Model

Perhaps one of the most difficult considerations in translating theories to practice is deciding which theories to use and how to use them in practice. Reason and Kimball (2012) proposed a theory-to-practice model (Figure 3.1) that combines four elements: formal theory, institutional context, informal theory, and practice. Formal theories are systematic descriptions of how college students develop. Most of the theories discussed in this book are examples of formal theories—they have gone through rigorous development and assessment by researchers. Informal theories, on the other hand, are implicit assumptions that student affairs educators make about the world that guide their practice. An example of an informal theory might be noticing that students in leadership positions at an institution are primarily members of the same fraternity and sorority. A student affairs educator might surmise that these students had leadership positions while in high school, which makes access to future leadership positions more natural or easier to attain.

The institutional context describes "the way in which environment informs institutionally supported student development goals and provides guidance to student affairs professionals about how these goals are best achieved" (Reason & Kimball, 2012, p. 368). The final component of Reason and Kimball's model, practice, underscores the translation of informal and formal theories into specific actions to affect student outcomes. One important component of this model is its feedback loop, in which student affairs educators use practice to then inform future theories about college students' development. At the centerpiece of this feedback loop is the notion of using reflection to guide

FIGURE 3.1. REASON AND KIMBALL'S (2012) THEORY-TO-PRACTICE MODEL

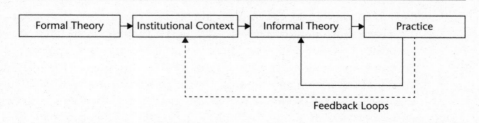

Source: Reason and Kimball (2012), p. 367.

practice, whereby educators actively contemplate decisions and theories and continually reassess their actions based on this reflection.

The institutional context is a critical component of Reason and Kimball's (2012) model. When considering this component, student affairs educators cannot apply theories without considering their particular contexts, students, institutional norms, cultures, and values. This important caution stresses the importance of understanding the students who attend an institution, as well as the values and beliefs held by institutional members. Finally, sharing the limitations and benefits of using certain theories in practice also bolsters and supports what Reason and Kimball refer to as reflexive practice.

In sum, a trial-and-error approach sometimes results in beneficial outcomes, but it can also result in problematic decisions. Theory, however, cannot meaningfully exist in a vacuum. To be of any utility, it must be related to practical situations found in real-life settings. Reason and Kimball's (2012) model provides a helpful way of examining how theory might work in practice, specifically, by also seeing how practice informs theory. Thus student affairs educators' implicit observations based on their daily work with students, as well as the formal theories they use to work with students, both feed back into a loop that then informs future theory and practice.

Theoretical Borderlands

Inspired by Gloria Anzaldúa, Abes (2009) recommended adopting a theoretical borderlands philosophy. Because students are complex, a theoretical borderlands approach recognizes this complexity and rather than reducing students to single categories, embraces "saying yes to the messiness, to that which interrupts and exceeds versus tidy categories" (Lather, 2006, p. 48). Another way to describe this theoretical borderlands approach is engaging in bricolage, or blending the various theories in this book to develop a deeper understanding of students. As Kinchloe and McLaren (2005) explained:

> The bricolage exists out of respect for the complexity of the lived world and complications of power. The task of the bricoleur is to attack this complexity, uncovering the invisible artifacts of power and culture, and documenting the nature of their influence on not only their own works but on scholarship in general. (p. 317)

We recommend that educators see themselves as bricoleurs and embrace the complexity of students, and therefore use theories in combination to understand students more holistically. This does not mean educators will ever understand the full complexity of students' experiences, but bricolage calls for acknowledging how context, power, and culture all influence students' experiences and ultimately their development.

Elisa Abes (2009) suggested that "more instances in student development theory research where research is conducted within theoretical borderlands ought to push the current boundaries of how student development theory is generally understood" (p. 143). Readers might perceive the ways we have structured this book to contradict Abes's argument and the stance for which we advocate in this book, since what follows this chapter is the presentation of singular theories of student development. A tension exists in that in order to effectively blend multiple theories, educators must first understand the depth that exists within each theory singularly. Hence we have chosen to clarify the key features of each theory. Understanding the theories individually first will be useful for uncovering where limitations exist, prior to determining what a theoretical borderlands, or bricolage, approach might offer.

Listening to Stories

A final integrative approach for using the theories in this book is focusing on students' stories. As Robert Coles (1989) wrote, "the people who come to see us bring us their stories. They hope they tell them well enough so that we understand the truth of their lives. They hope we know how to interpret their stories correctly. We have to remember that what we hear is *their story*. . . . I hadn't quite thought of my patients as storytellers" (p. 7). If student affairs educators see college students as storytellers, then this means educators provide the necessary scaffolding for students to share their stories, listen to these stories, and understand the context in which students' stories. Students will likely not share all aspects of their story in one, two, or even several meetings. This means paying attention to the parts of the story a student shares and working to connect those parts over time. For example, a student might share, during one meeting, that she is struggling to engage in dialogues in her ethnic studies class because she is used to relying upon correct answers and dualist perspectives, and then in a different meeting she might share learning about her Whiteness for the first time during this class. An educator listening to this student's story can begin to piece together various parts to make sense of this student's whole development. Knowing this student is attempting to reconcile dualist perspectives in the context of holding a privileged racial identity can prompt the educator to ask thoughtful questions that might help this student reflect more on her development. But without taking the time to hear the stories in various encounters, an educator would miss understanding how these different challenges connect to inform the student's development.

Coles (1989) offered more guidance: "In a manner of speaking, Dr. Ludwig added, we physicians bring *our* stories to the consultation room—even as, he pointedly added, the teachers of physicians carry *their* stories into the consulting rooms where 'supervisory instruction' takes place. Sometimes our knowledge and our theories (the two are not to be confused with each other!) interfere with or interrupt a patient's momentum" (p. 24, emphasis in original). Educators should focus on their own stories, too, as they interpret students' stories through their own lenses and understanding of development. As Coles conveyed, educators need to be aware of their own assumptions so they can hear students' stories in the ways students tell them. For example, when reading the theories in this book, thinking about how they apply to educators' own holistic development will provide possibilities for considering how students might be making sense of their own development. Then relying upon multiple theories to make sense of the stories educators hear from students will facilitate a more holistic view of students. Although educators will likely never get the full story, listening to students' stories over time and in multiple contexts will foster deeper understanding of their development and the resources they need to promote more developmental growth.

Integrative Approaches to Using Student Development Theory: An Application

At the end of this book, we provide several fictional portraits of students with diverse and complex characteristics and developmental experiences. We encourage readers to use these scenarios—as well as their own educational autobiographies—to consider how to apply multiple theoretical perspectives simultaneously. Here, we offer an abbreviated scenario to demonstrate the necessity of considering and applying multiple perspectives.

Luke's Story

Luke is a junior on the track team, with a full scholarship based on his athletic talent. He is also a pre-med biology major and Honors College student. Last year, he was vice president of his hall government, led an Alternative Spring Break trip (to New Orleans, where his group worked in a clinic serving people living with HIV and AIDS), and completed a summer internship in a hospital near his home. Luke enjoyed doing research at the hospital and is learning a great deal in his advanced science courses as a junior. He comes from a Latino family that keeps traditional Catholic values about gender roles (men take care of and protect women, for example) and sex outside marriage (not permissible under any circumstances). It is important to Luke to follow the teachings of his faith and not to disappoint his family.

At college, Luke has begun to explore his sexual orientation by talking to his Resident Assistant and one of his professors, who is gay. Luke is "pretty sure" he's gay, but hasn't ever "done anything" with a man, so he doesn't know for certain. He also doesn't know any gay Latinos—or even *know of* any other than Ricky Martin—and he's trying to figure out how the pieces of his identity fit together, or if he has to choose sexuality over ethnicity, religion, and family. Even with all of these thoughts and feelings, the most important thing on Luke's mind this year is staying connected to teammates and other friends on campus while he prepares medical school applications.

Applying Student Development Perspectives to Luke's Story

A careful read of Luke's story reveals a number of developmental processes in play. He is growing intellectually as he stretches himself in school and as a researcher. He is engaging in service and active on campus as an athlete and student leader—all are contexts with possibilities for intercultural development, leadership growth, and ethical decision-making. His gender identity and understanding of Latino masculinity are features of his life, as is his exploration of sexual identity. Faith, family, and friends are components of his daily life as well. Clearly, one student development theory is not enough to describe, explain, or predict Luke's developmental trajectories.

Using the theory-to-practice model (Reason & Kimball, 2012), an informal theory one of Luke's advisors might have is that he seems to rely heavily upon his family and his faith for making decisions about his life. This perspective connects to student development theory that specifies students might exhibit externally defined behaviors, whereby they rely upon authority figures for the answers about complex information. Luke's advisor, however, should reflect on her assumption about the need for students to separate from their families upon entering college, as this perspective reflects Westernized notions of development. Hearing how Luke talks about his sexual orientation, Luke's advisor can begin to connect this piece to other aspects of his life (Coles, 1989); for example, how sexual orientation connects to Luke's faith and notions of masculinity and ethnic identity.

In the absence of any apparent crisis, however, it can be hard to know where to begin in thinking about theoretical applications related to Luke and his college experiences. Depending on the professional context, different aspects might rise to heightened salience. The academic advisor for student athletes or pre-medical advisor may focus most on Luke's intellectual development, ensuring that he encounters adequate challenge to keep him engaged with science and medicine. The RA or the professor to whom he has talked about his emerging gay identity might focus on issues of gender and sexuality, providing resources that meet Luke's level of exploration. The advisor to the Catholic Student Association, who also went on the New Orleans service trip, may be aware of how multiple pieces fit together for Luke in relation to faith, service, commitment to family, and personal identities as a gay Latino scientist.

No one of these people is responsible for all of Luke's experience, education, or development. But each has the opportunity to look beyond the one most salient perspective for their context. An academic advisor who considers social identities, a coach who asks about academics and family, an RA who attends to intellectual development as well as social integration of students on the floor—all have the opportunity to consider using student development theories in combination to address multiple aspects of Luke's (or any student's) education and development.

Conclusion

Appropriate use of theories requires tentative use rather than prescriptive application, keeping the potential for individual variations in mind. No two students are alike, and no one theory is likely to explain the development of every aspect of any one student. Integrating concepts from several theories can often provide a more comprehensive understanding of development. To those unfamiliar with the many theories of student development, learning them all in enough detail to use effectively in practice may seem daunting. Terminology that is unfamiliar can prompt hesitant educators to think that learning a new language is a prerequisite to incorporating theory in their work. Those who teach students about theories need to be mindful of the legitimate nature of such reservations and present theory to others in an accessible manner. Educators have an intellectual and ethical responsibility to study theories in order to better understand students, colleagues, and environments, and they have an obligation as well to make appropriate use of their expertise.

In this chapter, we discussed the role of theory in the work of student affairs educators and how they might evaluate the utility of theory. Coles (1989) explained that "[Dr. Ludwig] gave me a stern lecture on my increasingly opaque way of talking about my patients, and he ended with a plea for 'more stories, less theory.' He urged that I err on the side of each person's particularity: offer *that* first, and only later offer 'a more general statement'—adding as a qualifier, 'if you want to, if you need to'" (p. 27). The integrated approaches we introduced in this chapter remind readers to keep students' stories in the forefront and use the theories in the following chapters as ways to make sense of students' lives, remembering that theories are observations of reality—how people interpret what is happening in students' lives in more systematic ways. Student affairs educators have a responsibility to students, one of which is using theories judiciously to guide their observations of students and their own practices. New and seasoned student affairs educators should understand their own stories and assumptions, reflect on the theories in this book, use them in their work, and then let their practice shape theories as well (Reason & Kimball, 2012). As educators read each theory individually, they should consider how they might be used with other theories throughout this book. Finally, we encourage educators to ask themselves: how will using these theories in combination enable me to better make sense of students' development? This is the integrative perspective we hope readers will adopt as they read in order to see the complexities of students' lives.

Discussion Questions

1. What is the role of theory—in particular, student development theory?
2. What is the difference between informal theory and formal theory? Give examples and describe their relationship.
3. How do higher education and student affairs educators evaluate theory?
4. As student affairs educators, what is our role in extending and strengthening the use of student development theory in higher education?
5. Describe the context of the institution where you study, teach, or practice student development theory. How will this context make a difference for the ways in which you apply developmental theory to students experiences?
6. How will you address the cautions for applying student development theory in your own work? Be specific.
7. Clearly articulate the challenges involved in applying student development theory and how you will overcome them in your practice.
8. How can Reason and Kimball's theory-to-practice model inform your practice? How does this relate to how you use theory in practice?
9. How might a borderlands approach or simply listening to students' stories be useful for integrating theories to inform practice? Provide examples.
10. Give practical examples of innovative approaches to using student development theory.

PART TWO

SOCIAL IDENTITY DEVELOPMENT

Regina is learning a lot in her first semester, and she is finding that in many cases, student development theory helps her understand and work effectively with students. But some dimensions of development that are important to the students she works with in Multicultural Student Affairs have not yet been addressed—namely, dimensions of social identity. The students Regina advises are diverse. Ethnically, they come from varied backgrounds and cultures: Latino, Indian, Japanese, Native American, and Arab American, to name a few. But even students with similar cultural backgrounds identify differently from one another. Marisela, for example, sees herself as Mexican American, and proudly displays her heritage in her daily life. Rudolfo, by contrast, identifies as Latino. His mother emigrated from Cuba and his father comes from Belize. Identifying as Latino makes more sense to him than choosing one aspect of his heritage over another. And Anita, who is also of Latino heritage, knows almost nothing about Latino culture and identifies as Latino only on required official documents.

Race is another matter. Many of Regina's advisees have been negatively affected by institutional and societal racism. Curtis, for example, was actively discouraged from going to a four-year college by his high school guidance counselor, who believed that someone from an underresourced, predominantly Black high school in Washington, DC, would never succeed at a predominantly White university like Prescott, which has historically attracted a number of students from wealthy communities. The guidance counselor amplified this racism by making assumptions about Curtis's potential based on his social class as well. Mike, who is a member of the Crow nation in Montana, recounts the derogatory remarks he and his friends heard every time they left their reservation. Yuko, who is of Japanese heritage, has had to deal with the stereotype that she will naturally excel in math and science, because Asian Americans are supposed to be good in these fields. In actuality, Yuko is not particularly interested in these areas and is an accomplished artist. And then there is Paul. His heritage is a mix of white, African American, and Latino. Because he is multiracial, he has often felt pressured by peers to identify with only one of his identities, African American, due to his darker complexion.

Sexual orientation issues have also come up for Regina's students. Vijay recently confided to Regina that he is gay. He is concerned about his parents' reaction, as he comes from a traditional family who expects him to marry a woman. Because he knows that many of his peers do not approve of gay, lesbian, and bisexual people, Vijay has not told anyone other than Regina about his sexual identity. Her first suggestion to Vijay was to attend a meeting of the LGB student organization to meet other students, but he is apprehensive because he does not want to draw public attention to his sexual identity.

Gender identity issues are also evident for many of Regina's students. Marisela struggles with the traditional gender roles within her Mexican American family, particularly when other students comment to her about how much time she devotes to going home to see them. She wants to remain committed to her family but also wants to fit in at college. And Regina was caught off guard when Les revealed that he had never really felt comfortable as a man and was considering a transition in his gender identity.

Regina is also wondering about the role of spirituality and religion, which is a concern at the forefront for many of her students. As a Muslim, Mariama fields frequent questions about why she wears a hijab and what she believes. Regina observes that many of the peers who ask are curious and do so kindly, but she has also heard students tell Mariama that she should convert to Christianity to be saved from eternal damnation. Yet when Regina questions some of her Christian students, like Curtis, about why he believes what he does, all he can tell her is that he believes what his parents and pastor tell him is right.

Finally, Regina is concerned about Robert, a student who recently talked with her about his learning impairment. Robert has not been medically diagnosed but is certain he needs assistance with completing his academic work. Regina is now in touch with a representative from the Disability Services Office to figure out possible strategies to assist Robert and to shift the learning environment to ensure his success. She is also helping Robert find student organizations for students with learning disabilities, who could be a source of peer support and group identification if he is interested.

Regina is relieved that the next part of her student development text focuses on social identity development. She needs some assistance with all the identity issues her students are sharing with her and, she acknowledges to herself, with the impact of her own social identities.

◆ ◆ ◆

Social identity development, the theme of Part Two, is the process by which people come to understand their social identities (ethnicity, race, gender, sexual orientation, and others) and how these identities affect other aspects of their lives (McEwen, 2003b). What makes these aspects of identity "social" is that other people, as well as the individual involved, evaluate a person and make judgments based on these identities. Time and place influence social identities, which are constantly shifting. The concepts of privilege and oppression underlie interpretations of social identity. Some identity groups are privileged in the United States and others are oppressed. Social identities influence how people see themselves, how they interact with others, how they make decisions, and how they live their lives. Ideological, social, and economic decisions are also contingent on how various social identity groups are perceived.

The first chapter in Part Two, Chapter Four, "Social Identity: Concepts and Overview," provides an introduction to concepts underlying social identity and its development, including an in-depth examination of oppression and privilege. We then discuss several manifestations of privilege, including White privilege, social class privilege, gender privilege, heterosexual privilege, ability privilege, and Christian privilege. We anchor the chapter with a discussion of multiple identity development, which explains how a person's privileged and oppressed social identities come together and influence each other and the person's overall self-concept, as explained by the theories of Jones and McEwen (2000) and Abes, Jones, and McEwen (2007). We highlight how theory can be beneficial in understanding not only how students develop but also how experiences shape their identities within a framework of power and privilege.

In Chapter Five, "Racial Identity Development," we present the concept of race as a social construction, and the tenets of critical race theory (CRT) in which privilege and oppression are embedded (Delgado & Stefanic, 2001), as precursors to an examination of racial identity development theories. Specifically, the chapter includes Sue and Sue's (2003) racial and cultural identity development (RCID) model, designed to apply to any minoritized identity; Cross and Fhagen-Smith's (2001) life-span model of Black identity development; Helms's White racial identity development model (1995) and the White racial consciousness model of Rowe, Bennett, and Atkinson (1994); as well as models of Latino identity development (Ferdman & Gallegos, 2012), Asian American identity development (Kim, 2012), and American Indian identity development (Horse, 2012). Multiracial identity development is gaining more attention in the United States as the number of individuals born to interracial/interethnic couples is increasing. We examine multiracial identity development, particularly how multiracial identity has been historically viewed and treated in the United States, and focus specifically on Renn's ecological approach (2004), the first model to specifically address college students.

Chapter Six, "Ethnic Identity Development and Acculturation," focuses on these two processes as experienced in the United States. Defined by Phinney (1995) as "a multicultural construct, involving ethnic feelings, attitudes, knowledge, and behaviors" (p. 58), ethnic identity has both an internal component that involves how individuals see themselves, their values, and their feelings and attitudes about their ethnicity and an external component that includes active involvement in their ethnic community, the language they speak, the foods they eat, and so forth (Isajiw, 1990). Acculturation refers to the process by which members of an ethnic minority group adapt to a dominant culture with which they come in contact (Berry, 1993). This chapter includes a review of Phinney's (1993) model of ethnic identity formation; Torres's Bicultural Orientation Model and Influences on Latino Identity (1999, 2003); the application of ethnic identity and acculturation models to Asian American, Indigenous, African American and Afro-Caribbean, and European American identity groups; and scholarship on measuring ethnic identity development.

"Sexual Identity Development," Chapter Seven, includes an examination of how individuals come to view themselves as lesbian, gay, bisexual, heterosexual, or asexual. Gay and lesbian identity development has been studied systematically since the introduction of Cass's (1979) stage theory. Finding Cass's stage theory too rigid, Fassinger (1998) and her colleagues introduced a model of gay, lesbian, and bisexual identity development that separated this process into two aspects: internal identification and group identification. D'Augelli (1994a) used a lifespan approach to suggest that development occurs in six different areas of one's life at varying times as a result of how individuals interpret their experiences and the decisions they make, their interactions with others who are important to them, and the cultural, historical, and geographical circumstances in which they find themselves. More recently scholars have examined heterosexual identity development.

Worthington and his colleagues (2002) considered both the individual and social processes involved in defining sexual needs, values, and behaviors. In their model, Worthington and his colleagues also take into consideration the development of individuals' attitudes and beliefs about those who identify as gay, lesbian, and bisexual. In this chapter, we adopt a universal approach to sexual identity and present Dillon, Worthington, and Moradi's (2011) unifying model of sexual identity development. The unifying model fits any sexual identity, and disrupts the presumption that heterosexual people do not experience a sexual identity process. The unifying model acknowledges and explains how all people experience sexual identity development.

Chapter Eight, "Gender and Gender Identity Development," offers definitions of concepts such as sex, gender, and gender identity to provide clarity about how they differ and interrelate. We present Lev's (2004) dismantling of the assumption that gender is binary (that there are only two genders and that one is either a man or a woman). We then discuss what it means to be cisgender (that is, the gender roles one assumes align with one's biological sex) and transgender (that is, one's gender identity does not align with one's biological sex). We briefly highlight Bem's (1983) gender schema and Bilodeau's (2005, 2009) work on transgender identity development. In order to capture the various intersecting components of gender identity, we present Bussey's (2011) social-cognitive theory of gender identity development to account for the personal, behavioral, and environmental characteristics that shape gender identity. This theory works equally well regardless of an individual's gender identity and is an inclusive model for diverse genders among college students.

In Chapter Nine, "Development of Faith and Spirituality," we share the work of developmental theorists such as James Fowler and Sharon Daloz Parks. Cognitive structural, psychosocial, and integrative theories influenced their approaches to understanding faith. Parks's theory integrates cognitive, affective, and environmental dimensions in considering development and suggests ways in which college campuses can become mentoring communities to students during their faith journeys. This chapter also features the groundbreaking work of Astin, Astin, and Lindholm (2011), which provides a contemporary perspective on student development in relation to religious and spiritual development. We discuss religious identity development, as a concept related to but distinct from spirituality, and highlight emergent theories of Muslim and atheist identities. We summarize the burgeoning literature on college students' spiritual and religious development and associated college outcomes.

Chapter Ten, "Disability Identities and Identity Development," provides information on the various approaches and models that have developed over time in relation to people with disabilities, including the moral, medical, functional limitations, social, minority group, and social justice approaches. Given the manner in which society constructs disabilities, we discuss how people with disabilities are minoritized and explain how their experiences are different from and similar to other minoritized populations. We provide further detail on disability identities through Johnstone's (2004) ecological approach to disability identity and two-stage models of disability identity: Gibson's (2006) model and Forber-Pratt and Aragon's (2013) social and psychosocial identity development model for college students with disabilities.

In Chapter Eleven, "Social Class and Identity," we delineate the difference between social class and socioeconomic status and describe prevailing myths that promote inequities and make conversations about social class a taboo topic. We then share brief descriptions of social class identities in college including first-generation, low-income/poor, working-class, middle-class, and affluent students, and describe how social class constructions shape and influence college experiences and ultimately development. The theories highlighted in this chapter include Bourdieu's (2000) theory of social reproduction and forms of capital and Yosso's (2005) community cultural wealth model. While neither theory describes a developmental process, both critically examine the inequities that stem from social class. In particular, Yosso's model captures the intersectionality of experience for minoritized groups in the educational system. Together, these theories have significant implications for how educators understand student development when issues of social class emerge. We conclude the chapter by presenting relevant research focusing on social class and student development, including belongingness, retention, involvement, and intersectionality.

Chapter Twelve, "Emerging Theoretical Perspectives on Student Experiences and Identities," is devoted to a discussion of the growing literature on diverse student populations in relation to digital, national, feminist, veteran, and athletic identities. Although student identities related to these phenomena are not themselves "emergent" (that is, there have been international students, feminists, veterans, and student athletes on campus for over a century), scholars are catching up in providing theories to explain these identities, as well as in describing how digital contexts produce and influence social identities. We provide a brief explanation of why we believe theories are emerging in these categories and provide relevant literature, models, and assessments where appropriate. We then describe the implications of these identities within the campus environment and the potential impact on student development.

CHAPTER FOUR

SOCIAL IDENTITY: CONCEPTS AND OVERVIEW

Identity development was named in the landmark document "The Student Personnel Point of View (SPPV)" (American Council on Education, 1937/1994a), and since then student affairs professionals and scholars have been working with the concept to enhance student learning and development. In the eight decades since the *SPPV* was written, social identity has remained central to student development. Indeed, as we describe in this chapter, evidence suggests that it is even more significant in the twenty-first century than it was in 1937.

In this chapter we provide a brief history of social identity as an organizing concept of the self and within higher education. We describe oppression and privilege based on social identities, which are important contexts in which to understand the development, enactment, and ongoing construction of social identities. As a precursor to subsequent chapters in which we describe specific domains of identity (for example, race, social class, gender), we conclude this chapter with a discussion of intersecting and multiple identities.

Definition and Historical Context

The notion of social identity emerged through the last half of the twentieth century as a central organizing concept for understanding self in society and, in the context of higher education, as a foundation for understanding student development. Torres, Jones, and Renn (2009) stated, "Enhancing the development of students has long been a primary role of student affairs practitioners. Identity development theories help practitioners understand how students go about discovering their 'abilities, aptitude and objectives' while assisting them to achieve their 'maximum effectiveness' (American Council on Education, 1937, p. 69)" (p. 577). But what exactly is social identity, why does it matter in college student development, and from what intellectual traditions are common theories drawn and/or born?

The study of identity takes place in a number of academic disciplines on which student affairs educators rely: psychology, sociology, social psychology, history, and anthropology, among others. The most commonly cited authors among college student development scholars tend to be psychologists and social psychologists, though sociological and human ecology approaches are becoming more visible in the student affairs literature (Torres et al., 2009). Vignoles, Schwartz, and Luyckx (2011) noted "identity is one of the most commonly studied constructs in the social sciences" and "the number of publications on 'identity' has steadily increased in the past few decades" (p. 1) across psychological, sociological, and related fields.

Vignoles et al. (2011) provided an integrative view of identity at four levels: individual, relational, collective, and material. *Individual* or *personal identities* are self-definitions at the individual level of goals, values, beliefs, and other individually held self-evaluations and expected future selves. *Relational identities* include roles (for example, child, student, coworker) that one establishes in relationship with and to others, in the interpersonal space created by social interactions. *Collective identities* are an individual's sense of self within or outside social categories such as ethnicity, race, religion, gender, sexual orientation, and so forth. *Material identities* are social entities beyond the self, consisting of geographic places and material artifacts of modern life. So a college student may understand herself as having individual-level values ("I hold traditionally conservative views about how government should address an economic downturn"), relational identities ("I am captain of the basketball team"), collective identities ("I am Arab American and Muslim"), and material identities ("I am a proud Michigan native who drives a Detroit-made car"). These identities interact in ways that yield innumerable unique outcomes for individuals and that change over time. The student here will likely end her term as basketball captain but may retain an athletic identity after college; she may not always live in Michigan but may retain her sense of "home" there and loyalty to local industries. Any college campus has as many unique identity combinations as it has students, faculty, and other employees.

Vignoles et al. (2011) also pointed out that cultural and historical definitions of what identities mean change over time; for a student to be conservative, a women's team captain, Arab American, Muslim, and native Michigander takes on different meanings at different points in time and in different places. Importantly, they noted, "The range of identity categories available in a given social context, and the meanings that are given to them, are constructed through a confluence of social processes over historical time" (p. 4). In other words, not everyone has access to every identity category at every point in time and in every context. This concept connects to ecological approaches to understanding student development, which stipulate that person-environment interactions shape core elements of the person and affect the direction of development (see Bronfenbrenner's Ecological Model in Chapter Two).

Postsecondary educators—and student affairs professionals in particular—have built on the tradition of attending to students' social identity development. Initially, they relied primarily on identity theories from psychology, over time expanding to sociological, social psychological, and ecological models. Researchers created these models in parallel with important social movements that drew attention to the diversity of human experience and identities, and student affairs professionals and scholars responded to increased diversity on campus. Professionals use social identity theories in their work with individuals, groups, and intergroup dynamics.

The earliest identity models used in higher education came from the Freudian and Eriksonian traditions and their focus on resolving a series of developmental crises toward healthy growth (see Chapter Thirteen). Chickering brought this approach firmly into the higher education context in his 1969 book *Education and Identity,* providing a foundation from which to consider the processes of identity development. At the same time, both within and outside the college context, social identities—and in particular those identities not in the majority—became more visible through the civil rights movement, women's liberation, and early gay rights organizing.

Researchers responded with new ways of thinking about the development of race, gender, and sexual orientation identities. African American scholars developed models of Black identity (for example, Cross, 1971) highlighting the contrast between Black identity and White identity. The 1970s spawned the women's movement and models related to gender (Gilligan, 1977; Josselson, 1973) and eventually feminism (hooks, 1981). The 1974 declassification of homosexuality as a mental illness and the increasingly visible gay rights movement led to the development of homosexual identity models (Cass, 1979), later expanded to include lesbian, gay, and bisexual identities (D'Augelli, 1994a). In the 1980s, theorists sought synthesis of individual racial and ethnic group models designed to encompass the experiences of all minoritized group members, such as the minority development model (Atkinson, Morten, & Sue, 1989) and the multiethnic model (Banks, 1984). As the twentieth century came to a close, White (Helms & Carter, 1990), Latino (Ferdman & Gallegos, 2001), Asian (Kim, 2001), ethnic (Phinney, 1990), and bi/multiracial (Renn, 2000, 2004; Root, 1990) frames and explanations for the identity development of their respective groupings followed. Scholars paid less attention to the development of gender identity per se, though studies of differences between men's and women's development and experiences became common (Baxter Magolda, 1989, 1992).

From the 1970s through the 1990s, most theories used to describe college students' social identities came out of the psychological tradition. Few theorists used samples of college students to derive their models, leading to a body of "student development theory" that was related to social identities but not specific to the collegiate context. The theories also tended to focus on single social identities, leading to depth in understanding racial, ethnic, or sexual orientation identity development but limiting consideration of identity development across a range of domains. Theories that are specific to one domain of identity are necessary for understanding individuals and groups, but they are not sufficient for the broader task of examining development across multiple domains. In response, researchers addressed both of these issues—basing theories on college students and addressing identity holistically.

During the 1990s and into the twenty-first century, scholars delved deeper into the complexity of multiple identities and their extensive overlapping influences and formations (Abes & Jones, 2004; Abes, Jones, & McEwen, 2007; Jones, 1997, 2009; Jones & Abes, 2013; Jones & McEwen, 2000; Reynolds & Pope, 1991). The introduction of legal theorist Kimberlé Crenshaw's (1991) concept of *intersectionality* into higher education scholarship resulted in a host of studies exploring its utility as developmental theory. Originally based on understanding the subjectivity of African American women in the judicial system, intersectionality theory after 25 years now covers intersections of race, class, gender, sexual orientation, nationality, and other identities that locate power and privilege in some categories at the expense of members of other categories. Like others (Cho, Crenshaw, & McCall, 2013; Torres et al., 2009), we do not consider intersectionality itself a developmental theory, as it does not describe or predict individual growth in the direction of developmental complexity, but we advocate for its use as a lens for understanding how the intersecting identities of individuals contribute to development and how development unfolds within the broader societal context of interlocking systems of privilege and oppression (Collins, 1991). Awareness of intersectionality theory and models of multiple dimensions of identity specific to college student development (see Jones & Abes, 2013) has led the field of student development to view identities as intertwined, interactive, and unique for each individual.

In the last two decades, the social identity literature expanded rapidly, as did foundational knowledge related to privilege, oppression, and multiple identities all outlined in this chapter. This expansion signifies a shift away from the dominance of mostly positivist psychosocial and cognitive structural theories to guide student development, toward inclusion of a wider range of research methods and social science disciplines, such as sociology and developmental ecology. To enhance college students' development, student affairs professionals in general—and counselors, social justice educators, and the staff of multicultural, women's/gender, and LGBT resource and cultural centers in particular—have also begun to seek out ways to work with students on issues of oppression, privilege, and power as they address multifaceted identity issues (see Black & Stone, 2005; Hanna, Talley, & Guindon, 2000; Patton & Chang, 2011; Patton, Kortegast, & Barela, 2011; Pope, Reynolds, & Mueller, 2004; Zúñiga, Nagda, Chesler, & Cytron-Walker, 2011).

Harnessing the complexity of multidimensional individual, relational, collective, and material identities in changing social contexts brings both the interpersonal and intrapersonal components of development to the foreground. In addition, much of the foundation of the social identity literature is methodologically grounded in social constructivism and less so in the more positivist tradition of a number of theories we discuss later in this book. How individuals and groups make meaning of the world they occupy is vital to understanding social identity, which makes social constructivism a worldview and method appropriate to consider these ideas. Recognizing the burgeoning availability of resources on these topics, we first review selected literature tied to the key concepts of oppression and privilege and then examine specific research linked to these and related concepts in the higher education literature.

Oppression

While scholars disagree about the meaning of oppression, inequities in power are a key component of most definitions (Sensoy & DiAngelo, 2012). Oppression consists of a family of concepts and conditions, including roadblocks to holistic development (Young, 2000) and, on campus, the creation of a negative climate for members of minoritized groups (Hurtado, Dey, Gurin, & Gurin, 2003), making it an important consideration for student affairs.

Bohmer and Briggs (1991) defined oppression as "those attitudes, behaviors, and pervasive and systemic social arrangements by which members of one group are exploited and subordinated while members of another group are granted privileges" (p. 155). Oppression includes injustices perpetrated, sometimes unconsciously, by members of privileged or majoritized groups (in the United States, those groups include those who are middle or upper class, White, Christian, heterosexual, cisgender, men, and without obvious mental, physical, or emotional impairments) against members of oppressed or minoritized groups (basically, anyone *not* in all of the aforementioned categories). Research has shown that individuals place themselves in various locations along an oppressed-oppressor continuum, "depending upon the contexts, time, and social and legal relationships involved in their interactions" (Sonn & Fisher, 2003, p. 117). An individual may be privileged along some dimensions but not along all (for example, a cisgender gay Black man is privileged by his gender but oppressed based on his race and sexual orientation). To recognize and eliminate oppression, it is important to inspect the visible and invisible interaction of privilege and oppression.

Though perpetuated through individual actions, oppression is a systemic issue. Sensoy and DiAngelo (2012) noted, "Oppression involves institutional control, ideological domination and the impositions of the dominant group's culture on the minoritized group. No individual member of the dominant group has to do anything specific to oppress a member of the minoritized group; prejudice and discrimination is built into the society as a whole and becomes normalized and taken for granted" (p. 40). Oppression, therefore, is woven into the fabric of tacit societal assumptions and is both a structural and a political issue. Indeed, oppression has long been an element of the dominant culture in the United States (Torres, Howard-Hamilton, & Cooper, 2003), and exposing its invisible, toxic nature heightens awareness and may encourage members of majoritized groups to change their perspective and take social action to address more equitable change.

Oppression can take many forms, including exploitation, marginalization, powerlessness, cultural imperialism, and violence (Young, 2000). Microaggressions, the "constant and continuing everyday reality of slights, insults and invalidations, and indignities visited upon marginalized groups by well-intentioned, moral, and decent" others (Sue, 2010, p. xv), also contribute to oppression. The outcomes of oppression on individual students span personal and relational or interpersonal domains. Minority stress theory (see Meyer, 2003) posits that experiencing prejudice and discrimination leads to negative health and mental health outcomes that could have deleterious effects on college students' performance, learning, and development. Systematic oppression keeps people from some social groups out of higher education altogether, and it creates negative, hostile, or unwelcoming climates for those minoritized individuals who do enter college (see Hurtado et al., 2003). Under certain conditions the interaction of minority stress and negative campus climate might become a catalyst for the development of agency and resilience, but it also could easily impede student development, learning, and success. Harvey (2000) claimed that "we need more adequate concepts of power, and an analysis of hidden power, in our own relationships and in social structures on the large scale" (p. 187) to take appropriate first steps toward dismantling oppressive structures that perpetuate cycles of power and privilege for some people at the expense of others.

Privilege

In the United States, a centuries-old democracy, the notion of privilege had been largely ignored, but McIntosh's (1989, 2003) articulation of the myth of meritocracy made widespread inequities more difficult to ignore on campus. Such inequities include: One in two offspring of families earning $90,000 or more per year attains a college degree by age 24, but only one in 17 offspring of families earning $35,000 or less per year does (Lott, 2012); women faculty and administrators are underrepresented at more prestigious institutions, overrepresented at less prestigious ones, and earn less on average than men (Lee & Won, 2014); unlike their peers with disabilities, nondisabled students can choose to live anywhere on campus without regard to building access; college calendars follow a schedule based on Christian holidays but rarely on the holidays of other faiths; and White students are more likely than Black and Latino students to attend institutions with more resources for learning and student development (John & Stage, 2013). Privilege is "defined in relational terms and in reference to social groups, and involves unearned benefits afforded to powerful social groups within systems of oppression" (Case, Iuzzini, & Hopkins, 2012). Most privileged individuals in U.S. society either cannot see or refuse to see the power they hold, leaving privilege invisible and intact for those who possess it (McIntosh, 1989, 2003, 2012, 2013; Robinson & Howard-Hamilton, 2000). Many people with privilege unknowingly take advantage, often devoid of any thought about the inequity their privilege enacts in the lives of people without privilege (McIntosh, 1989, 2003).

In her classic 1989 article, "White Privilege: Unpacking the Invisible Knapsack" Peggy McIntosh described the concept of white privilege in a way that was accessible to many readers; in it she listed 26 everyday occurrences in which White people carry privileges that people of color in the United States often do not have (for example, "I can turn on the television or open to the front page of the newspaper and see people of my race widely represented" and "If a traffic cop pulls me over or if the IRS audits my tax return, I can be sure I haven't been singled out because of my race," p. 11). The notion of the "invisible knapsack" took hold in student affairs circles, and there is a number of lists of privileges in different social categories (including gender, sex, sexual orientation, nationality, religion) that circulate through professional networks, training, and online resources.

McIntosh (1989, 2003, 2012) discussed two kinds of privilege: *unearned entitlements* or privileges everyone should possess, such as feeling safe on campus and in the workplace, and *conferred dominance*, giving one group power over another. Conferred dominance bestows privilege on a single group, simultaneously making individuals who are members of this group pivotal as oppressors with power. Many people in the United States have advantages because of some part of their status (for example, being socioeconomically secure, heterosexual, cisgender man, or Christian). However, they do not see dismantling privilege as their responsibility because they do not see themselves as oppressors. Furthermore, some individuals see their privileged status (for example, White, wealthy) outweighed by an oppressed status that is also part of their identity (for example, lesbian woman) and never recognize the privilege they hold. McIntosh (2012, 2013) advocated for teaching about privilege as a way to help individuals move beyond this ignorance to act on their privileged status as allies to members of oppressed groups (see also Case et al., 2012).

The unbalanced social structure of the United States "bestows privilege in a manner that impacts relationships between people who would otherwise be peers" (Rocco & West, 1998, p. 177). The intricate connections between self, others, and environment shape awareness and lack of awareness of privilege. Privilege comes in many seen and unseen manifestations in U.S. society, yet "The study of privilege adds a whole new dimension to analysis of social systems and individual experiences. It changes everything" (McIntosh, 2013, p. xii). In order to shed light on some of these often-invisible privileges, we discuss them here, followed by a short review of selected literature examining privilege in university contexts. In enumerating a handful of categories of privilege, we wish to avoid the implication that these are the only—or most important—ones operating in higher education. Readers can extend these examples into other categories of social privilege and oppression.

White Privilege

White privilege in the United States derives from historical, cultural, and political forces of domination and control by White people over indigenous people, voluntary immigrants of color and their children, and those people of color brought forcibly as slaves and captives (who might be called "involuntary immigrants"). Individuals who are perceived as having lighter skin and the phenotypical features expected in people with ancestors from Europe possess white privilege. Whiteness studies scholar Tim Wise (2011) uses "White" or "White folks" to describe "those persons, typically of European descent, who by virtue of skin color or perhaps national origin and culture are able to be perceived as 'White,' as members of the dominant racial group in the Western world" (p. xii). As a shifting social construction, definitions of the White population have varied throughout U.S. history, and no consensus has emerged for "the optimal term one should use to describe American descendants of European and Middle Eastern immigrants" (McDermott & Samson, 2005, p. 247). The U.S. census coined the term White, the most common one in use, though other terms, such as Caucasian, European American, and Anglo, are also used by White people to place themselves in an ethnic or racial category.

As an identity construct, whiteness is "ill-defined, illusory (as an identity marker) and elusive" (Jackson, 1999, p. 52). By contrast, white privilege is explicitly defined as a "system of benefits, advantages, and opportunities experienced by white persons" bestowed solely because of skin color (Donnelly, Cook, Van Ausdale, & Foley, 2005, p. 6). White privilege is often hard for White people to recognize, while easy for non-White people, to see and experience its deleterious effects. Wise (2014) described white privilege as "any advantage, opportunity, benefit, head start, or general protection from negative social mistreatment" (¶ 11) that people perceived as White enjoy but which are not available to people not perceived as White. These benefits may be material, social, or psychological. Lund and Colin (2010) stated, "White privilege is viewed by many as a birthright and is in essence an existentialist norm that is based upon the power and privilege of pigmentation" (p. 1).

Since McIntosh wrote about the invisible knapsack, White privilege has increased rapidly as a topic for discussion in myriad bodies of literature, including counseling (for example, Israel, 2012; Mindrup, Spray, & Lamberghini-West, 2011), higher education (for example, Cabrera, 2014; Wolfe & Dilworth, 2015), psychology (for example, Case et al., 2012; Sue, 2013), and student affairs (for example, Bondi, 2012; Edwards, Loftin, Nance, Riser, & Smith, 2014). She offered a fitting metaphor for white privilege, describing it as "a weightless knapsack of special provisions, assurances, tools, maps, guides, codebooks, passports, visas, clothes, compass, emergency gear, and blank checks" (McIntosh, 1989, p. 2).

Since the majority of college students in the United States are White, they are the group most often used as subjects in research conducted on campus—in psychology, marketing, medicine, and so forth. They may begin to see themselves reflected back, whereas racially minoritized students may remain invisible to them because, as Tatum (2000) noted, "dominant access to information about subordinants is often limited to stereotypical depictions of the 'other'" (p. 12). Yet there is also evidence that awareness of white privilege can be a stepping-stone to anti-racist action; White people can move from "acceptance of oppression to naming oppression (the feeling of guilt), to reflection and redefinition (learning from guilt), to multiperspective integration (to act on what one has learned from guilt)" (Arminio, 2001, pp. 246–247).

Social Class Privilege

Socioeconomic status (SES) and social class are related but distinct concepts. Rubin, Denson, Kilpatrick, Matthews, Stehlik, and Zyngier (2014) explained, "SES refers to one's *current* social and economic situation, and consequently, it is relatively mutable, especially in countries that provide opportunities for economic advancement. In contrast, social class refers to one's sociocultural *background* and is more stable, typically remaining static across generations" (p. 196). SES and social class influence self-perceptions, attitudes, and behaviors.

Social class privilege attaches to individuals who have a higher socioeconomic status in relation to individuals of lower socioeconomic status. In the United States, "the rich are supported by a general ideology that equates success with hard work and individual merit" (Lott, 2012, p. 654). The ideas that "intelligence and ambition will elevate our socioeconomic position" and that "class privilege is deserved" (Lott, 2012, p. 654) reinforce the myth of meritocracy and mask the effects of class privilege. Even in higher education, which may appear to be an engine for promoting social class equity by, for example, conferring degrees on first-generation college students, social class privilege operates to perpetuate societal inequity (Rubin et al., 2014; Seider, 2008)

For individuals, social class has three components: "a social class of origin, a current felt social class and an attributed social class" (Barrett, 2011, p. 7). When a shift in class occurs, identity can change, and felt and attributed social classes can be at odds with each other. A sharp social class contrast experience in college can lead to attrition of working-class students (Barrett, 2011;

Langhout, Drake, & Rosselli, 2009). Ignoring these inequities and others saturating contemporary economic and social systems perpetuates class privilege and class oppression.

Class privilege is also shaped by intersections with other domains of identity including "race, gender, sexuality, and geography" (Borrego, 2003, p. 4). An individual's social connections and experiences, often referred to as cultural capital, open doors and extend power. Though social class is often measured with criteria like income, occupation, and education, "class rests on other people's evaluation of our presentation of self" (Kimmel, 2003, p. 7), or what Barrett (2011) called attributed social class.

Most people think of class as "the kind of work they do, income they earn and their education" (Ostrander, 1984, p. 4). In contrast, members of the upper class frame their assets as "ownership of wealth, exercise of power, and membership in an exclusive network" (Ostrander, p. 5). Wealth, power, and a closed social network keep class distinctions in the hands of the rich who preserve class invisibility and maintain the social class status quo. At elite higher education institutions that fully fund all admitted students, regardless of their ability to pay, classism and social class privilege operate to create differential access to resources and opportunities such as unpaid summer internships, study abroad, and high-priced recreation during breaks (see Aries & Seider, 2005, 2007; Seider, 2008). Across diverse institutions the differential effects of social class privilege and oppression shape transition to college, experience in college, and college outcomes (Langhout et al., 2009; Radmacher & Azmitia, 2013).

Research on students' social class identities and experiences is relatively new in the field, though there is evidence that college students can learn to talk about their social class and its role in privilege and oppression (Barrett, 2011; Hurtado, Alvarez, Guillermo-Wann, Cuellar, & Arellano, 2012; Sanders & Mahalingam, 2012). For example, Sanders and Mahalingam (2012) found that a structured intergroup dialogue program created opportunities for students to explore class as a racialized phenomenon, to overturn taboos about social class discourse, and to break down class-based stereotypes.

Gender Privilege: Male Privilege and Cisgender Privilege

There are at least two types of gender privilege operating in higher education. The first relates to the power that men retain, even now that women are a majority among U.S. undergraduate enrollments, to shape campus culture and discourse. The second relates to the power that cisgender people who conform to a binary notion of gender (that is, male/man and female/woman) have over individuals who are transgender, who experience gender fluidity, or who otherwise express gender in a nonbinary way (by, for example, wearing clothing and hairstyles typical for women while also wearing facial hair typical for men). These two types of gender privilege are enactments, respectively, of sexism and genderism (the expectation that every individual fits into one and only one of two genders; see Bilodeau, 2009).

McIntosh's (1989) work on white privilege emerged from her observations of male privilege when she was the associate director of the Wellesley College Center for Research on Women. In the opening of the "Invisible Knapsack," she stated, "Through work to bring Women's Studies into the rest of the curriculum, I have often noticed men's unwillingness to grant that they are over-privileged, even though they may grant that women are disadvantaged" (McIntosh, 1989, p. 10). In the quarter century since she made this observation, women have made progress in higher education in terms of representation across academic fields, yet they still operate at a disadvantage in the student body, administration, and faculty, where male privilege remains strong.

Male privilege is "a special status conferred on males in societies where male supremacy is the central social organizing feature" (Phillips & Phillips, 2009, p. 683). College men—and particularly White men—benefit from privilege on campus in a number of ways, including feeling safe most of the time to walk alone, being able to wear what they choose without worrying that their character will be judged, seeing people like themselves participating in nationally televised sporting events, and setting campus norms for socializing, without fearing they will be sexually assaulted at a student party. They can participate in what sociologist Michael Kimmel has dubbed "Guyland," a culture in which norms of heterosexual masculinity govern all aspects of campus life, from academics to athletics to parties (see Kimmel, 2008; Kimmel & Davis, 2011). On most campuses, male students will also take most of their courses with male faculty and have a man leading the institution and board of trustees. Even though women make up the majority of students in higher education, across institutional sectors and types, male privilege is pervasive, often not visible, and instrumental in shaping the experiences of students of all genders.

Cisgender privilege includes "the collective advantages that are accepted, most often unknowingly, by those who are not positioned in opposition to the dominant ideology of the gender binary" (Taylor, 2010, p. 268). Taylor continued, "Simply put: A person who is able to live in a life and/or body that is easily recognized as being either man/male or woman/female generally needs to spend less energy to be understood by others. The energy one need not expend to explain their gender identity and/or expression to others is gendered privilege" (pp. 268–269). Citing McIntosh's invisible knapsack metaphor, Taylor listed dozens of privileges available to cisgender people, including "being able to find a safe public bathroom, seeing people of one's gender expression in media, and expecting to be able to find doctors willing to provide urgent medical care" (p. 269). Other cisgender privileges include not having to tell others what pronouns to use in referring to oneself, being able to shop for clothing without being questioned or considered suspicious, and being able to participate in intercollegiate and international athletic leagues without a physical examination or genetic test to "prove" one is competing in the "correct" gender. Binary gender normativity is so pervasive that even with growing awareness of transgender individuals in society and on campus, genderist microaggressions, discrimination, harassment, and violence remain substantial obstacles to student success (Bilodeau, 2009; Nicolazzo, 2015).

Heterosexual Privilege

Like the other categories of privilege we discuss here, heterosexual privilege is pervasive and largely invisible in U.S. society, though lesbian, gay, and bisexual activism for equal rights to serve in the military, to be protected from employment discrimination, and to marry someone of the same gender have brought attention to some of the legal privileges and protections from which heterosexual people benefit. Feigenbaum (2007) explained that "heterosexism is not about individuals or how comfortable they are around queers"; rather, "dominance, and the practices that support it are often replicated, reinforced, and reflected by the attitudes, behaviors and practices of even our best-intentioned allies" (p. 7). An "invisible knapsack" list of heterosexual privilege might include items such as "I can hold hands with my partner in public without fear of harassment or violence," "I don't have to worry about being fired from my job if people find out my sexual orientation," and "I feel confident that my healthcare providers are not judging me based on my sexual orientation."

As with other privileged identities, many people who identify as heterosexual do not think about their sexual orientation until they recognize their relationship to others who do not identify as heterosexual (Evans & Broido, 2005). Participants in a qualitative study of heterosexual college students described times when they became aware of heterosexism and homophobia and attempted to distance themselves from it, even when it occurred in faith-based settings that were important to them (Mueller & Cole, 2009). They were aware of discrimination against gay and lesbian people, but felt largely incapable of interrupting heterosexism, in part because as one student said "So much in our culture assumes your straightness" (Mueller & Cole, 2009, p. 330). They discussed some of the more visible political movements (military service, same-gender marriage), but were less able to articulate the everyday privileges of being heterosexual, one of the most fundamental being "these students had rarely or ever thought about their sexual orientation" (p. 333). These students reflected the dominant culture that rarely perceives heterosexuality as a social identity and takes heterosexual privilege for granted (Evans & Broido, 2005).

There is some evidence that interventions can increase awareness of heterosexual privilege in college students. Mueller and Cole (2009) reported that their participants appreciated the opportunity to talk about their heterosexual identity and its meaning, which also caused them to reflect on privileges associated with it. Kim Case and colleagues (Case, Hensley, & Anderson, 2014; Case & Stewart, 2009, 2010) demonstrated that participants in an undergraduate diversity course in Kentucky increased their awareness of heterosexual privilege, and Walls et al. (2009) documented graduate students in social work as they learned about heterosexual privilege.

Ability Privilege

Examining attitudes toward people with disabilities and their treatment throughout history reveals that ability privilege and the psychological, social, emotional, and economic freedom it bestows on its holders is very real (see Evans, 2008; Evans, Assadi, & Herriott, 2005; Griffin, Peters, & Smith, 2007). Wolbring (2014) stated, "Ability privilege is based on the *reality* that one has certain advantages if exhibiting certain abilities, and individuals enjoying these advantages are unwilling to give up these advantages" (p. 119, italics in original). Historically, disability has been viewed as "a sign of spiritual depravity, a cause for ridicule, a genetic weakness to be exterminated, something to be hidden away, a source of pity, a community health problem, and a problem to be fixed" (Evans, 2008, p. 11). Language used to describe people with disabilities indicates that nondisabled people view them as "less than" normal (Marks, 1999). Terms such as "learning disabled," "hearing impaired," or "brain injured" suggest that the individual so described cannot function at the level or in the way that society expects (Evans & Herriott, 2009). Meanwhile people who live with ability privilege find themselves represented in all forms of media, reflected among public figures, and are free to live, study, and work where they wish, with little regard to their ability to access necessary facilities, programs, and services.

By assuming one normative way to do things (move, speak, learn, and so forth), society privileges those who carry out these functions as prescribed and oppresses those who use other methods (Evans & Herriott, 2009; Wolbring, 2014). "Ableism"—the "pervasive system of discrimination and exclusion that oppresses people [with] ... disabilities on ... individual, institutional, and societal/cultural levels" (Rauscher & McClintock, 1997, p. 198) is an evident form of privilege in society and on college campuses (Evans, 2008).

In reality, the causes of disability and enablers of ability privilege are environmental conditions and attitudes, not physical and mental impairments (Griffin et al., 2007; Wolbring, 2014). The physical barriers that prevent people from accessing buildings, separate individuals in educational settings, fail to provide alternative methods of consuming information (for example, visual captioning for those with hearing loss), and so on place people with disabilities at a disadvantage. Nondisabled people are equally responsible for often discounting the talents and skills of anyone with a disability (Evans & Herriott, 2009).

Christian Privilege

Around the world, religious traditions differ regionally, as do degrees of homogeneity of religious and spiritual practices. In general, whatever religion predominates in a specific location is privileged, in that it is recognized and honored while other religious traditions are at best ignored and at worst outlawed and persecuted. Christian men founded the United States at a time when Christianity was the dominant religious tradition in Europe, and the majority of residents of the United States who practice a religion today are Christian. As a result, Christian privilege is ingrained in national history, law, society, and culture. Seifert (2007) defined Christian privilege on campus as "the conscious and subconscious advantages often afforded the Christian faith in America's colleges and universities" (p. 11).

The dominant religious groups in the United States include, but are not limited to, Roman Catholics, mainstream Protestant groups (for example, Lutherans, Methodists, Presbyterians), evangelical Christian groups (including Pentecostals, Southern Baptists, Assembly of God), Eastern Orthodox followers (for example, Greek, Russian), and those who belong to smaller denominations, including members of the Church of Jesus Christ of Latter-day Saints (LDS) and Seventh-Day Adventists. Non-Christian religions (for example, Buddhism, Hinduism, Judaism, and Islam) are relatively small in number in the United States and their members face oppression, prejudice, and discrimination (Schlosser, 2003). Atheist (see Mueller, 2012) and agnostic students are also subject to living in a Christonormative society in which they are doubly disadvantaged by not belonging to the Christian majority and not subscribing to a faith tradition.

Christian privilege is embedded in the academy (Seifert, 2007). The first colleges in the British colonies that would become the United States were founded to train ministers for Protestant congregations. Ritual, symbols, and practices representative of Christian privilege in U.S. higher education are clearly delineated examples of assumed Christian "cultural markers" (Seifert, p. 11). Christian privilege includes having academic calendars arranged around major Christian holidays; seeing public representations of Christianity such as Christmas trees on campus; and not having to explain the importance of major religious holidays to faculty in order to reschedule an examination or be excused from class. Christian students typically do not pray five times a day, as observant Muslim students do, and thus do not have to plan academic schedules to accommodate their religious observances. Similarly, Christian student athletes are not often expected to compete on Sunday morning, the traditional time for Christian worship, whereas Jewish, Muslim, and Hindu student athletes may be expected to compete on their religious holy days.

As with all of the privileges we discuss in this section, Christian privilege and religious oppression intersect with other aspects of identity; few students carry privilege across all domains of identity, and sometimes awareness of one oppressed identity can lead students to understanding and empathy with other groups (McIntosh, 2013). McIntosh (2012) called on scholars and educators to continue to pursue the field she called privilege studies in order to unmask additional areas of privilege and to develop effective strategies to interrupt cycles of privilege and oppression.

Summary

We have described six categories of privilege, but there are privileged and oppressed categories in nearly every social identity category. In the chapters that follow, we describe the ways that experiences of privilege and oppression shape identities and identity development, catalyze resistance and agency, and influence student learning and outcomes. We noted at the outset of this section that we were isolating social identity categories in order to highlight specific features of privilege and oppression in each, but any individual's iden-tity is made up of multiple, intersecting, mutually constituting, and mutually influencing categories. The highly personalized—if not unique—array of privileges and oppressions that individuals experience influences their life patterns and possibilities. In the next section we describe contemporary models of multiple social identities.

Multiple Identities

Returning to Vignoles et al.'s (2011) four-level, integrative view of identity (as individual, relational, collective, and material), and considering contexts of multiple, interlocking systems of privilege and oppression, it becomes clear that an inclusive model of identity development must account for the complexity of students' backgrounds, characteristics, beliefs, and aspirations. Traditional, linear stage theories of identity, mostly derived from Erikson (1959/1980) as we describe in Part Three of this book, were once the foundation for understanding college student identities. Yet social constructions of identities such as class, ethnicity, race, gender, sexual orientation, religion, geography, and ability play an important role in understanding identity dimensions (McEwen, 2003b). Some identity dimensions, like geography and material goods, are not developmentally grounded, yet they play a critical role in self-definitions.

The study of intersecting identities emerged in student affairs and other fields at the end of the twentieth century and expanded rapidly in the twenty-first century. Delworth (1989) was one of the first student affairs scholars to raise the issue of the intersection of gender and ethnic identity while raising questions about the lack of consideration given to the convergence of identities. Reynolds and Pope (1991) then described multiple identities and oppressions in the context of counseling. Based on an analysis of the scholarship on multiple identity constructs of race, class, gender, and sexuality, sociologist Weber (1998) concluded that the intersection of multiple identities is a socially constructed, contextual phenomenon enacted in everyday life that motivates action to create a more equitable society. This discourse has become more visible as research in student affairs (for example, Abes, 2012; Abes et al., 2007; Jones & Abes, 2013; Jones, Kim, & Skendall, 2012; Jones & McEwen, 2000; Stewart, 2008, 2009), and related disciplines like psychology (Brook, Garcia, & Fleming, 2008; Stanley, 2004) and counseling (Greene, 2012; Robinson & Howard-Hamilton, 2000; Williams, 2005), has illuminated the concept of multiple identities and their corresponding privileges and oppressions. The influence of intersectionality theory (Cho et al., 2013; Crenshaw, 1991) is also visible in recent and emerging research on college student development, though as we stated earlier, intersectionality is not a development theory per se.

Jones and McEwen (2000) first articulated a conceptual model of multiple dimensions of identity based on a grounded theory study of ten undergraduate women of diverse racial and cultural backgrounds. Portrayed at the center of the three-dimensional model is the core sense of self (one's personal identity), including personal attributes and characteristics, and other factors important to the individual. Surrounding and enveloping the core is the context within which identity occurs; special attention is given to family background, sociocultural conditions, current experiences, and career decisions and life planning. The model depicts significant identity dimensions (race, culture, gender, family, education, sexual orientation, social class, and religion) as intersecting circles surrounding the core identity. Dots located on each of these intersecting circles represent the importance of the identity dimension to the individual. The closer the dot is to the core, the greater the importance of that identity dimension to the individual at that time. Like Reynolds and Pope (1991), Jones and McEwen (2000) added to the research by offering an alternative to linear development, describing and illustrating their model as "a fluid and dynamic one, representing the ongoing construction of identities and the influence of changing contexts on the experience of identity development" (p. 408).

Based on Abes and Jones's (2004) study of lesbian identity development and meaning making, Abes, Jones, and McEwen (2007) reconceptualized Jones and McEwen's (2000) model of multiple identity dimensions. They drew on concepts of self-authorship theory (see Chapter Sixteen) and feminist theoretical conceptualizations of multiple identities (for example, Anzaldúa, 1987/1999) to create a model that incorporates interpersonal, intrapersonal, and cognitive elements (self-authorship) and recognizes the concurrent, nonhierarchical experience of multiple identities (Abes et al., 2007; Knight, 2002). Abes et al. (2007) embraced a postmodern approach of understanding identities as variable in meaning across contexts, mutually constructing, and performative (Butler, 1990). For example, a Latina, Catholic lesbian woman will experience her identity differently in different campus contexts and over time; her ethnic, gender, sexual orientation, and religious identities will influence one another; and she constructs her identity through performing it in daily interactions and in how she presents herself to others. As she does so, "repetition creates a sense of self, including a core sense of personal values, however fluid that sense of self might be" (Abes et al., 2007, p. 15). None of the relationships depicted in the Reconceptualized Model of Multiple Dimensions of Identity (RMMDI) stand alone, as all dimensions must be understood in relationship to each other.

The original Model of Multiple Dimensions of Identity (MMDI) (Jones & McEwen, 2000) depicted a core of personal characteristics, attributes, and identity, around which orbited identity dimensions such as race, gender, religion, social class, sexual orientation, and culture. Distance from the core represented salience of these dimensions at any given point in time. The "atom model," as it was dubbed for its resemblance to a two-dimensional depiction of an atom, was embedded within a context of family background, sociocultural conditions, current experiences, and career decisions and life planning. Student affairs educators and scholars quickly incorporated the MMDI into their work in the early 2000s.

At the same time, self-authorship theory (see Chapter Sixteen) was gaining traction among student affairs and student development professionals, and the concept of meaning making became important in understanding how students thought about their own and others' identities (see Abes & Jones, 2004; Pizzolato, Chaudhari, Murrell, Podobnik, & Schaeffer, 2008; Torres & Baxter Magolda, 2004; Torres & Hernandez, 2007). Abes et al. (2007) incorporated key constructs of self-authorship theory into the RMMDI to explain how individuals process contextual influences such as "peers, family, norms, stereotypes, and sociopolitical conditions" (p. 7) vis-à-vis their sense of self and identity. They inserted what they called a "meaning-making filter" between these contextual influences and the self-perceptions of multiple identity dimensions. The meaning-making filter acts as a sieve, and "depending on complexity, contextual influences pass through to different degrees" (Abes et al., 2007, p. 7), influencing identity self-perceptions. Increased cognitive complexity and more _____ ated meaning making result in more nuanced messag__ _____ sieve and interacting in the core of the __ _____ identity development process (see

_____ ussed the model using portraits of _____ le dimensions of identity through _____ le), transitional meaning making _____ d foundational meaning making _____ d perception of identity is com-_____ 00) multiple dimensions model _____ portrayal of not only *what* rela-_____ l and social identities, but also _____ . 13). The RMMDI captures _____ nd cognitive development in

_____ MDI, its application, and its _____ intersectionality, queer the-_____ book *Identity Development of College Students:*

FIGURE 4.1. RECONCEPTUALIZED MODEL OF MULTIPLE DIMENSIONS OF IDENTITY

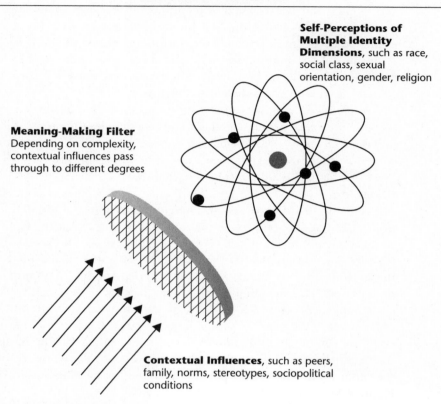

Self-Perceptions of Multiple Identity Dimensions, such as race, social class, sexual orientation, gender, religion

Meaning-Making Filter Depending on complexity, contextual influences pass through to different degrees

Contextual Influences, such as peers, family, norms, stereotypes, sociopolitical conditions

Source: Abes, Jones, & McEwen (2007).

Advancing Frameworks for Multiple Dimensions of Identity, and it seems likely that they will continue this line of research and theory development. We include examples of multiple dimensions of identity throughout this book when we describe theories and practical applications. Studies of intersecting identities (for example, gender and race, race and sexual orientation, or religion and race) are commonplace in contemporary literature and deepen knowledge about the complexity of lived experiences in higher education and society. Overarching models, such as the MMDI, which explain multiple dimensions of identity, provide useful heuristics for understanding how the various pieces may fit together and influence one another.

Future Directions

Social identities, oppression, and privilege are key concepts in understanding college student learning and development in the United States. Equally important is understanding how students make meaning of multiple, intersecting identities in the early twenty-first century. Student affairs educators and researchers have the benefit of drawing from early models of student identity that, while limited in their generalizability, provided a language for describing important intrapersonal, psychosocial identity development during college. Educators can also draw from the tradition of "single category" theories that provide insight into specific social identities (gender, race, sexual orientation, ability, and so forth) and enhance and deepen understanding of environments that are inclusive and optimal for growth. With attention now on multiple dimensions of identity, educators can use knowledge of early models with insights from the single category theories to explore the ways that identities develop over time and in varying contexts. As a set, all of these theories illuminate college student experiences of privilege, oppression, and intersecting social identities.

Jones and McEwen (2000) developed one of the first holistic models of student development for application in the academy, yet the first clarion call for attention to the whole student came over eight decades ago in "The Student Personnel Point of View (SPPV)" (American Council on Education, 1937/1994a). Continued work on single identity categories such as race, sexual orientation, and ability—and within them, on specific identities such as African American, heterosexual, nondisabled—is vital to continued understanding of the identities and experiences of students. Research that focuses on combinations of identities (such as White Muslims, people who are biracial and bisexual, and working-class Jews) will enhance the ability of student affairs educators to serve students effectively. And studies that press forward with holistic approaches to understanding identity in the context of interpersonal and cognitive development and in relation to multiple dimensions of identity will provide empirical evidence to support effective programs and services in higher education.

Understanding the development of social identities, particularly how students of different social identities learn about themselves and one another, is important to student affairs educators. King and Baxter Magolda (2005) offered a developmental model of intercultural maturity that provided guideposts for scholarship and practice in this area. King, Perez, and Shim (2013) found that students benefitted from sustained exposure to differences, a feeling of safety, and using an array of approaches to engage in intercultural learning. Additional studies that explore how privilege, oppression, and intercultural learning operate in academic settings can enhance higher education practice and enrich student outcomes. In setting forth an agenda for the future of Privilege Studies, McIntosh (2012) urged scholars to elicit "personal testimony about privilege and disadvantage … [because] [e]ach of us contains some of the data we need in order to know ourselves. Listening to others' testimonies allows us to know ourselves even better, know others better, and recognize the matrices of power we are all in" (p. 203).

Discussion Questions

1. Why do social identities matter in higher education and college student development?
2. In what disciplinary traditions did many of the social identity theories that are used in student development originate? Why do disciplinary traditions matter in understanding how to interpret and use a theory?
3. What are the four levels of social identity? Give examples of each.
4. Describe the evolution of social identity development models from the 1960s through today.
5. How would you explain the concepts of oppression and privilege to a group of undergraduate students?
6. Name three categories of privilege. Describe what they have in common and what is different about them.
7. Why did Jones and McEwen create the Model of Multiple Dimensions of Identity? Describe its key components.
8. What did Abes, Jones, and McEwen change when they introduced the Reconceptualized Model of Multiple Dimensions of Identity?
9. Describe three ways that you could use the RMMDI in your work with students.
10. What forms of privilege and oppression do you experience? What key steps will you take to become aware of how they shape your interactions with students as you work to create environments that facilitate development?

CHAPTER FIVE

RACIAL IDENTITY DEVELOPMENT

W. E. B. Du Bois (1903) accurately predicted, "The problem of the Twentieth Century is the problem of the color line" (p. vii). His prophetic words remain relevant in the twenty-first century. College mascots presumed to represent American Indian tribes, annual Halloween parties hosted by sorority and fraternity members donning costumes that negatively depict racially minoritized groups, images of U.S. immigrants constructed solely around Latino populations and referencing them as "illegal aliens" unworthy of citizenship, and erroneous accusations from White people exclaiming that affirmative action is reverse discrimination or that we live in a post–racial world—each represents issues that keep race and racism at the center of public thought and discourse, both on and beyond college campuses.

Race is socially constructed and devoid of any biological premise (Cokley, 2007; Ladson-Billings, 1998; Muir, 1993). Omi and Winant (2004) reference race as "an unstable and 'decentered' complex of social meanings constantly being transformed by political struggle" (p. 116). The meaning systems that undergird race result in material consequences such as the creation and maintenance of racial categories, the assignment of particular bodies to racial groups, and White racial domination over all racial groups. The most detrimental consequence of race is the oppressive system of racism, which is infused in law, politics, education, and everyday interactions. "Race is an organizing principle that cuts across class, gender, and other imaginable social identities" (Leonardo, 2004, p. 140). Race and racism influence worldviews, the treatment of people, life opportunities, and racial identity.

Racial identity theories highlight the role of race and the extent to which it is incorporated into self-concept. Racial identity is "a sense of group or collective identity based on one's perception that he or she shares a common racial heritage with a particular racial group" (Helms, 1993b, p. 3). An underlying presupposition about race is that people experience domination or oppression based upon the racial group with which they identify or are perceived to belong.

While race and racism prevail in the United States, little attention has been placed on them in theories of student development. Some would argue that race remains undertheorized in student development theories because they often omit race and are cloaked in "racelessness" (Patton, McEwen, Rendón, & Howard-Hamilton, 2007). Critical race theory (CRT) frames our introduction to the racial identity models presented in this chapter. As noted in Chapter Two, CRT—an interdisciplinary movement of scholars committed to challenging and deconstructing the interplay of race, racism, and power—is based on several key tenets (Delgado & Stefancic, 2001). First, racism is normal and systemically embedded, allowing it to go unnoticed; student development theories are no exception (Delgado, 1995; Delgado & Stefancic, 2001). In addition, the voices of communities of color are legitimate and central to challenging racialized discourses rooted in White racial domination; hence the need for racial identity theories that center experiences of people of color and disrupt the perceived normalcy of whiteness (Delgado, 1995; Solórzano, 1998). Third, the dominant culture will concede to advances for people of color only when there is also a benefit for them; this is referred to as the *principle of interest convergence* (Bell, 1995; Delgado, 1995; Ladson-Billings, 1998). Fourth, notions of colorblindness and neutrality must be challenged (Bonilla-Silva, 2014; Solórzano, 1998). When colorblindness is used as the dominant script, it renders the experiences of people of color invisible (Ladson-Billings, 1998).

In this chapter, we provide an overview of racial identity development models. We begin with a general discussion of models that provided a foundation for contemporary explorations on racial identity development. We also offer descriptions of several specific theories that depict development for Black, White, Latino/a, Asian American, Native American, and multiracial individuals. We close the chapter by discussing implications for these theories in informing student affairs practice, as well as the need for more research and scholarship that delves into racial identity development.

Racial Identity Development Models

Racial identity development of people of color and White people has attracted increasing attention in the student affairs literature (McEwen, 2003b). Building on the work of Erikson (1950, 1968) and Marcia (1966, 1980), researchers began to examine racial identity development (for example, Cross, 1978, 1991; Helms, 1993a; Kim, 1981) and build models to better understand how identity issues are resolved.

The Atkinson, Morten, and Sue (1979, 1989, 1993, 1998) minority identity development model was introduced in the late 1970s. Sue and Sue (2003) revised the model, calling it the racial and cultural identity development (RCID) model. It comprises five stages. In *conformity*, individuals identify with White culture, internalize negative stereotypes about themselves or their racial/ethnic group, and have no desire to learn about their cultural heritage. In *dissonance*, individuals' experiences contradict their White worldview. They begin a journey of questioning the dominant culture and gaining an increased interest in learning more about their own racial/ethnic group. *Resistance and immersion* involves conscious exploration of one's racial/ethnic identity. Individuals reject White culture and learn about themselves and their cultural group, leading to the formation of a new identity. In the *introspection* stage, individuals grapple with finding a balance between the dominant culture and their own cultural heritage and the role of both in shaping their identity. Those who continue this intensive exploration move to *synergistic articulation and awareness*, in which they integrate their knowledge and experiences into a new identity whereby they accept themselves, appreciate the contributions of other groups, and balance their racial/ethnic identity with other aspects of their identity.

The RCID serves as a foundation for understanding the stages and orientations found in other identity development models presented in this chapter, including models of Black (Cross & Fhagen-Smith, 2001), White (Helms, 1995; Rowe, Bennett, & Atkinson, 1994), Latino (Ferdman & Gallegos, 2001), Asian American (Kim, 2001), American Indian (Horse, 2001) and multiracial identity development (Renn, 2000). Research and application literature on most of these racial identity models is largely absent. As a result, our review of research is limited to scholarship related to Black identity development and multiracial identity development, and discussion of application is brief. We close with critique and suggestions for future work.

Cross and Fhagen-Smith's Model of Black Identity Development

Many models of Black identity development exist (Helms, 1990; Jackson, 2001; Sellers, Smith, Shelton, Rowley, & Chavous, 1998). Cross, Smith, and Payne (2002) describe Black identity as "the passing down from one generation to the next the learned experiences and identity activities that facilitate black adjustment and humanity under conditions often framed by race, racism, and the proactive dimensions of Black culture" (p. 94). William Cross's theory of psychological Nigrescence is the best known theory of Black identity development. The French term *Nigrescence* refers to the "process of becoming black" (Cross, 1991, p. 147). In 1971, Cross presented a five-stage Nigrescence theory, but in 1991 he condensed it to four stages and introduced three central concepts: personal identity (PI), reference group orientation (RGO), and race salience. *Personal identity* refers to the traits and characteristics that one's personality comprises, whereas *reference group orientation* describes what a person values, how the individual sees the world, and the lens through which the individual's philosophical and political views are filtered. *Race salience* "refers to the importance or significance of race in a person's approach to life" (Vandiver, 2001, p. 168).

William Cross and Peony Fhagen-Smith (2001) approached Black identity development using a life span perspective to reposition the original Nigrescence theory within the larger discourse on human development and to account for racialized experiences during childhood. The Nigrescence life span approach is composed of three patterns. *Nigrescence Pattern A* describes a process in which individuals develop a Black identity resulting from "formative socialization experiences" (Cross & Fhagen-Smith, 2001, p. 243). In this pattern, individuals establish their Black identity through interaction with parents and significant others from birth toward adulthood. Nigrescence Pattern A represents most Black people because, by adulthood, they have adopted one of several Black identities. *Nigrescence Pattern B* represents the conversion experience described in Cross's (1991) earlier work. Black people who are not socialized toward Blackness or who have not formed a healthy Black identity usually experience a conversion during adulthood. Whether African Americans experience Nigrescence Pattern A or Nigrescence Pattern B, Nigrescence Pattern C will occur. *Nigrescence Pattern C* involves *Nigrescence recycling*, an expansion or modification of Black identity throughout adulthood. The Cross and Fhagen-Smith life span model (2001) has six sectors encompassing all three Nigrescence patterns.

Sector One: Infancy and Childhood in Early Black Identity Development. In Sector One, factors including family income, traditions, and practices; social networks such as school and church; and historical events contribute to the early socialization experiences of Black children. These aspects make up the human ecologies of Black children who are unaware of racism or a racial identity (Cross & Fhagen-Smith, 2001).

Sector Two: Preadolescence. Development is fostered through parental teachings and their reinforcement outside the home. Through parental socialization, three identity types emerge: *low race salience, high race salience,* and *internalized racism.* Children with low race salience receive few or no messages from parents about race and place no significance on being Black with the exception of physical features. The importance of race is instilled in high race salience children. They are taught to view Black culture as an important aspect of self-concept. The internalized racism identity develops when children see patterns of negativity toward being Black or toward Black people in their immediate family. They begin to adopt these negative ideas and believe stereotypes about Black people as a result of the (mis)education they receive. These internalized ideas can lead to self-hatred. Despite the presence of these three emergent identity types in preadolescence, they are not fully developed identities until the onset of adolescence.

Sector Three: Adolescence. Using Marcia's (1966) identity statuses as a framework (see Chapter Thirteen), Cross and Fhagen-Smith (2001) pointed out that as they enter adolescence, many Black children accept without critical reflection the identity they have developed as a result of the socialization they received to this point (that is, their identity status is foreclosed). They move into moratorium as they begin the exploration process necessary to establish a personally created self-concept. Adolescents reach an achieved identity status by determining that their Black self-concept is truly based on their own beliefs. Their authenticated identity may reflect low race salience, high race salience, or internalized racism.

Cross and Fhagen-Smith (2001) clearly differentiated between the Black identity changes that occur in adolescence (Sector Three) and those that occur in adulthood (Sector Four). Authentication is related to adolescence, while Black identity *conversion* is related to adult development. The original Nigrescence theory assumed Black people entered adulthood with no idea of their Blackness and had to reconstruct their self-concept into one that placed salience on race and Black culture. In the current model, Cross and Fhagen-Smith assumed that most adolescents possess some awareness of a Black self. Black adolescents who enter moratorium with low race salience or internalized racism patterns may have an experience similar to the adult conversion if they move beyond these patterns and develop a healthy Black self-concept with high race salience.

During moratorium, Black youth for whom race has low salience may confirm low race salience self-concepts. Instead of exploring Black identity, these individuals explore the non-race identities that emerged while they were preadolescents (for example, being American, not African American; or focusing on a nondominant sexual or gender identity). For Black youth who approach adolescence with an internalized racism identity pattern, their negative Black self-concepts are likely to be maintained and strengthened if the assumptions they have previously internalized are not challenged or dispelled.

Overall, development in the adolescence phase can be linear, but it is not absolutely predictable. Thus it is highly possible that children who entered adolescence with low race salience will transition out of this sector with low race salience. However, it is also possible that children may have an experience that prompts progression toward adopting high race salience. Similarly, children who enter adolescence with high race salience could solidify a race salient identity but might also experience challenges to their Blackness that could lead to de-emphasizing race and Black culture, and shift focus toward a non–race salient identity.

Sector Four: Early Adulthood. The three identity types that emerged in preadolescence and were potentially explored during adolescence are present in early adulthood. Black people with high race salience identities typically represent the largest number in this sector. These adults have established a clear reference group orientation that values race and Black culture. Thus the changes that may result in their identity occur during Nigrescence Recycling (Sector Six). Persons who did not critically consider their reference group orientation in adolescence (that is, they maintained a foreclosed identity) may need to expand their understanding of their Black self-concept. In short, the Nigrescence experience is not a conversion per se for these individuals, because they already have a high race salience, but Nigrescence helps them personalize their sense of Blackness.

Black adults with low race salience still see race as nonessential and construct diverse identities across an array of categories. They can continue to live in environments where their identities are maintained and their race is never acknowledged. However, they are highly susceptible to adult Nigrescence, particularly if they experience a critical event that causes them to examine their race.

Internalized racism continues into adulthood as well. The same prevalent issues that existed in earlier stages of life remain embedded. To move toward a more corrective self-concept, these individuals have to experience adult Nigrescence. In other words, a conversion is necessary for them to establish a healthy Black identity and race salience.

Black adults who have low race salience or internalized racism may never experience adult Nigrescence. Race can potentially remain nonessential, and feelings of self-hatred may persist throughout adulthood. Similarly, those with high race salience may remain stagnant without having renewed or refreshed their Black self-concept. All of these individuals have *unchanged identities* (Cross & Fhagen-Smith, 2001).

Sector Five: Adult Nigrescence. This sector represents Cross's (1991) original model. Nigrescence involves four stages: pre-encounter, encounter, immersion-emersion, and internalization/internalization commitment. *Pre-encounter* represents two identity types previously mentioned: low race salience (pre-encounter assimilation) and internalized racism (pre-encounter anti-Black). The *encounter* stage occurs when Black people experience an event that causes a conflict in their understanding of their racial identity. Cross (1991) noted that an encounter is an unexpected situation, which can be one traumatic experience or a series of events that prompts a turning point.

Immersion-emersion has two developmental processes. In discussing the earlier Cross (1971) model, Vandiver (2001) stated, "Individuals immerse themselves in black culture to the point of romanticizing it" (p. 166). They become deeply entrenched in the immersion process and ultimately adopt a Black nationalist or pro-Black identity. A pro-Black identity embraces everything Black and strongly opposes White people. Cross (1991) explained that upon entering immersion, individuals have a clear sense of the identity they wish to shed but have little information about the identity they wish to assume. Individuals go through an "in between" phase in which they connect themselves to symbols of Black identity (that is, hairstyle, clothing, music, language; Cross, 1991). However, as they move away from an anti-White perspective toward a pro-Black vision, they begin to focus on nurturing a connection and commitment to Black people. In *emersion,* individuals begin their transition toward stage four, internalization, by reexamining, through a more balanced and focused lens, the coalescing of the affective and cognitive aspects of Black identity. They move beyond the superficiality characterized in the immersion phase toward a more authentic understanding of Black identity.

Although the immersion-emersion stage is a critical point in this model, Cross (1991) explained that negative outcomes might occur, such as *regression, continuation/fixation,* and *dropping out.* Regression toward pre-encounter can occur when individuals have negative experiences that are growth inhibiting or when they are unsuccessful in coping with the push toward a new identity and seek the comfort of the old identity. Individuals who harbor overwhelmingly negative perceptions of White people and remain fixated on these ideas exhibit continuation/fixation. Individuals who become exhausted, depressed, and stressed may drop out of dealing with being Black. Others may drop out once they have established a comfortable sense of Blackness and feel compelled to move on to examine other pressing matters in life.

Internalization represents dissonance resolution and is composed of three different perspectives: Black Nationalist, bicultural, and multicultural. Individuals with a *Black Nationalist identity* consider being Black their most salient identity and commit themselves to political and social platforms to advance the Black community. Individuals who have a *bicultural* reference group orientation concern themselves with infusing their Black identity and their American identity. Individuals who accept a *multicultural* perspective focus on a wide range of identities; thus in addition to being Black, they explore other identities and worldviews and push for social justice.

Black adults who experience a conversion through adult Nigrescence represent *Nigrescence Pattern B.* These individuals have a reinterpreted framework of Blackness. The Nigrescence process can be corrective, particularly for Black adults who exhibit self-hatred. This sector involves coming to race consciousness and establishing a more authentic and balanced comprehension of being Black.

Sector Six: Nigrescence Recycling. Cross and Fhagen-Smith reworked Parham's (1989) model of Nigrescence recycling to be more applicable to their life span model. *Nigrescence recycling* occurs when one's preexisting Black self-concept is called into question. Having no explanatory power to resolve emergent questions regarding their identity, adults reflect on and subject their identity to close scrutiny as they seek resolution. This examination results in an identity that has been enhanced or changed in some way. Throughout adulthood, African Americans will continuously be prompted to address issues or questions of identity, and through resolution they may reach *wisdom,* or a complex and multidimensional understanding of Black identity.

Cross and colleagues expanded Nigrescence theory by further exploring the functionality of Black identity in daily life. Strauss and Cross (2005) suggested three patterns of negotiation that influence the socialization of Black people. These patterns include promotion of "transactional competence in racist situations (transactions with oppression), in all-Black situations (transactions with African Americans), and mainstream circumstances (transactions with the larger and increasingly multicultural American society)" (p. 68). Each pattern represents the types of experiences Black people face daily, whether it be contending with racism, feeling a sense of pride in being Black, or understanding the importance of being successful in the larger society. In sum, Cross's expansion of Nigrescence theory emphasizes the lived experiences of Black people and represents not only how Black identity is performed but the manner in which Black people are taught to perform it (personal communication October 2, 2013). Strauss and Cross suggested five identity enactments or transactions common among Black people. As these enactments occur, identity remains the same across situations, but how individuals respond to a given stimulus in the environment shifts, based upon the level of integration in their Black identity.

Buffering, the first transaction, refers to the protective strategies that individuals use to either shield themselves from or respond to racist or oppressive interactions. Buffering is a reactive behavior enacted to address an immediate threat.

Code-switching is a transaction in which Black people successfully maneuver interactions within the larger mainstream and Black cultural life. Individuals can adeptly shift between the two as needed, suggesting a form of "bicultural competence" (Strauss & Cross, 2005, p. 70). While code-switching could be used as a buffering strategy, it is less associated with threat, because people make conscious choices out of necessity to place themselves in particular situations. Code-switching is a proactive method to address lifelong situations that arise, such as maneuvering the work environment to gain or maintain employment and promotion and striving toward a positive educational trajectory.

Bridging reflects the ability to foster close and meaningful interpersonal relationships with others, whether they are Black or not. This transaction represents a comfortable sense of identity and willingness to embrace people from various walks of life.

Bonding/attachment refers to the central, daily enactments that Black people use to remain connected to and grounded within Black social and cultural life. It represents the way in which Black people maintain deeply felt connections to other Black people and communities.

Individualism is an enactment in which Black people are "being themselves" and express less of a collectivistic affinity toward other Black people. They see themselves as simply "American" or as an "individual" (Strauss & Cross, 2005, p. 99).

The first three enactments—buffering, code-switching, and bridging—are strategies Black people use to navigate interactions with other groups, particularly White people. However, they are also enacted through intragroup relations around "issues such as social status, colorism, and differences in political ideology" that can cause intragroup conflict (Strauss & Cross, 2005, p. 99). One's sexual orientation is another aspect that can shape the extent to which they buffer, code-switch, and bridge within Black interactions and in the mainstream if they identify as gay, lesbian, bisexual, transgender, or queer. Embracing any identity that challenges perceived norms could prompt these three enactments. The bonding enactment is less about the external world and reflects a sense of belongingness and affinity with Black people. Bonding represents the promise of continuity and connection with other Black people. All four of these enactments "are race- and culture-sensitive identity operations that … give meaning to the term *collective identity*" (Strauss & Cross, p. 99). Individualism differs from the other enactments because its related actions reflect a minimization of race-salience and a prioritizing of individualistic thinking over a collectivistic perspective.

The identity enactments, while reflective of the many daily activities of Black people, also represent variation in relation to the stages of Nigrescence theory as described in Sector Five. For example, individualism tends to be more closely tied to the pre-encounter stage (Strauss & Cross, 2005). Individuals in the internalization stage who have adopted a Black Nationalist identity will enact buffering and code-switching when dealing with White people. They are also more likely to minimize bridging with White people and engage in individualism. Their primary enactment would reflect bonding with other Black people. Black people with a multicultural or bicultural identity will engage in all of the transactions (Cross, Smith, & Payne, 2002). For individuals who identify as Black and Biracial/Bicultural or Multicultural, these same enactments occur, but in more complex ways. These individuals may enact "dual-bonding" in which they foster strong connections to Black and mainstream society. Similarly, they may enact buffering and code-switching to address doubts about Black authenticity or to combat others who abide by a monoracial mindset.

Helms's Model of White Identity Development

Highly influenced by the work of William Cross, in 1990 Janet Helms introduced the people of color and the White identity development (WIDM) models (Helms, 1995). The WIDM is widely known and the most researched theory of White identity development. It was created to raise the awareness of White people about their role in creating and maintaining a racist society and the need for them to act responsibly by dismantling it (Helms, 1992).

Helms (1995) contended that all people in the United States have a racial identity that is experienced within a framework of power and privilege. She noted that U.S. residents experience and respond differently to their race and their designated racial group.

Helms (1992) explained that White identity development occurs in two sequential phases. The first is *abandonment of racism* or the process of moving from oblivious or naïve conceptions of race. Upon encountering a racial dilemma that causes dissonance, individuals grapple with the idea of relinquishing idealized notions of whiteness and acknowledging their complicity in maintaining a racist society. The *evolution of a non-racist identity*, the second phase, involves deeper reflection and attempts to interact with other racial group members that are often superficial and/or paternalistic. In this phase, people spend a significant amount of time devising a way to "be White without also being bad, evil, or racist" (Helms, 1992, p. 61). This phase progresses as individuals begin a quest toward understanding themselves as racial beings and the racism and privilege associated with being White, as well as redefining for themselves what it means to be White and taking ownership of racial privilege and how it affects others. Individuals continuously work toward abandoning White privilege and learning about other racial groups.

Rowe, Bennett, and Atkinson's White Racial Consciousness Model

Wayne Rowe, Sandra Bennett, and Donald Atkinson (1994) introduced the White racial consciousness model (WRCM) in response to four key concerns with White racial identity (WRID) models, including Helms's model. They took issue with the fact that many WRID models suggest White people and people of color have parallel identity development processes. Secondly, they asserted that rather than focusing on the development of a White identity, WRID models "mainly describe how Whites develop different levels of sensitivity to and appreciation of other racial/ethnic groups (i.e., racial attitudes)" (p. 131). A third problem is that WRID models assume an arbitrarily assigned linear process that has yet to be verified empirically. The fourth concern is that WRID models, namely Helms's theory, are contextualized strictly through a Black-White framework, with no consideration for other racial groups. Rowe et al. offered an alternative model that explains "the role of White attitudes toward their own and other racial groups … and can consequently describe the phenomena more accurately, predict relationships better, and provide a more stable base for assessment" (p. 133).

White racial consciousness involves "one's awareness of being White and what that implies in relation to those who do not share White group membership" (Rowe et al., 1994, pp. 133–134). Rowe et al. assumed that White racial consciousness and racial awareness are related and that dissonance and the manner in which it is resolved is the primary cause for change in racial attitudes. The model, derived from the ethnic identity stage model introduced by Phinney (1989; see Chapter Six), is composed of "types" of attitudes that White individuals may possess. The types are grouped into two categories: *unachieved White racial consciousness* and *achieved White racial consciousness*. It is important to note that the types are not stages and have no linear sequence. Instead, individuals may transition from one type to another contingent upon the experiences they encounter. Transitions result from significant dissonance, needed to move between the unachieved and achieved White racial consciousness types. The experience of dissonance, positive or negative, can determine to which type individuals move.

Unachieved White racial consciousness is composed of three attitude types: avoidant, dependent, and dissonant. *Avoidant* attitudes represent individuals' lack of conscious thought about their race or other's racial experiences. White people dismiss, ignore, or avoid race until forced to address their denial.

Dependent attitudes exist when individuals commit to superficial forms of White consciousness. Awareness of being White exists without ownership of it. Individuals depend on others to gauge their own views and opinions and will continue this dependence until they engage in meaningful reflection. *Dissonant* types have high levels of uncertainty about being White and the experiences of people of color. They are open to learning but may experience confusion due to the disconnection between previous and newfound racial knowledge.

Achieved White racial consciousness is composed of four types: dominative, conflictive, reactive, and integrative. *Dominative* type attitudes are ethnocentric, rooted in stereotypes, and emphasize racial superiority over people of color. Dominative attitudes can be "passive or active" (Rowe et al., 1994, p. 138). Passive dominative attitudes are expressed through avoiding interactions with people of color and denial of racist attitudes. Active dominative attitudes are overtly expressed through the use of racial slurs, violence, and discrimination.

White people who possess *conflictive* attitudes "are opposed to obvious, clearly discriminatory practices, yet are usually opposed to any program or procedure that has been designed to reduce or eliminate discrimination" (Rowe et al., 1994, p. 138). Individuals may espouse equality but disagree with measures to achieve it because they think equal opportunity exists. People of color are blamed for the challenges they face in society.

Reactive racial attitudes represent beliefs that inequities exist and people of color bear the brunt of these issues in their life experiences. White people understand they are afforded unearned privileges and benefits that perpetuate inequality. They work toward recognizing and addressing discrimination, while attempting to connect with people of color. Reactive attitudes may be passive or active. Those with passive attitudes intellectualize issues facing people of color and may present genuine concern in the presence of other White people, while having no real interactions with people of color. Those with reactive attitudes can be paternalistic in their approach to people of color, often using a White framework. Their concern is genuine as they wrestle with tensions between connecting with people of color and challenging the White status quo.

White people who see the realities of living in a racialized society demonstrate *integrative* racial attitudes. They understand the complexities associated with race and come to terms with being White. Their more integrated view of identity in relation to people of color fosters a commitment to social change. They have genuine interactions with people of color and may engage in social activism. "This type of racial awareness should not be construed as a state of racial self-actualization or transcendence, but more as a process" (Rowe et al., 1994, p. 141).

Ferdman and Gallegos's Model of Latina and Latino Ethnoracial Orientations

Ferdman and Gallegos (2001) stated, "The racial constructs that have predominated the United States do not easily apply to Latinos, and when they are forced to fit, they truncate and distort Latino realities" (p. 44). They offered three considerations for understanding how Latinos experience race and racism. First, while being Latino involves racial, cultural, and ethnic distinctions, race is secondary for these populations. However, skin color remains pertinent among Latinos, and racism may manifest itself in the devaluing of those with darker skin (that is, people with African and indigenous backgrounds) (Ferdman & Gallegos). Second, Latinos often come from mixed heritages and represent a wide range of skin colors, making it difficult to place them in finite racial categories. Third, Latinos respond in various ways to the racial categories in which they are placed in the United States. Some identify as White, while others reject this classification and use Latino as a racial and an ethnic category. Such distinctions can either be "imposed or self-imposed" (Ferdman & Gallegos, p. 45). A number of factors, including familial reference group, educational experiences, peer interaction, and physical appearance, contribute to how people develop their identities.

Bernardo Ferdman and Placida Gallegos (2012) offered a model of Latino identity that "focuses on the ways Latinos come to think about themselves in a diverse and ever-changing society against the backdrop of a wide range of historical and cultural influences" (p. 56). They discuss development within the racial system that permeates the United States and extends to more globalized contexts. They also acknowledge intersectionality of identity, the complexities embedded in discourses that conflate race and ethnicity, and the predominance of racial categories situated within a Black/White binary.

Ferdman and Gallegos avoided the use of stages to describe the identity process and instead provided six different "orientations" that serve as "lenses" through which Latinos may view themselves. The orientations are constructed based upon five features: "one's 'lens' toward identity, how individuals prefer to identify themselves, how Latinos as a group are seen, how Whites are seen, and how 'race' fits into the equation" (p. 49). The model is neither cyclical nor linear. Latinos may relate to several orientations in their lives or remain within one orientation throughout life. In later work, Ferdman and Gallegos (2012) expanded their thinking by prefacing the original model with a set of five critical questions to provide a more nuanced perspective on Latina/o identity development:

1. How does identity orientation affect Latinos' interactions with each other and with non-Latinos as well as the ways in which Latinos see themselves as similar to or different from other Latinos?
2. How are acculturation and enculturation filtered through a racially tinted lens?
3. Under what conditions will Latinos see themselves as linked to the larger community around them? When will they make the effort, for example, to bridge their neighborhoods … with the larger world? For Latinos embedded in a highly Latina/o community: when will they venture out and for what purposes? For those Latina/os embedded in a mostly non-Latino context, what will trigger … them to reconnect (or connect) to the Latino world? And how do they feel about those connections?
4. When and how do Latinos see (and experience) their differences from others as an advantage and value, rather than as a hindrance? How do they make attributions of difference?
5. How do Latinos understand and explain discrimination? (p. 63)

Ferdman and Gallegos's six orientations follow and are intended to reflect the utility of each orientation, the pressing societal expectations and demands influencing development of the orientations and the emergence of the orientations and instances that prompt development among the orientations. The updated model (2012) includes important developmental issues that individuals may face based upon their given orientation.

White-Identified Individuals in this orientation adopt a White racial identity and live as White people. They see other racial groups, including Latinos, as inferior and have minimal association with other Latinos. These individuals may have been exposed to negative, rather than positive, stereotypes and imagery of Latinos, and the consistent exposure inhibits them from developing a positive Latino identity. Their lens is entirely constructed around White culture, and they avoid or remove themselves from "ethnoracial" situations to lessen their vulnerability; by doing so, their identity remains unexamined.

Undifferentiated/Denial In this orientation, individuals have a narrow lens and adopt a color-blind ideology in which they claim that neither race, culture, nor ethnicity matter. They possess "the absence of negative or positive attitudes toward Latino identity," due to limited or no exposure to their culture (p. 68). Individuals do not connect with other Latinos and have a more individual-centered mindset. Movement within and beyond this orientation would involve greater exposure to culture and acknowledgment of both assets and limitations the culture represents.

Latino as Other Individuals with this orientation do not identify with being Latino because they may not know their specific background or heritage within the Latino community. However, they also do not see themselves as White and are likely to connect with other people of color because of their physical attributes (skin color) and the manner in which race is socially constructed. They do not place themselves in a rigid racial category or identify with any particular group, including White and Latino. Learning about their cultural group and making thoughtful decisions regarding the value of cultural knowledge is an important challenge for those with this orientation.

Subgroup-identified Subgroup-identified Latinos identify with their specific subgroup of origin and may view other subgroups, including Latino subgroups, as "inferior." They do not view themselves within a larger pan-Latino framework; instead, they have "a more narrow and exclusive view of their groupness," rarely engaging with Latino groups beyond their own (Ferdman & Gallegos, 2001, p. 52). Many Latinos maintain this orientation throughout their lives. The challenge is understanding that other subgroups exist and also have valuable cultural traditions, as well as galvanizing with other subgroups to push political and social agendas that move all Latinas/os forward.

Latino-identified Individuals in this orientation assume a "pan-Latino" identity (the entire Latino community encompasses one Latino race). These individuals have awareness of subgroups but may minimize these differences. They connect with all Latinos in an effort to promote group solidarity, realizing that some circumstances may require broad Latina/o support, while others may benefit from greater emphasis on subgroup voices.

Latino-integrated Persons with this orientation have a holistic self-concept that successfully incorporates their Latino identity with other identities. They understand racial complexities and see themselves as contributing within a larger multicultural framework inclusive of all people. Development in this orientation stems from exposure to various cultures among and beyond Latina/o identities and perspectives.

Kim's Asian American Identity Development Model

Based on research examining the experiences of Japanese American women, Jean Kim (1981, 2001, 2012) introduced the Asian American racial identity development model (AARID). Kim's model specifically emphasizes racial identity to highlight the "social and psychological consequences" of being racially minoritized in the United States (2012, p. 155). Ethnic identity, she notes, is also of critical importance, but regardless of one's ethnic identification, Asian Americans as a collective must deal with racism in this country. "It is their racial membership, not their ethnic membership, that impacts how Asian Americans feel about themselves in this country" (2012, p. 156). The AARID model addresses how Asian Americans come to terms with their racial identity and resolve racial conflicts in a society dominated by White perspectives. Kim (2001) presented three key assumptions to explain how racialized populations manage their identities in a White racist society. First, Asian American identity and White racism are not mutually exclusive entities. The insidious nature of racism and the press of the external environment influence the development of an Asian American self. Second, Asian Americans must consciously work to unlearn and challenge the negative messages and stereotypes they previously adopted without question. Third, a positive Asian American identity is contingent upon one's capacity to grapple with identity crises and transform previous negative experiences into constructive, growth-enhancing ones (Kim, 2001).

Kim's (2012) later work expounds on the AARID. The author noted that AARID has close similarities to other theoretical perspectives on racial identity in that the process occurs throughout the lifespan and stages, once accomplished, may be "revisited" based upon how individuals respond within a given environment. Kim (2012) also contends the AARID model is of critical relevance to understanding how Asian Americans deal with the psychological effects of racism in the United States. She explained, "One such psychological cost is racial identity conflict" (2012, p. 143). Many Asian Americans struggle with feelings about their racial selves and managing the expectations that stem from external perceptions of who they are and specific expectations from the groups (group orientation) to which they belong. Such experiences heavily influence their internal perceptions of themselves (Kim, 2012). Overall, the identity processes and challenges that some Asian Americans face are largely dictated by living in a racist society, in which the lives of racially minoritized populations carry little value. Kim (2012) explained that shifting political contexts, intergenerational differences and shifts in the structure of Asian American families, and the need for research within these respective areas influence the discourses surrounding Asian American identity. However, the model of AARID has remained consistent over the years and reflects the experiences of many Asian Americans.

Kim's model "describes a developmental process that progresses through five stages of perception and relation to one's racial group and the dominant group" (Kim, 2012, p. 148–149).

Ethnic Awareness. Individuals at this stage view their identity through their families and have not yet had any schooling experiences. As they develop, those who live in predominantly Asian American communities begin to gain greater awareness of their culture and ethnicity and develop a positive self-concept. Those who live in predominantly White communities experience confusion about being Asian American and feel "neutral" about their ethnicity. The primary experience in this stage is discovery of ethnic heritage; thus increased exposure has positive consequences for positive identity development (Kim, 2001; 2012).

White Identification At this point, children have begun their schooling experiences and may have learned several cultural norms such as enduring suffering quietly, avoiding public shame, and valuing a collective group orientation (Kim, 2001). At a very early age, Asian Americans are exposed to others who point out or make insensitive comments about how Asian Americans are different, fueling the development of shame for being Asian American (Kim, 2012). Due to the "collective orientation" (Kim, 2001, p. 74) among Asian American communities, individuals will react by attempting to fit in or denying racism exists. The desire to be accepted leads to the rejection of their Asian identity and internalization of White standards, "especially regarding standards of physical beauty and attractiveness" (Kim, 2001, p. 74).

This stage is characterized by both active and passive White identification. Asian Americans who experience *active White identification* are usually raised in predominantly White environments. As a result they forgo their "Asianness," adopt a White identity, and take measures to erase or downplay Asian identity (including language, physical features, food). Asian Americans who exhibit *passive White identification* likely have positive Asian ethnic awareness due to being raised in a predominantly Asian community. They do not view themselves as White, but internalize White culture and experience moments of "fantasizing about being white" (Kim, 2012, p. 147). Moving beyond this stage requires individuals to dismiss the belief of full assimilation into a White world.

Awakening to Social Political Consciousness   In this stage, Asian Americans no longer blame themselves for being treated differently and realize that their negative experiences are the result of racist social structures. They experience a paradigm shift through which whiteness is no longer treated as superior. For individuals in this stage, "passing" for White is unacceptable because they are astutely aware of the political and social implications of racism for Americans of Asian descent. In fact, "White people become the antireferent group, people they don't want to be like" (Kim, 2012, p. 147). Asian Americans in this stage feel more connected to having a minoritized group status.

Redirection to Asian American Consciousness   In this stage, Asian Americans move beyond the oppressed group designation, consciously identify with being an Asian American, and establish a sense of self-pride (Kim, 2001). This transition occurs with the support of family, friends, and the Asian American community, as well as through exploration of self and Asian culture, history, and heritage. Learning about the historical marginalization of Asian Americans produces feelings of fury and anger, but individuals move past these reactions in an effort to reconcile feelings about themselves as both Asian and American. Movement to the next stage is possible when individuals define what it means to be Asian American and the politics embedded in espousing this identity and embracing a sense of pride in being themselves.

Incorporation   The incorporation phase involves establishing a strong sense of "confidence in one's Asian American identity" (Kim, 2012, p. 148). Asian Americans in this stage have a positive self-concept. They move beyond immersion in strictly Asian American communities, can successfully connect with other populations, and can focus on other aspects of their identity without abandoning their newly redefined racial identity.

Horse's Perspective on American Indian Identity Development

American Indians represent a diverse array of peoples, tribes, and cultures. In order to understand their racial identity, it is important to recognize the role of colonization. "Colonization refers to both the formal and informal methods (behaviors, ideologies, institutions, policies, and economies) that maintain the subjugation or exploitation of Indigenous Peoples, lands, and resources" (Waziyatawin & Yellow Bird, 2005, p. 2). In the face of colonization, such as efforts by White people to "civilize" Indigenous peoples and force them into hegemonic cultural assimilation (Wright, 1988), Native Americans consistently have fought to preserve their culture. While cautioning against the generalization of American Indian identity, Horse (2001) offered several perspectives that often prevail in the establishment of a healthy identity for members of Native populations.

Perry Horse's (2001, 2012) model of Indian racial identity is grounded in what he termed individual and group "consciousness" (p. 100). This consciousness captures the unique and collective experiences of American Indians within a psychosocial context (Horse, 2012). Horse (2012) offered additional considerations for thinking about American Indian consciousness across generations and time. He explained that "contemporary influences of racial awareness, the legal status of Indians, and potential loss of native languages and culture will all figure into the Indian identity equation" (p. 110).

There are five cross-generational themes that Horse used to characterize consciousness.

First, knowledge of native language and culture reinforces a sense of consciousness. Language is central in American Indian culture and helps individuals to establish a sense of self, while also providing a vehicle through which cultural traditions, values, and behaviors are transmitted (Horse, 2001). Second, consciousness is grounded in the validity of one's genealogical heritage as Indian. It is important for individuals not only to understand tribal history but also to embrace teachings throughout life about being Indian. Third, consciousness also exists through adopting a worldview that respects the traditions and philosophical values of Indian ways (Horse). The extent to which individuals see themselves as Indian people is the fourth aspect of consciousness. The fifth element of consciousness is one's status as a member of an officially recognized tribe.

Horse's later thinking about native consciousness was shaped by his belief that it is a product of "eras of change" (2012, p. 109). These eras of change shift notions of Indian culture and identity, as well as facilitate Native American people's orientation toward race consciousness, political consciousness, linguistic consciousness, and cultural consciousness. Orientation toward race consciousness highlights the historical trajectory of Indian conceptions of race over time. He notes that many Native Americans tend to see themselves in terms of tribal affiliation rather than race. Orientation toward political consciousness focuses on the legal and political issues surrounding Native communities and their relationship with the U.S. government, particularly sovereignty rights. Orientation toward linguistic consciousness deals with the preservation of Indigenous languages, "the most potent aspect of one's tribal identity," but also the aspect most in danger of extinction (Horse, 2012, p. 114). Orientation toward cultural consciousness emphasizes a commitment to native culture and rests upon Native people's desire for and actions toward preserving and renewing forms of cultural expression that breathe life into native identity.

Research

Research related to racial identity development has largely centered on Black identity. With regard to student populations, much of the research on Black racial identity examines the phenomenon in counseling situations (Bradby & Helms, 1993; Carter, 1993; Helms, 1993a). Little attention has focused on how racial identity affects students' daily lives and decisions. However, one study examined the relationship between Black students' racial identity and their participation in cultural (Black-oriented) and noncultural campus organizations (Mitchell & Dell, 1992). As the researchers hypothesized, students whose scores on the RIAS-B (Parham & Helms, 1981; an instrument based on Cross's [1978] early work on Black identity) indicated they were in encounter, immersion, or internalization stages were more likely to be involved in cultural organizations, while students in the pre-encounter stage were not.

Using the RIAS-B and the African American Acculturation scale (AAAS), Pope-Davis, Liu, Ledesma-Jones, and Nevitt (2000) found significant positive correlations between the constructs of acculturation and racial identity among 187 African American students. A study of Black college students using Cross's early model provided partial support for the hypothesis that racial identity stage and self-esteem are related (Parham & Helms, 1985). The study found that Black college students in pre-encounter and immersion stages tend to have low self-esteem, whereas those in encounter tend to have positive self-esteem. In a later study, racial identity was a significant predictor of the psychological health of 136 African American college students at a predominantly White institution, endorsing the theoretical concepts offered by Cross's revised model (Pillay, 2005). Gilbert, So, Russell, and Wessel (2006) also used the RIAS-B to examine racial identity and psychological symptoms among Black students at Historically Black Colleges and Universities (HBCUs).

Research indicates that racial identity is not a predictor of grades or academic outcomes for college students (Awad, 2007; Lockett & Harrell, 2003). However, Sanchez and Carter (2005) reported significant relationships between racial identity attitudes and religious orientation among Black college students. Spurgeon and Myers (2010) used the RIAS-L to examine the relationship of racial identity, wellness, and college type among African American men attending predominantly White institutions (PWIs) and HBCUs. While no significant relationship was found, they were surprised to learn that men at PWIs had higher internalization scores, and they noted that PWI environments, though seemingly negative, may actually facilitate opportunities for men to connect with other men of color in solidarity. Men at HBCUs had high social self-wellness, suggesting a welcoming climate at HBCUs.

When the Nigrescence theory was expanded, researchers began to use the Cross Racial Identity Scale (CRIS) to examine racial identity. For example, Cokley (2002) used the CRIS to measure the relationship between racial identity and internalized racism among African American college students at an HBCU. He found that those in earlier stages (pre-encounter and immersion-emersion) were more likely to hold negative stereotypes of Black people, including intellectual inferiority and sexual prowess, whereas those in latter stages did not. Scholarship on the relationship of racial identity in Black college students to several other variables continues to grow and remains primarily based on Cross's contributions. These studies examine racial identity in relation to moral judgment (Moreland & Leach, 2001), stereotype threat (Davis, Aronson, & Salinas, 2006), perceptions of racial bias (Jefferson & Caldwell, 2002), psychosocial development (Pope, 1998; Taub & McEwen, 1992), racial socialization (Thompson, Anderson, & Bakeman, 2000), college racial composition (Cokley, 1999), coping (Neville, Heppner, & Wang, 1997), involvement (Taylor & Howard-Hamilton, 1995), psychological health (Whittaker & Neville, 2010), adjustment to college (Anglin & Wade, 2007), and perfectionism (Elion, Wang, Slaney, & French, 2012).

Application

A few scholars have encouraged faculty to learn more about their own and their students' racial identity development. Tatum's work (1992) has been particularly helpful over time since she used many examples to explain racial identity theory and its utility. Ortiz and Rhoads (2000) offered a multicultural education framework that could be used in programming to explore and deconstruct whiteness. They asserted that the only way to "displace white racial identity as the universal norm is by challenging ourselves and our students to name it" (p. 82).

Clayton and Jones (1993) recommended workshops that focus on unlearning racism for student affairs administrators and students in graduate preparation programs. These experiences allow White students to shift from viewing other racial groups as invisible, or in a stereotypical way, to respecting, appreciating, and celebrating racially different people. Such workshops can contribute to the eradication of racism in the academy.

The promotion of racial identity development and general knowledge of how racism operates in society is sorely needed at colleges and university. Incidents of racial violence (verbal, physical, and psychological) on college campuses and beyond are too numerous to avoid. Student affairs educators have a responsibility for facilitating dialogues and hosting programs that encourage students to examine race, racism, and racial identity. They also have an obligation to work collaboratively with academic affairs to provide opportunities in classrooms and other learning environments that allow students to grapple with racist assumptions, beliefs, and ideologies. Such opportunities can be critical in helping students come to terms with how their general understanding is a manifestation of their racial identity, as well as the extent to which they are privileged or oppressed due to their racial identity.

Any of the theories mentioned in this chapter thus far could be used to frame programs and services that promote racial identity development. For example, revising the curriculum in ways that incorporate diverse voices from various racial groups is one way to expose to students the marginalization of some racial groups. Research indicates that diversity-related courses have benefits when intentionally planned (Chang, 2002). In addition, culture centers and multicultural affairs offices are important campus spaces that allow racially minoritized students to learn about themselves, reflect on their culture, and develop into racially conscious individuals (Patton, 2010; Stewart, 2011). These centers can also be helpful to white students who wish to move beyond their comfort zone, engage in cross-racial interactions, and move toward a more developed understanding of their white identities (Benitez, 2010). Overall, fostering racial identity development could serve as a major tool in prompting students to consider their contributions to a racially just society as well as, the actions in which they might engage to disrupt racism on campus, and in society upon graduation.

Mixed Race And Multiracial Identity Development

While early theories of racial identity were significant contributions to understanding the process of development for racially marginalized groups, these theories presume a monoracial experience and fail to account for populations of people who identify with two or more racial categories. Nearly 7 million people (2.4% of the population) indicated on the 2000 U.S. census that their ancestry included more than one race (Jones & Smith, 2003). Based on data from that census, Jones and Smith described the multiracial population of the United States as young, reflecting an increase in multiracial births and more mixed heritage individuals claiming multiracial identities. The mixed race population is also diverse, with the largest percentage (32.3%) indicating they are White and "some other race" (Jones & Smith, p. 5).

In this section we review key theories related to multiracial identity development. While the terms biracial, multiracial, mixed race, and blended commonly refer to individuals whose racial and/or ethnic heritage is mixed, Stephan (1992) correctly pointed out "mixed heritage" is more accurate because it avoids the biological assumption of the term "race." In this chapter, terms used by various authors are retained, with the caveat that "mixed heritage" is a more accurate label.

Acceptance of "multiracial" as an identity is difficult for those who view races as discrete and cannot fathom people legitimately belonging to more than one group (Root, 2003a; Zack, 1995). For many, mixed race people are, first and foremost, not White (Gordon, 2004; Root, 1990). Such thinking stems from the "hypodescent or 'one-drop' rule," which was legally used to categorize mixed heritage individuals as Black "regardless of the proportion of black ancestry or the person's physical appearance" (Davis, 1995, p. 115). The rule was used to prevent children of White slave owners born to Black enslaved women from having any of the privileges associated with their paternity (Root, 1995) and operated as a strategy to maintain the White male power structure, ensuring that property, voting, and inheritance rights stayed in White hands (Wijeyesinghe, 1995).

In both historical and present day contexts, refusal to accept multiracial individuals has been manifested not only by White but also by non-White persons (Renn, 2012; Root, 1990; Song, 2003). For example, opponents of multiracial identification argue that such identification would obscure important racial differences and make it impossible to track progress on efforts to eliminate racial discrimination (Staples, 2007; Wu, 2006). Challenges such as these can have a tremendous impact on development of a secure identity.

Approaches to Mixed Race and Multiracial Identity Development

Identity development is a complex process for individuals from mixed race backgrounds (Kerwin & Ponterotto, 1995). Not only must they deal with prejudice similar to that experienced by people who are members of non-White ethnic and racial groups, but they must also decide "how to reconcile the heritages of both parents in a society that categorizes individuals into single groups" (p. 200).

Several approaches have been used to explain the process of identity development for mixed race individuals. *Deficit approaches* presume that bi- and multiracial individuals are "confused, distraught, and unable to fit in anywhere in the American racial landscape" (Wijeyesinghe, 2001, p. 131). Identity issues are believed to be internal rather than the result of societal pressures (Gibbs, 1987; Stonequist, 1937). *Stage theories* attempt to present multiracial identity development as normal (Wijeyesinghe, 2001). Patterned after stage theories of Black and White identity development (for example, Cross, Jackson, Helms, Hardiman), these approaches (Collins, 2000; Kerwin & Ponterotto, 1995; Kerwin, Ponterotto, Jackson, & Harris, 1993; Kich, 1992; Poston, 1990) include an immersion-like stage, strong emotional content, and greater self-awareness and self-appreciation in later stages (Wijeyesinghe, 2001). Critics note that stage theories may not be as appropriate for multiracial people as they might be for monoracial individuals, since multiracial individuals have more than one heritage to reconcile, a process that is varied and complex rather than linear (Renn, 2004). In addition, Standen (1996) suggested that the choice of a single multiracial identity could be viewed as a "forced choice" (p. 247) and therefore not necessarily positive.

Typology approaches suggest there are multiple ways for mixed heritage individuals to develop. Cortés (2000) and Daniel (2002) both rejected the idea that an integrated multiracial identity is the only healthy identity for mixed race individuals. They proposed that, depending on background and environmental influences, a number of options exist for how an individual may choose to identify. Cortés (2000) identified five identity patterns among mixed race individuals of various backgrounds: (1) *single racial identity,* where one aspect of the individual's heritage is favored; (2) *multiple racial identity,* in which individuals identify with each race that makes up their heritage (for example, Black and White); (3) *multiple racial–multiracial identity,* where individuals identify with each aspect of their heritage while also viewing themselves as multiracial; (4) *multiracial identity,* in which this identity is the primary one chosen rather than one or more specific racial identities, and (5) *nonracial identity,* where a person has no sense of racial identity (for example, a recent immigrant from a country in which race has little or no meaning).

Daniel (2002) hypothesized a continuum of identity for individuals with mixed Black and White heritage, ranging from integrative to pluralistic. On this continuum, Daniel (2002) saw three identity types: (1) synthesized identity, (2) functional identity/European American orientation, and (3) functional identity/African American orientation. A weakness of the approaches introduced by Cortés (2000) and Daniel is that both are based on anecdotal data only. Also, while both Cortés and Daniel expanded how multiracial identity is conceptualized, neither theorist examined factors that influence the identity choices individuals make.

Ecological approaches include an examination of external factors that affect how individuals decide to identify racially and/or ethnically, as well as how and why an initially chosen identity may change over time and place (Root, 2003a). A number of theorists writing about multiracial identity development adopted an ecological perspective, including Stephan (1992), Wijeyesinghe (2001, 2012) and Root (1996, 2003a, 2003b). A weakness of these three approaches is that the theorists did not conduct follow-up research to validate their findings. They also failed to consider the various identities that individuals chose. Maria P.P. Root's (1996, 2003a, 2003b) ecological model addressed these issues by outlining the variety of identity choices that mixed heritage individuals make, in addition to delineating factors that influence identity development. Her model is based on empirical research conducted during the 1990s.

Root (1996) first described four ways that mixed race individuals negotiate their identities as "border crossings" (p. xx). They are: (1) accept the identity assigned by society, (2) choose a monoracial identity, (3) choose a mixed-race identity, or (4) create a new racial identity. Later she added a fifth identity type: select a White identity (Root, 2003a, 2003b). Root (2003a) suggested persons understand themselves within the context of their environments, which change throughout life and can lead individuals to alter how they identify. Root (2003a) also noted that people might label themselves in more than one way depending on context.

Root (1995, 2003a, 2003b) identified a number of external factors that influence ethnic and racial identity development of mixed race individuals. The first five influences are contextual and therefore may not be obvious: the history of race within one's geographical region, generation, sexual orientation, gender, and class. More apparent factors are family functioning, family socialization, community, personal attributes, and physical appearance.

A number of studies (Brown, 2001; Hall, 1992; Kilson, 2001; Mass, 1992; Rockquemore & Brunsma, 2002; Wallace, 2001) have found that mixed heritage individuals choose a variety of labels when identifying themselves, as Root (2003a) suggested, and that the identity choices of multiracial individuals change over time and are contingent on the social context (Brown, 2001; Kilson, 2001; Standen, 1996). Researchers have also determined that identity development is affected by Root's (1995, 2003a, 2003b) personal and contextual factors (Brown, 2001; Hall, 1992; Hall & Cooke Turner, 2001; Korgen, 1998; Mass, 1992; Pinderhughes, 1995; Rockquemore, 2002; Rockquemore & Brunsma, 2002; Root, 1997, 2001; Talbot, 2008; Twine, 1996) as well as family and community influences (DeBose & Winters, 2003; Hall & Cooke Turner, 2001; Kilson, 2001; Miville, Constantine, Baysden, & So-Lloyd, 2005; Rockquemore & Brunsma, 2002; Shih, Bonam, Sanchez, & Peck, 2007; Wallace, 2003; Williams, 1996). Few of these studies, other than those conducted by Root herself, were explicitly designed to validate Root's theory, and a limited number have been based on the experiences of college students (Kilson, 2001; Rockquemore, 2002; Rockquemore & Brunsma, 2002; Twine, 1996; Wallace, 2001, 2003). While Root's theory has been supported by a reasonable amount of research, no specific applications to higher education could be found. Renn's ecological theory of mixed race identity development addressed this concern.

Renn's Ecological Theory of Mixed Race Identity Development

Noting that very little research on biracial identity had been completed in college settings, Kristen Renn (2000, 2003, 2004) conducted three increasingly complex studies examining both the identity development process and outcomes experienced by mixed race college students of various racial/ethnic backgrounds, generating an ecological model of mixed race identity. Renn's theory focuses on both ecological factors that influence multiracial identity development and the various labels individuals with mixed heritages use to identify themselves. Renn's (2000) study revealed the importance of space and peer culture on multiracial identity development. The concept of space included both physical and psychological elements. Students were influenced by the extent to which they found places where they saw themselves fitting in, either in formal organizations or in informal peer groups. Seeing parallels between her findings and Bronfenbrenner's (1979, 1993) ecology model of human development, Renn (2003, 2004) used the four components of Bronfenbrenner's (1979, 1993, 1995) person-process-context-time (PPCT) model (see Chapter Two) as a framework to discuss her mixed race participants' experiences.

Renn (2003) found that for biracial individuals the following aspects of the *person* component of the model applied: family background and heritage, extent of cultural knowledge, degree of experience with individuals of one's own heritage and other cultural backgrounds, and physical appearance. Secondly, Renn (2003) noted that in Bronfenbrenner's model the "key to development is the increasing complexity of interactive *Processes* [italics added] in which the individual is engaged" (p. 392). The college environment provides many such options for multiracial students to grapple with the cognitive demands of making sense of race (Renn, 2003, 2004).

Within the *context* of the college environment, Renn (2003, 2004) identified the following settings that influenced the identity development of mixed race students: (1) microsystems that encouraged face-to-face interactions with either positive or negative racial overtones, including monoracial and multiracial student organizations; (2) mesosystems of campus culture that sent positive or negative messages, including the "permeability of group boundaries and the desirability of identifying with various groups within the campus environment" (Renn, 2003, p. 394); (3) the exosystem that affected students' awareness of racial identity, including policies for identifying one's race/ethnicity on forms required by the college, and attention paid in the curriculum to racial issues; and (4) the aspects of the macrosystem that were influential in the students' development, including how the students viewed race and culture and their own roles in these systems as influenced by the existing belief systems about individuals with mixed race backgrounds. *Time*—the sociohistorical context—greatly influenced the macrosystem, in that debates about the racial and ethnic categories to be included on the 2000 census were very prevalent during these students' formative years. Renn (2003) correctly pointed out that Bronfenbrenner's model does not provide a sense of individual development over time.

Identity Patterns

Renn (2004) illustrated the variability and fluidity of identity among mixed race college students. Her participants chose various ways of identifying racially, and many presented different identities depending on the situation and context. Indeed, Taylor (2005) suggested that the most important finding from Renn's (2004) study is that a single identity may be neither possible nor desirable for mixed race students. Renn (2004) described five fluid and nonexclusive "identity patterns" (p. 67), all of which she viewed as healthy: (1) monoracial, (2) multiple monoracial, (3) multiracial,

(4) extraracial, and (5) situational. Different life experiences may lead individuals to change how they identify at various times in their lives. Following is a discussion of each of these patterns.

Monoracial Identity Close to half (48%) of Renn's (2004) participants claimed a monoracial identity; if one of their parents was White, the identity they chose generally represented their nondominant ancestry. Claiming a monoracial identity was easiest for students whose appearance and cultural knowledge were congruent with that identity. Cultural knowledge was greatly influenced by the presence or absence of family representing that heritage. Once in college, peer microsystems affected the degree to which students could easily assume a monoracial identity and have it accepted.

Multiple Monoracial Identities Almost half (48%) of the students Renn (2004) interviewed identified using multiple monoracial identities, most representing their parental heritages (for example, White and Latino; African American and Asian). These students often were equally knowledgeable about each aspect of their heritage or sought more information in college. They exhibited a strong desire to label themselves rather than be labeled by others. Students' ability to successfully identify with more than one monoracial group was contingent on how accepting their peers were of such a label.

Multiracial Identity Most of the students (89%) in Renn's (2004) study identified using a term that represented their unique mixed race background (for example, multiracial, biracial, hapa, mixed). They saw themselves as "existing outside of the monoracial paradigm" (Renn, 2004, p. 156) and sharing common experiences with other mixed race students regardless of heritage. For some students this was a privately held identity; others used it openly. On campuses that had either formal or informal groups where mixed race students interacted, public identification as mixed was more common. Being exposed to racial identity issues in classes and other educational settings also contributed to identification as multiracial.

Extraracial Identity Students in this pattern either opt out of racial categorization completely or do not adhere to the categories used in the United States (Renn, 2004). About one quarter of Renn's (2004) interviewees fit this pattern. Many had been raised outside of the United States, and about half attended an institution where they were exposed to postmodern perspectives and the idea that race is a social construction rather than a biological reality—ideas that contributed to their decision not to identify racially. All but one of the students who chose this identity were juniors and seniors. None of the students solely identified in this manner, which might suggest that "holding such an approach to racial identity is a difficult stance to maintain in the face of powerful forces on campuses that are organized in part around racial identities" (Renn, 2004, p. 78).

Situational Identity Over half (61%) of Renn's (2004) participants identified differently in different contexts, including all of the students who identified extraracially. They considered racial identification fluid and contextually driven. Shifting among identities was sometimes unconscious and other times deliberate. This process was easy for some students and stressful for others. The rigidity of racial boundaries on campus was a factor. Renn (2004) argued that rather than being problematic, as stage theorists would suggest, "the ability to read contexts and construct identity in relation to specific contexts is a highly evolved skill requiring emotional maturity and cognitive complexity" (p. 80).

Research

Renn (2004) identified trends with regard to identity choice among various student populations. In addition, researchers have found patterns of identity labeling similar to Renn's (2004). Factors influencing identity choice—in particular, the importance of the college years for multiracial identity development—have been documented.

Trends in Identity Choice

Renn (2004) reported some trends with regard to the five identity patterns. Women identified with more patterns on average than men. Men were more likely than women to select only one monoracial identity. Students whose parents were both people of color were less likely than students with a White parent to identify monoracially, more likely to select multiple monoracial identities, and very much more likely to select situational identities. Students with one White parent and one Black parent were less likely to select an extraracial identity, perhaps because of peer pressure to identify racially.

Identity Pattern Trends

While not directly based on Renn's (2004) theory, a number of research studies support some or all of the identity patterns she found. These include Wallace's (2001) study of high school and college students of mixed race background and Kilson's (2001) study of biracial youth. Wallace (2001) found that 14 of the

15 students in her study used at least two labels to identify themselves, consistent with Renn's (2004) finding that many students identify in more than one way. However, fewer of Kilson's (2001) participants (10 of 52) chose more than one label. Participants in a study conducted by Miville Constantine, Baysden, & So-Lloyd or Miville, Darlington, Whitlock, and Mulligan (2005) reported both a private multiracial identity and a public identity that was most often monoracial. They also exhibited an ability to adapt their identities to their social surroundings and expectations of others, as Renn (2004) suggested.

Identity Development Influencers

Identity development for the individuals in Miville, Darlington, Whitlock and Mulligan's (2005) study was influenced by significant others, particularly parents; specific places, especially school environments; and critical time periods, especially elementary school years, high school years, and college—findings that support Renn's (2004) ecological perspective. Renn (2004) also found differences in identification based on the specific institution the students attended, indicating that the culture and curriculum of the institution had an influence on how students saw themselves. In their study of 47 racially mixed college students of various heritages at two state universities in California, one more racially diverse than the other, Phinney and Alipuria (1996) discovered that 80% of the students chose a monoracial identity label when asked for their race on an open-ended question. Students with a White parent were more likely to identify as White, rather than mixed or the race of their other parent, on the predominantly White campus (45.5%) than on the ethnically diverse campus (5.9%), demonstrating the influence of context on identity, similar to Renn's (2003, 2004) findings concerning the differential impact of campus environments.

The Impact of College

Paralleling Renn's (2004) findings, researchers have found that college is a particularly challenging time for biracial individuals (Brown, 2001; King, 2008a; Korgen, 1998; Twine, 1996; Wallace, 2003). College is a major transition for mixed heritage students in that they leave the direct influence of their families and enter an environment in which peer interaction and friendships become especially important. Brown (2001) found that since her Black and White biracial participants were not given an opportunity to identify as biracial on application forms and therefore indicated that they were Black, they were recruited into Black organizations, where many found a home but others felt pushed to be something they were not and to choose between Black and White cultures. The Black and White biracial students at UC Berkeley who participated in Twine's (1996) study reported that the politicized racial environment pressured students who had any Black ancestry to assume a Black identity, date Black partners, and join Black student organizations. Korgen's (1998) and Harris's (2015) respondents also felt pressured to choose between the Black and White communities on campus, particularly by monoracial Black students, and to perform blackness in order to be accepted.

In the college setting, "cultural legitimacy and loyalty" (Wallace, 2003, p. 89) are key factors in acceptance and greatly influence the identity development of mixed heritage students. If their appearance is ambiguous and/or if their name or language does not reflect their ethnic identity, students may have a particularly difficult time being accepted by monoracial groups of color (Wallace, 2003). At the same time, biracial students are assumed by whites to be "of color" and are therefore excluded from White peer groups. The degree of fluency that mixed heritage students have with their racial/ethnic cultures greatly influences the extent to which they are eventually accepted by and see themselves as belonging to groups reflecting their background (Wallace, 2003).

King's (2008b) findings supported those of Wallace (2003). She identified the two major challenges facing multiracial students in her study: (1) how other students perceived their racial identities, based on the multiracial student's appearance, and (2) pressure from peers to conform to specific ways of being, based on their perceived racial heritage. King (2008a) reflected that "as a light-skinned multiracial woman with a racially ambiguous appearance and no knowledge of what [her] actual racial identity is because [she is] adopted," finding an answer to the question, "What are you?" was an ongoing concern. King (2008a) also reported another poignant example of being spoken to in Spanish because individuals perceived that she was Latina and the awkward result when she was unable to understand them.

College experiences led many individuals in Brown's (2001) study to reconsider and modify how they identified racially, and they left college "more firmly grounded about who they were" (p. 92). The women in Twine's (1996) study noted that taking courses in Black and ethnic studies helped them learn about their heritage and influenced their identity decisions. In addition, the establishment of multiracial groups on campuses provided a critical space for mixed heritage students to explore identity issues (King, 2008a, 2008b; Wallace, 2003).

Application

A strength of Renn's (2004) work is the number of implications she offered for higher education practice. Her suggestions relate to assessment, policy changes, programs, structural diversity, curriculum, and boundary crossing. In terms of assessment, Renn (2004) stressed the need to assess the campus climate experienced by mixed race students and accurately determine their enrollment numbers in colleges and universities and the various ways in which they identify. Institutional policy on how racial and ethnic data are collected must be reviewed and changed (Renn, 2004). For multiracial students, being able to indicate their mixed heritage, by either selecting more than one race/ethnicity or being able to choose "multiracial" as a way of identifying, gave students in Renn's (2004) study a feeling of inclusion, whereas having to "check one box only" was viewed as exclusionary. Renn and Lunceford (2002) reported that only 17.3% of the 127 randomly sampled institutions provided students the option to indicate more than one race and/or ethnicity. Not only does limiting students to only one racial/ethnic choice result in inaccurate data, but it also unfairly forces students to negate part of their heritage—an arbitrary decision with significant emotional ramifications for many (Cortés, 2000). Currently, institutions are required to offer the opportunity to indicate more than one race.

Scholars (Cortés, 2000; Renn, 2004; Williams, Nakashima, Kich, & Daniel, 1996) also stressed the importance of creating welcoming spaces for multiracial students by establishing student organizations for mixed heritage students to help them find others with common experiences. Orientation presentations, speakers' series, and awareness workshops, as well as providing opportunities for multiracial students to participate in cultural events, are other ways of creating a feeling of inclusion among mixed race students (Renn, 2003, 2004). Wong and Buckner (2008) provided an overview of emerging student services and practices for working with multiracial students, and Gasser (2008) discussed the role played by social networking sites, wikis, blogs, and other technology in supporting this population.

Structural diversity is also important for multiracial students. Multiracial faculty and staff should be visible and available to interact with multiracial students. Increasing the numbers of students of color on campus also increases the likelihood that the number of mixed race students will increase to the critical mass necessary to create informal and formal networks. Renn (2000, 2003) also pointed out the importance of including information about multiracial issues and identity in classes to enable all students to learn more about this topic, create a more inclusive environment for students of mixed heritage, and assist multiracial students in developing a sense of their own identity. In addition, Williams et al. (1996) stressed that courses on multiracial topics are important for social and political purposes in that they legitimize multiracial identity. Finally, Renn (2004) argued for environmental design that allows students to cross boundaries between peer cultures. In this process, it is helpful to ensure diversity in student groups over which the university has some control—such as orientation groups, advising groups, and course sections—and to make sure that physical space is used in ways that promote interaction among students of different backgrounds. Faculty and student affairs staff can also encourage boundary crossing in one-on-one conversations, leadership education programs, and student group advising.

Critique and Future Directions

While it is encouraging to see a number of racial identity development theories appearing in the literature, the lack of research available to validate the theories discussed in this chapter as well as others (for example, Hardiman, 2001; Jackson, 1976, 2001) is problematic (Burrow, Tubman, & Montgomery, 2006). Moreover, the research studies of racial identity that do exist rarely address the applicability of the models to higher education or student affairs specifically. To further complicate matters, existing models do not account for the complexity of development, and they characterize identity "in relationship to other groups and, in particular, the dominant majority" (Casas & Pytluk, 1995, p. 166), with little attention to other aspects that can influence development (for example, history of racism, other social identities).

Despite this complexity, ecological theories of multiracial identity development seem to provide a closer representation of reality than other theories that can be found in the literature. Further research is needed, however, to validate these approaches. Existing research, while supportive of the ecological theories of Root and Renn, is mostly atheoretical (Miville, 2005). Existing research on multiracial identity is also limited in that it tends to be based on biracial individuals of mixed Black and White heritage; studies have used small, regional, self-identified samples; they have been mostly qualitative and therefore are not generalizable; they have lacked consistent definitions of racial identity variables; and data analysis procedures have not been clearly discussed (Miville, 2005; Miville, Constantine, Baysden, & So-Lloyd, 2005; Rockquemore & Brunsma, 2002; Spencer, 2006). Also, most of the studies have focused on children and adolescents rather than college students or adults (Miville).

Not only is there an increased need for theoretical perspectives that address diverse student populations, but closer scrutiny of racial identity theories for people of color also is necessary to better understand the rapidly growing student populations that are becoming the majority in U.S. higher education. More must be known about the identity processes of diverse students from a "dynamic perspective—the affective and cognitive manifestations and their implications for an individual's psychological well-being and personality and/or characterological development from both a short- and a long-term perspective" (Casas & Pytluk, 1995, p. 176). In addition, most racial identity theories imply that oppression is at the core of identity, rather than factors—such as language, country of origin, and culture—that can also shape identity (Sue & Sue, 1990).

Racial identity models have highlighted individual differences among students. Yet the theories and models available represent only a tiny portion of what student affairs educators need to know to create healthy environments that promote racial identity exploration. If student affairs work is to be grounded in theory, the lack of applicable racial identity development theories and accompanying research serves as a call to action to validate existing theories and create new theories that represent the array of students on campus. While much remains to be learned about Black and White racial groups, it is also important to consider other racial groups, including Latinos/as, Asian Americans, and Native Americans, and validate their unique experiences. For example, Sanchez (2013) argued: "the process of identity development for Dominican and Puerto Rican Latino college students is markedly different from that of Whites in the United States" (p. 497). The continued focus on Black and White creates a binary in which other racial groups remain understudied (Chen, LePhuoc, Guzmán, Rude, & Dodd, 2006; Delgado, 1998).

This Black/White binary, a result of institutionalized racism, has particular consequences for mixed-heritage individuals and how they are treated in society. For example, Rockquemore and Brunsma (2002) argued persuasively that assimilation of any racial or ethnic population into White culture is possible and even desired, except for African Americans. Rockquemore and

Brunsma pointed out that people "with one quarter or less Native American, Mexican, Chinese, or Japanese ancestry are treated as assimilating Americans [*sic*]" (p. 110). In contrast, White people, Black people, and biracial individuals with Black ancestry have consistently been influenced by the one-drop rule, a norm intended to keep undesired assimilation from occurring. By challenging this rule, the recent multiracial movement has contributed to increasing tension among these groups over the identity of mixed race individuals. Rockquemore and Brunsma argued that the one-drop rule will not disappear until prejudice and discrimination are significantly reduced. However, multiracial individuals who resist using a single racial category to identify themselves are pushing against this norm and the racial biases associated with it (Rockquemore & Brunsma). To fully understand the identity development process among mixed race individuals, this important difference based on racial heritage must be kept in mind.

Student affairs professionals who use theory to inform their work must proceed with extreme caution, given the lack of research currently available. Institutions of higher education are increasingly more diverse, and the failure of student affairs educators and faculty to understand fully students' racial identity development "can lead to inappropriate and ineffective responses to volatile racial situations on campus" (Hardiman & Jackson, 1992, p. 21). In fact, how students even conceptualize race remains a topic to be studied. Johnston's (2014) work is particularly instructive here, as he found distinct ways that students defined race, ranging from seeing race as tied to biology or genetics to identifying race as a social or cultural construction to viewing race as connected to issues of power, privilege, and oppression. Some students even held these different views simultaneously. How students view race has implications for the work that student affairs educators do to promote their racial identity development.

Helping White individuals find avenues for exploring their identity can help curb, and disrupt, racism and other discriminatory practices against racially minoritized groups (Cabrera, 2012). Furthermore, educators must recognize their role in providing opportunities for all students and staff to explore racial identity. Most important, educators need to participate in their own racial self-exploration to better understand themselves and then work collectively toward helping others to do the same. There is no one path that people follow in forming their identities and presenting themselves. Students' lives are shaped by their parents and family, neighborhoods, school, friends and strangers, work experiences, love and romance, and other forces. All of these influences combine in different ways to shape individuals' belief systems and sense of themselves, and how they choose to present themselves in various settings, including college and university campuses.

Discussion Questions

1. Define racial identity and articulate its significance in the lives of minoritized and majoritized individuals.
2. Discuss how critical race theory frames a robust discussion of race and racism.
3. Describe the five sectors of Cross and Fhagen-Smith's Model of Black Identity Development and its relevance for Black students on your campus.
4. How can you use the models introduced by Helms and by Rowe, Bennett, and Atkinson to inform your interactions with White students?
5. What is the role of student affairs educators in enhancing the identity development of White students and encouraging students' reflection on their White privilege?
6. Create a chart to compare and contrast Ferdman and Gallegos's Latino identity, Kim's Asian American identity, and Horse's perspective on American Indian identity. How can student affairs educators use these theories to inform the development of programs and services that facilitate the racial identity of all minoritized students on your campus?
7. Describe current theoretical approaches to multiracial identity development and Renn's ecological theory of mixed race identity development. What trends did Renn identify in her research on identity choice?
8. Outline steps academic and student affairs educators can take to make your campus more welcoming for students who want to explore their racial and/or mixed race identity(ies).
9. How can current events that deal with race and racism be used in the classroom or programmatic efforts to bring greater awareness to students while also facilitating development?
10. What rationale would you provide to White students who do not see themselves as having a distinct identity? How would you help them to explore their whiteness and white identity?

CHAPTER SIX

ETHNIC IDENTITY DEVELOPMENT AND ACCULTURATION

There is a broad and deep literature on ethnic identities and ethnic identity development. The preponderance of literature on the topic resides in four areas of social science: anthropology, sociology, psychology, and counseling, although education, the arts, political science, and religion also increasingly address the topic. Some anthropological and sociological perspectives are based on ethnicity and nationalism, often examining how minoritized groups assimilated into a national identity (Fuller-Rowell, Ong, & Phinney, 2013), but more perspectives, particularly those in psychology and counseling, examine individual or group ethnic identity. Much of what we present in this chapter originates from these later sources.

In this chapter, we examine ethnic identity and describe its varied meanings, research, measurement, and application to college students. Partially due to its dynamic, fluid, multidimensional, and context-specific form (Burton, Nandi, & Platt, 2010), no consensus exists on a universal definition of the concept of ethnic identity or how the term is perceived and used (Cokley, 2015). Still, ethnic identity is a central organizing concept of the self in the United States and may be beneficial to psychosocial wellbeing (Umaña-Taylor, 2011). There are useful models for understanding students' ethnic identification and identity development, and we present several in this chapter. First we frame ethnic identity within several academic disciplines. Next, we consider college students' ethnic identity and discuss acculturation and its tie to students' ethnicity. Then we review universal models, highlight ethnic identity related to several major ethnic groups in the United States, and examine some of the more commonly used instruments designed to measure the concept. We conclude the chapter with a critique and offer future directions for studying college students' ethnic identity.

Just as there is no one definition of ethnicity, there are a number of ways to group and name various ethnicities. In this chapter we use the term Indigenous Peoples in the United States to reference Native American, American Indian, Native Hawaiian, and Native Alaskan. We use Native American and American Indian interchangeably, a practice supported in the literature (Native American Journalists Association, 2014). In addition, in this chapter we use the term European American instead of the more generic "White," which represents a racial category, not an ethnicity. If scholars use other terms, such as White or Caucasian, when reporting their research or presenting a model, then we use their original language.

Framing Ethnic Identity

Social scientists agree that ethnicity is a culturally and socially constructed phenomenon rather than a biological one. Psychologists, counselors, researchers, student affairs educators, and the general public often use the term ethnicity synonymously with race (Cokley, 2005; Spencer, 2014). Some scholars argue for a conceptual conflation to "race/ethnicity" because for many communities these terms are in effect identical (Grosfoguel, 2004). Scholars also defend the interchange of racial and ethnic identity as a natural evolution of language in which popular speech becomes integrated into "official definitions" (Quintana, 2007, p. 259). Others consider ethnic and racial identity related but different constructs (Cokley, 2007; Spencer 2014). For clarification, in this chapter *ethnicity* means a pattern of culture, traditions, customs, and norms unique to, but also shared within, an ethnic community. *Race* (see Chapter Five) is socially constructed as an "arbitrary classification system based in positions of power and privilege" (Inman & Alvarez, 2014, p. 289). As an example of these distinctions, in the United States many people consider "Asian or Asian American" to be a racial category, while within this racial grouping, people of Hmong descent may celebrate their ethnicity differently from people of Han Chinese or Gujarati Indian heritages.

Ethnic identity is "the identity that develops as a function of one's ethnic group membership" and "is conceptualized as a component of one's overall identity," varying "in its salience across individuals" (Umaña-Taylor, 2011, p. 792). Developing through experiences of similarity and difference, ethnicity ties the individual to the group in important ways: "Ethnicity, when it matters to people, really matters ... Ethnicity depends on similarity and difference rubbing up against each other collectively: 'us' and 'them' " (Jenkins, 2004, p. 65). Seen through a psychosocial lens, ethnic identity is grounded primarily in the theoretical underpinnings of ego identity (Erikson, 1968; Marcia, 1980) and social identity (Tajfel, 1981). Much of the research in this chapter was influenced by these perspectives.

Positive ethnic identity is important for healthy psychological functioning and enhanced self-esteem (Richardson, Bethea, Hayling, & Williamson-Taylor, 2010; St. Louis & Liem, 2005; Umaña-Taylor, 2004, 2011; Umaña-Taylor & Shin, 2007). From this perspective, researchers suggest "ethnic identity is a multidimensional construct, involving ethnic feelings, attitudes, knowledge and behaviors" (Phinney, 1995, p. 58). Some key identifiable elements of the construct are "self identification as a group member; attitudes and evaluations relative to one's group; attitudes about oneself as a member; extent of ethnic knowledge and commitment; and ethnic behaviors and practices" (p. 58).

Ethnic Identity and College Students

In 1969, Chickering posited that college students must resolve the developmental task of defining their identity by answering the question, "Who am I?" For students who identify with one or more minoritized ethnic groups, addressing this question is more complicated and perhaps more urgent than it is for members of majoritized groups, as they may face some form of stereotyping and discrimination on campus (Cronin, Levin, Branscombe, van Laar, & Tropp, 2012; Ortiz & Santos, 2009). Many White students ignore their cultural heritages and fail to consider issues of ethnicity unrelated to their experiences in a homogeneous dominant culture that does not discriminate against them (McIntosh, 1989). For example, White students often resist social justice learning for reasons that may include a fear of examining their privilege (Jones, 2008). In contrast, many college students raised outside the dominant culture are highly attuned to their culture and ethnicity in both positive and negative ways (Ortiz & Santos, 2009). Yet for all students, the opportunity to explore, question, understand, and deepen ethnic identity in college can contribute to positive overall development.

Ethnic identity development is the subject of a well-established but still limited literature. As in other areas of student development theory, student affairs educators draw on a mix of theories, some specific to college students and others brought into the field for the purpose of informing practice, policy, and research. There are, as we present in this chapter, "broad" theories that describe the development of ethnic identity of any person, not specific to one group (for example, Phinney). There are also models specific to particular ethnic groups that take into account the history and contemporary experiences of the group. We present several of these models in this chapter, acknowledging that we cannot include models that cover the full ethnic diversity among college student populations. In addition, the development of some ethnic identities (for example, many Indigenous Peoples) is under-researched; in those cases we offer insights into cultural beliefs and worldviews that may assist student affairs educators in understanding experiences and development of students in those groups. As with all of the theories we present in this book, we remind readers that there is substantial in-group variation in experience and development; given the diversity of cultures encompassed within broad categories (for example, Asian, Latino/Chicano, Native American), it is especially important to keep this guidance in mind.

Components of Ethnic Identity and Acculturation

Ethnic identity and acculturation have different saliency for different groups depending on their "relative isolation" (Phinney & Baldelomar, 2011, p. 173) from other groups. For example, when society is dominated by one group "such as the Han Chinese in China, European Americans in the United States, or Mestizos in Costa Rica" (p. 173), ethnic identity is *less salient* to them. Many European Americans in the United States give ethnicity little to no meaning in their lives (Waters, 2000) and are not likely to feel motivated to explore it unless they are in social contexts that identify them as a minoritized group.

Some scholars have classified ethnic identity as possessing external and internal components (Breton, Isajiw, Kalbach, & Reitz, 1990). In this schema, external ethnic identity refers to recognizable social and cultural behaviors like ethnic language, media, and traditions; friendship with other ethnic group members; and involvement in ethnic group functions and activities. More complex in nature, internal ethnic identity incorporates cognitive, moral, and affective dimensions. The cognitive dimension incorporates individuals' self-images, images of the group, and knowledge of the ethnic group's heritage and values. The moral dimension encompasses an obligation to the ethnic group resulting in commitment to the group's cohesion (Isajiw, 1990). Finally, individuals' feelings of attachment to a particular ethnic group include an affinity for similar ethnic group members and cultural patterns of the group.

Acculturation refers to changes in beliefs, values, and behaviors of ethnic individuals as a result of contact with, and desired or undesired adaptation to, the dominant culture (Berry, 1993). It is "a process of cultural and psychological changes that involve various forms of mutual accommodation, leading to some longer-term psychological and sociocultural adaptations between both groups" (Berry, 2005, p. 699). Although there is a relationship between acculturation and ethnic identity, the internal and external components of ethnic identity vary independently (Sodowsky, Kwan, & Pannu, 1995).

Visible elements like behaviors related to an ethnic group are more affected by acculturation, while invisible elements of ethnic identity such as cultural values can resist change over time (Rosenthal & Feldman, 1992; Sodowsky & Carey, 1988). For example, individuals may conform their outward behaviors, such as celebrations of culturally significant events, to the dominant norm over time, but they may retain deeply held beliefs and worldviews during the process of acculturation. Students with strong ethnic ties may experience this phenomenon at predominantly White institutions, modulating their cultural expressions and adopting those of the dominant group while maintaining rich cultural affiliations and expressions in campus communities with same-ethnicity peers (for example, a student organization based on shared culture, nationality, or religion). The degree to which individuals adopt Whiteness (acculturation) and the strength with which individuals retain their culture of origin reveal ethnic identity as a bidirectional system (Sodowsky et al., 1995). This way of examining acculturation allows individual movement over time and across contexts; we describe it in more detail later in this chapter.

The acculturative process begins at the moment of "contact and interaction between two or more autonomous cultural groups" (Mena, Padilla, & Maldonado, 1987, p. 207). Intercultural contact between parties creates a need to negotiate in order for both parties to reach successful outcomes (Berry, 2005). Berry (1984, 1993) outlined four distinct acculturative strategies college students in minoritized ethnic groups can use to relate to the dominant culture. They can "*assimilate* (identify solely with the dominant culture and sever ties with their own culture), *marginalize* (reject both their own and the host culture), *separate* (identify solely with their group and reject the host culture), [or] *integrate* (become bicultural by maintaining aspects of their own group and selectively acquiring some of the host culture)" (Farver, Xu, Bhadha, Narang, & Lieber, 2007, p. 187). Those pursuing an integration strategy experience less stress and better adaptations than those pursuing marginalization, while those who choose to assimilate or separate experience moderate levels of stress and adaptation (Berry, 2005). It seems clear that students whose group is outside the dominant culture face obstacles that culturally privileged students do not.

Evidence shows that most immigrants experience conflict within their group or with other groups, producing acculturative stress (Born, 1970). Mena and colleagues (1987) laid a foundation for studies of acculturative stress among college students. They identified the factors ranked most stressful related to students' perceptions of discrimination and their lack of a sense of belonging (Mena et al., 1987). Paradoxically, the stronger students' ethnic identity, the more stress and less self-esteem they reported. Students used a number of strategies, including planning appropriate action and talking with others, to combat acculturative stress. In the nearly 30 years since Mena and colleagues published this study, hundreds of other studies have used this framework for understanding acculturation of minoritized groups—from within the United States and outside it—to U.S. higher education.

Overall, some scholars conceptualize ethnic identity development as a component of the acculturation process, and studying it is a "subfield of acculturation/enculturation research" (Yoon, 2011, p. 145), while others see ethnic identity as a concept that is parallel to, though separate from, racial identity (Chae & Larres, 2010; Cokley, 2015). However, most agree that ethnic identity and acculturation are nonlinear processes requiring contact with unfamiliar and unknown others. Familiarity with both concepts is essential for understanding college student experiences in the United States, where majoritized and minoritized individuals from the United States and around the world come into contact with one another. Student affairs educators have a nearly unparalleled opportunity—and responsibility—to create environments that support healthy ethnic identity development for *all* students. Descriptions of useful concepts, models, and theories follow.

Models of Ethnic Identity Development

Ethnic identity constructs focus on what people learn about their culture from family and community (Fuller-Rowell et al., 2013; Torres, 1999) passed down from one generation to the next (Spencer & Markstrom-Adams, 1990; Umaña-Taylor, 2011). Ethnic identity, which is a multidimensional concept that can change for an individual over time, develops from sharing culture, religion, geography, and language with individuals who are often connected by strong loyalty and kinship (Umaña-Taylor, 2011). Theories of ethnic identity formation examine how students "understand the implications of their ethnicity and make decisions about its role in their lives, regardless of the extent of their ethnic involvement" (Phinney, 1990, p. 64). As part of the process of committing to an ethnic identity, ethnically minoritized youth must resolve two basic conflicts: (1) stereotyping and prejudice on the part of the majoritized European American population toward the minoritized group and (2) clashing value systems between majoritized and minoritized groups. Resolution of these conflicts typically requires minoritized adolescents to negotiate a bicultural value system (Ozer, 2015; Nguyen & Benet-Martínez, 2012; Torres, 1999), which can influence their self-concept and sense of ethnic identity.

Phinney's Model of Ethnic Identity Development

One of the earliest theorists to develop and test a general ethnic identity development model was Jean Phinney (1990, 1993, 1995), a counseling psychologist. Her model has been tested and studied more than any other related to ethnic identity. Phinney (1990) maintained that the issue of ethnic identity is important to the development of a positive self-concept for minoritized adolescents. Based on Erikson's (1964, 1968) theory, Phinney's model is consistent with Marcia's (1966, 1980) much-examined identity model (see Chapter Thirteen). In a foundational article, Phinney (1990) described the development of her theoretical model of ethnic identity. She based it on growing evidence that revealed commonalities across ethnic groups rather than by placing each group (for example, Latino, Asian American, European American) and their dissimilarities under a microscope. Phinney's (1993) three-stage model of ethnic identity formation describes a linear model of ethnic identity achievement.

Stage 1: Unexamined Ethnic Identity (Diffusion − Foreclosure). Individuals in the first stage of ethnic identity development have not explored feelings and attitudes regarding their own ethnicity. Ethnicity may be seen as a nonissue, which leads them to neither explore identity nor commit to one (diffusion), or individuals may acquire attitudes about ethnicity in childhood from significant others, leading them to commit to an identity with no exploration (foreclosure). Adolescents who accept negative attitudes displayed by the majority group toward the minority group are at risk of internalizing these values. However, for the most part, this stage is marked by disinterest in ethnicity.

Stage 2: Ethnic Identity Search/Moratorium. During the second stage of ethnic identity development (Phinney, 1990, 1993), students become increasingly aware of ethnic identity issues as they face situations moving them to exploration. Adolescents tend to examine the significance of their ethnic background as this new awareness increases. The experience may be harsh, such as an encounter with overt discrimination or harassment, or it may be more indirect, such as gradual recognition (as a result of less dramatic incidents) that their ethnicity is perceived as "less than" by the dominant cultural group. As a result of this awakening, adolescents begin an ethnic identity search, where they seek more information about their ethnic group while attempting to understand the personal significance of ethnic identity. They actively explore but are not yet committed to the identity (moratorium). Characterized by emotional intensity, this stage encompasses anger toward the dominant group and guilt or embarrassment about individuals' own past lack of knowledge of racial and ethnic issues.

Stage 3: Ethnic Identity Achievement. In the final stage of ethnic identity development, students achieve a healthy bicultural identity. They resolve their identity conflicts and come to terms with their ethnicity in the sociocultural and historical context in which they live. As students accept membership in cultures that are minoritized in the United States, they gain a sense of ethnic identification while being open to other cultures. The intense emotions of the previous stage give way to a more confident demeanor.

Phinney and her colleagues continue to shed light on a pivotal developmental issue for college students: the process of ethnic identification. Her substantial research covers a number of issues relevant to college students and their ethnic identity, including, but not limited to, acculturation and self-esteem (Phinney, 1995; Phinney & Alipuria, 1996; Phinney, Chavira, & Williamson, 1992), ethnicity as an important identity issue in minoritized students' lives (Phinney, 1993), parental support and academic achievement (Ong, Phinney, & Dennis, 2006), positive intergroup attitudes and intercultural thinking (Phinney, Jacoby, & Silva, 2007), college choice for ethnically minoritized students (Phinney, Dennis, & Osorio, 2006), a mentoring program for first-year Latino students (Phinney, Torres Campos, Padilla Kallemeyn, & Kim, 2011), national identity of and perceived discrimination against Latino college students in their ethnic identity commitment (Fuller-Rowell et al., 2013), and identity development in multiple cultural contexts (Phinney & Baldelomar, 2011). Phinney's impressive body of research makes a highly significant contribution to the literature on the theory underlying the ethnic identity of college students.

Latino and Latina Ethnic Identity in College Students

In the past twenty years, research on the ethnic identity of Latinos (a term used in this chapter to include Latinas and Latinos) has increased substantially. Naming this ethnic identity is not a simple matter (Torres, Howard-Hamilton, & Cooper, 2003). Students call themselves Chicana or Chicano, Latina or Latino or Latin@, Hispanic, Mexican American, *Puertorriqueña* or *Puertor-riqueño*, Dominican, and more; researchers use a number of designators, often seeking one term to define this diverse group of students, whose families of origin come from parts of the Caribbean and Latin and Central America, with the majority in the United States coming from Mexico (Torres, 2004). Individuals living in the United States are often identified simply by their ancestral geographical roots—Puerto Rican, Cuban, Chilean, and so on—not always hyphenated with "American" (for example, Schwartz, Donovan, & Guido-DiBrito, 2009). To further complicate discussion of Latino identities, the U.S. government maintains that "Hispanic or Latino" is an ethnicity (not a race), but a substantial portion of Latino adolescents consider it a racial category (Harris & Sim, 2002). In short, Latinos are a heterogeneous group when examining race, ethnicity, region, socioeconomic, and other identity categories, a reality that challenges researchers to describe the process of "Latino identity development" in a meaningful way (Miville, 2010). For the purposes of this chapter, we will discuss cultural aspects of Latino ethnic identity development.

In an early study of Chicano identity that demonstrates the importance of generational heritage in the United States, Keefe and Padilla (1987) surveyed Mexican American students to examine cultural awareness (that is, awareness of Mexican people and culture), ethnic loyalty (attitudes and feelings about Mexican culture), and ethnic social orientation (preference for interacting with those who identify as Mexican and for Mexican food) as aspects of a Chicano identity. Four-generation families in the United States demonstrated a steady decrease in cultural awareness, with the biggest shift occurring between the first and second generations. Keefe and Padilla identified only a slight decrease in ethnic loyalty between the first and second generations. Third- and fourth-generation participants scored higher on ethnic loyalty than cultural awareness, which may have meaning for current students, as some have lost the language of their ancestors but maintain a sense of pride in their heritage. Although sociocultural contexts have changed in the three decades since the study occurred, the key constructs of cultural awareness, ethnic loyalty, and ethnic social orientation remain fundamental to understanding Latino ethnic identity in U.S. college students (see Torres et al., 2003).

Torres's Bicultural Orientation Model and Influences on Latino Identity

Vasti Torres has conducted a methodologically diverse program of research on the ethnic identity development of Hispanic (her early term; later she changed to Latino) college students. One of her first studies (Torres, 1999) validated the bicultural orientation model (BOM), demonstrating a correlation between acculturation and ethnic identity among Hispanic college students using demographic data and other ethnic scales and measures (for example, Marin, Sabogal, Marin, Otero-Sabogal, & Perez-Stable, 1987; Phinney, 1992; Ramirez, 1983). Four cultural orientation quadrants frame Torres's model and parallel other acculturation models. Torres categorized individuals demonstrating high levels of acculturation and ethnic identity as bicultural; that is, signifying a preference for both Hispanic and Anglo cultures. High-level acculturation and low-level ethnic identity represent an Anglo orientation, signifying a preference for Anglo culture. Low-level acculturation and high-level ethnic identity embody the Hispanic orientation, indicating a preference for the Hispanic culture. Finally, low-level acculturation and ethnic identity point to a marginal orientation, describing the inability to function effectively in either the Anglo or Hispanic cultures.

In a grounded theory study, Torres (2003) explored the influences on Latino students' ethnic identity development during their first two years in college. Two salient categories emerged from this study: *situating identity* and *influences on change*. Conditions for situating identity are the environment where students grew up, family influence and generational status, and self-perception of status in society. Influences on change include cultural dissonance and relationship changes within the environment. Based on this research, Torres (2003) introduced a conceptual model that describes the influences on Latino ethnic identity through the sophomore year in college. In the first year of college, three influences are apparent:

Environment Where the Student Grew Up. Considered a continuum, this dimension ranges from being raised in a diverse environment to being raised in a predominantly White environment. Latino students at the former end of the continuum are secure in their ethnicity and open to those from other cultures. Students from predominantly White environments prefer the company of those from the dominant culture, though they are not likely to discard the culture of their ancestors.

Family Influence and Generational Status. Two dimensions encompass this category. Initially first-year Latino students likely use the same label their parents assigned to their culture of origin. Torres (2003) found that less acculturated parents of first-generation Latino students expected their children to consider parental desires, which sometimes conflicted with collegiate expectations. Not surprisingly, Latino students who were second-generation and beyond, with more acculturated parents, found less stress in the collegiate environment as the students' two worlds more smoothly intertwined.

Self-perception and Status in Society. This influence centers on Latino students' perceived privilege in their culture of origin. Though a correlation may exist, this privilege is not necessarily related to socioeconomic status. Students who grew up feeling some privilege often believed negative stereotypes about Latinos, but these students did not apply these stereotypes to their own lives. In contrast, Latino students voicing no perceived privilege in their youth were more open to the experiences of others and recognized racism in their everyday lives. There are two possible processes that can signal change in a student's ethnic identity: conflict with the culture or a shift in relationships within the environment. Positive and negative changes are associated with both processes:

Cultural dissonance. Behaviors reflecting cultural dissonance reveal "conflict between one's own sense of culture and what others expect" (Torres, 2003, p. 540). Depending on the student's issue and how it is approached and resolved, different outcomes can occur. For example, exploration of the Spanish language can resolve a cultural conflict for some students, while others may retreat from their culture of origin when in conflict with parental cultural expectations.

Changes in relationships. Shifts in relationships, mainly with peer group members, appear to produce a comparable interaction. If Latino students find congruence between their old and new beliefs within their peer groups, positive relationship outcomes are possible. If conflicts are not resolved, relationships are likely negative.

A number of follow-up studies use Torres's (2003) model as a foundation. In a grounded theory study that also drew on self-authorship theory (see Chapter Sixteen), college students who reconstructed their identity in more complex ways to reduce their vulnerability to stereotypes developed a stronger ethnic identity (Torres & Baxter Magolda, 2004). Torres and Baxter Magolda concluded that although self-authorship theory emerged from a homogenous, predominantly White sample, its holistic foundation makes it an appropriate lens for examining Latino ethnic identity change.

Qualitative findings from a study conducted to examine Latino college students' ethnic identity and its influence on holistic development (Torres & Hernandez, 2007) also found characteristics similar to those that Baxter Magolda (2001) identified in research on self-authorship among White students. Additional developmental tasks revealed a matrix of holistic development that featured specific Latino cultural choices, including cognitive, intrapersonal (ethnic identity), and interpersonal (cultural orientation) factors. Following the contours of self-authorship theory, Latino students exploring their ethnic identity moved from *external formulas* traced through geography, family, and a belief in negative stereotypes, to a comfort with cultural difference and demonstration of cultural choice and behavior as students moved to a solid internal foundation. At *the crossroads*, a pivotal developmental moment, students cognitively recognized expansion of views, including racism, as well as stereotypes about the group; they then made intentional choices related to their feelings of discrimination. *Becoming an author of one's life* required integrated daily cultural choices—in other words, creating an informed Latino identity, as well as advocating for others of similar ethnic origin, before moving to an integrated sense of self in a diverse environment. Torres and Hernandez concluded that Latino students need meaningful support as they face the developmental tasks associated with confronting racism, lest their growth stagnate or regress. This study was significant in acknowledging the experience of racism and its meaning in students' lives as a major developmental factor.

Even with these models of Latino college student identity development in place, Torres and her colleagues recognized a need to learn more about the experiences of adult Latinas in higher education. Comparing Latinas to White women and men and to Latino men, additional issues Latinas must consider include limited financial resources, an array of academic matters, gender-role stereotyping, and obligations to family and their expectations (Rodriguez, Guido-DiBrito, Torres, & Talbot, 2000). The limited research on the gendered experiences of Latinas in a college or university environment left a vacuum to fill in understanding how ethnic identity influences their family, work, education, and life experiences.

With this need in mind, Torres and her colleagues focused their research on adult Latinas, an increasing number of students nationally, who reformulate their identity while enrolled in an undergraduate or graduate program (Martinez et al., 2012). This study disclosed the role of ethnic identity connected to major life events for Latinas such as "family, childbearing, and negotiating relationships with family members as culture is transmitted across several generations" (Martinez, Torres, White, Medrano, Robledo, & Hernandez, 2012, p. 190). Another study by Torres and her colleagues (Torres, Martinez, Wallace, Medrano, Robledo, & Hernandez, 2012) used qualitative methods to examine what it means to be Latino. Using Marcia's identity statuses (2002; see Chapter Thirteen) and Helms's (1995) racial identity model (see Chapter Five) as a theoretical base, these scholars explored the ethnic identity development process for Latinos and recognized a revisiting of this process in adults, a process they named *looping*. For Latinos in their study, identity was repeatedly reshaped based on the context and events of their lives. This looping process demonstrates the social construction and reconstruction of identity and includes refinements to identity rather than fundamental questioning of it or regression to earlier identity development.

Additional Research on Latino Ethnic Identity

Several studies highlight ethnic identity development among Latino students and connect ethnicity to other variables for understanding and promoting student success in college. One longitudinal study (over eight semesters) demonstrated that "ethnic identity is a group-based coping response that can emerge over time in response to perceptions of discrimination, and that activism can be conceptualized as an additional group-based response that leads to increases in ethnic identification, activism, and well-being during later years" (Cronin et al., 2012, p. 404). Another study revealed that considering ethnic identification and ethnic stereotypes in combination predicted academic achievement identification in a sample of Latino students (Devos & Cruz Torres, 2007). If a student is tied to a group that values academic achievement, identifying with this group promoted academic achievement. In addition, if academic achievement is not a value connected to a certain group, it is less likely a student from that group will value it.

Guardia and Evans (2008) conducted a phenomenological study to examine the ethnic identity development of Latino fraternity members at a Hispanic-serving institution (HSI). Applying a fluid racial identity orientations model (Ferdman & Gallegos, 2001; see Chapter Five), examined through the lens of Bronfenbrenner's (2005) bioecological theory of human development, this study revealed six influences: family, the HSI campus, other Greeks and Greek affairs policies, gender, language, and involvement. The study also found that students engaged in Latino fraternity life view the environment of the fraternity as multicultural, providing members with *hermandad*—"a family atmosphere and Latino unity" (Guardia & Evans, p. 177). For students in this study, many aspects of the HSI, such as interactions with Hispanic faculty, were conducive to enhancing ethnic identity.

Highlighting the importance of culture and ethnic community for Latino college students at predominantly White institutions (PWIs), Cerezo and Chang (2013) found that "cultural fit and connection with ethnic minority peers affect[ed] college GPA for Latinos navigating this dominant culture environment" (p. 82). Cerezo and Chang found ethnic pride and support from ethnically similar peers crucial to Latino academic success. They encouraged postsecondary educators to create a cultural element in programs that support academics.

Ethnic Identity of Asian Americans

In the 2010 U.S. Census, 4.8% of the population (14.6 million people) reported that they were Asian American (Humes, Jones, & Ramirez, 2011). One of the fastest-growing racial and ethnic communities in the United States, Asian Americans represent three expansive yet distinct groups including East Asians from China, Taiwan, Japan, Philippines, and Korea; South Asians from India, Pakistan, Bangladesh, Sri Lanka, Nepal, Bhutan, and the Maldives; and Southeast Asians from Vietnam, Laos, Hmong, and Cambodia (Tewari, Inman, & Sandhu, 2003). Rhoads, Lee, and Yamada (2002) referred to this Asian American panethnicity as "a collective identity organized around broad commonalities rooted in a variety of particular ethnicities traceable to points in Asia (that is, Chinese American, Japanese American, Indian American, Taiwanese American, Vietnamese American, etc.)" (p. 877). But other scholars warn of the danger of such categorization (McCubbin & Dang, 2011), as substantial contrasts in culture, language, customs, and heritage defy uniform categorization of Asian Americans (Kawaguchi, 2003). We encourage readers to keep both viewpoints in mind when focusing on ethnic identity development among people whose race is Asian American.

In an early iteration of the ethnic identity processes of Asian Americans, Sodowsky, Kwan, and Pannu (1995) described it as "a social psychological phenomenon" that "provides relevant explanations to group interactions in pluralist societies, in which salience, ethnicity, and out-group status have an impact on an individual's identity process" (p. 134). In portraying Asian ethnic identity, some scholars offer a bi-axial systems model of acculturation; one axis examines questions of a shared ethnic existence, values, and attachment;

the other axis questions one's ethnic identity within White society (Sodowsky et al., 1995). The 2x2 design of this model resembles others described in this chapter and answers questions related to these two concepts (i.e., ethnic identity and dominant [White] identity). It includes the following four combinations of answers to questions about strong Asian ethnic identity and strong relationships to the dominant (White) culture: bicultural identity (yes, yes), strong ethnic identity (yes, no), strong U.S. White identity (no, yes), and identity of cultural marginalization (no, no). These four ethnic identity orientations depict a nonlinear pattern over time and across situations. They are fluid and allow movement in an unpredictable fashion instead of a stage journey in the predictable way of more linear models.

The diversity of Asian ethnic identities makes broad generalizations about identity development unwise. Evidence suggests that linear ethnic identity models applied to some other groups are not as applicable to Asian Americans (Yeh & Huang, 1996). Ethnic identity for Asian Americans, including students, is not only an internal process but one heavily influenced by others in external processes (Kim, 2012; Kodama, McEwen, Liang, & Lee, 2001; Yeh & Huang). For example, some cultural influences, such as Confucianism in East Asia, may have particular significance in ethnic identity development of Chinese, Japanese, and Korean individuals (see Chae & Larres, 2010). The importance of family in many Asian cultures exerts another developmental press on ethnic identification (Kodama et al., 2001; Umaña-Taylor, Bhanot, & Shin, 2006).

Umaña-Taylor (2001; Umaña-Taylor & Fine, 2004) used an ecological model of ethnic identity formation based on Bronfenbrenner's ecological approach (see Chapter Two). Umaña-Taylor, Bhanot, and Shin (2006) later used this model to understand adolescents' ethnic identity and the role of families in Chinese, Filipino, Vietnamese, Asian Indian (that is, South Asian), and Salvadoran Americans' identity development (Salvadorans are Latino, included in this study to extend Umaña-Taylor and colleagues' research beyond Mexican Americans). Using existing and new instruments to measure family ethnic socialization (FES; Umaña-Taylor, 2001) and ethnic identity achievement (Phinney, 1992), they found that the ecological approach explained ethnic identity achievement, and family influences were critically important to these youth. Influences also varied based on length of time family had been in the United States, demonstrating the intergenerational effects of immigration patterns on youth from these ethnic groups. Extending this study to other Asian ethnic groups might yield similar results or demonstrate that even within a pan-ethnic view of Asian Americans, differences exist by cultural group.

Asian American college students from different ethnic groups may share common cultural influences on ethnic identity or they may not, depending on their individual family and cultural history as well as regional and campus-based differences among groups. Student affairs educators should be aware of these potential differences and sensitive to how they play out across and within student communities. As with students from different Latino ethnic groups, long histories of cultural differences exist among ethnicities within these larger categories.

Ethnic Identity of Indigenous Peoples

Native American scholars do not appear to agree on a single term to name their group of origin; most identify either as Native American (see Jackson, Smith, & Hill, 2003; Lundberg, 2007) or American Indian (see Brown & Robinson Kurpius, 1997; Cajete, 2005). The Native American Journalists Association (2014) considers both acceptable, as we do in this chapter. Some Native scholars used the term *indigenous scholars* to identify themselves within the academy (Mihesuah & Wilson, 2004). In this section, we refer to indigenous people living in the United States as either Native American or American Indian (describing the peoples of what became the Continental United States), Native Hawaiian (native peoples of Hawaii), or Native Alaskan (native peoples of Alaska). Indigenous Peoples of the United States link their heritage to the land and to other native peoples around the globe. There is limited literature available to guide college student educators regarding the ethnic identities and identity development of native and indigenous peoples, though recent research has produced important work.

Identifying the ethnic identity of American Indians, Native Hawaiians, or Native Alaskans as one population is neither viable nor desirable, because it masks the unique histories of these indigenous groups. The broad diversity among tribes also precludes generalization of ethnic characteristics to the entire population, as each group and/or tribe has its own customs, traditions, language, history, myths, religion, culture, and symbols. Yet as Horse (2001) pointed out, there is a sense of Native American cultural pride: "In the context of ethnicity—as opposed to race—Indian people are intensely proud of their respective cultures" (p. 105). Although there are similarities among Native peoples' beliefs and values, customs and traditions are tribe-specific and frame "Indianness" for each group, making a universal description unlikely due to "the missing homogenous worldview" among Native peoples (Choney, Berryhill-Paapke, & Robbins, 1995, p. 75). In addition to being counted as a racial category in the United States Census and comprising hundreds of tribal ethnic identities, Native Americans and American Indians represent distinct political entities as sovereign nations entering into treaties with national and state governments. On the 2010 U.S. Census, 5.2 million people identified as American Indian and Alaskan Native either alone or in combination with another race; of this number, 2.9 million identified as being American Indian and Alaska Native alone (Norris, Vines, & Hoeffel, 2012). As of 2003, they are part of 562 federally recognized tribes in the United States, 229 of which are located in Alaska (National Congress of American Indians, n.d.) and numerous nations (for example, Apache, Sioux, Cherokee, Navajo, and Tewa) whose people speak over 252 languages (Herring, 1990). Native Hawaiians embrace similar diversity though, as of 2008, they "do not have tribal status" and "are not recognized as a sovereign entity" (McCubbin & Dang, 2011, p. 270), thus extending their history of oppression and colonization.

Native American/American Indian Identity

For many Native Americans, identity centers on who they are in relation to others—their family and tribe. Standing in opposition to Western individualistic epistemologies, this focus on community enhances Indigenous Peoples' identity. Cajete (2005) explored the "origins, nature, and methods of coming to know" (p. 69) in American Indian culture. At the heart of nearly every Native way of knowing, he found symbolic constructs reflecting epic metaphors that "present the Nature-centered orientation of indigenous epistemologies in the Americas" (p. 73). These myths, which appear in the vast majority of Native American languages, include Tree of Life, Earth Mother, Sun Father, and Sacred Directions. This worldview and way of being centers around Indigenous ways of knowing. Understanding the differences between individualism, embraced by dominant Western culture, and communalism, a way of life embraced by Native American, Native Alaskan, and Native Hawaiian cultures, sheds light on cultural differences in worldviews and identity. In a study that confirms communalism as central to indigenous identities and cultures, Waterman and Lindley (2013) found that Native American women most valued community, family, tradition, and cultural integrity.

Choney, Berryhill-Paapke, and Robbins (1995) presented a model that has held up for more than 20 years as an anti-deficit approach to understanding Native American acculturation, ethnic identity, and health outcomes. This fluid, nonlinear model consists of five concentric circles to depict Native

American acculturation. The five circles of the model represent levels of acculturation: traditional, transitional, bicultural, assimilated, and marginal. Levels of acculturation may vary within each circle. In contrast to many other Western-based models, however, "no value judgments are placed on any level of acculturation, nor is any dimension of personality emphasized more than another" (Choney et al., 1995, p. 85). Each distinctive level describes coping mechanisms developed based on environmental and social contexts.

Choney et al. (1995) also divided the model into four quadrants based on the four essential elements of the Native American medicine wheel and representing four psychological areas of human development: cognitive, behavioral, affective/spiritual, and social/environment. Outside the concentric circles but inside the four quadrants lies mainstream culture, representing the enveloping influence of the dominant culture in the lives of American Indians. The underlying and unique assumptions of this model include: Native American strengths, which are apparent at each level of acculturation, serve as coping skills in the stress of daily life; values at each level have no positive or negative valence, while movement between and among levels does not precede positive mental health; and stress during acculturation does not necessarily occur, although it can (Choney et al., 1995).

Higher education's dominant culture and discriminatory practices are at odds with the underlying cultural beliefs of American Indian students and may interfere with students' learning, development, and persistence toward achieving their educational goals. The reasons institutions are unsuccessful at recruiting and retaining Native students include potential issues related to development, such as blatantly racist treatment (Brown & Robinson Kurpius, 1997; Jackson, Smith, & Hill, 2003) and structures and philosophies of higher education embedded with cultural bias (Garrett & Pichette, 2000; Mihesuah, 2004; Pewardy & Frey, 2004; Tierney, 1992; Waterman, 2012). One study, which compared 67 American Indian college students' ethnic identity and beliefs about education with a sample of 96 European American undergraduate students, found clear differences between these two groups of students (Okagaki, Helling, & Bingham, 2009). The Native American students placed much more importance on their ethnic identity and connection to their ethnic group than did their dominant culture peers. Additionally, the students in this study credited their mothers' emphasis on cultural practices as a critical influence on their ethnic identity. In another study, Waterman (2012) found that contrary to theories that suggest that engagement *in the college setting* is critical to student success (for example, Astin's (1984) involvement theory; Tinto's (1993) departure theory), Native American students who went home frequently were as successful as Native American students who remained on campus.

Native Alaskan Identity

Native Alaskan identity, similar to Native American identity, often has a genetic connection to a tribe (Dixon & Portman, 2010). Obtaining legal tribal status is important to preserve the historic heritage and unique traditions of each Native Alaskan tribe. Although some tribal members receive membership through the U.S. government, others self-identify as Native Alaskan or Native American. Elders of the tribe teach children about their cultural identity, and tribal identity develops over a lifetime. Perhaps due to substantial differences in language, culture, beliefs, and oral traditions among Native Alaskan tribes, there is no identity development model for this group (Dixon & Portman, 2010). However, a shared set of values portrays traditional Native culture across tribes and geography (Herring, 1994; Sue & Sue, 2008). Some of these shared characteristics are valuing cooperation, viewing the community as an extended family, respecting elders, communicating primarily through the nonverbal, and living in the present and harmoniously with nature (Dixon & Portman, 2010).

Native Hawaiian Identity

Native Hawaiian identity is influenced by historical, sociopolitical and cultural contexts of colonization by missionaries and capitalists, and widespread slavery and oppression of indigenous peoples (McCubbin & Dang, 2011). These influences continue in the twenty-first century, in which some institutions or programs (for example, some schools) that accommodate only Hawaiians who live on the islands and comply with colonial standards continue to receive funding and favorable legislative policy decisions. The greatest challenge for the Native Hawaiian in developing an identity "is to strive for a balance between cultural heritage, ancestral knowledge, and his or her current adaptation with imperial and colonial laws and practices under the hegemonic doctrine of race" (McCubbin & Dang, 2011, p. 276). Under these oppressive conditions for Native Hawaiian peoples, applying Marcia's (1966) and Phinney's (1990) frameworks of identity development suggests that foreclosure may result, inhibiting growth and development. Instruments designed to measure Native Hawaiians' cultural identity and affiliation (e.g., Bautista, 2003; Rezentes, 1993) have as their base acculturation, culture, and enculturation perspectives (McCubbin & Dang, 2011) but do not focus specifically on identity.

Kupo (2010) added to the sparse literature on Native Hawaiian identity by exploring Native Hawaiian college women's identities through the lenses of Tribal Critical Race Theory (TribalCrit) (Brayboy, 2006), intersectionality, and identity performance. Through storytelling and narrative, eight Native Hawaiian college women disclosed that of all their identities, their strongest was their Hawaiian cultural identity. Other scholars also have reached similar conclusions (Kana'iaupuni & Malone, 2006).

Ethnic Identity of African and Afro-Caribbean Americans

Black Americans who can trace their ancestral origins to the African continent draw from an abundance of custom, language, history, tradition, religion, and other cultural legacies. However, for generations, colonialism and enslavement stripped Black communities of their cultural heritages. The long-term effects of these conditions still prevent most individuals with African ancestry from identifying many of the particulars of their ethnic heritage. For the purposes of this chapter, we use the term African American to refer to those people in the United States whose ancestors hail from Africa, and Black, a global term unattached to national identity, to refer to identities more closely tied to race than to ethnicity. For example, college students may identify racially as Black and ethnically as Haitian, or as African American with Zulu heritage. Black immigrants to the United States from the Caribbean may identify as Black and Afro-Caribbean, but not African American.

Just as for Latino and Asian ethnicities, there is no universal ethnic identity model for all Black or African American people, a reflection of the variety of worldviews and perspectives traced to origins in each African tribe or kinship. In this context the concept of identity "is always a question of producing in the future an account of the past, it is always about narrative, the stories which cultures tell themselves about who they are and where they came from" (Hall, 1995, p. 5). Linked to stories that were altered over time, "identity shifts with the way we think and hear them and experience them" (p. 8).

From the enslavement period until recently, African Americans in the United States knew their identities were uprooted and replaced with "an unrelenting institutionalized disenfranchisement and discrimination as the standard reality" (Richardson, Bethea, Hayling, & Williams-Taylor, 2010, p. 228). Basically, racial identity trumped any notion of ethnic identity because White oppressors denied this exceptionally broad range of people, descended from Africa, any acknowledgment of their individual ethnic identities. Thus some scholars propose that the larger social context (that is, racism) dictates the "content, shape, and form of Black identity" (Richardson et al., p. 229).

The ethnic identity of African American and Afro-Caribbean college students is often framed in terms of racial identity (Torres et al., 2003), which obfuscates understanding the phenomenon. Much of this research uses the labels "racial identity" and "ethnic identity" interchangeably, which makes understanding these concepts difficult and context specific. More scholars have written about Black racial identity (Cross, 2012; Jackson, 2012) than about African American ethnic identity (Cokley, 2007). Yet there are some studies about ethnic identities of Black and African American students that can inform practice. For example, Phelps and colleagues examined the relationship of ethnic identity to racial identity and self-esteem (Phelps, Taylor, & Gerard, 2001) and the relationship between encouragement and ethnicity (Phelps, Tranakos-Howe, Dagley, & Lyn, 2001). An earlier study (Day-Vines, Barker, & Exum 1998) examined the impact of diasporic travel on ethnic identity development.

European American Identity/White Ethnic Identity

As with other broad identity groups we discuss in this chapter, European American identity is complicated by racial categorization, history, and immigration, among other factors. Over centuries through the decennial census and immigration policies, the United States government has shifted its definition of White (see Painter, 2010), and there are multiple ways that scholars identify who is a member of this larger social group (McDermott & Samson, 2005). Although there are racial identity development models that include White individuals (see Chapter Five), there is little literature to explain ethnic identities of people in this racial group.

Throughout U.S. history, individuals from more privileged White ethnic groups—typically those of Protestant, Anglo-Saxon heritage—held positions of power and influence, which enabled them to define and monitor the acceptability of members of less-privileged groups (for example, Catholic immigrants fleeing famine in Ireland or trying to rise out of poverty in Italy and Portugal). Over time, for many people from these European American groups, the transition from their country of origin to the United States allowed for varying degrees of assimilation and acculturation. As the children (first generation), grandchildren (second generation) and great grandchildren (third generation) of these immigrants coalesced into a dominant cultural racial group (D'Andrea & Daniels, 2001), many of their customs and much of their once prized heritage lost out to a new "American" identity (McDermott & Samson, 2005;

McGill & Pearce, 2005). In effect and over generations, some White groups have shifted from identification as an ethnic group to attainment of a place in the privileged dominant racial group in the United States. This movement demonstrates the fluidity of ethnicity and race as socially constructed phenomena. For purposes of this discussion, we use European Americans to describe these migrating people unless a scholar's use of a different term is warranted in a specific context.

European immigrants were 61% of the 64 million immigrants who came to the United States between 1820 and 1998. Throughout much of U.S. history, recent and not-so-recent, immigrants were categorized by hierarchies generally favoring those from northern and western Europe over those from southern and eastern European countries (Banks, 2008). Recent European American immigrants represent 53 nationalities ranging from the most represented (German American) to least represented (Cypriot American) (McMahon, Paisley, & Skudrzyk, 2014). Most of the European refugees in the twenty-first century come from Russia and other former Soviet Union countries (for instance, Ukraine and Moldova) and the former countries of the Socialist Republic of Yugoslavia (Bosnia-Herzegovina, Serbia, and Montenegro).

Some values embedded in the worldviews and perspectives of European American ethnic identity perpetuate their groups' belief that White people are not racist (McMahon, Paisley, & Skudrzyk, 2014). In fact many Whites claim color-blindness (Bonilla-Silva, 2010), which indicates a lack of awareness of how race is socially constructed in social, political (McDermott, 2015), economic, educational, and religious life. On the 2011 American Community Survey (an annual federal survey) participants were asked to answer an open-ended question: "What is this person's ancestry or ethnic origin?" Thirty-eight percent of non-Hispanic White respondents answered "White," "American," or "United States," or left the box empty; the other 62 percent responded with a European ethnicity (McDermott, 2015, p. 8). McDermott (2015) suggested that rather than a connection to an identity emphasizing national origin, White people in the United States increasingly affiliate with an unmarked (White) racial identity instead. This study demonstrates a conflation of identities indicated by White, "American," and European ethnic heritage.

Several hallmark cultural values in the European American tradition offer an explanation of the context in which this sense of singular American identity developed (McMahon, Paisley, & Skudrzyk, 2014) from an array of diverse cultures. The first of these values is the metaphor of a "melting pot," the process of combining all European American ethnic attitudes and beliefs in the United States and creating "a new, virtuous (i.e., White American) culture" (p. 389). A number of scholars, activists, and educators have critiqued the melting pot concept as ethnocentric (and, in particular, centered on White, Western, and European American values) and offered alternative metaphors such as the *salad bowl* or *gumbo* (Jacoby, 2004; Lee, 2012), a mix of ethnic flavors in which each remains distinctive but together create a whole larger than the sum of its parts. Nevertheless, the concept of melting pot holds sway in the story of twentieth-century U.S. immigration. Another American value cherished as a manifestation of a singular cultural identity is the American Dream. Reinforcing the idea of the United States as a utopian mecca, it highlights U.S. political and social structures, embraces the nation's founding principles of life, liberty and the pursuit of happiness, explains the success of the American people, and justifies why others do not succeed (Johnson, 2006). Finally, the creation of an American heritage is the third value feeding the idea of a singular American identity. The U.S. school system is designed to teach history to U.S. students in line with its American heritage, and it perpetuates and propagates the myth of the American Dream and values associated with the dominant culture. The ability of people of European ethnic groups to assimilate into and conform to these three values (melting pot, American Dream, singular American identity) explains, in part, why increasingly fewer White individuals feel the need to develop a strong ethnic identity. Instead, "American" identity acts as a combined national and ethnic identity.

Measuring Ethnic Identity

Over 25 years ago, a number of scholars engaged in efforts to measure ethnic identity and ethnic identity development. Measures of these multidimensional, global phenomena typically focus on the intensity of an individual's attachment to their culture of origin and attachment to the dominant culture of the society in which they are now living. Scholars and professionals attempt to measure and track ethnic identity formation and the process of ethnic identity unfolding "in interaction with the cultural context" (Phinney & Baldelomar, 2011, p. 174).

In alignment with her scholarship on ethnic identity development, Phinney introduced the Multigroup Ethnic Identity Measure (MEIM) (Phinney, 1992). She designed it to assess a sense of belonging, identity achievement, and ethnic practices. Researchers originally revealed the MEIM as a single factor structure, but eventually Phinney and Ong (2007) recognized a multiple factor structure and revised the instrument. The newly revised instrument became the MEIM-R and highlights two factors, exploration and commitment, across six items (Yoon, 2011). Preliminary findings support the MEIM-R as a reliable measure of ethnic identity.

Extensive use of the MEIM and MEIM-R has led to a number of findings linking ethnic identity to college student experiences and outcomes (Miville, 2010). These experiences and outcomes include acculturation to Anglo culture (Cuéllar, Nyberg, Maldonado, & Roberts, 1997), career decision self-efficacy (Gushue & Witson, 2006), ethnocentrism (Negy, Shreve, Jensen, & Uddin, 2003), negative perceptions of the university environment (Castillo, Conoley, Choi-Pearson, Archuletta, Phoummarath, & Van Landingham, 2006), proactive coping (Umaña-Taylor, Vargas-Chanes, Garcia, & Gonzales-Backen, 2008), and ethnic identity of Native American students at Diné College, the first Tribal College (McNeil, Kee, & Zvolensky, 1999). Although minority stress theory is relatively new in the literature on college students, there are some studies that combine it with studies of ethnic identity that use the MEIM-R (for example, understanding minority stress, depression, and Latino/a ethnic identity; Arbona & Jimenez, 2014).

Scholars have used the Native American Acculturation Scale (NAAS) (Garrett & Pichette, 2000) to understand college student identities and development. One study employing the instrument (that is, Reynolds, Sodano, Ecklund, & Guyker, 2012) examined Native American undergraduate students representing a wide range of tribal cultures from universities across the United States. Study data revealed three correlated dimensions of Native American acculturation consisting of Core Self, Cultural Self-Expression, and Cultural and Community Engagement (Reynolds et al., 2012). A second sample supported the validity of the NASS's correlated three-factor model. Giving more multidimensional meaning than that offered by the previous single factor model, the three factors sculpt a richer model for understanding Native American students.

Critique and Future Directions

As postsecondary education increases in ethnic diversity, understanding the ethnic identities of college students remains an area ripe with research possibilities. Educators need to know more about how ethnicity and its development enhance identity in all ethnic groups during the college years (Phinney & Ong, 2007). Increased research on ethnic identity development may lead to improved educational practice that will enhance student development and create healthy, diverse campus environments that encourage it. We offer several specific suggestions.

First, the substantial cultural differences among Latino, African American, Afro-Caribbean, Native American, Native Hawaiian, Native Alaskan, and European American ethnic groups leaves ample room for research opportunities to explore how best to serve the needs of students from these groups. Relatively few studies exist to guide practice in relation to understanding how students from different ethnic groups within one racial category (for example, Hmong, Vietnamese, and Thai students) may experience higher education and/or their ethnic identities differently. Similarly, the diversity among Latino students (for example, Mexican, Guatemalan, and Chilean) highlights a need to examine groups in a disaggregated fashion.

Visibility of growing populations of some ethnic groups on campus calls attention to the need for better understanding of these students, their cultures, and their experiences. For example, facing increased discrimination since the terrorist attacks on the United States on September 11, 2001, the diverse and expanding Arab American college population in the United States needs more examination (Shammas, 2009). Arab Americans and Middle Eastern Americans are individuals who can trace their ancestors geographically to areas of the Saudi Arabian peninsula that historically identify as Islamic, although not all members of this ethnic group are Muslim (Nassar-McMillan, 2003; Nassar-McMillan, Gonzalez, & Mohammad, 2014; Salameh, 2011).

There are other ethnic groups about which little is known in relation to campus experiences, identities, and ethnic identity in particular. In addition to Arab Americans, there are other students of Middle Eastern descent. Recent African immigrants—from Nigeria, Egypt, Cape Verdes, and Somalia, for example—represent another group of ethnicities whose experiences in higher education are not well known. Students of Central Asian (for example, Afghanistan) and Eastern Asian (for example, Iran and Iraq) heritage are also among this group of understudied ethnic identities.

Because of the particular conflation of White racial identity with "American" nationality and European ethnic heritage, research into White ethnic identities and identity development could provide insight into the role of White students in perpetuating cycles of privilege and oppression on campus. Understanding how European national and ethnic groups arrived in the United States and assimilated—typically by shedding the culture of their country of origin and accepting the White, Protestant culture of their new home—may help White students see that acceptance by the dominant culture in U.S. society meant, and for the most part still means, giving up traditions and customs practiced for generations and constructing a racial hierarchy that is difficult to dismantle. Research on the worldviews and culture of European American students helps them better understand how their everyday lived experience is qualitatively different from that of those in the academy who are ethnically and racially minoritized in the United States.

Longitudinal studies of ethnic identity formation and change are long overdue. Researchers need to examine the functional form of "trajectories of ethnic identity ... over the adolescent and early adult years" (Phinney & Ong, 2007, p. 279). To do so, researchers need more sophisticated methodological tools and resources to conduct multiyear studies in order to explain in greater detail the process of ethnic identity during late adolescence and into adulthood. More varied methodological tools based in numerous paradigms and theoretical perspectives (see Chapter Two) generally would be helpful in better grasping the meaning and impact of this pervasive, varied social phenomenon.

International students come to the United States with national and ethnic identities. Knowing how these identities develop while attending a U.S. institution could be very useful in providing services to international students, to enriching their experience in the United States, and to promoting intercultural education. In Chapter Twelve we discuss national identities as an important element of college student development, and research on ethnic identity in international students would be a complement.

Finally, the intersections of ethnic identity with other social identities such as race, class, gender, sexuality, and religion (McCall, 2005) represents a cutting-edge area for investigation (Phinney, 2010). Rather than study components of student identities in isolation, ethnic identity examined from the intersections of other social identities gives a broader snapshot of growth (Jones & Abes, 2013). Knowledge about how identities intersect, shape the individual, and are shaped by the individual can be useful in designing programs, policies, and curriculum that support holistic development. To whatever extent they acknowledge and identify with their ethnic heritage, all students have one. Higher education is a context in which they can explore, extend, and commit to this aspect of identity.

Discussion Questions

1. Describe the characteristics of ethnic identity and what makes it different from but related to racial identity.
2. What happens when someone from a minoritized ethnic group encounters the dominant culture in a society?

3. What are some features of the acculturation process for minoritized ethnic group members on a college campus? What happens for members of majoritized groups?

4. Explain Phinney's ethnic identity development model, and develop a metaphor that represents this process.

5. Think about your own ethnic heritage group(s). How did you learn about this ethnicity? What does it mean to you to be a member(s) of this (these) groups?

6. What are some of the more visible ethnic groups on your campus? What groups are less visible or at the margins? How does invisibility and dominance affect the interaction of these ethnic groups?

7. How do members of different ethnic groups on your campus relate to one another? Is it different within racial categories (for example, students from different Asian ethnic groups) or across racial categories (for example, Korean American students interacting with Afro-Caribbean students or Cuban Americans)?

8. How do students you know describe their ethnic identity? How do they describe their development in the context of your campus?

9. What does (or can) your institution do to support students' ethnic identity development on campus?

CHAPTER SEVEN

SEXUAL IDENTITY DEVELOPMENT

Sexual identity is a complex construct that includes sexual orientation, attractions, emotions, desires, and behaviors. It is "the name and meaning individuals assign to themselves based on the most salient sexual aspects of their life—such as sexual attractions, fantasies, desires, and behaviors" (Savin-Williams, 2011, p. 671). Labels that contemporary college students may use for sexual identity include, but are not limited to, straight or heterosexual, gay or lesbian, bisexual or pansexual, asexual, and queer. Many students begin or accelerate exploration of their sexual identities when they are emerging as adults (Savin-Williams, 2011), a time that coincides with college-going for a large number of undergraduates. As such, it is critical for student affairs educators to understand the challenges that sexual identity development poses to students of all backgrounds, genders, sexual orientations, and ages.

For lesbian, gay, bisexual, or queer (LGBQ) students who knew earlier in their lives that they are not heterosexual, college is often seen as a safer environment in which to explore and express sexual identity than was their high school. Campus organizations and sexuality studies curricula provide social, interpersonal, and academic contexts for learning about the diversity of sexual identities, orientations, and expressions. Although harassment of LGBQ people remains a problem in postsecondary education (see Rankin, Blumenfeld, Weber, & Frazer, 2010), colleges and universities are generally less hostile to LGBQ students than were the secondary schools from which they came (see Kosciw, Greytak, Palmer, & Boesen, 2014). There is work to be done to improve campus climate, but higher education offers opportunities for LGBQ students to understand themselves and their sexual identities. Growing awareness of other non-heterosexual identities, such as asexual or pansexual identity, provides additional space for exploration and expression of minoritized sexual identities (for discussion of asexual college students, see McAleavey, Castonguay, & Locke, 2011; for pansexual, see Callis, 2014).

Sexual identity development is a "universal process" not limited to LGBQ or asexual individuals (Dillon, Worthington, & Moradi, 2011, p. 649). As noted in Chapter Four, heterosexual students also find college an opportune time to explore and solidify their sexual values, needs, and attitudes (Chickering & Reisser, 1993; Mueller & Cole, 2009). However, heterosexuality has only recently received attention in the developmental literature. Bieschke (2002), Mueller and Cole (2009), and Worthington, Savoy, Dillon, and Vernaglia (2002) stressed the importance of bringing sexual identity development into the awareness of heterosexuals to clarify important aspects of their sexuality as well as the privilege bestowed on heterosexuals by society.

In this chapter, we present Dillon et al.'s (2011) unifying model of sexual identity development. We then discuss the bodies of research that underlie this model and some applications of it in the college setting. We close the chapter with implications and suggestions for future directions. Although sometimes included in discussion of lesbian, gay, and bisexual identities, *transgender* identity is gender-based and discussed with gender theories in Chapter Eight.

Sexual Identity Development Concepts and Models

Student development scholars and student affairs educators have used the terms *sexual identity, sexual orientation,* and *sexual orientation identity* somewhat interchangeably and in nonspecific ways to mean the same thing: the sense individuals have of themselves as gay, lesbian, bisexual, heterosexual, asexual, or some other term. Here, we use sexual identity as a term that encompasses both sexual orientation and sexual orientation identity. Sexual orientation conveys "an individual's patterns of sexual, romantic, and affectional arousal and desire for other persons based on those persons' gender and sex characteristics" (Dillon et al., 2011, p. 650). Sexual orientation identity, then, is the individual's "conscious acknowledgement" (Dillon et al., p. 650) of sexual orientation and the ways that the individual relates to others in community and social settings. Sexual identity encompasses sexual orientation and sexual orientation identity, as well as "sexual behaviors, ... social affiliations with LGB[Q] and/or heterosexual individuals and communities, emotional attachment preferences for men and/or women, [and] gender identity" (Dillon et al., p. 650).

The debate about whether sexual identity is biological and fixed (the essentialist stance) or socially constructed and fluid (the constructionist stance) appears to be resolving in the direction that it is both (Diamond, 2008; Dillon et al., 2011; Savin-Williams, 2011; Vrangalova & Savin-Williams, 2010, 2012). Patterns of relationships, emotions, and affiliations may be fluid, whereas the elements of sexual orientation described in the previous paragraph may be more stable in an individual across time (Dillon et al., 2011). Whatever combination of fixed and fluid elements contribute to sexual identity, student affairs educators adhere to professional standards that view diverse sexual identities as part of holistic student development and do not support scientifically unproven attempts to "change" someone's sexual orientation or identity.

Early studies of "homosexual identity development" (for example, Cass, 1979, 1983–1984) represented a shift away from viewing non-heterosexual identities as pathological and separated the concept of sexual identity from sexual acts. The term "homosexual identity" is found in earlier literature and generally refers only to sexual behavior. Based on a sample of gay men, Cass proposed a linear model depicting homosexual identity development from lack of awareness of self as gay through stages of identity confusion, comparison, tolerance, acceptance, pride, and synthesis. From the 1970s through the 1990s, a number of other scholars proposed models of identity development for people who were not heterosexual. Variably focused on gay males, lesbian females, bisexual people, or some combination, these early models of identity development can be loosely grouped into two categories: the sociological, which focus on the impact of community, development of social roles, and managing stigma or on the coming out process (Coleman, 1981–1982; DuBay, 1987; Lee, 1977), and psychological theories, including those of Plummer (1975) and Troiden (1989), which concentrate on internal changes, such as growing self-awareness, formation of a gay/lesbian/bisexual self-image, and personal decisions about identity management, experienced by individuals as they come to identify as non-heterosexual. Levine and Evans (1991) identified four general developmental levels common to these models: first awareness, self-labeling, community involvement and disclosure, and identity integration.

Over time, scholars (see Bilodeau & Renn, 2005; McCarn & Fassinger, 1996; Reynolds & Hanjorgiris, 2000) criticized these models for their reliance on individuals coming out publicly, the failure to differentiate personal identity development from development of identity as a member of the gay and lesbian community, and the assumption that to be mentally healthy, a person must publicly identify as gay or lesbian and be active in the community (as in Cass, 1979, 1996). In addition, the linear progression included in many models failed to represent the observed variability in the timing of milestone events in the lives of gay men and lesbians, such as first awareness of same-sex attraction, labeling self as gay or lesbian, and becoming involved in the gay/lesbian community (see Diamond, 2008; Diamond & Savin-Williams, 2000; Maguen, Floyd, Bakeman, & Armistead, 2002; Parks, Hughes, & Matthews, 2004; Rosario, Schrimshaw, & Hunter, 2004). Scholars (Bilodeau & Renn, 2005; Diamond, 2008; Reynolds & Hanjorgiris, 2000; Worthington et al., 2002) criticized the body of theories on sexual identity development for its lack of generalizability to lesbian women, bisexuals, people of color, and heterosexuals. Finally, Fukuyama and Ferguson (2000) noted that a White Eurocentric bias is evident in most existing models of gay, lesbian, and bisexual identity development. They noted that sexual orientation itself is a Western concept not found in all cultures; the assumption that lesbian, gay, or bisexual people are always stigmatized does not hold in some cultures; coming out may be in direct conflict with the community and family values of many cultures; and integrating two central identities—such as race, religion, social class, or ability with sexual orientation—makes the process of identity formation more complex for people of color than it is for White individuals.

In the 1990s a few scholars proposed alternatives that addressed some of these criticisms. Arguing against the essentialist notion of a linear identity development process, Anthony D'Augelli (1994a) introduced a life span model of gay, lesbian, and bisexual identity development based on the idea that identity is a "social construction," shaped to varying degrees by social circumstances and environment and changeable throughout life. D'Augelli (1994a) pointed out that the social invisibility of sexual orientation and the social and legal penalties associated at the time with same-sex sexual expression represented two unique and powerful barriers to self-definition as gay, lesbian, or bisexual. He proposed six identity development processes: exiting heterosexual identity, developing personal LGB identity status, developing an LGB social identity, becoming an LGB offspring, developing an LGB intimacy status, and entering an LGB community.

Ruth Fassinger attempted to provide a more accurate model of lesbian identity development than that provided by earlier models. The model was later validated for men as well (Fassinger & Miller, 1997). Fassinger and her colleagues (Fassinger & Miller; McCarn & Fassinger, 1996; Mohr & Fassinger, 2000) sought to address the criticism that Cass and other stage theorists equated identity disclosure and activism with higher stages of identity development. Their work also took into account cultural and contextual influences on development to a greater extent than many earlier stage theories, particularly those developed by psychologists (Fassinger, 1998). They hypothesized two parallel processes of identity development: one related to individual sexual identity and the other focusing on group membership identity (Fassinger, 1998).

Although D'Augelli's and Fassinger's models addressed earlier weaknesses in understanding the development of minoritized sexual identities, they remain focused on lesbian, gay, and bisexual identities, to the exclusion of other minoritized sexual identities (for example, asexual, queer). They were not designed to explain heterosexual identities, but models of sexual identity development have emerged that address a wide range of sexualities in fluid contexts. We present one of those models in the next section, and as we explain, the theorists relied on Fassinger's foundational work on lesbian and gay identity development and on D'Augelli's lifespan focus. This integrated model focuses on processes and applies flexibly to understanding college students' development regardless of their sexual identities.

Unifying Model of Sexual Identity Development

For many years, student affairs educators relied on the stage-based, psychological models of gay and lesbian identity development—which were substantially based on an individual "coming out" to others (for example, Cass, 1979, 1996)—to inform their work with lesbian, gay, and bisexual students. While definitely advanced in comparison to previous approaches to working with students with minoritized sexual identities, the models had limitations and failed to describe how students across a spectrum of sexual identities, including heterosexual, developed. In this section, we introduce a unifying model of sexual identity development. In following sections, we present research on sexual identity development and applications of theory to practice.

Drawing on nearly four decades of research—their own and others'—Dillon et al. (2011) proposed a unifying model to describe the determinants and processes of sexual identity development that can apply to students of any sexual identity. The unifying model includes "two parallel, reciprocal developmental determinants: (a) an individual sexual identity development process and (b) a social identity process" (p. 657). The two processes occur within five sexual identity development statuses based on key concepts that James Marcia (1966, 1980; see Chapter Thirteen) introduced to describe identity development more broadly. Ruth Fassinger and colleagues (Fassinger, 1998; Fassinger & Miller, 1997; McCarn & Fassinger, 1996; Mohr & Fassinger, 2000;

Moradi, Mohr, Worthington, & Fassinger, 2009) pioneered the use of parallel processes and identity statuses to understand sexual identity formation of lesbians, then applied the model to other sexual identities. Notably, Worthington and colleagues (Worthington, Navarro, Savoy, & Hampton, 2008; Worthington et al., 2002) proposed and tested a model of heterosexual identity development that aligns closely with Fassinger's. The unifying model (Dillon et al., 2011) combines and extends these bodies of work. We present the unifying model and the five identity statuses here.

Parallel Processes of Sexual Identity Development

Dillon et al. (2011) mapped three main determinants of sexual identity development: biopsychosocial processes, individual identity, and social identity (see Figure 7.1). Individual identity comprises two elements: sexual orientation identity (described earlier in this chapter) and dimensions of human sexuality (such as sexual needs, behaviors, and values). Social identity also comprises two elements: group membership identity and attitudes toward sexual identity groups. Biopsychosocial processes influence individual identity and social

FIGURE 7.1. DETERMINANTS OF SEXUAL IDENTITY DEVELOPMENT

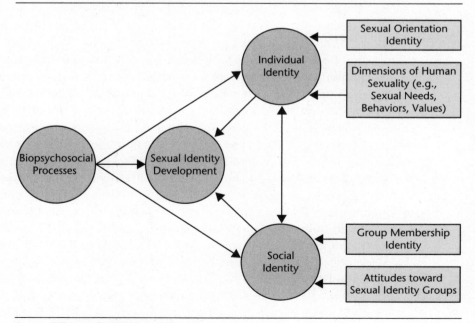

Source: Dillon et al. (2011), p. 657.

identity and also directly influence sexual identity development. Individual and social identities influence one another and also directly influence identity development. A heterosexual man, then, may undergo biopsychosocial processes that lead him to understand himself as a straight man, attracted to women, who belongs to a community that he believes to be made up mostly of other heterosexual students. A bisexual man may understand himself as attracted to women and to men, and he may participate in a community of other students who identify as lesbian, gay, bisexual, or pansexual (that is, attracted to individuals without regard for gender).

Individual identity and social identity may be consonant or divergent. Students whose sexual orientation is lesbian or gay but who have not talked with others about this identity may not participate in groups of LGBQ students on campus, but they are no less lesbian or gay than students who are "out and proud" on campus or at home. Similarly, straight allies may participate in LGBQ activism on campus and be very clear that their individual identity is as a heterosexual person. Intersecting identities of gender, race, social class, and religion may influence how LGBQ students engage with social identities related to sexuality; they may experience chilly subclimates within LGBQ groups on campus, or they may hold views about minoritized sexual identity groups that make it impossible for them to consider themselves part of one of those groups.

Sexual Identity Statuses

Synthesizing Fassinger's research on lesbian, gay, and bisexual identities and Worthington et al.'s (2002) research on heterosexual identity development, Dillon et al. (2011) proposed that the two processes (individual identity and social identity) occur in five sexual identity development statuses (see Figure 7.2). The statuses are not linear, but there is some order implicit in the model. The statuses derive from Marcia's (1966, 1980) concepts of identity exploration (crisis) and commitment that we describe in detail in Chapter Thirteen. Marcia's work and abundant research supporting this approach to identity development support the idea that an individual may be in a state of commitment without exploration (foreclosed), commitment following exploration (achieved), exploration with no commitment (moratorium), or no exploration and no commitment (diffused). Applied to college students' sexual identity development in both individual and social processes, these statuses provide a way to understand behaviors, emotions, and values regardless of expressed sexual orientations and identities.

FIGURE 7.2. PROCESSES OF SEXUAL IDENTITY DEVELOPMENT

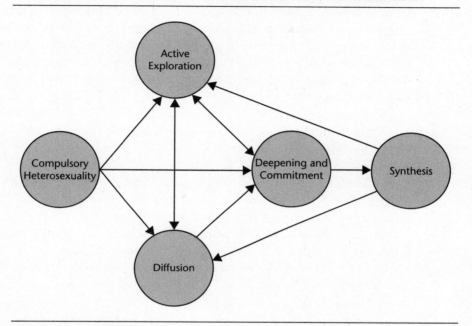

Source: Dillon et al. (2011), p. 658.

The first status is *compulsory heterosexuality,* a term introduced by Adrienne Rich (1980) to describe presumed—and socially sanctioned—sexual identity from birth. This status represents commitment to the dominant culture's assumption of heterosexuality without exploration of that assumption or identity—akin to a foreclosed status in Marcia's (1966, 1980) model. Individuals of any sexual orientation may "accept and adopt the compulsory heterosexuality as a sexual orientation identity that is institutionalized and required by socialization in many cultures" (Dillon et al., 2011, p. 659). For youth and college students who are heterosexual, this status may be invisible and unfelt, unmarked as an identity needing exploration. Adults who have never considered any alternative to heterosexuality have no developmental need to explore further. For people who are gay, lesbian, bisexual, asexual, and other identities, biopsychosocial determinants may lead to awareness that compulsory heterosexuality does not match emotions, behaviors, and values. Yet for a variety of reasons, they may retain the status of compulsory heterosexuality ascribed to them by society. Dillon et al. (2011)

noted that movement out of this status "is likely to be permanent because entry into one of the other statuses ultimately precludes the type of naïve commitment to sexual identity [that is] characteristic of this status" (p. 659). In other words, once individuals understand that so-called compulsory heterosexuality is not, in fact, universal and compulsory, they cannot fully return to a state in which they were unaware of the socially dictated, foreclosed identity.

From the presumption of heterosexuality, an individual may enter *active exploration* of individual and social sexual identities (exploration, no commitment; like Marcia's moratorium), *diffusion* (unexplored identity, with no commitment; Marcia's diffusion), or *deepening and commitment* (committed; like Marcia's identity achievement, with a key difference we describe shortly). The route to *synthesis* (which does not have a corollary in Marcia's model) goes through deepening and commitment. An individual can move among active exploration, diffusion, and deepening and commitment before reaching synthesis. Identity synthesis is not necessarily a permanent state, and individuals may move into active exploration or diffusion. The model describes sexual identity as fluid across the lifespan, with the potential for someone to be in different identity statuses in the individual and social processes already described.

The *active exploration status* is characterized by exploration that is cognitive, behavioral, or both. It is purposeful and directed toward the goal of exploring sexual identity. In this status, individuals actively question socially dictated aspects of compulsory heterosexuality. College students who are not heterosexual may question and experiment with emotions, thoughts, attractions, and behaviors related to same-sex or other-sex individuals (Fassinger & Miller, 1997). But Dillon et al. (2011) stressed that this questioning and experimenting can also be done by heterosexual individuals who are exploring societal, cultural, and family norms about heterosexuality, such as the preferred or sanctioned race, ethnicity, religion, social class, or physical abilities of the individuals with whom they are expected to partner. Active exploration of individual sexual identity is therefore "inclusive and flexible enough to account for between and within-group differences exhibited by same-sex and other-sex-oriented individuals" (p. 660).

Active exploration is also a status in which individuals may explore their social identity process. Students might use campus, local, and online resources and organizations to learn about the diversity of sexual identities and expressions. They might also experiment with different ways of expressing identities themselves as members of sexual identity communities, such as social or activist clubs for students with minoritized identities. Anti-gay attitudes and actions by individuals of any sexual orientation may be part of active exploration (see Moradi, van den Berg, & Epting, 2009; Mohr, 2002; Szymanski, Kashubeck-West, & Meyer, 2008), but there is also evidence that heterosexual, gay, lesbian, and bisexual individuals in active exploration showed positive associations with LGB-affirming attitudes and negative associations with measured homonegativity (Worthington, Dillon, & Becker-Schutte, 2005; Worthington & Reynolds, 2009). It is important to remember that individual sexual identity and social identity may not always be congruent (D'Augelli, 1994a; Diamond, 2008; Fassinger & Miller, 1997; McCarn & Fassinger, 1996; Savin-Williams, 2011); the processes are parallel but not necessarily aligned. Dillon et al. (2011) posited that individuals might leave active exploration by making a commitment and entering the deepening and commitment status or retreating from active exploration and entering diffusion.

Lack of purposeful exploration and lack of commitment to a sexual identity define the *diffusion status*. Dillon et al. (2011) describe two types of diffusion in the general literature on identity development and diffused status: diffused diffusion and carefree diffusion. In terms of sexual identity, people in carefree diffusion are "expected to indicate low levels of commitment or exploration, and apathy regarding commitment and exploration (e.g., "I don't care")" (p. 662). A carefree diffuser is not distressed by this status, whereas a diffused diffuser may "reflect an underlying uncertainty or insecurity and is more likely to be distressed by lack of commitments" (p. 662). In either case, the diffusion status lacks the intentionality of active exploration but also departs from the prescribed commitments, values, and expectations of compulsory heterosexuality.

College students of any sexual orientation could be in the diffused status. Based on research in psychology and counseling, Dillon et al. (2011) suggested that individuals in diffused diffusion may be experiencing stress related to exploration and commitment related to sexual identity, and could benefit from intervention. An individual might leave either type of diffusion through engaging in active exploration or, possibly, by returning to a commitment to compulsory heterosexuality, if not a full embrace of the original naïve state.

Deepening and commitment status involves "movement toward greater commitment to … identified sexual needs, values, sexual orientation and/or preferences for activities, partner characteristics, and modes of sexual expression" (Dillon et al., 2011, p. 663). There are two routes into this status. Individuals may move here from active exploration, creating a status akin to Marcia's (1966, 1980) achieved identity status that requires both exploration and commitment. But the unifying model of sexual identity development also posits that individuals may bypass exploration and move directly from compulsory heterosexuality to deepening and commitment, a concept (commitment, no exploration) not included in Marcia's identity statuses, but one that makes sense in the context of contemporary sexual identities and societal norms and expectations. Dillon et al. called this movement to *committed compulsory heterosexuality,* which is "characterized by a more profound commitment to compulsory heterosexuality" (p. 663).

Heterosexuals might also enter deepening and commitment following a period of active exploration, in which case they are more likely to question personal and societal values and norms related to heteronormativity and denial of equal rights and treatment for people of all sexual orientations. Lesbian, gay, bisexual, and asexual individuals are most likely to enter the deepening and commitment status from active exploration, which results in knowledge of self and personal identities (McCarn & Fassinger, 1996). Individuals of any sexual orientation who enter deepening and commitment by way of active exploration will have questioned and possibly abandoned the aspects of compulsory heterosexuality that foster anti-LGB attitudes. Thus internalized negative attitudes such as homophobia or biphobia may be reduced among LGB people. People of any sexual orientation may leave the deepening and commitment status to enter (or reenter) active exploration, diffusion, or synthesis.

Dillon et al. (2011) proposed that the deepening and commitment status is the only way to *synthesis.* In the synthesis status, "Individual sexual identity, group membership identity, and attitudes toward dominant and marginalized sexual orientation identity groups merge into an overall sexual self-concept, which is conscious, congruent, and volitional" (p. 664). Sexual identity is likely to be connected, coherent, and consistent with managing multiple dimensions of identity (see Abes, Jones, & McEwen, 2007). The unifying model suggests that individuals who move directly from compulsory heterosexuality to deepening and commitment to synthesis may not fully demonstrate all qualities of synthesis, having bypassed exploration and questioning of social values related to heterosexual privilege. But individuals of any sexual orientation who have at some point engaged in active exploration are likely to be more flexible and open in their thinking about sexual identities and groups when they reach synthesis status. Because sexual identity remains fluid over the lifespan, individuals may cycle back to active exploration or diffusion from synthesis.

The Unifying Model

In the unifying model, straight college students might move directly from presuming themselves as heterosexual to deepening and commitment to synthesis as straight identity. Or they might engage in active exploration before deepening and commitment and synthesis. Similarly, gay, lesbian, bisexual, or asexual students might exit compulsory heterosexuality, commit to an identity, and then move to identity synthesis status. Or they might explore and then commit to identity and reach synthesis. Any student might enter diffusion, either carefree or diffused, to step away from (or avoid) active exploration and commitment. The multiple developmental pressures and messages that students receive about sexual values, attitudes, and behaviors from peers, educators, and media may create an environment in which opting out of exploration or commitment is preferable. Or students may feel so conflicted about sexual feelings and deeply held values that they are in some distress, no longer fully experiencing compulsory heterosexuality and attendant expectations but not able to engage in active exploration. Of course, sexual identity development is under way before students enter college at whatever age, during their higher education experience, and afterward. Individually and as a student population, they are likely to be at different statuses across both processes over time.

A major benefit of this hypothesized model is that it assumes that all individuals—not just those with minoritized sexual identities—undergo some process of sexual identity development, which may include exploration or diffusion before commitment and synthesis. A second benefit lies in the fluidity of the statuses and the assumption that an array of biopsychosocial factors influences sexual identity at individual and social levels. Sexual identity is not defined by "coming out" as something other than heterosexual, and it exists for everyone, regardless of changes in sexual identities over time. This model also appears to be one that may prove durable as societal understanding of sexual orientations and identities evolves and expands.

Research Support for the Unifying Model of Sexual Identity Development

Dillon, Worthington, and Moradi (2011) proposed the unifying model of sexual identity development as a hypothetical, without specific testing of this model as a whole. However, they reference and describe the rich body of empirical literature that supports the tenets, assumptions, processes, and statuses in the model. They also credit the intellectual history of bodies of work, including that of Marcia (1966, 1980) and Fassinger and colleagues (Fassinger, 1998; Fassinger & Miller, 1997; McCarn & Fassinger, 1996; Mohr & Fassinger, 2000). Indeed, they cite work that specifically connects their thinking in this model to work done in collaboration with Fassinger (Moradi, Mohr, Worthington, & Fassinger, 2009). It is not unusual in social science research for teams of scholars working in various combinations over time to collaborate and develop ideas to provide empirical support for a new theoretical model such as the one Dillon et al. (2011) proposed; knowing the intellectual history of components can aid in understanding the overall concepts and underlying research. In this section, we describe some of the studies that contributed to the ideas synthesized in the unifying model of sexual identity development.

The unifying model is based in large part on the work that Fassinger and colleagues did to establish the key concepts of parallel processes and identity statuses for lesbian, gay, and bisexual people. Research she and her colleagues conducted supports the validity of their model. McCarn (1991) studied identity development among a group of 38 lesbians who were diverse with respect to age, education, race, ethnicity, and occupation; Fassinger and Miller (1997) explored the applicability of the model for a similarly diverse group of 34 gay men. In both studies, they found support for each of the two processes as well as a four-phase sequence they posited within each process (awareness, exploration, deepening/commitment, internalization/synthesis). In their longitudinal study of two first-year students, Evans and Herriott (2004) also reported evidence of separate internal and external developmental processes similar to those in Fassinger's model. Working with Fassinger, Risco (2008) validated the Same-Sex Orientation Identity Questionnaire (SSOIQ) with a racially and ethnically diverse sample. The SSOIQ measures location in the sexual minority identity formation process, using the parallel processes of individual sexual identity and group membership identity development.

Building out their work on heterosexual identity development (Worthington et al., 2002), Worthington and colleagues created the Measure of Sexual Identity Exploration and Commitment (MoSIEC) and validated it with national adult samples (Worthington et al., 2008; Worthington & Reynolds, 2009). They based the MoSIEC on Marcia's two dimensions of identity exploration and commitment, and it yielded four factors: commitment, exploration, sexual orientation identity uncertainty, and synthesis/integration. These factors "represent constructs from the unifying sexual identity development model: (a) active exploration indicated by the exploration factor, (b) compulsory heterosexuality and deepening and commitment represented by the commitment factor, (c) and synthesis characterized by the synthesis/integration factor" (Dillon et al., 2011, p. 665). The sexual orientation identity uncertainty factor aligns with Marcia's moratorium status, which also corresponds to exploration without commitment in the active exploration status. The diffused status in the unifying model has no direct correspondent on the MoSIEC, and it needs more empirical support, especially related to the question of carefree versus diffused diffusion and the level of distress individuals in diffusion may experience. Worthington and Reynolds (2009) used the MoSIEC to support the proposition in the unifying model that among individuals with minoritized sexual orientations (for example, lesbian, gay, bisexual), there are significant between-group differences in sexual identity development.

The MoSIEC offers potential for comparing the sexual identity development processes of gay, lesbian, bisexual, and heterosexual individuals with the unifying model of sexual identity development. Preliminary research suggests that they are different. For example, in a study using a measure of Marcia's (1966) ego identity statuses, Konik and Stewart (2004) found that heterosexually identified college students scored higher on identity foreclosure and moratorium than students who identified as gay, lesbian, or bisexual, while the former scored higher on identity achievement. Heterosexual students were also less likely than LGB students to see sexual identity formation as a process requiring effort and intentionality. Morgan, Steiner, and Thompson (2010) found that all sexual minority men but only half of heterosexual male college students questioned their sexual orientation. In a related study, two-thirds of heterosexual women had thought about or questioned their sexuality (Morgan & Thompson, 2011). But in a qualitative study, Mueller and Cole (2009) found that heterosexual students had rarely considered their sexual identity. These findings support tenets of the unifying model.

Another tenet of the unifying model, that sexual identity development is fluid across the lifespan and that individuals may cycle back to exploration or diffusion, has longstanding support in the research literature (see D'Augelli, 1994b; McCarn & Fassinger, 1996; Savin-Williams, 1995). In a study of gay men in college, Stevens (2004) found that sexual identity development is nonlinear and varies depending on context and the sense that gay men make of their situations. In particular, interactions with different people (peers, staff, faculty) led to revisions in the participants' identity. Critical incidents reported by the participants "centered around disclosure of their gay identity and assessment of their surroundings" (p. 201). The men reported that incidents of heterosexism and homophobia in the campus environment, as well as supportive statements and actions, had a significant effect on their willingness to disclose.

Consistent with a number of earlier theories, the unifying model posits that sexual behavior does not define sexual identity. Thompson and Morgan (2008) found that sexual behaviors do not necessarily differ across individuals in different sexual identity development statuses. And support for the proposition that individuals of any sexual orientation who have gone through exploration before deepening and commitment (and then to synthesis) are more open-minded about their own and others' sexual identities, derives from research using the MoSIEC in combination with measures of attitudes toward members of different social identity groups and individuals holding different ages and levels of religiosity and sexual conservatism (Worthington & Reynolds, 2009; Worthington et al., 2005; Worthington et al., 2008). Triangulating across studies of sexual identity statuses, self-identified sexual identity, and attitudes toward members of different groups, Dillon et al. (2011) were able to support the propositions underlying the unifying model. Additional research on the model as a whole, in particular with respect to college student identity development, will add empirical support and/or draw aspects of the model into question.

Application

The unifying model of sexual identity development, and the research that underlies its assumptions and concepts, suggests several applications in student affairs practice. First, the separation of individual and social group identities reinforces the idea that students may be in different statuses with their personal self-identification and their public social group affiliations. Membership in a student organization or peer group of people with minoritized sexualities does not indicate LGBQ or asexual self-identification, and avoidance of or lack of interest in such groups does not mean that the student holds a heterosexual identity. Even holding homonegative attitudes or engaging in homophobic speech or actions does not mean that the student is heterosexual. This knowledge can be useful in advising student organizations, helping students resolve personal conflicts with peers, and dealing with bias incidents on campus. It may also be useful in planning academic and career-related programs, taking into consideration that students will be in all statuses of individual and social sexual identity development.

Tomlinson and Fassinger (2003) explored the relationship of lesbian identity development, perceived campus climate, and career development for 192 lesbian and questioning college women. Their findings indicated that campus climate and, to a lesser degree, lesbian identity development status influence vocational development. They suggested that lesbian and questioning students might feel freer to explore both their sexual and vocational identities in an environment that is supportive. Thus career counselors need to create a visibly welcoming environment for LGBQ students, whether or not they believe students with minoritized sexual identities will be present.

A second key concept with applications to student affairs practice is that sexual behaviors do not determine sexual identity. Sexual behaviors, values, needs, and orientation are components of individual identity, but they do not act alone. Savin-Williams (2011) further posited that contemporary youth, regardless of sexual identity, eschew the need to affix labels to themselves. Providing health education messages to, or conducting research with, populations defined by the labels straight, gay, lesbian, or bisexual becomes more challenging when students do not identify with these terms. In addition, the increasing visibility of college students who identify on an asexual spectrum (sometimes calling themselves "ace-identified") calls on new ways of thinking about how to reach individuals who do not identify as lesbian, gay, bisexual, or heterosexual (McAleavey et al., 2011).

The unifying model incorporates research that positions sexual identity development in social environments. This third key concept is central in creating campus environments that support healthy exploration and expression of all sexual identities. Measuring and addressing campus climate for LGBQ students is the subject of a number of studies and professional networks (for example, Brown & Gortmaker, 2009; Rankin et al., 2010; Woodford, Chonody, Kulick, Brennan, & Renn, in press; Woodford, Kolb, Durocher-Radeka, & Javier, 2014). Some of the critical elements are an inclusive approach that addresses campus policies, provision of campus support services and resources specifically for sexually minoritized students, programming for heterosexual as well as LGBQ students, inclusion of content about LGBQ topics in the curriculum, supportive faculty and staff who are willing to act as advocates and role models, and active intervention to address homophobic acts (Dessel, Woodford, Routenberg, & Breijak, 2013; Rankin et al., 2010; Renn, 2010). D'Augelli (1994a) considered "safe zone" and other ally programs (Evans, 2002; Poynter & Tubbs, 2008; Woodford et al., 2014)—that is, networks of individuals who identify themselves as available to provide personal support and information to sexually minoritized students—to be important in identity development. These programs also provide visible signs of support that can make the climate appear more positive to LGBQ people.

The unifying model and studies underlying it also suggest strategies for creating campus environments that support active exploration of heterosexual identities. Worthington et al.'s (2002) model of heterosexual identity development can provide guidance in working with students who identify as heterosexual, to point out that exiting compulsory heterosexuality and exploring their own identities is a valuable undertaking. Heterosexual counselors and student affairs educators would also benefit from having a clearer understanding of their own sexual identity development process in order to more clearly understand the sexual diversity of individuals with whom they work (Hoffman, 2004). Being around others who are secure in their sexual identity and affirmative of sexual diversity provides the necessary context and motivation for the self-exploration and commitment Worthington et al. (2002)

have suggested as precursors to achievement of a synthesized heterosexual identity. Thus, focusing on development of an affirmative environment in which individuals can explore and grow is as important as working with the individuals themselves.

Critique and Future Directions

In recent years, research and theory about sexual identity development have increased, both in quantity and quality. Models are more sophisticated and inclusive than were the initial attempts to describe the formation of sexual identity. The unifying model of sexual identity development represents the most ambitious attempt to date to provide a framework for understanding parallel processes of individual and social identities, with flexibility across statuses, incorporating personal and environmental determinants, and applicable to any sexual identity. A reasonable body of research undergirds the proposed model, but more empirical work on the full model is needed before fully accepting it for use with college students.

As Renn (2010) pointed out, studies of college student sexual identities are often based on small samples on single campuses. Longitudinal studies of identity development are rare, and retrospective self-report does not always capture the richness of lived experiences. It is difficult to draw any firm conclusions about developmental processes based on cross-sectional studies. Tillapaugh (2012, 2013, 2015) launched a longitudinal study on the multiple identities of gay men, and this line of research promises to advance theory and method. More effort needs to focus on development of assessment techniques and research designs to validate models of sexual identity development. The MoSIEC instrument (Worthington et al., 2008) and the SSOIQ (Risco, 2008) are promising advances in this regard, as are efforts such as the National Study of LGBTQ Student Success (www.lgbtqsuccess.net), which includes a longitudinal study of self-identified LGBTQ students who entered college in fall 2013.

Researchers also need to continue to consider the interaction of sexuality and other social identities. Developmental theorists, particularly Abes (2009, 2012; Abes & Kasch, 2007), Jones and McEwen (2000), and Abes, Jones, and McEwen (2007), have demonstrated the importance of considering identity development as an integrated process. Researchers need to explore the roles that gender, ethnicity, religion, race, disability, class, and other identities play in sexual identity formation (see Tillapaugh, 2012, 2013, 2015).

In response to the invisibility of people of color in much research on LGBQ students, a number of higher education scholars have investigated sexual identity development, experiences, and expression of students minoritized by sexual identity and race, ethnicity, or nationality. The experience of Black gay men has been the subject of a number of studies: Means and Jaeger (2015) employed quare theory (see Means & Jaeger, 2013) to understand a Black gay male student's spiritual journey; Mitchell and Means (2014) synthesized literature on Black gay and bisexual men at predominantly White institutions; Patton (2011) analyzed the experiences of gay and bisexual men at an historically Black college; Squire and Mobley (2014) examined the college choice process of Black gay males; and Strayhorn and Mullins (2012) investigated Black gay men's experiences in residence halls. Research on LGBQ Black women and on students from other racial and ethnic groups has not yet been as plentiful, though a few scholars have begun to inform the field; for example, Peña-Talamantes (2013) described lesbian and gay Latino/a students' identity negotiation; Strayhorn (2014a) described Korean American gay men's experiences; Vaccaro and Mena (2011) discussed mental health of queer college students of color; Walker and Longmire-Avital (2013) explored religious faith and resilience in Black lesbian, gay, and bisexual emerging adults; Tillapaugh's (2012, 2013) study of multiple dimensions of identity included gay males with a number of different identifications; and Patton and Simmons's (2008) study of Black lesbian students attending an historically black college.

In addition to studying intersections between college students' racial, ethnic, and sexual identities, a handful of scholars have investigated other intersections. For example, Harley, Nowak, Gassaway, and Savage (2002) concluded that "LGBT college students with disabilities have been relegated to a status of invisibility" (p. 525), in part because "persons with disability have been desexualized" (p. 527). Gold and Stewart (2011) explored LGB students coming out at the intersection of spirituality and sexuality, and Love, Bock, Jannarone, and Richardson (2005) studied this intersection as well. As noted earlier, the research agenda built by Abes, Jones, and McEwen has contributed substantially to understanding the interactions between multiple dimensions of identities including spiritual, racial, ethnic, social class, and other identities. We expect these and other scholars will continue to probe the diversity within sexual identity groups and their findings will enrich and inform the use of the unifying model of sexual identity development.

A review of this chapter underscores the limited number of studies that have examined sexual identity development in college settings or ways that sexual identity development theory can contribute to intentional design of strategies to enhance identity formation. We encourage higher education scholars to build on the research that is available and to develop and evaluate interventions to facilitate the sexual identity development of students.

Discussion Questions

1. What is sexual identity and why is it important in the development of college students?

2. What were the characteristics of early models of minoritized sexual identities (that is, lesbian, gay, and bisexual identities)? Why did researchers believe a unifying model was necessary?

3. What one identity development theory and two sexual identity development theories did the authors of the unifying model bring together?

4. Describe the two parallel processes of the unifying model. What determinants go into these processes?

5. Describe the five identity statuses of the unifying model. What areas of exploration and commitment are associated with each?

6. Consider a college student with a particular sexual identity (for example, heterosexual, gay, lesbian, bisexual, asexual) and map the student's trajectory in different paths through the unifying model. What might cause the student to follow different paths of individual sexual identity and group membership identity?

7. What programs, services, interventions, or environmental cues could you employ to work with students with different sexual identities at different identity statuses?

8. What identities, processes, or statuses seem to be missing from the unifying model? Are there sexual identity development experiences that the model does not describe or explain? How might you modify it to include these experiences?

CHAPTER EIGHT

GENDER AND GENDER IDENTITY DEVELOPMENT

This chapter provides an introduction to important concepts related to sex, gender, and gender identity. It introduces research and theories related to how individuals come to understand their gender identity, whether they are cisgender (that is, their gender identity matches the sex observed at birth; see Green, 2006) or transgender (their gender identity is different from their observed sex at birth). We present applications of research to college students and offer suggestions for future directions.

Foundational Concepts: Sex, Gender, and Gender Identity

Although the words are sometimes used interchangeably and the concepts are closely related, *sex* and *gender* are distinct. Psychologist Kay Bussey (2011) pointed out that "Sex has typically been used when referring to biologically based differences between males and females and gender when referring to socially influenced differences" (p. 604). The World Health Organization (WHO, 2014) provided a more detailed definition of sex as "biological and physiological characteristics that define men and women" (¶ 2), whereas they stated gender "refers to the socially constructed roles, behaviours, activities, and attributes that a given society considers appropriate for men and women" (¶ 3). The WHO (2014) describes sex categories as "male" and "female"; gender categories as "masculine" and "feminine" (¶ 5). Some social scientists (see Bussey, 2011) now suggest that distinctions between sex and gender blur when considering there are both biological and sociological influences that result in observed differences between men and women.

When working with college students it is important to recognize that sex and gender, while very closely related, are not synonymous, and students' gender cannot be assumed in all cases to match what is expected based on their sex. Research over several decades (see Bem, 1981b, 1983; Bussey, 2011; Deaux, 1985; Kohlberg, 1966; Stiver, 1991; Zosuls, Miller, Ruble, Martin, & Fabes, 2011) provides evidence that in most cases *gender identity*, or sense of self as masculine, feminine, both, or neither (Bussey, 2011; Diamond, Pardo, & Butterworth, 2011; Lev, 2004; Wilchins, 2002), begins developing in early childhood, and then perhaps intensifies in early adolescence (Galambos, Almeida, & Petersen, 1990), well before students enter college. But college is also a context in which students can explore their understanding of masculinity, femininity, gender identity, gender expression, and adult gender roles (Berkowitz, 2011; Bilodeau, 2005, 2009; Dugan, Kusel, & Simounet, 2012; Edwards & Jones, 2009; Henry, West, & Jackson, 2010; McGuire, Berhanu, Davis, & Harper, 2014; Stevenson & Clegg, 2012). Emerging models posit that no matter one's gender identity, it is "not fixed in any point in time, but rather is an ongoing process that transforms over the life course" (Bussey, 2011, p. 604); this perspective reinforces the importance of attending to all students' gender identity development.

The relationships between and among the concepts of sex, gender, and gender identity are important to understand before knowing more about how cisgender and transgender students experience and explore gender identity. Noted queer theorists (for example, Bornstein, 1994; Butler, 1990, 2004; Jagose, 1997) have explained the ways these categories, as well as sexual orientation, have been posed as binaries; that is, common understandings of sex and gender, for example, have been framed around the binaries of male/female and masculine/feminine. Gender in a binary system is either "man" or "woman," gender identity is "masculine" or "feminine," and sexual orientation is "heterosexual" or "homosexual" (based on one's sex, gender, and gender identity in relation to the sex, gender, and gender identity of the persons to whom one is attracted). In such a binary system, sex, gender identity, gender role (the enactment of gender), and sexual orientation are assumed to align and to lead to the next, as in Figure 8.1.

In Lev's (2004) binary model, "if a person is a male, he is a man; if a person is a man, he is masculine; if a person is a masculine male man, he will be attracted to a feminine female woman; if a person is a female, she is a woman; if a person is a woman, she is feminine; if a person is a feminine female woman, she will be attracted to a masculine male man" (p. 94).

FIGURE 8.1. LEV'S (2004) CONCEPTUALIZATION OF BINARY SYSTEMS OF SEX, GENDER IDENTITY, GENDER ROLE, AND SEXUAL ORIENTATION

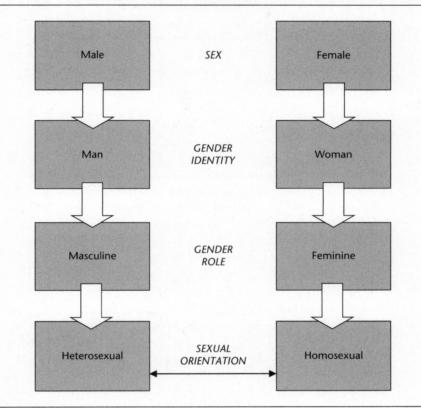

Source: Lev (2004), p. 94.

As an alternative to this set of fixed binary categories, linked to one another by assumptions of causal relationships (sex causes gender, which leads to "appropriate" gender role and sexual orientation), Lev (2004) proposed a model in which each element is on a continuum and exists in interaction but not causation with other elements. Such a model provides for the reality that some people are born "intersex," or have biological (for example, genetic, physical) traits of males and females (Fausto-Sterling, 1993). Their internal sense of gender may not be exclusively as a man or as a woman, their gender role may be both masculine *and* feminine, and their sexual orientation may be toward individuals of more than one sex, gender, and gender role (for example, bisexual or pansexual) (see Bem, 1983, 1995, and Bussey, 2011). Lev also proposed

FIGURE 8.2. RELATIONSHIP AMONG SEX, GENDER, GENDER ROLE, AND SEXUAL ORIENTATION WHEN ALL ARE FLUID AND ON A CONTINUUM

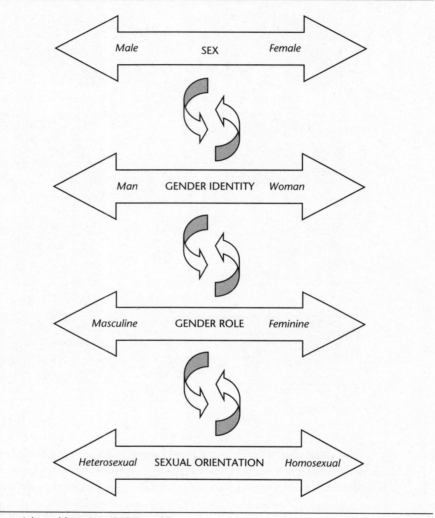

Source: Adapted from Lev (2004), p. 97.

that "in any category people can change their behavior, presentation, or identity and none of these categories represents an immutable entity" (p. 96). This fluidity within and across categories, both in the present and across time, represents the predominant thinking among contemporary social scientists about gender identity and its relationship to sex, gender, and sexual orientation.

Gender Identities

Bussey (2011) explained that "gender identity involves the self-representation of a gendered self, mediated by self-regulatory processes. Gender identity is informed by knowledge of one's biological sex and of the beliefs associated with gender, how one is perceived and treated by others depending on one's gender, and an understanding of the collective basis of gender" (p. 608). When gender identity aligns as traditionally expected with biological sex assigned at birth (that is, a female identifies as a girl or woman or a male as a boy or man), it is a cisgender identity (Bilodeau, 2009; Green, 2006). Transgender identity may occur when gender identity aligns differently from what would be traditionally expected based on biological sex assigned at birth (Bornstein, 1994; Diamond et al., 2011; Lev, 2004; Wilchins, 2002). An individual may identify with the "opposite" gender from assigned birth sex, sometimes defined as transsexual identity (see Diamond et al., 2011) such as Female-to-Male (FtM), Male-to-Female (MtF), transmasculine, or transfeminine (see Beemyn & Rankin, 2011), or in a way that blends masculine and feminine identities into a "genderqueer" or other nonbinary identity (Diamond et al., 2011; Saltzburg & Davis, 2010).

From here forward in the chapter, we use the term *trans** as an inclusive term for identities other than cisgender. As noted by Tompkins (2014),

> The asterisk (*), or star, is a symbol with multiple meanings and applications that can mark a bullet point in a list, highlight or draw attention to a particular word or phrase, indicate a footnote, or operate as a wildcard character in computing and telecommunications. In relation to transgender phenomena, the asterisk is used primarily in the latter sense, to open up transgender or trans to a greater range of meanings. (p. 26)

Many trans* activists and scholars use the asterisk to be inclusive of diverse gender identities, as well as to interrupt the viewer's or reader's attention momentarily, to draw attention to genderist assumptions about identities.

It is important to note that some trans* individuals do not reference themselves by any of the terms we have listed, and there may be additional ways of considering gender identity that fall between or beyond these categories. In the cisgender/trans* approach to gender identity, which itself replicates a binary identity construction, individuals who are male and identify as men or who are female and identify as women are cisgender; individuals who are male but who do not identify as men (they may identify as women, as gender fluid, as both men and women, or outside traditional notions of gender), or who are female but do not identify as women, are trans*.

Scholars have contributed evidence of more variation within than across gender categories (Bussey, 2011; Carrera, DePalma, & Lameiras, 2012). Masculinity and femininity, for example, vary widely among men as they do among women (Bem, 1981b). Masculinity and femininity, then, are not wholly reliable predictors of an individual's gender identity. A female student with strong masculine traits may identify as a cisgender woman, just as a feminine male student may identify as a man. Students may experience their gender identities as fluid or situational, defying a simplistic, fixed notion of gender identity before, during, or after college. Decoupling gender roles from sexual orientation, as Lev (2004) suggests, these students may be heterosexual, lesbian, gay, or bisexual. Their gender identity does not determine their sexual orientation.

Trans* Students

The higher education setting may provide opportunities for trans* students to explore and express gender identity in ways that were not possible elsewhere in their lives before college. Yet similar to the rest of society, college campuses are governed by a set of assumptions that Bilodeau (2009) called "genderism," which call on all members of a community to express their gender identities in ways that (1) align as expected with their observed sex and (2) subscribe to a gender binary that allows for masculine (male) men and feminine (female) women. Students whose gender expression—the ways in which they publicly enact gender roles through clothing, grooming, speech, posture, and other behaviors—does not conform to the expectations of peers and faculty report being subjected to alienation, harassment, and violence (Beemyn, 2005; Bilodeau, 2005, 2009; Rankin, Blumenfeld, Weber, & Frazier, 2010). Even allowing for within-gender variation, the penalties for stepping beyond the boundaries of what is considered acceptable can be harsh.

Trans* students are increasingly visible in U.S. higher education, and their experiences are the subject of an increasing empirical, theoretical, and practical literature (for example, Beemyn, 2005; Beemyn & Rankin, 2011; Bilodeau, 2005, 2009; Dugan, Kusel, & Simounet, 2012; Marine, 2011a, 2011b; Marine & Nicolazzo, 2014; Nicolazzo, 2015; Nicolazzo & Marine, 2015). This literature suggests trans* students may find college a place for identity exploration or for expression of a gender identity that they had not previously named or expressed publicly. Increasingly, trans* youth are connecting digitally with one another and other trans* people through social media (Nicolazzo, 2015; Singh, 2013). When they come to campus they may for the first time find an in-person community of other trans* people, and they may experiment with gender expression, trying on masculine and/or feminine expression.

However, the operation of genderism (Bilodeau, 2009) may constrict opportunities for students' gender identity exploration. The ongoing separation of men and women on athletic teams, in some campus activities (for example, fraternities and sororities), and in public facilities (locker rooms, restrooms) may pose challenges to trans* students who are exploring new modes of gender expression (see Beemyn, 2005, 2012). Some features of campus life—such as residence hall rooms assigned by sex—may be unavoidable, even if other single-sex/gender venues are managed through avoidance (by, for example, changing at home instead of using a locker room that is designated for males or females).

Cisgender Students

Genderism's twin values—gender expression conforming to expectations based on observed sex and a firmly etched gender binary—influence the college experiences and identities of cisgender students as much as they do for trans* students. Historically, "college men" and "college women" fulfilled clear gender and social roles (see Horowitz, 1987). The claim that traditional gender roles and expectations continue to play a central role in the lives of undergraduate students is supported by abundant and persistent evidence on gender-related phenomena, including college, academic major, and career choices (Harris & Harper, 2008; Shapiro & Sax, 2011); dating, socialization, and sexual activity (Handler, 1995; Holland & Eisenhart, 1990; Owen, Rhoades, Stanley, & Fincham, 2010); body image and eating disorders (Cash, Morrow, Hrabosky, & Perry, 2004; Cole, Davidson, & Gervais, 2013); alcohol use (Harper, Harris, & Mmeje, 2005; Wagoner, Blocker, McCoy, Sutfin, Champion, & Wolfson, 2012); and attitudes related to rape (McMahon, 2010; Nagel, Matsuo, McIntyre, & Morrison, 2005).

For cisgender students, violating gender norms by being a "too masculine" woman or "too feminine" man has consequences. For example, harassment of and violence against lesbian, gay, and bisexual (LGB) students, regardless of their gender identities, are attributed in part to outwardly directed reactions of hatred and fear generated by LGB students' apparent lack of conformity to expected sex/gender identity/gender role/sexual orientation linkages (Kimmel, 1994; Rankin et al., 2010). Anti-gay epithets, invoking female body parts to insult men, and the use of gendered terms such as "bitch" as all-purpose put-downs provide additional evidence of the ways that gender—and commenting on others' gender—operate on campus to reinforce expected roles and norms (Davis, 2002; Hamilton, 2007; Kimmel, 2010; Kimmel & Davis, 2011). Although gender roles and norms are reinforced on campus, students by and large come to higher education with the process of gender identity development well under way and with their own sense of gender identity well established (Bussey, 2011). There is some evidence, however, that the college experience may also influence perceptions of gender roles. The next section describes how gender identity develops before *and* during college.

Gender Identity Development

As stated earlier, gender identity development begins in early childhood and scholars believe it is well established before traditional-age college students arrive on campus (see Bem, 1981a, 1983; Davis, 2002; Deaux, 1985; Galambos et al., 1990; Harris & Harper, 2008; Kohlberg, 1966; Stiver, 1991). Yet recent literature (Beemyn & Rankin, 2011; Bussey, 2011; Diamond, Pardo, & Butterworth, 2011) emphasizes the lifelong nature of gender identity development, and suggests certain aspects of college life may challenge the identities students bring to campus or reinforce existing gender identities. There is no predominant model of gender identity development that applies to college students. Much of the literature on gender identity development relates to clinical populations of trans*-identified youth and adults. Contemporary theory and student affairs practice move away from these clinical models to a more inclusive understanding of gender fluidity within and across the categories of trans* and cisgender identity; some approaches (Bussey, 2011) question the delineation of trans* from cisgender, positing that everyone's gender identity is in continual development. We include theories that delineate these categories, in order to bring visibility to the particular needs of the trans* minoritized populations on campus.

The complexity of the sex/gender identity/gender role triad and the lack of a unified language (some authors use *sex* and *gender* interchangeably; some use different terms from others for the same concept) confound attempts to identify a single model that describes gender identity development in college students. Yet theories converge on the idea that one's sense of one's masculinity and femininity and the person-environment interactions related to gender roles and expression are key components of gender identity, and gender identity is related to other aspects of overall psychosocial identity. Thus this section describes a social-cognitive theory of gender identity development as a lifelong process involving personal and environmental factors, gendered experiences on campus, trans* identity development, and gender as a domain within models of multidimensional and intersecting identities.

Social-Cognitive Theory of Gender Identity Development

In keeping with ecological (for example, Bronfenbrenner, 1995, 2005; Renn & Arnold, 2003) and other person-environment approaches to understanding development, a social-cognitive theory of gender identity development takes into account three interacting components: personal, behavioral, and environmental (Bussey, 2011; Bussey & Bandura, 1999). Personal components include biological characteristics, self-concept, self-perception, and regulation. Behavioral factors are gender-related activity patterns. Environmental components include families, peers, educational settings, media, and digital contexts. Interactions occur among these components when students present themselves in gendered ways through, for example, clothing, hairstyle, makeup, and posture, and then act in ways considered "masculine" or "feminine" in their campus context. How students present themselves provokes reactions from peers and faculty that then cause students to repeat, cease, or change these gendered presentations to provoke desired reactions. If a cisgender woman wears her hair very short and goes to a campus coffee shop where she is addressed as "Sir," she may not care about this reaction, or she may begin to wear makeup and clothing that will indicate more clearly that she is a woman (with short hair). A female-to-male trans* student may wear men's slacks and shirts, wingtip shoes, and a bow tie to reinforce his masculine gender identity and deflect hostile stares as he enters the men's restroom. Students may experiment with gender expression to see what kind of reactions they receive in different contexts on and off campus. Or they may conform to local standards of gender expression to ensure that others see them in the way that they identify. Local (sometimes national) stereotypes of gendered identity expressions continuously evolve for subcultures of students on campus (for example, "jock," "prep," "sorority," "nerd"), and some students' behaviors demonstrate their membership in or identification with clearly gendered communities.

Gender remains a powerful enough organizing concept in most contemporary societies to have a substantial interactive effect on individuals and their self-perception, self-regulation, gender expression, and gender identity. Bussey (2011) stated, "Gender identity is conceptualized as an ongoing process that may change across the life span and as societal views about gender change" (p. 608). So the three interactive components operate within dynamic social environments that differ across time, place, and culture. Among others, Bem (1983) proposed that individuals filter information through gender schema that are formed at an early age but are not immutable. Students process information about themselves and their environments through gender schema and then interact with their environments informed by those schemas, toward identifying with or outside of different genders, even as societal views about those genders shift over time and across cultures.

The case of international students in a U.S. context provides a clear illustration of these phenomena. Some international students may come to college with different gender schema from their local peers, and part of the adjustment to the new environment is in understanding how to interpret local expressions of gender and gender diversity. For example, in many Middle Eastern nations, some of which are quite conservative regarding gender roles and sexuality, it is common to see men holding hands in public. This gesture is interpreted as one of friendship, with no romantic inference. In the same society, a man and a woman would rarely be seen holding hands in public, because that gesture would infer a looseness of her (hetero)sexuality. It is common on many campuses to see students of different genders touching in public, but still fairly rare to see students who appear to be of the same gender holding hands; in the United States, these gestures have different meanings associated with gender and sexuality. Through what social-cognitive processes do new international students come to understand gender and gender identity in the United States? Three levels of analysis may guide their process:

1. Is the new culture strongly and exclusively binary? Or is the new culture one in which gender fluidity and flexibility are visible?
2. What are the typical ways to express masculinities, femininities, and androgynies within the binary or fluid context? How does one express one's gender?
3. How much tolerance is there for diverging from expected gender norms? Is the penalty high or relatively modest for individuals who do not conform to typical expressions? Is the penalty the same for men, women, and trans* individuals, or is it more harsh for some genders than others?

Students from any culture must understand both the nature of gender in the college context and the varied expression of masculinities, femininities, and androgynies within it; because gender is such a strong organizing force, students will be subjected to gender influences in the environment and in interpersonal interactions even as they are figuring out the new culture vis-à-vis gender. The cognitive demands of this task may not be conscious, but they are real. A social-cognitive approach accounts for personal learning and environmental interactions, and thus lends itself to understanding the development of gender identity among college students.

Research Related to Social-Cognitive Factors of Gender Identity on Campus

If Bussey's (2011) articulation of a social-cognitive model is taken as a guide to understanding personal, behavioral, and environmental influences on gender identity, aspects of campus life can be considered in light of how they challenge or reinforce the gender identities that students may bring with them to college. Assuming that students of all ages have long since developed gender schema that shape their perceptions, social-cognitive theory predicts that college students will express gender identity through their decisions, behaviors, attitudes, and interactions within the environment (Bussey, 2011; Bussey & Bandura, 1999). Research provides evidence of gender in interactions in academic (for example, majors, faculty mentoring), career planning, and student life (for example, social, cocurricular, athletic, leadership, judicial) contexts, among others.

Earlier theories, such as Bem's (1983) gender schema theory, would predict these interactions to be mutually reinforcing, with students' perceptions shaping—and being shaped by—the gender schemas they hold. Students would then act in ways that would positively reinforce their own and others' conformity to the expected gender norms and inhibit behaviors and attitudes that were gender nonconforming. As noted earlier, heterosexism and homophobia are part of the reinforcement/inhibition mechanism. Despite the cultural dominance of genderism (Bilodeau, 2009) and its adherence to a strict gender binary, there is emerging evidence that some students act against gender schema to explore and express identities other than the traditional two (Beemyn & Rankin, 2011; Diamond et al., 2011; Renn, Nicolazzo, Brazelton, Nguyen, & Woodford, 2014; Saltzburg & Davis, 2010). At the same time, gender schema enacted in a genderist context may compel other students more firmly toward culturally sanctioned expressions of masculinity and femininity on campus. In this section we provide research-based examples of both phenomena.

Academic and Curricular. Academic contexts (classes, majors) are central to any discussion of environmental factors influencing gender identity development on campus. Women became the majority of college students in 1979 and have remained so (National Center for Education Statistics [NCES], 2014). Yet they also remain the minority in science, technology, engineering, and mathematics (STEM) fields (NCES, 2014). Men are underrepresented in teaching, nursing, social work, and allied health fields (NCES, 2014). Given assertions that these fields are essential to the twenty-first-century workforce and that many of them are experiencing personnel shortages (Beede, Julian, Langdon,

McKittrick, Khan, & Doms, 2011), why does gender imbalance persist? If, for example, women pursued engineering majors at the rate that men do, the supply of U.S. engineers would likely be robust; the same can be said for teachers and nurses if men pursued these majors at the same rate as women.

Social-cognitive and gender schema theories suggest that students come to college with predetermined ideas about what majors and careers are appropriate for people of different genders. Students who go against schema to enroll in an academic program where they are in the gender minority find themselves one of a few men or women in class. Faculty are disproportionately of a different gender from these students (NCES, 2014), and even textbooks may reinforce gender stereotypes of who belongs in an education, nursing, or engineering classroom (Bell-Scriber, 2008). Evidence suggests that persistence of minoritized genders in these majors is lower than persistence of students of the majoritized genders, so in upper-level classes the effects may be exaggerated (Gayles & Ampaw, 2014).

Faculty mentors may be a buffer against the effects of gender stereotyping in academic majors. There is some debate about whether same-gender mentors are necessary to maximize buffering effects (see Avery, Tonidandel, & Phillips, 2008; Blake-Beard, Bayne, Crosby, & Muller, 2011; Fassinger & Hensler-McGinnis, 2005; Patton, 2009), but the dearth of female STEM faculty and male education, nursing, and human service faculty renders the debate less meaningful. The question often comes down to whether having *any* faculty mentor is more effective than *no* mentor, and the answer is a resounding endorsement of the role of mentoring and role models in the academic success and persistence of students who are minoritized for their gender in academic majors (Herzig, 2004; Smith, 2007). The exact operation of the mentoring effect is not clear, but some evidence (Benishek, Bieschke, Park, & Slattery, 2004; Fassinger & Hensler-McGinnis, 2005; Patton, 2009; Strayhorn & Saddler, 2009) points to the power of mentors and role models to challenge—directly, by example, or both—students' gender schema: *If Professor Tina (or José) can be a physicist (or elementary educator), then maybe I can too.* Students who are in the majority gender in their academic majors, on the other hand, may have their gender identities validated as they find themselves among like-others, just as they expected (Bryant, 2003b).

Gender is also a factor in student experience at the individual course level. Studies show that students of different genders may engage more or less actively in various academic settings. Pérez (2014) found that gender and ethnic identity served as a catalyst and cultural resource for many high-achieving (GPA above 3.75) Latino males at predominantly White institutions (PWIs).

In contrast, Wood (2014) found that Black men in community colleges reported hesitance to engage actively in classroom discussions, a finding Wood attributed to gender role conflict and related beliefs about masculine identity and gender expression. Sáenz, Bukoski, Lu, and Rodriguez (2013) found that Latino men in community colleges were reluctant to seek academic help, citing gender and pride/machismo as a contributing factor, and Gardenhire-Crooks, Collado, Martin, and Castro (2010) noted the same phenomenon among a sample of men of color. In all of these studies, men (it is not known if they were cisgender or trans*) demonstrated motivation and academic talent to be successful, but personal factors interacted with the environment to produce behaviors that did not promote positive outcomes. Decades of scholarship on ostensibly cisgender women's experiences in academic settings have established a similar pattern: Social-cognitive factors related to gender identity influence talented and motivated female students to behave in ways that are contrary to what learning theories predict promote optimal engagement and learning (see Crawford & MacLeod, 1990; Crombie, Pyke, Silverthorn, Jones, & Piccinin, 2003; Hall & Sandler, 1982; Rocca, 2010; Salter & Persaud, 2003; Tatum, Schwartz, Schimmoeller, & Perry, 2013).

It is not yet clear if or how trans* identities interact with student engagement in academic settings, though a national report on campus climate (Rankin, Blumenfeld, Weber, & Frazer, 2010) indicated that a majority (62%) of trans* students had been harassed on campus, and of that group, 55% reported that the harassment happened in class. Fifteen percent feared a bad course grade because of a hostile classroom environment. Additionally, Nicolazzo (2015) found trans* student academic experiences varied widely based on academic discipline, participants' gender identities, and other salient identities (for example, race, disability, sexuality). Although not intended to be generalizable, Nicolazzo's study highlighted the need for further focus on the varied experiences of trans* college students in the classroom, and the fact that not all these experiences are negative. Therefore, given the link between campus climate and student outcomes (see Chang, Milem, & Antonio, 2011), it is reasonable to assume that trans* identities interact with academic environments in ways that influence gender identity as well as learning processes and outcomes. Conversely, the National Study of LGBTQ Student Success found that trans* students were more engaged with their campus LGBT centers than were their cisgender LGBQ peers (Brazelton, Renn, & Woodford, 2013). Without further research, it is not clear whether trans* students are less than, more than, or similarly engaged in college, compared to cisgender peers.

Career Planning. Just as gender expectations play a role in choices of academic majors, they factor into career planning for women and for men. Little has changed in the scholarly literature on gender and career choice since Phillips and Imhoff (1997) reviewed ten years of research on women and career development. They concluded that females have more flexible self-concepts and consider a wider domain of life contexts than do males; women's vocational aspirations can be traced to both individual and social factors, including race, class, and gender; women have higher self-efficacy (belief that they will be successful) in sex-typed careers than in cross-sex-typed careers; and reducing children's gender stereotypes produces higher aspirations among girls and boys. Scholarship in the subsequent decade has not produced different results (see Coogan & Chen, 2007), though examination of environmental factors such as the presence of same-gender role models demonstrates that they may influence women's self-efficacy, which could positively influence persistence in atypical career paths (BarNir, Watson, & Hutchins, 2011).

Student Life. Research has repeatedly shown peer culture to be one of the most powerful influences on student development and college outcomes (see Astin, 1977; Kaufman & Feldman, 2004; Kuh, 1995; Pascarella & Terenzini, 2005). The residential, co-curricular, student employment, athletic, and other student life contexts in which peer culture operates play critical roles in reinforcing and/or challenging gender schema and sex-role stereotypes (Sax, 2008). Cisgender women may choose campus involvement that is consistent with their sense of self as nurturing, care-taking, and relational while cisgender men may choose involvement that reinforces a masculine self-concept that is assertive, competitive, and independent. Of course, these are broad stereotypes, but there is evidence that nearly twice as many female than male students are interested in community service and study abroad (Desoff, 2006; Hurtado et al., 2007; Li, Olsen, & Frieze, 2013; Salisbury, Paulsen, & Pascarella, 2010), areas that draw on "feminine" characteristics such as concern for community and cross-cultural awareness.

Campus social life is a highly gendered context within the overall college environment. In 1990, Holland and Eisenhart wrote that college women were being "educated in romance," a phrase they coined to describe highly heterosexualized campus climates where women's concern about how they ranked as desirable to men outweighed their concern about friendships, academic life, and personal development. Little seems to have changed in over two decades. In 2003, Bank and Yelon reported that even at a single-sex institution, gender roles and heterosexual desirability were powerful influences on women students' decisions. Davis (2002) found evidence that gender role conflict occurred for men as they interacted in the social milieu of campus life at the turn of the twenty-first century, and factors contributing to the "hooking up" phenomenon of casual sexual activity differ by gender (Owen et al., 2010).

Scholars (Hamilton, 2007; Harris & Harper, 2014; Harper & Quaye, 2009; Kimmel, 2010) single out the fraternity and sorority system as a social context in which gender is particularly salient. Involvement in fraternities and sororities has been shown to increase the strength of previously held ideas about gender and sex roles (Pascarella & Terenzini, 2005), although some members may act counter to specific stereotypes of fraternity men (Harris & Harper, 2014). Perhaps over time gender norms in the fraternity and sorority system will become more flexible; participants in the 2013 National Study of LGBTQ Student Success (see Renn et al., 2014) included female-to-male trans* identified members of traditional men's fraternities who reported positive experiences in their respective brotherhoods.

Men are accused of and found responsible for student misconduct at much higher rates than are women (Harper et al., 2005). Their overrepresentation in campus judicial systems has been attributed in part to a male socialization process that purportedly impedes "the emotional development of boys and men" (Ludeman, 2011, p. 194) and leaves them unable to cope with strong emotions in socially acceptable ways. Harper et al. (2005) proposed a theoretical model to explain the overrepresentation of men among students who misbehave on campus. Their person-environment model included six factors: precollege socialization, male gender role conflict, developing competence and self-efficacy, social construction of masculinities, context-bound gendered social norms, and environmental ethos and corresponding behaviors. Taken as a set, these factors illustrate how the persistent effects of pre-college gender schema interact with the three factors of social-cognitive gender identity development to have a profound impact on attitudes and behaviors of college men.

Overall Effect of College on Gender Identity Development. Evidence over three decades confirms that college attendance has a generally liberalizing—that is, less constricting—effect on students' gender-role attitudes (see Pascarella & Terenzini, 1991, 2005; Stevenson & Clegg, 2012). The specific constellations of student experiences (their environment or ecology), including work, major, course-taking patterns, and involvement in activities mediate this effect (Bryant, 2003b). For example, taking women's studies courses and participating in diverse friendship groups are likely to increase egalitarian attitudes toward women, while playing football, being in a sorority or fraternity, and being in a major that matches one's sex-type are likely to decrease egalitarianism (Bryant, 2003b). Comparing these findings to social-cognitive theory, it could be said that students whose personal beliefs about gender lead them to sex-typed academic and co-curricular behaviors may be more likely to have those beliefs reinforced in the environment; those students who reject the genderist assumption of two and only two genders, of which everyone must choose just one, are more likely to move toward a less clearly defined masculine or feminine view. This proposition has not been tested, though studies like Bryant's that use egalitarian attitudes toward women as a dependent variable offer promising models for how to go about doing so.

Men's gender socialization before and during college is a growing area of study, with results indicating that gender role conflict may play some role in men's higher attrition rates (see Gardenhire-Crooks et al., 2010; Harper et al., 2005; Harris & Harper, 2008, 2014; Sáenz et al., 2013; Wood, 2014). It is important to remember that there appears to be more variation within sex (male or female) than between the two groups, so college effects on gender identity must not be considered categorical characteristics of cisgender men and women. There is also insufficient research evidence to support generalizable claims about the specific effects of college on trans* identity development.

Trans* Identity Development

In the early 2000s, higher education professionals and researchers relied mainly on medical and clinical psychological perspectives on trans* identity to understand the experiences and development of the newly visible population of trans* students on campus. Trans* activists and educators resisted the medical/clinical perspective, in favor of one that did not position trans* individuals as having a mental illness on the basis of their gender identity (see Carter, 2000; Wilchins, 2002). Realizing that the medical perspective was insufficient to describe what they and their higher education colleagues were seeing in practice, scholars began to study trans* students from other perspectives with samples drawn from nonclinical populations. Positive psychology and postmodern, feminist, and queer theoretical perspectives on gender and gender identity provide alternatives to the clinical approach (see Bilodeau & Renn, 2005).

Genderism and the debate about the gender binary poses an interesting challenge to understanding trans* student experiences and identities. Diamond et al. (2011) described "a general divide between individuals (such as transsexuals) whose experiences revolve around and reinforce a gender binary by seeking the physical presentations of gender that correspond to their psychological sense of gender, and those whose experience of transgender straddles, rejects, or collapses the binary" (p. 635). In other words, one approach to trans* identity development is unlikely to work for understanding all trans* students. Some students will seek to express themselves within traditional masculine or feminine norms (for example, a female-to-male trans* student joining a men's fraternity) while others seek to express themselves outside the gender binary (for example, mixing "men's" and "women's" apparel, hairstyle, and footwear simultaneously). The social-cognitive approach to gender identity does not predict an outcome for these developmental moments or value one type of gender identity (cisgender, trans*, binary, nonbinary), but it provides a way to examine the three factors (personal, environmental, behavioral) that interact in relation to gender identity development and expression. One way to explore how gender identity evolves for an individual student is to explore their reaction to and understanding of how the behaviors of joining the fraternity or dressing in a particular way draw reactions from the environment.

The identity development of trans* college students receives modest but steady attention from researchers and student affairs educators who subscribe to nonmedical approaches. Studies of trans* identity in college students (Bilodeau, 2009; McKinney, 2005; Nicolazzo, 2015; Pusch, 2005; Dugan et al., 2012) generally take a human development perspective that emphasizes person-environment interactions in the higher education context. These studies fit easily into a social-cognitive interpretation of trans* identity development.

Brent Bilodeau (2005), for example, adapted the six identity processes that Anthony D'Augelli (1994a) proposed as a lifespan model for LGB development to describe the experiences of transgender college students (Bilodeau used the term *transgender* in the original, so we retain it here). Bilodeau thus framed transgender identity development as:

1. *Exiting a traditionally gendered identity* by recognizing that one is gender variant, attaching a label to this identity, and affirming oneself as transgender through coming out to others.
2. *Developing a personal transgender identity* by achieving stability that comes from knowing oneself in relation to other transgender people and challenging internalized transphobia.
3. *Developing a transgender social identity* by creating a support network of people who know and accept that one is gender variant.
4. *Becoming a transgender offspring* by coming out as transgender to family members and reevaluating relationships that may be disrupted by this disclosure.
5. *Developing a transgender intimacy status* by creating intimate physical and emotional relationships.
6. *Entering a transgender community* by making a commitment to political and social action through challenging transphobia and genderism. (p. 26)

Viewing the identities of trans* college students through these six processes allows for a multidimensional, fluid model for how identities are context-specific and influenced by reciprocal relationships with others in the context. Another strength is that the model emphasizes a lifespan approach consistent with the social-cognitive model, demonstrating that gender identities are not fixed and immovable by the time a student enters college.

A limitation of scholarship on trans* student identity is that it is typically based on small samples on one or a few campuses. Exceptions include the Multi-Institutional Study of Leadership (see www.leadershipstudy.net; Dugan et al., 2012), the National Study of LGBTQ Student Success (see www.lgbtqsuccess.net; Renn et al., 2014), and the National Campus Climate study (Rankin et al., 2010), which have hundreds of trans* participants from a range of institutional types and geographic regions. Other studies of trans* identity development have included college students among a larger sample of youth or adults (for example, Beemyn & Rankin, 2011; Grossman, D'Augelli, & Frank, 2011), providing additional evidence of the fluidity of gender identity and the resilience of trans* college students in the face of genderist pressures, discrimination, harassment, and even violence. Further empirical studies of the experiences and identities of transgender college students could provide much-needed support for improving campus climate for trans* students.

Application

As is clear throughout this chapter, gender identity begins forming well before college, influences the college experience, and may modestly be influenced by the college environment. For cisgender students, a challenge may lie in helping them see gender as a central shaping force in their lives and reconsider long-held gender stereotypes. For trans* students, the role of the educator may lie more in creating a welcoming and equitable learning and living environment through appropriate programs, services, and policies that include students of all genders. As in many areas of campus life, gender and its implications for all campus constituents provide opportunities to apply theory to practice to promote optimal developmental opportunities.

Regardless of whether a campus has a women's center or similar office dedicated to educational and academic programming related to women's and gender issues, programs and services that address the curriculum, co-curricular activities, and career exploration can provide venues for students to explore their ideas about gender and sex roles. Research (for example, Bryant, 2003b; Pascarella & Terenzini, 1991, 2005; Shapiro & Sax, 2011; Stevenson

& Clegg, 2012) has shown that academic and co-curricular interactions can influence gender-related attitudes. Thoughtful curriculum and programming presented in the classroom and in appealing nonacademic settings can help students uncover tacit expectations they hold for themselves and others. Explicit use of the Bem Sex-Role Inventory (Bem, 1981a) or another tool that measures gender expectations can enrich career exploration, values clarification, and academic advising with language related to gender and gender roles. Programs that introduce role models and provide peer support for students in nontraditional majors and careers for their gender have the potential to provide buffers against negative reactions they may receive in those settings or about their decision to enter those majors and careers (BarNir, Watson, & Hutchins, 2011). In short, though college student gender identity development research may have some limitations, it also provides a way to introduce students to the unseen operation of gender in their lives on and off campus.

Supporting trans* students may take more active attention, in part because they represent a small population only recently becoming visible on some campuses and in part because higher education operates in a system of genderism that reinforces a gender binary to which all members are expected to adhere (Bilodeau, 2009). Beemyn (2005) recommended educational programs for and about trans* students, to raise awareness and visibility; support services such as discussion groups in resource centers for lesbian, gay, bisexual, and trans* students; campus nondiscrimination policies that include gender identity and expression as protected categories; gender-inclusive (sometimes called "gender neutral") housing options that do not assume that all students are male or female, or that they remain the same gender throughout their time at the university; locker room and restroom facilities that provide adequate privacy (for example, single stall, lockable, unisex) for individuals who do not choose to undress and shower in full view of other facility users, for fear of discrimination, harassment, or violence; counseling and healthcare that are trans*-inclusive and sensitive to the needs of trans* people; and record-keeping that permits changing gender and legal and preferred name in institutional systems in ways that do not place an undue burden on the individual.

As is often the case when recommendations are made to improve the quality of life for a minoritized population, several of these recommendations could benefit cisgender people as well. For example, gender-inclusive housing could benefit mixed-gender groups of friends who wish to share residence hall suites. Convenient unisex, single-stall bathrooms benefit anyone who lives or works near that facility who does not have to go farther to locate a designated men's or women's restroom, as well as anyone seeking more privacy than is available in shared public restrooms. Many locker room users might prefer the privacy of shower curtains and changing room stalls to the "gang shower" model prevalent in university recreation centers built in the mid-twentieth century. And education about human diversity can be seen as a benefit to all community members, not only to those who fall into the group on which the educational program is focused. By viewing the campus environment—physical, social, and policy—through the lens of gender, educators may discover other ways that genderism operates on their campuses to constrain the gender identities and life decisions of all community members.

Critique and Future Directions

Researchers have not articulated a clear, comprehensive understanding of how gender identity develops during college in cisgender or trans* students. Social-cognitive gender identity theory (Bussey, 2011) provides one way to understand the identities that students bring with them to college, and a rich literature, as highlighted earlier, explores the ways that personal, environmental, and behavioral aspects interact to continue to shape gender identity during and after college. Student outcomes research (see Pascarella & Terenzini, 2005) explores differences between college men and women; in these studies sex (sometimes labeled as gender) is frequently used as a binary independent variable and differences emerge in choice of academic majors, student life, academic behaviors, and career development. These ongoing gender differences in majors and career choices point to the persistent, unspoken power of gender to shape students' lives; understanding more clearly how gender does so could benefit educators and students.

Additional studies of trans* identity and identity development in college are also warranted. The few existing studies specific to trans* students provide some guidance for practice, but they are based on limited samples, are not longitudinal, and cannot be assumed to apply broadly. Some scholars make claims about trans* student experiences based on deficit-model studies of LGBT populations, which may have implications for sample bias and study focus. Locating representative samples of a population that is small and widely dispersed is not easy, but will be important as educators seek to provide evidence-based support to trans* students. In their studies that included trans* college students as part of larger samples, Beemyn and Rankin (2011) and Renn et al. (2014) found that these students defy easy categorization, do not always identify as "transgender" or "genderqueer," and use an ever-evolving set of self-labels within and outside existing concepts of gender itself.

Gender is at once ever-present and largely invisible in the lives of cisgender college students. Personal, environmental, and behavioral components influence and are influenced by gender schemas formed and intensified long before students come to campus and operate to filter what possibilities students see for themselves and what expectations they place on others for conforming to gender norms. Students who violate those norms face correction in the form of teasing, discrimination, harassment, and violence. Whether they are cisgender, trans*, or something else, students are expected to fall in line and to hold others in line in higher education institutions that mirror society's powerful system of genderism (Bilodeau, 2009).

Discussion Questions

1. What is gender identity and why is it important in the development of college students?
2. Name at least four gender identities that researchers have found among college students.
3. What are the differences among sex, gender, and sexual identities? How do these identities interact within an individual's experience?
4. What does the term "gender binary" mean?
5. Define genderism and give three examples of how it operates in higher education.
6. Where do you see differences by gender in academic, social, and co-curricular contexts at your institution?
7. How do other identities such as race, ethnicity, or social class intersect with students' gender identities? For example, how might students' understanding of acceptable expressions of masculinity and femininity differ across other identities?
8. Describe how your gender identity affects your interactions with students of similar and different genders.
9. How do students on your campus treat students who express a fluid gender identity? How can your campus demonstrate support for these students?

CHAPTER NINE

DEVELOPMENT OF FAITH AND SPIRITUALITY

Spirituality, faith, belief, and religion—in the United States these concepts are often used interchangeably. College students frequently struggle with articulating these concepts (Craft & Bryant Rockenbach, 2011), as do many student affairs educators. We have selected research-based definitions to clarify the differences among these concepts. Astin, Astin, and Lindholm (2011) described *spirituality* as "our sense of who we are and where we come from, our beliefs about why we are here—the meaning and purpose that we see in our work and our life—and our sense of connectedness to one another and to the world around us" (p. 4). Fowler (1996), whose theory we describe later in this chapter, defined *belief* as conscious intellectual agreement with particular doctrines or ideologies, while *religion* consists of many beliefs and practices of a collective group of people existing over a period of time. *Faith,* in Fowler's perspective, underlies both belief and religion but is also inclusive of secular worldviews: It "is our way of finding coherence in and giving meaning to the multiple forces and relations that make up our lives" (Fowler, 1981, p. 4).

How the aforementioned definitions inform development depends a great deal on how individuals make sense of their identities. Whether a particular identity is personal or collective depends on its function to the individual. Personal identities are those identity components or characteristics people believe are more unique to themselves rather than shared with a group. In contrast, a collective identity (similar to the social psychological concept of social identity) is shared by a group of people with some characteristic(s) in common; for example, native language, country of origin, or religion (Ashmore et al., 2004;

Côtè, 1996). It includes category membership, shared beliefs, perceived closeness to other members of the group, and behavioral enactments such as meeting attendance.

Based on this distinction, we consider a religious identity as a collective identity. Religion is "an organized system of beliefs, practices, rituals and symbols designed (a) to facilitate closeness to the sacred or transcendent (God, higher power or ultimate truth/reality) and (b) to foster an understanding of one's relationship and responsibility to others living together in a community" (Koenig, McCullough, & Larson, 2001, p. 18). Individuals with a religious identity believe they are members of a religious group; their identity can vary in terms of their acceptance of belief systems, and their endorsement of the importance of religious values, commitment to the religious group, and practices associated with the religion.

In contrast, we consider a spiritual identity as a personal identity. It consists of spiritual characteristics unique to the individual rather than shared with a group. Spiritual identity is not associated directly with feelings of belonging to a valued religious group, though an individual may experience spiritual identity in the context of a religious tradition.

Although the first colleges in the United States were created to train clergy and ensure that youth received an education that was religiously grounded (Thelin, 2011), public higher education in the last century has been reluctant to address the spiritual and faith development of students (Tisdell, 2003). Speck (2005) identified three factors that have contributed to avoidance of spirituality as a topic for discussion in public higher education: (1) the erroneous belief that the constitutional requirement of separation of church and state precludes any mention of matters that could be construed as religious; (2) the emphasis in higher education on objectivity and rationality; and (3) the lack of preparation that most educators have to address the topic of spirituality. The second and third factors apply equally to many private institutions as well.

While some students reject the concepts of religion and spirituality altogether (Goodman & Mueller, 2009), research suggests others are increasingly interested (Higher Education Research Institute, 2004). Some follow a traditional path within the context of organized religion; others are attracted to nondenominational evangelical groups, while many choose to pursue spirituality in nontraditional ways that are not connected to mainstream religion (Coomes, 2004; Dalton, Eberhardt, Bracken, & Echols, 2006; Hartley, 2004; Kuh & Gonyea, 2005).

Despite the reluctance of public and most nonsectarian private institutions to be involved in activities that focus on spiritual development, a plethora of books and articles addressing the topic of spirituality in higher education settings have appeared in recent years (for example, Bryant & Craft, 2010; Bryant Rockenbach & Mayhew, 2014; Chickering, Dalton, & Stamm, 2006; Hoppe & Speck, 2005; Mayhew, Bowman, & Bryan Rockenbach, 2014; Miller & Ryan, 2001; Radecke, 2007; Rogers & Dantley, 2001; Welch & Koth, 2013; Zajonc, 2003), supporting Tisdell's (2003) assertion that educators see this topic as timely. Each of these writings presents excellent examples for considering the integration of spirituality into the life of colleges and universities. While clear definitions of spirituality were lacking in previous scholarship, many scholars are making concerted efforts to discuss spirituality in general, as well as provide definitions of the concept and a theoretical base for their arguments (see Astin et al., 2011; Dalton, 2006a; Love, 2001; Stamm, 2006; Strange, 2001). In this chapter we discuss theories of faith, religious, and spiritual development that are research-based and have applications in student affairs practice. We begin with the work of James Fowler and Sharon Daloz Parks. We then explain more recent research from Alexander Astin, Helen Astin, and Jennifer Lindholm, as well as Lori Peek and Jesse Smith.

Fowler's Theory of Faith Development

James W. Fowler, trained as a Methodist minister, was among the first to address faith using a developmental approach in his 1981 book *Stages of Faith*. Subsequent iterations were published between 1978 and 2000. Fowler based his theory on semistructured interviews with 359 individuals, ranging from 3.5 to 84 years old, which he conducted from 1972 to 1981 in areas around Boston, Toronto, and Atlanta. The sample was 97.8% White and evenly divided between men and women. Protestants constituted 45% of the sample; 36.5% were Catholic, 11.2% were Jewish, 3.6% were Orthodox, and 3.6% identified other belief systems. Fowler vetted his theory in presentations to religious practitioners and educators, using their feedback in his revisions (Fowler, 1996).

To Fowler, faith and religion are distinct, with faith being "both broader and more personal" (p. 18) than religion. He argued that faith was universal (Fowler, 1981, 2000) but each person's faith expression is unique. Fowler (1981) stressed the relational nature of faith and interpreted it as a process of imagination, or internal representations of particular situations, or events that evolve as individuals mature.

In the first iteration of his theory, Fowler (1978) stressed the distinction between content and structure, pointing out that individuals at the same stage can hold beliefs that are vastly different (content) while their ways of thinking about and making sense of their beliefs (structure) are similar. As in other cognitive-structural models, Fowler's stages of faith are invariant, and some individuals never reach the more advanced stages (Fowler, 1996). He described development as movement that is like a spiral, with each proceeding stage as a more complex and comprehensive way of understanding one's religious tradition (Fowler, 1981, 2000). Influenced by Kegan, and unlike other cognitive-structural theories, Fowler (1981) did not separate cognition and affect, nor did he claim universality for his stages, but he suggested their descriptions were generalizable and testable across cultures.

Stages of Faith

These descriptions come from the 1981, 1986, and 2000 iterations of Fowler's theory.

Pre-stage 1—Primal faith (labeled *undifferentiated faith* in earlier versions of the model). A prelinguistic manifestation of faith arises in the person's first years in the context of relationship with primary caretakers. These relationships shape one's first images of God.

Stage 1—Intuitive-projective faith. This stage manifests around age two with the emergence of language; children begin to construct their first images of God, based on "perception, feelings, and imaginative fantasy" (Fowler, 2000, p. 42) that result from stories, pictures, and images shared with the young child by significant others.

Stage 2—Mythic-literal faith. During early elementary school years (ages six and seven), children begin to see perspectives other than their own and follow, make sense of, and remember stories told by family and significant others. These narratives are accepted literally and form the basis of their beliefs. Adults and children may function at this stage, as well as those to follow.

Stage 3—Synthetic-conventional faith. During early adolescence, individuals develop the ability to think abstractly and integrate ideas from various sources, including school, media, and religious community. Their faith is still meaningful, but they do not view it critically and require external validation to affirm decisions (Fowler, 1996).

Stage 4—Individuative-reflective faith (initially labeled *individuating-reflexive*). This stage is initiated when: (a) self-definition becomes self-authored, and (b) a coherent and explicit meaning-making system evolves from beliefs, values, and commitments. While Fowler (1981) suggested stage 4 thinking "most appropriately takes form in young adulthood" (p. 182), he later (see Fowler, 2000) indicated this transition usually occurs between ages 30 and 40, typically resulting from changed relationships or challenges in one's environment.

Stage 5—Conjunctive faith (labeled *paradoxical-consolidative* initially). This stage takes place at midlife or beyond and involves increasing awareness of life's complexities and unconscious influences on one's behavior and attitudes. Symbolism is meaningful and individuals are more deeply aware of their convictions. Individuals are more accepting of other faith traditions yet hold deep commitment to theirs.

Stage 6—Universalizing faith. Persons in this final stage experience a "radical decentration from self," accepting and "knowing" the world through others different from them, and valuing God and others "from a standpoint more nearly identified with the love of the Creator for creatures" (Fowler, 2000, pp. 55–56). Fowler claimed that it is rare to find individuals in this stage; his example included Mahatma Gandhi, Martin Luther King, Jr., and Mother Teresa of Calcutta. Despite criticism that little evidence supports the existence of this stage (see Broughton, 1986; Moran, 1983), Fowler (2000) modified his theory, stating that conjunctive faith (stage 5) is the end point of a natural progression of development but "in partnership with Spirit," any person has the potential to experience universalizing faith. (Fowler, 2000, p. 61)

Faith Development

"Biological maturation, emotional and cognitive development, psychosocial experience, and religio-cultural influences" (Fowler, 1996, p. 57) affect faith development. The process is triggered when individuals' experiences create dissonance that cannot be addressed effectively by their current meaning-making strategies (Fowler, 1981, 2000). A new stage results, consisting of change in one's belief system and sense-making process. Three phases are evident during transition between stages: endings, the neutral zone, and new beginnings (Fowler, 1996). Endings happen when the individual disengages from a relational context, shifts sense of self, and grieves the loss. The neutral zone is experienced as "a time out of ordinary time" (Fowler, 1996, p. 74). Individuals struggle through disintegration of their previous way of life, attempting to develop a new way of sense-making. Eventually, exploration prompts the new beginnings phase. Fowler (1996) cautioned that new beginnings should not be rushed, noting that therapy, religious communities, and spiritual guides can create "holding environments" (p. 74) that enable individuals to explore fully the potential new paths they are considering.

Lifespan Development and Vocation.

Fowler (2000) furthered these ideas by linking his model to the idea of vocation, which he viewed as more than work, occupation, or career. In his view, vocation involves every aspect of the person's life and is therefore a desired, but not automatic, developmental end goal. It is influenced by environmental conditions that one must address. He suggested one's faith community plays an important role in determining the extent to which a sense of vocation is formed and carried out during one's life.

Research

Fowler's initial research (Fowler, 1981) validated aspects of his theory. Stages corresponded to ages as predicted by the model, particularly the earlier stages. At later ages, individuals exhibited a range of stages from stage 2 to 6. Stage 5 was evident starting in the middle to late years of life, and only one person was at stage 6. A relationship between age, gender, and stage of faith was somewhat evident, with more women than men at stage 3 and fewer women than men at stages 4 and 5 in younger age groups. However, more women than men were in stage 5 in the older age groups. Fowler (1981) stressed that a larger, more representative sample was needed to verify this finding.

> Lee (2002) has also contributed to the validation of Fowler's theory. She conducted a narrative qualitative study to examine faith development among Catholic students. Lee discovered that participants were progressing toward intuitive-reflective faith, assuming responsibility for their own beliefs and decisions while simultaneously being challenged by social and academic aspects of their environments.

As noted, Fowler based his theory on semistructured interviews. In an attempt to develop an easier assessment method, Leak, Loucks, and Bowlin (1999) constructed the Faith Development Scale (FDS), a forced-choice measure with one response indicative of stages 2 or 3 in Fowler's model and the other response reflecting stages 4 or 5. In a longitudinal study of students from their first year to their senior year using the FDS, Leak (2003) found that students demonstrated increased faith development, as Fowler (1981) discussed. A cross-sectional study conducted by Leak also suggested seniors exhibited higher scores on the FDS than did first-year students.

Applications

Published applications of Fowler's theory within higher education settings focus on counseling and teaching. Lownsdale (1997) and Genia (1992) both found value in Fowler's theory for therapists and counselors because it provides a framework to understand clients' ideas about faith and to develop therapeutic interventions that align with clients' belief systems, particularly those experiencing crises of faith. Erwin (2001) argued that to address spiritual issues counselor trainees should understand spirituality in their own lives, and suggested supervision interventions for students in each of Fowler's (1981) stages to encourage faith awareness and growth.

Parker (2011) also wrote about the value of Fowler's theory in counseling contexts. He suggested the theory would be helpful because it depicted developmental changes in spirituality and religion, it is comprehensive and captures experiences relative to religious and nonsectarian beliefs, and it emphasizes growth rather than pathology. Parker offers several case studies, centered on the experiences of adolescents and young adults dealing with life events such as grieving loss or general transitions, to explore how Fowler's theory can be successfully applied.

Critique

While Fowler's theory has stood the test of time and provided the basis for research and later theory building, a number of scholars have also criticized his work because the theory was a priori and his sample was too homogeneous (Broughton, 1986; Nelson & Aleshire, 1986; Watt, 2003). Others have criticized his definition of faith as too generic and prescriptive (Dykstra, 1986), lacking a core understanding of faith as commitment and thus indistinguishable from other developmental theories (Fernout, 1986), incompatible with some forms of Christian faith (Hiebert, 1992), biased in favor of Protestant Christianity (Moran, 1983), theistic rather than nonreligious (Broughton, 1986), male-centered (Anderson, 1994; Harris, 1986), and conformist to a Western cultural perspective (Broughton). Other critiques focus on the model as a whole, as some scholars found little support for the stages (Fernout, 1986), Fowler's assumption that individuals should be pushed toward higher stages (Batson, Schoenrade, & Ventis, 1993; Moran, 1983), and the existence and definition of stage 6, universalizing faith, since few examples exist of individuals reaching this stage and its discontinuity with prior stages (Broughton, 1986; Moran; Parks, 1986b).

Parks's Theory of Faith Development

The contributions of Sharon Daloz Parks to the faith development literature include two books: *The Critical Years: The Young Adult Search for a Faith to Live By* (1986a) and *Big Questions, Worthy Dreams: Mentoring Young Adults in Their Search for Meaning, Purpose, and Faith* (2000). Her theory is based on her experiences as a teacher, counselor, and researcher in college, workplace, and religious environments (Parks, 2000).

The premise underscoring Parks's (1986a) work is that young adulthood prompts self-conscious reflection on life's meaning. She defined faith as "the activity of seeking and discovering meaning in the most comprehensive dimensions of our experience" (Parks, 2000, p. 7). Faith is validated through lived experience, making "itself public in everyday acts of decision, obedience, and courage" (Parks, 2000, p. 26). Thus it is much broader than religious belief.

Parks (1986a) set out to explore how higher education influences the development of faith for young adults. Like Fowler, she drew on the work of developmental psychologists, including Piaget, Erikson, Kohlberg, Gilligan, Perry, and Kegan. While similar to Fowler's theory, Parks's theory (1986a, 2000) differs in two important ways. First, Parks (1986a) focused on the connection between the structure and content of faith, as well as the role of affect and imagination, while Fowler concentrated mainly on structure and symbolism in development.

Second, Parks (1986a, 2000) argued that an important stage was missing from Fowler's theory—that of young adulthood. In this stage, individuals begin the process of taking responsibility for themselves, including their faith. Parks (1986a; 2000) noted this stage rarely occurs until at least age 17, and many people never reach it.

Parks (1986a, 2000) explained that during young adulthood, individuals are consumed with questions regarding purpose, vocation, and belonging. They are also concerned with the world, desiring to make it a better place, but worrying about their ability to do so. A sense of ambivalence pervades this time period. Parks (1986a) identified three forms of development—*cognition, dependence, and community*—that contribute to the process of faith development throughout adulthood, and she presented a developmental model in which each form of development consisted of four increasingly complex stages that contribute to a more comprehensive understanding of faith. In her later work, Parks (2000) revised and expanded her initial model, identifying four periods associated with development: adolescence or conventional, young adult, tested adult, and mature adult. She also modified and relabeled many of the models' stages. In this chapter we highlight her more recent model.

Forms of Knowing

Parks (2000) identified five forms of knowing that occur within the four periods of development.

Authority-bound. In this early adolescent stage, which parallels Perry's dualistic stage, individuals place their trust in known authorities, such as parents, religious leaders, or teachers, or impersonal authorities, such as media, cultural figures, or custom. Individuals see life in rigid terms and have little tolerance for ambiguity.

Unqualified relativism. As trusted authorities are found to be fallible, adolescents begin to realize that many forms of reality exist. This shift occurs gradually or abruptly, in an uncomplicated manner or through more challenging processes. Eventually, persons come to view all knowledge as relative. Moving through this stage, individuals begin to see that not all opinions are equally valid and that those based on evidence tend to have more substance.

Probing commitment. Young adulthood is characterized by tentative, short-term commitments based on "serious, critically aware exploration" (Parks, 2000, p. 67). These commitments often center on future plans related to relationships, vocation, and faith.

Tested commitment. As individuals advance in adulthood, their commitments become more secure.

Convictional commitment. In midlife, a new form of deep commitment may arise that many have labeled wisdom. It results from actively exploring the complexity and mystery of life. At this stage, individuals possess both a deep commitment to their understanding of truth and the ability to recognize and appreciate the truth of others.

Forms of Dependence

Parks (2000) stressed that emotion plays an important role in faith development. She believed that examining changes in dependency on others provides a way to evaluate the role of affect in faith development.

Dependent/counterdependent. In adolescence, individuals rely on authorities to determine how they should feel about life events. This reliance is challenged when the truth they have been taught is deemed fallible or they grow uncomfortable and want to explore other possibilities. Their response, counterdependence, is still a variation of dependence, because they are reacting against the positions of authorities rather than creating new truth for themselves. As such, authorities still have the power to determine one's reactions. If benevolent authorities encourage one to explore, this process can be relatively smooth. If the bonds to authorities are tighter or if authorities resent one's pulling away, the process can be more difficult and upsetting.

Fragile inner-dependence. In young adulthood, fragile inner-dependence develops. Parks made an important distinction between inner-dependence and independence, criticizing the overemphasis that Western culture has placed on being able to function completely on one's own without connection to others. Inner-dependence balances the views of others with one's own views. Since individuals at this stage are particularly vulnerable and need support, mentors are needed to guide and reinforce their new identities (Parks, 2000).

Confident inner-dependence. With the passage of time and as individuals receive encouragement while developing their sense of self and faith, they become increasingly confident in their ability to shape their destinies. Parks noted that confident inner-dependence is a necessary precursor to interiority—that is, inner dialogue—and stressed the importance of inner dialogue and reflection in "the formation of conscience and the ethical life" (Parks, 2000, p. 84).

Interdependence. Around midlife, a strong and confident sense of self leads to new understandings of faith in which individuals come to see the value in others' beliefs and perspectives without experiencing them as a challenge to their own values. They recognize the interconnections among self, others, the world, and "God."

Forms of Community

Parks (2000) explained that individuals need familiar and dependable networks of people, places, and communities to explore themselves and their values. Everyone experiences tension between the need to establish agency and the need to be in relationship with others. At different points in one's life, this tension is resolved in different ways—Parks's forms of community.

Conventional community. In adolescence, when individuals are dependent on others to define themselves and their faith, communities of importance generally consist of face-to-face relationships. Individuals adhere to the values and cultural norms of the significant people and groups in their lives.

Diffuse community. As adolescents begin to explore new ideas and ways of being, their familiar social groups become uncomfortable. Relationships can be difficult to maintain when one's views are constantly changing.

As the inadequateness of this position is recognized, individuals search for new relationships to confirm their tentative new choices, which leads them to a new form of community.

Mentoring community. Parks stressed the importance of a mentoring community for young adults that recognizes and encourages their potential. Often these communities are ones that support young adults as they distance themselves from the conventions and beliefs of their pasts.

Self-selected group. Tested adults seek out communities that share their beliefs and make meaning in similar ways, since they prefer relationships with others like themselves.

Open to the other. A deepening awareness of "otherness" can lead to further transformation. A community that truly values different perspectives is most likely to be sought past midlife.

The Nature of the Model

Parks cautioned that her model, rather than being linear and fixed, as some might perceive from the description, is actually dynamic and multidimensional. She suggested that a spiral model might be a more accurate portrayal of her thinking. In her earlier book, Parks (1986a) also explained that the three forms of development do not remain separate but rather are interwoven to form a unified whole.

Imagination

Defined as "the highest power of the knowing mind" (Parks, 2000, p. 104), imagination includes three components: (1) "a process" (p. 104), (2) "an act of naming" (p. 105) one's experiences, and (3) a way of participating in "the ongoing *creation* of life itself" (p. 105). In explaining the role of imagination in faith development, Parks (2000) cited Loder, who described how imagination evolves. In his model, five key elements, which Parks (1986a) called moments, are involved in the process of imagination: conscious conflict, pause, image, repatterning and release of energy, and interpretation. Individuals move through these processes as they feel dissonance in their current situation (conscious conflict), clarify the issue and let it rest (pause), have an "Aha!" moment of clarity (image), move ahead with new conviction (repatterning and release of energy), and verbalize the new insight to others as testimony (interpretation). *At this final point in the imagination process,* feedback from one's community tests one's insights.

Mentoring Communities

Parks (1986a, 2000) argued that the higher education community is a place in which young adults benefit greatly from mentoring relationships. Mentors provide young adults with recognition, support, challenge, and inspiration (Parks, 2000). Mentoring is not always a long-term, face-to-face experience. It can occur at a distance, in a moment, through observation, or via technology. Because one-on-one mentoring may not always meet the needs of young adults, Parks (2000) stressed the importance of mentoring communities in which trusting relationships can be formed.

A mentoring community is a "network of belonging" (Parks, 2000, p. 135) in which young adults' imaginations are supported. Such a community allows them to consider big questions that will shape their future lives: "questions of meaning, purpose, and faith" (Parks, 2000, p. 138). Young adults may raise these questions, or members of the mentoring community may pose these questions. Mentoring communities also provide opportunities for young adults to develop a willingness to consider different perspectives and interact with others not like themselves—interactions that can lead to awareness that people who are different from them may nonetheless share similar feelings and responses to various situations. To be successful in encouraging faith development, mentoring communities must foster particular "habits of mind" (Parks, 2000, p. 142): (a) dialogue, (b) critical thought, (c) connective-systemic-holistic thought, and (d) a contemplative mind. Mentoring communities also assist young adults in developing "worthy Dreams" (Parks, 2000, p. 146), which Parks defined as "imagined [possibilities] that [orient] meaning, purpose, and aspiration" (p. 146). A sense of vocation or calling is the most complete and spiritual form of the Dream. Parks uses a capitalized D to help readers understand that she is not merely referencing "night dreams" (p. 146). She explained, "The formation of a worth Dream is the critical task of young adult faith" (p. 146).

Young adults need access to appropriate images to develop worthy dreams, and mentoring communities provide such images (Parks, 2000). Images of truth about the world's suffering and beauty and of "transformation [and] hope for renewing the world" (p. 150) are important, as are "positive images of self" (p. 151), as well as "images of the other as both similar and unique" (p. 152). Finally, mentoring communities offer "images of interrelatedness and wholeness" (p. 153).

Parks (2000) listed a number of potential mentoring communities in the lives of young adults, such as the workplace, families, and religious institutions, but gave higher education an especially prominent role. Parks (2000) viewed faculty as having major responsibility for guiding students' spiritual lives by creating communities of imagination where students' ideas can be both challenged and supported. Parks (1986a; 2000) also stressed the responsibility of higher education as a whole to create communities in which students feel welcomed and safe while being provided with experiences that will encourage them to explore and address conscious conflicts, have opportunities for pause, and be supported as they clarify, confirm, and test their new images.

Research

A number of scholars reference Parks's (2000) theory in their own theoretical writing (for example, Chickering, Dalton, & Stamm, 2006; King & Baxter Magolda, 2005), but relatively few empirical studies use it as a theoretical foundation. Buchko (2004) investigated the faith development of college students, reporting that women, more so than men, have close relationships to God and with spiritual advisors; these results may indicate that the affective dimension of faith proposed by Parks (2000) is more important to women than to men. Buchko's use of a measure of religiosity rather than faith, as well as her references to religious practices, does call her interpretations regarding faith into question, however. Lee (2002) reported that participants in her study of the faith development of Catholic college students described their development in terms similar to Parks's (2000) hypotheses. During college, the students "redefined themselves" (Lee, p. 355) within the context of their previous religious identity rather than giving up that identity completely. Bryant Rockenbach, Roseboro Walker, and Luzader (2012) found in a phenomenological study that students had what Parks called "shipwreck" experiences, or life crises, that created disruptions and disequilibrium in spirituality, faith, and meaning making.

Patton and McClure (2009) used Parks's theory and Black feminist thought (BFT) to explore spiritual coping mechanisms among 14 Black undergraduate women. The authors noted the strength of Parks's theory in acknowledging the role of the college environment in influencing faith development, but also noted the limitations of Parks's theory for capturing the intersectionality of spirituality, race, and gender, hence their use of BFT. Findings from their study revealed that college prompted participants to break away from the authority figures of home to forge their own paths, some leading to the participants' choosing a nondenominational Christian affiliation. Participants also relied on their "spiritual way of knowing" to navigate environments they perceived as racist, sexist, and lacking in support of these women. Finally, the participants struggled to articulate how they made meaning of the relationships between the concepts of faith, religion, and spirituality. Additional empirical research to validate Parks's (2000) theory would benefit the literature.

Applications

A number of authors have suggested applications of Parks's theory. Love (2001) stressed the importance of student affairs professionals being comfortable with their own spirituality. Using Parks's (2000) theory as a foundation, Love (2001) suggested staff development focus on how student affairs professionals make meaning, the role of relationships in this process, and examination of one's communities, using critical reflection, journaling, and other processes that allow individuals to look inward. He also advocated recognition of spirituality in students' lives, inclusion of spiritual development theories in the study of student development and use of these theories in settings such as judicial affairs, development of mentoring communities and assessment of existing organizations for their potential as mentoring communities, and bringing spirituality into higher education in an open manner.

Building on Parks's (2000) concept of a mentoring community and Nash's (2002) levels of community, Dalton (2006a) offered a number of suggestions for developing personal, campus, societal, and global communities within higher education settings. Strange (2001) suggested that Parks's (2000) criteria for mentoring communities could be used to guide student affairs graduate programs in developing educational environments that focus on assisting students in making meaning of their experiences. Based on Parks's concepts, Strange stressed creating networks of belonging and presenting students with "big enough questions" (p. 61), helping students understand cultural differences, encouraging dialogue and critical thinking, assisting students as they develop "worthy dreams" (p. 63), and providing access to images of "truth and goodness" (p. 64) to enhance the "spiritual dimensions of … students' lives" (p. 65).

Critique

Big Questions, Worthy Dreams (Parks, 2000) receives generally positive reviews (Bowman & Wessel, 2002; Brinkman, 2000; Mussi, 2001). Comparing Parks' (2000) theory with other spiritual and cognitive development theories, Love (2002) concluded that Parks's (2000) integration of affective, social, and cognitive processes in her discussion of development made it particularly useful for examining "both the structures and the content of meaning making" (Love, 2002, p. 373).

However, Watt (2003) argued that while claiming to attend to both cognitive and affective aspects of faith development, Parks (2000) in actuality emphasized the cognitive. As such, her theory may not be as useful in working with African American women, whose faith development process is often affective in nature (Watt). Watt also criticized Parks for ignoring the role of ethnicity in the faith development process. Anderson (1994) expressed concern that Parks (2000) failed to consider the unique aspects of women's faith development.

Stamm (2006) noted that by using Fowler's (1981) theory as a foundation for her work, Parks failed to consider whether stage theories are appropriate for understanding development across cultures. Stamm argued that stage theories are based on Western cultural assumptions of independence and individualism, ignoring the values of community and the common good that are found in many other cultures.

Astin, Astin, and Lindholm's Spiritual and Religious Measures

Both Fowler and Parks discuss the challenges embedded in students' spiritual and faith trajectories. However, neither fully captured how college students struggle with their religious beliefs, spirituality, and triggers that prompt struggle or growth. Moreover, these theories are limited in that they do not specifically address spirituality as it pertains to having a minoritized identity versus identities that are privileged in society and on college campuses. Finally, the theories do not delve deeply into associated outcomes of spirituality. To date, new theories of spirituality have not emerged. However, a burgeoning body of research on this topic has major implications for the construction of a theory on spiritual growth and development in college. A significant amount of this research stems from the UCLA Higher Education Research Institute's (HERI) Spirituality in Higher Education Project.

In 2011, Astin et al. published *Cultivating the Spirit: How College Can Enhance Students' Inner Lives.* Based upon results from the College Students' Beliefs and Values (CSBV) Survey, the book highlights their empirically grounded study about "how students change spiritually and religiously during the college years, and to identify ways in which colleges can contribute to this developmental process" (p. 9). Three studies comprise the CSBV. The pilot study, conducted in 2003 and including roughly 3,700 students, was used to develop constructs to measure spirituality and religion. The Fall 2004 study (Higher Education Research Institute, 2004) included more than 112,000 students, 15,000 of whom completed a follow-up survey in 2007. Astin et al. (2011)

designed the 2004 and 2007 surveys to capture longitudinal data to assess changes in spirituality and religion among students during their first three years of college. In addition to the surveys, the researchers conducted focus group and individual interviews with students and select faculty across 11 campuses. From the surveys, focus groups, and interviews the researchers collected sufficient data to support the following assertions:

1. Students' religious engagement declines in college, but their spirituality increases.
2. Students grow in their connections to others and willingness to be more open-minded and accepting.
3. Growth in spirituality is linked to other positive college outcomes including the facilitation of strong student leaders, improved academic ability, and college satisfaction.
4. College environments are critical to the facilitation of spiritual growth, particularly through opportunities such as study abroad, service learning, and in-depth self-reflection, which provide exposure to diverse worldviews and people and prompt critical thinking about important life questions.
5. Too much engagement in activities (e.g., too much television) that hinder deep engagement with the life of the campus can deter students' spiritual development.

Astin et al. generated ten constructs and used them to document spirituality and religion among college students. We briefly summarize each construct here.

Measures of Spirituality

1. *Spiritual Quest* rests at the center of spiritual development and represents students' journey toward answering questions such as "Who am I?" and "What is my purpose in life?" Students' quest focuses on finding peace within themselves and developing a personal life philosophy, as well as communing with others and engaging in acts that benefit the greater good. Astin et al. explained that the spiritual quest is closely linked to other constructs. For example, finding a sense of inner peace has implications for equanimity. Similarly, acting for the greater good has implications for charitable involvement and ethic of caring. Astin et al. found that students were more willing to engage in a spiritual quest by the time they reached their junior and senior year in contrast to their first year in college.

2. *Equanimity* involves being able to push forward in the face of life's difficulties. It represents an ability not only to deal with such difficulties, but also to center the self and remain focused, despite the odds that may be presented. Those exhibiting equanimity can maintain optimism through challenging times, even when they feel conflicted, and use these experiences as learning moments.

3. *Ethic of Caring* refers to the capacity to "care *about* others" (p. 63). It entails a level of dedication and concern for the well-being of others and can be reflected in caring for people who are sick or suffering, demonstrating interest and action for those who are treated inequitably, or sharing concerns for the surrounding community.

4. *Charitable Involvement* emphasizes one's ability to express "caring *for* others" (p. 63). Charitable involvement is action-oriented and involves the demonstration of caring behaviors.

5. *Ecumenical Worldview* represents "a sense of connectedness to all beings" (p. 63). It reflects a "world-centric" perspective in which students feel part of a larger whole and are committed to accepting and valuing others for who they are.

Measures of Religiousness

6. *Religious Commitment* refers to one's level of commitment to and the centrality of their religion in one's life. It is "the degree to which the student seeks to follow religious teachings in everyday life; finds religion to be personally helpful; and gains personal strength by trusting in a higher power" (p. 84).

7. *Religious Engagement* represents the level of involvement students have in the actual practices of their religion or faith. Engagement is reflected in the behaviors students exhibit such as "attending religious services, praying, singing/chanting, and reading sacred texts" (p. 84). Students' level of engagement will ultimately affect their religious commitment; thus engagement is critical to maintaining connection with one's religion.

8. *Religious/Social Conservatism* denotes the level of conservatism present in one's religious beliefs. It captures students' level of disagreement on issues such as premarital sex and their belief in the condemnation of those who do not purport a religious belief in God (such as atheists). Students may also engage in fundamentalist beliefs.

9. *Religious Struggle* entails the challenges students face when their religious beliefs conflict with new experiences and changing beliefs. Students struggle with making important life decisions in college, particularly defining a career path, and as a result they may rely on their religious beliefs and

practices to help them. Other struggles might include questioning God and attempting to better understand their relationship with God.

10. *Religious/Skepticism* is the antithesis of religious commitment and engagement. It can emerge as "a form of indifference" toward religion or "the rejection of the idea that either science or religion alone can explain everything." (p. 110).

Religious Identity Development and Diverse Worldviews

We noted earlier in the chapter that many public and private higher education institutions are reluctant to engage in student development theory and practice related to religious identity. Yet, the Pew Forum on Religion and Public Life (2008) noted that 84% of people in the United States claim a religious identity and 92% report a belief in the existence of a God or "universal spirit." Among others (for example, Bowman & Small, 2012; Nash & Scott, 2008; Subbiondo, 2006), Eboo Patel (2007), founder and president of the Interfaith Youth Core, argued that higher education ignores students' religious identities as critical aspects of individual and group diversity. This line of reasoning suggests that the emphasis on spiritual development is laudable but the avoidance of religious identity itself is a grave error and a disservice to students and society. In partial response to this call, in this section, we provide an overview of key concepts in theories of religious and nonreligious identity development and provide two examples of theories.

Key Concepts in Religious Identity Development

Religious identity is a collective identity, whereas spiritual identity is an individual identity (Templeton & Eccles, 2006). If identities exist on a continuum from assigned (ascribed) to chosen, religious identity may begin as assigned to a young person who grows up in a family that practices a particular religion, then move to the middle when the adolescent is given freedom to explore, and then to a chosen identity, if and when the individual chooses to become (or continue as) a member of a given religious community (Templeton & Eccles, 2006). Collective religious identity may also emerge from a foreclosed status (Marcia, 1980; see Chapter Thirteen) in which individuals commit to identities ascribed to them without exploration.

A number of scholars have identified emerging adulthood, adolescence, and/or traditional college years a key time in the development of religious identity (DeHaan & Schulenberg, 1997; Kimball, Mannes, & Hackel, 2009;

Meeus, Iedema, Helsen, & Vollebergh, 1999; Roehlkepartain, Benson, & Scales, 2011; Sanders, 1998; Serpe & Stryker, 2011; Templeton & Eccles, 2006). The exploration that characterizes Marcia's identity statuses of moratorium (exploring, no commitment) and achievement (explored, with commitment) often occurs during the time when young people begin to have freedom to question beliefs, norms, and values. These findings align with the scholarship on spiritual development also discussed in this chapter, locating key developmental processes and milestones during many students' college years.

Religious identities are connected to spirituality, ethnicity, culture, race, and nationality. Mattis, Ahluwalia, Cowie, and Kirkland-Harris (2006) pointed out, "In many contexts, national identity, ethnic identity, and religious identity are inextricably intertwined. In these contexts, religious and spiritual identity may be determined exclusively by one's national and ethnic identities (i.e., to be Malay is to be Muslim)" (p. 286). In religiously pluralist contexts, children's religious identity typically aligns with that of their parents or guardians or, in cases of mixed-religious families, the religion that the parents or guardians decide for them. After childhood in religiously diverse societies, individuals may undergo a process of religious identity exploration and commitment as described earlier. Research connecting religious identity or orientation with ethnic, racial, national, and sexual identity shows they may be mutually constructing, even when seemingly contradictory or conflicting (Mattis et al., 2006; Sanchez & Carter, 2005; Rodriguez, 2009; Rodriguez & Ouellette, 2000).

In this section, we provide two examples of identity development models that incorporate the key concepts outlined earlier for religious and nonreligious people. The first provides a model for understanding Muslim identity; though it is specific to the experiences of Muslim American students, its general contours could inform an understanding of other religious identities, both dominant (i.e., Christian) and minoritized in the United States (e.g., Jewish, Hindu, Buddhist, Baha'i, and others). The second model describes how people come to an atheist identity. Its contours might also be useful in understanding students who are questioning their fundamental beliefs and worldviews, regardless of the outcome.

Peek's Model of Muslim Identity Development among College Students

Peek (2005), a sociologist of religion, undertook a substantial qualitative study of second-generation Muslim American college students' religious identity processes and development, immediately following the September 11, 2001 terrorist attacks, in part to understand the role of a crisis event in the development of an identity made salient by that crisis. From interviews, focus groups, and participant observation with 127 Muslim students in New York and Colorado, she created a three-stage model of religious identity development.

Stage One: Religion as Ascribed Identity. Most participants were raised in Muslim homes, and their religious identity was ascribed to them by family and community. As children they took their religious identity for granted. Peek (2005) noted that being born into a religion does not mean that young people understand it or any restrictions it might place on them as a minoritized religion, other than perhaps not being able to do some things (for example, eat certain foods) that other children do. Children take up religious customs (dress, ritual) as they are socialized into the norms, values, and behaviors of their family and community.

Stage Two: Religion as Chosen Identity. This stage is an introspective one in which Muslim youth become aware of values, norms, and beliefs of their faith. According to Peek (2005), participants described it as "'Only natural' to begin to contemplate more important life questions and their religious backgrounds, and hence [they] re-examined that aspect of their identities" (p. 227). In college, on-campus religious organizations helped them create self-formed Muslim identities.

Stage Three: Religion as Declared Identity. In response to a crisis—the September 11 attacks on the World Trade Center and Pentagon—students deepened their faith and religious identity. Like many non-Muslim peers of all faiths, the crisis caused "many students to pray more often and increased their need for a spiritual anchor" (Peek, 2005, p. 231). Negative media portrayals of Islam and learning how non-Muslims viewed these students caused them to identify more with their religion; they experienced increased identity salience. As they faced more questions than usual about their faith and religious beliefs, they studied their own religion, which made them feel like they became "better Muslims" (p. 231). From ascribed identity to chosen identity to declared identity, these students experienced development of religious identity, commitment, and knowledge.

The development of majoritized and other minoritized religious identities might take a similar path, from the identity ascribed in childhood to a chosen identity emerging out of introspection about values, beliefs, norms, and behaviors. Some students may have a reason—a crisis, a challenge, or perhaps some joyful catalyst—to reach a point of declared identity in which they deepen their religious knowledge and identity. We are cautious in applying a theory developed for one population to one or more others, but we believe that the contours of this model, from ascribed to chosen to declared, may be useful in understanding the experiences of non-Muslim students as well as the Muslim students in Peek's study. At a minimum, we recognize that students with other minoritized religious identities may travel a similar pathway.

Smith's Model of Atheist Identity Development

Smith (2011) proposed a model of identity development for self-identified atheists. The model emphasizes how individuals come to see themselves as atheists in a predominantly theistic society. Theism is heavily embedded in society and culture, making it difficult even for those who are not religious to reject the notion of an existent God (Smith). Smith argued that current research shares little about individuals "who divest themselves of a religious identity altogether ... [or] the active process of developing a non-religious identity" (p. 217). The Atheist Identity Development model emerged from a qualitative study in which Smith conducted interviews and observations with 40 individuals, ages 18 to 92. While participants ranged widely in age, the overwhelming majority were White and college educated. Atheist identity development is comprised of four components. While these components may be viewed as stages, Smith reminds us that identity is "a fluid and dynamic process" (p. 219). The stages are as follows:

The starting point: the ubiquity of theism. In this stage, most individuals espouse *belief* in God and have *certainty* of God's existence. Such belief and certainty are filtered through religious doctrine and practice that was present during childhood. In making sense of religion and religious identities during childhood and adolescence, individuals feel as if these ideas were imposed upon them, leaving little opportunity for them to choose whether religion was appropriate for their lives. As a result, theism remains unquestioned in the current context. Overall, whether individuals express low or high levels of religious beliefs, there is still an inherent expression of belief in God. These beliefs were fostered through family or the cultural milieu of theism in the United States.

Questioning theism. Individuals begin to question theism when they have interactions in different settings and contexts. In particular, exposure to different viewpoints and people from diverse backgrounds was prevalent during the college years. Smith stated, "most started experiencing significant doubts about the existence of God" upon leaving for college (p. 222). Meeting diverse others, particularly those who were also questioning, served as the impetus for individuals to question God and previously held theistic beliefs. Questioning ultimately leads to a gradual process of "unlearning" all of the religious instruction in which they have been indoctrinated over their life span. Unlearning includes educating oneself on different viewpoints, learning to articulate one's concerns with theistic beliefs, and using new understandings to challenge religious ideologies. While the fostering of doubts about God is central to this stage, questions about the "centrality of morality" are crucial. Many individuals, through their reexamination of biblical scripture, begin to doubt God, view religious people they know as hypocritical, separate themselves from religious beliefs, and no longer conflate morality with religion. In expressing their discontent with religion, individuals realize that "atheism not only allows for morality, but is potentially superior to the religious understanding of morality" (p. 227).

Rejecting theism: "Not theist, or atheism as a rejection identity." In this stage, individuals transition from exploration and questioning to actively and "explicitly" rejecting the idea of God and religion. Their worldview is filtered through "the lens of science and secular thinking" (p. 227). People in this stage are not compelled to believe in God. While they admit having no evidence of God, they do not claim certainty that God does not exist. What is clear, however, is their rejection of all theistic belief. This stage is also characterized by a process of "not-self" or "constructing an identity out of the rejection or negation of something, in this case theism" (p. 228). In other words, their atheist identity is shaped by the boundaries they create, particularly beliefs they no longer have and actions in which they no longer participate. They also begin to use these boundaries to guide decisions about their relationships and overall life decisions.

"Coming out" atheist. This stage is characterized by full self-acceptance of an atheist identity. Individuals are progressively able to express what it means for them to be atheist, internally and externally. In conversations and general interactions, they are able to grapple with the inherent tensions between "the stigmatized and deviant status of atheism" (p. 229) and their desire to fully acknowledge beliefs that contradict normalized notions of God and religion. Their increasing ability to claim atheism is empowering and prompts them to develop a stronger self-acceptance. "Publicly adopting the label and coming out as atheist [is] an important step toward a new self-concept and feeling of independence and empowerment" (p. 230). While this process may elicit discomfort, individuals eventually come to resolve these feelings and see the entire process as affirming and liberating.

While Smith's model suggests a generally positive experience stemming from the process of "coming out" atheist, it is important to acknowledge the environment in which this entire process occurs. While individuals may feel a sense of identity resolution and comfort with being atheist, they still must embrace this identity in a society that is not only unsupportive of atheism, but lacks a more sophisticated understanding of it. As a result, atheists may face ongoing pushback, particularly from individuals with theistic beliefs.

Research on College Student Spirituality and Religion

In this section, we highlight some of the extensive research that has been conducted on spirituality and religion. While most of this research is from CSBV data, we also incorporate qualitative studies and findings from other surveys to capture the wealth of information in this area.

Spirituality, Religion, and Well-Being

Small and Bowman (2012) examined CSBV data to discuss five key areas that play a significant role in student development and well-being: religious affiliation (or lack thereof), institutional religious affiliation, interplay between student and institutional affiliations, college experiences, and campus religious climate. They noted that evangelical or "born again" Christians experience the greatest spiritual and religious development, particularly related to spiritual quest, religious commitment, and religious engagement, all of which contributed to their overall positive well-being. Conversely, double religious minority (minority in society and on campus) and nonreligious students experienced fewer gains or no gains at all, respectively. The lack of gains among nonreligious students may be because they choose to identify as spiritual rather than nonreligious, since many of them believe in God, but do not identify with a particular religion (Small & Bowman; see also Bowman & Small, 2012).

Institutional affiliation appears to matter in students' experiences of spirituality and religion. Non-Catholic Christian institutions provide the most gains for students in religious commitment, spiritual identification, and spiritual quest. Students at Catholic schools fall in the middle, while students at non-religiously affiliated or secular schools show the least religious and spiritual development. Overall, religious students at religious schools have greater gains in their development (Small & Bowman, 2012). Double religious minority students were more adversely affected by the campus environment at Catholic institutions in relation to spiritual identification, spiritual quest, religious skepticism, and well-being (Small & Bowman), while Catholic students thrived in these same environments. Overall, non-Catholic Christian schools appear to be an environment where students, regardless of affiliation, experience developmental benefits. While this literature reveals some general information about religious affiliation of institutions, it is important to note that in many instances the affiliation may exist in name only; a religiously affiliated college may not actually engage in practices and behaviors that promote the religion and may be more secularized. As a result, students in these institutions may hold a particular religious belief but not be sufficiently educated about the religion (see Craft & Bryant Rockenbach, 2011).

Small and Bowman (2012) also noted the benefits of interacting with like-minded students within the campus setting. Such interactions decreased skepticism and enhanced religious commitment, religious engagement, spiritual quest, spiritual identification, and well-being. Small and Bowman opined that as students experience struggle they may seek out faculty support (see also Small & Bowman, 2011). Interactions with faculty to receive support on issues of a spiritual nature increased spiritual identification and spiritual quest, as well as religious skepticism and religious struggle.

The campus religious climate, or an institution's ecumenical worldview, provides a glimpse into the level of inclusivity fostered within the environment (Small & Bowman, 2012). Small and Bowman explained, "If students at a particular campus generally endorse and appreciate religious diversity, then the result will likely be an overall positive religious climate" (p. 72). As a result, a positive religious climate leads to positive well-being for students. Bryant (2011a) noted when students held positive perceptions of the religious and spiritual climate on campus, their spiritual struggles decreased and their ecumenical worldview grew (see also Bryant, 2011b). Moreover, as students experience religious struggles their ecumenical worldview expands.

Bryant, Wickliffe, Mayhew, and Bartell Behringer (2009) developed the Collegiate Religious and Spiritual Climate (CRSC) Survey to address the "nuanced historical, structural, behavioral, and psychological dimensions of campus climate for religion and spirituality" (p. 9). While the survey does not measure development, it is important to recognize the significance of the college environment to student development as noted in the following discussion on institutional affiliation (for more information about the CRSC, see Bryant & Craft, 2010; Bryant Rockenbach & Mayhew, 2013, 2014; Mayhew & Bryant, 2013; Rockenbach, Mayhew, Davidson, Ofstein, & Clark Bush, 2015).

Spiritual Struggle

Bryant and Astin (2008) offered a perspective on student spirituality, focusing specifically on the concept of *spiritual struggle*. Their work on spiritual struggle adds more depth to Fowler's and Parks's discussion of dissonance, disequilibrium, and tensions that arise in people's lives. Bryant Rockenbach, Roseboro Walker, and Luzader (2012) noted that spiritual struggle is much more complex than the traditional understandings rendered by Fowler and Parks because it captures the multiple ways in which students negotiate emotions such as fear, manage their changing perspectives on their various identities, and search for meaning and purpose in life. In their view, spiritual struggle is composed of five elements, which include: "questioning one's religious/ spiritual beliefs, feeling unsettled about spiritual and religious matters; struggling to understand evil, suffering, and death; feeling angry at God; and feeling disillusioned with one's religious upbringing" (p. 2).

Bryant and Astin (2008) explained that minoritized students were more likely to experience spiritual struggle due to their identities. In other words, minoritized religions primarily outside of traditional Christianity (e.g., Buddhism, Islam, Unitarian), women, people of color, and LGBTQ populations are more prone to spiritual struggle, and students possessing multiple minoritized identities may experience significant "spiritual wrestling" (Bryant Rockenbach et al., 2012, p. 71). Certain campus contexts, particularly religiously affiliated institutions and the manner in which students engage on campus, are also related to spiritual struggle. For example, students who majored in psychology experienced more struggle, given the nature of the field. Students had spiritual struggles as a result of activities such as "converting to another religion; being on a spiritual quest; discussing religion/spirituality with friends; and discussing politics" (Bryant & Astin, 2008, p. 14). These activities interrupt students' lives not only by causing disequilibrium, but also by prompting their vulnerability and reflection on critical issues or ideas about which they are less familiar (Bryant & Astin). Spiritual struggle can affect psychological well-being, but it can also help students expand their viewpoints, ultimately leading to an enhanced ability to be reflective and introspective (Bryant & Astin, 2008; Bryant et al., 2012; Bryant, 2011c).

Religious/Nonreligious Worldviews

Students represent a range of religions and worldviews that contribute to the campus environment and opportunities for interactions with diverse others (Rockenbach & Park, in press). Despite this great diversity, most research tends to group students together. Bowman, Felix, and Ortis (2014) examined religions/worldviews in relation to student success but disaggregated students representing diverse minority religions to account for Buddhists, Hindus, Jews, Muslims, Protestants, and non-affiliated students and examined various outcomes in college such as satisfaction, friendships, and grade point average. They found that how students identify is predictive of the aforementioned outcomes. In addition to outcomes, scholars are especially interested in examining how students with diverse worldviews make meaning of spirituality. For example, Mayhew (2004) examined spirituality among eight students, each with diverse worldviews (agnosticism, atheism, Buddhism, Hinduism, Judaism, Muslim, Protestantism, and Roman Catholicism) and found that while worldviews differed, students viewed spirituality as a meaning-making process in which people work to understand themselves and their connections to the larger world. He noted, "spirituality carries personal meaning for all students, even those who identify themselves as nonreligious" (p. 667).

While the resurgence of interest in spirituality and religion increasingly grows, a promising aspect of this work is that it focuses not only on students who are religiously affiliated but also on students who have been marginalized because they belong to nonmajority or non-Christian religions (i.e., Hindus, Sikhs, Buddhists) and those who follow no religion at all. Based upon data from the CSBV, Bryant (2006b) explained that Christian-based groups exhibit stronger levels on the constructs including "spirituality, religious commitment and engagement, and religious/social conservatism" (p. 5). Conversely, students labeled as religious minorities showed higher levels of "pluralistic openness and stronger commitment to an ethic of caring and charitable involvement" (p. 5). Using this information as a starting point, Bryant examined first-year students with six diverse worldviews, including those belonging to "non-Christian traditions" and nonreligious students, to learn about their demographics, practices, beliefs, and attitudes. General findings indicated a substantial range of diversity among the groups in terms of their religious behavior and spiritual beliefs, with Muslims being the most religious. With the exception of a few issues, students in these groups were less inclined toward conservative ideologies. While most of the students believed they were engaged in a spiritual quest, Jewish and nonreligious students were less likely to think of themselves as spiritual. Unitarian Universalists were the most open toward other religious groups. Finally, all of the students felt quite firm in their religious beliefs, with the exception of Unitarian Universalists and nonreligious students. While most students felt a sense of security in their religious beliefs and were likely to retain these beliefs, they also acknowledged the possibility of grappling with spiritual struggles as they continued to make sense of their experiences.

Given the wide range of diversity in student worldviews, literature has also captured these students' experiences in diverse campus contexts and the impact on development within a framework of privilege and oppression (Small & Bowman, 2012; Seifert, 2007). For example, Stubbs and Sallee (2013) found Muslim students experienced numerous challenges as religious minorities on campus, such as "lack of accommodation for religious practice, social expectations that conflict with Islamic values and behavior, and incidents of discrimination and prejudice in and out of the classroom" (p. 463). Yet they also manage to successfully navigate such environments (Stubbs & Sallee; Cole & Ahmadi, 2010; Ribeiro & Saleem, 2010).

While they possess different worldviews from Muslims and other religious minority groups, atheists' experiences appear more frequently in the literature. Goodman and Mueller (2009) began an important line of research examining the experiences of atheist students. Mueller's (2012) qualitative study of 16 undergraduate students who identified as atheist revealed their awareness of negative stereotypes ascribed to atheists such as "hedonistic, unhappy ... dangerous, devil-worshippers" (p. 259). While they generally felt welcomed in conversations about religion, some participants avoided the conversation out of respect for their religiously affiliated peers. They also felt as if they could blend in with their campus, which tended to be more secular in nature. Regarding overall findings, Mueller stated, "being an atheist is part of their identity structure and they experience not only marginalizing effects of Christian privilege, but also religious privilege as well" (p. 261).

Intersections with Spirituality, Gender, Sexual Orientation, and Race

Scholars have studied the role of gender in relation to religion and spirituality (Bryant, 2003a; Bryant, 2003b; Bryant, 2007; Astin et al., 2011). In terms of gender differences, women tend to experience greater spiritual growth in comparison to their male counterparts (Bryant, 2007). In her 2007 study, Bryant found women demonstrated more religious commitment, greater conservatism, spiritual quest and charitable engagement, and equanimity. On the other hand, men tended to be more skeptical and had lower levels of spiritual struggle. Men's academic experiences, particularly majoring in sciences and amount of time spent studying in a given week, were negatively associated with their spiritual development. Men's religious identity was also more strongly correlated to spirituality in comparison to women. Bryant found that discussions related to spirituality were beneficial for both men and women because they exposed students to diverse viewpoints and perspectives. Peer interactions also affected women's and men's spirituality; if they had peers who were engaged in religious activities, they too were more engaged, though women were engaged at a higher level.

Examinations of gender within specific collegiate religious subcultures have also emerged, particularly focusing on evangelical students (Bryant, 2011c). Bryant (2006a) explored the gender climate among evangelical students, focusing on their gendered beliefs and behaviors. She found while the students rarely broached the topic of gender in an explicit fashion, the subculture was rooted in masculine standards, especially in terms of "leadership, language, and images of God" (Bryant, 2006a, p. 629). They also believed in "essential gender differences ... designed by God" (p. 629), which shaped men's and women's behavior and beliefs, having lasting consequences for women who felt pressured to adhere to stringent cultural norms.

Gender also plays a prominent role for undergraduate women of particular religious groups, such as Muslim women who choose to veil (Seggie & Sanford, 2010). For example, findings from Cole and Ahmadi's (2003) examination of veiling practices among Muslim undergraduate women indicated participants wanted to be perceived as good Muslims and committed to their religion, hence their decision to wear the *hijab* (veil). Their decisions were also closely linked with expectations stemming from their religion, family, and culture, many of which reinforced veiling. Moreover, they deemed the hijab a reflection of modesty and respect. Due to their outward expression of their religion, some participants in this study felt alienated on campus, but "often interpreted intolerant encounters as ineffectual toward altering their veiling practice" (p. 65).

With regard to sexual orientation, the research literature remains limited. Love, Bock, Jannarone, and Richardson (2005) conducted a qualitative study of spirituality among seven lesbian and five gay male students. While some students shared the challenges they faced in reconciling their spirituality and sexual identities, others were still actively engaged in the process, and some had not broached the process. Their participants saw themselves as spiritual beings, were aware of the interactions between the two identities, and could distinguish between the concepts, though they used them interchangeably. Gold & Stewart (2011) also produced findings from their study of 47 LGB students, indicating that spirituality was linked to acceptance, personal relationships, and nature and a reflective process of reconciliation between sexual identity and spirituality. Abes (2012; Abes & Jones, 2004; Abes & Kasch, 2007) has made substantial contributions to understanding lesbian students' spiritual identity in the context of multiple social identities, finding that race, class, religion, gender, and sexuality intersect to form and re-form in dynamic fashion over time and contexts.

Race also plays a role in spiritual and religious development, but until recently it had not received much attention in the literature. Gehrke (2008) found that from their first year of college through junior year Black, Asian, and Latino/a students had greater gains in their ecumenical worldview. In a later study, Gehrke's (2014) findings revealed that students of color showed significantly higher gains in ecumenical worldview than White students and recommended the incorporation of prosocial involvement experiences (such as leadership and activism) to increase the development of ecumenical world-views among students.

Park and Millora (2010) examined linkages between spirituality and religion and psychological well-being, with emphasis on race. Using the CSBV Survey, they arrived at conclusions similar to those of Bryant and Astin (2008); that is, when students grapple with tough questions associated with religion (for example, spiritual struggle), they have decreased levels of well-being. In comparison to their White counterparts, Black, Latino/a, and Asian students benefit from self-reflection, an important aspect of spirituality. Moreover, Black students' psychological well-being was enhanced when they engaged in religious mission trips. Latinos/as who identified as Catholic had higher religious engagement, which contributed to psychological well-being. On the other hand, institutional affiliation was also important because Latino/a students' psychological well-being was decreased at private, secular schools. Asian American students' psychological well-being was predicted by their intellectual self-concept, but not by spiritual or religious identity.

Paredes-Collins and Collins (2011) also paid particular attention to how racial differences emerge when examining spirituality and religion. Using CSBV data, they explored these differences within the context of evangelical institutions and found that White students experienced increased religious commitment but decreased ethic of caring in comparison to their racially minoritized counterparts. The researchers explained that White students may embrace a strict doctrine as the center of their religious identity and may be more conservative and focused on individualistic understandings of religion rather than linkages of their religious values with larger communities. The sentiments of these students are not surprising, given that evangelical institutions are predominantly White and the majority of the sample in this study was White. Paredes-Collins and Collins also found that students of color scored higher on ethic of caring, supporting the notion that they have a more socially just framework for guiding their religion and spirituality. They issued a call for "predominantly White evangelical schools to work toward diversifying their student body, and to continue to educate students around faith-based mandates toward justice, which appear to be minimal from the traditionally White evangelical perspective" (p. 94).

Overall, Julie Park's scholarship has been most critical to the growing research on spirituality and religion, particularly how they intersect with diversity, race and ethnicity, social capital, and cross-racial interactions, as well as the resulting complexities (Park 2011, 2012a, 2012b, 2012c, 2013). For example, Park conducted a study of the experiences of Korean American students in relation to religion and diversity and found that religion facilitated ethnic identity among Korean American students as they decided whether they would be involved in the InterVarsity Christian Fellowship (IVCF) or the Korean American Christian organizations at a California university (Park, 2011, p. 193).

Park has geared much of her effort toward encouraging university professionals to pay closer attention to the role of intersectionality in cross-racial interactions (Park 2012a). Such an emphasis is important, given her findings that Protestant and Jewish students are least likely to have interracial friendships. The same is true for students with high religious salience (Park 2012a). Her research has also suggested that involvement in religious student organizations is negatively linked to cross-racial interactions (Park 2012a; Park & Kim, 2013). Park (2012b) examined how Black students experienced the IVCF at the same university where she studied Korean American student experiences. She found that while Black students remained involved with IVCF, their participation came at a significant cost. She noted, "Black students had to be willing to experience some marginalization in the fellowship for IVCF to retain its diversity, on top of the marginalization they already felt" (p. 585) at the institution. Despite some of their positive experiences, Black students dealt with racial battle fatigue. Their willingness to remain involved was largely related to the faith commonalities they held with other students in the IVCF. Moreover, the IVCF was one of the few organizations that encouraged Black students to join and had a willingness to deal with issues of race and social justice. In another study Park found positive cross-racial interaction links for Black, White, and Asian American students with high religious identities and students associated with minoritized religions (Park & Bowman, 2015).

Critique and Future Directions

The work of Fowler and Sharon Daloz Parks added important dimensions to the study of student development. Parks's theory is particularly relevant given her attention to the college environment. The more recent work of Astin, Astin, and Lindholm and the burgeoning research on religion and spirituality among college students have been critical in addressing many of the previous theoretical shortcomings, including the lack of clarity in terminology, longitudinal data, attention to minoritized religions and nonreligious identities, intersectionality, and diverse methodologies. All of these issues have been addressed in recent research, bringing a more in-depth understanding of how spirituality and religion function in the lives of students, contribute to their development, and shape the campus environment. Because scholars have offered clearer definitions of faith and spirituality, a better sense of the different ways in which students make meaning of these concepts, and the factors that contribute to their development, will help student affairs professionals work more effectively with students. Moreover, the addition of longitudinal data provides clearer information on how students make meaning of these various concepts over the duration of their college experiences. The inclusion of voices that have typically been silenced in the research literature is a major contribution that can disrupt the marginalization of particular groups. Finally, research studies grounded in both quantitative and qualitative methodologies are more readily available and provide both broad and more nuanced perspectives on spirituality and religion. The theories and theoretical constructs in this chapter have advanced the knowledge on spirituality and religion immensely, but more needs to be done.

In terms of research, more scholarship is needed on how students' race and social class mediate spirituality and religion on campus and vice versa. Relatively little is known about nonreligious, racially minoritized students, students from low-income backgrounds, LGBTQ students, or students with disabilities. Furthermore, the research on gender is extremely limited and does not account for trans* identities and experiences. Given that much of the research described herein accounts for institutional religious affiliation and the religious and spiritual climate of campuses, more research about historically Black colleges and universities, tribal colleges, and other minority-serving institutions as well as community colleges is warranted.

In terms of practice, there is a renewed interest in spirituality and religion, but not all institutions are invested in student development in these areas. Astin et al. (2011) noted, "To ignore the spiritual side of students' and faculty's lives is to encourage a kind of fragmentation and a lack of authenticity, where students and faculty act either as if they are not spiritual beings, or as if their spiritual side is irrelevant to their vocation or work" (p. 7). They recommend colleges and universities avoid this culture of fragmentation and direct more concerted energy toward enhancing the curriculum and developing opportunities for all members of the campus community to grapple with existential questions that engage the mind and spirit and expand beyond conventional ways of examining spirituality.

Dalton (2006b) argued that student affairs must do a better job of addressing students' spirituality. Dalton et al. (2006) offered a number of suggestions for creating a spiritual context within higher education settings, which include designating spaces on campus for meditation and reflection; offering programs on spirituality; promoting opportunities for dialogue with individuals of different faiths; incorporation of spirituality into appropriate courses; and art, music, and drama with spiritual themes. They went on to offer strategies for responding to the increasing interest in spirituality on campus: awareness and advocacy of spirituality as an important aspect of student development, creation of supportive environments that encourage spiritual development, education programs, and staff and faculty development to help educators work effectively with students in the area of faith development. Dalton (2006c) took his ideas further, developing a comprehensive set of institutional principles and practices for enhancing the spiritual growth of students.

As educators are called to focus more on the spiritual development of students, Gilley's (2005) cautions are important to keep in mind. He stressed that educators have a responsibility to "do no harm" (p. 96), which can be accomplished only by actively preparing through reading and study to address spirituality and faith development issues with which students may be dealing. He went on to caution, "Issues of the spirit may require more preparation than those more temporal" (p. 97). A learning environment in which the meaning making associated with spiritual development can occur must include a careful balance of care, support, and challenge. Craft and Bryant (2011) also reminded educators that matters of faith development are not always associated with religion and spirituality and that classrooms are excellent environments, whether at religious or secular institutions, to promote students' development and meaning making around larger questions of life.

Along with these elements, educators must remain mindful of the role privilege and oppression play in conversations about spirituality and faith (Goodman, 2009). Seifert and Holman-Harmon (2009) pointed out that, "Despite well-meaning efforts and intentions to define spirituality in an inclusive manner, the root word, spirit, conveys a construct that does not resonate with all students or all student affairs practitioners" (p. 13). Unfortunately, the terms spirituality and faith are often used to signify beliefs connected to Christianity or other organized religions, resulting in a discourse of exclusivity for those who identify as atheist or agnostic or hold beliefs beyond mainstream thinking.

Nash (2003) offered a "modest proposal" in which he not only discussed the growing religious pluralism on campus, but also encouraged colleges and universities to engage in "all-inclusive religious-non-religious dialogue" (p. 20). The work of Smith (2011) as well as Goodman and Mueller (2009) and Mueller (2012) is critical within higher education, particularly the capacity of their research findings to shatter traditional notions of faith and spirituality and expand beyond a theistically privileged context. More important, their perspectives help educators to understand the challenges and developmental processes of embracing a stigmatized identity in a world that consciously and unconsciously pressures individuals to hold theistic beliefs.

Seifert and Holman-Harmon (2009) recommended that educators not only recognize the privilege embedded in faith and spirituality discourses but also work to change the discourse to minimize confusion among the various terms and focus more intently on students' meaning-making processes as they discover their life purpose. Lastly, they recommended that student affairs educators engage in their own exploration of their life journey, come to terms with their own religious or spirituality-related biases, and consider their critical role in the holistic development of students.

Student affairs educators could also benefit from Stewart and Kocet's (2011) competency model for addressing spirituality, secularism, religious pluralism, and interfaith cooperation (CMSSRIC). They offered this model because student affairs professionals focus on students' holistic development, and nonsectarian colleges and universities rarely have a campus ministry. Educators should use this model, composed of 12 competencies, as a way to consider religion and spirituality in larger conversations about diversity. They should also expand their knowledge and awareness of diverse religions and worldviews; consider how spirituality, religion, and secularism influence identity development; remain consciously aware of and disrupt issues of privilege and oppression embedded in these areas; understand their own worldviews and their impact on practice; and educate others about diverse worldviews.

Discussion Questions

1. Discuss empirically derived definitions of spirituality, belief, faith, and religion. Compare and contrast these definitions.
2. Why are spirituality and religion important in understanding student development?

3. Compare and contrast Fowler and Parks's theories of faith development. Draw diagrams of each theory to visualize these concepts.

4. Describe the measures of spirituality and religion for college students generated by Astin, Astin, and Lindholm. In what ways do these measures resonate with your college experience or with students you know?

5. Describe Peek's model of Muslim identity and discuss how this process might resonate for other minoritized religious students. How does your campus support the religious identity development of students from minoritized religious groups?

6. Outline and compare the model of identity development for self-identified atheists to the processes of religious and spiritual development. How do they differ?

7. What are ways in which institutions of higher education, public and private, can support the religious and spiritual development of such diverse U.S. college students? How does your institution enhance the religious and spiritual development of students?

8. Draw a picture or image of how spirituality and religion intersect with other identities you have studied so far (for example, racial, ethnic, sexual, and gender). Give examples from your life or from the lives of students you know.

CHAPTER TEN

DISABILITY IDENTITIES AND IDENTITY DEVELOPMENT

At least one in ten postsecondary students reported having some type of disability—physical, psychological, or learning (Snyder & Dillow, 2012). Because of increased educational equity for elementary and secondary students with disabilities, combined with improved pathways to college for students from all backgrounds, enrollment of college and university students with disabilities continues to grow. In fact, Newman, Wagner, Cameto, Knokey, and Shaver (2010) documented that between 1990 and 2005 the percentage of secondary school graduates with disabilities who went on to postsecondary education increased from 26% to 46%. Understanding the identities and development of students with disabilities is important in providing access to higher education and working toward more equitable academic, social, and professional outcomes.

The landmark federal Americans with Disabilities Act (ADA) of 1990 required higher education institutions to align legally with other educational programs in creating access and accommodations for students with disabilities. The ADA provided this definition:

> the term "disability" means, with respect to an individual - (A) a physical or mental impairment that substantially limits one or more of the major life activities of such individual; (B) a record of such an impairment; or (C) being regarded as having such an impairment (ADA 42 U.S. C. Sec. 12111, 1990)

Further, a college student with a disability is a postsecondary student

> with a disability who, with or without reasonable modifications to rules, policies or practices, the removal of architectural, communication, or transportation barriers, or the provision of auxiliary aids and services, meets the essential eligibility requirements for the receipt of services of the participation in programs or activities provided by a public entity. (ADA 42 U.S. C. Sec. 12111, 1990)

In 2008, after several years of implementation of the ADA, legal challenges to institutions that failed to provide reasonable accommodations to students, and attempts by institutions to skirt the existing law, the law was amended to define disability to include broad coverage and to avoid extensive analysis of disability status. It counts in "major life activities" a number of activities crucial to student success, including reading, communicating, concentrating, and thinking (see Equal Employment Opportunity Commission, 2011; Simon, 2011). The intention of the amendments was to make it easier for individuals to establish that they have a disability as considered within the ADA.

The legal definitions are important, as are interpretations of the statutes (see Simon, 2011), but in the lives of students and educators, it is equally significant to understand that college students come with an array of diagnosed, undiagnosed, acknowledged, and unknown abilities and disabilities that may be physical impairments (for example, blindness or visual impairments, deafness or hearing loss, amputated limbs, traumatic brain injury, chronic illness, and autoimmune diseases), psychological impairments (living with depression, anxiety, post-traumatic stress disorder, panic disorder, eating disorder), or learning impairments and developmental disorders (dyslexia, attention deficit disorder, autism spectrum).

Some students come to college with several years of experience working with their impairments within an educational setting. Other students will acquire a permanent or temporary impairment while in college (for example, losing sight or hearing, or a broken limb). Still others will learn of their impairment while in college (for example, a high-achieving student who struggles with a new subject in college and is then diagnosed with a learning disability that had not previously manifested).

While one study suggested that the percentage of all college students who report a disability was 11.1% (Raue, Lewis, & Coopersmith, 2011), the federal statistics on students with disabilities count only those students who identify themselves to their institutions. Since a number of studies have indicated that students with disabilities failed to disclose their impairments to avoid the stigma associated with such disclosure (Baker, Boland, & Nowik, 2012; Denhart, 2008), it is likely that the number of students with disabilities is much higher. Specifically, Newman et al. (2010) estimated that approximately 55% of students in high schools who had individualized education programs (IEPs) indicating that they were eligible for accommodations and who enrolled in postsecondary education failed to inform their colleges that they had an impairment that qualified them for disability services.

In this chapter, we focus on disability identity and identity development. First we describe different approaches and models related to understanding disabled college students. We then discuss disability identities and provide theoretically grounded perspectives on identity development, sharing ecological and stage models. We close with critique and application of existing theory and implications for the future.

Before proceeding, it is important to clarify some of the language we use in this chapter. As with all minoritized groups, individuals have preferences for how they should be addressed. Some prefer "disabled" people, while others prefer "people with disabilities." We realize that no correct/all encompassing solution exists, because individuals are extremely diverse. Throughout this chapter we use these terms interchangeably, recognizing that when we use "disabled" we are clearly acknowledging that disability is a condition forced upon people, not one they create. We use "people with disabilities" to acknowledge that they are people, and each person represents a range of roles and unique characteristics that make up their identity. We also use "nondisabled" to refer to groups whose experiences are privileged within campus environments.

Approaches to Understanding College Students with Disabilities

Evans, Broido, Brown, and Wilke (forthcoming) summarized the historical construction of disability as moving from a moral model (if one is disabled, it is the result of someone's moral lapse), to a medical model (disabilities are defects of the body that may or may not be cured or fixed by medical personnel), to a functional limitations approach (the inability of the person to perform specific functions—such as walking, working, or living independently—as a result of an underlying impairment), to a social model (disability is a social construction, in which society creates boundaries and barriers for people with impairments), to a minority group model (disability derives from discrimination directed at people with disabilities who are part of a community that is marginalized by the constraints of the environment and the attitudes of nondisabled people in society), and finally to the ableist or social justice approach (people with disabilities are an oppressed minority who are denied resources available to nondisabled people and must work to achieve equity in society for all people). In higher education, disability historically has been conceptualized through a medical model that situates it as "deviance from the norm, as pathological condition and as deficit" (Linton, 1998, p. 144). The medical model and the rehabilitation model both situate the disability within the *person* (Hahn, 1991; Kaplan, 2005). The medical model was the result of the advance of science and medical technology in the late nineteenth century (Braddock & Parish, 2001; Hahn, 1991), a time when disability was perceived as something to be cured, and people with disabilities were considered physically or mentally deficient. The functional limitations model followed with the development of the field of rehabilitation, whose goal is to enable individuals to gain the ability to function in society (Drum, 2009).

Meade and Serlin (2006) pointed out that definitions and understanding of disability are located in time and culture. Slowly, and with some resistance, there has been a move toward the recognition that disability is a function of the social and physical environment rather than being a characteristic housed within the person (Fougeyrollas & Beauregard, 2001). The postmodern or social construction model of disability, which provides an umbrella for the minority group, social, and ableist models of disability (Drum, 2009), necessitates placing disability within the larger context of society. It situates disability *outside* the person and *within* the physical environment and attitudes of those who are nondisabled (Asch & Fine, 1988; Braddock & Parish, 2001; Hahn, 1991; Jones, 1996; Kaplan, 2005; Linton, 1998). This perspective requires individuals to reorganize their thinking, and institutions and individuals to look for solutions in the redesign of spaces, materials, technology, and thought (Bowe, 2000; Braddock & Parish, 2001; Brinckerhoff, Shaw, & McGuire, 1993; Jones, 1996; Linton, 1998).

The articulation of disability identity and its development has lagged behind those for other minoritized groups in higher education. There are differences between disabled people and other minoritized groups, such as acceptance (at least by some disabled people) of separate but equal (for example, separate "accessible" building entrances, residence hall rooms, restrooms, and on some campuses, sections of courses) that have been rejected in discourse and legal precedent for people of different races (Olkin, 1999). Another difference is in the expression of pride in one's racial, ethnic, sexual orientation, and nationality, but rarely in disability status; though "a non-tragic view of disability and impairment which encompasses positive social identities, both individual and collective, for disabled people grounded in the benefits of lifestyle and life experience of being impaired and disabled" is steadily emerging (Swain & French, 2000, p. 569). On the other hand, there are a number of similarities between disability identity and other minoritized identities, including being expected to conform to the majority and experiencing more negative educational outcomes (Olkin, 1999). These differences and similarities offer opportunities to consider disability identities and identity development alone and in the context of multiple dimensions of identity.

Disability Identities

As with the other socially constructed categories of identity that we describe in this book, disability identity is a matter of individuals, their environment, and the interactions between the two. Given the diversity of visible, noticeable, and invisible conditions that disabilities comprise, and variations in the extent to which an individual may experience limitations and possibilities within each condition, unsurprisingly there is no single widely accepted disability identity development model for college students (or anyone else). We present two ecological approaches to disability identity and two proposed stage models.

When exploring disability identity, it is important to take into account the whole student, with multiple identities, and the student's context on and off campus in family, peer groups, living situation, academic settings, and so forth. Equally significant is understanding that developing and integrating a disability identity may be different for someone who is born with or develops an impairment early in life compared to someone who acquires an impairment after other aspects of holistic identity are well formed (see Charmaz, 1994, 1995). College students may be in either of these groups.

Ecological Approaches to Understanding Disability Identity

Noting that the diversity of experiences of people with disabilities across time defies a unitary description of "disability identity," Johnstone (2004) presented six categories of disability identity he observed in the literature. The first category is *externally ascribed, disempowering identities*. In this category, identities are imposed on students from other sources, labeling them with stigmatizing terms and limiting their opportunities for self-discovery of identity. The second category is *overcompensating identities*. Students with overcompensating identities typically have disclosed their impairment to others and feel compelled to perform at high levels to overcome obstacles and prove to others they are not impaired or deemphasize the weight of the impairment. The third category

Johnstone observed was that of *identities that shift the focus away from disability*. He located Deaf culture within this category, noting its emphasis on linguistic and social bonds rather than rehabilitation.

The fourth category is *empowering identities*. Like the "pride" or "immersion" aspect of other minoritized identities, this category includes a focus on reclaiming the body and legitimizing the experience of being a person with a disability. *Complex identities* is Johnstone's fifth category, locating disability within multiple identity domains including race, class, gender, and sexual orientation. Finally, the *common identity* category accounts for the feelings of commonality and shared experience—sometimes culture—that disabled people have with others. Common identity among students may be shared across types of disability, and it may be accentuated within communities of students with the same, or similar, impairments.

Johnstone (2004) explained that individuals might experience different categories of identity and that disability identity formation is both personal and social. Disability identity may be imposed (ascribed) by others and "thus delimiting; or it can be self-ascribed and empowering" (Johnstone, 2004, p. 39). This approach to understanding disability identity—not as a stage model through which individuals progress, but in relation to the world and to how others see the individual—is similar to ecological approaches to understanding bi- and multiracial student identity (Renn, 2004; Wijeyesinghe, 2001, 2012; see Chapter Five) that include interactions between individuals and those around them.

In their model, Davidson and Henderson (2010) offered four "sense-making discourse clusters, or repertoires" (p. 155) they located in autobiographies and narratives of college students on the autism spectrum (AS). Repertoire one was *keeping safe*, which related to self-protection in disclosure. Repertoire two was *qualified deception*, which focused on the complex nature of nondisclosure at different levels to different people. Repertoire three was *like/as resistance*, in which individuals located their experiences of disclosure on the spectrum as similar to the coming-out experiences of LGBTQ and Deaf individuals. Repertoire four was an *education* approach, in which individuals build community as part of disclosure. These repertoires were all based on personal agency rather than imposed or ascribed identities and relate to the processes through which students with disabilities may elect to express their identities, particularly if those identities are not immediately visible. Davidson and Henderson (2010) based their research on students on the autism spectrum, but it seems sensible to extend these four repertoires to other disabled students with impairments not immediately visible to others.

An advantage of the Johnstone (2004) and Davidson and Henderson (2010) approaches is that they account for an array of variables within the experience and identity process of a student with a disability. Johnstone's six categories provide a way to understand and describe how students may present their disabilities and identities in different contexts. Davidson and Henderson provide four clusters that illuminate the ways students with invisible disabilities may handle disclosure of their disabilities, or "coming out" to others. Collectively, these two approaches provide an ecological overview of disability identity in students.

Stage Models of Disability Identity

Similar to other areas of minoritized identities, there are also stage or stagelike models that offer descriptions of a progression that may be typical for individuals in that identity group. Models describing the developmental trajectories of disabled students focus on how individuals come to understand themselves inclusive of their disability and in relation to others with disabilities. The existence of a reference group or culture, such as an active community of athletes with disabilities or local and online Deaf culture, into which individuals enter is another common feature of stage models. We present two stage models here.

Gibson (2006) offered a three-stage disability identity model to guide practitioners. Her audience was psychologists, though the model translates to other areas of student services in higher education. Stage 1: *Passive Awareness* typically occurs during the first part of life and can continue to adulthood. In this stage, the individual's medical needs are met, but the person has no role model, is taught to deny social aspects of disability, avoids attention, and avoids associating with other disabled individuals. An incident that brings the disability to salience prompts movement to Stage 2: *Realization.* Gibson located this transition most often in adolescence or early adulthood. In this stage, individuals begin to see themselves as having a disability and may experience self-hate, anger (why me?), and concern about how others see them. In Stage 2, students with disabilities may develop what Gibson called a "superman/woman complex," which Johnstone (2004) labeled overcompensating. Stage 3: *Acceptance* has parallel stages among other minority identity development models (for example, see Chapter Five on racial identity). In this stage, which Gibson locates most commonly in adulthood, individuals understand their differences in a positive way, integrate into the "majority (able-bodied) world" (p. 8), incorporate others with disabilities into their lives, and sometimes involve themselves in disability advocacy and activism.

Although Gibson's model unfolds in three stages, she stated that "identity development of persons with disabilities can be fluid" (p. 8). She also noted that individuals may revert from Stage 3 to Stage 2 under circumstances that trigger anger ("Why me?"). In the lives of college students, there are several common occurrences that could prompt reversion and recycling through previous stages. For residential students with disabilities, coping with the transition to close communal living and the intimacy of shared bedrooms and bathrooms could prompt a reversion from Stage 2 to Stage 1 (avoiding attention, not associating with others with disabilities) or from Stage 3 to Stage 2 (why do I have to deal with these additional obstacles to transition?). For any student with a disability, navigating the physical campus, learning where there are accessible building entrances, approaching faculty to request accommodations on assignments, or dealing with inaccessible online learning and social media could lead to a reversion to a previous stage.

Conversely, the campus may offer opportunities to enhance the developmental trajectory of disabled students, gain confidence in self-advocacy, and navigate complex physical and organizational systems. Students may advance developmentally in the transition from a parent- (or guardian-) based system of educational support, required by law for students with disabilities in the K–12 school system and known as the individualized educational program (IEP), to reliance on themselves to locate and activate systems of accommodation and support. Communities of other students with disabilities provide outlets for finding role models, engaging in advocacy and activism, and participating in social, recreational, and educational activities with other students with disabilities. Any of these opportunities might catalyze movement from Stage 1 to Stage 2 in Gibson's (2006) model, or from Stage 2 to Stage 3.

Forber-Pratt and Aragon (2013) proposed a similar, but more complex, model for social and psychosocial identity development for college students with physical disabilities. They focused their model on how college students with disabilities enter disability culture. They based their model on a single-campus study in which they conducted 30 hours of observations in a residence hall for students with severe disabilities and a resource center for persons with disabilities, combined with interviews of four students with disabilities. They conducted the study at the University of Illinois, which they stated is "known as one of the world's most disability friendly campuses" (p. 11). Although there are limits to generalizing such a study to the entire population of college students with disabilities, the proposed model holds promise for describing the broader experience of how students at other institutions enter into disability culture.

The Forber-Pratt and Aragon (2013) developmental trajectory into disability culture has four stages. As illustrated in Figure 10.1, the first stage is *Acceptance Phase.* The authors contend that whether individuals are born with a disability or acquire it, they undergo a process of acceptance. According to this model, accepting an acquired disability may entail going through stages of grief as outlined by Kübler-Ross and Kessler (2005): denial, anger, bargaining, depression, and acceptance. The individual accepts the disability, as do important others such as family, friends, and educators.

Stage 2 is the *Relationship Phase.* In this stage of entering disability culture, students meet other people with disabilities and create relationships. They learn the norms and activities of the group and begin to feel a connection with others. Forber-Pratt and Aragon's research design may have had a particular influence on identifying this stage, because they made observations in campus locations where students were likely to encounter others, especially those with visible disabilities (for example, students using wheelchairs). Building relationships with other students with disabilities contributed to forward progress into the campus disability culture.

In Stage 3: *Adoption* students internalized the "core values of disability culture: independence and social justice" (Forber-Pratt & Aragon, 2013, p. 9). For students with physical disabilities, independence involves navigating the world and managing personal hygiene. Participating in disability culture provides a peer group with whom to discuss these topics with others who understand them from personal experience and to share strategies and advice. Social justice varies from individual self-advocacy to collective activism on behalf of the disabled community.

The fourth stage is the *Giving Back to Community Phase.* Students in this stage integrate the values of independence and social justice to become leaders and role models in the campus disability culture. As in one aspect of Gibson's (2006) acceptance stage, students in this stage integrate disability identity into their lives and feel an obligation to give back to others—particularly youth and other college students—with disabilities. To Forber-Pratt and Aragon (2013), "this stage is truly about identity synthesis and embracing one's disability" (p. 12). They identified a division in disability culture between those students who believed that they "got it," meaning that they had reached stage four, and those students who were deemed by the group that "got it" to have "not gotten it yet." This phenomenon appears in other minority identity models, in which students who have achieved X identity judge other students whom they believe belong to the same identity category and find their peers lacking in recognition and "proper" enactment of X identity.

FIGURE 10.1. MODEL OF SOCIAL AND PSYCHOSOCIAL IDENTITY DEVELOPMENT FOR POSTSECONDARY STUDENTS WITH PHYSICAL DISABILITIES

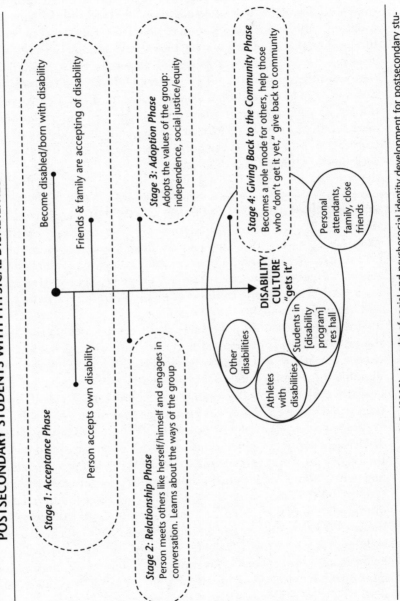

Stage 1: Acceptance Phase

Become disabled/born with disability

Friends & family are accepting of disability

Person accepts own disability

Stage 2: Relationship Phase
Person meets others like herself/himself and engages in conversation. Learns about the ways of the group

Stage 3: Adoption Phase
Adopts the values of the group: independence, social justice/equity

Stage 4: Giving Back to the Community Phase
Becomes a role mode for others, help those who "don't get it yet," give back to community

DISABILITY CULTURE "gets it"

Other disabilities

Athletes with disabilities

Students in [disability program] res hall

Personal attendants, family, close friends

Source: Forber-Pratt, A. J., & Aragon, S. R. (2013). A model of social and psychosocial identity development for postsecondary students with physical disabilities. In M. Wappett & K. Arndt (Eds.), *Emerging perspectives on disability studies (pp. 1–22). New York: Palgrave-MacMillan*

Students on campuses without a strong disability culture might experience these four stages differently, or they might find alliances with other minoritized students. They may also seek disability culture in online communities, which provide opportunities to experience several of the in-person activities that Forber-Pratt and Aragon (2013) observed. Students with other types of impairments (such as learning, chronic illness, or mental health) might experience a similar progression if they were able to identify a disability culture of like others. While based on a specific context and disability type, this model provides a road map for future research and for understanding some common experiences of disabled students. Taken with the ecological perspectives and the Johnstone (2004) model, it provides insight into the experiences and identities of students with disabilities.

Critique, Application, and Future Directions

As we noted earlier, disability identity theories have been a relatively recent arrival in student development literature compared with theories for other aspects of identity (for example, race, ethnicity, sexual orientation). Following a pattern seen in the creation of theory for different groups, we observed that the models available for describing college student disability identity and identity development were limited and somewhat speculative, based on small studies on single campuses or drawn from clinical experience. To be clear, we believe that the four models we present in this chapter are useful for understanding the identities of students with a variety of impairments. But we would like to see more empirical testing of these models and the creation of additional models based on more robust research designs.

In a positive development, more researchers are exploring intersections of disability experiences and identities with other salient aspects of student experiences. Lombardi, Murray, and Gerdes (2012) found interaction effects of first-generation student status and disabilities; first-generation college students with disabilities fared worse academically than other first-generation students without disabilities or continuing generation students with disabilities. Harley, Nowak, Gassaway, and Savage (2002) studied LGBT college students with disabilities and found that they were accommodated for their disabilities while being marginalized based on sexual orientation. More research on students minoritized by race, ethnicity, and nationality would be valuable additions, as would a deeper understanding of the ways gender interacts with disabilities in student identity development.

In terms of application, unlike students in some other minoritized groups, students with disabilities have legal protection not only from discrimination but also for reasonable accommodations necessary for them to participate in higher education. Section 504 of the Rehabilitation Act of 1973 mandated that postsecondary institutions open their doors to students with disabilities and provide them equal access to an education, including the support necessary for them to undertake that education. In 1990 the Americans with Disabilities Act (ADA) and the 2008 amendments expanded and clarified the civil rights of student with disabilities in higher education (Evans & Herriott, 2009), paving the way for continued support.

Yet abundant barriers remain for college students with all types of disabilities. Even where where strong institutional support services exist and campus climate welcomes the full diversity of students with disabilities, students must identify themselves to administrators, counselors, and/or faculty in order to obtain accommodations necessary to succeed in higher education. Not having a disability identity may hold some students back from seeking accommodations to which they are entitled and that might help them be most successful in college (Lightner, Kipps-Vaughan, Schulte, & Trice, 2012; Marshak, Van Wieren, Ferrell, Swiss, & Dugan, 2010). This phenomenon may be especially common among students with hidden impairments (for example, a student with an unapparent medical condition such as diabetes or epilepsy) (Valeras, 2010). These students may elect to "pass" as nondisabled rather than identify themselves within a minoritized group. For example, only two-thirds of students on the autism spectrum identify themselves as having a disability (Shattuck et al., 2014); the remaining third may never avail themselves of necessary support services, because they do not see themselves as being disabled.

It is critically important for all campus educators to be alert and knowledgeable about opportunities to inform disabled students of programs and services available to them, and to be as inclusive as possible in disrupting the disabling nature of many campus environments. Educators are in a position to break the silence around diverse impairments including mental health diagnoses, naming chronic illnesses as potential barriers to student success, and discussing the autism spectrum as a reality for many students. Being alert to the ways that campus policy, architecture, organization, and people create barriers for students of different abilities is another important role for student affairs educators. Understanding that "one accommodation does not (equally) fit all" is also important; an American Sign Language interpreter is no more helpful in the education of a deaf international student who speaks British Sign Language than the interpreter is to a visually impaired student. What helps a student with a learning disability succeed will be different from what a student using a wheelchair needs in terms of access to academic buildings.

Helping students understand the possibilities for disability identity is another valuable role. Introducing role models—other students, faculty, staff, or community members—can facilitate identity development and a sense of belonging to disability culture. Whether a student grew up with an impairment and has integrated that identity into their self-concept, or a student acquired an impairment shortly before or during college, the postsecondary setting may bring opportunities to revisit earlier stages of disability identity development or to encounter people and environments that prompt new ways of seeing the self in relation to ability, disability, and communities.

Discussion Questions

1. Students come to higher education with a range of abilities, some of which are legally considered disabilities. What are some categories of disabilities likely to be seen on college campuses?

2. How are disabilities constructed in society, and how can such constructions minoritize certain students and affect their holistic development?

3. What attitudes and conditions in higher education create obstacles to success for students with disabilities?

4. What resources on campus facilitate success for students with disabilities?

5. What are the six categories of disability identity in Johnstone's model? In this model, what is the difference between an identity imposed by others and one ascribed to self?

6. How are Johnstone's categories similar to and different from Davidson and Henderson's four sense-making clusters or repertoires found among students on the autism spectrum?

7. In Gibson's stage model and Forber-Pratt and Aragon's developmental trajectory model, what are the resting points and the catalysts for movement from one stage to the next?

8. How does an understanding of disability identity development facilitate the work of student affairs professionals in different contexts (for example, residence life, admissions, academic advising, orientation, multicultural affairs)?

9. Think of a student you have known with a disability. How does Johnstone's theory inform your work with students who are similar?

CHAPTER ELEVEN

SOCIAL CLASS AND IDENTITY

Sullivan et al. (2015) noted that, "Over the past four decades, wealth inequality has skyrocketed, with nearly half of all wealth accumulation since 1986 going to the top 0.1 percent of households. Today the portion of wealth shared by the bottom 90 percent of Americans is shrinking, while the top 1 percent controls 42 percent of the nation's wealth" (p. 5). These figures reveal a great deal about social class and resulting inequities, and have multiple implications when considering the tremendous disparities that shape wealth, income, health, and education. In this chapter, we differentiate between social class and socioeconomic status and share prevailing myths associated with social class. We then highlight social class identities in relation to the college environment and offer two theoretical perspectives for considering social class and its influence on college student development. We close with relevant research on college student experiences and social class and offer recommendations, critiques, and future directions for social class, social class identities, and college student development.

Defining Social Class

Social class "consists of a large group of people who share a similar economic and/or social position in society based on their income, wealth, property ownership, job status, education, skills, or power in the economic and political sphere in relation to those who have more and those who have less"

(Yeskel, 2008, p. 3). While related and often treated as synonymous concepts, social class differs from socioeconomic status. Socioeconomic status represents objective dimensions such as household income, occupational status, and educational status. Social class, on the other hand, "is an experience of shared economic circumstances and shared social and cultural practices in relation to positions of power" (Zandy, 1996, p. 8). Social class is socially constructed, fluid, subjective, and relationally bound. It represents the role of power dynamics in determining the "haves and have-nots" among various populations. While an individual's understanding of class is used to draw conclusions about others, it is important to note that the conclusions one draws about class status and oneself can significantly differ from one's "material conditions" (Sanders & Mahalingam, 2012, p. 114).

Social class has a profound effect on higher education, influencing who has access to college, which colleges individuals attend, whether or not college is affordable, and whether college is an option at all (Paulsen & St. John, 2002). It also affects the transition to college, determining college readiness, academic preparedness, and performance on standardized tests (such as ACT or SAT). Social class shapes classroom discourses as well, including the curriculum, course content, and pedagogical processes. Social class is everywhere, yet it remains understudied, some argue, because of identity politics that have shifted more toward race, gender, and sexuality (Kandal, 1996; Nesbit, 2004; Ostrove & Cole, 2003; Pearce, Down, & Moore, 2008). Social class also remains understudied due to the tremendous downplaying, silence, and invisibility that surrounds it (Borrego, 2003; Schwartz, Donovan, & Guido-DiBrito, 2009; Sanders & Mahalingam, 2012; Seider, 2008). Plainly stated, many people avoid discussions of class, deeming them a private matter (hooks, 1989; Ostrove & Cole, 2003; Zandy, 1996). In higher education, studying class and class inequities can prove challenging, especially when the system presumed to help reduce inequities is complicit in reproducing and reinforcing them (Fine & Burns, 2003; Martin, 2012; Yeskel, 2008).

To date, there are no specific theories regarding social class identity development among college students. Borrego (2003) argued that social class identity has been literally ignored and unexamined in student affairs. However, social class exerts a powerful influence on both how students develop and the choices they make in getting to and through college (St. John, Paulsen, & Carter, 2005). Moreover, social class influences the collegiate contexts in which development occurs. Yeskel (2008) offered a helpful discussion of social class identity:

> Social-class identity is based on the presence or absence of income (a yearly measure of money coming into your life), wealth (the amount of investment or ownership with monetary value

that has accumulated over time), status (relative social position or standing), and cultural capital (both who you know and what you know), in relation to those with more or those with less ... it influences how we feel about ourselves in relation to others who have more or less economically privileged positions. (p. 3)

Higher education contexts are relevant and appropriate spaces for examining class and class inequities (Langhout, Rosselli, & Feinstein, 2007). Ostrove (1993) stated, "For people who attend college, that context seems to be a very useful place to explore the psychological implications of class as people from a variety of social class backgrounds (as well as geographical regions, religious backgrounds, racial/ethnic groups, etc.) enter a common environment that is itself shaped by particular social class and regional mores" (p. 772). The college environment may be a useful place to explore social class, but Stewart and Ostrove (1993) argued that colleges, themselves, represent different social classes; thus aspects such as physical structures and buildings, types of courses taught, location, and focus could very well delineate a highly selective elite college from a community college. More specifically, scholars (Pearce et al., 2008; Green, 2003) reference colleges and universities as middle-class entities, which communicate and normalize middle-class values. Elite institutions are imbued with values that are more likely to create avenues for lucrative opportunities, networks, and prestige for their graduates—avenues not experienced by students at other types of institutions.

Those from low-income and working-class backgrounds are presumed to bring in values that differ from and conflict with higher education, while upper-class and more affluent students are rewarded because their values align with the institutional culture. Overall, individuals' social class can dictate how and whether they access college and thrive and succeed there. The more selective the college, the greater the likelihood that students from low-income and working-class backgrounds will face challenges, while those from middle and upper-class backgrounds will experience greater success (Aries & Seider, 2005; Lehmann, 2014).

Conversely, institutions can exert an influence on how students experience social class (Seider, 2008; Aries & Seider, 2005). For middle-class and more affluent students, college is an expectation and "the ultimate symbol of independence" (Stephens, Fryberg, Markus, Johnson, & Covarrubias, 2012). Stephens, Townsend, Markus, and Phillips (2012) explained that colleges and universities in the United States promote the value of *in*dependence. Such a value feels natural and normal for more affluent students who have also been socialized to embrace *in*dependence. Similarly, students from low-income families, with limited resources have likely had to conduct their lives based on *inter*dependent expectations and as a result may experience a "cultural mismatch" between their own *inter*dependent experiences and the *in*dependent push in the campus environment.

Myths Regarding Social Class

A number of myths govern discourses on social class. One myth is that the US is a classless society; thus individuals, regardless of income, adopt the title of "middle class" because it is a comfortable status that suggests neither overwhelming wealth nor extreme poverty (Ortner, 1998; Ostrove & Cole, 2003; Yeskel, 2008; Zandy, 1996). Matusov and Smith (2012) stated, "While working class folks are born in struggle for survival and upper class folks are born into native-born entitlement, middle class folks are born into the anxiety of not slipping back into the working class (or slipping out of their tenuous privilege status born from educational attainments)" (p. 279).

Another myth is that education serves as the "great equalizer"—the key to upward mobility—and is central to achieving a successful life (Ostrove, 1993; Martin, 2012; Yeskel, 2008; Fine & Burns, 2003; Walpole, 2008). Many believe that education has the singular power to place individuals on equal footing, ensuring access to any and all opportunities regardless of background. The third myth is that everyone has the same opportunities and begins at the same starting point. Unfortunately, this myth dismisses the fact that despite similar opportunities, there are a variety of factors ensuring that only some individuals can benefit from such opportunities (Yeskel).

A fourth myth is that issues of class are individual rather than systemic (Ostrove & Cole, 2003). This myth, rooted in meritocracy, is fueled by the simplistic idea that if individuals work hard and put forth their best effort, they will succeed and be rewarded. This myth fuels the notion that success is based upon individual talents, ambition, and drive. Those who succeed are deserving of their success because of the fruits of their labor, while those who are less successful are considered lazy or simply not to have worked hard enough (Adair, 2005; Ostrove & Cole).

Social Class Identities

In literature focusing on social class, authors typically reference "working-class" and "middle-class" students, statuses that sit toward the middle of the class continuum. Research on "low-income" students is usually associated with "first-generation" college students, while discussions of "affluent and upper-class" students receive only minimal attention.

First-Generation, Low-Income/Poor Students, and Working-Class Students

Given their complexity, no single definition captures what it means to be first-generation, low-income, or working class. Collectively, Borrego (2003) described these groups as "academic immigrants." Most often, low-income or working-class students are also first-generation students (Aries & Seider, 2005; Harackiewicz, Canning, Tibbetts, Giffen, & Hyde, 2014). First-generation students are those whose parents did not earn a college degree (Sáenz, Hurtado, Barrera, Wolf, & Yeung, 2007; Stephens, Townsend, Markus, & Phillips, 2012). Stephens et al. noted that first-generation students often have a more difficult time adjusting to college in comparison to their continuing-generation peers whose parents attended college. However, not all first-generation students are working-class or low-income (Borrego). A working-class or low-income background could be characterized as having "lack of power, limited cultural capital, economic vulnerability, and a low level of education" (Borrego, p. 3).

Adair stated, "The widening chasm between the economically stable and the poor is a gap most often predicated on the distinction between those who have an education and those who do not" (p. 222). Because educational status is often used as a predictor of social class (Harackiewicz et al., 2014; Hurst, 2007), individuals without a college degree are likely to earn less money, placing them in a lower-class status. Affordability plays a major role in whether college is even possible. Most first-generation, low-income, and working-class students view college as "financially prohibitive" (Schwartz, Donovan, & Guido-DiBrito, 2009, p. 51). Moreover, they have less information about the college-going process and have limited finances to support a college education. Research suggests first-generation, low-income college students may receive encouragement from their parents to attend college but limited guidance in navigating the process (Auerbach, 2004; Pascarella, Pierson, Wolniak, & Terenzini, 2004). Once they enter college, these students may experience it as an "alien" environment and have difficulties with adjusting to the exclusive culture of higher education (Orbe, 2008; Ostrove & Long, 2007). They rarely attend selective institutions; they earn lower grades and are less involved (Ostrove & Long, 2007; Pascarella et al., 2004).

How low-income and working-class people are constructed in the literature is not only limited but also rooted in hegemonic, masculine ideals.

Adair (2005) argued, "The working class is most often imagined as unmarked in terms of race and as consisting of families with male heads of household" (p. 824) who work hard, keep order, and exercise independence. This image is less than reflective of a reality in which women, while quite instrumental, are negatively racialized, treated as if their survival depends on male guidance, and chided for consistently making poor decisions.

Adair's (2001) work focuses specifically on women in college, particularly those who are low-income, welfare recipients, and mothers. She argued that for this population "the academy becomes a place of fear and diminished value, rather than a site of empowerment" (p. 234). Her emphasis on these women's college experiences is crucial, given that "the poorest families are headed by single mothers" (Adair, 2005, p. 820). Low-income women experience class anxiety, being demeaned and humiliated by faculty, and feeling devalued and underprepared. These feelings reflect a collegiate culture that communicates to low-income students in general that they do not belong in college—a sentiment contradictory to the belief that higher education is necessary for emerging from poverty or a low-income status.

Some working-class students view colleges and universities as foreign, alienating places and feel less secure about attending or navigating these institutional spaces (Aries & Seider, 2005; Borrego, 2003; Hurst, 2007; Langhout et al., 2007; Lehmann, 2014; Ostrove, 1993; Ostrove & Long 2007; Stewart & Ostrove, 1993; Stephens et al., 2012). These students often do not know the "rules" of the academy or how to strategically maneuver within academic spaces (Borrego). Moreover, Lehmann (2014) noted that for working class students, college can be "a period of profound confusion that includes feelings of inferiority vis-à-vis their well-traveled, better read, privately educated, well-spoken, articulate, and generally more privileged peers (and faculty)" (p. 3). These students must negotiate living in two conflicting worlds: the environment in which they grew up and the environment in which they are pursuing their postsecondary education (Lee & Kramer, 2013). As students attend college, embrace the idea that they do indeed belong, and gain a greater awareness of the culture and norms of their institution, they often find that these norms conflict with the cultural milieu and values that have shaped their worldview and relationships with family and friends. Hurst argued "those moving between the working class and the middle class through participation in higher education are faced with making a *choice* between loyalty to the working class or socially recognized success through bourgeois assimilation" (p. 83). When students ineffectively negotiate between these competing worlds, they may have an adverse reaction that could prohibit their college retention.

Middle-Class Students and Upper-Class/Affluent Students

Middle class status suggests that individuals have worked hard to attain their societal positioning and in many cases have used education to pave the way. Thus there is a desire to remain in this status or move up to greater affluence. For the middle class, moving down the class ladder is a transition riddled with anxiety, as moving in this direction is generally not a chosen option. "Class anxiety is the middle name of the middle class" (Matusov & Smith, 2012, p. 279). For middle- and upper-class students, class salience is often minimized, allowing them to avoid or (un)consciously ignore what those with fewer resources experience daily. Students with a low-income or working class status may experience feelings of exclusion at the expense of more affluent students, many of whom are taught to exert power over resources and space to which they feel entitled. Ostrove (1993) argued that affluent students use their class privilege to protect and maintain the status quo by isolating themselves from students they deem to have lower-class status.

"The lack of discourse—manifested as taboos restricting discussions of money or economic status—prevents economically advantaged individuals from critically reflecting on their privileges, rendering those privileges invisible, and further renders economically disadvantaged individuals mute and unable to discuss their lived experiences" (Sanders & Mahalingam, 2012, p. 113). While those hailing from more affluent backgrounds avoid discussions about social class, they also benefit from their class status in that they have access to more resources and information to make decisions that lead to increased successful outcomes. Not only do they possess more resources, they also can expect to receive "greater returns" on investment of these resources (Martin, 2012). These students usually have parents who attended college and can be more involved and influential in assisting these students in the college process; a significant difference from first-generation, low-income, and/or working-class families (Cabrera & La Nasa, 2001).

Theories of Class and Capital

As previously noted, theories that describe the developmental process of a class identity among college students, do not exist. However, some current theories can be useful for gaining a sense of the contexts in which development occurs and the inequitable structures that ultimately shape how individuals view their class identity. In this section, we share Bourdieu's theory of social reproduction and follow with Yosso's community cultural wealth theory and highlight studies in which these theories have been used.

Bourdieu's Theory of Social Reproduction

Pierre Bourdieu introduced a theory of social reproduction to explain enduring socioeconomic inequality. He argued that education is primarily responsible for legitimizing and creating hierarchies that both reward those at the top and disenfranchise those at the bottom. In other words, education creates, maintains, and reproduces inequality (Moi, 1991; Swartz, 1977). As Moi explains, "the function of the education system ... is above all to produce the necessary social *belief* in the *legitimacy* of currently dominant power structures or in others: to make us believe that our rulers are ruling us by virtue of their qualifications and achievements rather than by virtue of their noble birth or connections" (p. 1023).

Bourdieu described a range of concepts to explain social reproduction. Concepts in this chapter include field, habitus, and capital. "Field" is a term Bourdieu used to explain various spheres of social life in which individuals, from dominant and subordinated groups "play the game" of life in arenas such as education, sports, travel, music, economics, politics, and so on. All fields are in some way interrelated and "characterized by their own particular regulative principles" (Edgerton & Roberts, 2014, p. 195). Within each field, individuals compete for power using unspoken rules. Different social groups attempt to legitimize their preferences, tastes, and culture to exert power and prioritize what they value within a given field over all other groups. The desire to make one's group preferences the norm translates into capital that dominant groups can use to serve their own interests and needs (for example, creating and maintaining rules), while simultaneously delegitimizing the interests and needs of others (Moi, 1991).

The legitimacy of any given field is grounded in habitus. "Habitus" "is a system of lasting, transposable dispositions which, integrating past experiences, functions at every moment as a matrix of perceptions, appreciations, and actions" (Bourdieu, 2000, pp. 82–83). Habitus refers to the dispositions that compose one's worldview and behaviors within a given field. It describes the system of thought or cognitive schemas that govern how people's thoughts and actions translate within social relations to determine one's level of taste and practices that communicate a "class-specific lifestyle" (Joppke, 1986, p. 61). In other words, habitus is one's understanding and ability to define and enact rules of the game and represents the tacit norms that govern people's actions.

Bourdieu explicates three fundamental types of capital—economic, cultural, and social—that shape social class structures. These forms of capital are significant in that they can be strategically deployed in ways to increase one's status, wealth, and power in a world of competition over scarce resources. "Economic capital" refers to resources that are "immediately and directly convertible into money" (Bourdieu, 2002, p. 281). Economic capital influences all other forms of capital because it represents financial assets and money flow.

"Cultural capital" describes "cultural knowledge as a resource of power used by individuals and social groups to improve their positions in society" (Joppke, 1986, p. 57). It refers to an internal disposition toward cultural knowledge that is valued within society. Forms of cultural capital are not evaluated equally; some forms are more meaningful than others. All individuals have a particular disposition (the aforementioned habitus) toward accessing cultural capital. How individuals access cultural capital is predicated on what they acquire during their upbringing and their social class. For example, one's degree of cultural capital might shape postsecondary institutional choice and be the difference between selecting a community college versus a four-year state institution or more elite university. Such a decision would be based upon one's access to and knowledge of the college-going process. Cultural capital can also refer to externally derived material resources such as art, books, and talents, the products of which can be converted into economic capital. Individuals may be born into and/or socialized through processes that foster cultural capital. Cultural capital becomes institutionalized through symbols such as titles and academic degrees.

"Social capital" refers to "the aggregate of the actual or potential resources which are linked to possession of a durable network of more or less institutionalized relationships of mutual acquaintance or recognition" (Bourdieu, 2002, p. 286). Plainly stated, social capital consists of the resources individuals possess to form and maintain networks or participate and build relationships as members of a given social group (for example, based upon acquired credentials, the family to which an individual belongs, or affiliation with a particular school or other institution). The value of social capital depends upon the reach of one's network and the capacity of individuals to use membership to accrue greater rewards and resources (Portes, 1998). In a collegiate setting, such networks might include legacy students who have a long generational line of family members who previously attended an elite Ivy League institution. Another network might be affiliation with a sorority or fraternity on campus that benefits significantly from alumni giving. Overall, social capital is determined by one's level of connection—whether "material or symbolic"—with others and the amount of resources that can be accrued through the relationship (Dika & Singh, 2002, p. 33; Sobel, 2002).

These forms of capital are connected and mutually shaping in several ways. Edgerton and Roberts (2014) explained, "Economic capital affords the time and resources for investment in the development of children's cultural capital, which is associated with future educational and occupational success and, in turn, contributes to the accumulation of economic capital [which is] associated with greater social capital in that one's social network becomes broader, more influential, and more conducive to opportunity and further enhancement of one's other capital stocks" (p. 195).

Forms of capital not only shape one another but also can be exchanged or converted in given situations based upon what is or is not valued in society. For example, education is valued in society; thus becoming a schoolteacher is generally a respected occupation. However, becoming a schoolteacher does not translate into greater economic capital in comparison to a doctor or lawyer, because the medical and legal fields garner greater societal positioning. Thus doctors and lawyers might typically have larger networks (social capital) and greater income (economic capital). As a result, doctors and lawyers can use the forms of capital they possess to accrue increased capital. Bourdieu (1987) shared that collectively, the forms of capital create "symbolic capital;" that is, "the form the different types of capital take once they are perceived and recognized as legitimate" (p. 4). In other words, individuals within a social group must have mutual agreement regarding what is valued in the relationship. Thus capital is best understood in three dimensions: the amount of capital individuals possess, the factors that compose one's capital, and the capacity of the capital to help individuals transcend their position in society (Bourdieu, 1987). Overall, the relative level of capital and one's power to exercise and reproduce greater capital shapes how class structures get reified and further rooted in inequality and persistent inequities.

Bourdieu directly addressed the role of higher education in reproducing class structures. He argued that "the higher educational system is part of a more general theory of cultural transmission … that links knowledge, power, socialization, and education" (Swartz, 1977, p. 547). As a result, colleges and universities tend to give preference to the kind of cultural capital that is more readily available to middle-class and affluent groups rather than what is readily available to poor or working-class groups.

Given the popularity of Bourdieu's work, it has been used to frame studies related to college students and their experiences in postsecondary settings. Sanders and Mahalingam used Bourdieu's concepts of habitus and discourse to frame their study of class-based privilege among college students in an intergroup dialogue course. They analyzed 102 final papers from students enrolled in the course, which focused on social class. While the majority of students described having a greater awareness of class, the authors highlighted three themes prevalent in students' responses regarding why their class salience was low. First, students' class was often conflated with race and by what they saw in the media. For example, students of color who were also working-class were able to tease apart race and class distinctions, while White students who were middle class or upper class were less capable of doing so. Second, students wrote that conversations about social class were taboo and a personal matter. Moreover, students attempted to minimize social class, believing it inappropriate to point out that such differences exist between upper-class and working-class people. Third, students demonstrated low class salience to avoid association with negative stereotypes. For example, low-income students did not want to be pitied or perceived as less than, while upper-class students wanted to avoid perceptions that they were "spoiled" and "wasteful," given their privilege.

Martin's (2012) study revealed clear differences in campus involvement based on social class. Upper-class students were involved in a range of activities and had the financial means to participate in activities such as study abroad, while their middle-class counterparts were significantly less involved and spent more time working to pay for college. Martin suggested that cultural capital (or lack thereof) was central to how students from different social classes were involved on campus.

Grounded in Bourdieu's work on cultural capital and habitus, Lehmann examined how working-class students attain success in college despite the challenges embedded in the campus environment and found that these students were successful once they were more integrated into the campus environment, particularly through campus employment. Employment opportunities in residence life and in the admissions office as a tour guide were integral to students' success. The experiences offered by participants in his study countered the dominant narrative that working-class students always struggle in college and revealed how these students experienced college as a positive transformational experience in which they negotiated their working-class background with newer forms of understanding themselves, including their political views. Scholars also use Bourdieu's concept of habitus to examine the role of social class in college students' plans for attending college or delaying enrollment, as well as the influence of college on interactions between low-income students and their family and friends (Lee & Kramer, 2013; Wells & Lynch, 2012).

Yosso's Community Cultural Wealth Model (CCWM)

While Bourdieu's work is used in research both within and beyond higher education, it is not without its critics. Some researchers critique Bourdieu's perspective; others critique the use (or what they deem the misuse) of

Bourdieu's concepts (see Lamont & Lareau, 1988; Lareau & Weininger, 2003). One of the major critiques of Bourdieu's work mirrors an underlying assumption rooted in much of the literature on low-income and working-class students; that is, they enter college as "disadvantaged" or "lacking" in some capacity. As Lehmann (2014) articulated, these students may not have the financial means or in-depth knowledge of college, yet many experience success. Thus focusing on what students lack ignores the values and culture that working-class and low-income students take along as they enter college. Tara Yosso (2005) introduced a conceptual framework of community cultural wealth grounded in critical race theory to challenge the idea that "people of color 'lack' the social and cultural capital required for social mobility" (p. 70). While Yosso credited Bourdieu with offering a structural analysis of societal hierarchies and how they operate, she also challenged the narrow scope he used to describe assets and resources that are valuable in society. Moreover, she challenged the manner in which his work has been presented to suggest that communities of color are culturally deprived while predominantly White communities are culturally rich. She stated, "This interpretation of Bourdieu exposes White, middle class culture as the standard, and therefore all of the forms and expressions of 'culture' are judged in comparison to this 'norm'" (p. 76). Yosso outlined six forms of capital that compose community cultural wealth, as follows:

"Aspirational capital" defines an individual's capacity to remain hopeful and optimistic despite the presence of obstacles. It represents resilience and belief in the possibility of rising above one's current state and grasping hold of the possibilities of a brighter future. "Linguistic capital" refers to the ability to communicate in one or more languages. It also captures the growth in knowledge and in maneuvering social situations through the use of diverse languages and communication styles. Linguistic capital represents the richness of various communication forms (storytelling, oral history, and various art) that allow communities of color to communicate with a range of people. "Familial capital" comprises the various forms of knowledge individuals gain through interactions with immediate and extended family. These interactions are filled with "a sense of community history, memory and cultural intuition" (p. 79). Yosso likens familial capital to the idea of "pedagogies of home" because it represents "kinship" ties that extend into the community and fosters life lessons about education, surviving, responsibility, and consciousness. These life lessons serve as capital that contributes to and shapes students' ways of knowing.

"Social capital" refers to "networks of people and community resources" which serve as support mechanisms for students (p. 79). Social capital is important in helping them to negotiate their presence in academic spaces and processes (for example, completing a college application, applying for financial aid, choosing a college). "Navigational capital" comprises the skill set that students use to traverse diverse institutional settings, particularly those that are unwelcoming due to oppressive structures. Navigational capital "acknowledges individual agency within institutional constraints" (p. 80). It also recognizes the resilience of students of color who strategically foster success despite situations that place them in vulnerable predicaments. "Resistant capital" consists of "knowledges and skills fostered through oppositional behavior that challenges inequality" (p. 80). It involves disrupting the dominant and debilitating narratives that threaten communities of color. It also provokes conscious awareness of oppressive structures and enactment of forms of resistance (speaking out, counterstorytelling, building coalitions) to challenge them. Yosso contends that these forms of cultural wealth overlap and complement one another. Moreover, they are dynamic and constitute a strategy to challenge dominant discourses that shape social class, particularly notions of capital. Finally, community cultural wealth not only acknowledges class-based notions of inequality, but also recognizes the intersecting nature of classism and racism in society.

Yosso's work has been increasingly used in research on college students, particularly Latina/o students, to describe the forms of capital they use to negotiate access to higher education. Pérez Huber (2009) used the CCWM to frame her study of ten Chicana college students attending a major university. Participants in this study relied on familial, navigational, resistant, and social capital to navigate the racist and nativist terrains of their institutions. Liou, Antrop-Gonzalez, and Cooper (2009) used the CCWM to guide their study of college-going networks among Latina/o students at an urban high school. They found students used community-based organizations (social capital) to support their desire to attend college, particularly when they perceived their schools as failing to provide adequate information about college. Through their involvement, they received tutoring and mentoring. The students also used linguistic capital to seek out and foster relationships with high-achieving students of diverse racial backgrounds. The students used navigational capital, particularly their spiritual and faith-based connections, to practice resilience and access critical information about college. Luna and Prieto (2009) also found community cultural wealth to be central for Latina/o undergraduates who were considering graduate school. Through mentoring and support from family and community, the graduate school process was demystified and served as a pathway for the students to pursue graduate school.

Research

The research on social class and higher education is expanding. The review of literature that follows highlights some of the directions in which much of the research is going.

Retention, Attrition, Academics, Sense-Making of Identity

Hurst (2007) conducted an ethnographic study, spanning two years, in which she interviewed 21 working-class college students about their experiences in college and perspectives on social class. She placed the students' responses to social class on a continuum from "loyalists" to "renegades." Loyalists remained committed to and reaffirmed their working-class backgrounds as they negotiated the college culture and environment. They saw the structural oppression that governs class and attempted to resist the dominant status quo. Renegades adopted middle- and upper-class values and norms. They made sense of their working-class values through a deficit-based lens and attempted to relinquish their working-class background as a strategy toward upward mobility. Renegades believed that working-class people were dysfunctional and lazy. They expressed shame and frustration with working-class people and believed upper-class people had earned what they had through hard work. They bought into the belief that by acting middle class, they could achieve the American Dream. Loyalists, on the other hand were interested in getting an education to improve themselves and contribute to improving their familial and background conditions. They expressed pride in their ability to survive college and use their struggles as teachable moments. Hurst suggests that the stories of loyalists should not be viewed as good stories versus bad stories. Instead, Loyalists represented the promise of higher education to be a transformative space. Renegades represented "internalized classism." Through no fault of their own, these students are bombarded with convincing images in the media and elsewhere that communicate individualism and the promise of the American Dream, a story difficult to reject.

Aries and Seider (2005) examined how institutional type influenced the class-based identity of students, particularly low-income. Students who had at least one parent who went to college still faced financial obstacles and revealed marked distinctions between themselves and their upper-class peers. They expressed feeling inferior, powerless, and intimidated, and they shared concerns about how they articulated ideas, realizing "the language of home was often not the language spoken in the academy" (p. 427). They felt a sense of shame in discussing their parents' blue-collar occupation and their lack of cultural exposure through travel abroad. In their 2007 study, Aries and Seider (2007) found that social class background influenced students' post-college aspirations. Study participants from upper-class backgrounds who attended an elite private institution aspired to high-paying and powerful positions in law, medicine, and business. Low-income students at the same institution aspired to careers that would promote upward mobility, but these careers (such as, teaching) were not as lucrative when compared to their upper-class peers. Only a few of these students sought more lucrative positions. In the same study, none of the low-income students attending a state college aspired to lucrative careers, opting instead to be teachers and social workers or seeking entry-level positions in business and industry. The study participants were certain they would achieve their aspirations. However, their choices reified "the class system, not only in their anticipated positions, but also in the satisfaction they expressed with their specific goals … these students added a measure of legitimacy to the growing class divide in the US and through their college experiences, helped to reproduce that very class system" (Seider, 2008, p. 47).

Ostrove and Stewart (1998) studied the perceptions and consequences of class among a sample of Radcliffe College alumnae from the 1964 graduating class. Though these women had gone on to productive lives, they spoke vividly about how class shaped their experiences, noting that they felt the impact many years later. Study participants noticed the class stratification on campus. In particular, students from low-income backgrounds indicated that Radcliffe was their first opportunity to interact with someone from the upper class. The responses from women with a working-class background revealed the exclusion that some felt on campus due to cliques, while responses from women with upper-class backgrounds reflected how they consorted only with individuals who shared their class affiliation. Many mentioned feeling bad about the elitist and exclusive culture of the campus and how it made others feel inferior and less confident.

Engagement and Involvement

Martin's (2012) study of social class and student involvement at highly selective private universities revealed differences in levels of involvement among students from different social classes. He found that upper-class students entered these institutions and had immense involvement, while middle- and lower-class students were less involved and participated less in social activities such as Greek life, intramural sports, and study abroad, due to working part-time jobs to fund their education. As a result of fewer opportunities to get involved, these students were less satisfied with their experience. Martin's findings are similar to those of Walpole (2003), who found that students from lower-income backgrounds were less involved, tended to work during college, and were less likely to attend graduate school.

Stuber's (2009) findings also confirm that students with more affluent backgrounds had resources at their disposal before and during college to enhance their involvement in multiple activities including study abroad, Greek life, and internships. For example, upper-class students entered college with a disposition toward and belief in the value of involvement as a way to expand their social networks. Conversely, working-class students entered with fewer social networks and resources, which ultimately limited their involvement in comparison to upper-class students. Working-class students were involved with residence life and other leadership opportunities but were not as interested in study abroad opportunities. Their disposition was more closely linked to remaining near family, especially given that they had little travel experience. The major difference between upper-class and working-class students was that the former entered college with the assumption that involvement was important and necessary, whereas the latter did not readily view out-of-class activities as beneficial. Instead, they focused on earning good grades and working hard as the pathway to a successful future.

Belongingness

Ostrove (2003) conducted a study of 193 alumnae from Smith and Radcliffe colleges to examine how social class background influenced their perspectives of these elite institutions. In particular, she used social class as a framework to explore belongingness and alienation for women who attended Smith and Radcliffe. She found working-class and middle-class women experienced feelings of exclusion and felt academically underprepared in comparison to upper-class women. On the other hand, upper-class women felt as if they were continuing their family legacy. All of the women were aware of the looming class differences that shaped their college experiences. A later study by Ostrove and Long (2007) also emphasized the role of class in moderating students' sense of belongingness. Stating that race, class, gender, and ability have a strong relation to class and shape who belongs (as well as who does not belong), the researchers conducted a study of social class at a selective liberal arts college. Survey responses from their 324 participants revealed a strong relationship between social class and sense of belonging. In particular, this relationship correlated to students' "adjustment to college, quality of experience at college, and academic performance" (p. 381).

Intersections of Class, Race, and Gender

It is easy to proceed with an examination of class and forgo mention of other identities. One-dimensional analyses such as these rule out more critical and complex understandings of not only class but also other identities. "The psychological experiences of social class cannot be meaningfully understood outside of the context of race and other social identities with which class interacts" (Ostrove & Cole, 2003, p. 682). For example, Warr (2006) discussed how popularized notions of social capital fail to account for how capital is gendered. Social capital is presented as "inevitably positive, and rarely acknowledge[s] the ways in which it is likely to fortify economic privilege and exert exclusionary effects" (p. 500).

Ostrove and Cole (2003) discussed the intersections of class and race, noting that much of the terminology used to describe people is "class-coded," while language used to describe social class is "racially-coded" (p. 681). For example, "urban" typically equates to people of color and "rural" equates to White people, and in either case these individuals are likely working-class or poor. Similarly, a term like "undocumented student" suggests a person who is of color and poor, while a term like "sorority girl" suggests a woman who is White and middle or upper class and also has gendered implications. Attending to the intersections of identity is critical to understanding college student development.

It is impossible to discuss class without acknowledging its intersections with other identities. As noted, race and class are often simultaneously examined. One challenge to dissecting the obtuse nature of class deals with issues of racial divisions in the United States. "Class has been racialized, but class does not equal race" (Yeskel, 2008, p. 9). The racialization of class is rooted in the large number of racially minoritized people who are often disadvantaged in the system of social class. Yeskel (2008) suggested that it is further fueled by people—some poor, White people, in particular—who refuse solidarity and coalition building with people of color in the same social class due to their adoption of negative racial ideologies.

In general, class studies that address intersectionality are few and far between. Walpole (2008) noted that few studies focus on the role of social class in the college experiences and outcomes for African Americans. In her study, she found that low-income African American students were low on several indicators of college success, including low involvement, infrequent interactions with faculty, and lower grades than their peers. Nine years later, these students had "lower incomes, lower rates of degree attainment, lower aspirations ... and were less likely to have attended graduate school" (p. 237).

Similarly, Parks-Yancy (2012) found that low-income African American students rarely used university resources related to career development because they were unaware that such resources and interactions with individuals at these offices would be beneficial to achieving their career goals. The authors described differences in social capital between African American students and their White counterparts, who receive support, advice, and information about career management and also know to seek it out. Parks-Yancy encouraged college and university personnel to make information and resources more explicit to low-income African American students. Issues of race and class also collide for Black ethnic groups such as Haitians and others with Caribbean identities. Clerge (2014) stated, "The boundaries of race render black native and foreign-born individuals in the USA unassimilable and marginal despite their increasing class status" (p. 959). Thus, despite one's income level, one's racial identity will often be "stigmatized" as low-income or poor (Clerge).

In their study of five self-identified Mexican male college students, Schwartz, Donovan, and Guido-DiBrito (2009) touch on the intersections of class, ethnicity, and gender. They found four themes that revealed how participants experienced social class. First, students were aware of the "cultural rules" governing social class, such as demonstrating certain behaviors related to dress and language. They could also clearly delineate upper-class students by their material resources, wastefulness, and lack of appreciation for what they had. For the participants, working their way through school was necessary to support themselves and family. Similar to participants in Hurst's (2007) study, the men saw college as an avenue toward opportunities and as a way to give back to their families. Participants described the intersection of gender, ethnicity, and class in that their families expected them to succeed in order to provide for their immediate family and future family—an expectation different from that felt by Mexican women, who might have been pressured to stay home instead of attending college. Finally, despite many of the pressures participants faced, they remained optimistic about their future.

Implications for Social Class and Student Development

A developmental theme throughout these studies is change and stagnation. Students, regardless of their societal positioning, are likely to experience moments of development that facilitate personal change. Similarly, they also endure experiences in which growth is slow or nonexistent. For low-income and working-class students, a significant developmental process includes navigating one's background in an environment that often runs counter to the values embedded in one's upbringing. Similarly, a person's developmental trajectory can be linked to desires for class and social mobility for financial, personal, or familial reasons. Perhaps the largest implication for student development in relation to social class is the notion of *choices*. Early psychosocial theorists such as Erikson and Marcia discuss development in terms of choices, particularly vocational (see Chapter Thirteen; Matusov & Smith, 2012). "Constructing an identity involves occupational choice, but those choices are shaped by the people who are available in one's environment for identification as well as the work opportunities" (Aries & Seider, 2007, p. 138). In other words, social class has the potential to place boundaries on individuals' career aspirations and choices as well as the opportunities throughout life that shape these aspirations and choices. A more in-depth examination of such choices might reveal that *how* development is understood within theories is rooted in and reproduces middle-class values of making "smart choices" (Matusov & Smith).

Matusov and Smith (2012) argue that choices are the "capital" of the middle class and that schools operate as "a choice machine." They contend that while identity development is certainly about the choices individuals make, identity discourses manufacture the notion of choice to ensure that choices are not actually our own and that choices available to some are not available to others.

These authors suggest that identity is often treated as if it results from the choices people make. In other words, people *are* their choices. Yet there is a failure to recognize these choices are manufactured through structural inequality, which ensures that only certain groups of people have access to certain choices. Class inequality is reproduced to maintain stratification and inequitable differences between the lower and upper classes. The "smart choices" the middle class make keep them invisible and promote the myth of a classless society. "Although identity achievement involves choice, power and privilege are what dictates the choices one has" (Aries & Seider, 2007, p. 138).

Critique and Future Directions

One of the major critiques of social class research related to college students is that it tends to focus on White students. In attempts to understand students and the role of social class in their experiences, difficulties can arise because the dominant narrative tends to capture a White and often male experience. As a result, the voices of students representing an array of backgrounds get silenced in the research and discourse surrounding college, development, and social class. Moreover, emphasizing class alone ignores the complicated and intersecting dynamics that exist when race, gender, and sexuality as well as other identities are fully considered.

Another critique of the literature on college students and social class is the attention typically focused on low-income and working-class students. Currently there is a failure to consider the development (or lack thereof) of students who occupy a more affluent social class status. Surely there are opportunities to assist these students in understanding their class privilege and the ways in which they use this privilege, whether consciously or not, to oppress others.

A third critique of the literature is a focus primarily on Ivy League or elite institutions. While it is understood that the class culture permeating these institutions is critically important, it is also important to consider the operation of class and class inequality across institutional types. Moreover, considering intragroup class differences is important. For example, how do class differences play out within different racial groups? How do class differences operate within LGBT groups? In addition to differences, what similarities exist, and how does this information inform how students develop, particularly in terms of their class consciousness?

Student affairs professionals and educators play a tremendous role in fostering and facilitating student development. However, they are not immune to social forces grounded in social class. Educators often unintentionally promote classed discourses that value the middle and upper classes and discount working-class values. They also engage in exclusive behaviors and may unintentionally communicate that being included and involved comes with a cost. For example, the belief that T-shirts should be purchased to show solidarity among a residence hall floor or student groups is prominent on college campuses, as are potlucks and social gatherings where everyone is expected to contribute a dish. Professionals who oversee programs and other social opportunities should consider the class implications in this common practice, particularly the fact that some students may not be able to afford to purchase a T-shirt or contribute to a potluck. In addition, major opportunities to promote student involvement and engagement should be assessed to consider the differential impact that may be placed on students of different social class backgrounds with the understanding that costs as well as classed assumptions can make some students feel accepted, while others feel excluded.

Serving diverse students in college and helping them to develop successfully will require institutions and those working within them to focus less on changing students and forcing them to adapt to dominant social class mores and values. Instead, efforts must be directed toward creating a more welcoming environment that embraces individuals from different social class backgrounds. These efforts should be focused on increasing social class diversity among students at institutions to promote cross-class interactions and disrupt obstacles that prevent greater interactions between a diverse array of students (Park & Denson, 2013). "It is essential that colleges and universities develop programs that include innovative, responsive, and challenging curricula and a range of academic, cultural, and family supports" (Adair, 2001, p. 236). Moreover, such efforts must be geared toward disrupting structural barriers (for example, policies, norms, and taken for granted ways of conducting programs and services) that often exclude populations that are typically marginalized (for example, first-generation, low income, racially minoritized).

Educational leaders should also be proactive in acknowledging the invisibility of social class. Langhout et al. (2007) challenged institutions of higher education to create campus climates where classism and classist behaviors are unacceptable. Doing so requires bringing greater awareness of these issues. Schwartz et al. (2009) also suggested that student affairs educators facilitate dialogues about social class to break the silence surrounding this topic. They also recommended that institutions do more to get students involved by offering opportunities for involvement that also provide financial assistance for students who must work through college to support their education. Another suggestion was to create programs and initiatives that help students maintain familial ties as they get integrated into campus life. Most important, colleges and universities must do more to ensure that students are aware of all of the opportunities available on campus as well as helping students capitalize on these opportunities (see Duffy, 2007). Museus and Neville (2012) noted that institutional agents were essential in facilitating social capital for students of color. Their findings reveal the promise of student affairs educators in serving students across social classes. Based on what they found, it is important for professionals to share common ground with students, which means not only shared identities but also a willingness to learn about students' backgrounds and points of connection. Educators should provide holistic support by going beyond the call of duty and work genuinely to support students by acknowledging their humanity and fostering strong relationships with them. Finally, educators must be proactive and thoughtful about students' needs and how class can shape their futures, rather than being reactive. Doing so requires thoughtful and strategic communication with students and other diverse university constituents.

Discussion Questions

1. Define social class and discuss why it is important in higher education and how it can affect students who are first-generation, low-income/poor, working class, middle class, or affluent/upper class.

2. Name some of the myths surrounding social class and state why they need debunking. Why do these myths persist? How will you help disrupt these myths for students and colleagues?

3. Define Bourdieu's theory of social reproduction and specify Yosso's forms of capital that community cultural wealth comprises. In what ways do Bourdieu's and Yosso's perspectives diverge? What commonalities do you see? Use the forms of capital to provide examples of how social class differences are evident on your campus.

4. Discuss what the increasing literature on college students and social class is revealing about the college experience. How can these issues be addressed at your institution in and out of the classroom?

5. In what ways does social class hinder or encourage students' development in college? Explain with clear examples.

6. Social class is rarely discussed in public in the United States and U.S. higher education. How would you facilitate a program to shatter the myths around social class and discuss this difficult topic to increase understanding among colleagues and students?

7. Create a collage of how social class is experienced differently for students from different social class backgrounds. Ask a colleague from a different social class background to do the same and compare. What is the meaning of the differences and similarities that appear in your visual representations?

8. Examine your social class roots. How do they resonate with the theory discussed in this chapter? What social class aspirations for the future do you hold for yourself and your students?

CHAPTER TWELVE

EMERGING THEORETICAL PERSPECTIVES ON STUDENT EXPERIENCES AND IDENTITIES

There is no shortage of conversations, and there are likely multiple meetings, in which educators strategize to serve the increasingly diverse populations represented on their campuses. College and university professionals emphasize the implementation of programs and initiatives that will not only retain diverse students but also facilitate their identity development. In this chapter, we discuss the growing literature on "emergent" student identities and experiences in higher education. In particular, we highlight (1) digital, (2) national, (3) feminist, (4) student veteran, and (5) student athlete identities and experiences.

We reference these identities as "emergent" for several reasons. First, some of these populations, such as veterans and athletes, have existed on campuses for decades, yet little attention has been devoted to their identity development in a student affairs context. Second, the notion of "borders" is quickly redefining who has access to higher education. College students are no longer confined to "traditional age" borders wherein a specific generational cohort of 18-year-olds serves as the primary default for understanding development. Today, college students range in age, ethnicity, gender, and so on, and as such, the term "traditional age college student" is becoming obsolete. Moreover, our sense-making around "borders" is changing. Today's global context and the policies and transactions within it are swiftly allowing for cross-national transactions between students from diverse countries, prompting a discourse around national identities. Furthermore, technology is ultimately redefining borders and offering individuals the opportunity to think about themselves beyond a physical realm and embrace digital identities.

Currently, the student development literature is devoid of substantive information about the developmental trajectories associated with the identities we explore in this chapter. For some identities there is existing theory, but it is located in publication venues beyond the field of higher education. However, we provide a summary of available developmental theories. For other identities, no developmental theory exists, but we share relevant literature, which clearly boasts developmental implications.

Digital Experiences and Identities

Without question, college students of any age interact with technology on a regular basis to communicate, participate in social media, complete course assignments, and engage in digital recreation (for example, online gaming, streaming video, listening to music). Research on digital experiences and identities of college students is a rapidly growing field and one in which it can be difficult to keep up; indeed, some studies seem out of date before they are published online or (especially) in print. In this book, we consider students' digital environments as part of their developmental and learning ecologies. This section focuses on the specific topic of "digital identity," which we define as the ways students understand themselves in digital contexts, rather than the technical meaning of digital identity as the sum of one's online data (see Windley, 2005). We are concerned with how students understand the expression and construction of self online.

Traditional-age college students are well within the generation that Prensky (2001a, 2001b) dubbed the digital natives; adult learners belong to the group he called digital immigrants, because they have to enter the digital world as opposed to being born into and raised in it. Because Prensky did not base his original claims about digital natives and immigrants on empirical data, the concept has some substantial criticism (see Bennett, Maton, & Kervin, 2008), and debates continue about the extent to which so-called digital natives think and construct self differently from previous generations. Prensky (2009) argued these distinctions will become less relevant over time. Still, the concept that a generation of students has grown up with technologies that shape communication, self-presentation, and education seems to hold some weight with student affairs educators who see new behaviors—or old behaviors conducted in new, digital forums—on campus. Digital natives, many now old enough to be student affairs professionals themselves, grew up with, around, and in technologies that enable—perhaps even require—the maintenance of a digital presence through communication tools (for example, an email account or text message platform such as WeChat or iMessage), digital social media (Facebook, Twitter, Tumblr, Instagram), and online learning (the learning management system on their campus, whether classes are fully online, hybrid, or in person with resources stored online; research for assignments; class projects presented in online venues). To be sure, the digital native title does not equally apply to all, because social class, gender, and culture may play a role in students' pre-college experiences with and access to technology (Cleary, Pierce, & Trauth, 2006). Adult learners (so-called digital immigrants) and other students with less online experience than their peers may also come to college with different levels of comfort, facility, and motivation to explore digital identities (Hsu, Wang, & Hamilton, 2011).

A handful of researchers have examined how college students (typically those in the digital natives generation) construct digital selves. For example, Martinez-Alemán and Wartman (2008) conducted an online ethnography of Facebook to explore gender and ethnic identity on campus. Grasmuck, Martin, and Zhao (2009) studied "ethno-racial identity displays" on the same social media platform. Lee (2012, 2014, 2015) examined Facebook usage and outcomes among African American and Latino students. From each of these studies, interconnections among and mutual co-creation of psychosocial identities, their online expression, and stand-alone digital identities are so tight that it is impossible to separate them—as some scholars once attempted—into "in person" and "online" identities.

As we noted earlier, scholarship on online identities, and identities expressed online, is an area that is growing exponentially; it is nearly impossible to capture the field in a static source such as this book. There is not yet a consensus on whether the development of digital identities, per se, will become an area of scholarship; perhaps such a consensus will emerge and with it a theory to explain how students develop digital identities distinct from other identities. We advise readers interested in this area to follow scholarship emerging from such reliable sources as the Pew Research Center on Internet, Science, and Technology (www.pewinternet.org) and the non-profit EDUCAUSE association (www.educause.edu).

National Experiences and Identities

Students from the United States and international students in the United States have experiences and identities related to their nationality. Most scholarship to date has focused on the experiences of international students in the United States, and some on U.S. students studying abroad (Renn, Brazelton, & Holmes, 2014). Most of the former relates to students who come to the United States for full degree programs; most of the latter focuses on study abroad for a year, a semester, or less, in the context of a U.S.–based degree program (Renn et al., 2014). But there are also important elements of nationality related to undocumented students in U.S. colleges and universities, immigrant students, and students in their home countries attending a branch campus of a foreign institution (for example, an Emirati student at New York University's Abu Dhabi campus). We introduce scholarship and theory about these related—but distinct—concepts of national experience and identity.

National identity may not be especially salient for most White domestic students who are legal U.S. citizens and who study on a U.S. college campus, but racially and ethnically minoritized students and undocumented U.S. residents attending college in the United States may experience national identity differently. For example, Weisskirch (2005) found that Asian American and Latino students with high levels of ethnic identity did not see themselves as being "typical Americans" (p. 355). Some minoritized students may feel fully "American" but feel that students from other ethnic groups do not see them that way (Cheryan & Monin, 2005). Acculturation literature generally supports a bifurcation of ethnic and national identity, but it also points to some instances where ethnicity comes to be seen as part of national identity (see Gong, 2007). Regional differences in the distribution of ethnic communities may contribute to the sense of national identity inclusion or exclusion.

U.S. students of any ethnicity who study abroad may experience their national identity differently as they encounter other cultures, people of other nationalities, and people who have expectations about them as residents of the United States. Dolby (2004, 2007) explored U.S. students' "American" identities in the context of study abroad in Australia, and found among other things that students became aware of the distinction between the meanings of "United States" and "America," examined their feelings of patriotism, and questioned the dominance of the United States in a globalized society. Research on pre-service teachers (education majors intending to teach in K–12 schools) also indicates that U.S. students who study abroad experience their national identity in new ways (Malewski & Phillion, 2009; Walters, Garii, & Walters, 2009). More evidence is needed to create something like a model of how study abroad or other international experiences influence national identity development among U.S. students, but it is clear that these experiences do have some effect on national identity.

There is a growing awareness of "third culture kids" (TCKs in the literature on the topic) in higher education. These are individuals who, typically, have parents who are U.S. citizens and who grew up and took some or all of their K–12 education outside the United States in international schools (see Pollock & Van Reken, 1999). Pollock and Van Reken (1999) found that TCKs are highly adaptable, making themselves feel at home anywhere, adjusting easily, and moving often. Most research on TCK college students is currently based in counseling frameworks. After surveying conflicting literature, Fail, Thompson, and Walker (2004) concluded that TCKs' sense of belonging may be more about relationships than physical space. They found that TCKs may experience marginality, either "encapsulated" or "constructive," which sets them permanently apart from whatever culture in which they find themselves. In a study of 15 female TCK college students, Choi, Bernard, and Luke (2013) found that their research participants had three patterns of close friends—socially connected, emotionally connected, and functionally connected—describing friends respectively as playmates, nurturers, or resources. The development of TCKs' national, trans-national, or other identity in relation to citizenship and residence has not yet been the center of much research in higher education.

Undocumented students in U.S. higher education are constantly reminded that their national identity, which may be rooted in the United States, does not match their citizenship (see Pérez Huber, 2010). They may find themselves with what Torres and Wicks-Asbun (2014) called "in-between" identities as they negotiate postsecondary access, finances, and success. The larger context of public discourse related to immigration and the right to education for undocumented students keeps this issue at the forefront of media, politics, and campus climate in ways that are likely to contribute to heightened salience of national identities for these students.

Documented immigrants—including "1.5 generation" students who came to the United States as children and have grown up partly in the United States, partly elsewhere—make up a significant portion of students in higher education, and of adult learners at many community colleges in particular. Legal status contributes to a sense of national identity for these students (see Cebulko, 2014), as do language, culture, and family history (see Lee, Sleeter, & Kumashiro, 2015). Community colleges in many regions are the postsecondary home, or starting point, for immigrants from all regions of the world and all conditions—voluntary immigrants, refugees, and displaced people (see Tarrow & Raby, 2014). Higher education can be a location for acculturation and the construction of an "American" or a "hyphenated-American" identity as students come to understand themselves and their national identity/identities.

Finally, there is a growing literature on international students in the United States (Renn et al., 2014). National identity and acculturation are two areas within this literature, which also focuses heavily on language, adjustment, and mental health. Studies of international students may combine undergraduate and graduate/professional students, and sometimes these combine students from all nations in their sample. Many are small-scale qualitative interview studies, but there are also survey-based quantitative studies, usually based on a single campus. It is therefore difficult to build something like a theoretical model for the national identity development of international students in the United States. There are, however, some common themes relating to how international students adjust to living and learning in a new country. Reviewing acculturation literature vis-à-vis international students in Western countries, Smith and Khawaja (2011) identified stress and coping, cultural learning, and social identification perspectives. They further parsed stressors into language, educational (academic), sociocultural, discrimination, and practical stressors (for example, finances). The coping category in the literature includes "cognitive appraisal of life changes" (p. 705), responding to acculturative stressors, and underutilization of student counseling services. Buffers to acculturative stress include social support, friendships with co-nationals, and (more effective as a buffer) friends from the host country. The effects of being an international student on the student's own national identity during and after the degree program are much less well studied.

Theory on college students' national identity is an area that is likely to grow in the coming decade as higher education around the world becomes increasingly internationalized and globalized. The movement of students, scholars, and educational institutions across national borders—and the ways that technology renders distance and national borders increasingly irrelevant to one's identity—is likely to create new ways of thinking of self in a national and global context.

Feminist Experiences and Identities

In 1985, Downing and Roush introduced a model of feminist identity development for women. Noting the paucity of literature on women's development, particularly from a feminist perspective, the authors argued for a model that would capture the lived experiences of women while acknowledging the oppression they face in society. Given that women face gender discrimination,

Downing and Roush suggested that existing models of development on marginalized groups could be used to inform a model of women's development. They used Cross's (1971) Black identity development model (see Chapter Five) as a guide for women's identity because of its non-deficit-based emphasis on identity and its "heuristic value for the development of a model of positive feminist identity" (Downing & Roush, 1985, p. 698). In this section, we describe the five stages of the feminist identity development model.

Stage One: Passive Acceptance. In this stage, women lack awareness of the structural and systematic ways in which they experience gender-based oppression. Women do not accept the idea of discrimination as a reality in their lives and follow dominant male standards and expectations of womanhood. Women in this stage maintain a state of denial, and in doing so prevent interactions that might cause dissonance or challenge traditional, oppressive notions of womanhood. Women with a passive acceptance perspective embrace the idea of male superiority and think traditionally conceived ideas of womanhood are acceptable. Transition out of this stage is characterized by a sense of "readiness, a receptivity or openness to change or risk" (p. 698). This readiness is prompted by increased self-confidence and experiences that facilitate movement to the next stage.

Stage Two: Revelation. This stage occurs as the result of an experience or set of experiences that cause disequilibrium for women. Events such as "consciousness raising groups, realization of discrimination against female children, ending of a relationship, divorce, or denial of credit or job application" are all powerful enough to cause women to question their conventional understanding of womanhood (Downing & Roush, 1985, p. 698). While any of these events may be life-changing, a woman's readiness level will determine how she handles these crises in preparation to move to the next stage. Such events may occur simultaneously, or over an extended period of time, each with greater magnitude and depth, requiring women to change their outlook. The revelation stage is particularly difficult for women due to "perceptual distortions," or the ways in which women are socialized to distrust their perceptions and feelings. Furthermore, there are few national events of significance that have galvanized women to embrace a more critical and conscious perspective. In order to transition to the next stage, women must examine themselves, paying particular attention to how they contribute to the very system that oppresses them. The Revelation stage is an emotional period in which women feel angry, hurt, and guilty in recognizing the systemic nature of sexism. This stage is also representative of dualistic thinking and strongly held opinions, whereby women are placed on a pedestal and men are negatively viewed. While their actions and ideas may be externally perceived as strong and mature, internally, women in this stage are still grappling with negative ideas they have about women rather than reaching a point of affirming the positives associated with being a woman.

Stage 3: Embeddedness-Emanation. Women in this stage attempt to reconcile their deep desire for greater "gender consciousness" while also negotiating their intricate connection to dominant culture through marriage, motherhood, and career. In an effort to deal with these embedded relationships, women seek support mechanisms to express themselves. Support may come from various women's groups, attending events sponsored by the women's center, or taking courses focusing on women. All of these activities help women to develop bonds with other women and establish affirming relationships that reflect who these women wish to become. Emanation, the second phase in this stage, is characterized by women's willingness to accept more diverse perspectives. Women's understanding that emotional disdain alone is ineffective for disrupting the status quo prompts transition into emanation. It is also prompted by their desire to lose their prior selves and rise above the culture of disrespect for women that surrounds them. Women in this latter portion of the stage still interact with but have apprehensions about men.

Stage 4: Synthesis. This stage is characterized by women who positively view being women and value the qualities that their identity comprises. Women are able to move past traditional, oppressive ideas and make sound judgments about men that are not grounded in stereotypes. Women consciously acknowledge the challenges women face in society but also embrace the fullness of being women who have a positive self-concept.

Stage 5: Active Commitment. Women in this stage transition into a more cohesive and solid identity, which shapes their behaviors and actions toward changing the status of women in society. They practice a commitment to challenging the predominant narrative of gender roles and want not only to change society, but also use their knowledge and skills to educate others toward women's empowerment. As women mature, they experience a recycling through the various stages of this model, "each time experiencing the challenge of that stage more profoundly and using previously learned skills to work through the particular stage again" (p. 702).

How each woman moves through the stages in this model is inevitably shaped by her surroundings and the interactions she has with others. While Downing and Roush created their model based on the work of Cross, they also note similarities between the feminist identity development model (FIDM) and Erikson's work (see Chapter Thirteen) as well as Kegan's theory (see Chapter Sixteen). Since the creation of the FIDM, a range of studies have been conducted to examine feminist identity in relation to eating disorders, stress, self-esteem, and anxiety (Blue & Berkel, 2010; Carpenter & Johnson, 2001; Sabik & Tylka, 2006; Snyder & Hasbrouck, 1996), benefits of women's and gender courses (Bargad & Hyde, 1991; Eisele & Stake, 2008; Stake, Roades, Rose, Ellis, & West, 1994; Yoder, Fischer, Kahn, & Groden, 2007), sense-making and validation of feminism and feminist attitudes (Eisele & Stake, 2008; Fischer, Tokar, Mergl, Good, Hill, & Blum, 2000; Liss & Erchull, 2010; Liss, O'Connor, Morosky, & Crawford, 2001; Quinn & Radtke, 2006), and romantic partners (Backus & Mahalik, 2011).

Student Veteran Experiences and Identities

Student veterans are prominent on college campuses across the country. Vacchi (2012) describes this group as "any student who is a current or former member of the active duty military, the National Guard, or Reserves regardless of deployment status, combat experience, legal veteran status, or GI Bill use" (p. 17). The GI Bill of 1944 following World War II ushered these students to campus in mass numbers and provided several benefits including housing and education. The Post-9/11 GI Bill offers more expansive educational opportunities for college than previous versions (Rumann, Rivera, & Hernandez, 2011). DiRamio, Ackerman, and Mitchell (2008) noted that student veterans came to represent a unique population shortly following the Vietnam War, and their presence on campuses continues to increase. Despite the many veterans in pursuit of higher education, research on their experiences is limited. Earlier research focused mainly on academic performance and mental health issues (DiRamio et al., 2008). In the past several years there has been an increased interest among educators and researchers to examine how student veterans experience college, the capacity of institutions to support these students, and their transitional experiences particularly following deployment and combat (Ackerman, DiRamio, & Garza Mitchell, 2009; Demers, 2011; Elliott, Gonzalez, & Larsen, 2011; Jones, 2013; Mangan, 2010; Zinger & Cohen, 2010).

The bulk of current research focuses on veteran students and their transition experiences, and researchers use Schlossberg's transition theory as a framework (Goodman, Schlossberg, & Anderson, 2006; see Chapter Two). DiRamio et al. (2008) conducted a multicampus study to learn about the experiences of students who had served in the Iraq and Afghanistan conflicts. They were interested in exploring how these students transitioned from military to civilian life and more important, from "active duty to college student" (p. 74). They argued the usefulness of Schlossberg's theory because student veterans face a number of transitions, namely having one's education interrupted due to active duty deployment, especially combat, and then returning home to continue college. Such major life transitions can have a tremendous impact on how students navigate their identities in two extremely different contexts, but university administrators and leaders may not have a clear understanding or sound strategies to help students navigate transitions.

DiRamio et al.'s (2008) study of 25 student veterans yielded 16 themes, which the authors framed using Schlossberg et al.'s "moving in, moving through, and moving out" model (Goodman et al., 2006). DiRamio et al. found student veterans to be more mature than traditional-age, civilian college students. They were more willing to join the military due to their patriotic beliefs, the educational benefits, and family tradition. Though committed to service, the students experienced many interruptions and mentioned the toll it took in the continuing uncertainty in their education due to the prospect of being called up to service. As students moved through their military transitions, they dealt with significant experiences that were "astounding, horrifying, and gratifying" (p. 83). These experiences prompted their interest in continuing college. Moving out of the military was characterized by students' participation in military transition programs and the support they received, as well as dealing with their adjustment to life with family, college preparation, and college affordability due to limitations in military benefits.

Once the veterans arrived on campus, they dealt with finding ways to connect with other students there, because their experiences were vastly different. As a result, student veterans blended in and avoided calling attention to themselves. Finally, these students dealt with health concerns related to PTSD and other documented disabilities that affected their experiences. DiRamio et al. recommended that institutions take a holistic approach to serving student veterans, which includes identifying who these students are by creating a registry, providing an orientation to the campus and support services, assisting them with financial aid, providing a mentor or "transition coach," and offering counseling and advising services to promote student success.

Rumann and Hamrick (2010) also used Schlossberg's theory to examine the transitions of student veterans, post–war zone deployment. Their attention to identity for student veterans and to the complexities associated with making sense of one's identity, given the diverse contexts in which student veterans find themselves, is important for understanding this population. Rumann and Hamrick identified three role incongruities their participants faced: "military and academic life, the incompatibilities of lingering stress and anxiety with returning to college, and enacting aspects of the 'student' role during deployment and aspects of the 'military' role during college" (p. 440). While some participants drew no significant distinctions between college and the military, others dealt with stressors stemming from their deployment. Similar to DiRamio et al., students in this study exhibited greater maturity and believed their deployment was a motivating factor to complete college. They also dealt with negotiating relationships, as some friendships had drifted during deployment. Finally, students dealt with "identity re-negotiation." For example, they tried to make sense of how they were perceived by others when they wore their uniforms. Their uniforms made them feel different, but also as if they had accomplished something while deployed.

Several other studies focus on student veterans' experiences, but few pay particular attention to identity negotiation within the military and on campus. Identity development for student veterans is important given the context of college campuses versus the military. The college campus is not as structured as the military (Rumann et al., 2011; Vacchi, 2012). Moreover, the military places a high value on the roles and responsibilities of their members, and these roles may be underappreciated or misunderstood in a civilian context like college campuses. The military also teaches values of self-sufficiency, which may not translate on a college campus. Student veterans either feel uncomfortable seeking help or do not realize they need help because they learned to solve life-and-death issues in the military.

Intersectional experiences with race and gender also play a role in veterans' identity. Smith (2014) discussed the importance of intersectional perspectives in making sense of her campus experiences as a Black female veteran who was medically discharged. She discussed the silence, both in the military and on campus, surrounding intersectional experiences among veterans with multiple oppressed identities. With regard to gender, the military is perceived as having a masculine or macho atmosphere. For men, gendered expectations that play out in the military can affect their experiences on the college campus, particularly their psychological well-being and capacity to seek help (Alfred, Hammer, & Good, 2014; Livingston, Havice, Cawthon, & Fleming, 2012). For women, this type of environment may have prompted them to hide their "femaleness" and take on more masculine traits; such actions would not be expected in a campus environment (Baechtold & De Sawal, 2009; Vacchi, 2012).

Some student veterans come to college with physical impairments associated with their military deployment; others return to campus with learning impairments that were present prior to deployment (DiRamio & Spires, 2009; Elliott et al., 2011; Madaus, Miller, & Vance, 2009). However, these students are less likely to seek assistance (Burnett & Segoria, 2009; Shackleford, 2009). This may be because they do not want to face societal stigmas associated with disabilities and do not want to be perceived as incapable in any way (Burnett & Segoria). Aside from counseling centers and disability services, many campuses are not prepared to support these students, creating an unwelcoming, isolating, and oppressive campus environment. Branker (2009) suggested that institutions consider a universal design framework to assist student veterans with disabilities because, given the contributions of these students, the "constant threat and uncertainty" of combat should not be something they experience on campus (p. 60).

While the study of student veterans is a burgeoning area of research, Vacchi (2012) cautions against "mischaracterizations" suggesting that all student veterans have some form of impairment or that they all struggle with transitioning to college. Such ideas are presumptuous and limit the scope of how college campuses might serve this diverse student population. As campus services and support continue to increase, institutions may be recognized as "veteran-friendly," but seeking such status may prove unimportant to veterans who simply want a campus environment that has intentionally and thoughtfully developed programs, services, and support to facilitate their development and success (Vacchi).

Branker (2009) argued that for many service members turned students, college life is about seeking new purpose and reclaiming their adult lives, "lives they began in the military to become civil, productive and responsible citizens" (p. 60). In their study of student veterans, Vance and Miller (2009) found participants wanted opportunities to connect with other student veterans, avoid bureaucracy, receive accurate referrals for assistance, have an advocate to communicate their needs and assist them, and establishment of a centrally located office to seek services. Across the literature, scholars have offered recommendations for how student veterans should be supported. Many of these recommendations align with participants' voices in the Vance and Miller study.

Rumann and Hamrick (2010) suggested that colleges and universities collaborate with veterans' organizations to create seamless transition experiences. They also recommended that campuses provide opportunities for campus constituents to gain increased awareness of student veteran populations. This might include providing professional development for staff and speaking with veterans' representatives about what students need. Campus organizations for student veterans may also prove helpful for students' sense of belonging and provide opportunities to connect with other student veterans (Burnett & Segoria, 2009; Summerlot, Green, & Parker, 2009). Moreover, student veterans' organizations can serve as strong vocal advocates and provide information to students as they navigate campus. Students can also be valuable as participants in peer counseling programs to help new and returning veterans establish a sense of trust on campus (Church, 2009; Whiteman, Barry, Mroczek, & Wadsworth, 2013). Burnett and Segoria identified several collaborative efforts that should occur on college campuses. In addition to the aforementioned recommendations, they suggested collaboration between disability student services and the veterans services officer (VSO) on campus as well as connecting college and university faculty and staff with military backgrounds to current student veterans.

Student Athlete Identities and Experiences

The proper role of athletics in higher education—and particularly in revenue-generating sports at NCAA Division I institutions—is the subject of much controversy (see Clotfelter, 2011). Regardless of one's opinion in this debate, the reality that hundreds of thousands of college students participate in intercollegiate athletics requires that student affairs educators consider their experiences and identities in a developmental context. It is important to remember that the student athlete experience varies considerably across institutions and NCAA competitive divisions, which specify how institutions treat student athletes from the time they are considered as prospects through to the time they leave the institution (for details on these policies, see http://www.ncaa.org/compliance). And not all institutions are NCAA members, so there are student athletes competing in other contexts including community college leagues. An emerging literature centers the development of college student athletes as a topic for research that can be used to guide practice, whether one works primarily with student athletes or with a general or specific (for example, students of color, LGBTQ students, fraternity/sorority members) student population that includes student athletes. In this section we provide an overview of this literature.

The foundation for much research on athletic identity in collegiate and noncollegiate settings lies in the work of Brewer and colleagues (Brewer & Cornelius, 2001; Brewer, Van Raalte, & Linder, 1993). Brewer et al. (1993)

defined athletic identity as "the degree to which an individual identifies with the athlete role" (p. 237). They developed and tested a 10-item Athletic Identity Measurement Scale (AIMS), which Brewer and Cornelius (2001) revised into a seven-item scale. The AIMS (original and revised) is widely used in studies of college students across cultures and contexts, including women's colleges and HBCUs (see Mignano, Brewer, Winter, & Van Raalte, 2006; Steinfeldt, Reed, & Steinfeldt, 2010; Visek, Hurst, Maxwell, & Watson II, 2008). The AIMS contains three first-order factors: social identity ("I consider myself an athlete"), exclusivity ("Sport is the most important thing in my life"), and negative affectivity ("I feel bad about myself when I do poorly in sport") (Brewer & Cornelius, 2001). These factors subordinate to one higher-order athletic identity factor. The AIMS is not a developmental model; it is a measure of athletic identity at one point in time. Researchers have used it to understand student athletes' career planning (see Cox, Sadbury, McGuire, & McBride, 2009; Lally & Kerr, 2005; Navarro, 2014) and to illuminate athlete identities in relation to other identities (for example, gender: Steinfeldt & Steinfeldt, 2012; Steinfeldt, Steinfeldt, England, & Speight, 2009; race: Beamon, 2012; Bimper, 2014; Harrison, Sailes, Rotich, & Bimper, 2011).

The AIMS is also useful in understanding the developmental ecology of college student athletes. For example, Weight, Navarro, Huffman, and Smith-Ryan (2014) compared varsity student athletes to students participating in lifetime fitness courses at the same universities. They found that students who were not intercollegiate athletes indicated more ability to pursue university opportunities; among student athletes, those in revenue-generating sports (for example, football, basketball, ice hockey) indicated even less ability to do so than did students in non-revenue-generating sports. Student athletes scored higher on measures of achievement striving, teamwork, leadership, valor/ bravery/courage, and perseverance. But nonathletes who had participated intensely in sport before college scored similarly to college student athletes, indicating that these personality constructs may be established before college. So even a one-time measure of athletic identity, conducted across subpopulations, may provide some information about student athlete development.

The extent to which student athletes at the collegiate level have already established their identities as athletes prior to college, and what—if any—influence college has on that identity, is not known. We believe it is reasonable to assume that at the most competitive levels of intercollegiate athletics, students come to college with strong athletic identities, like the ones that Weight et al. (2014) found. They also found that former student athletes entered college with strong athletic identities, though what happens to the identities of students who are no longer formally involved in competition is not known. Given the importance of sport in the personal experiences of student athletes—and continued physical activity in the experiences of students who are not intercollegiate athletes—we believe that research on the development, maintenance, and evolution of athletic identity among college students is warranted.

Future Directions

In this chapter, we highlighted five emergent identities and experiences related to college students, campus environments, and development. We are certain we could have identified several more populations that are either invisible in the student affairs and higher education literature or simply treated as invisible on college campuses. We chose to focus on these particular identities given the current contexts of society and our campuses. The developmental literature on these identities is limited, as is the role of the campus in shaping these identities. More research is needed to provide more robust perspectives on college student development for these diverse populations. Overall, more substantive attention needs to be directed to the aforementioned groups as well as others that could be deemed "emergent." Such attention could be directed toward research that broadens understanding of how these different identities develop, as well as how they intersect. Researchers and educators might ask, what might we better understand about the intersections between digital identity and feminist identity, and what are the developmental implications for a student who possesses these identities? How might research findings (current and future) inform the creation and implementation of initiatives designed to promote and support development? In general, we encourage readers to think critically about the wide range of identities present on campus and consider how they might contribute to increasing, enhancing, strengthening, and, in some cases, challenging our limited knowledge of "emergent identities."

Discussion Questions

1. What characterizes a digital native? How do these characteristics interact with the college environment to shape development?
2. What should student affairs and other postsecondary educators consider in creating environments for learning and development that include students from different digital generations? How can higher education be inclusive of learners from all digital generations?

3. For domestic and international students, how does national identity shape the college experience in the United States, and how does the college experience in the United States shape national identity?

4. How do international education experiences influence national identity?

5. What features of U.S. postsecondary education interact with national identity for documented and undocumented immigrant students? For Third Culture Kids (TCKs)? For international students?

6. Name and describe the five stages of Downing and Roush's feminist identity development model (FIDM). In what ways is the FIDM similar to and different from other stage models of minoritized identity development?

7. What milestones mark student veterans' experiences on campus?

8. How do veterans' multiple dimensions of identity influence their experiences?

9. What are the three constructs of the Athletic Identity Measurement Scale (AIMS)?

10. How do the AIMS constructs contribute to overall athletic identity?

PART THREE

PSYCHOSOCIAL, COGNITIVE-STRUCTURAL, AND INTEGRATIVE DEVELOPMENT

Regina is several weeks into her graduate assistantship in Multicultural Student Affairs. She now has an established relationship with the 16 students for whom she is the primary multicultural affairs advisor. To offer a range of experiences, her supervisor has assigned her students in all four undergraduate classes, with majors ranging from art to chemical engineering. While she finds the work exciting, she is amazed at the diversity of the students with whom she works. For example, Marisela and Vijay, both first-year students, are wondering if they can make it in college and have no idea what they will major in, while some of the older students, including Rudolfo and Anita, are already talking about internships to help them decide if the career direction they have chosen is going to work out for them. Two of the seniors, Mariama and Andre, recently made life commitments to their partners and are considering how they will balance their committed relationships and career plans.

Regina has also noticed that students don't think about these issues in the same way. One of her students, Luisa, expects Regina to tell her what to do and assumes there is one right answer for every question. Another student, Paul, doesn't seem to want to have anything to do with her and declares to anyone around him that his answers are as good as anyone else's, including Regina's. A few of the older students, especially Isabel and Mike, appear to be able to weigh the pros and cons of their decisions and are willing to adjust their perspectives when they encounter new information.

Making sense out of moral issues is another area in which Regina has noticed differences among her students. In processing a recent situation in which a student in their first-year seminar was charged with plagiarizing a paper, one student, Nikki, stated that rules are rules and the student should be punished for his actions. Another student, LaToya, jumped to the defense of the charged student, feeling sure that he did not mean to hurt anyone through his actions. A third student, Les, wanted to know more about the situation before making any judgments.

In making decisions, for example, her students often seem to be influenced by their emotions and the people around them, rather than just using cognitive reasoning processes to decide what to do. For example, Regina has had numerous discussions with Andre regarding his plans for the future. A consulting company on the East Coast has offered Andre a lucrative position that his partner and his parents are urging him to take, but he has set his heart on using his marketing degree to work for a nonprofit organization devoted to assisting indigenous people in Central America develop their own businesses. Logical thinking does not appear likely to help Andre make this decision.

The lockstep nature of many of the stage theories bothers Regina as she considers how to think about these students. The process for her students does not seem to be that orderly. "Life" frequently gets in the way of moving smoothly along a clear developmental path. LaToya, for example, just learned that her father lost his job when the small business he worked for declared bankruptcy. The family was already stretched financially to afford college for their two children, and LaToya works 20 hours a week at two jobs—a work-study job on campus, another one off. LaToya was set to graduate with honors next year and planned to go on to graduate school in social work, but now she isn't even sure if she can come back to school next semester. At the beginning of the semester, LaToya seemed to have everything under control; now she often bursts into tears at unexpected moments and can't seem to concentrate on anything. Regina is at a loss as to how to support her during this difficult time.

Another aspect of the psychosocial and cognitive structural theories that bothers Regina is their strong focus on internal processes. What about the environment? She really liked the idea that development is fostered through interactions between the person and the environment, but none of the theories she has studied so far talk much about the role that the environment plays in the developmental process. Her student Devon, who is a student-athlete, comes to mind. The athletic department seems to have a strong influence on his decisions, and Regina thinks they do not always have Devon's best interests in mind. For example, Regina believes that Devon really should be doing an internship related to his major next summer, but he is being advised by his coaches to stay in town and work out with the team. Devon has a shot at starting next year and does not want to displease his coaches. Regina's advice seems to carry little weight in comparison to that of his coaches and teammates.

◆ ◆ ◆

Part Three, "Psychosocial, Cognitive-Structural, and Integrative Development," includes theories that expand understanding of student development to include psychological changes in students' lives, how they make meaning, their thinking processes, their moral reasoning and decision making, and a number of developmental aspects (cognitive and affective) that occur individually and simultaneously.

Psychosocial theorists examine the *content* of development; that is, the important issues people face as their lives progress, such as how to define themselves, their relationships with others, and what to do with their lives. Not all issues are equally important throughout a person's life. Rather, development takes place across the lifespan within a series of age-linked sequential stages. In each stage particular issues, called developmental tasks, arise and present compelling questions that must be resolved (Erikson, 1959/1980). Each new stage occurs when internal biological and psychological changes interact with environmental demands, such as social norms and roles expected of individuals at certain ages in particular cultures. How successful the individual is in developing appropriate coping skills influences resolution of developmental tasks. Regression to earlier stages, readdressing of developmental tasks, and relearning of coping skills frequently occur when individuals find themselves in new and stressful situations (Erikson, 1968). Psychosocial theories are helpful in understanding the issues facing individuals at various points in their lives.

The first chapter in Part Three, Chapter Thirteen, "Psychosocial Identity Development," begins with an examination of Erik Erikson's (1959/1980) theory of psychosocial development. We then discuss the work of theorists who followed him, specifically examining identity development of men (Marcia, 1966) and women (Josselson, 1978/1991, 1996). Chickering's theory of identity development, the first major theory to specifically examine the development of college students (Chickering, 1969; Chickering & Reisser, 1993), follows next.

"Epistemological and Intellectual Development" is the focus of Chapter Fourteen. Rooted in the work of Piaget (1952), cognitive structural theories examine the process of epistemological and intellectual development during the college years. These theories focus on *how* people think, reason, and make meaning of their experiences. In this approach, the mind is thought to have structures, generally called stages. These structures act as sets of assumptions by which persons adapt to and organize their environments. They act as filters or lenses for determining how people perceive and evaluate experiences and events. Cognitive structural stages arise one at a time and always in the same order. The age at which each stage occurs and the rate of speed with which the person passes through it are variable, however. Each stage derives from the previous one and incorporates aspects of it; thus each successive stage is qualitatively different from and more complex than the stages before it. As individuals are exposed to new information or experiences that create cognitive dissonance, they first attempt to incorporate the new data into their current way of thinking (assimilation). If the new information cannot fit into the person's existing structure, a new, more complex structure will be created (accommodation) (Wadsworth, 1979). Piaget (1952) stressed the importance of neurological maturation in cognitive development but also noted the significant role played by the environment in providing experiences to which the individual must react. Social interaction with peers, parents, and other adults is especially influential in cognitive development.

In this chapter, we examine Perry's theory of intellectual and ethical development, the first cognitive structural theory to focus on the intellectual development of college students. Then we present two cognitive structural theories whose authors incorporated and built upon the work of Perry. We first discuss the work of Belenky and her colleagues (1986), who studied women's ways of knowing, demonstrating that the cognitive development process of women in their study differed from that of the men who served as research participants in Perry's initial study (1968). Finally, we focus on the reflective judgment model of Patricia King and Karen Kitchener (1994), who examined how individuals respond to ill-structured problems—problems that have no clear solution.

Chapter Fifteen, "Moral Development," includes an overview of the work of Lawrence Kohlberg (1976) as well as a discussion of two theorists who expanded theory about moral reasoning. James Rest and his colleagues (Rest, Narvaez, Bebeau, & Thoma, 1999) developed the Defining Issues Test, an instrument to assess moral reasoning level, and refined Kohlberg's theory based on their research. Carol Gilligan (1982, 1993) introduced the idea of gender-related moral reasoning based on the concept of care rather than Kohlberg's concept of justice. Knowledge of students' reasoning processes will help student affairs professionals understand students' decision making with regard to their own lives as well as their interactions with others.

A criticism of many of the aforementioned theories is that they separate the developmental process into discrete categories: cognitive, moral, psychosocial, and so forth. In conducting research and considering this criticism, several researchers recognized that affective, cognitive, and interpersonal processes are intertwined in student development. They urged an integration of these processes into more holistic theories of development and change.

In Chapter Sixteen, "Development of Self-Authorship," we highlight the work of Robert Kegan, who was among the first to write about integrative developmental processes. In examining the meaning-making process, he argued that both cognitive and affective components are involved (Kegan, 1982, 1994). He also viewed the evolution of meaning-making as involving changing interpretations of the relationship between the self and others, thus bringing the interpersonal dimension into play in the developmental process.

We then examine Marcia Baxter Magolda's (1992) theory of epistemological development, which was based on interviews with both male and female students over a four-year timeframe and included gender-related patterns of meaning making. The later work of Marcia Baxter Magolda (for example, 2001, 2007, 2008), who continued a longitudinal study of development in young adulthood, led her to the conclusion that three processes are involved in student development: (1) an epistemological, meaning-making component; (2) an intrapersonal dimension—how individuals view themselves; and (3) an interpersonal component—how interactions with others influence how individuals see themselves (Baxter Magolda, 2001). The goal of development in her approach, self-authorship, integrates these factors in a way that enables individuals to take control of their lives and decisions.

CHAPTER THIRTEEN

PSYCHOSOCIAL IDENTITY DEVELOPMENT

Psychosocial theorists examine the *content* of development; that is, the important issues people face as their lives progress, such as how to define themselves and their relationships with others, and what to do with their lives. Not all issues are equally important throughout a person's life. Rather, development takes place across the lifespan within a series of age-linked sequential stages. In each stage, particular issues, called developmental tasks, arise and present compelling questions that must be resolved (Erikson, 1959/1980). Each new stage occurs when internal biological and psychological changes interact with environmental demands, such as social norms and roles expected of individuals at certain ages in particular cultures. Resolution of developmental tasks is influenced by how successful the individual is in developing appropriate coping skills. Regression to earlier stages, readdressing developmental tasks, and relearning coping skills frequently occur when individuals are placed in new and stressful situations (Erikson, 1968).

Psychosocial theories are helpful in understanding the issues facing individuals at various points in their lives. In this chapter, we present theories based on the research of Erik Erikson, James Marcia, Ruthellen Josselson, and Arthur Chickering and Linda Reisser. We provide a background on the theories and associated research. We also discuss the application of these theories and share critiques and future directions for students' psychosocial development.

Erikson's Identity Development Theory

Erik Erikson (1959/1980, 1963, 1968) was the first clinical psychologist to address the identity development journey from adolescence through adulthood. He placed the developing person in a social and historical context and addressed the influences of significant others and social institutions across the life span (1959/1980), going beyond earlier theories that focused only on childhood. Basing his research on Freud's psychoanalytic perspective of individual development, Erikson opined that both external environments and internal dynamics influenced development (Widick, Parker, & Knefelkamp, 1978). Erikson's perspective on development is grounded in the *epigenetic principle*: "Anything that grows has a ground plan, and ... out of this ground plan the parts arise, each part having its time of special ascendancy, until all parts have arisen to form a functioning whole" (Erikson, 1968, p. 92).

Erikson (1968) described eight stages of development, each distinguished by a *crisis*, or "turning point," that individuals resolve by balancing the internal self and the external environment. While the concept may suggest otherwise, a crisis is not necessarily a negative experience. Instead, it serves as a catalyst for development. A crisis represents an experience or set of experiences that prompt developmental changes. How individuals negotiate developmental changes will shape how they grapple with later life encounters.

The first four stages of Erikson's theory capture childhood and one's transition into adolescence and emerging adulthood. The fifth stage represents the basis of identity development. The remaining three stages represent the culmination of adulthood.

Stages One through Four

Stages One through Four encompass early childhood development into early adolescence. In *Stage One: Basic Trust versus Mistrust*, children develop and maintain trust levels and learn the process of reciprocity with family and caregivers. In *Stage Two: Autonomy versus Shame and Doubt*, children explore their environments and rely on encouragement from caretakers to help them build confidence. In *Stage Three: Initiative versus Guilt*, children's schooling experiences begin and they engage in more extensive social interactions. They also begin to determine socially acceptable behaviors, which entails accepting responsibility and possibly guilt as a result of their decisions. In *Stage Four: Industry versus Inferiority*, children continue to expand beyond the sole influence of their parents and have multiple interactions with other adults and children at school. Children work toward developing a "sense of industry," where they master different skills to feel a sense of competency (Erikson, 1959/1980). Collectively, how children advance through these stages shapes their transition into adolescence and early adulthood. Positive experiences such as the establishment of trusting relationships, opportunities to explore and build a sense of confidence, engaging with diverse others, and feeling supported while also contributing in some way are critical building blocks toward healthy identity development. When children lack trust in and support from adults, teachers, and peers, they may enter adolescence and early adulthood without the necessary tools to develop a strong sense of self.

Stage Five: Identity versus Identity Diffusion (Confusion)

Stage Five: Identity versus Identity Diffusion represents a watershed moment in Erikson's theory (Marcia, 1993a, 1993b). It signals a transition between childhood and adulthood and a push to define oneself. Marcia's (1966) identity statuses and Josselson's (1978/1991) theory of women's identity development, which we discuss later in this chapter, flow from this fifth stage in which adolescents begin to develop their core sense of self. They become more independent, as they experience the complexities of life and discover answers to the question, "Who am I?" Côté and Levine (1987) explained four criteria to describe an identity crisis. First, individuals should have reached a certain point in their cognitive development. Second, they should have experienced puberty. Third, they should be physically presenting adult characteristics. Fourth, they should feel mounting societal pressures to define their identity.

Individuals may struggle with role confusion as they delineate between how others see them and how they view themselves. Those who experience struggles with developing their core sense of self may feel confused or insecure about themselves and their relationships. Erikson (1959/1980) labeled this state "identity diffusion" to represent the point when individuals lack a clear sense of self or purpose. When they have no clear understanding of their role in life, they may over-identify with others who have been influential in their lives and demonstrate intolerance toward those they view as unfamiliar or different. Erikson (1959/1980) stressed that identity "connotes both a persistent sameness within oneself (selfsameness) and a persistent sharing of some kind of essential character with others" (p. 109). Identity is ever-changing from birth to death, but as each crisis is successfully resolved, commitment to an established identity becomes stronger. Identity formation embodies "commitment to a sexual orientation, an ideological stance, and a vocational direction" (as cited in Marcia, 1980, p. 160).

Stages Six through Eight

Stage Six: Intimacy versus Isolation represents the first of three that Erikson (1959/1980) identified as adulthood. Adults work toward establishing committed relationships and friendships, as well as severing unhealthy relationships. Adults need a strong sense of identity to foster strong relationships. Otherwise they may have difficulty connecting with others, leading to emotional stress or isolation. In *Stage Seven: Generativity versus Stagnation*, adults reach a midlife point during which they are concerned with generativity or cultivating the next generation, which includes raising children, mentoring, and contributing to one's community. They contribute to society and determine their legacy by directing energy toward productive life activities. However, lack of a strong identity could result in stagnation and withdrawal from others.

Stage Eight: Integrity versus Despair emerges in late adulthood, a time when adults age and experience significant body and mental changes. They examine their lives and reflect on choices, failures, and successes. Those who established a strong sense of identity are pleased with their lives and have little regret. They experience a sense of integrity, which Erikson (1959/1980) defined as "the acceptance of one's own and only life cycle and of the people who have become significant to it as something that had to be and that, by necessity, permitted of no substitutions" (p. 98).

Marcia's Ego Identity Statuses

Erikson's stages are hard to study empirically. Grounding his research in Erikson's stage theory, psychologist James Marcia (1966) was the first to create a "prototype of needed empirical study" (Widick et al., 1978, p. 11) on the identity development of young adults. Focusing specifically on the identity versus identity diffusion stage, Marcia (1966, 1975, 1980) introduced identity statuses to explain how young adults experience and resolve crises. There are two critical variables in identity formation: *exploration (crisis)* and *commitment*, which occur in the contexts of political, religious, and occupational decision-making (Marcia, 1980). Marcia's research had been primarily based on the experiences of white men. Schenkel and Marcia (1972) added sexual decisions as a fourth context and incorporated women in their study.

Exploration (Marcia, 1980) involves questioning values and goals defined by parents or other authority figures and weighing various identity alternatives. Individuals seek resources and advice from knowledgeable others (teachers, friends) to explore their options (Waterman & Archer, 1990). Exploration can begin with excitement and curiosity, but as pressures mount, fear and anxiety may prompt the need to reach a resolution (Waterman & Archer, 1990). *Commitment* refers to attaching ownership to pronounced choices, values, and goals (Bilsker, Schiedel, & Marcia, 1988), about which individuals are confident and optimistic.

Marcia (1966) identified four identity states, or ways of handling crisis and commitment, though Erikson never endorsed the statuses (Marcia, 1993a). Marcia (1980) stated, "The identity statuses were developed as a methodological device by means of which Erikson's theoretical notions about identity might be subjected to empirical study" (p. 161). The statuses offer additional ways to understand how individuals within the identity versus identity diffusion stage resolve identity crisis (Marcia, 1980). Unlike Erikson's stages, Marcia's identity statuses are not progressive or permanent. Both healthy and unhealthy choices shape how crises are resolved. Marcia's (1966, 1980) identity statuses include foreclosure, moratorium, achievement, and diffusion.

Foreclosure (No Crisis/Commitment)

In this status, individuals accept parental values and experience few crises because authorities direct their path. Some were raised in a homogenous environment with little exposure to diversity and no encouragement to challenge the status quo. They may also shy away from attempts to go in a direction different from authorities in their lives; this reluctance could result in their failure to establish a true life purpose (Waterman & Archer, 1990). As long as they have strong authoritative influences in their lives, individuals will remain in this status. Dealing with major life experiences in the absence of authority can cause major challenges, due to their inability to adapt and handle a crisis on their own. Individuals in this status follow the rules, maintain conventional relationships, and typically demonstrate inflexible thinking (Marcia, 1994). Marcia (1994) explained that foreclosure is the most common identity status and usually occurs prior to other statuses. However, it is important to note the statuses do not occur in a specific order.

Moratorium (Crisis/No Commitment)

Moratorium is the "most engaging among the statuses" (Marcia, 1994, p. 75). Individuals question parental values in order to form their identity; however, their crisis or exploration comes without commitment. They are seen "either as sensitive or anxiety-ridden, highly ethical or self-righteous, flexible or vacillating" (Marcia, 1980, p. 161). The vacillating occurs as they grapple between resistance and conforming to authority and "can generally be expected to move into Identity Achievement" (Marcia, 1989b, p. 289; 1994). Out of the four statuses, individuals experience moratorium for the shortest period, during which they exhibit high moral sensitivity (Marcia, 1980).

Identity Achievement (Crisis/Commitment)

Achievement status comes after an extensive period of crisis (exploration) in which individuals sort through alternatives and make crucial choices that lead to strong commitments in setting goals and establishing a firm foundation (Crocetti, Rubini, Luyckx, & Meeus, 2008; Schwartz, Zamboanaga, Luyckx, Meca, & Ritchie, 2013). Individuals in this status experience more crises than in other statuses because their identity foundation is secure enough to investigate multiple alternatives, engage in risk-taking, and clearly articulate choices (Marcia, 1994). Achievement is viewed as the healthiest psychological status indicating successful navigation of Erikson's Identity vs. Identity Diffusion stage (Marcia, 1980, 1994).

Diffusion (No Crisis/No Commitment)

In diffusion, individuals either refuse or are unable to firmly commit and have not experienced significant crisis. In other words, their exploration of life choices has been limited primarily due to their lack of interest (Schwartz et al., 2013). They simply "go with the flow," taking no account of consequences

FIGURE 13.1. MARCIA AND JOSSELSON'S STATUSES

	Search/Exploration	No Search/Exploration
Commitment	Identity-Achievement (Marcia) Identity Achievements: Pavers of the Way (Pathmakers) (Josselson)	Foreclosure (Marcia) Foreclosures: Purveyors of the Heritage (Guardians) (Josselson)
No Commitment	Moratorium (Marcia) Moratoriums: Daughters of the Crisis (Searchers) (Josselson)	Diffusion (Marcia) Identity Diffusions: Lost and Sometimes Found (Drifters) (Josselson)

(positive or negative) that may affect them personally. Submitting to external, rather than internal authority, they also tend to conform, have difficulty with intimacy, are easily manipulated, and lack cognitive complexity (Marcia, 1989b, 1994; Waterman & Archer, 1990).

Josselson's Theory of Women's Development

In 1971, Ruthellen Josselson set out "to understand the internal and developmental roots of identity formation in women" (1978/1991, p. 33). She explored the internal differences among the four identity statuses described by Marcia (1966) to explain why some women resolve their identity crisis while others avoid creating identity or fail to move beyond crisis. Over a three-year period, Josselson gathered data from 60 randomly selected women college seniors between 20 and 22 years of age from four different colleges and universities and reported their experiences in her book, *Finding Herself.* Curious about the accuracy of her predictions for these women after 10 years of presenting and examining her findings, she conducted follow-up studies of 30 women from the original study (Josselson, 1996). Her research spanned 22 years as she observed their development unfold from age 21 to age 43 (Josselson, 1996). She interviewed the women in three phases; as college seniors, during their thirties, and during their forties. In her follow-up study, which was published in the book *Revising Herself,* Josselson (1996) was especially concerned with two things: how women "revise their lives as they grow from late adolescence to mature adulthood" and how changes in societal ideas regarding gender roles affected "women who were coming of age in the midst of such wrenching changes" (p. 5).

Josselson explained the following patterns that she identified in two studies. Each identity status reflects the original pathway she assigned in her 1978 study; the designation given in her 1996 publication follows in parentheses.

Foreclosures: Purveyors of the Heritage (Guardians)

In this pathway, women graduate from college with identity commitment but have experienced no identity crisis. They make choices with little doubt or questioning of messages received during childhood and adopt standards about sexual morality, occupation, and religion based on parental beliefs (Josselson, 1978/1991). Women interviewed 12 years later still exhibited foreclosure patterns and were unable to imagine a life different from their childhood. Josselson described them as "hardworking, responsible, and capable" (1978/1991, p. 60). Their careers represented a "preoccupation with the care of others" but their main focus was "in their private worlds" (Josselson, 1978/1991, p. 59). These women sought security in relationships, chose partners who shared their perception of family life, and were psychologically tied to the centrality of family. When interviewed in their forties, these women had experienced important changes such as allowing themselves freedom to explore new opportunities, albeit in a restricted manner. Sometimes they did not experience crisis until their thirties or forties as they reflected on why they did not engage in more exploration and risk-taking. Ultimately, they were able to find the inner strength to move beyond boundaries without crumbling to pressure (Josselson, 1996).

Moratoriums: Daughters of the Crisis (Searchers)

The moratorium state is an unstable time of experimenting and searching. After internalizing family values, these women are convinced of the rightness of these values, but upon learning of other legitimate ways of being, are pulled into a tailspin. Many who remain in moratorium at the end of college are caught in identity conflict and need additional time beyond college to resolve the conflict by continuing to search, regressing to a previously prescribed self-identity, or moving on to identity achievement (Josselson, 1996).

In college, women on the moratorium pathway indicated they had overprotective mothers. Most did not consciously want to be like their mothers, yet they were closer to their mothers as adults than any other identity-status group. While rejecting identification with their mothers, they idealized their fathers, who represented a romantic notion of strength and success. More than any other group, women in moratorium dreamed of reaching amazing accomplishments in the future, such as discovering a cure for cancer.

Following college graduation, these women remained in a state of exploration and uncertainty. During the next decade of their lives, they searched for a suitable life pathway. By midlife, most had some semblance of a path and slightly resembled identity achieved women. The difference is that women in moratorium maintain a sense of ambivalence and uncertainty about their lives. "Revision over the course of life for these women has often been focused on tempering impossibly high standards for themselves in the face of which they could only feel inadequate" (Josselson, 1996, p. 141). As they progressed, these women realized their lives were not as they imagined, but they appreciated who they became.

Identity Achievements: Pavers of the Way (Pathmakers)

In this pathway women break the psychological ties to their childhood and form separate, distinct identities. During adolescence, they create identity after considering who they were and who they want to become. Rather than experience major crisis, many test their options internally. They want to feel pride in themselves rather than external affirmation of their worth.

Interaction with others outside the family, such as teachers and peers, serve as opportunities to explore without fully abandoning the old self. As traditional college students, they are likely to be saddened by the psychological separation from parents. As adults, they mature and relationships become primary. They structure relationships based on partnership needs rather than societal expectations and balance among work, relationships, and interests.

By the end of college, some were dissatisfied with their career choices and initiated change by obtaining work opportunities that promoted a more harmonious identity. Although this may seem inconsistent with identity achievers, other research (see Schenkel & Marcia, 1972) has demonstrated "that for women occupational identity is less predictive of overall identity status than is ideological and interpersonal identity" (Josselson, 1978/1991, p. 101). In short, once they commit to who they are in relation to others, occupational identity becomes a way to express the self. The success of women in this status is their ongoing capacity to construct their identity. They move through their lives despite the anxiety engendered by new challenges and continue to use their experiences to revise themselves (Josselson, 1996).

Identity Diffusions: Lost and Sometimes Found (Drifters)

Marked by lack of crisis and commitment, college women on this path are a varied and complex group. Evidence suggests that they score lowest among the four identity status groups "on all measures of healthy psychological functioning" (Josselson, 1978/1991, p. 140). Little is known about why women in this status experience difficulty, but one commonality among them is a tendency to withdraw from challenging situations (Bourne, 1978a, 1978b).

When interviewed as college seniors, women in identity diffusion were a diverse group who demonstrated diverse patterns. Some experienced psychological trauma and were "unable to make identity commitments because of the instability and unreliability of their capacity to organize and integrate their experiences" (Josselson, 1987b, p. 142). Some felt conflicted about life choices and perplexed by complicated philosophical questions about the meaning of life. Others drifted through life waiting passively for someone else to take over.

As women with diffused identities graduated from college, they still had little sense of direction—a condition still present 20 years later. As they reached their forties, they had a more stable life, due to either decisions they made or decisions made for them by others. However, they were "still very much anticipating that their real lives will yet begin and are starting over, hoping for better outcomes" (Josselson, 1996, p. 144). Their families provided the most stability for them throughout life. As they aged, their outlook became more realistic, although they continued to optimistically seek options that would make the difference.

Chickering's Developmental Vectors and Educationally Influential Environments

In his theory of psychosocial development, Arthur Chickering (1969) provided an overview of the developmental issues faced by college students and identified environmental conditions that influence development. Building on Erikson's discussion of identity and intimacy (1959/1980), Chickering saw the establishment of identity as the core developmental issue with which college students grapple. Resolution of a number of issues contributes to a person's growing sense of identity, allowing the person to successfully address concerns arising later in the developmental process. Chickering also identified key aspects of the college environment that influence development and suggested ways to enhance student growth. Chickering's theory has been widely used in student affairs since its introduction in 1969. It has been instrumental for extensive research as well as practical application.

Chickering's theory was first outlined in his landmark book *Education and Identity* (1969). The theory is based on research Chickering conducted between 1959 and 1965 while he was employed at Goddard College (Thomas & Chickering, 1984). At Goddard, Chickering was responsible for evaluating the impact of innovative curricular practices on student development. He administered 16 hours worth of achievement tests, personality inventories, and other instruments to students at the end of their sophomore and senior years. He also asked selected students to keep diaries of their experiences and thoughts and conducted detailed interviews with other students. He began writing *Education and Identity* in 1963 in an attempt to provide a conceptual framework for his findings as well as other research that had been conducted on college students.

Chickering targeted faculty in the preparation of his book to provide them with ideas for the organization of educational programs to enhance student development more systematically (Thomas & Chickering, 1984). In fact,

Chickering noted, "student affairs professionals as an audience were not in my mind at all ... it was entirely by chance that *Education and Identity* made a significant contribution to those professionals" (Thomas & Chickering, 1984, p. 393). As a result of invitations during the late 1960s and early 1970s to speak to professionals in student affairs, Chickering learned about the field that would come to have the most impact on his later thinking and would do the most to implement his ideas in practice (Thomas & Chickering, 1984).

Working with Linda Reisser, Chickering revised his theory to incorporate new findings from research. The revised edition (Chickering & Reisser, 1993) adhered to the basic premises of the original work but included 90% new material (Schuh, 1994).

The Seven Vectors

Chickering (1969) proposed seven vectors of development that contribute to the formation of identity. He used the term *vectors of development* "because each seems to have direction and magnitude—even though the direction may be expressed more appropriately by a spiral or by steps than by a straight line" (p. 8). In other words, the progression is not necessarily linear. He called these vectors "major highways for journeying toward individuation" (Chickering & Reisser, 1993, p. 35). Chickering noted that students move through these vectors at different rates and may deal with issues related to more than one vector at the same time, that vectors can interact with each other, and that students often find themselves reexamining issues associated with vectors they had previously worked through, a process of recycling. Although not rigidly sequential and not intended to be stages, vectors do build on each other, leading to greater complexity, stability, and integration as the issues related to each vector are addressed. Chickering's work takes into account emotional, interpersonal, ethical, and intellectual aspects of development.

Developing Competence Chickering and Reisser (1993) likened competence to a three-tined pitchfork, with the tines being intellectual competence, physical and manual skills, and interpersonal competence. The handle of the pitchfork, necessary if the tines are to do their work, is "a sense of competence [that] stems from the confidence that one can cope with what comes and achieve goals successfully" (p. 53). Intellectual competence involves acquisition of knowledge and skills related to particular subject matter, development of "intellectual, cultural, and aesthetic sophistication" (Reisser, 1995, p. 506), and increased skill in areas such as critical thinking and reasoning ability. Physical competence comes through athletic and recreational activities, attention to wellness, and involvement in artistic and manual activities. Interpersonal competence includes skills in communication, leadership, and working effectively with others.

Managing Emotions In this vector, students develop the ability to recognize and accept emotions, as well as to appropriately express and control them. In addition, students learn to act on feelings in a responsible manner. Chickering's (1969) original theory focused on aggression and sexual desire. His more recent work addresses a more inclusive range of feelings including anxiety, depression, anger, shame, and guilt, as well as more positive emotions such as caring, optimism, and inspiration.

Moving Through Autonomy toward Interdependence This aspect of development results in increased emotional independence, which is defined as "freedom from continual and pressing needs for reassurance, affection, or approval from others" (Chickering & Reisser, 1993, p. 117). Students also develop instrumental independence that includes self-direction, problem-solving ability, and mobility. Finally, they come to recognize and accept the importance of interdependence, an awareness of their interconnectedness with others. Chickering's revised theory places a greater emphasis on the importance of interdependence. To underscore this change, he and Reisser renamed this vector, which was previously titled "developing autonomy."

Developing Mature Interpersonal Relationships This vector, which in the original version of the theory was titled "freeing interpersonal relationships" and followed the "establishing identity" vector, was placed earlier in the sequence to acknowledge that experiences with relationships contribute significantly to the development of a sense of self (Chickering & Reisser, 1993). The tasks associated with this vector include development of intercultural and interpersonal tolerance and appreciation of differences, as well as the capacity for healthy and lasting intimate relationships with partners and close friends. Reisser (1995) noted that both tasks "involve the ability to accept individuals for who they are, to respect differences, and to appreciate commonalities" (p. 509).

Establishing Identity Establishing identity builds on the vectors that come before it. In Chickering's revised theory, this vector took on added complexity to acknowledge differences in identity development based on gender, ethnic background, and sexual orientation. Identity includes comfort with body and appearance, comfort with gender and sexual orientation, a sense of one's social and cultural heritage, a clear self-concept and comfort with one's roles and lifestyle, a secure sense of self in light of feedback from significant others, self-acceptance and self-esteem, and personal stability and integration (Chickering & Reisser, 1993).

Developing Purpose This vector consists of developing clear vocational goals, making meaningful commitments to specific personal interests and activities, and establishing strong interpersonal commitments (Chickering & Reisser, 1993). It includes intentionally making and staying with decisions, even in the face of opposition. The term "vocation" is used broadly to refer to paid and/or unpaid work within the context of a specific career or more generally as a person's life calling. Lifestyle and family influences affect the decision-making and goal-setting processes involved in developing purpose (Chickering & Reisser). The establishment of a secure identity will ultimately influence one's life purpose. Similarly, one's level of integrity is precipitated by a sense of identity and purpose in life.

Developing Integrity This vector includes "three sequential but overlapping stages" (Chickering & Reisser, 1993, p. 51): humanizing values, personalizing values, and developing congruence. First, students progress from rigid, moralistic thinking to the development of a more humanized value system in which the interests of others are balanced with one's own interests. Next, a personalized value system is established in which core values are consciously affirmed and the beliefs of others are acknowledged and respected. In developing congruence, values and actions become congruent and authentic, as self-interest is balanced by a sense of social responsibility (Chickering & Reisser).

Educationally Influential Environments

From 1964 to 1969 Chickering served as director of the Project on Student Development in Small Colleges (Thomas & Chickering, 1984). The data he obtained from studies of 13 dissimilar small colleges across the country focused on the influences of the college environment on development and were incorporated into the latter half of *Education and Identity*.

Chickering (1969) argued educational environments exert powerful influences on student development and proposed seven *key influences* (Chickering & Reisser, 1993):

Institutional Objectives Clear and specific objectives that personnel pay attention to and use to guide the development of programs and services have a powerful impact. They lead to greater consistency in policies, programs, and practices while making evident the values of the institution. Students and other constituencies are then able to agree with or challenge these values.

FIGURE 13.2. CHICKERING AND REISSER'S VECTORS

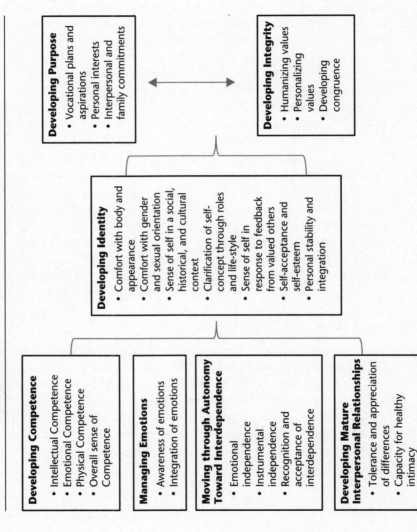

Objectives can influence the emphasis given to each vector and, therefore, the educational outcomes for students (Chickering & Reisser).

Institutional Size Chickering and Reisser (1993) argued "as the number of persons outstrips the opportunities for significant participation and satisfaction, the developmental potential of available settings is attenuated for all" (p. 269). They express concern about redundancy, wherein people become superfluous because of excessive numbers, resulting in fewer opportunities for personal development.

Student-Faculty Relationships Extensive and varied interaction among faculty and students facilitates development. Students need to see faculty in a variety of situations, which helps students perceive faculty as real people who are accessible and interested in them beyond the classroom. Chickering and Reisser (1993) identified four components of positive student-faculty relationships: accessibility, authenticity, knowledge about students, and the ability to communicate with students.

Curriculum A curriculum that recognizes individual difference, offers diverse perspectives, and helps students make sense of what they are learning is critical to foster development. In regard to selecting content, Chickering and Reisser (1993) recommended making it "relevant to students' backgrounds and prior experiences" (p. 362); recognizing "significant dimensions of individual differences between students" (p. 364); creating "encounters with diverse perspectives that challenge pre-exiting information, assumptions, and values" (p. 365); and providing "activities that help students integrate diverse perspectives, assumptions, [and] value orientations" (p. 367).

Teaching For development to occur, teaching should involve active learning, student-faculty interaction, timely feedback, high expectations, and respect for individual learning differences. Such teaching strategies affect cognitive development in the form of active thinking and integration of ideas. They also encourage interdependence, cooperation, and interpersonal sensitivity (Chickering & Reisser, 1993).

Friendships and Student Communities Chickering and Reisser (1993) noted, "A student's most important teacher is often another student" (p. 392). Meaningful friendships and diverse student communities in which shared interests exist and significant interactions occur encourage development along all seven vectors. Communities may be informal or formal groups. For the greatest positive benefits, the community should "[encourage] regular interactions between students," "[offer] opportunities for collaboration," be "small enough so that no one feels superfluous," "[include] people from diverse backgrounds," and "[serve] as a reference group" (Chickering & Reisser, 1993, p. 277).

Student Development Programs and Services Collaborative efforts by faculty and student affairs professionals are necessary to provide developmental programs and services. Chickering and Reisser "recommend[ed] that administrators of student programs and services redefine themselves as educators and refer to themselves as 'student development professionals'" (p. 278). They noted the importance of student development staff serving as advocates for "the education of the whole student" (p. 427).

Chickering and Reisser (1993) also introduced what they termed *three admonitions* (not to be confused with the seven key influences) that underscore the creation of educationally powerful environments:

Integration of Work and Learning Since most students today work as well as take classes, collaborative relationships are needed between business, the community, and institutions of higher education that will maximize the developmental potential of work and volunteer experiences (Chickering & Reisser).

Recognition and Respect for Individual Differences Chickering and Reisser (1993) stated, "It is clear that diversity will only increase in the years ahead. It is also clear that if we are unable to deal with it, we are likely to face increasing conflict, a two-tier society, and economic stagnation" (p. 473). Educators must be cognizant of the different backgrounds and needs of their students and adjust their interactions and services to address these differences.

Acknowledgment of the Cyclical Nature of Learning and Development Learning involves periods of differentiation and integration, equilibrium and disequilibrium. New experiences and challenges provide opportunities for new perspectives and more complex understanding to occur. Chickering and Reisser (1993) cautioned, "signs of discomfort and upset are not necessarily negative. On the contrary, they often signal that developmentally fruitful encounters are occurring, that stimuli for learning are at work" (p. 479).

Research

The bulk of research related to psychosocial maturity and identity development stemming from Erikson's (1959/1980, 1963, 1968) theoretical framework was conducted between 1950 and 1970. This research examined late adolescent men at prestigious colleges from an Eriksonian perspective and generalized the findings to women. Although Marcia's identity statuses have been the dominant topic of research on ego identity since the 1970s, with over 500 studies in existence (Bourne, 1978a; Kroger & Marcia, 2011; Marcia, 1994), little research has been conducted on women's psychosocial identity in general and even less research has been conducted using Josselson's work as a theoretical base. The research on Josselson's theory was conducted by the researcher herself in earlier studies (for example, Josselson, 1973, 1978/1991, 1982, 1987b). As noted later, most of the recent research on psychosocial identity development is based on findings from student populations in countries other than the United States. Research using Chickering and Reisser's vectors is also available, but again, the most recent findings are quite limited and somewhat outdated. In this discussion of research, we highlight investigations based on Marcia's and Josselson's identity statuses and Chickering and Reisser's vectors. Because some of the research discussed in this section was conducted much earlier, readers should use extreme caution in applying the results to today's students and collegiate contexts.

Research Involving Marcia's Identity Statuses

Research on Marcia's identity statuses has extended over 40 years (Kroger & Marcia, 2011; Marcia, 1994). Researchers have focused their efforts on determining whether the identity statuses as defined and measured by Marcia are robust enough measures of Erikson's identity stages. In addition, extensive research has examined the relationship of identity status to other psychological variables and outcomes. According to Marcia (1999), "These four identity statuses have become something like a psychological map for researchers" (p. 395). At least four scholars (Bourne, 1978a; Marcia, 1980; Matteson, 1975; Waterman, 1982) have given extensive consideration to the abundance of research on the identity status paradigm. Others have used the identity statuses to frame research in the following areas noted by Marcia (1993c): "personality characteristics of the identity statuses, developmental aspects of the statuses, gender differences, and cross-cultural studies" (p. 22).

More recent scholarship has emerged regarding the identity statuses and their relationship to adult development (Clark-Plaskie & Shaw, 2014; Marcia, 2002); barriers that affect ego identity status formation (Yoder, 2000); college drinking behaviors (Bentrim-Tapio, 2004); race, ethnicity, and gender (Alberts & Meyer, 1998; Branch, Tayal, & Triplett, 2000; Miville, Darlington, Whitlock, & Mulligan, 2005; Sanchez, 2013; Yip, Seaton, & Sellers, 2006); sexual identity (Archer & Grey, 2009); spiritual identity (Leak, 2009); political bias (Linvill, 2011); and the role of friendships on psychosocial development

(Jones, Vaterlaus, Jackson, & Morrill, 2014). In particular, Marcia's work has been highly influential in the development of Phinney's (1993) model of ethnic identity development (see Chapter Fifteen) and Dillon, Worthington, and Moradi's (2011) unifying model of sexual identity development (see Chapter Seven).

In the decade since 2005, neo-Eriksonian identity research has emerged. Much of this scholarship relies heavily on Marcia's identity statuses. According to Schwartz, Zamboanga, Wang, and Olthius (2009), neo-Eriksonian work derives primarily from Marcia, "because Erikson discussed identity in figurative and clinical terms, used a number of case examples, and spoke in highly abstract language" (p. 143). Seth Schwartz's scholarship (Schwartz, Zamboanga, Luycks, Mecca, & Ritchie, 2013; Schwartz, Zamboanga, Meca, & Ritchie, 2012) has been critical to the advancement of research on the identity statuses within a North American context. In addition to the increase in neo-Eriksonian research in the United States, several international scholars are using the statuses to explore identity development among college and university students in countries beyond the United States. Koen Luyckx, who has also collaborated with Schwartz and others, is at the forefront of the increasing number of publications focusing on the relevance and extension of Marcia's statuses to students in countries such as Belgium and Italy. Explication of this body of work is beyond the scope of this chapter. However, one example of Marcia's statuses is worth mentioning, given its influence on later neo-Eriksonian research. Luyckx, Goossens, Soenens, Beyers, and Vansteenkiste (2005) and Luyckx, Goossens, Soenens, and Beyers (2006) expanded Marcia's concepts of exploration and commitment with their research, which indicated that both concepts occur along two dimensions: (1) exploration in both breadth and depth, and (2) commitment making and identification with commitment. Exploration in breadth is reflective of Marcia's earlier description, in which individuals are forming life commitments. Exploration in depth is a more iterative process that involves not only making a commitment but also reflection, redefinition, and evaluation of individual identity commitments. Commitment making is also reflective of Marcia's contention that individuals make choices about their identity and take ownership in the process. Identification with commitment refers to "the degree to which adolescents identify with and feel certain about their choices" (Luyckx, Schwartz, Goossens, Soenens, & Beyers, 2008b, p. 597).

Collectively, the rise of neo-Eriksonian identity research has resulted in the creation of additional models or expanded versions of the statuses as previously noted to depict more nuanced explanations for how development occurs

(Crocetti, Rubini, Luyckx, & Meeus, 2008; Luyckx, Klimstra, Schwartz, & Duriez, 2013; Luyckx, Schwartz, Berzonsky, Soenens, Vansteenkiste, Smits, & Goossens, 2008a; Luyckx, Schwartz, Soenens, Vansteenkiste, & Goossens, 2010).

It should be noted that neo-Eriksonian research, while quite robust, has placed far more attention on Marcia's statuses and very little emphasis on Josselson's contributions. We identified only one recent study, conducted at a Belgian university, that accounted for Josselson's earlier research (Luyckx et al., 2008b). Luyckx et al. examined the relationship between identity and adjustment (for example, self-esteem and depressive symptoms), using a trajectory analytical approach. Overall, research concerning Josselson's model has not appeared in the literature since the early 1980s, making this area of research ripe for study.

Research Involving Chickering and Reisser's Vectors

Chickering's (1969) theory as well as his revised theory in collaboration with Reisser have generated significant research relevant to the field of student development.

Context and Student Populations. Researchers have examined the applicability of Chickering's theory to various institutional contexts and diverse student populations. With regard to context, Rogers (2004) explored the psychosocial development of community college students and found the developing competence and purpose vectors to be most meaningful in describing development among students at these institutions. Regarding specific student populations, Costello and English (2001) noted no statistically significant developmental differences between students who identified as having a learning disability and those who did not, with the exception that those with learning disabilities may place greater emphasis on academic success, which may contribute to fewer mature interpersonal relationships.

In terms of developmental differences between traditional and nontraditional students, Macari, Maples, and D'Andrea (2005–2006) found nontraditional students scored lower on the establishing purpose, developing autonomy, and developing mature interpersonal relationships vectors. Although nontraditional-age students scored lower on these vectors, Macari et al. (2005–2006) explained that these students are often "engaged in tasks and responsibilities outside of college that require a great deal of the individual's time and attention" (p. 294), which limits their campus involvement. Alessandria and Nelson (2005) found no significant differences in identity development when comparing first-generation U.S. students and continuing generation U.S. students. With traditional-age students, Cullaty (2011) noted that autonomy development increased when their relationships with their parents promoted autonomy-related behaviors, including redefinition of the students' relationships, with their parents allowing the student to be perceived and to behave as an adult, parents treating students as individuals who are responsible, and parents exercising support of, rather than overbearing control over, their students' decisions and affairs while in college.

Evans (2003) noted gender and cultural differences can have an impact on the ordering and importance of the vectors. How students experience the vectors differs based on social identities, such as gender, race, ethnicity, and sexual orientation. In terms of gender, researchers have found differences between women's and men's development, in the interpersonal relationships and developing autonomy vectors (in fostering other aspects of development; see Taub & McEwen, 1991). In particular women tend to develop mature interpersonal relationships prior to developing autonomy and score higher on intimacy than male students (Blackhurst, 1995; Foubert, Nixon, Sisson, & Barnes, 2005; Taub, 1995, 1997; Utterback, Spooner, Barbieri, & Fox, 1995).

Several writers have questioned the applicability of Chickering's theory for racially minoritized students. As Pope (1998) stated, theories such as Chickering's can be "insufficient" (p. 274) in explaining the development of students of color. In her study of 539 Black, Asian, and Latino Americans, Pope (2000) found it was crucial to pay attention to the interrelated constructs of race and racial identity when attempting to facilitate psychosocial development of racially minoritized students. For example, development of racial/ethnic identity is of particular importance to African American students, often taking priority over other aspects of psychosocial development (Cokley, 2001; McEwen, Roper, Bryant, & Langa, 1990; Taub & McEwen, 1992). Kodama, McEwen, Liang, and Lee (2001, 2002) offered insight into the psychosocial development of Asian American students, noting that Chickering's theory (Chickering & Reisser, 1993) does not adequately address development for this population and fails to consider fully the nature and impact of an oppressive society (Kodama et al., 2001, 2002). Other racial and ethnic differences have also been identified. White students score higher on intimacy than Native Americans, African Americans, and Hispanic Americans (Utterback et al., 1995). Asian international first-year students scored significantly lower than U.S. students, for whom race/ethnicity was not specified, in regard to establishing and clarifying purpose and developing mature interpersonal relationships and intimacy (Sheehan & Pearson, 1995).

Although Chickering and Reisser (1993) expanded the description of establishing identity to include becoming comfortable with one's sexual orientation, no recent research has been conducted to examine the suitability of Chickering's theory for lesbian, gay, and bisexual students. Certainly, vectors such as managing emotions, developing mature interpersonal relationships, establishing identity, and developing purpose would be affected by how individuals make sense of sexual orientation (Evans & D'Augelli, 1996).

Other College Variables. Researchers have investigated the relationship of psychosocial development and campus involvement. First-year students who remain on campus on weekends report higher levels of autonomy than students who leave campus (Fox, Spooner, Utterback, & Barbieri, 1996). Students who are more involved in extracurricular activities score higher on scales measuring confidence, developing purpose, developing mature interpersonal relationships, and intimacy (Hunt & Rentz, 1994). Foubert and Grainger (2006) found that student involvement increased developmental gains in the moving through autonomy toward interdependence and establishing purpose vectors. They noted greater development among student leaders and those who get involved earlier. Involvement is not always positively related to development, however. Students who participated in intercollegiate athletics scored lower than nonathletes in regard to educational plans, career plans, and mature relationships (Sowa & Gressard, 1993). Moreover, sophomore men in Greek-letter organizations scored lower in confidence than did non-members (Kilgannon & Erwin, 1992).

Relationships among Forms of Development. The interconnections of forms of development have also been considered in research. For example, researchers found connections between psychosocial development and career development in relation to autonomy, sense of purpose, vocational identity, and occupational information (Bowers, Dickman, & Fuqua, 2001; Long, Sowa, & Niles, 1995). A relationship also seems to exist between psychosocial development and moral development in that they appear to be parallel processes (Bruess & Pearson, 2000). Jones and Watt (1991) found students who viewed themselves as having both a high justice and low care moral orientation had higher scores in regard to psychosocial development (Jones & Watt, 1999). In a later study, Jones and Watt (2001) reported "increasing psychosocial development across class standing," meaning more senior students exhibited increased development in comparison to first-year students (p. 10).

They also found that whereas connectedness and relationships promoted identity development and autonomy for women, separation contributed to the same processes for men.

Application

An inclusive review of the literature uncovered a dearth of information related to applying the theories of Josselson and Marcia in practice. With regard to Josselson's theory, much of the research is nearly 40 years old and likely lacks applicability to today's college student. The literature on Marcia's work primarily focuses on testing the validity of and expanding the statuses rather than translation to practice. However, Marcia (1989a) offered insights into establishing psychological interventions to promote identity development that are easily adapted to present-day student affairs practice. From his perspective, identity statuses may not be as significant as exploration and commitment processes. Students face difficult decisions about ideology, occupation, sexuality, and relationships that lead to naturally occurring disequilibrium in their lives. Student affairs professionals can capitalize on this predictability and offer structured, intentional programming and services to assist students in their explorations. In order to make commitments, college students need nurturing environments that encourage risk-taking and provide a retreat to nurture their psychological health. Marcia (1989a) also stressed that educators must be nourished in supportive environments where they can address their own identity, intimacy, and generativity. This is easily translated to a student affairs context, as professionals must engage in their own identity development as well as that of the students. Failure to do so undermines the learning process.

Chickering's theory has generated a number of student affairs applications, particularly in the area of programming. Interventions to facilitate particular aspects of development have been introduced as well as general programming strategies. Chickering has also provided examples of ways that several of the key environmental influences can be implemented (Chickering & Schlossberg, 1995, 2001; Schlossberg, Lynch, & Chickering, 1989). Hamrick, Evans, and Schuh (2002) linked Chickering's theory to work related to college outcomes. The vectors and key influences provide information to aid in creating environments to facilitate student development.

Although earlier applications found in the literature remain relevant, use of Chickering's theory has decreased over time. Chickering's theory is still applicable for working individually with students, programming, and structuring environments to promote psychosocial development. An awareness of the developmental issues represented by the vectors can aid student affairs practitioners in their interactions with students on an individual level. For example, knowing that entering students are likely to be concerned about competency issues, practitioners can be prepared to suggest activities and institutional supports that can facilitate intellectual, physical, and social competence and a sense of competence. As another example, Moran (2001) suggested various ways student affairs practitioners can support students in developing purpose, such as investing quality time in meaningful activities.

In terms of programming, the theory can be used to inform programming and assessment in a variety of functional areas. For example, student affairs professionals might consider ways to promote development by using the vectors in residence hall programming (Krivoski & Nicholson, 1989). The managing emotions and developing competence vectors could be used to guide programming among student athletes, given the intense demands on these individuals and those who get injured (Harris, 2003; Valentine & Taub, 1999). Developing purpose could be a vector used to guide programmatic opportunities in career services. Given the broad nature of the vectors, the programming possibilities are endless. However, student affairs professionals should be aware that students do not or cannot always take advantage of developmentally appropriate programs and services; thus they should make special efforts to encourage involvement, rather than assuming that involvement will occur naturally.

Critique and Future Directions

The psychosocial theories in this chapter are clearly beneficial to educators. Erikson was the first psychologist to consider development across the lifespan; thus his theory has been foundational for other explorations of psychosocial development of adolescents and adults (Hamrick, Evans, & Schuh, 2002). Erikson recognized the importance of environment and context in human development. Although he did not specifically address the development of college students, the developmental issues he noted are clearly applicable to this population. Since Marcia focused on the resolution of identity in young adulthood, his theory also has great utility for individuals working with college students, although, like Erikson, he did not specifically focus on students. Marcia did identify the various issues that are central to identity development for men and the means that they use to resolve these issues—knowledge that is very useful to educators as they work with male students. In contrast, Josselson's research provides information about identity resolution among women, particularly the important role of relationships. Her participants were in college when she began her research, so it has direct applicability. A strength of her work is its longitudinal nature.

A number of critiques of psychosocial identity development theory exist. Erikson's initial work is often criticized as being overly general and complex (Coté & Levine, 1987), as well as biased against women (Gilligan, 1982; Josselson, 1996). As noted earlier, the stages in Erikson's theory are difficult to study empirically because they appear to be abstract and vague. While Erikson provides highly descriptive stages, he does not offer detailed information on specific catalysts for development. In other words, the theory provides little clarity about which experiences promote development and what specific knowledge or skills individuals must have at each stage to resolve crises. Furthermore, while Erikson indicates each stage builds upon the next, he does not explain how the resolution within one stage influences resolution at later stages. Erikson's theory has also been critiqued because he placed greater emphasis on the earlier stages, despite Erikson's portrayal of the theory as "lifespan" development. The theory may also be perceived as essentialist, allowing no room for variation in development across the lifespan, and suggesting instead that developmental crises unfold in an invariant, linear way.

Many critiques of Marcia's theory can be found in the literature as well. Marcia (1975) himself noted, "The problem with the statuses is that they have a static quality and identity is never static" (p. 153). Coté and Levine (1983, 1988a, 1988b) lodged several major critiques against Marcia's work. First, they challenged the assumption that Marcia's statuses are developmentally ordered on a continuum from a diffused identity to an achieved identity. While there have been some shifts in this continuum assumption, they asserted that the literature has failed to explicitly correct it. Second, Coté and Levine (1983, 1988a, 1988b) questioned the accuracy of Marcia's statuses in reflecting the Eriksonian concept of identity formation, contending that the statuses do not operationalize Erikson's theory. Moreover, they noted that while Marcia has implied that the identity statuses do not capture the overall complexity of Erikson's theory, he has not made this limitation clear in his work. Finally, Coté and Levine (1983, 1988a, 1988b) suggested that Marcia inappropriately used terminology from Erikson's theory within the identity statuses.

There is a paucity of research related to the identity development of women; in particular, research validating Josselson's findings is needed. In addition, Jones (1995) and Kroger (1985) pointed out a specific need for work that addresses the intersection of race and other identity domains with gender. Since psychosocial development is very much influenced by societal conditions and norms, ongoing research to determine whether findings from Josselson's earlier studies are still applicable or modern day replication of her study is warranted, given how rapidly gender norms continue to change. Findings from future studies could enhance general understanding of women's psychosocial development and gender differences in college.

The first version of Chickering's theory provided a good glimpse of the developmental tasks college students face. Chickering and Reisser's (1993) revisions did much to update the theory by incorporating women's development and the development of African American and Hispanic/Latino students, but was still limited in its attention to Asian American and Native American (Schuh, 1994). While empirically grounded, Chickering's theory lacks specificity and precision. Even in the newer version, definitions of vectors are often quite general. The developing integrity vector is particularly hard to grasp and therefore to measure. Chickering also failed to address how students grapple with issues or the process by which they accomplish developmental tasks. More research to test the validity of Chickering's theory is warranted and should focus on more than one or two vectors, to provide a more comprehensive view of development. Reisser (1995) acknowledged that more research is needed on the interrelationships among age, gender, sexual orientation, race, culture, and aspects of psychosocial development. She called for broad, inclusive theories rather than ones that are narrow and group-specific. However, much of psychosocial development is culture-specific. It is not possible to develop a theory that is totally valid for everyone.

Qualitative research approaches show promise for examining psychosocial development, particularly as it occurs for members of different multicultural populations. Torres, Howard-Hamilton, and Cooper (2003) asserted that "the important life question—'Who am I?'—is only partially addressed" (p. 16) in theories such as Chickering's. Pope, Reynolds, and Mueller (2004), while acknowledging that Chickering's theory has changed to accommodate diverse populations, reiterated that multicultural issues and concerns have not been effectively incorporated.

Chickering's theory has had a significant impact in student affairs. He has become perhaps one of the most highly regarded student development theorists to date. Higbee (2002) described the theory as one "that stands the test of time" (p. 33). Valentine and Taub (1999) maintained that despite concerns, this theory "remains arguably the most well known, widely used, and comprehensive model available for understanding and describing the psychosocial development of college students" (p. 166). For now, it remains important to use Chickering's theory with care, acknowledging its limitations while continuing to appreciate its utility when used appropriately.

Psychosocial development theories presented in this chapter are important, but for several reasons, their use and application has decreased over time. First, early work by Erikson, Marcia, and Chickering was based upon studies using primarily white, all male participants. While Josselson's work and Chickering's updated theory captured the experiences of women to some extent, collectively these theories have excluded participants who are women or who represent racially minoritized groups. The application of these theories is also limited because the theories are older; thus their applicability can become limited due to ongoing changes in society. For example, the theories presented in this chapter would fail to account for the burgeoning technological advances that undoubtedly shape how students understand and experience identity development (see Chapter Twelve on emergent perspectives on identities). Moreover, these theories, like many others presented in this text, treat gender as fixed (that is, man or woman). Today's societal context challenges the boundaries of gender and is slowly but surely grappling with trans* and non-gender-conforming students and their development (see Chapter Eight). Though still quite valuable and relevant in many instances, psychosocial theory has significant limitations. Therefore, it is extremely important for student affairs educators to appropriately contextualize psychosocial theories and view them as a product of their time with limited applicability in an ever-changing society.

Discussion Questions

1. The fifth stage of Erikson's theory is "Identity versus Identity Diffusion" and individuals ask "Who am I?" Reflecting on your own college experiences, identify two or three experiences that prompted you to ask "Who am I?"

2. Many of the psychosocial identity models in this chapter were developed several decades ago. Given today's higher education environment, how might Erikson's, Marcia's, Josselson's, and Chickering's work be expanded?

3. If you were creating psychosocial theory today, what additional considerations should be accounted for in these theoretical perspectives? For example, how would social media and digital identities affect psychosocial development?

4. How would today's college students experience crisis/commitment as originally framed by Marcia?

5. How could psychosocial theories be more inclusive of the diversity of today's college students—in terms of race, ethnicity, socioeconomic class, immigrant status, sexual orientation, and gender identity?

6. How are Josselson's research findings applicable to the diversity of today's college women? How would you incorporate her study into a program to support college women's development?

7. Examine the key influences on student development offered by Chickering and Reisser. How are these influences visible in your current work environment? For example, how does institutional size shape students' participation? How does teaching promote or hinder active learning opportunities?

8. How are other key influences and Chickering's admonitions at play within your current work environment or within your undergraduate college experience?

9. Create a diagram or drawing that compares and contrasts these four theories of psychosocial development—Erickson, Marcia, Josselson, and Chickering—and discuss your development (or that of a student you know well) within each one.

10. What do you think should be the focus of future examinations of psychosocial development ?

CHAPTER FOURTEEN

EPISTEMOLOGICAL AND INTELLECTUAL DEVELOPMENT

Structures that shape how people view their experiences form intellectual and ethical development (Perry, 1968). Since the mid-twentieth century, several theories have provided important contributions to knowledge about how students make meaning of their experiences. Perry's theory of intellectual and ethical development (1968); Belenky, Clinchy, Goldberger, and Tarule's study of women's ways of knowing (1986); and King and Kitchener's reflective judgment model (1994) build on one another, laying the groundwork for more contemporary cognitive models, specifically Baxter Magolda's theories of epistemological reflection (1992) and self-authorship (2001), discussed further in Chapter Sixteen.

This chapter describes the work of Perry, Belenky et al., and King and Kitchener and how their research formed the basis for contemporary knowledge about cognitive and intellectual development among college students, and examines their contributions to theory, research, and educational practice. The chapter also contains an overview of each of these three theories, a review of related research, and a discussion of the ways in which each theory is applied in student affairs and academic settings, while providing comparisons when applicable and a critique of each theory as well as suggestions for future directions.

Assumptions and Origins

Cognitive structural theories describe the process of epistemological and intellectual development during the college years. Rooted in the work of Piaget (1952), these theories focus on how people think, reason, and make meaning of their experiences. In this approach, the mind uses structures, generally called *stages*, which act as sets of assumptions by which individuals adapt to and organize their environments. Stages, and their counterparts, act as filters or lenses for determining how people perceive and evaluate experiences and events. Some theorists view cognitive structural stages as arising one at a time and always in the same order. However, the age at which each stage occurs and the rate at which the individual passes through are variable. Each stage is derived from the previous one and incorporates aspects of it; thus each successive stage is qualitatively different from and more complex than the stages before it. As individuals encounter new information or experiences that create cognitive dissonance, they first attempt to incorporate the new data into their way of thinking (assimilation). If the new information can no longer fit into their existing structure, they produce a new, more complex structure (accommodation; Wadsworth, 1979). Neurological maturation in cognitive development is central, but the role played by the environment in providing experiences to which the individual must react is also significant (Piaget, 1952).

Perry's Theory of Intellectual and Ethical Development

During the 1950s and early 1960s, while serving as the director of Harvard's Bureau of Study Counsel, William G. Perry, Jr., along with his associates, engaged in research examining how students interpreted and made meaning of the teaching and learning process. From this research, Perry and his colleagues formulated what he described as "the typical course of development of students' patterns of thought" (1981, p. 77) and "unfolding views of the world" (1968, p. ix). Perry (1968) acknowledged indebtedness to Piaget and other developmental psychologists, such as Kohlberg. Because little work had been done to address the adolescent-to-adulthood transition, Perry made particular mention of the influence of Sanford's (1962, 1966) and Heath's (1964) research in the higher education setting.

The Theory

Perry's (1968) theory of intellectual and ethical development begins with simplistic forms, in which individuals interpret the world in dichotomous, unqualified "terms of right-wrong, good-bad" (p. 3), and concludes with complex forms in which individuals seek to affirm personal commitments "in a world of contingent knowledge and relative values" (p. 3). The foundation for Perry's (1968) theory consists of nine positions outlined on a continuum of development. Perry chose "position" over "stage" for several reasons. First, "position" makes no assumption about duration. Second, since individuals may demonstrate some range in structures at any point in time, "position" can represent "the locus of a central tendency or dominance among these structures" (p. 48). Finally, "position" is consistent with the point of view individuals use as a lens to examine the world. Interestingly, in Perry's scheme, positions are static, with development occurring not in the positions, but during transitions between them. In this theory, development is the movement between positions, unlike a stage, which implies a stop along the way (Perry, 1981). One scholar noted that Perry "emphasized our need to understand students in motion and not imprison them in stages" (Knefelkamp, 1999, p. xii).

The positions in Perry's (1981) theory move on a continuum from duality to evolving commitments. The precision and more subtle differences that characterize the nine positions represent more detail than most educators need for the purpose of rendering Perry's scheme a usable tool for understanding and interacting with students. A simplified version of the theory—portraying the basic differences in the primary modes of meaning making, along with an explanation of the deflections that can delay cognitive growth—seems sufficient to facilitate active use of these ideas.

The three concepts that represent fundamental differences in the meaning-making process are *duality, multiplicity*, and *relativism. Commitment* signifies another important idea within the scheme. The following descriptions of these basic concepts in the Perry scheme are derived from Perry (1968, 1981), King (1978), and Knefelkamp and Cornfeld (1979).

Dualism represents a mode of meaning making in which individuals view the world dichotomously: good-bad, right-wrong, black-white. Learning is essentially information exchange because knowledge is seen as quantitative (facts) and authorities (including people and books) are seen as possessing the right answers. Dualistic meaning-makers believe that right answers exist for everything. The transition to multiplicity begins when cognitive dissonance occurs. For example, when experts disagree or when good teachers or authority figures do not have all the answers or express uncertainty, disequilibrium enters students' meaning-making process.

Multiplicity is sometimes misunderstood and described as an "anything goes" mode of making meaning. In reality, Perry characterized multiplicity as honoring diverse views when the right answers are not yet known. In such instances, all opinions are equally valid, from a multiplistic perspective. As individuals move through multiplicity, their conception of the student role shifts from that of one who works hard to learn what experts are teaching toward one who learns to think more independently. During this progression, peers become more legitimate sources of knowledge, and individuals are likely to improve their ability to think analytically.

For multiplistic thinkers, a recognition of what is needed to support opinions initiates the transition to *relativism*. All opinions no longer appear equally valid. Relativistic thinkers acknowledge that some opinions are of little value, yet reasonable people can also legitimately disagree on some matters. They view knowledge more qualitatively; knowledge is contextually defined, based on evidence and supporting arguments.

Dualistic and relativistic thinkers can resemble each other on the surface, as when a student appears to be oppositional in a class or group setting. Oppositional students may express some dichotomous views—for example, what's right is right and what's wrong is wrong. It seems important, however, to reach such a conclusion tentatively. Oppositional students' views appear less inclusive, and their mode of meaning making therefore may be assumed to be less complex. However, the content of individuals' views should not be confused with the degree of complexity of the thought process used to reach conclusions (Knefelkamp, Widick, & Stroad, 1976). Dualistic and relativistic thinking among students may be demonstrated as "strong" views. At issue is the degree of examination and reflection that formulates those views. If ideas are essentially "swallowed whole" from authorities such as parents, teachers, group advisors, or textbooks, if little or no questioning is part of the process of adopting these beliefs, then the process demonstrates a dualistic mode of thinking. By contrast, relativistic thinkers, when presented with ideas by an authority figure, may adopt them as their own. Along the way, they may critically examine ideas and perhaps even reject some for a period. The rationale for current adherence to the beliefs reflects a more complex process of coming to conclusions—a process that includes some questioning and a contextual basis for the stance taken.

The movement from relativism to the process of *commitment in relativism*, which involves making choices in a contextual world, exemplifies a shift away from cognitive development, because it does not involve changes in cognitive structures (King, 1978). This movement can be viewed as initiating ethical development rather than increasing cognitive complexity. The commitment process involves choices, decisions, and affirmations that are made from the vantage point of relativism. Affirmation of commitment is a time when individuals find their identity, which previously was difficult to pinpoint (Perry, 1981). Two aspects characterize students' thinking about commitments: area and style (Perry, 1968). Area refers to social content—decisions about academic major, career, religion, relationships, politics, and so forth. Style relates to balancing the external (for example, relative time use, nature of relationships) and the subjective (for example, action versus contemplation, and control versus openness).

Deflections from Cognitive Growth

Consistent with the notion that development does not occur in a linear fashion, three deflections from cognitive growth frame Perry's theory (1968). *Temporizing* represents a "time out" period when movement is postponed. Some temporizing may be needed to allow for horizontal *décalage* (defined as lateral growth or development within a particular position) or to provide a rest period. With temporizing, cognitive development is essentially put on hold, maintaining a plateau while the individual hesitates to take the next step (King, 1978). *Escape*, another deflection, involves an abandonment of responsibility characterized by alienation. Often, avoidance of responsibility is linked to making commitments in relativism. For example, a student in an interview with Perry described not having any consuming interest, but drifting and leading a hollow life (Perry, 1981). *Retreat*, the third deflection, involves a temporary return to dualism and can result from feelings of being overwhelmed or overly challenged. For example, students feeling weighed down by the job search process can look to an authority figure such as a faculty member or a career counselor to tell them what to do.

Research and Assessment

Perry's theory has generated a substantial body of research. This section covers only the development of assessment methods, as well as early, ground-breaking research, and studies that have examined outcomes within higher education settings.

Assessment. Several assessment methods, including both production and recognition formats, are available and have been used in research studies.

Production formats require respondents to generate their own answers, either verbally or in writing, while recognition formats have individuals select a response from alternatives provided. In the original study, Perry (1968) and his colleagues conducted open-ended interviews, beginning with a question such as, "Would you like to say what has stood out for you during the year?" (p. 7) and following up with probes seeking specific examples.

After the scheme was conceptualized from a qualitative analysis of early protocols, Perry and his colleagues developed a manual and independent judges conducted subsequent ratings (Perry, 1968). The time and expense involved in conducting interviews and rating protocols for assessment purposes limited any widespread use of the technique. As alternatives to the interview approach, several "paper and pencil" measures of the Perry scheme have been developed.

Knefelkamp (1974) and Widick (1975) developed and refined a production-oriented instrument that came to be known as the Measure of Intellectual Development (MID), which measures Perry's first five positions. Baxter Magolda and Porterfield's Measure of Epistemological Reflection (MER) (1985; Baxter Magolda, 1987), another production instrument, also measures the first five positions of the Perry scheme. Erwin's Scale of Intellectual Development (SID) (1983) represents an early effort to create a Perry measure comprised of recognition tasks. Another Perry measure that utilizes the recognition format is Moore's Learning Environment Preferences Measure (LEP) (1989).

Foundational Research. Perry and his colleagues replicated their original work with the Harvard-Radcliffe entering class of 1971 and again with the class of 1979 (Perry, 1981). Though some variations were noted when comparing these samples to the original, the scheme of cognitive and ethical development seemed to be a constant phenomenon in a pluralistic culture.

Heffernan was credited as being the first to use the scheme for research purposes by incorporating it into an outcome study of a residential college at the University of Michigan (Perry, 1981). King (1978) and Perry (1981) identified Kurfiss as a researcher who conducted early work based on the Perry scheme by examining conceptual properties and the comparative rates of development within individuals. Meyer (1977), who used Perry's theory in the early years, showed how an understanding of religious issues can serve as an indication of intellectual development (King, 1978).

Higher Education Outcomes. Use of Perry's scheme as an outcome measure is also represented in the research literature. For example, the MID was used to assess the influence on cognitive development of a program designed to enhance the professional identity of medical students (Swick, 1991); the SID was used to assess the effectiveness of a semester-long career-planning course for vocationally undecided students (Jones & Newman, 1993). The MID was also used to measure the impact of a year-long interdisciplinary program at Daytona Beach Community College (Avens & Zelley, 1992). In a later study using the MER, service-learning courses were found to have a positive influence on cognitive development, and those with a social justice emphasis had more impact than those without it (Wang & Rodgers, 2006).

An early and extensive use of the Perry scheme as an outcomes measure was made at Alverno College (Mentkowski, Moeser, & Strait, 1983). The researchers used Perry's scheme, along with other developmentally oriented instruments, as a measure of student growth at this small private liberal arts institution, which had an outcome-centered curriculum. Results of a five-year longitudinal study involving 750 women, ages 17 to 55, suggested that students do develop along the Perry trajectory during their time in college. Development occurred differentially, depending on the area (for example, career development versus classroom learning). The University of Maine at Farmington also used Perry's scheme to assess the piloting of the institution's four-credit first-year seminar and its effect on student retention and intellectual development in comparison to the institution's one-credit seminars (Barton & Donahue, 2009). Using the MID as a tool, researchers learned that no significant changes occurred in intellectual development between students in the four-credit hour course versus those enrolled in the standard one-hour course, or other transition courses.

Other studies in which Perry's scheme has been used focus on diverse academic programs. For example, Myers (2010) examined class participation among 202 undergraduates in two introductory communication courses. The students were identified as dualist, multiplist, and contextual relativist thinkers. Examples of class participation included speaking aloud in class, asking questions, and engaging interactively with others in class. Findings revealed that, while no differences existed with regard to speaking in class, multiplist students posed more questions in comparison to dualist students, and contextual relativist students engaged more interactively than their multiplist counterparts.

Two studies conducted by Carmel-Gilfilen and Portillo (2010, 2012) focused on intellectual development among architecture and design students using the MID, as well as other measures. Their findings supported the development proposed in Perry's scheme. In 2008, Hofer suggested achieving a more widespread understanding of epistemological development by engaging in a repetition of Perry's scheme using a cross-cultural lens focused on non-Westernized school systems. Roberts (2011) used markers proposed by Perry and by King and Kitchener to explore which modes and combinations of teaching strategies would best promote and advance cognitive and intellectual development.

In the sciences, Olson and Finson (2009) studied reflective practice among students in undergraduate elementary science methods courses and found that most students (28 out of 38) were dualistic thinkers. They proposed science method instruction be enhanced to promote higher levels of thinking among students and assist them in understanding the realities of teaching science, including the teacher's ability to articulate complex topics and to contextualize their instruction. Students in an organic chemistry course at Miami University experienced similar struggles with advancing their cognitive complexity (Grove & Bretz, 2010). Perry's scheme was used to examine development among students, most of whom presumed that a "straightforwardness of organic chemistry existed" (p. 210). Similarly, Grove and Bretz recommended adding more complexity to the course curriculum to challenge learners and promote their development.

Finally, Torres (2003), studying Latino college students, raised the possibility that the deflections of retreat and escape may result from dissonance felt by students in relation to their ethnic identity development. Her interpretation forms a connection between cognitive development and ethnic identity development.

Application

Perry's theory has been used extensively in higher education settings. This section explores the concept of informal assessment using this theory. Following informal assessment is the developmental instruction model and a discussion of classroom and student affairs applications.

Informal Assessment. The time, expense, and expertise required to implement production-oriented assessments typically render them impractical for applied uses in the classroom or in student affairs settings. By contrast, recognition-oriented assessments are likely to be viewed as more viable when formal assessment is desired in a context other than academic research. However, educators should consider the option of informal assessment, which combines the advantages of formal and recognition-oriented assessments.

Interactions with students in the classroom, the residence halls, student organizations, counseling relationships, and judicial conferences are likely to provide clues about how students make meaning. Such impressionistic information can be valuable in attempting to understand students' perspectives and work effectively with them. It is not necessary to conduct a formal assessment to form tentative impressions of students' cognitive development and to use Perry's theory as a support in responding. Assessors should use caution, however, as they run the risk of error in conducting informal assessments (King, 1990). Thus it is important to use such information tentatively and empathically while being willing to recognize the possibility of mistaken impressions.

The Developmental Instruction Model. The developmental instruction (DI) model (Knefelkamp, 1999) provides an invaluable resource to aid in operationalizing Perry's model. As "second generation" theorists, Knefelkamp and Widick can be credited with producing a model for instructional design grounded in an analysis of Perry's discussion of student learner characteristics, and usable in the classroom and other instructional settings. Four variables of challenge and support describe the model: structure, diversity, experiential learning, and personalism. Each variable can be viewed as existing on a continuum, which symbolizes greater or fewer numbers of these characteristics.

Structure refers to the framework and direction provided to students. The continuum represents the movement from a high degree to a low degree of structure. Following are examples of ways in which structure can be provided: placing the course in the context of the curriculum, affording an opportunity to rehearse evaluation tasks, giving detailed explanations of assignments, and using specific examples that reflect students' experience. Students in the earlier positions in Perry's model will value structure as a support; students who have advanced further may consider structure limiting and prefer a more open-ended approach that gives them latitude.

Diversity has to do with presenting, and encouraging students to consider, alternatives and perspectives. Two dimensions characterize diversity: quantity, which refers to numeric amount, and quality, which refers to complexity. Consequently, the two-dimensional continuum reflects these two dimensions and ranges from a few simple pieces of information to many highly complex concepts or tasks. Diversity can be introduced via variety in readings, assignments, points of view, and instructional methods.

Experiential learning relates to the concreteness, directness, and involvement contained in learning activities. This continuum ranges from direct involvement to vicarious learning. The purpose of experiential learning is to help students make connections to the subject matter. Methods include case studies, role-playing, and exercises that facilitate reflection on and application of the material. Students in the early stages of cognitive development are most in need of this form of support, which can be lacking in the traditional college classroom.

Personalism reflects the creation of a safe environment in which educators encourage risk-taking. This continuum moves from high to moderate, since an impersonal learning environment is not considered facilitative for any student. Personalism is manifested in an interactive environment in which enthusiasm for the material, instructor availability, and comprehensive feedback are exhibited. While personalism has value throughout the cognitive development process, it is especially important for students in the early stages.

By drawing upon these four challenge and support variables, faculty and student affairs educators can create learning activities and environments that connect with and support students' cognitive development processes. Another useful resource in the design process is the analysis of learner characteristics presented by Knefelkamp and Cornfeld (see Knefelkamp, 1999), who describe uses for curriculum development and course evaluations.

Belenky, Clinchy, Goldberger, and Tarule's Women's Ways of Knowing

Mary Field Belenky, Blythe McVicker Clinchy, Nancy Rule Goldberger, and Jill Mattuck Tarule began their research in the late 1970s when they realized women lacked confidence in their own ability to think, speaking often about holes in their learning. The authors cited the work of both Gilligan (1982) and Perry (1968) as influential in shaping their own efforts. Undertaking a study involving lengthy interviews with 135 women (some students or recent graduates and some affiliated with human service agencies providing support to female parents), these early theorists of women's knowing began to understand this thinking process. The results of their research are presented in their book, *Women's Ways of Knowing: The Development of Self, Voice, and Mind* (Belenky et al., 1986). Stanton (1996) claimed that Belenky et al.'s work "has contributed importantly to liberating women's voices" (p. 45).

The Theory

Belenky et al. (1986) referred to the different ways of knowing as "perspectives" rather than stages. They offered several disclaimers about the five perspectives, acknowledging that they may not be exhaustive, fixed, or universal; that by nature of their abstractness, they do not portray the unique and complex aspects of a given individual's thought process; that similar categories may be found in men's thinking; and that others might organize the observations in a different way. However, the authors stated with conviction their finding that, for women, the development of voice, mind, and self are "intricately intertwined" (p. 18). Goldberger (1996b) noted that since the publication of their initial theory the authors had become "much more alert to the situational and cultural determinants of knowing and to the relationship between power and knowledge" (p. 8), aspects that were only implicit in their earlier work.

From the study of women of "diverse ages, circumstances, and outlooks" (Belenky et al., 1986, p. 13) emerged five "epistemological perspectives from which women know and view the world" (p. 15): silence, received knowledge, subjective knowledge, procedural knowledge, and constructed knowledge. Clinchy (2002) later indicated that the authors came to prefer "knowing" rather than "knowledge" in naming these perspectives.

The perspective of *silence* is characterized as mindless, voiceless, and obedient. In this perspective, women find themselves subject to the whims of external authority. Though rare as a current way of knowing among the women at the time they were interviewed, some interviewees who were found through the social service agencies described in retrospect the perspective of silence. They were among "the youngest and most socially, economically, and educationally deprived" (pp. 23–24) of the women. Belenky later suggested using the term "silenced" to reflect the coercion inherent in the position (Goldberger, 1996b).

Listening to the voices of others is a predominant trait of *received knowing*. A lack of self-confidence is evident in the belief that one is capable of receiving and reproducing only knowledge imparted by external authorities. First-year students may exhibit traits of received knowing as most are primarily conditioned to this type of learning. Creating knowledge independently does not emerge for consideration in this perspective.

With the perspective of *subjective knowing*, the pendulum swings, and truth is now seen as residing in the self, a shift that is particularly significant for women (Belenky et al., 1986). Among the research participants, a frequently cited contributing element was a failed male authority figure, such as a father who committed incest or an abusive husband. Inherent in the process of subjective knowing for women is a quest for the self, often including the element of "walking away from the past" (p. 76).

The perspective of *procedural knowing* involves learning and applying objective procedures for taking in and conveying knowledge. Two approaches are evident. The first, *separate knowing*, uses impersonal procedures for establishing truth. Characterized by critical thinking, listening to reason, and an adversarial tone, separate knowing often involves doubting (Belenky et al., 1986). The second approach, *connected knowing*, is grounded in empathy and care. Truth emerges in the context of personal experience rather than being derived from authorities. Connected knowing often involves believing.

Constructed knowing involves the integration of subjective and objective knowledge, with both feeling and thought present. Belenky et al. (1986) asserted that "it is in the process of sorting out the pieces of the self and of searching for a unique and authentic voice" (p. 137) that women discover the two basic insights of constructivist thought: all knowledge is constructed, and the knower is an intimate part of what is known. Constructivists are often able to listen to others without losing the ability to also hear their own voices.

Research

Belenky et al.'s research (1986) spawned further investigation of the relationship of cognitive development to other factors, as well as those factors influencing cognitive development. As an example of the former, Weinstock and Bond (2000) found a relationship between college women's epistemological perspectives and their conceptions of conflicts with close friends. With regard to the latter, student-faculty interaction demonstrated support for the importance of validation, support, and sense of connectedness for women's intellectual and personal development (Sax, Bryant, & Harper, 2005).

Similarly, collaborative learning has a positive impact on college students' development (Cabrera, Crissman, Bernal, Nora, Terenzini, & Pascarella et al., 2002). In contrast, traditional approaches to teaching mathematics are biased toward separate knowers, which underscores the need for more attention to the connected learning perspective (Chapman, 1993). Finally, connected knowing is significantly related to approaches to learning wherein students embrace all responsibilities associated with successfully completing a course (Marrs & Benton, 2009). Examining reasons for continuing studies in their chosen field, two scholars applied Belenky et al.'s linear cognitive developmental progression to women studying nursing, through examination of their growth, self-confidence, motivation, and renewal (Dearnley & Matthew, 2007). Other scholars examining Belenky et al.'s study of women found several previously unexamined associations between "ways of knowing, epistemological beliefs, and learning" (Schommer-Aikins & Easter, 2006, p. 415), expanding the paradigm to include considerations of age, gender, and academic year position in order to achieve an academic-success predictor.

Application

Belenky et al.'s (1986) theory has relevance to classroom teaching and to student affairs settings. Advocating "connected teaching" (p. 214) to help women nurture their own voices, educators place emphasis on connection rather than separation, understanding and acceptance rather than assessment, and collaboration rather than debate. Connected teaching respects and supports first-hand experience as a source of knowledge and encourages student-initiated work patterns rather than imposing arbitrary requirements.

Belenky et al. (1986) suggested the role of teacher as midwife, an individual who assists students "in giving birth to their own ideas" (p. 217). Class discussions that encourage the expression of diverse opinions represent a means of implementing connected teaching. Connected teachers demonstrate belief and trust in their students' thinking. Ten years after the publication of *Women's Ways of Knowing*, Stanton (1996) reported that voice and connection were the most widely adapted of its concepts.

Utilizing principles of connected teaching in an undergraduate learning theory course taught at a women's college, one scholar included *Women's Ways of Knowing* as a text and used a discussion format, case studies, group presentations, a cooperative evaluation system, and a final paper rather than an exam (Ortman, 1993). Ursuline College, in an institution-wide application, introduced a core curriculum, the Ursuline Studies Program, based on the work of Belenky and her colleagues, which emphasized group discussions and collaborative learning in a freshman seminar (Gose, 1995).

Focusing on student affairs applications, development can be supported in any area of student affairs in which educators emphasize issues of connection when working with women (Forrest, 1988; Fried, 1988). One way to do so is by genuinely connecting with students and helping them produce their own ideas. In class or out, all students need to connect and build relationships helpful to their personal and professional development.

Nurturing both separate and connected knowing and their integration is best for intellectual development. Student affairs professionals should also be aware of the call for teaching developmentally oriented leadership (Belenky, 1996; Belenky, Bond, & Weinstock, 1997). Belenky et al. (1986) are cited as a helpful resource for providing effective mentoring to women (Egan, 1996). Finally, their work was also instrumental in the development of Asian American and Pacific Islander feminist epistemology (Yee, 2009).

King and Kitchener's Reflective Judgment Model

In their 1994 book, *Developing Reflective Judgment*, Patricia King and Karen Strohm Kitchener described how individuals understand the nature of knowledge and use that understanding to guide their thinking and behaviors. King and Kitchener cited several influences in the development of their model: individuals whom they interviewed about epistemic assumptions; their own interest in understanding the process of and rationale for the evolution of different forms of reasoning; and efforts to identify the differences between their own and other approaches. Dewey's ideas (1933, 1938/1960) related to reflective thinking and Piaget's assumptions (1956/1973) about stage-related development were both influential in King and Kitchener's work, as was Kohlberg's (1969) work on cognitive and moral development. Their model also builds upon previous theories developed by Perry (1968); Harvey, Hunt, and Schroder (1961); and Loevinger (1976). Central to King and Kitchener's model (1994) is the observation that "people's assumptions about what and how something can be known provide a lens that shapes how individuals frame a problem and how they justify their beliefs about it in the face of uncertainty" (p. xvi).

The Theory

In the development of the reflective judgment model (RJM), King and Kitchener (1994) adopted Dewey's (1933, 1938/1960) notion that people make reflective judgments to bring closure to situations that can be characterized as uncertain. Reflective thinking, then, focuses on epistemological assumptions and ill-structured problems. Ill-structured problems have no certain answers, in contrast to well-structured problems for which single correct answers can be identified. Hunger, overpopulation, pollution, and inflation are all examples of ill-structured problems (King & Kitchener, 1994).

Seven stages characterize the RJM. Each stage represents a distinct set of assumptions about knowledge and the process of acquiring knowledge, and each set of assumptions results in a different strategy for solving ill-structured problems. Increasingly advanced stages signify increasing complexity. The seven stages may be clustered into pre-reflective thinking (stages 1, 2, and 3), quasi-reflective thinking (stages 4 and 5), and reflective thinking (stages 6 and 7).

The stages of the RJM are qualitatively different and build on the skills of previous stages while also providing the groundwork for the increasing complexity of subsequent stages. Individuals typically display "reasoning that is characteristic of more than one stage at a time" (King & Kitchener, 2002, p. 45). Therefore individuals should not be portrayed as being in a single stage. The three clustered stages and their descriptions demonstrating reflective judgment are explained as follows:

Pre-reflective thinkers do not acknowledge and may not even realize that knowledge is uncertain. Consequently, they do not recognize the existence of real problems that lack an absolute, correct answer, nor do they use evidence in reasoning toward a conclusion. *Quasi-reflective thinkers* realize ill-structured problems exist and knowledge claims about such problems include uncertainty. Consequently, quasi-reflective thinkers can identify some issues as being genuinely problematic. At the same time, while they use evidence, they have difficulty drawing reasoned conclusions and justifying their beliefs. *Reflective thinkers* maintain that knowledge is actively constructed, and claims of knowledge must be viewed in relation to the context in which they were generated. Reflective thinkers maintain that judgments must be based upon relevant data, and conclusions should be open to reevaluation.

Research

King and Kitchener (1994) used the reflective judgment interview (RJI) to gather information about individuals' assumptions about knowledge and how it is obtained, as proposed in the RJM. The RJI consists of four ill-structured problems and a standard set of follow-up questions. A trained interviewer reads the problems, and interviewees are asked to explain and justify their own points of view on the issues. More than 1,700 people, representing varied student and nonstudent subgroups, participated in RJIs at the time of its creation (King & Kitchener, 1994).

On the basis of a ten-year longitudinal study conducted from 1977 to 1987, involving 80 participants of a wide range of ages, King and Kitchener (1994) concluded, "the development of reflective thinking as measured by the RJI evolves slowly and steadily over time among individuals engaged in educational programs" (p. 132). While the researchers did find a strong linear relationship between age and RJM stage, the role of age should not be overstated, because participants were actively involved in educational pursuits during the study's time period and demonstrated a high level of scholastic aptitude (King & Kitchener, 1994).

The researchers also found gender differences in the longitudinal study; however, 14 later studies investigating gender differences produced mixed results (King & Kitchener, 1994). Women and men may develop at different rates, and these rates may be different between cohorts of women and men. Differences in timing may also characterize developmental changes in women and men. Later studies by Jensen and Guthrie, King, and Palmer found no gender differences (as cited in King & Kitchener, 2002).

King and Kitchener (1994) were careful to note that the sample for their longitudinal study was restricted to white adolescents and adults from the upper Midwest, and the students involved possessed unusually high academic aptitude scores. At the same time, they concluded there was strong evidence to support the development of reflective thinking, and the observed changes in reasoning were consistent with the RJM. Numerous longitudinal and cross-sectional studies conducted later provided additional evidence that reflective judgment develops slowly and steadily over time, and increases in scores are not based on practice or selective participation (King & Kitchener, 1994). Limited research indicates that the RJM may be applicable to African American and Latino populations (King & Kitchener, 2002), in undergraduate majors such as teacher education (Badger, 2010; Bullough, Young, Hall, Draper, & Smith, 2008; Friedman & Schoen, 2009), in post-graduate studies such as dentistry (Boyd, 2008), and in peer feedback processes (Xie, Ke, & Sharma, 2008).

Finally, one study identified a relationship between reflective judgment and tolerance for diversity, with the participants reasoning at quasi-reflective and reflective thinking levels tending to hold tolerant views regarding race and sexual orientation (Guthrie, King, & Palmer, as cited in King & Kitchener, 2002). Service-learning activities also increased students' reflective thinking in multicultural education (Li & Lal, 2005). McAllister, Whiteford, Hill, Thomas, and Fitzgerald (2006), applying King and Kitchener's theory, studied the development of self-understanding as college students attempted to recognize, comprehend, and develop their own attitudes and assumptions toward groups in other cultures.

Application

King and Kitchener (1994) claimed that a primary goal of higher education is to teach "students to engage in reflective thinking and to make reflective judgments about vexing problems" (p. 222). They offered 11 suggestions to support the efforts of both faculty and student affairs practitioners, which include showing respect for individuals at any developmental level, honoring students' assumptions about knowledge, presenting ill-structured problems in the classroom, recognizing multiple perspectives, and providing challenge and support, to name a few. To aid in facilitating processes that promote reflective thinking, they proposed activities providing effective support and challenge in the classroom. One approach to promoting reflective thinking in multicultural education advocates for challenge and support in the classroom (King & Shuford, 1996); others advocate for using reflective journal writing to promote reflective thinking (Spaulding & Wilson, 2002).

Love and Guthrie (1999) identified several ill-structured problems in student affairs work and call on student affairs professionals themselves to engage in reflective judgment. For example, posing a question such as "Which student leader would make the most effective organizational president?" (p. 50) requires the ability to think across several categories of qualifications to determine the "best" answer. In this example, an activities advisor can best help students by giving them feedback on their responses, providing evaluation of students' arguments, and modeling advanced reasoning about such complex issues.

Critique and Future Directions

Theories discussed in this chapter have been used and found effective since their introduction in the 1970s, 1980s, and 1990s. At least one (Perry's) is more than twice as old as today's youngest traditionally aged college students, yet it remains relevant when assessing contemporary students' ability to think. Both strengths and weaknesses are evident in this review of Perry's theory. Legitimate concerns have been aired about the lack of inclusiveness of Perry's samples. Clearly, attempting to generalize from a study of primarily traditionally aged white males at a prestigious institution in the late 1960s is risky and unwise. Cautious use of Perry's theory in relation to women, people of color, and other minoritized groups is advisable; some tentativeness is in order even with white male students in the twenty-first century. At the same time, the general contours of Perry's ways of making meaning make sense, and student affairs practitioners readily recognize these modes in the students with whom they interact—and even in themselves.

Obvious limitations exist when comparing students of the 1950s and 1960s to more contemporary U.S. college students (Knefelkamp, 1999). Interestingly noted, the assessment procedures developed have made possible the measurement of "tens of thousands of students at all types of American colleges and universities" (p. xiv), and these results indicate that the theory is useful "with a wide range of diverse students" (p. xvi). However, other studies (for example, Durham, Hays, & Martinez, 1994) found differing patterns of sociocognitive development when comparing Chicano and Anglo students, adding to an understanding of similarities and differences among students.

Another concern arises as a consequence of Perry's scheme's inclusion of two constructs (intellectual and ethical development) rather than one. To combine these can result in confounding notions, particularly in terms of what is perceived as being a "more developed" person. The positions associated with Perry's commitment process are no longer measuring or portraying increased cognitive complexity (King, 1978). Structurally, positions beyond relativism do not represent cognitive change. Rather, these positions reflect the second construct of "ethical" growth or the development of commitment. Relatedly, evidence to support the existence of the most advanced positions, the "committed" positions, is limited (King, 1978). Whether this is a weakness of the measurement instruments or of the theory itself is uncertain. Another possible explanation is that most research has been on undergraduate college students, a population that seldom demonstrates post-contextual relativistic thinking (Moore, 2002).

The heuristic value of Perry's theory deserves mention. Perry's work influenced Belenky et al.'s research on women (1986), Baxter Magolda's examination of the cognitive development of both women and men in the college setting (1992), and King and Kitchener's development of the RJM (1994). In addition, Perry's influence can be seen in theories of faith development, such as that of Parks (2000; see Chapter Nine). With little doubt, "Nearly all the existing psychological work on epistemological beliefs can be traced to ... Perry" (Hofer & Pintrich, 1997, p. 90).

Clearly, Perry's work is of great value in gaining a basic understanding of how students make meaning. The concepts of dualism, multiplicity, relativism, and commitment in relativism are easy to grasp and to recognize, at least tentatively, in students. The possibility exists that the Perry scheme may be measuring students' socialization into Western liberal education—perhaps into the dominant vision of the faculty—rather than measuring growth (Moore, 1994). However, even if this is true, the theory is no less valuable as an aid in understanding college students' learning processes (Moore, 1994). Perry's theory presents three visions of learning that "enrich and broaden" (Moore, 1994, p. 59) the way in which learning is considered in today's colleges and universities: learning as intellectual and ethical development, learning as transformation, and learning as loss. Knefelkamp (1999) concluded, "Perry's thinking contributes significant and fundamental notions to our understanding of the nature of students and the natures of developmental models" (p. xii). Hofer (2008) suggests that Perry's scheme can be expanded and used as a resource for understanding foundational cultural worldviews in higher education outside Western cultures and to determine whether development follows the same paths in non-Western colleges and universities. The impact of how students make meaning can be felt in the classroom, in interactions with student affairs staff, and in their contacts with each other. In turn, Perry's theory can be used to support practice in any of these arenas.

Some may raise concerns that Perry's theory simply "labels" students and that efforts to facilitate development are misdirected. If Perry's descriptions are used empathically rather than judgmentally in relation to students, then faculty and student affairs practitioners may be able to avoid stereotyping students and instead attempt to understand how they make meaning and respond appropriately. With this knowledge, faculty and student affairs professionals can more effectively contribute to students' learning processes. Educators need to recognize that students cannot be pulled against their will through a developmental sequence. Students are agents on their own behalf and cannot be forced to grow. At the same time, many institutional mission statements make reference to developing character and producing responsible citizens; enhanced cognitive complexity supports such goals. Perry (1978) argued that the world is a complicated place and it is better to function in it with "a matching set of complicated ideas" (p. 269) rather than simple ideas that do not fit. Educators have an obligation to help students equip themselves with complicated ideas that are both self-supporting and inclusive of others.

Finally, it is important to note that all cognitive structural theories, including Perry's, will benefit from continuing research efforts inclusive of the diversity inherent in a twenty-first-century campus. Along with understanding student differences, understanding more about different contexts and their impact on students and vice versa warrants attention (Moore, 2002).

The theories presented in this chapter and the research supporting them certainly advanced the knowledge base regarding the cognitive development of students. Belenky et al. (1986) and Baxter Magolda (1992) outlined important gender-related differences in how students interpret their experiences. King and Kitchener (1994) identified the existence of more complex thought processes in response to ill-structured problems. The longitudinal and programmatic research conducted by Baxter Magolda and King and Kitchener provided a strong foundation for the theories they introduced. King and Kitchener's reflective judgment interview has also provided a useful means for assessing reasoning processes. All of these researchers expanded the student population base to which cognitive development theory is applicable.

Clearly a strength of the work of these scholars is the attention each has paid to the practical applications of their work in the classroom and in student affairs. Sensitivity to the need for differing instructional methods to facilitate the development of at least some women is a reasonable implication for practice that can be derived from Belenky et al.'s (1986) work. Student affairs practitioners may also benefit from using *Women's Ways of Knowing* as a framework for listening and responding in their interactions with all students, not only women. As Love and Guthrie (1999) pointed out, Belenky et al.'s work was important because "it focused on women, social classes, and differences that are significant in our society" (p. 17).

King and Kitchener's (1994) discussion of how educational practice, both within the classroom and beyond, can foster reflective judgment is important in promoting theory-to-practice connections. At least a fundamental understanding of pre-reflective, quasi-reflective, and reflective thinking, along with a grasp of how to challenge and support students demonstrating each process, would have value for educators.

Despite advances, critiques of this body of work can certainly be found, particularly with regard to methodological issues. Examining Belenky et al.'s (1986) study, King (1987) pointed out the lack of detail in the discussion of procedures used and the presentation of the data itself. Also, Evans (1996) noted that because the study was not longitudinal, the question remains as to whether the perspectives found are, in fact, sequential and hierarchical. Goldberger (1996a) has indicated that the four authors are not in complete agreement that the ways of knowing represent a developmental sequence.

In reviewing King and Kitchener's 1994 book, Liddell (1995) noted that the issue of gender differences in relation to the RJM merits further attention. While more research has been done, continuing efforts to examine potential differences in regard to reflective judgment based on gender (Liddell, 1995), race, and ethnicity would be valuable. In fact, a 2006 study did use King and Kitchener's model as a theoretical basis for examining self-reflection across cultural barriers and recommended it as a means to help students better understand cultural differences (McAllister, Whiteford, Hill, Thomas, & Fitzgerald, 2006).

In addition to the methodological issues noted, cognitive development cannot be separated from affective and interpersonal development. It is understandable that early researchers considered these aspects of development separately to gain a better understanding of each process. However, it is now time to examine the interaction of these components of development and how, together, they affect the college experiences of students (Baxter Magolda, 2001).

The three theories discussed in this chapter—those of Perry, Belenky et al., and King and Kitchener—address a large slice of the topic of cognitive and intellectual development covering nearly three decades at the end of the twentieth century. In fact these researchers laid the groundwork for Baxter Magolda's (2007, 2009) theory of self-authorship (see Chapter Sixteen). Ultimately, whatever higher education and student affairs professionals can glean about cognitive and intellectual development can help students inside and outside the classroom while in college. These three theories lay the groundwork for more contemporary research on the topic, yet the patterns apparent among them are strikingly similar as individuals move from silence and a dualist way of thinking to more complex ways of thinking, which encourages creation of more options. Ultimately, individuals are capable of selecting the best option under the circumstance, choosing from among a multitude of alternatives. Student affairs professionals who work closely with university students could benefit from clearly understanding these concepts and imparting them to all in the academy who help students make better decisions as they learn to think in more complex ways.

Discussion Questions

1. All of the theories in the intellectual and moral development chapters are considered cognitive structural theories. Describe the characteristics of cognitive structural student development theory, highlighting how these characteristics are evident in the theories discussed in this chapter.

2. Discuss representations and metaphors for all three theories and connect them to the college student experience.

3. Compare and contrast the three theories presented in this chapter (i.e., intellectual and ethical development [Perry], women's ways of knowing, [Belenky, Clinchy, Goldberger, and Tarule], and reflective judgment [Kitchener and King] with corresponding theories in the moral development chapter (that is, Kohlberg, Rest, and Gilligan).

4. Discuss the patterns and themes you can identify in the three theories presented in this chapter and how you might move students in one stage or level to the next stage or level.

5. In what ways can knowledge about cognitive and intellectual development inform student learning and development in postsecondary classrooms?

6. How can these theories, concepts and models best be applied to students' experiences outside of the classroom? What is the role of student affairs educators in this pursuit?

7. Think of your own cognitive development in the college classroom. What about these three theories resonates most strongly with your experience?

8. Outline the advantages and disadvantages of stage theory in describing college students' epistemological and intellectual development.

9. Describe examples of scenarios that might arise in the following offices and prompt the fostering of cognitive development: residence life, student activities, orientation, athletic academic support, judicial affairs.

10. Describe a program you would design to help students talk through societal issues that have no easy resolution, such as racism, heterosexism, classism.

CHAPTER FIFTEEN

MORAL DEVELOPMENT

College administrators have expressed concerns about the moral development of college students since the beginning of higher education, when
college presidents were responsible for the moral character of the young men
in their care (Thelin, 2011). Though colonial educators attached religious
beliefs to morality, contemporary educators and researchers understand that
morality and religion are separate constructs. Moral development in college
students describes the processes through which individuals develop more complex principles and ways of reasoning about what is right, just, and caring.

   Student affairs educators rely on the work of three leading psychological
theorists—Lawrence Kohlberg, James Rest, and Carol Gilligan—who conducted much of the earlier empirical research on college students' moral
development. Kohlberg's theory came first and focused on moral reasoning,
the cognitive component of moral behavior. He saw moral development as
"the transformations that occur in a person's form or structure of thought"
(Kohlberg & Hersh, 1977, p. 54) with regard to what is viewed as right or
necessary. Extending Kohlberg's notion of moral reasoning, Rest (1986b)
stressed that moral behavior consists of additional components: (1) *moral
sensitivity*—interpreting a situation involving the welfare of another as a moral
problem and identifying possible alternatives; (2) *moral motivation*—deciding
to follow the moral path; and (3) *moral action*—implementing and carrying
out a moral plan. Rest and his colleagues (1999) built on Kohlberg's theory
and sculpted the neo-Kohlbergian approach to moral development. Gilligan
(1977, 1982/1993) was one of the first to recognize and document what she

perceived as two different moral orientations: care and justice. In the last 30 years of the twentieth century, her research received praise and stirred controversy in academe and the general public over the moral orientations of women and men. Since encouraging moral behavior is an important developmental goal of higher education (Evans, 1987), understanding and facilitating the development of moral reasoning is an important goal for educators.

This chapter presents an overview of moral development focusing on the work of cognitive psychologists Kohlberg, Rest, and Gilligan and selected inquiry and critique that has followed their original research. We frame each theory within the context of its history before describing it. Then we highlight research and application of these theories in the college context, to showcase how student affairs educators can enhance students' moral development. When appropriate, we discuss these interconnected theories together. The chapter concludes with current theory critiques and suggestions for future research.

Kohlberg's Theory of Moral Development

Kohlberg's ideas were a dominant force guiding moral development research for over four decades (Rest, Narvaez, Thoma, & Bebeau, 2000). Based on both psychology (Piaget) and moral philosophy (Rawls), Kohlberg's theory is cognitive-developmental in nature. The empirical tie between moral and cognitive development is strong (Pascarella & Terenzini, 2005); thus a more advanced intellect is likely to demonstrate more developed moral reasoning. Focusing on the process of how individuals make moral judgments, not the content of these decisions, Kohlberg saw such judgments as having three qualities: (1) an emphasis on value rather than fact; (2) an effect on a person or persons; and (3) a requirement that action be taken (Colby, Kohlberg, & Kauffman, 1987).

Historical Overview

Kohlberg focused on the process of how individuals make moral judgments, not the content of these decisions, and he placed universalism and individualism at the center of his thinking. He was one of the first scholars to study the moral development of adolescents, and later of college students. Building on Piaget's (1932/1977) research, Kohlberg (1958) examined the moral reasoning of adolescent boys and found their reasoning proceeded through invariant and qualitatively different stages. He and his colleagues then embarked on a series of studies to validate the theory, establish the content and sequence of moral stages in other cultures (Kohlberg, 1979), and demonstrate the hierarchical arrangement of stages (Rest, 1969). The first comprehensive statement of Kohlberg's (1969) approach to moral reasoning emerged from these later inquiries.

Kohlberg's Theory

Kohlberg's (1981) stages represent "holistic structures that develop in an invariant sequence and constitute a hierarchy" (Walker, 1988, p. 38), which characterizes the theory as a "hard" stage model (Kohlberg, Levine, & Hewer, 1984). Three criteria frame Kohlberg's stage theory (Walker, 1988). The *structure criterion* is the most fundamental of the three characteristics. At a given stage, individuals exhibit a similar reasoning pattern regardless of the content or situation. The *sequence criterion* indicates that stages appear in a specific order, regardless of setting or experience. Not all individuals advance through all stages, nor will they move through the stages at the same rate. However, the sequence of stages is fixed. The final stage characteristic is the *hierarchy criterion.* This criterion states that each successive stage is more highly developed than the previous one because it incorporates aspects of all earlier stages. Individuals understand and use all stages of thinking below the stage at which they currently function, but never at higher stages.

Prerequisites for Moral Stage Development Two domains of cognition are related to moral reasoning: more general cognitive structures (Piaget, 1950) and social perspective-taking (Kohlberg, 1976). The ability to put oneself in another person's place, or perspective-taking, means understanding what someone is thinking (Selman, 1980). Kohlberg (1976) hypothesized that perspective-taking mediates between cognitive and moral development. Both cognitive structures and social perspective-taking are necessary, but not sufficient, conditions for moral development. Growth in these two domains can, with no guarantee, create "a state of readiness" for such development (Walker, 1988, p. 53).

Conditions Facilitating Moral Stage Development Two factors appear to contribute to moral stage development: exposure to higher stage thinking and disequilibrium (Walker, 1988). Earlier statements focusing on moral education (for example, Kohlberg, 1975) promoted the use of reasoning one stage above the thinking exhibited by the individual ("plus-one" reasoning) to enhance development. Theoretically, observing reasoning at a stage higher than the next one is incomprehensible to the individual and therefore has no impact on their development. One review of moral research, however, concluded that exposure to thinking at any stage higher than that presented by an individual is sufficient to foster development (Walker, 1988). Disequilibrium, or cognitive conflict, occurs when individuals are faced with situations arousing internal contradictions in their moral reasoning structures or when they find their reasoning is different from that of significant others (Kohlberg, 1976). Exposure to conflict, in both opinions and reasoning, also leads to moral development (Walker, 1983; 1988). For example, a study of moral reasoning among college students found that diversity courses in which students encountered ideas that challenged their current ways of moral reasoning promoted development (Hurtado, Mayhew, & Engberg, 2012).

Kohlberg's Stages of Moral Reasoning At the core of Kohlberg's theory is the claim that moral reasoning develops through a six-stage sequence grouped into three levels (Kohlberg, 1976). Each level, composed of two stages, represents a different relationship between the self and society's rules and expectations. At Level I (preconventional), individuals have not yet come to understand societal rules and expectations; their perspective is concrete and individually focused. Level II (conventional) is called the "member-of-society" perspective. At this level, individuals identify with the rules and expectations of others, especially authorities. Level III (postconventional, or principled) is labeled the "prior-to-society" perspective. Individuals separate themselves from the rules and expectations of others and base their decisions on self-chosen principles. Each level of Kohlberg's theory has two stages centered on judgments of rightness and obligation (Colby, Kohlberg, & Kauffman, 1987). Kohlberg (1976) and Colby et al. (1987) defined them as follows:

> ***Stage 1: Heteronomous Morality.*** In the first stage of the preconventional level, what is right is defined as obeying rules to avoid punishment and refraining from physical harm to others and their property. Individuals justify actions based on avoidance of punishment and the superior power of authorities. They do not consider the rights or concerns of others.
>
> ***Stage 2: Individualistic, Instrumental Morality.*** This is the second stage in the preconventional level. Individuals at this stage follow rules, if it is in their interest to do so. They understand that other people have needs and interests that may conflict with their own, so right is defined by what is fair, an equal exchange, or an agreement. They maintain a pragmatic perspective, which ensures satisfaction of their own needs and wants, while minimizing the possibility of negative consequences to themselves.

Stage 3: Interpersonally Normative Morality. At this stage, the first in the conventional level, right is defined as meeting the expectations of those to whom one is close and carrying out appropriate, acceptable social roles (for example, son, friend). Concern centers on maintaining a "good person" image and gaining others' approval. Shared feelings, agreements, and expectations take precedence over individual interests, but a generalized social system perspective does not yet exist.

Stage 4: Social System Morality. In this second conventional stage, individuals view the social system as made up of a consistent set of rules and procedures applying equally to all. Right is defined as upholding the laws established by society and carrying out the duties agreed upon. Individuals behave in a way that maintains the system and fulfills societal obligations.

Stage 5: Human Rights and Social Welfare Morality. In this first principled stage, laws and social systems are evaluated based on the extent to which they promote fundamental human rights and values. The social system is understood as a social contract freely entered into to protect members' rights and ensure the welfare of all. Moral obligations and social relationships are based on making, and being able to depend on, agreements.

Stage 6: Morality of Universalizable, Reversible, and Prescriptive General Ethical Principles. In the second principled stage, morality involves equal consideration of the points of view of all involved in a moral situation. Decisions are based on universal generalizable principles that apply in all situations; for example, the equality of human rights. The process by which a contract is made is viewed as equally important to the fairness of the procedures underlying the agreement.

Kohlberg was unsuccessful in empirically demonstrating the existence of Stage 6 (Kohlberg et al., 1984) in his longitudinal studies. He maintained, however, that it is a philosophical and theoretical stage necessary to bring his theory to a logical endpoint. Kohlberg based his definition of Stage 6 on a few individuals, such as Martin Luther King, Jr., with formal training in philosophy and a demonstrated commitment to moral leadership (Kohlberg et al.). Kohlberg's inability to articulate and empirically test this abstract moral apex is the root of substantial criticism of his theory.

Rest's Neo-Kohlbergian Approach

Rest (1979b; 1986a) developed an objective measure of moral development, the Defining Issues Test (DIT), and undertook a significant program of research. He and his colleagues (for example, Narvaez, 2005; Rest et al., 2000;

Thoma & Rest, 1999) adapted Kohlberg's theory to create a neo-Kohlbergian approach to moral thinking. The core aspects of Rest's moral development stages, however, are borrowed directly from Kohlberg. Rest (1979a) examined two elements in a person's thinking: how expectations about actions (rules) are known and shared and how interests are balanced. He identified the following central concepts for determining moral rights and responsibilities:

Stage 1: Obedience ("Do what you're told.")

Stage 2: Instrumental egoism and simple exchange ("Let's make a deal.")

Stage 3: Interpersonal concordance ("Be considerate, nice, and kind, and you'll get along with people.")

Stage 4: Law and duty to the social order ("Everyone in society is obligated and protected by the law.")

Stage 5: Societal consensus ("You are obligated by whatever arrangements are agreed to by due process procedures.")

Stage 6: Non-arbitrary social cooperation ("How rational and impartial people would organize cooperation is "moral.")" (Rest, 1979a, pp. 22–23)

Assumptions Underlying Rest's Theory

While grounded in many assumptions of Kohlberg's theory, a neo-Kohlbergian perspective differs in several ways (Rest et al., 2000). Rest viewed the moral development framework more broadly than Kohlberg did. First, Rest (1979a) questioned whether content and structure can be separated in moral reasoning. Rest focused on the kind of consideration an individual uses in making a decision, noting that both content and structural elements might be included. Kohlberg limited stage content to social institutions, whereas Rest fashioned his schemas around "institutions and role systems in society" (Rest et al., 2000, p. 387).

Next, Rest (1979a) rejected Kohlberg's hard stage model and proposed a more complex alternative. Based on his conception of development as a continuous process, Rest suggested that it is more appropriate to consider the percentage of an individual's reasoning at a particular stage of development rather than whether a person is "in" a particular stage. Rest believed a person may use or show forward movement in several stages at the same time. For instance, 20% of a person's thinking might rank at stage 3, interpersonal concordance, 50% at stage 4, law and duty to the social order, and 30% at stage 5, societal consensus. The percentage of thinking at the principled level (stages 5 and 6) is of most concern to researchers.

Third, Rest (1979a) rejected the idea of step-by-step development through the stages and instead "envision[ed] development as shifting distributions rather than as a staircase" (Rest et al., 2000, p. 384). Thus he referred to the development process as schemas (soft, more permeable stages), rather than hard stages as Kohlberg proposed.

Rest's Schemas

Rest and his colleagues (2000) proposed three schemas related to structures in moral reasoning development, examined by administration of the DIT (Rest, 1979a) and DIT-2 (Rest & Narvaez, 1998).

Personal Interest Schema Derived from Kohlberg's Stages 2 and 3, the personal interest schema develops in childhood and is no longer paramount by the time one acquires the reading level of a 12-year-old. In this schema, individuals consider "what each stakeholder in a moral dilemma has to gain and lose as if they did not have to worry about organising co-operation on a society-wide basis" (Rest et al., 2000, p. 387). What is morally right, in this schema, is that which appeals to the investment an individual holds in consequences of the action. Both individual concerns, as well as the concerns of those with whom one has close attachment, are prevalent in this schema. In short, the personal interest schema puts focus on the self and recognizes some awareness of the other in making moral decisions.

Maintaining Norms Schema Derived from Kohlberg's Stage 4, the maintaining norms schema is a first attempt to envision societal collaboration in this neo-Kohlbergian approach. The following elements are common: (1) a desire for "generally accepted norms to govern a collective," (2) a belief that norms apply to all who live in a particular society, (3) a need for "clear, uniform, and categorical" norms or rule of law, (4) a view of norms as reciprocal; if I obey the law, others will too; and (5) "establishment of hierarchical role orders, of chains of command and of authority and duty" (Rest et al., 2000, p. 387). Respect for authority is derived not from the authority's personal attributes, but from respect for society. Simply put, morality, in this schema, is "an act prescribed by the law, is the established way of doing things, or is the established Will of God" (Rest et al., 2000, p. 388). Thus, the neo-Kohlbergian approach focuses on a need for societal norms motivated by duty and embraced in uniform application (Narvaez, 2005).

Postconventional Schema Derived from Kohlberg's Stages 5 and 6, the postconventional schema places moral obligation on communal values such as shared ideals, reciprocity, and critical inspection in the form of logical consistency and debate. Incorporating more developmental complexity, the postconventional schema also is "more advanced in a normative ethical sense" (Narvaez, 2005, p. 122). Four elements critical to the postconventional schema include "primacy of moral criteria, appeal to an ideal, shareable values and full reciprocity" (Rest et al., 2000, p. 388). A feature of late adolescent development, the postconventional schema is a leading indicator of students' development in college (Narvaez; Pascarella & Terenzini, 2005).

Research on Moral Stage Development

There are thousands of studies based on Kohlberg's theory of moral development, with over 500 studies using the DIT (King & Mayhew, 2002; Rest, 1986b). Early studies by both Kohlberg's and Rest's research teams focused on validation of the theory and measurement issues related to their respective instruments (Rest, 1979a). Both the DIT and Kohlberg's Moral Judgment Inventory (MJI) (Kohlberg, 1984) are valid and reliable instruments. In addition, a number of scholars (among them Rest, 1979a, 1986b; Walker, 1988; Walker & Taylor, 1991) have demonstrated the basic constructs associated with Kohlberg's theory.

Factors Related to the Development of Moral Judgment

Review of the DIT research indicated that moral development increases with age and educational level, with educational level being the more powerful variable (Rest, 1986b). Pascarella and Terenzini (1991, 2005) summarized the quantitative research investigating moral development in college, including studies that used both the MJI and DIT. King and Mayhew (2005) conducted an in-depth exploration of theory and research on moral reasoning among college students. Research continues to reveal that individuals attending college show a significant increase in the use of principled reasoning (as measured by the DIT), beyond that related just to maturation.

Becoming more aware of the world in general and one's place in it does more to foster moral development than specific experiences (Rest, 1986b). Pascarella and Terenzini (1991, 2005) and King and Mayhew (2005) suggested, for example, that college may foster moral development by providing a variety of social, intellectual, and cultural experiences for students. An introduction to higher stage thinking provided by upper-class students in residence halls, courses providing conflicting perspectives on various issues, exposure to divergent ideas resulting from living away from home, and interactions with roommates are conditions that promote moral development (Hurtado, Mayhew, & Engberg, 2012; King & Mayhew, 2005; Mayhew & King, 2008; Rest & Narvaez, 1991). The extent to which individuals take advantage of such experiences is the most important factor leading to growth in moral reasoning.

The Impact of Educational Interventions

Evans (1987) presented a framework for intentionally designing interventions to foster moral development on college campuses, using policy, programming, and individual approaches. This model considers the target of the intervention (individual or institutional), the type of intervention (planned or responsive), and the intervention approach (implicit or explicit). Specific interventions designed to foster moral reasoning seem to have some impact on principled thinking, particularly those emphasizing discussion of moral dilemmas or overall psychological development (Rest, 1986b). This effect may be conditional (Pascarella & Terenzini, 1991); that is, such interventions may work for certain students (for example, formal reasoners who seek intellectual stimulation) but not for others (for example, concrete reasoners) (Pascarella & Terenzini, 2005). Other areas of identity—including Black identity development (Moreland & Leach, 2001), spiritual development (Power, 2005), psychosocial development (Jones & Watt, 2001), and cognitive development (King, 2009; Mayhew & King, 2008)—also affect moral development.

Cultural and Religious Differences

Research findings related to cultural and religious differences in moral development are mixed. While there is variation in the rate of development and the stage to which individuals may progress, scholars have established the universality of Kohlberg's stage model in various cultures generally and with college students in different cultures specifically (see Lind, 1986; Snarey, 1985). Values and principles upon which individuals base moral judgments (that is, their moral orientation) vary in different cultures and contexts. People descended from Asian cultures may demonstrate more altruism and concern for the law, while those from Western cultures may exhibit more individualistic values (Iwasa, 1992; Ma, 1989; Miller & Bersoff, 1992). Some researchers suggested that Kohlberg's theory may not adequately reflect the range of worldviews and values found in non-Western cultures (Heubner &

Garrod, 1993). The dilemmas used in the MJI, for example, may not be meaningful where concerns such as compassion and karma, rather than justice, are paramount. A study of adolescents from Israel, the United States, Taiwan, Turkey, and the Bahamas indicated there may be cultural differences related to autonomous versus heteronomous judgment (Logan, Snarey, & Schrader, 1990). Conceptions of justice and power influenced outcomes in a study of ethical decision-making in college students from China, Japan, Mexico, and the United States (Curtis, Conover, & Chui, 2012).

Adherence to a conservative versus a liberal religious ideology is moderately related to moral development, with those holding a liberal perspective scoring higher (Rest, 1986b). In an attempt to explain this finding, Dirks (1988) suggested the tenets of evangelical belief systems may foster unquestioning allegiance to a higher authority consistent with conventional rather than postconventional thinking. Offering a similar explanation for their findings, Good and Cartwright (1998) found no relationship between moral development and religious orthodoxy, intense religious training, or passionate religious devotion among students enrolled in state and Christian universities. Another study assessed the relationship between religious choice (which in this study was limited to Roman Catholic, Protestant, or none) and level of moral development of first-year college men (Tatum, Foubert, Fuqua, & Ray, 2013). As with similar studies, male students who indicated no religious affiliation scored higher in their moral development than those with a religious preference.

College Students

In recent years, Mayhew and colleagues have carried out a research agenda on moral development in college students. Studies of first-year students (Mayhew, Seifert, & Pascarella, 2012), pedagogy (Mayhew & King, 2008), diversity (Mayhew & Engberg, 2010), and institutional type (Mayhew, 2012) revealed findings pertinent to students' moral stage development. Other variables that may influence the development of moral reasoning in college include educational level, age, and academic major (King & Mayhew, 2005). Seeking influences on first-year college students' moral reasoning, Mayhew et al. (2012) found that "structuring and sequencing developmentally challenging and appropriate learning opportunities for first year students may help them achieve developmental gains in moral reasoning" (p. 37). It is clear from their review that students enter college at different levels of readiness for moral development, and student affairs educators cannot assume that a given student is at a particular stage.

Gilligan's Theory of Women's Moral Development

Prior to the popular and scholarly success of Carol Gilligan's (1982/1993) book *In a Different Voice*, human development theorists, for the most part, did not include women in psychological studies. Freud's (1905/1965) research began a snowball "portrayal of women as deviants" (Kuk, 1992, p. 26) and set men as the standard by which to judge what was normal. Using a theory based solely on male participants, Kohlberg (1981) concluded that women were unable to reach the same developmental pinnacle as their male counterparts. Kohlberg later included women in his research, but continued to find women "underdeveloped" (Gelwick, 1985, p. 29).

Historical Overview

In 1982, Carol Gilligan published her pathbreaking work, *In a Different Voice*, in which she presented research findings about women's moral development. She disputed previous models of human growth that did not accurately represent women's experience. The different voice she delineated is distinguished not by gender but by the themes of care and justice. Gilligan contrasted the voices of men and women by empirical observation to pinpoint "a distinction between two modes of thought and to focus a problem of interpretation rather than to represent a generalization about either sex" (Gilligan, 1982/1993, p. 2). Gilligan spent 30 years studying girls and their relationships, and her research has changed views on moral development. In her current research she deconstructs patriarchy for more equal treatment of women and men, and urges a feminist ethic of care as a means to resist injustice (Gilligan, 2011).

Gilligan's Theory: In a Different Voice

Gilligan's and Kohlberg's beliefs about how people make meaning of their world are quite different (Linn, 2001). Kohlberg's (1969) justice orientation focused morality on understanding rights and rules. His six-stage hierarchy reflects a progression from lower order to higher order moral thinking in which autonomy is prized and universal justice is the goal (Romer, 1991). In contrast, Gilligan (1986) observed "in women's thinking the lines of a different conception, grounded in different images of relationship and implying a different interpretive framework" (p. 326). The central tenet of Gilligan's care orientation is that for some individuals, often women, relationships with others carry equal weight with self-care when making moral decisions.

Gilligan (1977, 1982/1993) demonstrated that women in her study identified care and responsibility as their moral compass. Derived from responses of 29 women facing an abortion decision, Gilligan (1977) "formed the basis for describing a developmental sequence that traces progressive differentiations" in how women understand and judge "conflicts between self and others" (p. 183). She proposed that women's moral development proceeds through a sequence of three levels and two transition periods. Each level identifies a more intricate relationship between self and others. Each transition represents the achievement of a more sophisticated understanding between selfishness and responsibility.

Level I: Orientation to Individual Survival The individual is self-centered, preoccupied with survival, and unable to distinguish between necessity and desire. For example, one 18-year-old respondent in Gilligan's study affirmed "there was no right decision" to be made when it came to her abortion because she did not want to be pregnant. Growth and transition have potential to occur only if her dilemma compelled her to seek another moral option. The goal at this level is to fulfill individual desires and needs for the purpose of preserving the self.

First Transition: From Selfishness to Responsibility The most salient issue in the first transition is one of attachment and connection to others. The criteria used for judging moral dilemmas shifts from independence and selfishness to connection and responsibility. The conflict between necessity and desire (needing and wanting) is clear, giving the individual more choices for moral judgment. Questioning their self-concept, individuals in this transition consider the opportunity for doing the right thing. Responsibility and care are integrated into patterns of moral decision-making.

Level II: Goodness as Self-Sacrifice As the individual moves from a self-centered, independent view of the world to one of richer engagement with and reliance on others, survival is predicated on social acceptance. In fact, an individual may give up her own judgment in order to achieve consensus and remain in connection with others. Disequilibrium arises over the issue of hurting others. Although conflict exists, it is typically not voiced in public but rather in private.

Second Transition: From Goodness to Truth In the second transition, individuals question why they continue to put others first at their own expense. During this time of doubt, individuals examine their own needs to determine if they can be included within the realm of responsibility. However, the struggle "to reconcile the disparity between hurt and care" (Gilligan, 1977, p. 498) continues. At this time, individuals make moral judgment shifts from deciding in accordance with those around them to deciding by inclusion of their own needs on a par with others. For the first time, individuals view examination of their own needs as truth, not selfishness.

Level III: The Morality of Nonviolence   The individual raises nonviolence, a moral mandate to avoid hurt, to the overriding principle that governs moral judgment and action. The individual is elevated to the principle of care by a "transformed understanding of self and a corresponding redefinition of morality" (Gilligan, 1977, p. 504). Through this second transformation, which now includes respect for the self, the dichotomization of selfishness and responsibility disappears. Reconciliation opens the door for the individual to recognize her power to select among competing choices and keep her needs within the mix of moral alternatives.

Research on Gilligan's Theory of Moral Development

Gilligan has spent the better part of her career examining the relational aspects of moral reasoning. With continued modification and extension of her original work, Gilligan shifted from examination of primarily white, privileged women's moral development to a more inclusive examination of women's and girls' relationships and how cultural differences influence these relationships and their development (Taylor, Gilligan, & Sullivan, 1995). Other scholars have contributed to a better understanding of the care ethic; however, findings on gender-related moral orientation are not always consistent.

Gender Differences

In a Different Voice presented research from three studies: one explored identity and moral development of college students (Gilligan, 1981); another emphasized how women make decisions about abortion (Gilligan & Belenky, 1980); and finally, a rights and responsibilities study examined different ways of moral thinking and their relationship to different ways of thinking about the self (Gilligan & Murphy, 1979). Each study employed similar qualitative methods to reveal how different voices (that is, care and justice) reflect moral life. Gilligan and colleagues framed results using interview excerpts accompanied by the researchers' interpretations (Brabeck, 1983).

Hundreds of studies over two decades probed the question of gender differences in moral development and orientation. A comprehensive meta-analysis of quantitative studies found that empirical research largely does not support the hypothesis that there are differences in either the care orientation or the justice orientation; nearly three-quarters of the studies of these orientations demonstrate no meaningful differences (Jaffee & Hyde, 2000). Where there were statistically significant differences between sexes, the effect sizes were small. In an analysis of research on gender and morality, Walker (2006) concluded, "There is no support for the notion that Kohlberg's model downscores the reasoning of women and those with a care orientation," and "Gilligan's claim of gender polarity in moral orientations cannot be sustained in light of the small effect sizes in analyses of gender differences" (p. 109). Still, Walker acknowledged the important contribution that Gilligan made to the field in bringing attention to the ethic of care as a critical feature of the moral aspects of interpersonal conflict.

Cultural Differences between Care and Justice Orientations

Just as scholars sought to discover cross-cultural differences using Kohlberg's theory, scholars have examined cultural differences in relation to Gilligan's concepts of care and justice. As a whole, there is "no clear pattern of results concerning the differential effects of race and ethnicity on the development of undergraduate students' moral reasoning" (King & Mayhew, 2005, p. 392). A study of Gilligan's ethic of care in students from Brazil and Norway found no gender-related differences, but there were differences between countries, with Norwegian students measuring higher on ethic of care (Vikan, Camino, & Biaggio, 2005). It does seem clear that culture influences justice and care reasoning and the priority that individuals place on these values (Miller, 2006). There are some observed differences across gender and cultural contexts. For example, in a cross-cultural study of Mexican American and Anglo college students, Gump, Baker, and Roll (2000) found females scored higher than males and Mexican Americans scored higher than Anglos on the care measure. Other research reported gender differences in moral orientation and found differences recognizable across cultures (Stimpson, Jensen, & Neff, 1992). A questionnaire administered to female and male college students in Korea, Thailand, the People's Republic of China, and the United States revealed that in all four countries women showed a preference for an ethic of care. Similarly, a study conducted to explore the ethics of care and justice, using the Measure of Moral Orientation (MMO) (Liddell, 1995) among female nursing students at different educational levels, found a propensity toward the ethics of care (Wilson, 2000).

In contrast, research on the moral orientation of American Indian college students, utilizing the MMO (Liddell, 1995), sought objectively to identify the moral orientations of students from three tribal colleges (Little Big Horn College, Kootenai College, and Southwest Indian Polytechnic Institute) (Arvizu, 1995). The findings contrasted with the literature regarding women's care and justice scores in that female American Indian students score "higher on justice than either American Indian men or the Euro-American men in these studies" (p. 11).

Gilligan's Theory Applied to Student Affairs

For many student affairs educators, an ethic of care is embedded within their personal value system and translated daily into professional practice. Since the profession is premised on a long history of support for and care of students, a longstanding relationship exists between student affairs practice and moral reasoning based on care (Canon & Brown, 1985). A number of contemporary scholars call on an ethic of care as a central concept in student affairs practice and organizations (see Hirt, Amelink, McFeeters, & Strayhorn, 2008; Manning, Kinzie, & Schuh, 2013). Likewise, Gilligan's ideas concerning ethics of care and justice have been applied to college counseling (Frey, Beesley, & Miller, 2006; Griffin, 2007), residence life (Hirt et al., 2008; Simola, Barling, & Turner, 2010), career planning (Cabrera, 2007; McMahon, Watson, & Bimrose, 2014), service learning (Bernacki & Jaeger, 2008; Bowdon, Pigg, & Mansfield, 2014; Lies, Bock, Brandenberger, & Trozzolo, 2012), and leadership development (Begley & Stefkovich, 2007; Onorato & Musoba, 2015; Simola et al., 2010). This literature offers insight and practical suggestions for student affairs professionals who want to understand how care and justice may differently influence students' moral development. Student affairs professionals can apply Gilligan's theory in the contexts of community development, policy enforcement, conflict management, and team building.

Reframing Gilligan's Ethic of Care

Since the 1970s, Gilligan shifted the conversation about moral development, from self and morality to voice and relationships. Growing evidence of a paradigm shift in human development studies is recasting healthy maturation not as separating from others (for example, in the tradition of Kohlberg or Chickering), but as connecting with them. In fact, social and biological scientists see the clear connection between thought and emotion, and view separation as a way to "signal injury or response to trauma" (Gilligan, 2014,

p. 89). In reframing the conversation, Gilligan (2014) explains the shift in her thinking in the last three decades:

> Care is a feminist, not a "feminine" ethic, and feminism, guided by an ethic of care, is arguably the most radical, in the sense of going to the roots, liberation movement in human history. Released from the gender binary and hierarchy, feminism is neither a women's issue nor a battle between women and men. It is the movement to free democracy from patriarchy. (p. 101)

Simola (2014) presented a study that moves away from the limitation of gender specificity outlined in Gilligan's (1977) moral development theory and toward an ethic of care by examining moral courage through a feminist lens set within the context of business ethics and organizational dynamics.

Analyzing Qualitative Data: Gilligan's Listening Guide

Gilligan (2015) documented the method she used for collecting and analyzing the psychological data for her research on women throughout the last 30 years of her research. How an individual's voice interplays with the voices of others, the underlying forces of the research relationship, and the cultural environment of the inquiry all add to understanding the contextual framework for data interpretation. In a nutshell, as a way of exploring an individual's interchange of their inner and outer worlds, the Listening Guide starts with questions about voice and relationship, such as: "Who is speaking and to whom? In what body or physical space? Telling what stories about which relationships? In what societal and cultural frameworks?" (p. 69). Finally, these answers are framed through a psychological lens, examined in relationship to the movement of the speaker's voice throughout the transcripts, and highlighted by the voices that specifically address the researcher's questions. Relationships between researcher and research participants, not independence and autonomy, guide this method to a successful conclusion. Consistent with the notion of an ethic of care for moral decision-making, Gilligan articulated the ethical challenge as staying in relationship with oneself and others.

Measuring Care-Based Moral Development

Based on Gilligan's (1982) theory of moral development, Skoe (1998, 2008) developed the Ethic of Care Interview (ECI) to measure care-based moral development. The ECI measures five stages of care-based moral thought, which move from self-concern, to questioning self-concern as a singular criterion, to primary concern for others, to questioning a single criterion of concern for others, to a balance of concern for self and others. This progression demonstrates more complex interpretations of a hierarchy of interdependence and a clearer understanding of differentiation between self and others. Healthy adulthood requires care for oneself and care for others, which emerges as individuals deal with issues across the lifespan such as developing long-term relationships, parenting, and coping with mortality, as well as supporting children and aging parents simultaneously. Conflict and stress provide stimulation for positive growth, and a chaotic end to an intimate relationship or death of significant other can lead to this advancement. Across a lifetime, care-based moral thought may serve as a psychological tool in fulfilling the primary tasks of adulthood; for example, realizing intimacy (Chickering, 1969; Chickering & Reisser, 1993; see Chapter Thirteen) and creating generativity (Erikson, 1982). The challenges brought on by maturity and wisdom help move individuals to higher ECI levels.

Critique and Future Directions

Evidence strongly supports the claim that participating in postsecondary education enhances students' moral development (Pascarella & Terenzini, 2005). Liddell and Cooper (2012) called for a return to moral and ethical education as an intended outcome of higher education, as was the case in early U.S. higher education. They made a strong case for purposely designing learning opportunities that focus on college students' moral development. They contended that a moral crisis in higher education continues to deepen, and the moral credibility of its leaders has been called into question; these phenomena provide powerful, teachable moments everywhere in the academy—inside and outside the classroom. More and more of the curriculum in a wide range of disciplines is requiring students to study ethical and moral development to enhance professional decision-making (Liddell & Cooper).

Recommendations for continuing research on the moral development of college students abound. As the most widely used instrument to measure moral reasoning, the DIT and its validation of the neo-Kohlbergian approach are by far the most popular way of examining students' moral reasoning. Pascarella and Terenzini (2005) argued for using more sophisticated models with large-scale samples at different types of institutions as the next step in understanding students' moral development. We suggest other areas ripe for discovery.

More research is needed on how cultural ideology is transmitted and if it limits or facilitates moral development (Rest et al., 1999). Outside the classroom, students' exposure to diverse social and intellectual climates is likely to create development in higher-level moral thinking (Hurtado, Mayhew, & Engberg, 2012). Teasing out the nuances of all cultural groups to which students belong (for example, ethnicity, race, gender, social class, ability, and so on) and their intersection and impact on moral development would help as faculty and staff delve deeper into understanding how to facilitate moral growth. Not only is it important to know how culture influences moral development, but also how moral development influences and is influenced by other domains of student development (for example, cognitive and psychosocial).

Stewart (2012) recommended "educating for pluralism and social justice in promoting moral growth among college students" (p. 63). Detailing how student affairs educators can develop a "pedagogy of social justice education as well as strategies for resistance" (p. 68), Stewart discussed the hard work necessary for building trust and rapport across difference. Some suggestions for addressing inequities include awareness of power dynamics in relationships with students, acknowledgment of any privileged social group membership, and use of reflection and lived experience to stimulate learning. As institutions of higher education continue to become more diverse, modeling and teaching students to reason with moral intent is paramount for a democratic society to thrive, allowing minoritized groups a voice (Gilligan & Richards, 2009).

How students, faculty, and staff in postsecondary education morally reason within a community of scholars is vital to producing a society with individuals and groups who will use similar consideration in moral decision-making after college. Creating a campus climate conducive to facilitating moral development is an aspirational goal that needs constant evaluation and realignment with changing student populations, social contexts, and moral dilemmas both age-old (such as academic honesty) and of-the-minute (ethical relationships in cyberspace). The field of student affairs needs continued scholarship and theorizing about how to decipher the ways in which moral development manifests differently in each student, what policies and practices can create climates on campus to stimulate a diversity of ideas to promote moral behavior and decision-making, and how professionals can best help students from all cultural backgrounds increase their moral maturity.

Discusssion Questions

1. Think of a moral development dilemma a student might face based upon your functional area (for example, residence life, campus activities). Describe the student's journey through the dilemma, using Kohlberg's

preconventional, conventional, and postconventional levels (as a whole known as the justice orientation) and what the student's decisions might look like at each level (or stage).

2. How do theories of moral development differ from those of psychosocial development? How might intersections of knowledge in each area inform student affairs practice?

3. Rest's neo-Kohlbergian approach to moral development is based on Kohlberg's moral theory but differs in significant ways. Describe the differences.

4. Gilligan noted that women's decision-making processes appeared different from men's. Identify another student you know who is facing a moral dilemma right now. Using Gilligan's theory as a model, describe how this student might decide, using a care orientation.

5. Create a table or diagram that compares and contrasts the similarities and differences between decision-making that focuses on care and decision-making that focuses on justice orientations. Please address how each relates to gender.

6. Overall, when thinking about college students' moral development, describe a metaphor for the concept and draw an illustration of its meaning to you.

7. Compare and contrast the three theories presented in this chapter (including Kohlberg, Rest, and Gilligan) with the corresponding theories presented in the preceding epistemological and intellectual development chapter (including Perry; Belenky, Clinchy, Goldberger, and Tarule; and Kitchener and King).

8. Think about moral development through a lens of privilege and oppression. Provide examples of how issues related to moral development in college can affect populations minoritized by their race, gender, sexuality, religion, disability, and class.

CHAPTER SIXTEEN

DEVELOPMENT OF SELF-AUTHORSHIP

Since the early 2000s, the concept of self-authorship has become a central theory in understanding college students' ability to make meaning of the world and their lives in it. Self-authorship theory is holistic in that it includes epistemological/cognitive, interpersonal/relational, and intrapersonal/psychosocial dimensions of development. The processes related to developing the ability to self-author—to write one's own life—relate well to prevailing philosophies of higher education, including the cultivation of critical thinking and intercultural understanding.

This chapter describes the concept of self-authorship, "the internal capacity to define one's beliefs, identity, and social relations" (Baxter Magolda, 2008, p. 269). This concept aligns with theories in the "constructivist-developmental" category, which focuses on "the growth or transformation" of ways people "construct meaning" (Kegan, 1994, p. 199) regarding their life experiences. We present and examine two important constructive-developmental theories—those of Robert Kegan and Marcia Baxter Magolda.

Kegan's Theory of the Evolution of Consciousness

Kegan introduced his theory of self-evolution in his 1982 book *The Evolving Self*. In his later book *In Over Our Heads: The Mental Demands of Modern Life* (1994), he presented a revised version of his theory and further discussion of the implications of his work for society. Kegan (1982) noted that Piaget's work served as inspiration for his own. Pointing out that Piaget had attended very little to emotion or to the process and experience of development, Kegan sought to address these omissions, drawing on the work of object-relation theorists such as Kernberg (1966), who explored how interpretations of self-other relationships evolved over time, and psychosocial theorists, especially Erikson (see Chapter Thirteen). Kegan especially valued "building strong intellectual bridges" (Scharmer, 2000, n.p.) to educational practice, leadership, and organizational development.

Kegan's Theory

The focus of Kegan's (1994) theory is the "evolution of consciousness, the personal unfolding of ways of organizing experience that are not simply replaced as we grow but subsumed into more complex systems of mind" (p. 9). Growth involves movement through five progressively more complex ways of knowing, which Kegan referred to as stages of development in 1982, orders of consciousness in 1994, and forms of mind in 2000. The process of growth involves an evolution of meaning, marked by continual shifts from periods of stability to periods of instability, leading to ongoing reconstruction relationships between persons and their environments (Kegan, 1982). Each succeeding order consists of cognitive, intrapersonal, and interpersonal components.

Kegan (1982, 1994) saw the process of development as an effort to resolve the tension between a desire for differentiation and an equally powerful desire to be immersed in one's surroundings (Kegan, 1994). The evolutionary truces evident at each developmental stage of Kegan's (1982) model are "temporary solution[s] to the lifelong tension between the yearnings for inclusion and distinctness" (p. 107). While initially stating that his ways of knowing alternated between favoring autonomy at one stage and favoring embeddedness at the next (Kegan, 1982), he later modified his view, stating that "each order of consciousness can favor either of the two fundamental longings" (Kegan, 1994, p. 221) and that neither position is better than the other. He suggested that increased differentiation could mean finding new ways to stay connected. Paradoxically, as people make meaning in a more differentiated way, they also have the capacity to become closer to others.

Kegan (1982) was clear that the process of growth could be painful, since it involves changing one's way of functioning in the world. Borrowing from Winnicott (1965), Kegan (1982) introduced the idea of the "holding environment" (p. 116) to assist individuals with these changes. The holding environment has two functions: supporting individuals in their current stage of development and encouraging movement to the next evolutionary truce. Kegan (1994) equated a holding environment to an "evolutionary bridge, a context for crossing over" (p. 43) from one order of consciousness to the next, more developed, order. Student affairs educators have numerous opportunities to create these holding environments in which college students can evolve.

Descriptions of Kegan's levels of consciousness follow. They have had different names in different iterations of his theory. We provide the numerical "orders" (similar to a stage or phase) used in the 1994 version as well as the names used for the later orders in the 2000 version. In addition to describing each order, we provide Kegan's (1982) suggestions regarding ways to challenge and support development to the next order.

Order 0. Kegan (1982) described newborn infants as "living in an object-less world, a world in which everything sensed is taken to be an extension of the infant" (p. 78). As a result, when the infant cannot see or experience something, it does not exist. By the time infants are 18 months old, they begin to recognize the existence of objects outside themselves, propelling them into the next stage. Parents must remain constant as the child pushes against them to determine where the boundaries are between its self and the environment.

Order 1. Children develop order 1 meaning making at about age two, when they realize they have control over their reflexes (Kegan, 1982) and become aware of objects in their environment as independent from themselves (Kegan, 1994). Their thinking tends to be "fantastic and illogical, their feelings impulsive and fluid, [and] their social-relating egocentric" (p. 29) in that they are attached to whatever or whoever is present at the moment. Parents should support their children's fantasies while challenging them to take responsibility for themselves and their feelings as they begin to perceive the world realistically and differentiate themselves from others while moving into order 2.

Order 2: Instrumental Mind. Individuals in order 2 are able to construct "durable categories"—classifications of objects, people, or ideas with specific characteristics (Kegan, 1994). As a result, their thinking becomes more logical and organized, their feelings are more enduring, and they relate to others as separate and unique beings. Kegan, Broderick, Drago-Severson, Helsing, Popp, and Portnow (2001) noted that at this time, "rules, sets of directions, and dualisms give shape and structure to one's daily activity" (pp. 4–5). In this order, individuals develop a sense of who they are and what they want. "Competition and compromise" (Kegan,

1982, p. 163) are characteristic themes of order 2 and are often enacted within peer group settings. Support at this stage requires confirmation of the person the child has become. Challenge to develop further involves encouragement to take into consideration the expectations, needs, and desires of others.

Order 3: Socialized Mind. Cross-categorical thinking—the ability to relate one durable category to another characterizes the third order of consciousness. In this order, thinking is more abstract, individuals are aware of their feelings and the internal processes associated with them, and they can make commitments to communities of people and ideas (Kegan, 1994). Kegan and his colleagues (2001) noted that in this order of consciousness, "other people are experienced … as sources of internal validation, orientation, or authority" (p. 5). Because acceptance by others is crucial in this order, individuals pay particular attention to how others perceive them. Support is found in mutually rewarding relationships and shared experiences, while challenge takes the form of resisting codependence and encouraging individuals to make their own decisions and establish independent lives.

Order 4: Self-Authoring Mind. Cross-categorical constructing—the ability to generalize across abstractions, which could also be labeled systems thinking—emerges in order 4 (Kegan, 1994). In this order, self-authorship is the focus. Individuals "have the capacity to take responsibility for and ownership of their internal authority" (Kegan et al., 2001, p. 5) and establish their own sets of values and ideologies (Kegan, 1994). Relationships become a *part* of one's world rather than the reason for one's existence. Support at this stage is evident in acknowledgment of the individual's independence and self-regulation. Significant others who refuse to accept relationships that are not intimate and mutually rewarding encourage individuals to develop further.

Order 5: Self-Transforming Mind. In this order of consciousness, which Kegan (1994) asserted is infrequently reached and never reached before the age of 40, individuals see beyond themselves, others, and systems of which they are a part to form an understanding of how all people and systems interconnect (Kegan, 2000). They recognize their "commonalities and interdependence with others" (Kegan, 1982, p. 239). Relationships can be truly intimate in this order, with nurturance and affiliation as its key characteristics. Kegan (1982) concluded that only rarely do work environments and long-lasting adult intimate partnerships provide these conditions.

The Demands of Modern Life

Kegan (1982) argued that modern life, particularly within the contexts of the family and the work environment, places enormous stress on individuals. Kegan's (1994) book, *In Over Our Heads*, focused on the demands of modern society, or the "hidden curriculum" (p. 9). He argued that expectations of adult life—parenting, partnering, and working—require fourth order meaning making, and many adults have not attained that level.

Kegan (1994) hypothesized that postmodern life requires an ever more complex way of knowing, that of the fifth order, which very few people ever reach. He suggested that rather than demanding that people think in a way that is impossible, they would benefit more from support to help them reach self-authorship, the necessary first step on the path to fifth order meaning making. Kegan wrote about the demands of "modern life" before the Internet introduced manifold changes to how individuals access, process, and synthesize information as well as the conduct of interpersonal relationships and deployment of self and identity in face-to-face and online settings. These new ways of being, knowing, and relating in a digital society amplify the need for helping individuals achieve more complex orders of consciousness.

Research

Several studies have built on Kegan's theory. A four-year longitudinal study of 22 adults conducted by Kegan and colleagues using the subject-object interview (Lahey et al., 1988) revealed that "at any given moment, around one-half to two-thirds of the adult population appears not to have fully reached the fourth order of consciousness" (Kegan, 1994, pp. 188, 191). Drawing on 13 other studies conducted mainly by his doctoral students, Kegan (1994) reported that in the composite sample of 282 adults, 59% had not reached the fourth order. Findings from a longitudinal study of identity development of West Point cadets using Kegan's (1982, 1994) theory as a framework indicated that for most military cadets the challenge of college is moving from self-interest (order 2) to thinking in terms of being part of a community (order 3), a goal that must be accomplished before self-authorship can be considered (Lewis, Forsythe, Sweeney, Bartone, Bullis, & Snook, 2005).

In a study of adult basic education learners in their twenties—who were mostly non-White, non-native English–speaking, lower-income immigrants—participants interpreted and negotiated learning differently depending on their developmental level (Kegan et al., 2001). Students in the cohort played an important role as a holding environment in the learning process by challenging and supporting each other, partially because of the different ways of knowing they exhibited.

Application

Much of Kegan's 1994 book is devoted to understanding and addressing the demands of modern life using his theory as a framework. With regard to the college learning environment, Kegan (1994) suggested that while most students approach learning from an order 3 perspective, teaching is generally approached through the lens of order 4, creating a developmental mismatch. For instance, instructors expect students to be self-reflective, engaged, independent, self-directed, critical thinkers—skills that become evident only in order 4. Rather than assuming and treating students as if they are already self-authoring, Kegan (1994) stressed the importance of building a "consciousness bridge" (p. 278) between the point at which the student enters the classroom (generally order 3) and the level at which they are expected to perform in the classroom (order 4), noting that "the bridge builder must have an equal respect for both ends, creating a firm foundation on both sides of the chasm students will traverse" (p. 278).

Ignelzi (2000) used Kegan's concepts to discuss applications in traditional undergraduate classrooms. Noting that most undergraduate students use order 3 meaning-making and therefore look to their instructors and classmates to determine how they should think and the conclusions they should draw about the material being examined, Ignelzi (2000) suggested the following strategies for encouraging both learning and development: (1) value and support students' current ways of thinking, (2) provide structure and guidance in taking on unfamiliar tasks, (3) encourage students to learn from each other by working together in groups, and (4) acknowledge and reinforce students' successes in moving to a self-authored perspective while recognizing the challenges that are required to do so. These suggestions reflect Kegan's (1982) idea of an effective holding environment.

To assist students in moving from order 2 to order 3, Love and Guthrie (1999) raised the importance of letting students know what behaviors are expected of them and what their responsibilities are, working with them to understand how others' perspectives compare to their own and when the needs of others take priority, and encouraging self-reflection. The transition from order 3 to order 4 is often precipitated by a failed relationship around which individuals have constructed their life's meaning and the resulting need to develop independent goals and values. Love and Guthrie encouraged educators to recognize the pain associated with this transition and support students through the process by recognizing them as independent people, acknowledging their achievements, and encouraging them to get involved in activities where their talents will be valued.

Kegan's concept of coaching can easily translate into student affairs practice (Love & Guthrie, 1999). In the challenging college environment, student affairs staff can act as "sympathetic coaches" (p. 74), providing needed support for students to be who they are while also encouraging them to move beyond their current way of making meaning. Coaching can take the form of programs that keep students' developmental levels in mind and provide appropriate structure and communication in ways students understand, while also encouraging them to try new approaches to ideas.

King and Baxter Magolda (2005) introduced a multidimensional model focusing on the development of intercultural maturity as a pathway to self-authorship, which they described as consisting of a "range of attributes, including understanding (the cognitive dimension), sensitivity to others (the interpersonal dimension), and a sense of oneself that enables one to listen to and learn from others (the intrapersonal dimension)" (p. 574). They identified three intertwined, mutually influencing levels of development in each dimension. Educators will be more effective in promoting intercultural maturity if all the dimensions of development are considered and if the process is viewed as one that evolves over time, given appropriate experiences (King & Baxter Magolda, 2005).

Baxter Magolda's Self-Authorship Theory

Marcia Baxter Magolda's early research focused on the epistemological development of 101 Miami University students during the college years. She then followed a subset of 39 of these students during their twenties, and 30 of the 39 into their thirties. From this study she developed a model of epistemological reflection that was a precursor to her theory of self-authorship. She then presented a model of self-authorship development (Baxter Magolda, 2001) that contains at its core the movement from uncritically following external formulas to a crossroads that leads to self-authorship (Baxter Magolda, 2014). With Patricia King and other colleagues, Baxter Magolda has extended and explored self-authorship theory in the Wabash National Study of Liberal Arts Education (the Wabash study), providing a substantial empirical base for understanding this critical developmental task (see King, Baxter Magolda, Barber, Brown, & Lindsay, 2009). A host of additional studies, which we describe later in the chapter, further elaborate on the theory of self-authorship with diverse student samples and research methods. In this section we describe the model of epistemological reflection and Baxter Magolda's turn toward self-authorship as a central concept in student development theory.

Epistemological Reflection

Informed by both her own research and the work of Belenky et al. (1986) that we discussed in Chapter Fourteen, Marcia Baxter Magolda was struck by both the similarities and the differences that emerged from Perry's (1968) work on men's development and Belenky et al.'s work on women's development. Kitchener and King's (1981, 1990) research involving both men and women also influenced Baxter Magolda because of the differing conception of the nature of knowledge that emerged. However, because gender was not at the core of Kitchener and King's (1981, 1990) research, Baxter Magolda believed she had identified an important gap in the existing research—the need to address gender in a study of cognitive development that would include both men and women. From this realization came the longitudinal study that served as a basis for the most extensive treatment of Baxter Magolda's early work, *Knowing and Reasoning in College: Gender-Related Patterns in Students' Intellectual Development* (1992). As the longitudinal study progressed it became the empirical base for her self-authorship theory.

Baxter Magolda (1992) presented the results of a five-year longitudinal study of 101 students at Miami University. This volume reflects interviews begun in 1986, during the students' first year, and continuing annually through their first year after graduation. Baxter Magolda (1992) reported that the random sample of entering students included 51 women and 50 men. Ninety-eight of the 101 were white. Seventy students participated for the entire five-year period, including the three students of color.

Baxter Magolda (1992) identified six guiding assumptions underlying her model: (1) ways of knowing and patterns within them are socially constructed; (2) ways of knowing can best be examined using naturalistic inquiry; (3) students' use of reasoning patterns is fluid; (4) patterns are related to, but not dictated by, gender; (5) student stories are context-bound; and (6) ways of knowing appear as "patterns," a term suggested by Frye (1990) to "make sense of experience but stop short of characterizing it in static and generalizable ways" (p. 17).

The epistemological reflection model that resulted from Baxter Magolda's (1992) research contains four stages, with gender-related patterns reflected in the first three. Baxter Magolda (2004a) defined epistemological reflection as "assumptions about the nature, limits, and certainty of knowledge" (p. 31). In the first stage, *absolute knowing*, students view knowledge as certain. They view instructors as authorities with the answers, and the purpose of evaluation is to reproduce what one has learned so that the instructor can determine its accuracy. Baxter Magolda found two patterns, *receiving knowledge* and *mastering knowledge*, within this stage.

More women used receiving knowledge, a more private approach, in comparison to men who used mastering knowledge, a more public approach. Receiving knowledge involves "minimal interaction with instructors, an emphasis on comfort in the learning environment, relationships with peers, and ample opportunities to demonstrate knowledge" (Baxter Magolda, 1992, p. 82). While receiving knowers do have more independent perspectives, they do not always express them. Mastering knowledge is characterized by a verbal approach to learning, a willingness to be critical of instructors, and an expectation that interactions with peers and instructors will lead to the mastery of knowledge. Mastery knowers rely on logic and demonstrate a competitive style.

The second stage, *transitional knowing*, involves an acceptance that some knowledge is uncertain. A realization that authorities are not all-knowing is a turning point from absolute knowing. Transitional knowers expect instructors to go beyond merely supplying information to facilitate an understanding and application of knowledge. A utilitarian perspective motivates students, with investment in learning determined by perceived future usefulness of the information. Evaluation that focuses on understanding is endorsed over that which deals only with acquisition. *Interpersonal knowing* and *impersonal knowing* are the two patterns within this stage.

Interpersonal knowing, used more by women than by men, is characterized by interaction with peers to gather and share ideas, valuing of rapport with instructors to facilitate self-expression, a preference for evaluation geared to individual differences, and resolving uncertainty by employing personal judgment. Impersonal knowing, used more by men than by women, involves a desire to be forced to think, a preference for debate as a vehicle for sharing views, an endorsement of evaluation that is fair and practical, and the use of logic and research to resolve uncertainty.

In *independent knowing*, the third stage, students view knowledge as mostly uncertain. The instructor role that students prefer shifts to providing the context for knowledge exploration. Students value instructors who promote independent thinking and the exchange of opinions. Independent knowers believe evaluation should reward their thinking and not penalize views that diverge from those presented by instructors or in textbooks. This stage includes *interindividual* and *individual* patterns.

Interindividual knowing, used more by women, places value on one's own ideas as well as the ideas of others. Individual knowing, used more by men, also values interchange with peers and instructors, but more attention is given to the individual's own thinking. Baxter Magolda (1992) noted that for individual knowers, sometimes listening to others involves an element of struggle. Although interindividual knowers lean toward connection and individual learners toward separation, Baxter Magolda (1992) emphasized that they are moving closer together.

Contextual knowing, the final stage, reflects a convergence of previous gender-related patterns. Demonstrated only rarely among undergraduate students, contextual knowing involves the belief that the legitimacy of knowledge claims is determined contextually. While the individual still constructs a point of view, the perspective now requires supporting evidence. The role of the instructor now involves the creation of a learning environment that endorses contextual applications of knowledge, discussions that include evaluation of perspectives, and opportunities for mutual critiques by students and instructor. Students appreciate evaluations that measure competence contextually and permit mutual involvement of instructor and student. Because only 12% of the post-graduation interviews contained indications of contextual knowing, Baxter Magolda (1992) considered the data to be insufficient to explore gender patterns. Baxter Magolda (1995) later indicated, in the post-college phase of her study, that the relational and impersonal patterns of knowing that characterized the preceding stages become integrated in the contextual knowing stage.

Baxter Magolda (1992) found more similarities than differences between men's and women's ways of knowing. In addition, she stressed that variability exists among members of a particular gender. Therefore patterns are *related to, but not dictated by*, gender.

In regard to the evolution of ways of knowing, Baxter Magolda (1992) found that absolute knowing was most prevalent in the first year of college (68%). Among sophomores, 53% were transitional knowers. Transitional knowing was also the most prevalent mode among both juniors (83%) and seniors (80%). Independent knowing was most represented in the year following graduation (57%).

Epistemological reflection upholds one of the three dimensions of the more holistic self-authorship theory, which also includes interpersonal/relational and intrapersonal/identity dimensions. These dimensions appear in the model of epistemological reflection in less prominent forms, and particularly in relation to the role of others in individual sense-making and beliefs about sources of knowledge. As the longitudinal study continued past the first year in college, these dimensions became more apparent to Baxter Magolda, and she connected her work with Kegan's orders of consciousness to focus on the development of self-authorship.

Self-Authorship

After the study of 101 participants during their college years, 39 continued to participate in the study after graduation into their twenties and 30 continued into their thirties. Participants told Baxter Magolda that learning was not an appropriate framework to discuss their post-college development and suggested that they discuss their overall experience instead (Baxter Magolda, 2004a). In these interviews, Baxter Magolda (1998b, 1999a, 2001, 2004a, 2008) found evidence that her participants' epistemological development was intertwined with the development of their sense of self and relationships with others. Based on her research involving young adults in their twenties, Baxter Magolda (1998b, 1999a, 1999c, 2001) extended her theory to explain their development at this point in their lives—development that centered on achieving self-authorship. Drawing on Kegan's (1994) theory, Baxter Magolda (2008) defined self-authorship as "the internal capacity to define one's beliefs, identity, and social relations" (p. 269). Baxter Magolda (2008) explored the developmental process her participants experienced in their thirties, a time in which self-authorship becomes solidified.

Self-authorship theory undergirds Baxter Magolda's collaboration with colleagues on the Wabash National Study of Liberal Arts Education. In the Wabash study, annual interviews with 228 students at six campuses provided a substantial empirical foundation for verifying and deepening self-authorship theory (see Baxter Magolda & King, 2012; Baxter Magolda, King, Taylor, & Wakefield, 2012). Along with the relative explosion of empirical studies of self-authorship development among diverse participant samples, which we describe later in this chapter, the Wabash study led Baxter Magolda et al. (2012) to conclude with assurance that "development evolves from relying primarily on external sources for meaning making, through relying on a mix of external and internal sources (what Baxter Magolda called the Crossroads), to relying primarily on internally generated meaning making" (p. 420).

Based on evidence from the longitudinal sample from her original study, Baxter Magolda (2001) highlighted a number of developmental tasks and chal-lenges for young adults in their twenties, including values exploration, making sense of information gained about the world in previous years, determining the path one will take, and taking steps along that path. During this time, three major questions take precedence: "How do I know?" "Who am I?" and "How do I want to construct relationships with others?" (p. 15). The first question has to do with "the *epistemological* dimension of self-authorship—the evolution of assumptions about the nature, limits, and certainty of knowledge" (p. 15). The "Who am I?" question refers to the *intrapersonal* dimension—individuals' sense of who they are and what they believe. The relationship question reflects the *interpersonal* dimension—"how one perceives and constructs one's relationships with others" (p. 15). People soon learn that the answers to these questions are intertwined. They also learn that in a fast-paced and complex society with few clear formulas for success in career and relationships, a self-authoring perspective is key to being able to manage their own lives (Baxter Magolda, 2001, 2008).

Unfortunately, mixed evidence suggests that for some students college does not create the conditions necessary for self-authorship to develop. Baxter Magolda (2001) indicated that students in her study were only anticipating self-authorship as they finished their degrees: "They left college with an initial awareness that they would have to make their own decisions, but without internal mechanisms to do so" (p. 36). Other scholars (for example, Jehangir, Williams, & Pete, 2011; Pizzolato, 2005, 2007; Pizzolato, Nguyen, Johnston, & Wang, 2012) have identified collegiate contexts that appear to promote the development of self-authorship for some students of color and for some students who are the first in their families to attend college. Baxter Magolda and colleagues in the Wabash study identified some "long strides on the journey to self-authorship" among undergraduates (Barber, King, & Baxter Magolda, 2013, p. 866; Baxter Magolda, King, Taylor, & Wakefield, 2012), demonstrating that in a larger sample with more institutional and individual diversity than the one in her foundational study, and under the right conditions, movement toward self-authorship may in fact occur more often during college than the results of the first study indicated.

The Path to Self-Authorship. Baxter Magolda (2001) identified four phases in the journey toward self-authorship involving movement from external to internal self-definition. As we describe here, cognitive, intrapersonal, and interpersonal dimensions are associated with each of these phases.

Phase 1: Following Formulas In the first phase of the "journey toward self-authorship" (Baxter Magolda, 2001, p. 40), young adults follow the plans laid out for them by external authorities about what they should think and how they should accomplish their work, although they frame these formulas to sound like their own ideas. Likewise, they allow others to define who they are. Gaining approval of others is a critical aspect of relationship-building. Sources of external formulas include societal expectations, adults with whom they interact, and peers. Parents, significant others, and mentors are particularly influential. Baxter Magolda (1998b) equated this phase with the third order in Kegan's (1994) theory. Careers and personal lives were the main contexts in which individuals carried out these formulas. For example, decisions about careers and jobs "revolved around doing what one was supposed to do to be successful" (Baxter Magolda, 2001, p. 78), which often did not lead to meaningful work, since the formulas did not always reflect individuals' actual interests. In taking on adult roles, participants found it even more difficult to follow external formulas to satisfactory conclusions. Often formulas conflicted, such as "be in a relationship" and "devote yourself to your career." Not having a clear sense of self made it difficult to determine what to do, both personally and in relationships, and thus when one formula did not work out, other formulas were sought.

Phase 2: Crossroads As individuals progress along their journey, they discover that the plans they have followed do not necessarily work too well and that they need to establish new plans that better suit their needs and interests. They also become dissatisfied with how they have been defined by others and see the need to create their own sense of self. Individuals see that allowing the approval of others to dictate their relationships is limiting and that being more authentic would be preferable. In some cases, following external formulas leads to crisis, while in others the result is a general sense of unhappiness and lack of fulfillment. In each instance, however, young adults are not yet ready to act on their desires to be more autonomous, fearing reactions of others. Baxter Magolda (2001) determined that career settings often provided the impetus to question external formulas. In the workplace, her participants' developing inner voices often questioned their career paths. Relationships were also the focus of the Crossroads, as individuals attempted to resolve tension between what they wanted and what others wanted or expected. Establishing one's own beliefs rather than adopting those of others as they had done in the past was also a difficult experience in this phase for many young adults. A clearer sense of direction and more self-confidence marked the end of the Crossroads.

Phase 3: Becoming the Author of One's Life Similar to Kegan's (1994) fourth order of consciousness, this phase is characterized by the ability to choose one's beliefs and stand up for them in the face of conflicting external viewpoints (Baxter Magolda, 1998b, 2001). After choosing their beliefs, individuals feel compelled to live them out, which is often difficult. They are also aware that belief systems are contextual, can change, and are never as clear as one would wish. As a result of intensive self-reflection, individuals develop a strong self-concept. In relationships, renegotiation often occurs, as young adults weigh their needs and desires along with those of others around them. Individuals are also more careful in making relationship commitments to ensure that the commitment "honor[s] the self they [are] constructing" (Baxter Magolda, 2001, p. 140). The three dimensions of self-authorship are closely intertwined, and the saliency of each dimension differs depending on life circumstances and experiences.

Phase 4: Internal Foundation Young adults who successfully negotiate this stage are grounded—in their self-determined belief system, in their sense of who they are, and in the mutuality of their relationships. A "solidified and comprehensive system of belief" (Baxter Magolda, 2001, p. 155) now exists. At the same time, individuals are accepting of ambiguity and open to change. They experience feelings of peace, contentment, and inner strength. While aware of external influences, they are not greatly affected by them, because they trust their own feelings and act on them rationally. Life decisions are based on one's internal foundation. For some individuals, this leads to new directions in their careers; for others, changes are made in their personal lives. At the same time, their responsibilities to others, based on their own sense of those responsibilities, are clearly a part of their internal foundations. For many individuals, spirituality plays a role.

The Elements of Self-Authorship. Interviews with participants in their thirties uncovered three elements of self-authorship: *trusting the internal voice, building an internal foundation*, and *securing internal commitments* (Baxter Magolda, 2008). *Trusting the internal voice* involved participants' realizing that while they could not always control events external to them, they did have control over how they thought about and responded to events, which led to their becoming more confident of their internal voices. This process occurred in each of the different dimensions of development (that is, epistemological, interpersonal, and intrapersonal) and in different domains (such as work, relationships, self-awareness).

Once individuals learned to trust their internal voices, they began *building an internal foundation*, which Baxter Magolda (2008) defined as a personal philosophy or framework to guide one's actions. One participant in Baxter Magolda's study called this foundation the "core of one's being" (Baxter Magolda, 2008, p. 280). All the dimensions of development merge to create a "cohesive entity" (p. 280). As individuals experience different life events, they may reevaluate and adjust their foundation.

Once the third element of self-authorship, *securing internal commitments*, had been achieved, "participants felt that living their convictions was as natural and as necessary as breathing" (Baxter Magolda, 2008, p. 281). They integrated their internal foundations with the realities of their external worlds, which led to a sense of freedom to live their lives authentically.

The development of self-authorship is not a linear process but can follow many different paths influenced by the personal characteristics of individuals, the contexts in which they find themselves, and the challenges and supports they experience along the way (Baxter Magolda, 2008; Baxter Magolda & King, 2012). Self-authorship enhances rather than detracts from relationships and interactions with the external world. As people become more confident and clear about who they are, they are able to relate to others in a more honest and open manner.

Research on Self-Authorship

In addition to Baxter Magolda's foundational longitudinal research, which we have already described, a number of other studies have explored aspects of self-authorship.

Looking at the Crossroads within the Development of Self-Authorship

Several scholars have studied the concept of self-authorship as well as factors associated with its development. Jane Pizzolato (2005) explored factors associated with self-authorship by examining narratives written by 613 students in response to her experience survey (see Pizzolato, 2007) regarding important decisions they had made. Her findings indicated that experiencing a decision as a "provocative moment" (that is, one creating disequilibrium leading to reevaluation of one's goals or sense of self) (Pizzolato, 2005, p. 629) on the path to self-authorship was related to both characteristics of the student and of the situation. More important, however, was the student's purpose for making the decision. Pizzolato (2007) suggested that self-authored action may be dependent on whether the individual views the situation as supportive of self-authorship. She proposed four expressions of self-authorship, based on whether or not reasoning and/or action are self-authored.

Findings from the Wabash study indicated that the majority of students by their second year of college continued to be externally defined, with some entering the Crossroads, which signals the transition to ways of making meaning that are not dependent on others (Baxter Magolda, King, Taylor, & Wakefield, 2012). Baxter Magolda and King (2012) elaborated ten "milestones" from external to internal definitions, and Barber et al. (2013) identified college experiences that produced significant gains.

Self-Authorship in Diverse Populations

To extend Baxter Magolda's theory to more diverse populations, several scholars have investigated self-authorship in different settings. Baxter Magolda joined with Peggy Meszaros and Elizabeth Creamer to edit the volume *Development and Assessment of Self-Authorship: Exploring the Concept Across Cultures* (2012). Chapters address self-authorship in international and multicultural populations, including male and female Bedouin and Jewish adolescents, female undergraduates in Australia, and Japanese college students. Outside of this edited volume, however, the majority of studies on self-authorship among diverse college student populations comes from the United States, with substantial contributions through the research agenda of Jane Pizzolato and colleagues.

In an interview study, Pizzolato (2003) found that so-called high-risk college students often reached self-authorship prior to college as a result of experiencing challenging situations early in life that required them to make decisions and take action on their own, such as making the decision to attend college and needing to negotiate the admissions process without any guidance or encouragement from parents. Pizzolato (2004) discovered that although high-risk students entered college at the level of self-authorship (see Pizzolato, 2003), classroom and out-of-classroom experiences challenged this way of making meaning and led them to feel incompetent, misunderstood, and different from their peers. These feelings led to high levels of anxiety and dissonance, which caused students to reconsider their internal foundations and attempt to meet external expectations. Discomfort with this strategy eventually allowed them to return to a self-authored perspective. Pizzolato (2004) noted that acting in self-authored ways may require not only the ability to reason independently but also feeling supported to take action.

Pizzolato, Chaudhari, Murrell, Podobnik, and Schaeffer (2008) suggested that ethnic identity development and epistemological development are intertwined processes, with each process positively affecting the other. Together, ethnic identity development and epistemological development predicted college GPA almost as well as previous academic performance measured by SAT scores and high school GPA. In particular, capacity for autonomous action made a difference. In another study of 166 students of color at three large public research universities, Pizzolato, Nguyen, Johnston, and Wang (2012) found that experiencing identity dissonance and relationship dissonance were key catalysts in the development of self-authorship. Chaudhari and Pizzolato (2008) pointed to identity dissonance as a location for epistemological development among multiethnic students (that is, students whose parents are of different ethnicities).

In a longitudinal qualitative study involving Latino/a students from seven colleges and universities, Torres and Baxter Magolda (2004) found that ethnic identity development, an intrapersonal dimension of development, was interwoven with cognitive and interpersonal dimensions of development, with all three dimensions working together as students developed self-authorship. The challenge of cognitive dissonance caused by experiences of stereotyping and cultural oppression was a key factor in propelling students toward self-authorship, while support to address this dissonance was also a critical factor. Torres and Hernandez (2007) also reported that for the 29 Latino students they interviewed, recognizing and making meaning of racism was important in developing self-authorship.

Additional work on students with minoritized sexual orientation and first-generation students also enriches the literature. Abes and Jones (2004) discovered that how far along lesbian students were on the path toward self-authorship determined the extent to which external influences, such as family, peer group, social norms, and stereotypes, affected self-perceptions of sexual orientation identity, and other dimensions of identity, including religion, race, gender, and social class, as well as the intersections of the dimensions. Jehangir, Williams, and Pete (2011) studied the development of self-authorship among first-generation students participating in multicultural learning communities and concluded that interaction with diverse others and purposeful attention to reflection in a multicultural context created opportunities for first-generation students to move toward self-authorship.

These studies of self-authorship among diverse samples affirm the validity of using the theory across student populations. At the same time, the studies deepened scholarship on self-authorship and made substantive contributions to understanding the subprocesses within self-authorship development.

Assessing and Measuring Self-Authorship

Being able to assess students' level of self-authorship is important for understanding how best to use this theory in practice. Kegan (1994) set the stage for assessing his orders through detailed analysis of qualitative interviews. Following this tradition, initial assessments of self-authorship in higher education were qualitative, and that tradition continues. Baxter Magolda and King (2007) described two interview strategies to aid educators in assessing self-authorship. The first is the self-authorship interview (see Baxter Magolda, 2001), in which participants share their personal reflections on topics of importance to them. The second is the reflective conversation guide, which was part of the mixed methods Wabash study (see Baxter Magolda, 2008; Baxter Magolda & King, 2007, 2008, 2012). Welkener and Baxter Magolda (2014) assessed self-authorship through students' self-portraits, and a host of dissertation writers and other student researchers have used qualitative methods to explore various aspects of self-authorship and its development.

Pizzolato (2007) introduced and validated a short, quantitative measure of self-authorship, the self-authorship survey (SAS), consisting of four subscales: capacity for autonomous action, problem-solving orientation, perceptions of volitional competence, and self-regulation in challenging situations. The second half of the same instrument is the experience survey, which asks participants to write narratives about a significant decision they have made. Essays are scored on each of three dimensions: decision-making, problem solving, and autonomy. These narratives formed the basis for Pizzolato's claims related to provocative moments in the Crossroads (Pizzolato, 2005). She recommended using the two instruments together to get a more complete picture of participants' ability to self-author both their reasoning and their actions. Creamer, Baxter Magolda, and Yue (2010) used 18 items from the Career Decision Making Survey (CDMS) to measure the first three phases in the development of self-authorship, proposing that the instrument shows promise as an assessment of interventions. Strayhorn (2014b) developed the African American Student Success Questionnaire, which included seven items to measure the four key self-authorship subscales that Pizzolato (2005) identified. Quantitative measures of self-authorship and its development provide a more efficient strategy than qualitative interviews, which are not always possible or practical on a large scale. Taken together, studies using qualitative and quantitative assessments provide ways to understand self-authorship in context and the purposeful creation of environments to promote its development.

Self-Authorship and Other Student Outcomes

Research has also suggested relationships between self-authorship and other variables. In a longitudinal study of the relationships among student characteristics, students' academic and living environment, and self-authorship, Wawrzynski and Pizzolato (2006) found that the sex of the student, being a transfer student, strong academic performance prior to college, being a student of color, and living on campus significantly predicted several of the subscales on the SAS (Pizzolato, 2004). In a quantitative study of 140 African American first-year students at an HBCU (Historically Black College or University), Strayhorn (2014b) found that controlling for pre-college preparation (for example, GPA and standardized test scores), self-authorship accounted for 58% of variance in first-year GPA.

Pizzolato (2006) determined that students who worked with advisors who encouraged reflection in goal-setting and intentional planning and discussed with students their nonacademic life experiences were more likely to develop abilities and perspectives associated with self-authorship. Continuing to explore the developmental experiences of students in advising situations, Pizzolato and Ozaki (2007) investigated early movement toward self-authorship experienced by students who were part of an advising program modeled after the Learning Partnerships Model (Baxter Magolda, 2001) that was designed to enhance retention of students in academic difficulty. Their findings suggested that students entered the program using external formulas to make sense of the world. However, external pressures caused them interpersonal and intrapersonal stress, pushing them into the Crossroads in Baxter Magolda's (2001) model. As a result of participating in the program, they appeared to experience more rapid development than most students. They came to believe that they had control over the outcomes they experienced and that they personally played an important role in constructing knowledge and decision-making, precursors of self-authorship.

The authors of a study examining the relationship between self-authorship and women's career decision-making concluded that early in the process of self-authorship women still relied heavily on advice from people they trusted, usually parents, even though the women were aware that they were ultimately responsible for their own decisions (Creamer & Laughlin, 2005; Laughlin & Creamer, 2007). This finding supports Baxter Magolda's (2001) description of young adults' reliance on external formulas as they begin the journey to self-authorship.

Application

Much of Baxter Magolda's scholarship has focused on applications of her model to classroom and student affairs settings. She has argued that to adequately prepare students for the increasing complexities of adult life in the twenty-first century, self-authorship needs to be the basis for advanced learning outcomes in college (Baxter Magolda, 2007). Using the principles for learning and development that she initially proposed in her 1992 book and outlined in detail in several books and in numerous articles (see Baxter Magolda, 1998b, 1999a, 2001, 2002, 2003; Baxter Magolda & King, 2004), Baxter Magolda has suggested methods for measuring and promoting self-authorship in college settings. A number of other scholars join her in this effort, resulting in a robust body of literature to guide postsecondary educators. Baxter Magolda (2009) has also written a guidebook, *Authoring Your Life: Developing an INTERNAL VOICE to Meet Life's Challenges*, which, as the title suggests, engages the reader directly in reflection and action toward self-authorship.

Baxter Magolda (2002) stressed the need for students and educators to work together to develop student self-authorship, demonstrating respect for each other and actively sharing ideas and viewpoints. Classroom and co-curricular settings provide opportunities for this type of exchange. Opportunities for self-reflection in these settings also assist students in becoming clearer about what they know, why they hold the beliefs they do, and how they want to act on their beliefs (Baxter Magolda, 1999a, 2008). King et al. (2009); Barber, King, and Magolda (2013); and Pizzolato and Ozaki (2007) identified practices that might be especially effective in promoting self-authorship.

Baxter Magolda and King (2008) introduced the Wabash National Study Conversation Guide as an aid for engaging students in meaningful, reflective conversations. This guide is based on the interview protocol mentioned earlier. The purpose of the conversations for which the guide was constructed is to offer "students an opportunity to reflect on the meaning of their experiences and to help them develop reflective habits" (Baxter Magolda & King, 2008, p. 9). Advisors, faculty, supervisors of student employees, diversity educators, or other student affairs staff might initiate these conversations (Baxter Magolda, 2008).

Active involvement in meaningful activities and leadership positions is another variable that can foster development of self-authorship (Baxter Magolda, 1999a). Baxter Magolda (1999d) stressed that "students do not learn to behave in mature ways without practice" (p. 4). This process requires identifying situations that are safe, challenging, and doable for students who are at varying points along the journey to self-authorship (Baxter Magolda, 2003). Support is critical as students assume meaningful responsibility.

Learning Partnerships Model

Baxter Magolda was as concerned about the conditions that foster development of self-authorship as she was about the concept itself. Based on the findings of her longitudinal study of young adults and ideas first outlined in her 1992 book, she introduced the Learning Partnerships Model in

Making Their Own Way (2001) and elaborated on it in her book with Patricia King, *Learning Partnerships* (2004). Baxter Magolda (2001) stated that "environments that were most effective in promoting self-authorship" challenged dependence on authority. Three assumptions guided her approach: (1) "knowledge [is] complex and socially constructed," (2) "self is central to knowledge construction," and (3) "authority and expertise [are] shared in the mutual construction of knowledge among peers" (p. xx). These assumptions address cognitive, intrapersonal, and interpersonal aspects of development (Baxter Magolda, 2004b).

Building on these three assumptions, Baxter Magolda (2001) claimed that educational practice that encourages self-authorship is based on three principles: (1) "validating learners' capacity to know," (2) "situating learning in learners' experience," and (3) "mutually constructing meaning" (p. xxi), the same principles she introduced in relation to her original theory of epistemological development (Baxter Magolda, 1992). She noted that while the assumptions challenged students' meaning-making processes, the principles served as a bridge between their current level of development and self-authorship (Baxter Magolda, 2004b).

Examples of the Learning Partnerships Model in action in instructional settings and in student affairs practice appear in numerous books and articles (see Baxter Magolda, 2003; Baxter Magolda & King, 2004; Cardone, Turton, Olson, & Baxter Magolda, 2013; Meszaros, 2007). Some examples of its use in academic settings include framing faculty development (Day & Lane, 2014; Howson, 2015; Quaye, 2012; Wildman, 2004, 2007), undergirding curriculum development (Bekken & Marie, 2007), providing impetus for institutional development (Wildman, 2004), creating an urban leadership internship program designed to promote intercultural maturity (Baxter Magolda, 2007; Egart & Healy, 2004), structuring an international service-learning curriculum (Baxter Magolda, 2007; Yonkers-Talz, 2004), establishing a multicultural education class at a community college (Baxter Magolda, 2003; Hornak & Ortiz, 2004), developing a college honors program (Haynes, 2006), providing a guiding philosophy for student affairs graduate preparation (Baxter Magolda, 1999b, 2007; Rogers, Magolda, Baxter Magolda, & Knight Abowitz, 2004), and creating conditions for self-authorship in graduate education (Baxter Magolda, 1998a; Robinson, 2013; Wawrzynski & Jessup-Anger, 2014).

The Learning Partnerships Model has also been used in student affairs settings as an overall framework to structure the work of student affairs divisions (Baxter Magolda, 2007; Mills & Strong, 2004), to create community standards in residence halls (Baxter Magolda, 2003, 2007; Piper, 1997; Piper & Buckley, 2004), in conceptualizing developmental academic advising (Baxter Magolda, 2003, 2007; Pizzolato, 2006, 2008; Pizzolato & Ozaki, 2007), in providing a basis for career advising (Baxter Magolda, 2007), as a focus for training honors councils that adjudicate academic dishonesty cases (Baxter Magolda, 2007), and in professional student affairs staff development (Baxter Magolda, 2007).

In the final chapter of *Learning Partnerships* (Baxter Magolda & King, 2004), King and Baxter Magolda (2004) offered a framework for educators to decide whether and how to use the Learning Partnerships Model. It includes questions to ask oneself when considering whether to use the model and also offers ten specific steps for its implementation.

Critique and Future Directions

As both Kegan (1994) and Baxter Magolda (2008) have effectively articulated, the complexities of today's society make self-authorship a necessity. This concept, introduced by Kegan in the 1980s, has gained new life with the ongoing work of Baxter Magolda and later researchers, including Pizzolato, Torres, and the research team on the Wabash study.

Kegan's (1982, 1994) theory offered conceptual breakthroughs, particularly with regard to the interconnection of epistemological, intrapersonal, and interpersonal components of development, as well as the role of the environment in shaping development. However, his writing is often dense and psychoanalytic in tone, qualities with which student affairs educators may have difficulty. Kegan was also vague about the research foundations of his work, which can lead to skepticism about its validity. In his 1994 book, Kegan offered more in the way of suggestions for encouraging development in educational settings than he had earlier. The concepts of holding environments, evolutionary bridges, and sympathetic coaches all have meaning for those who work closely with students.

The importance of Kegan's theory as a description of developmental evolution over the lifespan cannot be overstated. However, it has been the work of Marcia Baxter Magolda that has popularized it within educational circles. The power of Baxter Magolda's scholarship lies in her longitudinal approach, depth of analysis, and careful attention to application of theory in practice. In each of these areas, her work is exemplary.

No other student development theorist has even considered interviewing the same participants yearly for a period of over 20 years. As one reads their stories as told in Baxter Magolda's books and articles, they become real people facing challenging life experiences. As a result, it is easy to relate to their circumstances and their meaning making. The shifts in perspective are clear as one follows them through time. The evidence from their narratives definitely validates Baxter Magolda's evolving theory. The narratives she provides and her careful grounded theory analysis have led to a carefully conceptualized theory that is easy to understand and therefore to use.

A major strength of Baxter Magolda's work is its utility. She and others have succeeded in explaining and giving guidance on ways in which her theory translates into practice, both in student affairs and in academic settings. The Learning Partnerships Model has been used in numerous settings and is making a difference in the lives of students, faculty, and student affairs professionals.

Research, including that described in this chapter, with samples more diverse than the one in Baxter Magolda's foundational study has overcome early criticism of self-authorship theory being based on a narrow population (white, mostly privileged individuals who were undergraduate students at Miami University in Ohio). Baxter Magolda (2004a) herself called for additional studies based on diverse populations of students in different institutional contexts, and she has conducted some of it in collaboration with a number of colleagues. Ongoing research into self-authorship and its development among diverse populations will further test and elaborate the model and its applications.

Discussion Questions

1. In what ways is a constructive-development theory similar to and different from the cognitive structural student development theories described in the previous chapters?
2. What features of contemporary collegiate and adult life require different responses at Kegan's different orders of consciousness? How would individuals in the second, third, and fourth orders respond differently to these features?
3. What is the relationship of Baxter Magolda's epistemological reflection and self-authorship theories to other theories that focus on cognitive and moral development (for example, Kohlberg, Gilligan, Perry, and Belenky et al.)?
4. Think about a key developmental issue in college that would facilitate self-authorship. What kinds of interactions might occur across the development of each dimension (intrapersonal, interpersonal, epistemological) of self-authorship?

5. Describe how an individual student moves from Baxter Magolda's following external formulas to the Crossroads and to establishing internal foundations.

6. Describe three strategies for postsecondary educators that are most likely to promote self-authorship among diverse student populations. Consider diversity across dimensions of student populations (for example, age, race and ethnicity, gender identity, academic major) and institutional types (for example, community college, research university, liberal arts college, online institution, HBCU).

7. Baxter Magolda and many others use metaphors of journey—including crossroads, milestones, good company for the trip—to describe self-authorship development. Evidence shows that the process is not necessarily linear. In what other ways can you describe the process?

8. Identify a population of students and describe the components of a program you would design to specifically cater to their development of self-authorship.

9. How might larger systems of societal oppression/privilege affect the self-authorship of minoritized populations? Majoritized populations?

PART FOUR

REFLECTING ON THEORY TO PRACTICE

Regina has come to the end of her course on student development theory. Throughout the semester she has studied a number of social, psychological, cognitive-structural, and integrative identity theories. She started with her own educational autobiography and tried to apply theories to her experience. She read Perry's original work and wrote a paper critiquing his book. She has considered the implications of each theory for diverse student populations and has interviewed several Asian American students to determine if the theories inform their experiences. She has examined research related to each theory and has even designed a study to investigate whether lesbian identity development is similar for African American and White women. She has considered how theory can be used in practice and has designed an orientation program for transfer students based on Chickering and Reisser vectors.

As she reflects on her experience, Regina is unsettled. She has been exposed to a lot of material and experiences designed to provide her with a comprehensive background in student development theory and its uses in practice. But somehow it is not all coming together. Maybe the final course projects will help her. They require her to write a reflective analytic paper based on her own developmental journey using formal theories. She will also give a class presentation on strategies for incorporating theory into practice and the importance of theory in promoting development in students' in and out of class experiences. In addition, she will present critiques of the knowledge base on to student development theory and make recommendations concerning future directions. Her projects are due in a week. Regina decides she had better get to work.

◆ ◆ ◆

Like Regina's, our work is drawing to a close. Parts One through Three included consideration of the concept of student development, review of the historical and philosophical underpinnings of the student development movement, the role of privilege and oppression in shaping identities, discussion of the uses of student development in practice, and review of the major identity theories. A step back from the details and a look at the big picture is now necessary. How do these ideas and theories come together to guide educational practice? What can be gained from all this knowledge?

In many respects the body of student development theory acts like a kaleidoscope. When the kaleidoscope is turned, the design changes. Likewise, when different theories form the lens through which to interpret the same situation, the interpretations vary. Thinking about situations through different theoretical lenses can provide a more comprehensive understanding of what is going on and can lead to a variety of possible strategies for addressing issues. Depending on the situation, some theories will fit better than others. Having a repertoire of theories to consider is helpful in finding the ones that are of most value.

Still, theory alone cannot always suggest the best solution. In some instances, theory is not yet sophisticated enough to be of much assistance. In other cases, it does not apply to the particular population under consideration. Sometimes it helps in describing the situation, but does not provide guidance in terms of how to proceed. Users of theory must recognize its limitations as well as the positive contributions it makes to educational practice.

All professionals are obligated to reflect upon the current state of their profession and the knowledge base that underpins it. Further, they must challenge themselves and their colleagues to test, refine, and extend that knowledge base. For student affairs educators, it is particularly important to examine student development theory critically and seek opportunities to add to the information that already exists about how students change and grow during the college years.

The two chapters that make up Part Four present possible responses to Regina's final exam. Chapter Seventeen, "Student Affairs Educators as Partners in Using Student Development Theory," addresses ways in which faculty, administrators, and other campus professionals can serve as advocates and partners in the learning process for students and one another. We also delve into the difficult dialogues that can ensue during conversations about theory, particularly when individuals must grapple with their own biases, assumptions, and privileges. We introduce the intergroup dialogues process broadly and in the context of difficult dialogues in the classroom and campus settings. We conclude the chapter by challenging educators to reflect on their own development with the intent of enhancing their professional knowledge and life-long learning.

Chapter Eighteen, the closing chapter, is entitled "Implications and Future Directions for Practice, Research, and Theory Development." It presents some final thoughts and recommendations for future work related to student development. The chapter begins with a review of the current status of developmental theory, research, and practice, looking at both its accomplishments and also its limitations. We then provide a list of recommendations to extend the student development knowledge base and enhance the work of student development educators.

CHAPTER SEVENTEEN

STUDENT AFFAIRS EDUCATORS AS PARTNERS IN USING STUDENT DEVELOPMENT THEORY

In this chapter, we offer readers a few suggestions for considering the application of student development theories in their roles as advocates and partners in the learning process. The primary goal of knowing and using student development theories is, ultimately, to provide the necessary scaffolding for students as they move through higher education. This scaffolding supports students' development and provides them with opportunities to learn and grow during college. Graduate students and others who are using this book to learn about student development theory may find this chapter, in conjunction with Chapter Three, helpful in contextualizing theories and considering how to use them; instructors using this book to teach about student development may find this chapter helpful in designing instruction on the use of theory and for learning how to handle some controversies related to theory. In this chapter we refer to readers of this book as students in some sections, and as educators in others, because we expect that students who read this book will be—or already are—educators in some capacity. We refer to faculty and others who use this book to teach courses or facilitate professional development workshops as instructors.

We begin this chapter with a discussion of how to engage students and colleagues in discussions about the various theories explored in the book. Then we shift to commentary on using the theories in classes and exploring how to engage in difficult dialogues about these theories. We close the chapter with a discussion of the importance of recognizing one's own developmental capacities as an educator, in order to support students in their development.

Engaging Students and Colleagues in Discussions About Theories

"I don't understand the point of these theories; they seem so detached from students' lives!" Many student affairs educators have heard graduate students make this or similar remarks in frustration. Perhaps they have also said it, or silently believed it, themselves. After considering the many theories in this book, readers may be overwhelmed and unable to see how they can use these theories in practice, given all of the competing demands placed upon them as educators. Additionally, educators might not see how these theories make sense in students' day-to-day lives. In Chapter Three we offered a number of suggestions for how to use theory in practice, yet the challenge of bringing colleagues into a discussion—and use—of theory remains.

In many ways, theories help simplify complex phenomena. Approaching conversations with colleagues about the role and relevance of theories can certainly be challenging but also can be quite rewarding. Such conversations provide a space to share real-world scenarios that can be helpful in expanding theoretical knowledge and awareness. One way to approach individuals who say they do not see the utility of student development theories is to encourage sharing of individuals' unique developmental journey in college. Educators might discuss the pivotal moments in their lives and how understanding those moments can be informed by theories or how making sense of their struggles theoretically might have enhanced their development.

In another approach, educators can have dialogues with their colleagues about challenges students face in navigating the college experience. Then they can identify theories that they use in their practice and how these theories manifest in real-world scenarios. Following this sharing, they can discuss what these theories contribute, how they are limited, and how other theories might work collectively to illuminate additional areas of development.

Alongside conversations about how theories work in real-life scenarios, educators can discuss how theories have evolved over time based on different populations arriving in higher education contexts. Educators might discuss the students with whom they work on campus and how certain theories might not be as applicable to their development. For example, many campuses continue to have an influx of international students. How might the existing theories be limited in their application to these students? These kinds of conversations invite educators to critique theories and consider the students on their campuses, what their needs may be, and how the theories in this book may be limited in their application. Such critical conversations also allow space for educators to describe the informal theories that they use to adapt to a changing student population.

How to Introduce Theories in Graduate Classes and Professional Settings

One of the primary ways student affairs educators learn about student development theories is during a graduate program in student affairs or higher education. In these programs, usually students will at least have an introductory course on student development theories and might also complete a more advanced course covering these theories in greater depth. Understanding and applying student development theory is a core competency in the student affairs profession (see Bresciani et al., 2010), and graduate programs are one formal opportunity to learn how to do so (Renn & Jessup-Anger, 2008).

There are numerous approaches that faculty implement to teach student development theory. One common way is to begin with psychosocial and cognitive theories, given their longer history; then continue with social identity theories, which are more recent; and close with holistic approaches to identity. Another common approach is to begin the class with an overview of holistic theories (for example, self-authorship) to give students an opportunity to consider development across the landscape prior to focusing on theories that highlight one aspect of identity (for example, gender). Then students learn about earlier theoretical work (for example, cognitive, psychosocial, moral) before returning to holistic theories at the end of the semester, which helps them return to viewing the theories in an integrated manner. Faculty might also begin from a standpoint of addressing issues of privilege and oppression in relation to student development. In the beginning they emphasize social identity theories and their intersections; midway through the course they shift to holistic theories, and they end with a review of earlier psychosocial and cognitive theories. There are, obviously, several other ways to structure a course, but these three are typical in contemporary graduate programs. Given the integrated approach to using theories that we suggested in Chapter Three, we believe it is important to stress that students learn to view theories holistically even if it is necessary to understand them individually prior to integrating them.

Understanding Your Own Story

Our experiences teaching student development theory in graduate programs leads us to suggest the following strategies. First, understanding one's own story provides a firm foundation not only for learning developmental theory but also for professional practice that reflects maturity and self-knowledge. Starting with their own stories is also an accessible approach for most students. We recommend giving students opportunities to think about their own stories—where they are from, their backgrounds, their prior experiences and education, their identities—and how these stories inform their privileged and marginalized identities. Strategies to provide these opportunities include using autobiographic writing, reflection papers, and multimedia representations of self and story.

Help Students See Themselves

We recommend activities that invite students to "see" themselves in the various theories about which they are reading. For example, instructors can ask students to plot their development in Abes et al.'s (2007) Reconceptualized Model of Multiple Dimensions of Identity prior to reading about the theories, midway through the semester, and again, at the end of the semester, to see how their models look at different points in their learning process. Their models will likely look more complex at the end of the semester, due in part to their active reading of theories and reflection on these ideas. Instructors could use this approach with other theories, letting students locate themselves and their development in the models.

Instructors can also pair students and have them work throughout the semester to assess their own development and discuss their developmental struggles and successes with their partner. Pairing students by different social identities can help them explore issues of privilege, power, and oppression as they consider the contextual influences within the theories they are studying. Dyads also provide a critical opportunity for students to see theory in other people's stories as well as their own, building a bridge from self-knowledge to external application of theories in practice.

Instructors can also have students interview other students (outside the graduate program) on campus and design tentative theories about their development based on these interviews. This exercise enables students to see how theories are developed and the challenges in making decisions about the various models they are studying. Such an exercise also provides insight into how theories reflect embedded assumptions of the theorist.

Encourage Critique and Deep Thinking

Finally, instructors should continually ask students to consider what resonates with them in the theories they are studying and what does not. What seems "true"? What does not seem to work? What is missing? Does the theory seem to fit some students but not all? Whose interests are served by different theories? Answering these questions helps students see what theories make sense to them and why certain theories may be limited in explaining the circumstances of students from marginalized populations (for example, racially minoritized students, low-income students, students with disabilities).

In professional settings, student affairs educators may not formally use theories in the same way as those who teach in classroom settings, but the application of these theories is nonetheless just as important. Student affairs educators might have refresher workshops or professional development retreats to help their colleagues understand theories and how they might apply to different populations. For example, racism, underage drinking, academic dishonesty, and sexual assault unfortunately occur on many campuses. These issues can serve as a catalyst for educators to use theory as a way to describe developmental issues and why they occur, explain appropriate and inappropriate behaviors among students, or create programs and services to change the prominence of such issues on campus.

As researchers continue to develop and share theories, student affairs educators can promote knowledge and application of theory by engaging their colleagues in conversations which focus on newer theoretical perspectives. They can also encourage colleagues to remain abreast through reading books, publications, and academic magazines. This approach would be particularly useful for educators who have a strong commitment to students but lack familiarity with formal theory. Individuals who supervise new professionals should also welcome professionals' enthusiasm in using and applying theories. Sometimes when new professionals enter work settings with an excitement about theories, supervisors who might feel intimidated by their own lack of knowledge may spurn these professionals' desire to use theories in their work by suggesting theories are time-consuming, lack applicability, or are irrelevant to practice.

Difficult Dialogues About Theory

Teaching and learning student development theory can lead to difficult dialogues in and out of class, as instructors and students encounter their own assumptions, biases, and experiences of privilege and marginalization. Discussions about social identities may raise open disagreement. They may also yield numerous microaggressions on the part of instructors and students. Understanding how to recognize these complexities and what to do about them is important not only for the learning environment in graduate school, but also—if handled effectively—for creating models that students can follow when they too, are working with organizations, teams, students, and colleagues on and off campus. The intergroup dialogue model provides a strong foundation for this process.

Intergroup Dialogues

Intergroup dialogues (IGD) are sustained face-to-face dialogues between two groups that have a history of conflict, oppression, or both (for example, White people and people of color; cisgender men, cisgender women, and trans* people). The goal of these dialogues is to explore the sources of conflict, speak from personal experiences, and work to build alliances across differences (Nagda & Maxwell, 2011). In the United States, some topics are hard to discuss because we fear saying the wrong thing, appearing ignorant, or offending someone. For example, given the history of race relations and slavery in the United States, race is a hard topic to discuss openly, particularly for White students who may be racially unaware and for racially minoritized students who are often called upon to serve as informants, experts, or the voice of a particular racial group. Given the tensions that arise in conversations about race, people often remain silent and experience deep-seated fear during these dialogues. The purpose of IGD is to provide people with the framework and language for having difficult dialogues.

One way in which these dialogues accomplish their goal is through cofacilitation by members who represent the groups in the dialogue. For example, a dialogue on race would have facilitators from racially minoritized groups as well as White facilitators. The facilitators represent the agent and the target groups. As we described in Chapter Four, agent identities are those that are historically privileged, whereas target identities are historically oppressed (Obear, 2007). These dialogues usually occur over the course of 8 to 12 weeks in order to move through the various stages in ways that enable participants to build the trusting relationships necessary for having dialogues in open, honest, and critical ways. There are various intergroup dialogue models; we describe Ximena Zúñiga's (2003) four-stage approach. We find this model to be user-friendly and helpful for students and student affairs educators alike; even when following the full process is not possible, the principles underlying each stage provide guidance for other interventions. Following the description of the model, we discuss how it can be tailored to engage in difficult dialogues about student development theories.

Stage 1: Creating an Environment for Dialogue The first stage, usually lasting two sessions, works to help participants build relationships and trust that will enable them to engage in open and honest dialogues. Participants at this stage discuss their hopes and fears for dialogue, what they hope to gain out of the dialogues, and ground rules for how they will have dialogue. The goal of this stage is to help participants become acquainted with each other in ways that build trust. Cofacilitators also share vulnerably as a way to break down some of their authority and connect on a deeper level with participants.

Stage 2: Situating the Dialogue: Learning about Differences and Commonalities of Experience In this stage, participants work to build the necessary language for engaging in dialogues about difficult topics. Zúñiga (2003) stated, "Participants explore the impact of prejudice, in/out group dynamics, discrimination, and privilege at the personal, interpersonal, intergroup, and societal levels. Students enter the dialogues with differing levels of awareness of social group distinctions as well as varying degrees of readiness to engage in conversations about social identity affiliation in the context of power and privilege" (p. 13). As Zúñiga noted, a distinguishing feature of this stage involves exploration of individual acts of oppression as well as larger systemic issues that exist in society. By working through the different terms people use, participants work to gain a deeper understanding of their own role in addressing, and sometimes being complicit in, these systemic inequities. Since participants are sharing from their own personal stories, some people from targeted groups might experience pain in these dialogues, while some agent members may not have the language to express their first experiences of understanding privilege and oppression. To provide models for participants, facilitators share from their own experiences about their own successes and missteps. This stage usually lasts two to three sessions.

Stage 3: Exploring Conflicts and Multiple Perspectives: Dialoguing about "Hot" Topics Having taken time to build trust and relationships and developing some shared language about difficult topics, in the third stage participants work to address contentious topics that they may have been avoiding or may not have had the language to address previously. For example, participants might discuss self-segregation and why, for example, Black students associate with their Black peers in higher education settings. Participants might discuss the role of identity centers in tandem with this larger discussion of self-segregation. Facilitators might also challenge participants to consider why racially minoritized groups are hyper visible on campus and why issues of self-segregation are not typically directed toward White students, who also associate with White peers. Facilitators can use a number of structured activities, including readings, videos, role-plays, or case studies, to help participants grapple with these hot topics. Through these conversations, facilitators help connect these topics to issues happening on campus and make the links stronger and more personal. Given the depth of information shared in this stage, ideally it lasts four to five sessions.

Stage 4: Moving from Dialogue to Action A persistent challenge in these IGD is what participants can do with what they learn through dialogue. Without application to campus and their lives, one may see these dialogues failing to fulfill a larger goal. Thus Stage 4 (ideally one or two sessions) attempts to support participants in making commitments to action beyond the dialogue space. Although action is sometimes construed as a protest or something more visible, facilitators work with participants to develop tangible actions, ranging from smaller (for example, doing more reading, challenging peers when they make oppressive jokes) to larger (for example, structuring a town hall meeting to address a campus issue). Facilitators also help participants understand that smaller actions may be seen as big for some participants, depending on their level of awareness prior to entering the dialogue space. Thus an important caution here is to not criticize the size of these actions but work with participants in finding ways to keep the momentum going outside of the dialogue space in addressing issues that are relevant and personal to them.

Using the IGD Model to Engage in Dialogues about Theories

Zuñiga's (2003) four-stage intergroup dialogue provides the foundation for engaging students in dialogues about the various theories discussed in this book. As a reminder, the major purpose of the IGD model is to help participants engage in structured dialogues about difficult topics with the support of cofacilitators providing activities and resources to guide participants in this process. Throughout this book we presented theories about how students develop holistically and across domains including cognitive, moral, and social identity. At the center of each of these theories is students' developmental readiness. Students are not able to develop in any domain if they do not possess the developmental capacity and readiness to do so. Educators therefore must provide the necessary scaffolding to foster students' developmental readiness.

An important observation from the IGD model is that in any given dialogue group, just as in any student organization or classroom, participants will enter the space with varied awareness and understanding of diversity-related issues. One of the most challenging tasks for facilitators is balancing the varied levels and needs of participants in these dialogue groups. Similarly, one of the challenges of student affairs educators in using theories is that students will have differing levels of developmental readiness based in large part on their prior experiences, as well as their privileged and marginalized identities. Typically, people have spent more time reflecting on the marginalized identities they hold, and less time actively reflecting on privileged identities, in part because they are rarely prompted to do so. Using IGD as a model provides instructors of student development theory courses and student affairs educators themselves key components for creating productive contexts for learning. In the following paragraphs we connect IGD stages to understanding and using student development theory. We did not place time constraints on timing or length of each stage, because every situation is dependent upon context. In a student development graduate course, educators may have an entire semester to implement these stages and explicitly link them to theory. In a week-long professional development training, educators may need to modify and condense activities to cover material in the book and frame it through the IGD process. Ultimately, educators and facilitators should engage in great intentionality to ensure the effectiveness of the IGD model, but they should also be realistic about what can be accomplished based upon group size, audience, and available time to conduct instruction.

Stage 1. Stage 1 of the IGD model involves building trust and relationships to set the stage for exploring controversial topics. Prior to using theories to make sense of students' experiences, at this stage educators should work with students to help them develop comfort in sharing their stories. Williams's (1997) reminder that behind every face is a story is an important point here. Educators must keep students' stories at the forefront, and at Stage 1, it is essential to take time to hear students' stories and let them share with others. At this stage, educators can share pieces of their own stories as appropriate in order to reciprocate the vulnerability they are asking students to demonstrate. Our suggestion to use autobiography and self-reflection as a means to understand student development theory connects closely with this stage in the IGD, as both rely on knowing oneself and coming to know and value the diverse stories of others.

Stage 2. In Stage 2, participants work to develop a shared language for difficult terms, such as privilege, power, and oppression. A challenge in this stage is the different levels of awareness about these issues that participants will have. Participants with more knowledge, especially when this knowledge derives from their experiences as members of marginalized groups, may feel frustrated with those who have less knowledge, particularly if participants with less knowledge are also from privileged groups. In thinking about student development theories, students with more privileged identities may believe they have nothing to contribute to dialogues about differences, given that they do not see how talking about their privileged identities would benefit other dialogue participants. At this stage, it is important for educators to remind participants to speak from their own experiences. Thus, educators can build from the knowledge and stories participants shared in Stage 1 and add complexity by asking participants to connect their stories to larger issues of systemic oppression and power. A question here might be: How does your [privileged/marginalized] identity connect to larger structures of oppression that exist in society? Educators can also share their own stories of how they came to learn about issues of power, privilege, and oppression in order to illustrate their own developmental journeys and struggles along the way. In the context of student development theory, it is important for individuals to understand their privileged and marginalized identities and their role as a student affairs educator in talking about power, privilege, and oppression. The ability to do so in service of students and their development is a hallmark of good student affairs practice.

Stage 3. One of the features of Stage 3 is discussing controversial topics. Educators can incorporate supplemental readings from venues such as *About Campus, The Chronicle of Higher Education,* and *Diverse Issues in Higher Education* to complement assigned chapters in the book. For example, in discussions about racial identity, students may raise the issue of campus culture centers and multicultural affairs and ask why some racially minoritized students "self-segregate" on campus. From a student development theory lens, educators might help students understand the stage in many racial identity development theories in which students of color choose to associate only with people who share their racial identity, which is a common aspect of identity development. Educators can work to help students see this inclination to gather with like-others as a form of solidarity and preservation for racially minoritized students within isolating, predominantly White campus environments, for example; these racially homogeneous groups support student development as they navigate their racial identities. Similarly, educators might also help students understand the embedded assumptions of "self-segregation," particularly the fact that White students also connect with other White students, but their actions are viewed as normal and rarely scrutinized. Educators might ask students to consider the role of societal racism in shaping how the actions of majoritized groups are deemed acceptable, while similar actions, when enacted by minoritized groups, are questioned and subjected to hypervisibility.

In this IGD stage, educators can also help participants grapple with how to work with varied levels of understanding about their own awareness of their identities, how their identities ultimately shape the types of questions they ask, and how experiences on campus shape their identities. Participants might for the first time recognize the existence of privilege and power, which can create a range of emotions including anger, frustration, embarrassment, shame, and guilt. Educators can work with participants to understand that these emotions are not unusual and represent the *crisis or turning point*, prevalent in most psychosocial theories. Educators can also explain that working through them is a way to keep moving forward toward commitment or resolution in their development. Participants might resist topics at this stage, and educators should be prepared to help them work through that resistance by normalizing it, and by reminding students that such topics will continue to emerge and students will be encouraged to grapple with them in relation to the theories. Student development theory explains some of the responses that individuals may have in Stage 3 of the IGD, and the strategies of IGD may be helpful as participants work on their own psychosocial, cognitive, and emotional development within a power, privilege, and oppression framework.

Stage 4. Finally, the last stage involves moving from dialogue to action. Educators can work with students to see what is necessary to take their next developmental steps and what kinds of actions will foster their holistic growth. For students still working through guilt based on their privileged identities, educators might ask students to examine their own development within the framing of a particular theory or set of theories (for example, social identities, self-authorship, cognitive). Educators can also assign accountability partners or encourage students to create small learning support groups to ensure that students continue to explore their identities throughout the course and possibly the semester or academic year. Finding members from various identity groups is also a way to keep participants working across differences to make sense of their development. Students may decide they want to keep exploring some aspects of their identity as a tangible action step, and educators can work with them to find ways that challenge and support them in this developmental growth, including peer-mentoring, journal reflection, reading, attending trainings, and blogging, to name a few. Just as student development theories can encompass lifelong learning and development, this stage in the IGD model asks individuals to commit to advancing themselves and provides scaffolding to do so.

Recognizing Educators' Own Developmental Capacities

Throughout this book, we have discussed student development theories that readers can use to understand, describe, and explain college students' development. Our focus has been on college students and their development, but we would be remiss if we did not address educators' own development. As faculty members and professionals, we often assume that student affairs educators have the knowledge, skills, and capacity to facilitate students' development. However, it seems likely—if not certain—that not all educators possess these qualities. In light of this, we advocate that student affairs educators continuously reflect on their own development in order to identify areas for growth, opportunities to learn new concepts and ways of working, and gaps in professional knowledge that need to be filled. We are not suggesting that educators must have all of the answers in order to promote students' development; to do so limits the possibility of lifelong learning, which we highly value. Rather, we encourage educators to consider their own development alongside that of students in graduate programs and students in the larger campus environment in order to understand the processes of development in a range of domains in the twenty-first century.

We recommend strongly that as educators read and consider the various theories, they assess their own developmental capacities and opportunities. In terms of social identities, we recommend that educators pay particular attention to understanding their privileged identities, for as we discussed in the previous section, those are likely the identities on which individuals reflect the least. We encourage educators to push themselves to develop in those areas in which they have the most work to do.

When considering self-authorship, for example, new professionals seeking approval and external validation as they make their way in new professional settings might see themselves in the description of people who "follow external formulas." Defined by their relationships (another hallmark of this position in self-authorship theory) and spending countless hours in direct service to undergraduates, they may well seek approval and affirmation from the very students with whom they work. ("It's important that they like me.") On one hand, this personal imperative to be likable could result in good relationships with students. But this situation could also yield difficulties with challenging students to reflect more deeply on multiple perspectives, since students sometimes resist and do not look favorably upon an educator challenging them. ("I don't want to push too hard because they won't like me anymore.") However, an educator who has developed an internal foundation would not need this approval in relationships, and thus might more confidently push students in the sometimes uncomfortable ways that are necessary for development. ("I want the students with whom I work to respect me, even like me, but my highest priority is that I can raise difficult topics when necessary to promote their development.") Educators who see themselves "following external formulas" might consider using supervisors, mentors, and trusted peers to create a plan for moving toward self-authorship. Although we used self-authorship theory in this example, educators can examine themselves in the context of any theory to see what assets and liabilities their current level of development might hold for professional practice.

Self-knowledge and reflection about developmental capacity may also contribute to good thinking about which theories to use in practice to promote student development. Drawing from their own developmental journeys, informed by theories and models that help describe and explain those journeys, educators may be able to assess the limitations and benefits of those theories. Students, of course, have their own experiences, different from one another and from the educators with whom they work, yet educators with a firm grasp of theory recognized through their own experiences may use it to see connections across differences.

Conclusion

In this chapter, we conveyed how student affairs educators can partner with students in the complex processes of development. Using the intergroup dialogue (IGD) approach, we made a case for how this framework can help educators use structured activities to promote students' development, while also focusing on their own developmental capacities. Given the large number of theories and the many personal topics they address, it can be challenging to teach about student development theory, as well as to work to promote students' development. It is important to remember that often the best one can do is to provide the scaffolding necessary for students to move forward in their development, listen to their stories, reflect on one's own developmental journeys, and share this information with students. Being present and weighing how assumptions and biases inform their perspectives and how they work with students—these are also important. For many professionals, sharing their own struggles along the way is a route to building trusting relationships that help foster developmental growth. We encourage educators to connect experience to theory and theory to practice that provides context for additional developmental experiences for students and themselves. In this approach, student development theories are one—but not the only—source of knowledge for good professional practice as student affairs educators.

Discussion Questions

1. In what ways can student affairs educators partner to facilitate maximum benefit from application of student development theory?
2. Outline the four stages of the intergroup dialogue (IGD) model, and identify what might be the easiest and most difficult components of the model for you to implement.
3. How would you talk with a colleague or student who does not see the value of student development theory about why it is important to use it in professional practice?
4. Choose two student development theories described in this book. Reflect on your own development in these areas and where you see yourself in the theories.
5. Based on your self-assessment in #4, what next step could you take to enhance and further facilitate your own development?
6. Think of a student with whom you have worked or are working. Using the theories you chose for #4, consider where that student is in those developmental domains. What is similar about your experience and the student's? What is different? What do the theories add to your understanding of that student, and how you are different and similar?
7. In your opinion, which contemporary topics related to identity might spark the need for a difficult dialogue in the classroom or professional settings? Based on the topic, how would you approach these conversations to account for diverse perspectives and needs among your audience?
8. What three approaches would you use to challenge resistance during difficult dialogues that emerge around theory and identity?
9. In addition to the suggestions offered here, what strategies would you recommend for strengthening arguments in favor of theoretically grounded student affairs practice?

CHAPTER EIGHTEEN

IMPLICATIONS AND FUTURE DIRECTIONS FOR PRACTICE, RESEARCH, AND THEORY DEVELOPMENT

In this book, we have illustrated the wide range of student development theories, from early-stage theories to more recent theories that highlight holistic, integrated development, many through an ecological lens. Although over 50 years have passed since the concept was first presented, student development is a relatively young idea, now coming into its own with a vast array of theories and models to examine college students' development. In a society filled with conflict and tensions that ultimately shape higher education, the need to understand how college students develop and to promote their development is critical.

The theory and research presented in this book embody the bulk of available knowledge on the topic, yet there is still much more to learn about student development. If a theory was not included in this book, that does not necessarily mean it is unworthy or lacks credibility for research or practice. Because student development research continues to expand, capturing all the theories in one volume is both difficult and unrealistic. We tried to be as inclusive as possible, realizing that we likely left out certain theories that some might deem important.

In this concluding chapter, we provide a glimpse at what has been achieved and some challenges to student development theory, followed by an overall evaluation of the current status of student development theory, research, and practice. We close with recommendations regarding future efforts to better understand how students develop and the impact of college on their experiences.

What Has Been Achieved?

In the 1980s, student affairs educators who were familiar with the work of Chickering, Perry, and Kohlberg considered themselves well versed in student development theory. Today, the theory base of the field has grown to include many important perspectives that challenge educators to expand their thinking, particularly related to gender, class, race, sexuality, ethnicity, age, disability, religion, spirituality, and so on, and how these identities intersect and influence each other. Student development is also about cognitive, psychosocial, and moral development and how these intersect with each other and social identities, too. Ultimately, the intersection of these developmental perspectives best describes who students are and who they can become.

There is a growing emphasis on foregrounding intersectional theories to capture the complex nature of student development. These theories have enabled educators to focus on how specific social identities, such as race, class, and gender, intersect to impact the experiences and development of college students. Equally as important, these theories have shifted attention to how particular contexts impact the salience of one's identities and the fact that identities are still always coexisting through their intersections. These theories have moved the field beyond stage-based theories toward more holistic examinations of students.

Indeed, student affairs educators who teach student development theory regularly face the challenging task of determining which theories to include and which to omit from their syllabi. Many student affairs graduate programs have expanded their offerings to include at least two classes examining student development theory, usually an introductory course and then a more advanced course that might focus on critical approaches to student development theory or the process of creating theory. These advanced classes have helped students understand the complexities involved in creating theories and useful considerations, such as who the theorists are and how their own stories and identities inform construction and interpretation of theories.

The application of student development theory to student affairs practice also has become more sophisticated and intentional since the turn of the century. Theory-to-practice models, such as that of Reason and Kimball (2012) discussed in Chapter Three, provide guidance for student affairs educators in using and applying theories as a foundation for their work. Examples reported in the literature and at professional conferences suggest that student affairs educators are creatively using theory as a tool for understanding the issues student face in today's postsecondary context and as a method of scaffolding to create a more positive campus environment to enhance student development. Theories provide insights into working effectively with individual students, to advising and training student groups and organizations, to designing classroom experiences, and to evaluating and developing policy and procedures on college campuses. Student development theories can help to meet the longstanding goal of educating the whole student (American Council on Education, 1994b).

Limitations of the Existing Theories

Although there have been several advancements in student development theories since the last edition of this book was published, there continue to be limitations in the existing knowledge base of theories. Noting these shortcomings helps put the ideas presented in this book in context and helps readers consider these limitations as they use theories in their work.

First, readers need to consider the limited nature of theory. We have tried to capture new and emerging theories in this book, but we recognize that theory is still growing; thus we have left out some populations that warrant attention. For instance, the presence of veteran students continues to increase on many campuses. Although these students may not have a common identity in the traditional sense, they do have shared experiences that reflect their veteran status. Also, students who have children form another population that warrants more attention, as these students navigate campuses where it is often difficult to balance parenting and student roles. Undocumented students certainly have unique developmental challenges and experiences, as do students who study abroad and return to the United States. The reentry shock these students experience impacts their identity in unexpected ways. In addition, international students continue to increase across many postsecondary institutions. Understanding the unique needs and challenges of these students would enable educators to be more mindful of these students' development (see Chapter Twelve for a fuller discussion of emergent populations). Finally, the dimension of social class (Chapter Eleven) continues to affect students, and although we discussed students with disabilities, more research is needed on this population, particularly when considering the intersections of these students' identities (see Chapter Ten).

In addition, existing developmental theories are, for the most part, based on the values of White, middle-class, and educated people, predominantly men. Such values may contribute to a limited sense of what is important in the lives of students, especially those from different backgrounds. As more research on marginalized and minoritized college populations is conducted, many identity research boundaries have expanded. This research expands our understanding of identity intersectionality and broadens the research on student groups not often studied. Readers should also consider our backgrounds as authors of this book. Although we have different racial, gender, sexual orientation, and religious identities, our ideas are filtered through our own stories and lenses.

Another important point to recall is that student development theory has its base in the field of psychology. As such, internal developmental processes tend to be emphasized, while insufficient attention is paid to the role of environmental forces (for example, racism, sexism, homophobia, xenophobia) that influence development. Additionally, student development theory is now based in more academic disciplines (for example, sociology and anthropology) and epistemological frameworks (for example, constructivism and feminism), making research on holistic development of college students complex but necessary for a more complete view of student development.

Stage theories, in particular, suffer from the problems just noted. Underlying assumptions upon which these theories are based imply that the developmental path is similar for all people, leading to an end point, at which time the person has achieved maximum growth. The descriptions of various stages reflect dominant White culture values and perspectives relevant at the time of their inception. Adaptation of these models may have value for future student development researchers, but generalizing theory to all people is unwise and does a disservice to understanding development.

Recommendations for the Future

Based on the critique of the student development knowledge base and research presented in the previous section, we offer recommendations for integrating student development theory, research, and practice. Even with the ever-increasing body of literature emanating from numerous disciplines, we make recommendations for how students and student affairs educators think about using and applying student development theories now and in the future.

Educators Must Consider Development in a More Holistic and Less Linear Manner

People are complex beings; therefore we must view development more complexly. In an article in the fiftieth edition of the *Journal of College Student*

Development, Baxter Magolda (2009) noted: "Thus higher education in general and student affairs in particular lack a holistic, theoretical perspective to promote the learning and development of the whole student" (p. 621). She went on to add: "Constructing a holistic theoretical perspective requires focusing on the intersections rather than separate constructs" (p. 621). In Chapter Three of this book, we advocated for looking at development more holistically. Even as certain identities might be more salient for students at particular times in their lives and within particular contexts, treating development more holistically and in an intersecting and integrated manner means looking at students as whole beings.

Educators Must Examine Development Through a Lens of Privilege, Power, and Oppression

The theories described in this book are sometimes written without considering how development happens within larger contexts that are oppressive and where power and privilege exist. For instance, students of color are often developing their racial identities in campus environments that are racist and oppressive and where power imbalances exist. Consequently, development should not be examined in a vacuum. Certain students, because of their privileged identities, have more freedom to develop their identities without pushback or pressure to assimilate to certain norms and standards. Plainly stated, power differentials impact individuals' development. As a result, developing identity, particularly minoritized identities, in the presence of opposition to the very existence of these identities will influence the manner in which development occurs.

Educators Must Examine Development Independent of Dominant Culture Models

Many people wonder how Chickering and Reisser's (1993) theory would be different if the population from which the theory was developed had been significantly more diverse. Although the knowledge base is expanding to consider the generalizability of developmental theories to students from diverse backgrounds, most often researchers and practitioners still begin from the existing theoretical base and examine how students of color, women, and other minoritized groups differ from or fare in comparison to that base. Implicitly, as Gilligan (1977) suggested, difference is viewed as deficient, and the White male dominant culture experience is still considered the norm. Although this book is evidence of the expanding nature of the literature, researchers need to explore the development of students from various racial and ethnic groups; gay, lesbian, bisexual students; transgender students; students with disabilities; and other students whose life experiences have shaped them in ways different from students from majoritized cultures. Qualitative research approaches—including phenomenological interviews, participant observation, visual methods including photovoice and video, and other techniques used in anthropology and sociology—are particularly appropriate for determining the nature of development over time for students from diverse backgrounds.

Educators Must Give Appropriate Attention to Underrepresented Groups

Related to the preceding recommendation, student affairs educators need to become more aware of the missing voices in the student development literature. How often do educators read about or consider the developmental experiences of students with disabilities, Jewish students, or Muslim students, for example? What about transgender students? What about students raised in poverty and those raised with extreme wealth and privilege? What about the children of migrant workers, veterans, or displaced factory workers returning to college? What about students who are first-, second-, third-, and fourth-generation in the United States with strong ethnic and cultural heritages? What about international students who come from nearly every country on the globe? For student affairs educators to be inclusive in creating meaningful experiences to facilitate development for all students, they must have a greater understanding of the role played by background and culture in the lives of students from diverse populations. Addressing issues of invisibility and voicelessness in the theory base may be the most pressing need. Educators cannot assume that development is the same process for all students or that the concepts derived from a narrowly defined group of students work equally well for others. Identifying what influences development by learning from students who have been previously overlooked will help in understanding the unique and diverse developmental challenges students face.

Educators Must Consider Development Across the Lifespan

No longer are college students all 18 to 22 years old. Nor does development end at age 22. If educators want to truly understand student development, they must learn more about the changes that occur later in life and the impact of those changes on the ways in which older students negotiate the college environment. Returning adult students face unique developmental challenges, and theories must reflect that. Understanding development across the lifespan is also crucial for student affairs educators to understand their own life experiences and effectively work with colleagues to enhance personal as well as professional development.

Educators Must Conduct More Longitudinal Research to Examine Development Over Time

Development is not a static variable. It cannot be studied in the same way researchers study topics such as who gets admitted to college and who graduates. Researchers must follow people as they move through their lives and see what unfolds in the process. While this kind of research is time consuming and difficult, the benefits are important. Baxter Magolda's (2008) research, which began when participants were in college and has now spanned into their careers and lives after college, enables readers to understand not only the process of development during college but also the impact of college experiences on later development. More longitudinal studies with students of color (for example, Torres & Baxter Magolda, 2004) are needed to understand the holistic development of college students from different backgrounds.

Educators Must Consider the Impact of the Environment on Development

As Lewin (1936) stated long before the advent of the student development movement, behavior is a function of the interaction of the person and the environment. For too long researchers have focused on the person by concentrating on internal maturational processes and downplayed the role of the environment in the determination of developmental outcomes. "Environment" has many meanings. As noted earlier, it can be the familial, cultural, and social circumstances of a person's life before college. Environment can be the type of institution in which a student is enrolled. For example, liberal arts colleges are more likely than other types of educational institutions to focus attention and resources on student development efforts. Faculty and student affairs educators in these institutions more easily make the personal connections with students that are so important for their development (Hirt, 2006). Also, research indicates that the development of African American students attending predominantly White universities is quite different from the development of their counterparts in historically Black universities (Fleming, 1984). Particular settings on college campuses must also be considered when examining the environment. In a study of the development of gay, lesbian, and bisexual students in residence halls (Evans & Broido, 1999), students reported very different experiences in various hall settings that either facilitated or enhanced the development of their identities.

Educators Must Generate Better Methods to Assess Development

More accessible and inexpensive assessment techniques are needed, particularly for large-scale evaluation studies. If educators are to determine whether programs, services, and other interventions are having an impact on students, they must have ways of measuring development. Programmatic efforts to develop and refine instrumentation, such as the work of Worthington and his colleagues (2005, 2008), Fassinger (1998), and Fassinger and Miller (1997) are crucial to advance progress in this area. Since the last edition of this book was published, studies employing qualitative methods have become more acceptable in student development research, which is helping researchers understand the the nuances of development in a different way. Qualitative approaches are particularly appropriate when building new theory and extending theory to previously unconsidered populations.

Educators Must Design Interventions Attuned to Specific Environments

The following scenario still happens far too often in student affairs: A student affairs educator attends a student affairs conference presentation in which the presenters outline a program they have implemented successfully on their campus. The educator is impressed. She believes that this program is just what is needed to address a similar issue on her campus. She comes home and tells her staff about the new program; they implement it the next year, and it fails. What the educator and her staff members did not consider is that each campus is unique. The issue may seem the same, but the environmental context matters (for example, institutional size, type, mission, culture, history). Programs cannot be transplanted without a careful assessment of the environment and modifications to adapt the program to each particular situation and context to promote development.

Educators Must Make Assessment and Evaluation a Part of Developmental Intervention

Interventions need to be intentionally planned and based on sound assessment data reflecting the needs of the student community. They also need to be carefully evaluated to determine their effectiveness. Focus groups, interviewing based on purposive sampling, examination of archival data, and other qualitative means of assessment can be used effectively in program evaluation along with more traditional quantitative approaches (Upcraft & Schuh, 1996). Few evaluative studies of theory-based interventions are available in the literature. Such work is extremely important for advancing the field. Evaluation studies, of course, provide information to student affairs educators about what efforts are worthy of continuation and where resources should be allocated. In addition, well-designed evaluation studies can also lead to refinement of theory and provide direction for future investigation. Student affairs educators and faculty can both gain from collaborative efforts to evaluate developmental interventions for students.

Educators Must Encourage the Use of Theory in Educational Practice

In an applied field such as student affairs, a knowledge base would seem valuable only to the extent that it informs practice. In the same way, theoretical information that can enhance the teaching and learning process is of limited value if it does not find a home in the classroom. Educators must disseminate information about how student development theory informs educational practice. Collaborative efforts between student affairs educators and faculty are particularly powerful in enhancing the climate for learning and development on college campuses. In this book, we have included student portraits as a resource to encourage theoretical analysis and promote critical thinking about the theory-to-practice connection.

Educators Teaching Student Development Must Be Aware of Theoretical Complexities

With an ever-increasing developmental knowledge base, it is important for faculty teaching student development to update constantly and be knowledgeable about the various theories related to college students. Faculty will be more proficient in teaching language, concepts, and ideas specific to developmental theory if they continually gain expertise through participation in professional development activities targeted at expanding knowledge of the vast range of traditional and contemporary student development theories. Although staying current in the field is time consuming, it is a crucial practice for student affairs educators teaching student development theory to graduate or undergraduate students. We encourage faculty and students alike to read widely and explore original sources of student development theory. Faculty and student affairs educators who engage in the study of student development over their careers will be able to better serve the diverse students entering higher education institutions.

Educators Must Take an Inclusive and Evolutionary Approach to Theory

The study of student development has moved from focus on several theories derived primarily from psychology to many theories derived from a host of academic disciplines and epistemologies. It is much easier to be familiar with and favor a handful of theories, usually those with more linear patterns and a structured developmental path. While, many theories contribute to knowledge of student development, educators must not limit their use to only a few. Adopting an intersectional framework here will help educators see how using multiple theories in combination can add to a more complex view of student development.

Educators Must Acknowledge Contextual Influences on the Development Trajectory

In some ways, this idea suggests that student development has features of both the positivist (in reference to a trajectory or path) and constructivist (in reference to the contextual influences) paradigms. In college, the trajectory of students' developmental path can resemble a line, curve, or arc, but in all cases is influenced by the environment. As student development research moves forward, the context of higher education needs more investigation, particularly as it pertains to the shape of the path for the development of diverse students.

Educators Must Acknowledge the Whole of Students' Development

In 1937, the American Council on Education offered a report that acknowledged the necessity of institutions of higher education attending to the needs of the whole student (American Council on Education, 1937/1994a). Since that time, and with the advent of the professionalization of student affairs, the attention to the developmental needs of all students has been paramount. In order to continue this tradition, researchers and student affairs educators must find a space to converse about the complexity involved in developing the "whole student" for the many diverse students who attend institutions of higher education. Thorough examination of students' developmental needs and the institution's environment is likely to uncover that the whole of student development is greater than the sum of its parts.

Conclusion

The many student development models and theories available to educators and researchers interested in facilitating student development can be a guide to students' growth processes. As times shift and more is learned, some theories receive more attention than others. For instance, Abes, Jones, and McEwen's (2007) model is one of the most cited theories in this book. As developmental research based in constructivism, its popularity has signaled a move away from stage models toward a more integrative lens of student development theories. Limitations in stage theories are evident in theories such as those that are purely cognitive, because affect and cognition cannot be separated; the two should be studied in tandem. Linear models are rigid and static and do not reflect the complexity inherent in human beings.

Since the beginning of the twenty-first century, much student development research and theory has reflected the integration of theory and intersection of identity through a constructivist lens. Future research is needed focusing on ecological approaches (for example, Bronfenbrenner, 2005), which are powerful in enhancing understanding of student/institution interaction. As our population ages and the numbers of traditional age students decline, longitudinal research based on the lifespan will expand the knowledge base regarding student populations. As institutions with predominantly White cultures seek to increase the diversity of their student populations, there is a need to learn more about racial and ethnic identity (for example, Phinney, 2007; Torres, 1999, 2003). Self-authorship as a developmental outcome increasingly finds its way into the literature (see Baxter Magolda, 2001, 2008; Pizzolato, 2004, 2006), creating a need to reexamine and extend Kegan's (1994) foundational work. As students' lives continue to become more complicated, further examination of spirituality is needed for students' success and development. And as students come from clearly distinguishable lower, middle, and upper social classes (Schwartz, Donovan, & Guido-DiBrito, 2009), more research can shed light on how student identity is shaped by class status and how class shapes other identities.

A consideration of integration and intersection of all parts of student development provides a warrant for new and creative ways to examine the whole student. Though more complex, student development studied from constructivist, postmodern, and critical lenses with new methodologies captures multiple, overlapping images of the development of the whole student. We owe our students nothing less.

Discussion Questions

1. What has been achieved in student development theory since the 1980s?
2. What are some of the limitations of current student development theory, and what is your responsibility to address them as you apply theory in your work environment and research?

3. In addition to those noted in this chapter, what recommendations for practice, theory, and research do you have for creating and applying student development theory in the future?

4. What are the responsibilities of higher education and student affairs educators for attending to the complex developmental needs of the most diverse student populations in U.S. higher education?

5. How would you describe the future of student development theory? Will it continue to grow? Remain salient?

6. How can student development theory continue to address the whole student in the future without seeking one unified theory?

7. Build a 50-year plan for student development theory. What do you think are possible issues students and student development educators will face in the next half century?

8. Make two lists, which indicate (a) what you now know about yourself and (b) what you now know about student development theory that was not known to you when you began reading this book. What general observations can you make about what these lists reveal?

9. What will you learn about student development theory next? Where do you think your developmental journey will take you in 5, 10, and 25 years?

AFTERWORD

As a proud contributor to the two previous editions of this book, I would like to begin by expressing appreciation to the current authors for undertaking a task that grows increasingly more challenging with each edition. A primary challenge resides in the task of deciding what previous information to retain, what to delete, and what new material to include, all while working to produce a volume that is comprehensive but also of a manageable length. This is no small feat. In addition, the challenge remains of presenting the content in a meaningful way.

Just as the second edition was a departure from the first, so is this edition a departure from the second. Such change is appropriate. The authors have engaged with the knowledge base of college student development theory as well as relevant related areas. They identified what they consider to be the most important information and presented this information in a manner that will engage readers and inform student affairs practice.

As an advocate of reflective practice, I have long believed that we need much more than our good intentions and instincts to guide our work in student affairs and as classroom teachers, to inform our work as educators. College student development theory is one of our most important knowledge bases. I am happy to see the good work produced by the authors of this edition in support of keeping college student development theory central and accessible to higher education professionals.

The authors do well in addressing both the content of theory and the process of using theory in practice. Their desire and effort to create an appendix of sketches to aid readers in seeing the relationships among various aspects of development for individuals within multiple identity contexts is noteworthy. The general discussion questions at the end of each chapter can provoke further reflection and serve as a stimulus for readers' generating additional questions of their own.

In conclusion, I applaud the outstanding work done by the authors of this edition. I respect their efforts and outcomes. They have produced a major contribution to the profession that reflects diversity within college student development. I hope future versions of *Student Development in College* will be produced and reflective of the caliber of this volume as well as the ongoing growth, complexity, and evolving contextual influences of student development. Our profession will benefit greatly from authors' continuing efforts to rise to the challenge.

Dea Forney
Professor Emeritus, Western Illinois University
Easton, PA

APPENDIX

CASE STUDY SCENARIO: INTRODUCING PRESCOTT UNIVERSITY'S SELECTED SAHE GRADUATE STUDENTS

On the first day of class, 25 students sit with eager anticipation in their College Student Development Theory course as their graduate studies in student affairs commence. The students, representing an array of unique life stories, wonder how their first year in the student affairs graduate program at Prescott State University will unfold. The Prescott program has a strong reputation and is highly regarded in the field for training educators who go on to make a difference in students' lives as college administrators, faculty, and social justice leaders. The chatter among the students is lively as they ask each other about their backgrounds, their undergraduate institutions, and how they came to enroll in the Prescott program.

In the midst of these informal connections, Dr. Joanne Greene, the professor these neophyte students met during interview days, and her graduate assistant appear in the front of the room. Dr. J begins, "Good morning and welcome to SAHE 610, College Student Development Theory. My name is Dr. Joanne Greene. I'm so pleased to meet you and look forward to working with you this semester." Dr. J. continues warmly, to lighten the obvious anxiety in the room: "New students often wonder about how I prefer to be addressed, and I tell them Dr. J, but you may call me Dr. Greene or Joanne, too." After reviewing the syllabus and course expectations, Dr. J turns the class over to her assistant to facilitate a brief community-building activity for everyone to get to know each other more formally. When the activity comes to a close, Dr. J notes, "I can see that this is going to be a stimulating class. Based on my observations, each of you has something important to contribute to and enrich this learning space.

While the emphasis for this course is the development of students in college, I want to acknowledge the transitions each of you are experiencing as you begin this rigorous program. I encourage you to view development in this course as a lifelong journey, which means, yes, each one of you has completed college, but your development is still occurring and will continue throughout your lifetime. One of my beliefs is that student affairs educators dare not attempt to facilitate the development of a student without having also engaged in critical reflection on their own development."

Revealing her own reflective path, Dr. J directs the students' attention to a newsprint size, hand-drawn map that depicts her developmental journey and the varied experiences contributing to her identity development. She shares how her experiences in a historically Black sorority helped shape her identity as a woman, and how the hazing death of a dear friend in another sorority accelerated her moral development. She also tells the students about her decision to attend college, how she changed her major three times, and what events led up to her major in psychology—each shaping her psychosocial development. She discusses her experiences with racism in the residence hall and how it prompted growth in her racial identity development as an African American woman. Finally, she discusses the philosophy course that challenged how she thought about virtually everything, a reflection of her cognitive development.

"As I pinpoint these critical life moments, college was not simply a series of isolated events. Instead, college was full of complexities and intersections reflecting individual, collective, and integrated experiences. Now that I've shared my college experiences with you, I would like to hear about your experiences. For the rest of this semester, we will focus on understanding student development in college and explore various theories related to social identities, psychosocial and cognitive development theories and integrative perspectives on theory. I realize that at this point, you have not received much guidance about the issues students are facing in college or how to go about addressing them in practice. I would venture to guess that many of you would rely on your own experiences to tackle the developmental issues students face. That said, for the first few weeks of this course, we will discuss the origins of student development theory, its foundations and how we can best implement theory to practice by adopting an integrative, holistic lens. We will then discuss families of theories throughout the remainder of the course, and we will wrap up with a focus on student affairs educators as learning partners and the future of student development theory.

"For the remainder of this class period, I want you all to take a moment and reflect on your own development and the experiences that helped shape your identity. Please take a moment and reflect on the following questions:

"Who am I?
What critical moments in college contributed to my development?"

"After reflecting, please identify a partner and share your responses. We will then come back together for a large group discussion."

Student Portraits

Here are the developmental portraits shared by 7 of the 25 students:

Drew

Drew, a 30-year-old Chinese American father and husband, was intrigued by Dr. J's questions because they made him think about his life experiences in addition to those in college. Drew and his wife are devout Protestant Christians who are active in their local church, serving as volunteers for annual events and programs. For the past few years, Drew has coordinated the college readiness summer camp at his church. The idea for the camp came from Drew's experiences in a similar program prior to entering college. While it was not a church-affiliated program, Drew thought many of the program activities could be beneficial to the large population of teens at the church. Drew facilitated the program so well that it garnered attention in the local newspaper, prompting the admissions director at a nearby college, and Prescott alumni, to reach out to him and encourage him to consider a career in student affairs.

The ultimate decision to pursue a student affairs degree was challenging for Drew because he took great pride in his ability to provide for his family, including their newly purchased home in an upscale community. His wife enjoyed shopping at high-end retail chains and grocery stores, and they both knew this would need to end if he left the lucrative field in which he had been working. Moreover, he truly enjoyed the nearby golf course, a place where he did plenty of networking to make business connections for the firm employing him. Support from his wife in agreeing to go without upscale material goods meant everything to Drew since he had initiated this radical change for his family.

As he reflected on college, Drew realized that while growing up he had never imagined then he could live life with the luxury he currently enjoyed. As the son of immigrants, he watched his parents struggle to ensure he and siblings received a solid education. Though his parents were not strong English speakers, they worked numerous jobs, which ultimately resulted in the purchase of a chain of small businesses. Fluent in English, Drew helped his parents manage their entrepreneurial enterprises. These meaningful childhood experiences were crucial influences on his decision to major in business as an undergraduate.

Now, having decided to pursue a career in student affairs, Drew recalled how the courses in the business school had prepared him for a profitable career. However, running a business failed to capture his intense passion for working and learning about diverse people and issues. As a first-generation college student, he always wondered how he could help others access college, but at the time he did not know how to pursue a degree in the field of student affairs. He felt confident about his performance in the business courses in which he enrolled and surprised himself when he excelled. However, Drew found other courses more challenging because they forced him to think about topics that had never crossed his mind. As a sociology minor, Drew took courses dealing with race, class, gender, and a range of other identity groups. He moved from seeing the world as composed of many right and wrong answers to understanding the context of the knowledge he was gaining. Among the courses that forced him to think in a different way were those focusing on religious and spiritual pluralism. These courses had a tremendous influence on how he chose to practice and maintain his Christian beliefs. Drew also took two courses on ethnic and racial identity. While he thought both courses tended to have a heavy emphasis on experiences pertaining to African American and Latino groups, he was pleased to see that instructors in each course spent much time during the semester addressing Asian American and Pacific Islander peoples. In these courses, he learned more about the vast array of peoples that comprised the Asian Diaspora. Craving more self-knowledge, Drew completed class assignments that allowed him to explore his own ethnic group in greater depth. After some time passed, Drew began to reject values he had unwittingly adopted from the dominant culture while supporting values of his Asian American cultural heritage. His fraternity brothers noticed a change but allowed him space to reflect on his ethnic identity and its importance in his life.

His college experiences, particularly involvement in a traditionally White fraternity, taught Drew a great deal about manhood. The fraternity's emphasis on men and leadership was what initially attracted him. He learned much through the many leadership development programs offered by the fraternity's national office, as he found them personally fulfilling while also complementing his major. He also learned about the man he did not want to become as he observed how a handful of his fraternity brothers mistreated women. Drew took those lessons, specifically those that focused on honoring traditional family values, and now uses them in raising his sons. Drew emphasizes to his offspring that they too must be providers for their family when they marry and have children. He believes that what he knows about manhood is the most important lesson he can impart to his boys. While this is admittedly a somewhat paternalistic idea, Drew also realizes his perspectives align with his religious beliefs, but he has come a long way from his father's views on gender. He insists he supports women's rights and views women as equal, but appreciates his wife for understanding his strong desire to be the primary provider in their household.

In college, Drew volunteered at a homeless shelter as part of a service-learning project. When the project ended, he extended his time so he could feel like he made a difference in the community. In addition, it reminded him of his own challenges of paying for college on an extremely limited income, which required him to work throughout his four years to avoid loans. As a first-generation college student, Drew often grappled with being in a fraternity among men who had financial means, while he barely made ends meet. He often felt as if his fraternity brothers entered college with the privilege of money and tools for success. In other words, he believed his college friends knew far more than he did initially about attending college. These diverse experiences led Drew to implement the college readiness summer camp at his church and helped solidify his decision to pursue a master's degree in student affairs.

Discussion Questions

1. With a timeline, trace Drew's life events and development since childhood. In what ways does his life reflect Schlossberg's transition theory?
2. Outline Drew's ethnic identity development. Explain its trajectory and Drew's behavior at each stage of development. How has his ethnic identity contributed to making him the person he is today? How might being a member of a White fraternity affect his ethnic identity as a student of color?
3. As renewed appreciation for his own ethnic group intensified, in what ways did Drew separate himself from the dominant culture? How have other students of color you have observed rejected dominant culture values? In what ways can colleges and universities support students with a strong ethnic identity and enhance their development while they reject the dominant culture?
4. Compare and contrast Drew's social class identity as a child and then after he graduated from college and became financially successful. From the

child of immigrants to upper middle class, what kind of identity changes could Drew have experienced? What theories, models, or research apply to his social class identity?

5. Examine Drew's cognitive development and discuss how it resonated with cognitive developmental theory. What would Drew be like in class, and how could his professors challenge him to increase his cognitive development?

6. Think about the religious issues Drew faced in college. If Drew were a student at your university, how might the student affairs division support his religious identity development?

7. Drew has a strong gender identity and exhibits gender characteristics similar to his father's. Explain how this could change as he grows and develops in this capacity.

8. Draw a diagram of Drew's intersecting identities and discuss how these multiple identities are uniquely illustrated by him. How is Drew's development different from and similar to that of other students in his cohort?

Amber

Amber, a 26-year-old single mother, welcomed Dr. J's questions. She was happy to be joining the program, having worked at Prescott for the past eight years. Amber's journey in higher education has been both tumultuous and rewarding. She grew up in a predominantly White, conservative town where she had limited contact with people who were not White. Having come of age as the youngest child and only daughter of working-class parents, Amber was overprotected and rarely thought about her pathway in life. Her parents made decisions for her with little input or protest from Amber.

By the time she was a teenager, Amber felt like her life was too confined. She craved more freedom but was unable to express this desire to her parents; hence she remained silent and followed the pathway they created for her. Her brothers received more attention and independence than she did, and this bothered her. For most of her life, she recalled weekends in which the family traveled to her brothers' sporting events and activities. While she did not question her parents' love, she was concerned about what she perceived as their unending attention to her siblings. Amber's parents thought she should be more socially refined and marry in a more prestigious social class. Thus, despite her true interest in Spanish, her parents enrolled her in French. In high school, she wanted to be a cheerleader, but was reminded that it was neither a "real" sport, nor a worthwhile endeavor. The one boy she liked in high school never met her parent's approval because he was Honduran and from a migrant worker family.

When Amber graduated from high school, she could hardly contain her composure as she thought about her upcoming freedom. For the first time in her life, she had made a decision with which her parents agreed. Prescott State University was the perfect place for Amber and could feed her desire to major in international studies and theatre.

The first two years of college went well for Amber. She earned outstanding grades, was elected to the executive board of the French Club, and completed a summer internship as a counselor for the theatre program's summer camp for kids. She also studied in Paris for one semester, becoming fluent in French. Finally, Amber felt a sense of control. Despite her parents' staunch disapproval of interracial dating, Amber was even in a relationship with Jerry, an African American student, who led Amber's group during the first-year orientation program.

Amber's life drastically changed as her fifth semester began. Not only did she experience a break-up with Jerry, but she was also pregnant. How could she tell her parents she was pregnant, and how would they respond knowing Jerry was the father? Amber was overwhelmed by fear as she prepared to tell Jerry and her parents. Jerry agreed to do his best to care for their child and unexpectedly insisted they get back together and share an apartment. Amber's parents were devastated and disappointed, quickly outlining a plan of action. Amber would move home, but remain in school until the baby was born. As long as her relationship with Jerry ended, her parents would help support the baby while she finished college. Within a matter of months, Amber was faced with difficult life choices. In the end, she complied with her parents' wishes, but she remained in touch with Jerry periodically.

Amber's working-class parents wanted nothing more for her than to graduate from college; they prayed over it often at the mega church in her small hometown. Amber loved singing in the choir and performing in front of a crowd, but never saw much point to the overly passionate behaviors of some evangelists with whom she interacted on Sunday. One later fell from grace for non-Christian behavior, which forced Amber to question what she believed about religion and spirituality in her stopout from college. Although she wanted to believe in God for her daughter's sake, Amber found organized religion and other forms of spiritual expression nonsensical. She became agnostic about the time she returned to college to begin her coursework again.

When Amber returned to finish her undergraduate degree, she took classes part-time. She kept her international studies major, but changed her minor to communication and culture. In her mind, the international studies degree would be more marketable with a communication minor. In her coursework, Amber went from seeing her parents and professors as the keepers of all knowledge to finding her own path to knowledge. Her interest in theatre waned as her daughter required more of her time, and she knew that pursuing a life in the theatre would be difficult, if not impossible, as a single mom. Amber's parents also assured her that finding a job in the arts would be hard; thus she needed to focus on a degree that could make her more immediately employable—because after her daughter's birth most of her decisions revolved around what she (and often her parents) saw as best for her daughter. She also worked as a student assistant in residence life, eventually serving as a student program coordinator for the Commuter Student Center (CSC).

As Amber increasingly voiced an interest in students and their success, the director of the CSC told her about the student affairs master's program at Prescott and suggested she apply. Despite her overwhelming interest, she decided to wait and work professionally before pursuing graduate school so she could support and spend time with her daughter. After college graduation, she held a position in the continuing studies department as an academic and career advisor. Amber worked in that role to gain valuable experience, and when she was ready for career advancement, she applied to Prescott University's student affairs master's program.

Discussion Questions

1. Amber's parents made many decisions for her during her college years. How did these decisions affect her moral, religious, and cognitive development? How would you analyze her development in each of these developmental dimensions? How are her experiences reflected in the theory around these three dimensions?
2. Describe and explain Amber's moral development through Gilligan's theory. In what ways does her decision to keep her child, even though her relationship with Jerry had ended, reflect on her moral development? How might this differ from someone who resonated with the ethic of justice?
3. How does the ethic of care change over the course of Amber's life, particularly after the birth of her daughter?
4. What role does racial identity play in Amber's relationship with Jerry?
5. How do racial and class identity intersect for Amber? In other words, how does being from White working-class roots influence her development as a college student?
6. Think of a student you know who has a similar background. Describe the issues the student faces at the postsecondary level. What could you do in your role on campus to help enhance this student's development?

7. In what ways does Amber's story resonate with psychosocial theory? Discuss her life in terms of crisis and commitment. How did her identity change in the course of her adult life?

8. Diagram Amber's cognitive and moral development. How do these developmental pathways parallel one another? How does Amber's journey to agnosticism parallel theory?

Cory

Cory was excited about pursuing a student affairs master's degree. He thought Dr. J's questions were a good way to begin the class, but he was less than enthused to share stories about his development so publicly. He rarely spoke of his learning disability or multiracial identity. Cory felt as if he had no issues with his identity but was unsure how sharing this information would influence his classmates' view of him. Nevertheless, he began to reflect, jot down his thoughts, and prepare to share with a partner.

Cory is a 23-year-old man. His mother is African American and Filipino American, while his father is Puerto Rican and White. He was born and raised in a middle-class neighborhood on the West Coast until he was 15 years old. His mother's job relocation meant a permanent move to the Midwest for his family. Growing up, Cory was diagnosed at a young age with dyslexia. While his teachers and parents encouraged him, Cory often felt uncomfortable at school because he did not learn at the same pace or in the same way as his classmates. To offset some of his anxiety, Cory worked extremely hard with his tutors to ensure that he would succeed academically. Eventually, he learned to feel comfortable and confident about himself and his learning style.

During his early adolescent years, Cory was popular and amassed a large group of friends. When he learned his family was moving away his junior year of high school, he hated the idea of starting over socially. He wondered who his new friends would be, whether they would notice his learning disability and, if so, whether they would judge him harshly for it.

Over time, Cory adjusted to his new life. He was a well-known star athlete—and secretly in a relationship with another male student at school. Cory never shared information about his boyfriend with his parents for fear they would not accept his sexuality because of their strong religious beliefs. He was raised Catholic, but he grew increasingly uncomfortable with the many teachings that decried homosexuality. Cory made many decisions that were important for him, especially around his coming out, reflecting his moral development. Most often he made these decisions thinking about a universal correct response and eventually made moral decisions based on consideration for himself and others affected by his decision. For example, at first he believed that keeping his sexual identity a secret from his parents and the football team was the right thing to do because he anticipated that if he revealed it, he and the football team would be punished for it. By the time Cory came out in college, he was ready to relate publicly to a community of individuals with a similar sexual orientation. He did so in consultation with his boyfriend first but ultimately made the decision for himself.

Cory chose to attend a small, private liberal arts college on an athletic scholarship. He believed this institution was a good choice because of its location and its status in his family as his mother's alma mater. By the time Cory entered college, he was excited about his various courses. During his first year, he was very inquisitive and participated in class discussions. In addition to seeking clarification from instructors, Cory often asked follow-up questions because he wanted to hear a range of perspectives in order to figure out his own opinion. By the time his junior year rolled around, his classroom interactions were different and so was his thinking. Now he could form his own opinion and support it with available evidence. He still respected other opinions and perspectives but could consciously weigh his level of agreement or disagreement. Moreover, he viewed his instructors as facilitators of learning, not there to tell him "the right answer" or what to think.

His development took off at this institution as he learned more than he thought possible about himself, including his discomfort with coming out and his growing atheism. Prior to college, he did not have the language or words to describe these burgeoning experiences. At least now he was beginning to grapple with disclosing his sexual identity and no longer felt pressure to practice his parents' religion. In college, Cory continued to be exclusive with his boyfriend from high school, but he insisted the relationship remain private. As a student-athlete, he could not risk public disclosure of his relationship with a man.

Cory also gained a better understanding of his racial identity. From time to time throughout his life, he had been asked, "What are you?" He would always reply, in the same order, "Black, Puerto Rican, and Filipino" without much reflection on why the question made him feel uncomfortable. Was it the order in which he shared his identities? Was it the pressure of feeling different somehow? Why did he always exclude his White identity? In some instances, others insinuated he should take the question as a compliment because he was so physically attractive. In college, this question increased exponentially and mirrored his growing uneasiness of feeling targeted and hyper visible. On the college football team, fellow teammates often cracked jokes about his multiracial background, with which he seldom expressed discontent. In his mind, this was normal culture in a men's locker room. Cory was not involved in any of the many cultural groups on campus because he did not want to feel forced to choose one of his many identities over another. His participation in sports was his excuse for his lack of involvement. However, he did connect with the director of the multicultural center on campus, who served as his mentor during his junior year in college and was the first person to recognize Cory's potential to work in student affairs. As he reflects on his identity, Cory is happy he chose this academic program, because he wants to support students who struggle with their multiracial and sexual identities. He is hopeful he can also mentor students and help them see their full potential.

Discussion Questions

1. Describe Cory's sexual identity development and compare it to the sexual identity models and theories described in this book.
2. Think of a student you know who grappled with their sexual identity development in college, particularly their gay identity and coming out. What types of decisions did the student make? How supported did the student feel? What does your current institution, or a prior one at which you worked or attended, do to support the sexual identity development of all students?
3. Think of students you know who come out about their sexual identity in comparison to those who do not. Is one "more" developed than the other? Explain.
4. What role should institutions play in nurturing and celebrating students' diverse sexual identities?
5. Cory was concerned about having dyslexia and how others would perceive him. What conditions exist on campuses to create disabling environments for students with dyslexia?
6. Cory's racial and ethnic identities are intimately intertwined and personal. Define and discuss the differences between racial and ethnic identity and how they are developing for him. How is Cory's mixed race development reflected in development theory?
7. Cory identified as "Black, Puerto Rican, and Filipino." What are characteristics of these racial and ethnic groups individually? How might they differ for someone who represents all of them like Cory?
8. Cory began making moral decisions in college, theoretically evoking Kohlberg and Rest's theories or the justice orientation of moral development. Before he graduated, he shifted his perspective and believed it was important to consider others' perspective, or a care orientation, in his

moral decision-making. Plot the trajectory from each of these perspectives and discuss the value of each moral orientation.

Merriam

The reflection required by Dr. J was a welcomed opportunity for 24-year-old Merriam, who grew up on the Navajo Reservation in the southwest. Her father died when she was two years old, so her mother and grandparents raised her. She was intricately connected in meaningful spiritual, psychological, and physical ways to the entire Navajo tribal community. Her intimate connection with the tribe and its spiritualism taught her the value of nature and the urgency of preserving it. Merriam's mother and grandmother made sure her beaded ceremonial apparel and all the treasures of her cultural heritage were made known to her and treated as sacred objects. Still, she had an insatiable curiosity about the world of people and ideas beyond the reservation.

In her childhood, Merriam loved to walk the backcountry, track a storm or an animal, and pick herbs she gave to her grandfather, the tribe's medicine man. Often, she wandered into the desert to find the one shade tree where she could sit and read for hours on a hot day. She read everything she could get her hands on. The world was an open book to Merriam, and she loved looking from the outside in. She desired to be of the world (i.e., from the reservation) *and* in the world (i.e., attend a non-Native college).

Merriam's family was rich, but not in the classic Western sense of monetary wealth. In fact, her family had limited income. Her family's wealth came in the form of *connection* to each other and the land, nature, and spirit, assets she suspected money would never buy. After high school graduation and two years at a local tribal college, she felt whole and grounded within the Navajo community, giving her enough confidence to leave the tribe to continue the education she sought and then return home to fulfill her dream of increasing educational opportunities for future generations of Navajo people.

Merriam loved learning in college and took advantage of every opportunity that crossed her path. She learned much from her fellow biology majors and her professors. In her first year she rarely spoke in class, but this changed as she became more comfortable with sharing her perspectives. She became active in the biology club almost immediately, arranging outdoor field trips and coordinating service-learning trips to a nearby elementary school to introduce children to everyday science. In her senior year, she co-wrote a grant with her professor to create a student-managed university xeriscape flower garden and an experimental herb garden for all food service venues on campus.

While Merriam appreciated her college experience and feeling like she was making a difference off the reservation, she also experienced some challenging moments. For example, she was interested in participating in a study abroad trip to broaden her knowledge and exposure to the world. While she was never concerned about her low-income background, she was devastated to realize the expenses associated with study abroad were too much and she could not afford participation. This was even more troubling since her roommate and good friend was going. Merriam was hoping to identify grants or a fellowship to help offset the costs but was unable to gather enough financial resources. Situations like these made Merriam miss her family, their language, easy access to nature, and the desert homeland of her indigenous ancestors.

Merriam always thought she would return to the reservation and marry Sam, the son of one of her mother's friends. During her second year in college, Sam and Merriam broke up. Through her involvement in the biology club, Merriam met Alex, a Dominican American male student, who was the student body president and a chemistry major. After some time passed, they became close friends and began to see similarities in their Afro-Latino and Native family stories of heritage, culture, ritual, history, and celebration; later they created a more intimate bond. Inseparable, they were extremely active on campus. After attending a "Careers in Student Affairs" program, they decided to pursue their graduate degrees together. For Merriam, the degree would serve as an opportunity to hone her programming and leadership skills. When she finishes her master's degree, her immediate plans are to return to the reservation and encourage younger generations of Navajo youth to attend college. She also plans to work with the reservation's tribal college to implement pre-college STEM programs.

Discussion Questions

1. Describe some of the artifacts representing Merriam's cultural heritage and the value they hold in the lives of her mother and grandmother. In what ways do they teach Merriam about the values important to her family's past? How are these artifacts and traditions connected to her ethnic identity?

2. Detail Merriam's racial identity and how it is different from her ethnic identity?

3. How is American Indian racial identity distinctive from the way other minoritized youths see themselves racially?

4. To Merriam, growing up in a family with a low-income was not a deficit, because of the value of what she experienced. Describe what Merriam

experienced and its connection to nature and her spirituality. Would you consider giving up your earthly possessions to be in close connection to nature?

5. Merriam's financial concerns mounted when she was unable to afford the study abroad trip. How would you help her make sense of the role of social class in her development? How would you support her?

6. In what ways is Native American spirituality different from and the same as other theoretical models of spiritual development?

7. Describe Merriam's journey to self-authorship and explain in relation to Baxter Magolda's theory.

8. The development of independence is a noted value in several theories. How does this value conflict with Merriam's desire to return to the reservation? What support would you provide to her as she remains committed to returning home following graduation?

Leslie

As he reflects on his identity development, Leslie, a trans* man, thinks back to his childhood and early schooling experiences, as well as how these experiences shaped his decision to attend and ultimately graduate from an urban university on the east coast. Leslie grew up in a working-class Jewish family in the northeast where little came easy. His father, a school teacher who instilled the values of volunteerism and activism, raised Leslie and his younger sister. In addition, Leslie received care from his maternal grandmother and other extended family members who wanted to make sure he and his sister were well cared for. Leslie remembers growing up with special moments to celebrate Jewish religion, connect with family, and learn his culture.

Throughout his early education, Leslie attended schools with large Jewish student populations. In those predominantly White settings, issues pertaining to race never emerged in a significant way. However, once he entered college, Leslie was forced to grapple with being perceived and treated as a White person. In other words, college was the first time Leslie was made aware of his White privilege. For much of his childhood, Leslie was taught to see himself as Jewish, not White. Similarly, Leslie had to deal with anti-Semitism in the residence halls. He dealt with what became an increasingly hostile Anti-Semitic environment in college as some peers denigrated his Jewish identity, made seemingly insensitive jokes, and acted unaware of his observance of Jewish holidays. Leslie's involvement with the Hillel group on campus helped to mediate some of the struggles around his Jewish identity. As a student leader, Leslie felt it important to take social action, and through Hillel he taught other faculty, students, and staff on campus about Judaism. As he matured and his ethnic and religious Jewish identities crystallized, he realized he was repressing a different and equally salient identity.

Leslie was assigned female at birth and was socialized as a girl until late adolescence. As young girls he and his sister learned how to handle household chores, cook, and clean. Following his mother's death and with the help of women in the family, Leslie learned to take on increasing responsibilities. As a young teenager, he (then "she") often received compliments that he would become an excellent wife and mother someday. The pressing issue was that Leslie never felt like a woman or connected to the socialization into womanhood that was a major part of his upbringing. While he always felt different growing up and more drawn to masculine activities, these gender differences were wrongly and unconsciously dismissed by his family as tomboy behavior. Although he tried to discount them, these same feelings intensified as Leslie entered high school and later college, particularly when trying to establish close or intimate relationships.

During college, Leslie's leadership in Hillel was no easy accomplishment. At the time of joining, Leslie barely noticed that most Hillel leaders were men and there was little encouragement for women to pursue more prominent roles in the organization. Leslie's perspective began to change while taking an introductory gender studies course. In Leslie's view, the instructor always asked a series of deep, rhetorical questions, to which Leslie seldom had a response. When initially asked whether patriarchy would ever end, Leslie could hardly articulate patriarchy as an issue, let alone identify a solution to end it. Toward the latter half of the semester and after deep class discussions, the instructor posed the question about ending patriarchy. This time, Leslie was able to openly discuss why patriarchy was a problem that had no easy solutions. The convergence of Leslie's experiences in the gender studies course and participation in the Hillel group positioned Leslie for leadership as she used the platform of a group meeting to discuss and respond to the recent anti-Semitic slander written in the residence halls. Some group members were angry; others were deeply wounded by the ordeal. All of them sat contemplating how to end this behavior and wondering whether it was even possible. Realizing that the issue of anti-Semitism would not be easily resolved, Leslie stood before the group and explained the realities of living in a world of difference. She noted the incident was horrible, but it was not a surprise, given the diverse religions on campus and the fact that everyone would not agree with Jewish beliefs. She encouraged them to galvanize and demonstrate activism on campus. Leslie led many of the efforts about which she spoke and was elected president the following year.

That same year, Leslie realized she could no longer live as a woman or a female and sought resources to learn more about sex reassignment surgery and communities on campus that could provide support. Leslie eventually joined the campus GLBTQ community and became an employee of the GLBTQ center. Leslie singlehandedly stocked the library with books and resources and created a presentation to serve as a resource on trans* and gender nonconforming identities in college. When Leslie was a college senior, a faculty member from the gender studies program in which he minored invited Leslie to coteach a course and participate on a research team, both focused on gender identity in the United States.

Following graduation, Leslie wanted to pursue a master's degree in student affairs but felt it more important to work full time to raise money for his medical expenses. He was hired as an advisor to the trans* student organization on campus and also served as a residence hall diversity educator. He continued to work with his professor and earned extra money through his participation on a research grant. These opportunities not only were gratifying but also helped Leslie pay for his surgery. Now, at age 29, Leslie is fully committed to his Jewish male identity and strongly values the decisions and experiences that have shaped his life. He is uncertain how his classmates will receive him because he is older and his life encompasses remarkably different experiences and expectations. However, he feels confident and looks forward to earning his master's degree in student affairs, while maintaining a strong commitment to activism and social justice.

Discussion Questions

1. Leslie experienced a great deal of gender socialization toward being a woman. Reflect on your gender identity. How were you socialized toward this gender? As trans* identity becomes more common and visible in U.S. society, how will institutions of higher education support these students' development during college?

2. How would you support a trans* student who came to you seeking advice and resources about gender identity? How can the theories provided in this book help frame your approach? What are their limitations?

3. Identify at least three developmental moments in Leslie's life. For each moment, identify a theory or set of theories to describe Leslie's development.

4. How beneficial are GLBTQ centers and other campus services with a mission to serve minoritized populations? Might Leslie have been able to seek

support elsewhere if there was no GLBTQ center? If so, where? How do identity centers support student development?

5. How would you articulate the differences and fluidity between gender and sexual identity? Though they are closely related, how would you disentangle these separate processes for students who struggle to make sense of them? How would your explanation be informed by theory?

6. Considering Leslie's story, how would you use theory to explain the convergence of his cognitive, psychosocial, religious, and gender identities?

7. Leslie grappled with his White identity and the conflation of White identity with Jewish identity. Describe how you would help Leslie or students with similar perspectives to challenge themselves and think more complexly about race. What racial identity or ethnic identity theory could inform your challenge to students?

8. Describe what developmental processes and decisions Leslie might have considered prior to moving forward with surgery and how these decisions contributed to self-authorship.

Selena

"Who am I?" Selena asked herself as she pondered Dr. J's questions. A 22-year-old woman, Selena grew up the daughter of undocumented Mexican immigrants. Her parents were migrant workers from Texas to Michigan, migrating eastward throughout her childhood. Her *abuela* (grandmother) and *tias* (aunts) also came to the United States, and eventually all of them reunited with extended family on the east coast. Not a day goes by that she does not think of the sacrifices made for her in her family's quest across the U.S. border to a better life. About the time Selena graduated from high school, her parents received citizenship. Not wanting to leave her family, Selena decided to attend community college first because it was affordable and would keep her close to home.

The importance of the church in Selena's life cannot be overstated. The Catholic church gave her the faith to believe all would work out well for her family and a deep sense of community with Spanish-speaking Mexicans in a place where White people held all the money and power. She felt the most at home with her family and church members, but she also experienced guilt about anything related to church doctrine with which she did not agree or that she did not live by. As she became more aware of her lesbian identity in high school, she denied and hid it. Once she completed community college, she chose to transfer to a state university. While attending this large public institution, Selena decided the Catholic church was not a good fit for her. Slowly, she admitted to herself she no longer wished to hide being gay, and she believed she could still have a spiritual connection with God, minus the strict doctrine of Catholicism.

In the last two years of her undergraduate studies, Selena learned it was "okay to be who you are" and during that time, she developed a relationship with another woman on campus, Kara, who was experiencing a similar developmental moment. Kara was also coming to terms with her identity and relied heavily on Selena's advice for how she should think about her lesbian identity. Selena had recently revealed her lesbian identity to her parents and *tias*. While they were surprised and clearly saddened by the news, her family continued to support her educational endeavors and see her as a clear indication of the family's successful legacy. After all, as the only family member to attend college, she is now pursuing an advanced degree. Selena majored in secondary education and minored in Latino studies. Working with Kara, and several other students who worked for the gender center on campus, Selena began to think deeply about how women, particularly women of color, were rarely included in conversations about sexual assault and violence on campus. Moreover, men who experience sexual assault and violence were also absent in these discourses. When she raised this concern with her friends, they suggested that she begin an awareness campaign to bring more voices into the current campus dialogue. Selena embraced the idea and her efforts seemed to gain traction, but she unfortunately received pushback from a few men on campus who argued that sexual assault violence was a women's issues and that any man who experienced sexual assault would not come forward because "that sort of thing just didn't happen." Selena was surprised by the responses to the campaign, especially given that she had recently befriended a man on campus who had experienced sexual assault. While Selena did not allow the interaction to deter her, she spent a great deal of time trying to make sense of why the men would feel that way. She also sought out various sources to help her better articulate why men should be critically involved in efforts to end sexual assault on campus. Moreover, the interaction solidified her decision to pursue a graduate education in student affairs so she could play a more substantial role in educating students.

As Selena came to understand herself better in college, she became unafraid to talk about both her passion for teaching and her newfound Chicana feminist identity. Her education prepared her to be a competent professional and role model, while portraying her authentic self. Selena could not stop thinking about how some of her college experiences paved the way for a fuller, richer life, which she would not have had otherwise. She was glad she found the strength to become the person and professional she believes she is meant to be.

Discussion Questions

1. Selena has a strong ethnic identity. Describe Selena's Latino ethnic identity, explaining several components of her rich cultural heritage and their influence. What aspects of ethnic identity development models can inform her development in college?

2. In what ways can the models and theories of religious and spiritual development be used to frame Selena's concern about her religion and separation from the Catholic church?

3. Describe Selena's psychosocial development (particularly her connection to her family) and her crisis and commitment journey through college. How do you think Selena would describe her sexual and religious identity journeys in terms of crisis and commitment to an identity?

4. Selena's multiple identities have a major impact on her relationships with her family and college experiences. Identify three theories that would be most informative in helping Selena make sense of her developmental process.

5. Selena began at a community college prior to transferring to a four-year institution. What theories would you use to guide the creation of a program to assist students in transition from two-year to four-year colleges? What developmental aspects would you include to ensure that the transition process is developmental and informative for students?

6. Selena's lesbian identity seemed to conflict with her family's beliefs and her religious beliefs. However, she made a thoughtful decision no longer to hide her identity and to embrace all its aspects. Use a cognitive-structural or integrative theory to explain what Selena's developmental trajectory may have been to prompt her identity commitment.

7. What are the diverse identities represented in Selena's portrait? Create a draft of a program to support student's diverse and intersecting identities. Describe a relevant theory that applies to each program component.

8. Briefly describe what steps might have occurred along Selena's pathway as a first-generation college student to guarantee her success academically and developmentally in college.

9. What examples of cognitive dissonance may have occurred for Selena while she attended college? What advice and support would you have offered her as she grappled with these challenging moments in college?

Elliott

Elliott thought deeply about Dr. J's questions because they forced him to reflect on who he is and who he will become upon graduation from the program. Elliott is a 25-year-old African American man who was born and raised in the urban south. He grew up the son of working-class parents. His father works in construction, while his mother is an aide at a nursing home. He is the eldest of four children, and his parents did all they could to teach them about life, including the harsh realities of racism and social inequalities. His parents emphasized academics and ensured that Elliott and his siblings were on the pathway to a strong education and a successful life. He grew up in a Baptist church, which he attended every Sunday. A church member and alumnus of a private, historically Black college encouraged Elliott to attend the same institution. Elliott visited in his junior year and decided that this institution was a good fit. He was enamored with the rich institutional culture and the opportunity to experience college in an environment where he genuinely mattered.

Elliott's college years brought a range of developmental experiences. He joined a national Black fraternity and was highly involved on the campus programming board. His fraternity membership was accompanied by unexpected, but welcomed attention from women on campus. Though Elliott remained highly involved, he realized he was focusing more on casual dating and hanging with his friends than on his academics, until he met Vanessa. Elliott and Vanessa became great friends and began a committed relationship. Elliott maintained his grades and involvement. The vice president of student affairs noticed Elliott's potential and told him to consider a student affairs graduate degree.

During his junior year, Elliott's college life came to a halt after being injured in a car accident that required amputation of his legs. Elliott survived but was forever changed. He left school for a year to heal. Elliott dealt with depression for months following his accident. He questioned his faith in God because he could not understand why the accident had happened to him. His feelings were intensified as the woman he deemed his best friend struggled to handle his leg amputation. Though she tried to remain committed, the relationship eventually faded. Again, Elliott questioned his religious and spiritual beliefs, and he felt completely overwhelmed. After months of wanting to drop out of life, and with encouragement from his family, he started to feel like he had something to offer the world and became his optimistic self again. His family convinced him he could succeed and they would help. During that time, he received many notes and calls of support from friends. Their support, along with his family, helped Elliott move past his depression and learn to navigate with leg prosthetics.

Upon his return to college, Elliott felt self-conscious about not having legs. However, his roommate and fraternity brothers showed tremendous support, while the Adaptive Educational Services Office staff provided resources to support his transition back to college. As Elliott returned, he realized how difficult it was to enroll in certain classes and events. Many of the physical spaces on campus could not accommodate his needs. Frustrated, Elliott focused his attention on obtaining an internship in the president's office and encouraging directed efforts for a campus that fully embraces universal design. The car accident signaled a turning point in Elliott's life and made him more grateful to be alive and finish college. Through his strong faith and religious beliefs, he accepted the result of the accident, and over time he realized he was the same individual and the loss of his legs did not define him. Elliott spent his final year applying to student affairs graduate programs. During his attendance at one of the national student affairs conferences, he met Dr. J and found their interaction was pivotal in his decision to attend Prescott's program.

Discussion Questions

1. What role did social class play in Elliott's upbringing? Did his social class indirectly play a role in his college choice?
2. Conduct a brief review of historically Black colleges and universities (HBCU) literature. What does the literature suggest about these campus environments that make Black students feel like they matter? How do such environments promote psychosocial development?
3. How might the HBCU environment promote positive racial identity development?
4. Which of Chickering and Reisser's vectors could help inform the developmental issues that Elliott faced?
5. Elliott identifies as a cisgender man. What contributed to this gender identity and how would a fraternity support it?
6. Elliott faced a significant spiritual struggle following his car accident and the dissolution of his relationship with Vanessa. Though the struggle was difficult for him, how might he have benefitted developmentally as the result of the struggle?
7. When Elliott returned to campus, he found that the campus presented a disabling environment, ultimately making it difficult for him to navigate. How would you use the theories on disabilities and identities to implement spaces, programs, and services to meet the needs of all students on campus?
8. Create a visual representation of Elliott's development. As you identify significant developmental moments, note the relevant theories that apply to his experiences.

What's Next?

The questions posed by Dr. Greene were ultimately thought provoking, but for these seven students—Drew, Amber, Cory, Merriam, Leslie, Selena, and Elliott—the questions served as the impetus for deep reflection spanning the course and far beyond. In contemplating their own backgrounds and experiences as undergraduate students at qualitatively different institutions of higher education, these first-semester, student affairs graduate students' stories laid the groundwork for knowing about and learning from each other. Using the content of this book, we invite readers to engage with these seven students' developmental journeys while simultaneously examining their own unique developmental trajectories. Use the theories described in this book to prompt reflection and further study of identity development. With increased understanding, use, and critique of theories and their content, educators will have a better understanding of themselves, students, and how growth and change occur in multifaceted ways while attending college.

REFERENCES

Abes, E. S. (2009). Theoretical borderlands: Using multiple theoretical perspectives to challenge inequitable power structures in student development theory. *Journal of College Student Development, 50,* 151–156.

Abes, E. S. (2012). Constructivist and intersectional interpretations of a lesbian college student's multiple social identities. *The Journal of Higher Education, 83,* 186–216.

Abes, E. S., & Jones, S. R. (2004). Meaning-making capacity and the dynamics of lesbian college students' multiple dimensions of identity. *Journal of College Student Development, 45,* 612–632.

Abes, E. S., Jones, S. R., & McEwen, M. K. (2007). Reconceptualizing the model of multiple dimensions of identity: The role of meaning-making capacity in the construction of multiple identities. *Journal of College Student Development, 48,* 1–22.

Abes, E. S., & Kasch, D. (2007). Using queer theory to explore lesbian college students' multiple dimensions of identity. *Journal of College Student Development, 48,* 619–636.

Abes, E. S., & Kasch, D. (2012). Queer theory. In S. R. Jones & E. S. Abes, *Identity development of college students: Advancing frameworks for multiple dimensions of identity* (pp. 191–212). San Francisco: Jossey-Bass.

Acevedo-Gil, N., Santos, R. E., Alonso, L., & Solorzano, D. G. (2015). Latinas/os in community college developmental education increasing moments of academic and interpersonal validation. *Journal of Hispanic Higher Education, 14,* 101–127.

Ackerman, R., DiRamio, D., & Garza Mitchell, R. L. (2009). Transitions: Combat veterans as college students. In R. Ackerman & D. DiRamio (Eds.), *Creating a veteran-friendly campus: Strategies for transition and success.* New Directions for Student Services, no. 126, pp. 5–14. San Francisco: Jossey-Bass.

Adair, V. G. (2001). Poverty and the (broken) promise of higher education. *Harvard Educational Review, 71,* 217–239.

Adair, V. G. (2005). US working-class/poverty-class divides. *Sociology, 39,* 817–835.

Ahmed, S. (2006). *Queer phenomenology: Orientations, objects, others.* Duke University Press.

Ahmed, S. (2009). Embodying diversity: Problems and paradoxes for black feminists. *Race Ethnicity and Education, 12*, 41–52.

Alberts, C., & Meyer, J. J. (1998). The relationship between Marcia's ego identity statuses and selected personality variables in an African context. *International Journal for the Advancement of Counseling, 20*, 277–288.

Alessandria, K. P., & Nelson, E. S. (2005). Identity development and self-esteem of first-generation American college students: An exploratory study. *Journal of College Student Development, 46*, 3–11.

Alfred, G. C., Hammer, J. H., & Good, G. E. (2014). Male student veterans: Hardiness, psychological well-being, and masculine norms. *Psychology of Men & Masculinity, 15*, 95–99.

Ali, S. (2009). Black feminist praxis: Some reflections on pedagogies and politics in higher education. *Race Ethnicity and Education, 12*, 79–86.

American College Personnel Association (ACPA) College Student Educators International. (1996). The Student Learning Imperative: Implications for student affairs. *Journal of College Student Development, 37*, 118–122. Retrieved from http://www.myacpa.org/sites/default/files/ACPA%27s%20Student%20Learning%20Imperative.pdf

American Council on Education. (1994a). The student personnel point of view (SPPV). In A. L. Rentz (Ed.), *Student affairs: A profession's heritage*. American College Personnel Association Media Publication no. 40, 2nd ed., pp. 66–77. Lanham, MD: University Press of America. (Original work published 1937)

American Council on Education. (1994b). The student personnel point of view. In A. L. Rentz (Ed.), *Student affairs: A profession's heritage*. American College Personnel Association Media Publication no. 40, 2nd ed., pp. 108–123. Lanham, MD: University Press of America. (Original work published 1949)

Americans with Disabilities Act of 1990, 42 U. S.C. § 12101 et seq. (1990).

Anchor, R. (1967). *The Enlightenment tradition*. Major Traditions of World Civilization Series. New York: Harper Row.

Anderson, C. (1994, November 11). *"How can my faith be so different?": The emergence of religious identity in college women*. Paper presented at the annual meeting of the Association for the Study of Higher Education, Tucson, AZ. (ERIC Document Reproduction Service No. ED375724)

Anfara, V. A., & Mertz, N. T. (2015). *Theoretical frameworks in qualitative research* (2nd ed.). Thousand Oaks, CA: Sage.

Anglin, D. M., & Wade, J. C. (2007). Racial socialization, racial identity, and Black students' adjustment to college. *Cultural Diversity and Ethnic Minority Psychology, 13*, 207–215.

Anzaldúa, G. (1999). *Borderlands, La frontera: The new mestiza*. San Francisco: Aunt Lute Books. (Original work published 1987)

Arbona, C., & Jimenez, C. (2014). Minority stress, ethnic identity, and depression among Latino/a college students. *Journal of Counseling Psychology, 61*, 162–168.

Arbuckle, D. S. (1953). *Student personnel services in higher education*. New York: McGraw-Hill.

Archer, S. L., & Grey, J. A. (2009). The sexual domain of identity: Sexual statuses of identity in relations to psychosocial sexual health. *Identity: An International Journal of Theory and Research, 9*, 33–62.

Aries, E., & Seider, M. (2005). The interactive relationship between class identity and the college experience: The case of lower income students. *Qualitative Sociology, 28*, 419–443.

Aries, E., & Seider, M. (2007). The role of social class in the formation of identity: A study of public and elite private college students. *The Journal of Social Psychology, 147*, 137–157.

Arminio, J. (2001). Exploring the nature of race-related guilt. *Journal of Multicultural Counseling and Development, 29*, 239–252.

Arvizu, D. R. (1995). The care voice and American Indian college students: An alternative perspective for student development professionals. *Journal of American Indian Education, 34*, 1–17.

Asch, A., & Fine, M. (1988). Introduction: Beyond pedestals. In M. Fine & A. Asch (Eds.), *Women with disabilities: Essays in psychology, culture and politics* (pp. 1–37). Philadelphia: Temple University.

Ashmore, R. D., Deaux, K., & McLaughlin-Volpe, T. (2004). An organizing framework for collective identity: articulation and significance of multidimensionality. *Psychological Bulletin, 130*(1), 80–114.

Astin, A. W. (1977). *Four critical years.* San Francisco: Jossey-Bass.

Astin, A. W. (1984). Student involvement: A developmental theory for higher education. *Journal of College Student Personnel, 25*, 297–308.

Astin, A. W., Astin, H. S., & Lindholm, J. A. (2011). *Cultivating the spirit: How college can enhance students' inner lives.* San Francisco: Jossey-Bass.

Atkinson, D. R., Morten, G., & Sue, D. W. (1979). *Counseling American minorities* (1st ed.). Dubuque, IA: William C. Brown.

Atkinson, D. R., Morten, G., & Sue, D. W. (1989). *Counseling American minorities: A cross-cultural perspective* (3rd ed.). Dubuque, IA: Brown.

Atkinson, D. R., Morten, G., & Sue, D. W. (1993). *Counseling American minorities: A cross-cultural perspective* (4th ed.). Madison, WI: Brown and Benchmark.

Atkinson, D. R., Morten, G., & Sue, D. W. (1998). *Counseling American minorities: A cross-cultural perspective* (5th ed.). San Francisco: McGraw-Hill.

Auerbach, S. (2004). Engaging Latino parents in supporting college pathways: Lessons from a college access program. *Journal of Hispanic Higher Education, 3*(2), 125–145.

Aulepp, L., & Delworth, U. (1976). *Training manual for an ecosystem model: Assessing campus environments.* Boulder, CO: Western Interstate Commission for Higher Education. Retrieved from http://www.campusecologist.org/files/tmem/home.htm

Avens, C., & Zelley, R. (1992). *QUANTA: An interdisciplinary learning community (four studies).* Daytona Beach, FL: Daytona Beach Community College. (ERIC Document Reproduction Service No. ED 349 073)

Avery, D. R., Tonidandel, S., & Phillips, M. G. (2008). Similarly on sports sidelines: How mentor-protégé sex similarity affects mentoring. *Sex Roles, 58*, 72–80.

Awad, G. H. (2007). The role of racial identity, academic self-concept, and self-esteem in the prediction of academic outcomes for African American students. *Journal of Black Psychology, 33*, 188–207.

Backus, F. R., & Mahalik, J. R. (2011). The masculinity of Mr. Right: Feminist identity in heterosexual women's ideal romantic partners. *Psychology of Women Quarterly, 35*, 318–326.

Badger, J. (2010). Assessing reflective thinking: Pre-service teachers' and professors' perceptions of an oral examination. *Assessment in Education: Principles, Policy & Practice, 17*, 77–89.

Baechtoldt, M., & De Sawal, D. M. (2009). Meeting the needs of women veterans. In R. Ackerman & D. DiRamio (Eds.), *Creating a veteran-friendly campus: Strategies for transition and success.* New Directions for Student Services, no. 126, pp. 35–43. San Francisco: Jossey-Bass.

Baker, K. Q., Boland, K., & Nowik, C. M. (2012). Survey of faculty and student perceptions of persons with disabilities. *Journal of Postsecondary Education and Disability, 25*(4), 309–329.

Bank, B. J. (with Yelon, H. M.). (2003). *Contradictions in women's education: Traditionalism, careerism, and community at a single-sex college.* New York: Teachers College Press.

Banks, J. A. (1984). *Teaching strategies for ethnic studies* (3rd ed.). Boston: Allyn & Bacon.

Banks, J. A. (2008). *Teaching strategies for ethnic studies* (8th ed.). Boston: Allyn & Bacon.

Banning, J. H. (Ed.). (1978). *Campus ecology: A perspective for student affairs.* Washington, DC: National Association of Student Personnel Administrators. Retrieved from http://www .campusecologist.org/files/Monograph.pdf

Banning, J. H., & Kaiser, L. (1974). An ecological perspective and model for campus design. *Personnel and Guidance Journal, 52,* 370–375.

Barber, J. P., King, P. M., & Magolda, M.B.B. (2013). Long strides on the journey toward self-authorship: Substantial developmental shifts in college students' meaning making. *The Journal of Higher Education, 84,* 866–896.

Bargad, A., & Hyde, J. S. (1991). A study of feminist identity development in women. *Psychology of Women Quarterly, 15,* 181–201.

Barnett, E. A. (2011). Validation experiences and persistence among community college students. *The Review of Higher Education, 34,* 193–230.

BarNir, A., Watson, W. W., & Hutchins, H. M. (2011). Mediation and moderated mediation in the relationship among role models, self-efficacy, entrepreneurial career intention, and gender. *Journal of Applied Social Psychology, 41,* 270–297.

Barrett, W. (2011). *Social class on campus: Theories and manifestations.* Sterling, VA: Stylus.

Barton, A., & Donahue, C. (2009). Multiple assessments of a first-year seminar pilot. *JGE: The Journal of General Education, 58,* 259–278.

Batson, C. D., Schoenrade, P., & Ventis, W. L. (1993). *Religion and the individual: A social psychological perspective.* New York: Oxford University Press.

Bautista, D. R. (2003). Da Kine Scale: Construction and validation of the Hawaii Local Acculturation Scale. *Dissertation Abstracts International, 64,* 7A.

Baxter Magolda, M. B. (1987). Comparing open-ended interviews and standardized measures of intellectual development. *Journal of College Student Personnel, 28,* 443–448.

Baxter Magolda, M. B. (1989). Gender differences in cognitive development: An analysis of cognitive complexity and learning styles. *Journal of College Student Development, 30,* 213–220.

Baxter Magolda, M. B. (1992). *Knowing and reasoning in college: Gender-related patterns in students' intellectual development.* San Francisco: Jossey-Bass.

Baxter Magolda, M. B. (1998a). Developing self-authorship in graduate school. In M. S. Anderson (Ed.), *The experience of being in graduate school: An exploration.* New Directions for Higher Education, no. 101, pp. 41–54. San Francisco: Jossey-Bass.

Baxter Magolda, M. B. (1998b). Developing self-authorship in young adult life. *Journal of College Student Development, 39,* 143–156.

Baxter Magolda, M. B. (1999a). Constructing adult identities. *Journal of College Student Development, 40,* 629–644.

Baxter Magolda, M. B. (1999b). *Creating contexts for learning and self-authorship: Constructive-developmental pedagogy.* Nashville: Vanderbilt University Press.

Baxter Magolda, M. B. (1999c). The evolution of epistemology: Refining contextual knowing at twentysomething. *Journal of College Student Development, 40,* 333–344.

Baxter Magolda, M. B. (1999d). Learner-centered practice is harder than it looks. *About Campus, 4* (4), 2–4.

Baxter Magolda, M. B. (2001). *Making their own way: Narratives for transforming higher education to promote self-development.* Sterling, VA: Stylus.

Baxter Magolda, M. B. (2002). Helping students make their own way to adulthood: Good company for the journey. *About Campus, 6* (6), 2–9.

Baxter Magolda, M. B. (2003). Identity and learning: student affairs' role in transforming higher education. *Journal of College Student Development, 44,* 231–247.

Baxter Magolda, M. B. (2004a). Evolution of a constructivist conceptualization of epistemological reflection. *Educational Psychologist, 39,* 31–42.

Baxter Magolda, M. B. (2004b). Learning partnerships model: A framework for promoting self-authorship. In M. Baxter Magolda & P. M. King (Eds.), *Learning partnerships: Theory and modes of practice to educate for self-authorship* (pp. 37–62). Sterling, VA: Stylus.

Baxter Magolda, M. B. (2007). Self-authorship: The foundation for twenty-first-century education. In P. S. Meszaros (Ed.), *Self-authorship: Advancing students' intellectual growth.* New Directions for Teaching and Learning, no. 109, pp. 69–83. San Francisco: Jossey-Bass.

Baxter Magolda, M. B. (2008). Three elements of self-authorship. *Journal of College Student Development, 49,* 269–284.

Baxter Magolda, M. B. (2009). *Authoring your life: Developing an internal voice to navigate life's challenges.* Sterling, VA: Stylus Publishing.

Baxter Magolda, M. B. (2014). Self-authorship. In C. Hanson (Ed.), *In search of self: Exploring student identity development.* New Directions for Higher Education, no. 166, pp. 25–33. San Francisco: Jossey-Bass.

Baxter Magolda, B. M., & King, P. M. (Eds.). (2004). *Learning partnerships: Theory and models of practice to educate for self-authorship.* Sterling, VA: Stylus.

Baxter Magolda, M. B., & King, P. M. (2007). Interview strategies for assessing self-authorship: Constructing conversations to assess meaning making. *Journal of College Student Development, 48,* 491–508.

Baxter Magolda, M. B., & King, P. M. (2008). Toward reflective conversations: An advising approach that promotes self-authorship. *Peer Review, 10,* 8–11.

Baxter Magolda, M. B., & King, P. M. (2012). Assessing meaning making and self-authorship— Theory, research, and application. *ASHE Higher Education Report, 38*(3), 1–138.

Baxter Magolda, M. B., King, P. M., Taylor, K. B., & Wakefield, K. M. (2012). Decreasing authority dependence during the first year of college. *Journal of College Student Development, 53,* 418–435.

Baxter Magolda, M. B., Meszaros, P. S., & Creamer, E. G. (Eds.). (2012). *Development and assessment of self-authorship: Exploring the concept across cultures.* Sterling, VA: Stylus Publishing.

Baxter Magolda, M. B., & Porterfield, W. D. (1985). A new approach to assess intellectual development on the Perry scheme. *Journal of College Student Personnel, 26,* 343–350.

Beamon, K. (2012). "I'm a Baller": Athletic identity foreclosure among African-American former student-athletes. *Journal of African American Studies, 16,* 195–208.

Beede, D., Julian, T., Langdon, D., McKittrick, G., Khan, B., & Doms, M. (2011). *Women in STEM: A gender gap to innovation* (Report No. 04-11). Washington, DC: U.S. Department of Commerce.

Beemyn, B. G. (2005). Making campuses more inclusive of transgender students. *Journal of Gay and Lesbian Issues in Education, 3,* 77–89.

Beemyn, G. (2012). The experiences and needs of transgender community college students. *Community College Journal of Research and Practice, 36,* 504–510.

Beemyn, G., & Rankin, S. (2011). *The lives of transgender people.* New York: Columbia University Press.

Begley, P. T., & Stefkovich, J. (2007). Integrating values and ethics into post secondary teaching for leadership development: Principles, concepts, and strategies. *Journal of Educational Administration, 45,* 398–412.

Bekken, B., & Marie, J. (2007). Making self-authorship a goal of core curricula: The Earth Sustainability Pilot Project. In P. S. Meszaros (Ed.), *Self-authorship: Advancing students' intellectual growth*. New Directions for Teaching and Learning, no. 109, pp. 53–67. San Francisco: Jossey-Bass.

Belenky, M. F. (1996). Public homeplaces: Nurturing the development of people, families, and communities. In N. Goldberger, J. Tarule, B. Clinchy, & M. Belenky (Eds.), *Knowledge, difference, and power* (pp. 393–430). New York: Basic Books.

Belenky, M. F., Bond, L. A., & Weinstock, J. S. (1997). *A tradition that has no name: Nurturing the development of people, families, and communities*. New York: Basic Books.

Belenky, M. F., Clinchy, B. M., Goldberger, N. R., & Tarule, J. M. (1986). *Women's ways of knowing: The development of self, voice, and mind*. New York: Basic Books.

Bell, D. (1995). Brown v. Board of Education and the interest convergence dilemma. *Harvard Law Review, 93*(3), 518–533.

Bell-Scriber, M. J. (2008). Warming the nursing education climate for traditional-age learners who are male. *Nursing Education Perspectives, 29*, 143–150.

Bem, S. L. (1981a). *Bem sex-role inventory: Professional manual*. Palo Alto, CA: Consulting Psychologists Press.

Bem, S. L. (1981b). Gender schema theory: A cognitive account of sex typing. *Psychological Review, 88*, 354–364.

Bem, S. L. (1983). Gender schema theory and its implications for child development: Raising gender-aschematic children in a gender-schematic society. *Signs, 8*, 598–616.

Bem, S. L. (1995). Dismantling gender polarization and compulsory heterosexuality: Should we turn the volume down or up? *Journal of Sex Research, 32*, 329–333.

Bengtson, V. L. (1996). Continuities and discontinuities in intergenerational relationships over time. In V. L. Bengtson (Ed.), *Adulthood and aging: Research on continuities and discontinuities* (pp. 271–303). New York: Springer.

Benishek, L. A., Bieschke, K. J., Park, J., & Slattery, S. M. (2004). A multicultural feminist model of mentoring. *Journal of Multicultural Counseling and Development, 32*, 428–442.

Bennett, S. J., Maton, K. A., & Kervin, L. K. (2008). The "digital natives" debate: A critical review of the evidence. *British Journal of Educational Technology, 39*, 775–786.

Benitez, M. (2010). Resituating Culture Centers within a Social Justice Framework: Is There Room for Examining Whiteness. In L. D. Patton (Ed.), *Culture centers in higher education: Perspectives on identity, theory and practice* (pp. 119–134). Sterling, VA: Stylus Publishing.

Bentrim-Tapio, E. M. (2004). Alcohol consumption in undergraduate students: The role of ego-identity status, alcohol expectancies, and drinking refusal self-efficacy. *NASPA Journal, 41*, 728–741.

Berkowitz, A. D. (2011). Successful judicial interventions with college men. In J. A. Laker & T. Davis (Eds.), *Masculinities in higher education: Theoretical and practical considerations* (pp. 161–176). New York: Taylor & Francis.

Bernacki, M. L., & Jaeger, E. (2008). Exploring the impact of service-learning on moral development and moral orientation. *Michigan Journal of Community Service Learning, 14*(2), 5–15.

Berry, J. W. (1984). Cultural relations in plural societies: Alternatives to segregation and their socio-psychological implications. In N. Miller & M. B. Brewer (Eds.), *Groups in contact* (pp. 11–27). New York: Academic.

Berry, J. W. (1993). Ethnic identities in plural societies. In M. E. Bernal & G. P. Knight (Eds.), *Ethnic identity: Formation and transmission among Hispanics and other minorities* (pp. 271–296). Albany: State University of New York Press.

Berry, J. W. (2005). Acculturation: Living successfully in two cultures. *International Journal of Intercultural Relations, 29*, 697–712.

Bieschke, K. J. (2002). Charting the waters. *Counseling Psychologist, 30*, 575–581.

Bilodeau, B. L. (2005). Beyond the gender binary: A case study of two transgender students at a Midwestern university. *Journal of Gay and Lesbian Issues in Education, 3*(1), 29–46.

Bilodeau, B. L. (2009). *Genderism: Transgender students, binary systems, and higher education.* Saarbrücken, Germany: VDM Verlag.

Bilodeau, B. L., & Renn, K. A. (2005). Analysis of LGBT identity development models and implications for practice. In Sanlo, R. L. (Ed.), *Gender identity and sexual orientation: Research, policy, and personal perspectives.* New Directions for Student Services, no. 111, pp. 25–39. San Francisco: Jossey-Bass.

Bilsker, D., Schiedel, D., & Marcia, J. (1988). Sex differences in identity status. *Sex Roles, 18*, 231–236.

Bimper, A. Y., Jr. (2014). Game changers: The role athletic identity and racial identity play on academic performance. *Journal of College Student Development, 55*, 795–807.

Black, L., & Stone, D. (2005). Expanding the definition of privilege: The concept of social privilege. *Journal of Multicultural Counseling and Development, 33*, 243–255.

Blackhurst, A. B. (1995). The relationship between gender and student outcomes in a freshman orientation course. *Journal of the Freshman Year Experience, 7*, 63–80.

Blake-Beard, S., Bayne, M. L., Crosby, F. J., & Muller, C. B. (2011). Matching by race and gender in mentoring relationships: Keeping our eyes on the prize. *Journal of Social Issues, 67*, 622–643.

Blue, E. L., & Berkel, L. A. (2010). Feminist identity attitudes, negative affect, and eating pathology in African American college women. *Journal of Black Psychology, 36*, 426–445.

Bohmer, S., & Briggs, J. L. (1991). Teaching privileged students about gender, race and class oppression. *Teaching Sociology, 19*, 154–163.

Bondi, S. (2012). Students and institutions protecting Whiteness as property: A critical race theory analysis of student affairs preparation. *Journal of Student Affairs Research and Practice, 49*, 397–414.

Bonilla-Silva, E. (2010). *Racism without racists: Color-blind racism and the persistence of racial inequality in the United States.* New York: Rowman and Littlefield.

Bonilla-Silva, E. (2014). *Racism without racists: Color-blind racism and the persistence of racial inequality in America* (4th ed.). Lanham, MD: Rowman & Littlefield Publishers.

Born, D. (1970). Psychological adaptation and development under acculturative stress: Toward a general model. *Social Science and Medicine, 3*, 529–547.

Bornstein, K. (1994). *Gender outlaw: On men, women and the rest of us.* New York: Routledge.

Borrego, S. (2003). *Class matters: Beyond access to inclusion.* Washington: National Association of Student Affairs Administrators in Higher Education.

Bourdieu, P. (1987). What makes a social class? On the theoretical and practical existence of groups. *Berkeley Journal of Sociology, 32*, 1–17.

Bourdieu, P. (2000). *Pascalian meditations.* Cambridge: Polity.

Bourdieu, P. (2002). The forms of capital. In N. Woolsey Biggart (Ed.), *Readings in economic sociology* (pp. 280–291). Malden, MA: Blackwell.

Bourne, E. (1978a). The state of research on ego identity: A review and appraisal. *Part I. Journal of Youth and Adolescence, 7*, 223–251.

Bourne, E. (1978b). The state of research on ego identity: A review and appraisal. *Part II. Journal of Youth and Adolescence, 7*, 371–392.

Bowdon, M., Pigg, S., & Mansfield, L. P. (2014). Feminine and feminist ethics and service-learning site selection: The role of empathy. *Feminist Teacher, 24*, 57–82.

Bowe, F. (2000). *Universal design in education: Teaching nontraditional students.* Westport, CT: Greenwood Publishing.

Bowers, P. J., Dickman, M. M., & Fuqua, D. R. (2001). Psychosocial and career development related to employment of graduating seniors. *NASPA Journal, 38*, 326–347.

Bowleg, L. (2008). When Black + lesbian + woman ≠ Black lesbian woman: The methodological challenges of quantitative and qualitative intersectionality research. *Sex Roles, 59*, 312–325.

Bowman, J., & Wessel, R. (2002). [Review of the book *Big questions, worthy dreams: Mentoring young adults in their search for meaning, purpose, and faith*]. *Journal of College Student Development, 43*, 420–421.

Bowman, N. A., Felix, V., & Ortis, L. (2014). Religious/worldview identification and college student success. *Religion & Education, 41*(2), 117–133.

Bowman, N. A., & Small, J. L. (2012). Exploring a hidden form of minority status: College students' religious affiliation and well-being. *Journal of College Student Development, 53*, 491–509.

Boyd, L. D. (2008). Development of reflective judgment in the pre-doctoral dental clinical curriculum. *European Journal of Dental Education, 12*, 149–158.

Brabeck, M. (1983). Moral judgment: Theory and research on differences between males and females. *Developmental Review, 3*, 274–291.

Bradby, D., & Helms, J. E. (1993). Black racial identity attitudes and White therapist cultural sensitivity in cross-racial therapy dyads: An exploratory study. In J. E. Helms (Ed.), *Black and White racial identity: Theory, research, and practice* (pp. 165–175). Westport, CT: Praeger.

Braddock, D. L., & Parrish, S. L. (2001). An institutional history of disability. In G. L. Albrecht, K. D. Seelman, & M. Bury (Eds.), *Handbook of disability studies* (pp. 11–68). Thousand Oaks, CA: Sage.

Branch, C. W., Tayal, P., & Triplett, C. (2000). The relationship of ethnic identity and ego identity status among adolescents and young adults. *International Journal of Intercultural Relations, 24*, 777–790.

Branker, C. (2009). Deserving design: The new generation of student veterans. *Journal of Postsecondary Education & Disability, 22*, 59–66.

Brayboy, B.M.J. (2006). Toward a tribal critical race theory in education. *The Urban Review, 37*, 425–446.

Brazelton, G. B., Renn. K. A., & Woodford, M. (2013). LGBTQ gendered participation with campus resources. Paper presented in the symposium College Men and Success: Intersections of Identities with Diverse Contexts of Masculinity, Association for the Study of Higher Education Annual Meeting, St. Louis, MO.

Bresciani, M., Todd, D., Carpenter, S., Janosik, S., Komives, S., Love, P., & Tyrell, S. (2010). *ACPA/NASPA professional competency areas for student affairs practitioners.* Washington, DC: American College Personnel Association and National Association of Student Personnel Administrators.

Breton, R., Isajiw, W. W., Kalbach, W. E., & Reitz, J. G. (Eds.). (1990). *Ethnic identity and equality.* Toronto: University of Toronto Press.

Brewer, B. W., & Cornelius, A. E. (2001). Norms and factorial invariance of the Athletic Identity Measurement Scale. *Academic Athletic Journal, 15*, 103–113.

Brewer, B. W., Van Raalte, J. L., & Linder, D. E. (1993). Athletic identity: Hercules' muscles or Achilles heel? *International Journal of Sport Psychology, 24*, 237–254.

Brinckerhoff, L. C., Shaw, S. F., & McGuire, J. M. (1993). *Promoting postsecondary education for students with learning disabilities: A handbook for practitioners.* Austin, TX: Pro-Ed.

Brinkman, A. (2000). [Review of the book *Big questions, worthy dreams: Mentoring young adults in their search for meaning, purpose, and faith*]. *Library Journal, 125*(19), 85.

Britzman, D. (1997). What is this thing called love?: New discourses for understanding gay and lesbian youth. In S. de Castell & M. Bryson (Eds.), *Radical in(ter)ventions: Identity, politics, and difference/s on educational praxis* (pp. 183–207). Albany: State University of New York Press.

Broido, E. M., & Manning, K. (2002). Philosophical foundations and current theoretical perspectives in qualitative research. *Journal of College Student Development, 43*, 434–445.

Bronfenbrenner, U. (1979). *The ecology of human development: Experiments by nature and design.* Cambridge, MA: Harvard University Press.

Bronfenbrenner, U. (1993). The ecology of cognitive development: Research models and fugitive findings. In R. H. Wozniak & K. W. Fischer (Eds.), *Development in context: Acting and thinking in specific environments* (pp. 3–44). Hillsdale, NJ: Erlbaum.

Bronfenbrenner, U. (1995). Developmental ecology through space and time: A future perspective. In P. Moen & G. H. Elder, Jr. (Eds.), *Examining lives in context: Perspectives on the ecology of human development* (pp. 619–647). Washington, DC: American Psychological Association.

Bronfenbrenner, U. (Ed.). (2005). *Making human beings human: Bioecological perspectives on human development.* Thousand Oaks, CA: Sage.

Bronfenbrenner, U., & Morris, P. A. (2006). The bioecological model of human development. In W. Damon & R. M. Lerner (Eds.), *Handbook of child psychology* (6th ed.), pp. 793–828. Hoboken, NJ: Wiley.

Brook, A. T., Garcia, J., & Fleming, M. A. (2008). The effects of multiple identities on psychological well-being. *Personality and Social Psychology Bulletin, 34*, 1588–1600.

Brookfield, S. D. (2005). *The power of critical theory: Liberating adult learning and teaching.* San Francisco: Jossey-Bass.

Broughton, J. M. (1986). The political psychology of faith development theory. In C. Dykstra & S. Parks (Eds.), *Faith development and Fowler* (pp. 90–114). Birmingham, AL: Religious Education Press.

Brown, L. L., & Robinson Kurpius, S. E. (1997). Psychosocial factors influencing academic persistence of American Indian college students. *Journal of College Student Development, 38*, 3–12.

Brown, R. D. (1972). *Student development in tomorrow's higher education—a return to the academy.* Alexandria, VA: American College Personnel Association.

Brown, R. D., & Gortmaker, V. J. (2009). Assessing campus climates for lesbian, gay, bisexual and transgender (LGBT) students: Methodological and political issues. *Journal of LGBT Youth, 6*, 416–435.

Brown, U. M. (2001). *The interracial experience: Growing up black/white racially mixed in the United States.* Westport, CT: Praeger.

Bruess, B. J., & Pearson, F. C. (2000). A study of the relationship between identity and moral development. *College Student Affairs Journal, 19*, 61–70.

Bryant, A. N. (2003a). Understanding women's spirituality in the context of a progressive campus-based Catholic community. *Religion and Education, 30*, 59–83.

Bryant, A. N. (2003b). Changes in attitudes toward women's roles: Predicting gender-role traditionalism among college students. *Sex Roles, 48*, 131–142.

Bryant, A. N. (2006a). Assessing the gender climate of an evangelical student subculture in the United States. *Gender and Education, 18*, 613–634.

Bryant, A. N. (2006b). Exploring religious pluralism in higher education: Non-majority religious perspectives among entering first-year college students. *Religion and Education, 33*, 1–25.

Bryant, A. N. (2007). Gender differences in spiritual development during the college years. *Sex Roles, 56*, 835–846.

Bryant, A. N. (2011a). The impact of campus context, college encounters, and religious/spiritual struggle on ecumenical worldview development. *Research in Higher Education, 52*, 441–459.

Bryant, A. N. (2011b). Ecumenical worldview development by gender, race, and worldview: A multiple-group analysis of model invariance. *Research in Higher Education, 52*, 460–479.

Bryant, A. N. (2011c). Evangelical Christian students and the path to self-authorship. *Journal of Psychology and Theology, 39*(1), 16–30.

Bryant, A. N., & Astin, H. S. (2008). The correlates of spiritual struggle during college years. *The Journal of Higher Education, 79*, 1–27.

Bryant, A. N., & Craft, C. M. (2010). The challenge and promise of pluralism: Dimensions of spiritual climate and diversity at a Lutheran college. *Christian Higher Education, 5*, 396–422.

Bryant, A. N., Wickliffe, K., Mayhew, M. J., & Bartell Behringer, L. (2009). Developing an assessment of college students' spiritual experiences: The collegiate religious and spiritual climate survey. *Journal of College & Character, 10*(6), 1–10.

Bryant Rockenbach, A. N., & Mayhew, M. J. (2013). How the collegiate religious and spiritual climate shapes students' ecumenical orientation. *Research in Higher Education, 54*, 461–479.

Bryant Rockenbach, A. N., & Mayhew, M. J. (2014). The campus spiritual climate: Predictors of satisfaction among students with diverse worldviews. *Journal of College Student Development, 55*, 41–62.

Bryant Rockenbach, A. N., Roseboro Walker, C., & Luzader, J. (2012). A phenomenological analysis of college students' spiritual struggles. *Journal of College Student Development, 53*, 55–75.

Buchko, K. J. (2004). Religious beliefs and practices of college women as compared to men. *Journal of College Student Development, 45*, 89–98.

Buehler, C. (1962). Genetic aspects of the self. *Annals of the New York Academy of Sciences, 96*, 730–764.

Bullough, R. V., Jr., Young, J. R., Hall, K. M., Draper, R. J., & Smith, L. K. (2008). Cognitive complexity, the first year of teaching, and mentoring. *Teaching and Teacher Education, 24*, 1846–1858.

Burnett, S. E., & Segoria, J. (2009). Collaboration for military transition students from combat to college: It takes a community. *Journal of Postsecondary Education and Disability, 22*, 53–58.

Burrow, A. L., Tubman, J. G., & Montgomery, M. J. (2006). Racial identity: Toward an integrated developmental psychological perspective. *Identity: An International Journal of Theory and Research, 6*, 317–339.

Burton, J., Nandi, A., & Platt, L. (2010). Measuring ethnicity: Challenges and opportunities for survey research. *Ethnic and Racial Studies, 33*, 1332–1349.

Bussey, K. (2011). Gender identity development. In S. J. Schwartz, K. Luyckx, & V. L. Vignoles (Eds.), *Handbook of identity theory and research* (pp. 603–628). New York: Springer.

Bussey, K., & Bandura, A. (1999). Social cognitive theory of gender development and differentiation. *Psychological Review, 106*(4), 676–713.

Butler, J. (1990). *Gender trouble: Feminism and the subversion of identity.* New York: Routledge.

Butler, J. (1993). *Bodies that matter: On the discursive limits of "sex."* New York: Routledge.

Butler, J. (1999). *Gender trouble: Feminism and the subversion of identity.* New York: Routledge.

Butler, J. (2004). *Undoing gender.* New York: Routledge.

Cabrera, A. F., Crissman, J. L., Bernal, E. M., Nora, A., Terenzini, P. T., & Pascarella, E. T. (2002). Collaborative learning: Impact on college students' development and diversity. *Journal of College Student Development, 43*, 20–34.

Cabrera, A. F., & La Nasa, S. M. (2001). On the path to college: Three critical tasks facing America's disadvantaged. *Research in Higher Education, 42*, 119–150.

Cabrera, E. F. (2007). Opting out and opting in: Understanding the complexities of women's career transitions. *Career Development International, 12*, 218–237.

Cabrera, N. L. (2012). Working through Whiteness: White, male college students challenging racism. *The Review of Higher Education, 35*(3), 375–401.

Cabrera, N. L. (2014). Exposing Whiteness in higher education: White male college students minimizing racism, claiming victimization, and recreating White supremacy. *Race Ethnicity and Education, 17*(1), 30–55.

Cajete, G. (2005). American Indian epistemologies. In M.J.T. Fox, S. C. Lowe, & G. S. McClellan (Eds.), *Serving Native American students.* New Directions for Student Services, no. 109, pp. 69–78. San Francisco: Jossey-Bass.

Callis, A. S. (2014). Bisexual, pansexual, queer: Non-binary identities and the sexual borderlands. *Sexualities, 17*, 63–80.

Canon, H. J., & Brown, R. D. (1985). How to think about professional ethics. In H. J. Canon & R. D. Brown (Eds.), *Applied ethics in student services.* New Directions for Student Services, no. 30, pp. 81–87. San Francisco: Jossey-Bass.

Cardone, T., Turton, E. S., Olson, G., & Baxter Magolda, M. B. (2013). Learning partnerships in practice: Orientation, leadership, and residence life. *About Campus, 18*(5), 2–9.

Carmel-Gilfilen, C., & Portillo, M. (2010). Developmental trajectories in design thinking: An examination of criteria. *Design Studies, 31*, 74–91.

Carmel-Gilfilen, C., & Portillo, M. (2012). Where what's in common mediates disciplinary diversity in design students: A shared pathway of intellectual development. *Design Studies, 33*, 237–261.

Carpenter, D. S. (1996). The philosophical heritage of student affairs. In A. Rentz (Ed.), *Student affairs functions in higher education* (2nd ed., pp. 3–27). Springfield, IL: Thomas.

Carpenter, S., & Johnson, L. E. (2001). Women derive collective self-esteem from their feminist identity. *Psychology of Women Quarterly, 25*, 254–257.

Carrera, V., DePalma, R., & Lameiras, M. (2012). Sex/gender identity: Moving beyond fixed and "natural" categories. *Sexualities, 15*, 995–1016.

Carter, K. A. (2000). Transgenderism in college students: Issues of gender identity and its role on our campuses. In V. A. Wall & N. J. Evans (Eds.), *Toward acceptance: Sexual orientation issues on campus* (pp. 261–283). Lanham, MD: University Press of America.

Carter, R. T. (1993). Does race or racial identity attitudes influence the counseling process in Black and White dyads? In J. E. Helms (Ed.), *Black and White racial identity: Theory, research, and practice* (pp. 145–163). Westport, CT: Praeger.

Casas, J. M., & Pytluk, S. D. (1995). Hispanic identity development: Implications for research and practice. In J. G. Ponterotto, J. M. Casas, L. A. Suzuki, & C. M. Alexander (Eds.), *Handbook of Multicultural Counseling* (pp. 155–180). Thousand Oaks, CA: Sage.

Case, K. A., Hensley, R., & Anderson, A. (2014). Reflecting on heterosexual and male privilege: Interventions to raise awareness. *Journal of Social Issues, 70*, 722–740.

Case, K. A., Iuzzini, J., & Hopkins, M. (2012). Systems of privilege: Intersections, awareness, and applications. *Journal of Social Issues, 68*, 1–10.

Case, K., & Stewart, B. (2009). Heterosexual privilege awareness, prejudice, and support of gay marriage among diversity course students. *College Teaching, 58*, 3–7.

Case, K. A., & Stewart, B. (2010). Changes in diversity course student prejudice and attitudes toward heterosexual privilege and gay marriage. *Teaching of Psychology, 37*, 172–177.

Cash, T. F., Morrow, J. A., Hrabosky, J. I., & Perry, A. A. (2004). How has body image changed? A cross-sectional investigation of college women and men from 1983 to 2001. *Journal of Consulting and Clinical Psychology, 72*, 1081–1089.

Cass, V. C. (1979). Homosexual identity formation: A theoretical model. *Journal of Homosexuality, 4*, 219–235.

Cass, V. C. (1983–1984). Homosexual identity: A concept in need of definition. *Journal of Homosexuality, 9*(2–3), 31–43.

Cass, V. C. (1996). Sexual orientation identity formation: A Western phenomenon. In R. P. Cabaj & T. S. Stein (Eds.), *Textbook of homosexuality and mental health* (pp. 227–251). Washington, DC: American Psychiatric Press.

Castillo, L. G., Conoley, C. W., Choi-Pearson, C., Archuleta, D. J., Phoummarath, M. J., & Van Landingham, A. (2006). University environment as a mediator of Latino ethnic identity and persistent attitudes. *Journal of Counseling Psychology, 53*, 267–271.

Cebulko, K. (2014). Documented, undocumented, and liminally legal: Legal status during the transition to adulthood for 1.5-generation Brazilian immigrants. *The Sociological Quarterly, 55*, 143–167.

Cerezo, A., & Chang, T. (2013). Latina/o achievement at predominantly white universities: The importance of culture and ethnic community. *Journal of Hispanic Higher Education, 12*, 72–85.

Chae, M. H., & Larres, C. (2010). Asian American racial and ethnic identity: Update on theory and measurement. In J. G. Ponterotto, J. M. Casas, L. A. Suzuki, & C. M. Alexander (Eds.), *Handbook of multicultural counseling* (3rd ed., pp. 253–267). Thousand Oaks, CA: Sage.

Chang, M. J. (2002). The impact of an undergraduate diversity course requirement on students racial views and attitudes. *The Journal of General Education, 51*(1), 21–42.

Chang, M. J., Milem, J. F., & Antonio, A. L. (2011). Campus climate and diversity. In J. H. Schuh, S. R. Jones, & S. R. Harper (Eds.), *Student services: A handbook for the profession* (5th ed., pp. 43–58). San Francisco: Jossey-Bass.

Chapman, O. (1993). Women's voice and the learning of math. *Journal of Gender Studies, 2*, 206–220.

Charmaz, K. (1994). Identity dilemmas of chronically ill men. *The Sociological Quarterly, 35*, 269–288.

Charmaz, K. (1995). The body, identity, and self. *The Sociological Quarterly, 36*, 657–680.

Chaudhari, P., & Pizzolato, J. E. (2008). Understanding the epistemology of ethnic identity development in multiethnic college students. *Journal of College Student Development, 49*, 443–458.

Chávez, A. F. (2009). Leading in the borderlands: Negotiating ethnic patriarchy for the benefit of students. *Journal about Women in Higher Education, 1*, 39–65.

Chávez, A. F., & Longerbeam, S. D. (2016). *Teaching across cultural strengths: A guide to balancing integrated and individuated cultural frameworks in college teaching.* Sterling, VA: Stylus.

Chávez, A. F., Ke, F., & Herrera, F. (2012). Clan, sage, and sky: Indigenous, Hispano, and Mestizo narratives of learning in New Mexico context. *American Educational Research Journal. 49*, 775–806.

Chen, G. A., LePhuoc, P., Guzmán, M. R., Rude, S. S., & Dodd, B. G. (2006). Exploring Asian American racial identity. *Cultural Diversity and Ethnic Minority Psychology, 12*, 461–476.

Cheryan, S., & Monin, B. (2005). "Where are you really from?" Asian Americans and identity denial. *Journal of Personality and Social Psychology, 89*, 717–730.

Chickering, A. W. (1969). *Education and identity.* San Francisco: Jossey-Bass.

Chickering, A. W., Dalton, J. C., & Stamm, L. (2006). *Encouraging authenticity and spirituality in higher education.* San Francisco: Jossey-Bass.

Chickering, A. W., & Havighurst, R. J. (1990). The life cycle. In A. W. Chickering & Associates (Eds.), *The modern American college: Responding to the new realities of diverse students and a changing society* (pp. 16–50). San Francisco: Jossey-Bass. (Originally published 1981)

Chickering, A. W., & Reisser, L. (1993). *Education and identity* (2nd ed.). San Francisco: Jossey-Bass.

Chickering, A. W., & Schlossberg, N. K. (1995). *How to get the most out of college.* Boston: Allyn & Bacon.

Chickering, A. W., & Schlossberg, N. K. (2001). *Getting the most out of college* (2nd ed.). Upper Saddle River, NJ: Prentice Hall.

Cho, S., Crenshaw, K. W., & McCall, L. (2013). Toward a field of intersectionality studies: Theory, applications, and praxis. *Signs, 38*(4), 785–810.

Choi, K. M., Bernard, J. M., & Luke, M. (2013). Characteristics of friends of female college third culture kids. *Asia Pacific Journal of Counselling and Psychotherapy, 4,* 125–136.

Choney, S. K., Berryhill-Paapke, E., & Robbins, R. R. (1995). The acculturation of American Indians: Developing frameworks for research and practice. In J. G. Ponterotto, J. M. Casas, L. A. Suzuki, & C. M. Alexander (Eds.), *Handbook of multicultural counseling* (pp. 73–92). Thousand Oaks, CA: Sage.

Church, T. E. (2009). Returning veterans on campus with war related injuries and the long road back home. *Journal of Postsecondary Education and Disability, 22*(1), 43–52.

Clark-Plaskie, M., & Shaw, J. P. (2014). Beyond stages: Mentoring as transitional identity space for adult learners. *Educational Research, 5*(2), 58–70.

Clayton, S. A., & Jones, A. (1993). Multiculturalism: An imperative for change. *Iowa Student Personnel Association Journal, 8,* 35–49.

Cleary, P. F., Pierce, G., & Trauth, E. M. (2006). Closing the digital divide: Understanding racial, ethnic, social class, gender and geographic disparities in Internet use among school age children in the United States. *Universal Access in the Information Society, 4,* 354–373.

Clerge, O. (2014). Balancing stigma and status: Racial and class identities among middle-class Haitian youth. *Ethnic and Racial Studies, 37,* 958–977.

Clinchy, B. M. (2002). Revisiting *Women's ways of knowing.* In B. K. Hofer & P. R. Pintrich (Eds.), *Personal epistemology: The psychology of beliefs about knowledge and knowing* (pp. 63–87). Mahwah, NJ: Erlbaum.

Clotfelter, C. T. (2011). *Big-time sports in American universities.* Cambridge University Press.

Cokley, K. (1999). Reconceptualizing the impact of college racial composition on African American students' racial identity. *Journal of College Student Development, 40,* 235–246.

Cokley, K. O. (2001). Gender differences among African American students in the impact of racial identity on academic psychosocial development. *Journal of College Student Development, 42,* 480–487.

Cokley, K. O. (2002). Testing Cross's revised racial identity model: An examination of the relationship between racial identity and internalized racialism. *Journal of Counseling Psychology, 49,* 476–483.

Cokley, K. O. (2005). Racial(ized) identity, ethnic identity, and Afrocentric values: Conceptual and methodological challenges in understanding African American identity. *Journal of Counseling Psychology, 52,* 517–526.

Cokley, K. O. (2007). Critical issues in the measurement of ethnic and racial identity: A referendum on the state of the field. *Journal of Counseling Psychology, 54,* 224–234.

Cokley, K. O. (2015). *The myth of Black anti-intellectualism: A true psychology of African American students.* Santa Barbara, CA: Praeger.

Colby, A., Kohlberg, L., & Kauffman, K. (1987). Theoretical introduction to the measurement of moral judgment. In A. Colby & L. Kohlberg (Eds.), *The measurement of moral judgment: Vol. 1. Theoretical foundations and research validation* (pp. 1–67). New York: Cambridge University Press.

Cole, B. P., Davidson, M. M., & Gervais, S. J. (2013). Body surveillance and body shame in college men: Are men who self-objectify less hopeful? *Sex roles, 69,* 29–41.

Cole, D., & Ahmadi, S. (2003). Perspectives and experiences of Muslim women who veil on college campuses. *Journal of College Student Development, 44*(1), 47–66.

Cole, D., & Ahmadi, S. (2010). Reconsidering campus diversity: An examination of Muslim students' experiences. *The Journal of Higher Education, 81*(2), 121–139.

Coleman, E. (1981–1982). Developmental stages of the coming out process. *Journal of Homosexuality, 7,* 31–43.

Coles, R. (1989). *The call of stories: Teaching and the moral imagination.* Boston, MA: Houghton Mifflin.

Collins, J. F. (2000). Biracial-bisexual individuals: Identity coming of age. *International Journal of Sexuality and Gender Studies, 5,* 221–253.

Collins, P. H. (1991). *Black feminist thought: Knowledge, consciousness, and the politics of empowerment.* New York: Routledge.

Collins, P. H. (1993). Black feminism in the twentieth century. In D. Clark Hine, E. Barkley Brown, & R. Terborg-Penn (Eds.) *Black women in the United States: An historical encyclopedia* (pp. 418–425). New York: Carlson.

Collins, P. H. (1996). What's in a name? Womanism, black feminism, and beyond. *The Black Scholar, 26*(1), 9–17.

Collins, P. H. (2009). *Black feminist thought:* Knowledge, consciousness, and the politics of empowerment (3rd ed.). New York: Routledge.

Committee on the Student in Higher Education (1968). *The student in higher education.* New Haven, CT: Hazen Foundation.

Coogan, P. A., & Chen, C. P. (2007). Career development and counseling for women: Connecting theories to practice. *Counseling Psychology Quarterly, 20,* 191–204.

Coomes, M. D. (2004). Understanding the historical and cultural influences that shape generations. In M. D. Coomes & R. DeBard (Eds.), *Serving the millennial generation.* New Directions for Student Services, no. 106, pp. 17–31. San Francisco: Jossey-Bass.

Cortés, C. E. (2000). The diversity within: Intermarriage, identity, and campus community. *About Campus, 5*(1), 5–10.

Costello, J. J., & English, R. W. (2001). The psychosocial development of college students with and without learning disabilities. *Journal of Postsecondary Education and Disability, 15*(1), 16–27.

Côté, J. E. (1996). Sociological perspectives on identity formation: The culture–identity link and identity capital. *Journal of adolescence, 19*(5), 417–428.

Côté, J. E., & Levine, C. (1983). Marcia and Erikson: The relationships among ego identity status, neuroticism, dogmatism, and purpose in life. *Journal of Youth and Adolescence, 12,* 43–83.

Côté, J. E., & Levine, C. (1987). A formulation of Erikson's theory of ego identity formation. *Developmental Review, 7,* 273–325.

Côté, J. E., & Levine, C. (1988a). A critical examination of the ego identity status paradigm. *Developmental Review, 8,* 147–184.

Côté, J. E., & Levine, C. (1988b). On critiquing the identity status paradigm: A rejoinder to Waterman. *Developmental Review, 8,* 209–218.

Council of Student Personnel Associations in Higher Education (1994). Student development workers in postsecondary education. In A. Rentz (Ed.), *Student affairs: A profession's heritage* (American College Personnel Association Media Publication No. 40, 2nd ed., pp. 428–437). Lanham, MD: University Press of America. (Original published 1975)

Cox, R. H., Sadberry, S., McGuire, R. T., & McBride, A. (2009). Predicting student athlete career situation awareness from college experiences. *Journal of Clinical Sport Psychology, 3,* 156–181.

Craft, C. M., & Bryant, A. N. (2011). Faith development within religion and philosophy courses at a college of the Lutheran church. *Journal of Student Affairs Research and Practice, 48,* 195–212.

Craft, C. M., & Bryant Rockenbach, A. N. (2011). Conceptualizations of spirituality, religion, and faith: Comparing biblical notions with the perspectives of Protestant Christian students at a Lutheran college. *Christian Higher Education, 10,* 444–463.

Craft, C. M., & Bryant, A. N. (2011). Faith development within religion and philosophy courses at a college of the Lutheran church. *Journal of Student Affairs Research and Practice, 48,* 195–212.

Crawford, M., & MacLeod, M. (1990). Gender in the college classroom: An assessment of the "chilly climate" for women. *Sex Roles, 23,* 101–122.

Creamer, E. G., Baxter Magolda, M. B., & Yue, J. (2010). Preliminary evidence of the reliability and validity of a quantitative measure of self-authorship. *Journal of College Student Development, 51,* 550–562.

Creamer, E. G., & Laughlin, A. (2005). Self-authorship and women's career decision making. *Journal of College Student Development, 46,* 13–27.

Crenshaw, K. (1989). Demarginalizing the intersection of race and sex: A black feminist critique of antidiscrimination doctrine, feminist theory, and antiracist politics. *University of Chicago Legal Forum, 139,* 139–167.

Crenshaw, K. W. (1991). Mapping the margins: Intersectionality, identity politics, and violence against women of color. *Stanford Law Review, 43,* 1241–1299.

Crenshaw, K., Gotanda, N., Peller, G., & Thomas, K. (Eds.). (1995). *Critical race theory: The key writings that formed the movement.* New York: The New Press.

Creswell, J. W. (2013). *Research design: Qualitative, quantitative, and mixed methods approaches* (4th ed.). Thousand Oaks, CA: Sage.

Crocetti, E., Rubini, M., Luyckx, K., & Meeus, W. (2008). Identity formation in early and middle adolescents from various ethnic groups: From three dimensions to five statuses. *Journal of Youth Adolescence, 37,* 983–996.

Crombie, G., Pyke, S. W., Silverthorn, N., Jones, A., & Piccinin, S. (2003). Students' perceptions of their classroom participation and instructor as a function of gender and context. *The Journal of Higher Education, 74,* 51–76.

Cronin, T. J., Levin, S., Branscombe, N. R., van Laar, C., & Tropp, L. R. (2012). Ethnic identification in response to perceived discrimination protects well-being and promotes activism: A longitudinal study of Latino college students. *Group Processes Intergroup Relations, 15,* 393–407.

Cross, W. E., Jr. (1971). Toward a psychology of Black liberation: The Negro-to-Black conversion experience. *Black World, 20*(9), 13–27.

Cross, W. E., Jr. (1978). The Thomas and Cross models of psychological nigrescence: A review. *The Journal of Black Psychology, 5,* 13–31.

Cross, W. E., Jr. (1991). *Shades of Black: Diversity in African American identity.* Philadelphia: Temple University Press.

Cross, W. E., Jr. (2012). The enactment of race and other social identities during everyday interactions. In C. L. Wijeyesinghe & B. W. Jackson, III. (Eds.), *New perspectives on racial identity development: A theoretical and practical anthology* (2nd. ed., pp. 192–215). New York: New York University.

Cross, W. E., Jr., & Fhagen-Smith, P. (2001). Patterns in African American identity development: A life span perspective. In C. L. Wijeyesinghe & B. W. Jackson III (Eds.). *New perspectives on racial identity development: A theoretical and practical anthology* (pp. 243–270). New York: New York University Press.

Cross, W. E., Jr., Smith, L., & Payne, Y. (2002). Black identity: A repertoire of daily enactments. In P. B. Pedersen, J. G. Draguns, W. J. Lonner, & J. E. Trimble (Eds.), *Counseling across cultures* (5th ed., pp. 93–107). Thousand Oaks, CA: Sage.

Crotty, M. (1998). *The foundations of social research: Meaning and perspective in the research process.* Thousand Oaks, CA: Sage.

Cuéllar, I., Nyberg, B., Maldonado, R. E., & Roberts, R. E. (1997). Ethnic identity and acculturation in a young adult Mexican-origin population. *Journal of Community Psychology, 25,* 535–549.

Cullaty, B. (2011). The role of parental involvement in the autonomy development of traditional-age college students. *Journal of College Student Development, 52,* 425–439.

Curtis, M. B., Conover, T. L., & Chui, L. C. (2012). A cross-cultural study of the influence of country of origin, justice, power distance, and gender on ethical decision making. *Journal of International Accounting Research, 11,* 5–34.

Dalton, J. C. (2006a). Integrating spirit and community in higher education. In A. W. Chickering, J. C. Dalton, & L. Stamm (Eds.), *Encouraging authenticity and spirituality in higher education* (pp. 165–185). San Francisco: Jossey-Bass.

Dalton, J. C. (2006b). The place of spirituality in the mission and work of college student affairs. In A. W. Chickering, J. C. Dalton, & L. Stamm (Eds.), *Encouraging authenticity and spirituality in higher education* (pp. 145–164). San Francisco: Jossey-Bass.

Dalton, J. C. (2006c). Principles and practices for strengthening moral and spiritual growth in college. In A. W. Chickering, J. C. Dalton, & L. Stamm (Eds.), *Encouraging authenticity and spirituality in higher education* (pp. 272–282). San Francisco: Jossey-Bass.

Dalton, J. C., Eberhardt, D., Bracken, J., & Echols, K. (2006). Inward journeys: Forms and patterns of college student spirituality. *Journal of College and Character, 7*(8), 1–21.

Daniel, G. R. (2002). *More than black? Multiracial identity and the new racial order.* Philadelphia: Temple University Press.

D'Andrea, M., & Daniels, J. (2001). Expanding our thinking about White racism: Facing the challenge of multicultural counseling in the 21st century. In J. G. Ponterotto, J. M. Casas, L. A. Suzuki, & C. M. Alexander (Eds.), *Handbook of multicultural counseling* (2nd. ed., pp. 289–310). Thousand Oaks, CA: Sage.

D'Augelli, A. R. (1994a). Identity development and sexual orientation: Toward a model of lesbian, gay, and bisexual identity development. In E. J. Trickett, R. J. Watts, & D. Birman (Eds.), *Human diversity: Perspectives on people in context* (pp. 312–333). San Francisco: Jossey-Bass.

D'Augelli, A. R. (1994b). Lesbian and gay male development: Steps toward an analysis of lesbians' and gay men's lives. In B. Greene & G. M. Herek (Eds.), *Lesbian and gay psychology: Theory, research, and clinical implications* (Psychological Perspectives on Lesbian and Gay Issues, Vol. *1,* pp. 118–132). Thousand Oaks, CA: Sage.

Davidson, J., & Henderson, V. L. (2010). "Coming out" on the spectrum: Autism, identity and disclosure. *Social & Cultural Geography, 11,* 155–170.

Davis, C., III, Aronson, J., & Salinas, M. (2006). Shades of threat: Racial identity as a moderator of stereotype threat. *Journal of Black Psychology, 32,* 399–417.

Davis, F. J. (1995). The Hawaiian alternative to the one-drop rule. In N. Zack (Ed.), *American mixed race: The culture of microdiversity* (pp. 115–131). Lanham, MD: Rowman & Littlefield.

Davis, T. L. (2002). Voices of gender role conflict: The social construction of college men's identity. *Journal of College Student Development, 43*, 508–521.

Day, D. A., & Lane, T. (2014). Reconstructing faculty roles to align with self-authorship development: The gentle art of stepping back. *The Canadian Journal for the Scholarship of Teaching and Learning, 5*(1), 5.

Day-Vines, N., Barker, J. M., & Exum, H. (1998). Impact of diasporic travel on ethnic identity development of African American college students. *College Student Journal, 32*, 463–471.

Dearnley, C., & Matthew, B. (2007) Factors that contribute to undergraduate student success. *Teaching in Higher Education, 12*(3), 377–391.

Deaux, K. (1985). Sex and gender. *Annual Review of Psychology, 36*, 49–81.

DeBose, H. L., & Winters, L. I. (2003). The dilemma of biracial people of African American descent. In L. I. Winters & H. L. DeBose (Eds.), *New faces in a changing America: Multiracial identity in the 21st century* (pp. 127–157). Thousand Oaks, CA: Sage.

DeHaan, L. G., & Schulenberg, J. (1997). The covariation of religion and politics during the transition to young adulthood: Challenging global identity assumptions. *Journal of Adolescence, 20*, 537–552.

Delgado, R. (Ed.). (1995). *Critical race theory: The cutting edge*. Philadelphia, PA: Temple University Press.

Delgado, R. (1998). The black/white binary: How does it work? In R. Delgado & J. Stefancic (Eds.) *The Latino condition: A critical reader* (pp. 369–375). New York: New York University Press.

Delgado, R., & Stefancic, J. (2001). *Critical race theory: An introduction*. New York: New York University Press.

Delgado, R., & Stefancic, J. (2012). *Critical race theory: An introduction* (2nd ed.). New York: New York University Press.

Delgado, R., & Stefancic, J. (Eds.). (2013). *Critical race theory: The cutting edge* (3rd ed.). Philadelphia, PA: Temple University Press.

Delgado Bernal, D. (2002). Critical race theory, Latino critical theory, and critical race-gendered epistemologies: Recognizing students of color as holders and creators of knowledge. *Qualitative Inquiry, 8*, 105–126.

Delworth, U. (1989). Identity in the college years: Issues of gender and ethnicity. *NASPA Journal, 26*, 162–166.

Demers, A. (2011). When veterans return: The role of community in reintegration. *Journal of Loss and Trauma, 16*, 160–179.

Denhart, H. (2008). Deconstructing barriers: Perceptions of students labeled with learning disabilities in higher education. *Journal of Learning Disabilities, 41*(6), 483–497.

Denzin, N. K., & Lincoln, Y. S. (Eds.) (2005). *The handbook of qualitative research* (3rd ed.). Thousand Oaks, CA: Sage.

Denzin, N. K., Lincoln, Y. S., & Smith, L. T. (Eds.). (2008). *Handbook of critical and indigenous methodologies*. Los Angeles: Sage.

Derrida, J. (1978). *Writing and difference* (A. Bass, Trans.). Chicago: University of Chicago Press. (Original work published 1967)

Desoff, A. (2006). Who's NOT going abroad? *International Educator, 15*(2), 20–27.

Dessel, A. B., Woodford, M. R., Routenberg, R., & Breijak, D. P. (2013). Heterosexual students' experiences in sexual orientation intergroup dialogue courses. *Journal of Homosexuality, 60*(7), 1054–1080.

Devos, T., & Cruz Torres, J. A. (2007). Implicit identification with academic achievement among Latino college students: The role of ethnic identity and significant others. *Basic and Applied Social Psychology, 29*, 293–310.

Dewey, J. (1933). *How we think: A restatement of the relation of reflective thinking to the educative process.* Lexington, MA: Heath.

Dewey, J. (1960). *Logic: The theory of inquiry.* New York: Holt, Rinehart, and Winston. (Original work published in 1938)

Diamond, L. M. (2008). *Sexual fluidity: Understanding women's love and desire.* Cambridge, MA: Harvard University Press.

Diamond, L. M., Pardo, S. T., & Butterworth, M. R. (2011). Gender identity development. In S. J. Schwartz, K. Luyckx, & V. L. Vignoles (Eds.), *Handbook of identity theory and research* (pp. 629–647). New York: Springer.

Diamond, L. M., & Savin-Williams, R. C. (2000). Explaining diversity in the development of same-sex sexuality among young women. *Journal of Social Issues, 56*, 297–313.

Dika, S. L., & Singh, K. (2002). Applications of social capital in educational literature: A critical synthesis. *Review of Educational Research, 72*, 31–60.

Dill, B. T., & Zambrana, R. E. (2009). Emerging intersections: Race, class, and gender in theory, policy, and practice. In B. T. Dill & R. E. Zambrana (Eds.), *Emerging intersections: Race, class and gender in theory, policy, and practice* (pp. 1–21). New Brunswick, NJ: Rutgers University Press.

Dillon, F. R., Worthington, R. L., & Moradi, B. (2011). Sexual identity as a universal process. In S. J. Schwartz, K. Luyckx, & V. L. Vignoles (Eds.), *Handbook of identity theory and research* (pp. 649–670). New York: Springer.

DiRamio, D., Ackerman, R., & Mitchell, R. L. (2008). From combat to campus: Voices of student-veterans. *NASPA Journal, 45*, 73–102.

DiRamio, D., & Spires, M. (2009). Partnering to assist disabled veterans in transition. In R. Ackerman & D. DiRamio (Eds.), *Creating a veteran-friendly campus: Strategies for transition and success.* New Directions for Student Services, no. 126, pp. 81–88. San Francisco: Jossey-Bass.

Dirks, D. H. (1988). Moral development in Christian higher education. *Journal of Psychology and Theology, 16*, 324–331.

Dixon, A. L., & Portman, T.A.A. (2010). The beauty of being native: The nature of Native American and Alaska native identity development. In J. G. Ponterotto, J. M. Casas, L. A. Suzuki, & C. M. Alexander (Eds.), *Handbook of multicultural counseling* (3rd ed., pp. 215–225). Thousand Oaks, CA: Sage.

Dixson, A. D., & Rousseau, C. K. (2005). And are we still not saved: Critical race theory in education ten years later. *Race, Ethnicity, and Education, 8*, 7–27.

Dolby, N. (2004). Encountering an American self: Study abroad and national identity. *Comparative Education Review, 48*, 150–173.

Dolby, N. (2007). Reflections on nation: American undergraduates and education abroad. *Journal of Studies in International Education, 11*, 141–156.

Donald, J. G. (2002). *Learning to think: Disciplinary perspectives.* San Francisco: Jossey-Bass.

Donnelly, D. A., Cook, K. J., Van Ausdale, D., & Foley, L. (2005). White privilege, color blindness, and services to battered women. *Violence Against Women, 11*, 6–37.

Downing, N. E., & Roush, K. L. (1985). From passive acceptance to active commitment: A model of feminist development for women. *Counseling Psychologist, 13*, 695–709.

Drum, C. E. (2009). Models and approaches to disability. In C. E. Drum, G. L. Krahn, & H. Bersani Jr. (Eds.), *Disability and public health* (pp. 27–44). Washington, DC: American Public Health Association, American Association of Intellectual and Developmental Disabilities.

DuBay, W. H. (1987). *Gay identity: The self under ban.* Jefferson, NC: McFarland.

Du Bois, W.E.B. (1903). *The souls of black folk: Essays and sketches* (3rd ed.). Chicago: McClurg.

Duffy, J. O. (2007). Invisibly at risk: Low-income students in a middle- and upper-class world. *About Campus, 12* (2), 18–25.

Dugan, J. P., Kusel, M. L., & Simounet, D. M. (2012). Transgender college students: An exploratory study of perceptions, engagement, and educational outcomes. *Journal of College Student Development, 53,* 719–736.

Durham, R. L., Hays, J., & Martinez, R. (1994). Socio-cognitive development among Chicano and Anglo American college students. *Journal of College Student Development, 35,* 178–182.

Dykstra, C. (1986). What is faith? In C. Dykstra & S. Parks (Eds.), *Faith development and Fowler* (pp. 45–64). Birmingham, AL: Religious Education Press.

Edgerton, J. D., & Roberts, L. W. (2014). Cultural capital or habitus? Bourdieu and beyond in the explanation of enduring educational inequality. *Theory and Research in Education, 12,* 193–220.

Edwards, K. E., & Jones, S. R. (2009). "Putting my man face on": A grounded theory of college men's gender identity development. *Journal of College Student Development, 50,* 210–228.

Edwards, K. T., Loftin, J. K., Nance, A. D., Riser, S., & Smith, Y. (2014). Learning to transform: Implications for centering social justice in a student affairs program. *College Student Affairs Journal, 32,* 1–17.

Egan, K. S. (1996). Flexible mentoring: Adaptations in style for women's ways of knowing. *Journal of Business Communication, 33,* 401–425.

Egart, K., & Healy, M. P. (2004). An urban leadership internship program: Implementing learning partnerships "unplugged" from campus structures. In M. Baxter Magolda & P. M. King (Eds.), *Learning partnerships: Theory and modes of practice to educate for self-authorship* (pp. 125–149). Sterling, VA: Stylus.

Eisele, H., & Stake, J. (2008). The differential relationship of feminist attitudes and feminist identity to self efficacy. *Psychology of Women Quarterly, 32,* 233–244.

Elder, G. H., Jr. (1994). Time, human agency, and social change: Perspectives on the life course. *Social Psychology Quarterly, 57*(1), 4–15.

Elder, G. H., Jr., Johnson, M. K., & Crosnoe, R. (2003). The emergence and development of life course theory. In J. T. Mortimer & M. J. Shanahan (Eds.), *Handbook of the life course* (pp. 3–17). New York: Kluwer Academic/Plenum Publishers.

Elion, A. A., Wang, K. T., Slaney, R. B., & French, B. H. (2012). Perfectionism in African American students: Relationship to racial identity, GPA, self-esteem, and depression. *Cultural Diversity and Ethnic Minority Psychology, 18,* 118–127.

Elliott, M., Gonzalez, C., & Larsen, B. (2011). U.S. military veterans transition to college: Combat, PTSD, and alienation on campus. *Journal of Student Affairs Research and Practice, 48,* 279–296.

Equal Employment Opportunity Commission. (2011). Regulations to implement the Equal Employment Provisions of the Americans with Disabilities Act, as Amended. *Federal Register.* Washington, DC: United State Government. Retrieved from https://www.federalregister.gov/articles/2011/03/25/2011-6056/regulations-to-implement-the-equal-employment-provisions-of-the-americans-with-disabilities-act-as

Erikson, E. H. (1950). *Childhood and society.* New York: Norton.

Erikson, E. H. (1963). *Childhood and society* (2nd ed.). New York: Norton.

Erikson, E. H. (1964). *Insight and responsibility.* New York: Norton.

Erikson, E. H. (1968). *Identity: Youth and crisis.* New York: Norton.

Erikson, E. H. (1980). *Identity and the life cycle.* New York: Norton. (Originally published 1959)

Erickson, E. H. (1982). *The life cycle completed: A review.* New York: Norton.

Erwin, T. D. (1983). The scale of intellectual development: Measuring Perry's scheme. *Journal of College Student Personnel, 24,* 6–12.

Erwin, T. M. (2001). *Encouraging the spiritual development of counseling students and supervisees using Fowler's stages of faith development.* (ERIC Document Reproduction Service No. ED4457473).

Evans, N. J. (1987). A framework for assisting student affairs staff in fostering moral development. *Journal of Counseling and Development, 66,* 191–194.

Evans, N. J. (1996). Psychosocial, cognitive, and typological perspectives on student development. In S. Komives & D. Woodard (Eds.), *Student services: A handbook for the profession* (3rd ed.). San Francisco: Jossey-Bass.

Evans, N. J. (with Reason, R. D.). (2001). Guiding principles: A review and analysis of student affairs philosophical statements. *Journal of College Student Development, 42,* 359–377.

Evans, N. J. (2002). The impact of an LGBT Safe Zone project on campus climate. *Journal of College Student Development, 43,* 522–539.

Evans, N. J. (2003). Psychosocial, cognitive, and typological perspectives on student development. In S. K. Komives, D. B. Woodard, Jr., & Associates, *Student services: A handbook for the profession* (4th ed., pp. 179–202). San Francisco: Jossey-Bass.

Evans, N. J. (2008). Theoretical foundations of Universal Instructional Design. In J. L. Higbee & E. Goff (Eds.), *Pedagogy and student services for institutional transformation: Implementing universal design in higher education* (pp. 11–23). Center for Research on Developmental Education and Urban Literacies, University of Minnesota.

Evans, N. J. (2011). Psychosocial and cognitive-structural perspectives on student development. In J. H. Schuh, S. R. Jones, & Harper, S. R. (Eds.), *Student services: A handbook for the profession* (5th ed., pp. 168–186). San Francisco: Jossey-Bass.

Evans, N. J., Assadi, J. L., & Herriott, T. K. (2005). Encouraging the development of disability allies. In R. D. Reason, E. M. Broido, T. L. Davis, & N. J. Evans (Eds.), *Developing social justice allies.* New Directions for Student Services, no. 110, pp. 67–79. San Francisco: Jossey-Bass.

Evans, N. J., & Broido, E. M. (1999). Coming out in college residence halls: Negotiation, meaning making, challenges, supports. *Journal of College Student Development, 40,* 658–668.

Evans, N. J., & Broido, E. M. (2005). Encouraging the development of social justice attitudes and actions in heterosexual students. In R. D. Reason, E. M. Broido, T. L. Davis, & N. J. Evans (Eds.), *Developing social justice allies.* New Directions for Student Services, no. 110, pp. 43–54. San Francisco: Jossey-Bass.

Evans, N. J., Broido, E. M., Brown, K. R., & Wilke, A. K. (forthcoming). *Disability in higher education: A social justice approach.* San Francisco: Jossey-Bass.

Evans, N. J., & D'Augelli, A. R. (1996). Lesbians, gay men, and bisexual people in college. In R. C. Savin-Williams & K. M. Cohen (Eds.), *The lives of lesbians, gays and bisexuals: Children to adults* (pp. 201–226). Fort Worth, TX: Harcourt Brace.

Evans, N. J., & Guido, F. M. (2012). Response to Patrick Love's "informal theory": A rejoinder. *Journal of College Student Development, 53*(4), 192–200.

Evans, N. J., & Herriott, T. K. (2004). Freshmen impressions: How a campus climate study shaped the perceptions, self-awareness, and behavior of four first-year students. *Journal of College Student Development, 45,* 316–332.

Evans, N. J., & Herriott, T. K. (2009). Philosophical and theoretical approaches to disability. In J. L. Higbee & A. A. Mitchell (Eds.), *Making good on the promise: Student affairs professionals with disabilities* (pp. 27–40). Lanham, MD: American College Personnel Association.

Fail, H., Thompson, J., & Walker, G. (2004). Belonging, identity and Third Culture Kids: Life histories of former international school students. *Journal of Research in International Education*, *3*, 319–338.

Farver, J. M., Xu, Y., Bhadha, B. R., Narang, S., & Lieber, E. (2007). Ethnic identity, acculturation, parenting beliefs, and adolescent adjustment: A comparison of Asian Indian and European American families. *Merrill-Palmer Quarterly*, *53*, 184–215.

Fassinger, R. E. (1998). Lesbian, gay, and bisexual identity and student development theory. In Sanlo, R. L. (Ed.), *Working with lesbian, gay, bisexual, and transgender college students: A handbook for faculty and administrators* (pp. 13–22). Westport, CT: Greenwood.

Fassinger, R. E., & Hensler-McGinnis, N. F. (2005). Multicultural feminist mentoring as individual and small-group pedagogy. In C. Z. Enns & A. L. Sinacore (Eds.), *Teaching and social justice: Integrating multicultural and feminist theories in the classroom* (pp. 143–161). Washington DC: American Psychological Association Books.

Fassinger, R. E., & Miller, B. A. (1997). Validation of an inclusive model of homosexual identity formation in a sample of gay men. *Journal of Homosexuality*, *32*(2), 53–78.

Fausto-Sterling, A. (1993). The five sexes: Why male and female are not enough. *The Sciences*, *33*(2), 20–25.

Feigenbaum, E. F. (2007). Heterosexual privilege: The political and the personal. *Hypatia*, *22*, 1–9.

Feldman, K. A., & Newcomb, T. M. (1969). *The impact of college on students*. 2 vols. San Francisco: Jossey-Bass.

Ferdman, B. M., & Gallegos, P. I. (2001). Racial identity development and Latinos in the United States. In C. L. Wijeyesinghe & B. W. Jackson, III (Eds.), *New perspectives on racial identity development: A theoretical and practical anthology* (pp. 32–66). New York: New York University Press.

Ferdman, B. M., & Gallegos, P. I. (2012). Latina and Latino ethnoracial identity orientations: A dynamic and developmental perspective. In C. L. Wijeyesinghe & B. W. Jackson, III (Eds.), *New perspectives on racial identity development: Integrating emerging frameworks* (2nd ed) (pp. 51–80). New York: NYU Press.

Fernout, J. H. (1986). Where is faith? Searching for the core of the cube. In C. Dykstra & S. Parks (Eds.), *Faith development and Fowler* (pp. 65–89). Birmingham, AL: Religious Education Press.

Ferraro, K. F. (2001). Aging and role transitions. *Handbook of Aging and the Social Sciences*, *5*, 313–330.

Fine, M., & Burns, A. (2003). Class notes: Toward a critical psychology of class and schooling. *Journal of Social Issues*, *59*(4), 841–860.

Fischer, A. R., Tokar, D. M., Mergl, M. M., Good, G. E., Hill, M. S., & Blum, S. A. (2000). Assessing women's feminist identity development: Studies of convergent, discriminant, and structural validity. *Psychology of Women Quarterly*, *24*, 15–29.

Fleming, J. (1984). *Blacks in college: A comparative study of students' success in black and white institutions*. San Francisco: Jossey-Bass.

Forber-Pratt, A. J., & Aragon, S. R. (2013). A model of social and psychosocial identity development for postsecondary students with physical disabilities. In M. Wappett & K. Arndt (Eds.), *Emerging perspectives on disability studies* (pp. 1–22). New York: Palgrave-MacMillan.

Forrest, L. (1988). [Review of the book *Women's ways of knowing: The development of self, voice, and mind*]. *Journal of College Student Development*, *29*, 82–84.

Fouad, N. A., & Kantamneni, N. (2011). Cultural validity of Holland's theory. In J. G. Ponterotto, J. M. Cassas, L. A. Suzuki, & C. M. Alexander (Eds.), *Handbook of multicultural counseling* (pp. 703–714). Thousand Oaks, CA: Sage.

Foubert, J. D., & Grainger, L. U. (2006). Effects of involvement in clubs and organizations on the psychosocial development of first-year and senior college students. *NASPA Journal, 43,* 166–182.

Foubert, J. D., Nixon, M. L., Sisson, V. S., & Barnes, A. C. (2005). A longitudinal study of Chickering and Reisser's vectors: Exploring gender differences and implications for refining the theory. *Journal of College Student Development, 46,* 461–471.

Foucault, M. (1978). *The history of sexuality: Vol. I. An introduction* (R. Hurley, Trans.). New York: Vintage Books.

Fougeyrollas, P., & Beauregard, L. (2001). An interactive person-environment social creation. In G. L. Albrecht, K. D. Seelman, & M. Bury (Eds.), *Handbook of disability studies* (pp. 171–194). Thousand Oaks, CA: Sage.

Fowler, J. W. (1978). Life/faith patterns: Structures of trust and loyalty. In J. Berryman (Ed.), *Life-maps: Conversations on the journey of faith* (pp. 14–104). Waco, TX: Word.

Fowler, J. W. (1981). *Stages of faith: The psychology of human development and the quest for meaning.* New York: Harper & Row.

Fowler, J. W. (1996). *Faithful change: The personal and public challenges of postmodern life.* Nashville, TN: Abingdon.

Fowler, J. W. (2000). *Becoming adult, becoming Christian: Adult development and Christian faith.* San Francisco: Jossey-Bass.

Fox, N. S., Spooner, S. E., Utterback, J. W., & Barbieri, J. A. (1996). Relationships between autonomy, gender, and weekend commuting among college students. *NASPA Journal, 34,* 19–28.

Freiler, T. (2008). Learning through the body. In S. B. Merriam (Ed.), *Special issue: Third update on adult learning theory. New Directions for Adult and Continuing Education,* no. 119, pp. 37–47. San Francisco: Jossey-Bass

Freire, P. (1997). *Pedagogy of the oppressed.* New York: Continuum. (Original work published 1970)

Freud, S. (1965). *Three essays on the theory of sexuality* (J. Strachey, Trans.). New York: Basic Books. (Original work published 1905)

Frey, L. L., Beesley, D., & Miller, M. R. (2006). Relational health, attachment, and psychological distress in college women and men. *Psychology of Women Quarterly, 30,* 303–311.

Fried, J. (1988). Women's ways of knowing: Some additional observations [Review of the book Women's ways of knowing: The development of self, voice, and mind]. *Journal of College Student Development, 29,* 84–85.

Fried, J., & Associates. (1995). *Shifting paradigms in student affairs: Culture, context, teaching, and learning.* Lanham, MD: American College Personnel Association.

Fried, J., & Associates. (2012). *Transformative learning through engagement: Student affairs practice as experiential pedagogy.* Sterling, VA: Stylus.

Friedman, A., & Schoen, L. (2009). Reflective practice interventions: Raising levels of reflective judgment. *Action in Teacher Education, 31*(2), 61–73.

Frye, M. (1990). The possibility of feminist theory. In D. L. Rhode (Ed.), *Theoretical perspectives on sexual difference* (pp. 174–184). New Haven, CT: Yale University Press.

Fukuyama, M. A., & Ferguson, A. D. (2000). Lesbian, gay, and bisexual people of color: Understanding cultural complexity and managing multiple oppressions. In R. P. Perez, K. A. DeBord, & K. Bieschke (Eds.), *Handbook of counseling and psychotherapy with lesbian, gay, and bisexual clients* (pp. 81–105). Washington, DC: American Psychological Association.

Fuller-Rowell, T. E., Ong, A. D., & Phinney, J. S. (2013). National identity and perceived discrimination predict changes in ethnic identity commitment: Evidence from a longitudinal study of Latino college students. *Applied Psychology: An International Review, 62,* 406–426.

Galambos, N. L., Almeida, D. M., & Petersen, A. C. (1990). Masculinity, femininity, and sex role attitudes in early adolescence: Exploring gender intensification. *Child Development, 61*, 1905–1914.

Gallegos, P. V., & Ferdman, B. M. (2012). Latina and Latino ethnoracial identity orientations: a dynamic and developmental perspective. In C. L. Wejeyesinghe & B. W. Jackson III (Ed.), *New perspectives on racial identity development: Integrating emerging frameworks* (2nd ed., pp. 51–80). New York: NYU Press.

Gamson, J. (2000). Sexualities, queer theory, and qualitative research. In N. K. Denzin & Y. S. Lincoln (Eds.), *Handbook of qualitative research* (2nd ed., pp. 347–365). Thousand Oaks, CA: Sage.

Gardenhire-Crooks, A., Collado, H., Martin, K., & Castro, A. (2010). *Terms of engagement: Men of color discuss their experiences in community college.* New York: MDRC.

Garland, P. H., & Grace, T. W. (1993). *New perspectives for student affairs professionals: Evolving realities, responsibilities, and roles.* ASHE-Eric Higher Education Report No. 7. Washington, DC: George Washington University School of Education and Human Development.

Garrett, M. T., & Pichette, E. F. (2000). Red as an apple: Native American acculturation and counseling with or without reservation. *Journal of Counseling and Development, 78*, 3–13.

Garriott, P. O., Flores, L. Y., & Martens, M. P. (2013). Predicting the math/science career goals of low-income prospective first-generation college students. *Journal of Counseling Psychology, 60*, 200–209.

Gasser, H. S. (2008). Being multiracial in a wired society: Using the internet to define identity and community on campus. In K. A. Renn & P. Shang (Eds.), *Biracial and multiracial college students.* New Directions for Student Services, no. 123, pp. 63–71. San Francisco: Jossey-Bass.

Gayles, J. G., & Ampaw, F. (2014). The impact of college experiences on degree completion in STEM fields at four-year institutions: Does gender matter? *The Journal of Higher Education, 85*, 439–468.

Gehrke, S. J. (2008). Leadership through meaning-making: An empirical exploration of spirituality and leadership in college students. *Journal of College Student Development, 49*(4), 351–359.

Gehrke, S. J. (2014). Dynamics of race and prosocial involvement experiences in developing an ecumenical worldview. *Journal of College Student Development, 55*(7), 675–692.

Gelwick, B. P. (1985). Cognitive development of women. In N. J. Evans (Ed.), *Facilitating the development of women.* New Directions for Student Services, no. 29, pp. 29–44. San Francisco: Jossey-Bass.

Genia, V. (1992). Transitional faith: A developmental step toward religious maturity. *Counseling and Values, 37*, 15–23.

Gibbs, J. T. (1987). Identity and marginality: Issues in the treatment of biracial adolescents. *American Journal of Orthopsychiatry, 57*, 265–278.

Gibson, J. (2006). Disability and clinical competency: An introduction. *The California Psychologist, 39*, 6–10.

Gilbert, S. C., So, D., Russell, T. M., & Wessel, T. R. (2006). Racial identity and psychological symptoms among African Americans attending a historically black university. *Journal of College Counseling, 9*, 111–122.

Gilley, D. V. (2005). Whose spirituality? Cautionary notes about the role of spirituality in higher education. In S. L. Hoppe & B. W. Speck (Eds.), *Spirituality in higher education.* New Directions for Teaching and Learning, no. 104, pp. 93–99. San Francisco: Jossey-Bass.

Gilligan, C. (1977). In a different voice: Women's conception of self and morality. *Harvard Educational Review, 47*, 481–517.

Gilligan, C. (1981). Moral development in the college years. In A. Chickering (Ed.), *The modern American college* (pp. 139–157). San Francisco: Jossey-Bass.

Gilligan, C. (1982). *In a different voice: Psychological theory and women's development*. Cambridge, MA: Harvard University Press.

Gilligan, C. (1986). Reply (to critics). *Signs: Journal of Women in Culture and Society, 11*, 324–333.

Gilligan, C. (1993). *In a different voice: Psychological theory and women's development*. Cambridge, MA: Harvard University Press. (Original work published 1982)

Gilligan, C. (2011). *Joining the resistance*. Cambridge, UK: Polity Press.

Gilligan, C. (2014). Moral injury and the ethic of care: Reframing the conversation about differences. *Journal of Social Philosophy, 45*, 89–106.

Gilligan, C. (2015). Introduction: The listening guide method of psychological inquiry. *Qualitative Psychology, 2*, 69–77.

Gilligan, C., & Belenky, M. F. (1980). A naturalistic study of abortion decisions. In R. Selman & R. Yando (Eds.), *Clinical-developmental psychology*. New Directions for Child Development, no. 7, pp. 69–90. San Francisco: Jossey-Bass.

Gilligan, C., & Murphy, J. M. (1979). Development from adolescence to adulthood: The philosopher and the "dilemma of the fact." In D. Kuhn (Ed.), *Intellectual development beyond childhood*. New Directions for Child Development, no. 5, pp. 85–99. San Francisco: Jossey-Bass.

Gilligan, C., & Richards, D.A.J. (2009). *The deepening darkness: Patriarchy, resistance, and democracy's future*. New York: Cambridge University Press.

Gold, S. P., & Stewart, D. L. (2011). Lesbian, gay, and bisexual students coming out at the intersection of spirituality and sexual identity. *Journal of LGBT Issues in Counseling, 5*, 237–258.

Goldberger, N. R. (1996a). Cultural imperatives and diversity in ways of knowing. In N. Goldberger, J. Tarule, B. Clinchy, & M. Belenky (Eds.), *Knowledge, difference, and power* (pp. 335–371). New York: Basic Books.

Goldberger, N. R. (1996b). Introduction: Looking backward, looking forward. In N. Goldberger, J. Tarule, B. Clinchy, & M. Belenky (Eds.), *Knowledge, difference, and power* (pp. 1–21). New York: Basic Books.

Gong, L. (2007). Ethnic identity and identification with the majority group: Relations with national identity and self-esteem. *International Journal of Intercultural Relations, 31*, 503–523.

Good, J. L., & Cartwright, C. (1998). Development of moral judgment among undergraduate university students. *College Student Journal, 32*, 270–277.

Goodman, J., Schlossberg, N. K., & Anderson, M. L. (2006). *Counseling adults in transition* (3rd ed.). New York: Springer.

Goodman, K. M., & Mueller, J. A. (2009). Invisible, marginalized and stigmatized: Understanding and addressing the needs of atheist students. In S. K. Watt, E. F. Fairchild, & K. M. Goodman (Eds.), *Intersections of religious privilege: Difficult dialogues and student affairs practice*. New Directions in Student Affairs, no. 125, pp. 55–63. San Francisco: Jossey-Bass.

Gordon, L. R. (2004). Race, biraciality, and mixed race—In theory. In L. Heldke & P. O'Connor (Eds.), *Oppression, privilege, & resistance: Theoretical perspectives on racism, sexism, and heterosexism* (pp. 422–439). New York: McGraw-Hill.

Gose, B. (1995, February 10). "Women's ways of knowing" form the basis of Ursuline curriculum. *Chronicle of Higher Education*, p. A25.

Grasmuck, S., Martin, J., & Zhao, S. (2009). Ethno-racial identity displays on Facebook. *Journal of Computer-Mediated Communication, 15*, 158–188.

Green, A. (2003). Learning to tell stories: Social class, narratives, and pedagogy. *Modern Language Studies, 33*(1/2), 80–89.

Green, E. R. (2006). Debating trans inclusion in the feminist movement: A trans-positive analysis. *Journal of Lesbian Studies, 10*, 231–248.

Greene, B. (2012). Intersections of multiple identities and multiple marginalizations: Clinical and paradigmatic considerations. In R. Nettles & R. Balter (Eds.), *Multiple minority identities: Applications for practice, research, and training* (pp. 81–91). New York: Springer.

Griffin, P., Peters, M. L., & Smith, R. M. (2007). Ableism curricular design. In M. Adams, L. A. Bell, & P. Griffin (Eds.), *Teaching for diversity and social justice* (2nd ed., pp. 335–358). New York: Routledge.

Griffin, W. (2007). Psychological first aid in the aftermath of crisis. In E. L. Zdziarski, II, N. W. Dunkel, & J. M. Rollo (Eds.), *Campus crisis management: A comprehensive guide to planning, prevention, response, and recovery* (pp. 145–182). San Francisco: Wiley.

Grosfoguel, R. (2004). Race and ethnicity or racialized ethnicities? Identities within global coloniality. *Ethnicities, 4*, 315–336.

Grossman, A. H., D'Augelli, A. R., & Frank, J. A. (2011). Aspects of psychological resilience among transgender youth. *Journal of LGBT Youth, 8*, 103–115.

Grove, N. P., & Bretz, S. L. (2010). Perry's scheme of intellectual and epistemological development as a framework for describing student difficulties in learning organic chemistry. *Chemistry Education Research and Practice, 11*, 207–211.

Guardia, J. R., & Evans, N. J. (2008). Factors influencing the ethnic identity development of Latino fraternity members at a Hispanic serving institution. *Journal of College Student Development, 49*, 163–181.

Guba, E. G. (1990). The alternative paradigm dialog. In E. G. Guba (Ed.), *The paradigm dialog* (pp. 17–30). Newbury Park, CA: Sage.

Guba, E. G., & Lincoln, Y. S. (1994). Competing paradigms in qualitative research. In N. K. Denzin & Y. S. Lincoln (Eds.), *Handbook of qualitative research* (pp. 105–117). Thousand Oaks, CA: Sage.

Guido, F. M., Chávez, A. F., & Lincoln, Y. S. (2010). Underlying paradigms in student affairs research and practice. *Journal of Student Affairs Research and Practice, 47*, 1–22.

Gump, L. S., Baker, R. C., & Roll, S. (2000). Cultural and gender differences in moral judgment: A study of Mexican Americans and Anglo-Americans. *Hispanic Journal of Behavioral Sciences, 22*, 78–93.

Gushue, G. V., & Witson, M. L. (2006). The relationship of ethnic identity and gender role attitudes to the development of career choice goals among Black and Latina girls. *Journal of Counseling Psychology, 53*, 379–385.

Hahn, H. (1991). Alternative views of empowerment: social services and civil rights. *The Journal of Rehabilitation, 57*(4), 17–19.

Hall, C.C.I. (1992). Please choose one: Ethnic identity choices for biracial individuals. In M.P.P. Root (Ed.), *Racially mixed people in America* (pp. 250–264). Newbury Park, CA: Sage.

Hall, C.C.I., & Cooke Turner, T. I. (2001). The diversity of biracial individuals: Asian-white and Asian-minority biracial identity. In T. Williams-León & C. L. Nakashima (Eds.), *The sum of our parts: Mixed-heritage Asian Americans* (pp. 81–91). Philadelphia: Temple University Press.

Hall, R. M., & Sandler, B. R. (1982). *The classroom climate: A chilly one for women?* Project on the Status and Education of Women. Washington, DC: Association of American Colleges.

Hall, S. (1995). Negotiating Caribbean identities. *New Left Review, 209*, 2–14.

Hamilton, L. (2007). Trading on heterosexuality: College women's gender strategies and homophobia. *Gender & Society, 21*, 145–172.

Hamrick, F. A., Evans, N. J., & Schuh, J. H. (2002). *Foundations of student affairs practice: How philosophy, theory, and research strengthen educational outcomes*. San Francisco: Jossey-Bass.

Handler, L. (1995). In the fraternal sisterhood: Sororities as gender strategy. *Gender & Society, 9,* 236–255.

Hanna, F. J., Talley, W. B., & Guindon, M. H. (2000). The power of perception: Toward a model of cultural oppression and liberation. *Journal of Counseling and Development, 78,* 430–441.

Harackiewicz, J. M., Canning, E. A., Tibbetts, Y., Giffen, C. J., & Hyde, J. S. (2014). Closing the social class achievement gap for first generation students in undergraduate biology. *Journal of Educational Psychology, 106,* 375–389.

Hardiman, R. (2001). Reflections on White identity development theory. In C. L. Wijeyesinghe & B. W. Jackson III (Eds.), *New perspectives on racial identity development: A theoretical and practical anthology* (pp. 108–128). New York: New York University Press.

Hardiman, R., & Jackson, B. W. (1992). Racial identity development: Understanding racial dynamics in college classrooms and on college campuses. In M. Adams (Ed.), *Promoting diversity in college classrooms: Innovative responses for the curriculum, faculty, and institutions.* New Directions for Teaching and Learning, no. 52, pp. 21–37. San Francisco: Jossey-Bass.

Hardiman, R., & Keehn, M. (2012). White identity development revisited: Listening to white students. In C. L. Wejeyesinghe & B. W. Jackson III (Eds.), *New perspectives on racial identity development: Integrating emerging frameworks* (2nd ed., pp. 121–137). New York: NYU Press.

Harley, D. A., Nowak, T. M., Gassaway, L. J., & Savage, T. (2002). Lesbian, gay, bisexual, and transgender college students with disabilities: A look at multiple cultural minorities. *Psychology in the Schools, 39,* 525–538.

Harper, S. R. (2009). Niggers no more: A critical race counternarrative on Black male student achievement at predominantly white colleges and universities. *International Journal of Qualitative Studies in Education, 22,* 697–712.

Harper, S. R., Harris, F., III, & Mmeje, K. A. (2005). A theoretical model to explain the over-representation of college men among campus judicial offenders: Implications for campus administrators. *NASPA Journal, 42,* 565–588.

Harper, S. R., Patton, L. D., & Wooden, O. S. (2009). Access and equity for African American students in higher education: A critical race historical analysis of policy efforts. *Journal of Higher Education, 80*(4), 389–414.

Harper, S. R., & Quaye, S. J. (Eds.) (2009). *Student engagement in higher education.* New York and London: Routledge.

Harris, D. R., & Sim, J. J. (2002). Who is multiracial? Assessing the complexity of lived race. *American Sociological Review, 67,* 614–627.

Harris, F., III, & Harper, S. R. (2008). Masculinities go to community college: Understanding male identity socialization and gender role conflict. In J. Lester (Ed.), *Gendered perspectives on community colleges.* New Directions for Community Colleges, no. 142, pp. 25–35. San Francisco: Jossey-Bass.

Harris, F., III, & Harper, S. R. (2014). Beyond bad behaving brothers: Productive performances of masculinities among college fraternity men. *International Journal of Qualitative Studies in Education, 27,* 703–723.

Harris, J. C. (2015). "Intrinsically interesting": The racialized experiences of multiracial women students at a predominantly White institution. Doctoral dissertation. Bloomington, IN: Indiana University

Harris, L. L. (2003). Integrating and analyzing psychosocial stage theories to challenge the development of the injured collegiate athlete. *Journal of Athletic Training, 38,* 75–82.

Harris, M. (1986). Completion and faith development. In C. Dykstra & S. Parks (Eds.), *Faith development and Fowler* (pp. 115–133). Birmingham, AL: Religious Education Press.

Harrison, L., Sailes, G., Rotich, W. K., & Bimper, A. Y. (2011). Living the dream or awakening from the nightmare: Race and athletic identity. *Race Ethnicity and Education, 14*(1), 91–103.

Hartley, H. V., III. (2004). How college affects students' religious faith and practice: A review of research. *College Student Affairs Journal, 23,* 111–129.

Harvey, J. (2000). Social privilege and moral subordination. *Journal of Social Philosophy, 31,* 177–188.

Harvey, L. J., Hunt, D. E., & Schroder, H. M. (1961). *Conceptual systems and personality organization.* New York: Wiley.

Haynes, C. (2006). The integrated student: Fostering holistic development to advance learning. *About Campus, 10*(6), 17–23.

Heath, D. (1968). *Growing up in college.* San Francisco: Jossey-Bass.

Heath, R. (1964). *The reasonable adventurer.* Pittsburgh, PA: University of Pittsburgh Press.

Helms, J. E. (1990). *Black and white racial identity: Theory, research, and practice.* Westport, CT: Greenwood Press.

Helms, J. E. (1992). *A race is a nice thing to have: A guide to being a white person or understanding the white persons in your life.* Topeka, KS: Content Communications.

Helms, J. E. (Ed.). (1993a). *Black and white racial identity: Theory, research and practice.* Westport, CT: Praeger.

Helms, J. E. (1993b). Introduction: Review of racial identity terminology. In J. E. Helms (Ed.), *Black and white identity: Theory, research, and practice* (pp. 3–8). Westport, CT: Praeger.

Helms, J. E. (1995). An update of Helms's white and people of color racial identity models. In J. G. Ponterotto, J. M. Casas, L. A. Suzuki, & C. M. Alexander (Eds.), *Handbook of multicultural counseling* (pp. 181–198). Thousand Oaks, CA: Sage.

Helms, J. E., & Carter, R. T. (1990). Development of the white racial identity inventory. In J. E. Helms (Ed.), *Black and white racial identity: Theory, research, and practice* (pp. 67–80). Westport, CT: Greenwood Press.

Henry, W. J., West, N. M., & Jackson, A. (2010). Hip-hop's influence on the identity development of Black female college students: A literature review. *Journal of College Student Development, 51,* 237–251.

Herring, R. D. (1990). Understanding Native-American values: Process and content concerns for counselors. *Counseling & Values, 34,* 134–138.

Herring, R. D. (1994). The clown or contrary figure as a counseling intervention strategy with Native American Indian clients. *Journal of Multicultural Counseling and Development, 22,* 153–164.

Herzig, A. H. (2004). Becoming mathematicians: Women and students of color choosing and leaving doctoral mathematics. *Review of Educational Research, 74,* 171–214.

Heubner, A. M., & Garrod, A. C. (1993). Moral reasoning among Tibetan monks: A study of Buddhist adolescents and young adults in Nepal. *Journal of Cross-Cultural Psychology, 24,* 167–185.

Hickling-Hudson, A. (1998). When Marxist and postmodern theories won't do: The potential of postcolonial theory for educational analysis. *Discourse: Studies in the Cultural Politics of Education, 19,* 327–339.

Hiebert, D. W. (1992). The sociology of Fowler's faith development theory. *Studies in Religion, 21,* 321–335.

Higbee, J. L. (2002). The application of Chickering's theory of student development to student success in the sixties and beyond. *Research and Teaching in Developmental Education, 18*(2), 24–26.

Higher Education Research Institute. (2004). *The spiritual life of college students: A national study of college students' search for meaning and purpose.* Retrieved January 3, 2007, from the University of California, Los Angeles, Spirituality in Higher Education Web site: http://www.spirituality .ucla.edu/spirituality/reports/

Hirt, J. B. (2006). *Where you work matters: Student affairs administration at different types of institutions.* Lanham, MD: American College Personnel Association (ACPA) and University Press of America.

Hirt, J. B., Amelink, C. T., McFeeters, B. B., & Strayhorn, T. L. (2008). A system of othermothering: Student affairs administrators' perceptions of relationships with students at historically black colleges. *Journal of Student Affairs Research and Practice, 45,* 382–408.

Hofer, B. F. (2008). Personal epistemology and culture. In M. S. Khine (Ed.), *Knowing, knowledge and beliefs: Epistemological studies across diverse cultures* (pp. 3–22). New York: Springer.

Hofer, B. K., & Pintrich, P. R. (1997). The development of epistemological theories: Beliefs about knowledge and knowing and their relationship to learning. *Review of Educational Research, 67,* 88–140.

Hoffman, J., & Peña, E. V. (2013). Too Korean to be White and too White to be Korean: Ethnic identity development among transracial Korean American adoptees. *Journal of Student Affairs Research and Practice, 50*(2), 152–170.

Hoffman, J. L., Iverson, S.V.D., Allan, E. J., & Ropers-Huilman, R. (2010). Title IX policy and intercollegiate athletics: A feminist poststructural critique. In E. J. Allen, S.V.D. Iverson, & R. Ropers-Huilman (Eds.), *Restructuring policy in higher education: Feminist poststructural perspectives* (pp. 111–128). New York: Routledge.

Hoffman, R. M. (2004). Conceptualizing heterosexual identity development: Issues and challenges. *Journal of Counseling and Development, 82,* 375–380.

Holland, D. C., & Eisenhart, M. A. (1990). *Educated in romance: Women, achievement, and college culture.* Chicago: University of Chicago Press.

Holland, J. L. (1966). *The psychology of vocational choice: A theory of personality types and model environments.* Waltham, MA: Blaisdell.

Holland, J. L. (1973). *Making vocational choices: A theory of careers.* Englewood Cliffs, NJ: Prentice Hall.

Holland, J. L. (1997). *Making vocational choices: A theory of vocational personalities and work environments* (3rd ed.). Odessa, FL: Psychological Assessment Research.

hooks, b. (1981). *Ain't I a woman: Black women and feminism.* Boston, MA: South End Press.

hooks, b. (1989). *Talking back: Thinking feminist, thinking black.* Boston: South End Press.

Hoppe, S. L., & Speck, B. W. (Eds.). (2005). *Spirituality in higher education.* New Directions for Teaching and Learning, no. 104. San Francisco: Jossey-Bass.

Hornak, A. M., & Ortiz, A. M. (2004). Creating a context to promote diversity education and self—authorship among community college students. In M. Baxter Magolda & P. M. King (Eds.), *Learning partnerships: Theory and modes of practice to educate for self—authorship* (pp. 91–123). Sterling, VA: Stylus.

Horowitz, H. L. (1987). *Campus life: Undergraduate cultures from the end of the eighteenth century to the present.* New York: Knopf.

Horse, P. G. (2001). Reflections on American Indian identity. In C. L. Wijeyesinghe & B. W. Jackson, III (Eds.), *New perspectives on racial identity development: A theoretical and practical anthology* (pp. 91–107). New York: New York University Press.

Horse, P. G. (2012). Twenty first century Native American consciousness: A thematic model of Indian identity. In C. L. Wejeyesinghe & B. W. Jackson III (Ed.), *New perspectives on racial identity development: Integrating emerging frameworks* (2nd ed., pp. 108–120). New York: NYU Press.

Howell, L. C., & Beth, A. (2002). Midlife myths and realities: Women reflect on their experiences. *Journal of Women and Aging, 14* (3/4), 189–204.

Howson, C. B. K. (2015). Feedback to and from students. In H. Fry, S. Ketteridge, & S. Marshall (Eds.), *A handbook for teaching and learning in higher education: Enhancing academic practice* (4th ed., pp. 123–138). New York: Routledge.

Hsu, J., Wang, Z., & Hamilton, K. (2011). Developing and managing digital/technology literacy and effective learning skills in adult learners. *International Journal of Digital Literacy and Digital Competence (IJDLDC), 2*(1), 52–70.

Hughes, J. A., & Graham, S. W. (1990). Adult life roles: A new approach to adult development. *The Journal of Continuing Higher Education, 38*(2), 2–8.

Humes, K. R., Jones, N. A., & Ramirez, R. R. (2011). *Overview of race and Hispanic origin: 2010* (C2010BR-02).

Hunt, S., & Rentz, A. L. (1994). Greek-letter social group members' involvement and psychosocial development. *Journal of College Student Development, 35*, 289–295.

Hurst, A. L. (2007). Telling tales of oppression and dysfunction: Narratives of class identity reformation. *Qualitative Sociology Review, 3*, 82–104.

Hurtado, S., Alvarez, C. L., Guillermo-Wann, C., Cuellar, M., & Arellano, L. (2012). A model for diverse learning environments. In J. C. Smart & M. B. Paulsen (Eds.), *Higher education: Handbook of theory and research* (pp. 41–122). Springer Netherlands.

Hurtado, S., Dey, E. L., Gurin, P. Y., & Gurin, G. (2003). College environments, diversity, and student learning. In J. C. Smart (Ed.), *Higher education: Handbook of theory and research, Volume XVIII* (pp. 145–189). Dordrecht, Netherlands: Springer.

Hurtado, S., Mayhew, M. J., & Engberg, M. E. (2012). Diversity courses and students' moral reasoning: a model of predispositions and change. *Journal of Moral Education, 41*, 201–224.

Hurtado, S., Sax, L. J., Saenz, V., Harper, C. E., Oseguera, L., Curley, J., … Arellano, L. (2007). *Findings from the 2005 administration of Your First College Year*. Los Angeles: Higher Education Research Institute.

Ignelzi, M. (2000). Meaning-making in the learning and teaching process. In M. B. Baxter Magolda (Ed.), *Teaching to promote intellectual and personal maturity: Incorporating students' worldviews and identities into the learning process*. New Directions for Teaching and Learning, no. 82, pp. 5–14. San Francisco: Jossey-Bass.

Inman, A. G., & Alvarez, A. N. (2014). Individuals and families of Asian descent. In D. G. Hays & B. T. Erford (Eds.), *Developing mulitcultural counseling competence: A systems approach* (2nd ed., pp. 278–312). Boston: Erford.

Isajiw, W. W. (1990). Ethnic-identity retention. In R. Breton, W. W. Isajiw, W. E. Kalbach, & J. G. Reitz (Eds.), *Ethnic identity and equality* (pp. 34–91). Toronto: University of Toronto Press.

Israel, T. (2012). Society of Counseling Psychology presidential address: Exploring privilege in counseling psychology: Shifting the lens. *The Counseling Psychologist, 40*, 158–180.

Iwasa, N. (1992). Postconventional reasoning and moral education in Japan. *Journal of Moral Education, 21*, 2–16.

Jackson, A. P., Smith, S. A., & Hill, C. L. (2003). Academic persistence among Native American college students. *Journal of College Student Development, 44*, 548–565.

Jackson, B. W. (1976). Black identity development. In L. H. Golubchick & B. Persky (Eds.), *Urban social and educational issues* (pp. 158–164). Dubuque, IA: Kendall Hunt.

Jackson, B. W., III. (2001). Black identity development: Further analysis and elaboration. In C. L. Wijeyesinghe & B. W. Jackson III (Eds.), *New perspectives on racial identity development: A theoretical and practical anthology* (pp. 8–31). New York: New York University Press.

Jackson, B. W., III. (2012). Black identity development: Influences of culture and social oppression. In C. L. Wijeyesinghe & B. W. Jackson, III (Eds.). *New perspectives on racial identity development: A theoretical and practical anthology* (pp. 33–80). New York: New York University Press.

Jackson, R. L., II. (1999). White space, white privilege: Mapping discursive inquiry into the self. *Quarterly Journal of Speech, 85,* 38–54.

Jacoby, T. (Ed.). (2004). *Reinventing the melting pot: The new immigrants and what it means to be American.* New York: Basic Books.

Jaffee, S., & Hyde, J. S. (2000). Gender differences in moral orientation: A meta-analysis. *Psychological Bulletin, 126,* 703–726.

Jagose, A. (1997). *Queer theory: An introduction.* New York: New York University Press.

Jefferson, S. D., & Caldwell, R. (2002). An exploration of the relationship between racial identity attitudes and the perception of racial bias. *Journal of Black Psychology, 28,* 174–192.

Jehangir, R., Williams, R., & Pete, J. (2011). Multicultural learning communities: Vehicles for developing self-authorship in first-generation college students. *Journal of The First-Year Experience & Students in Transition, 23,* 53–73.

Jenkins, R. (2004). *Social identity* (2nd ed.). London: Routledge.

Jessup-Anger, J. E. (2012). Examining how residential college environments inspire the life of the mind. *The Review of Higher Education, 35,* 431–462.

John, G., & Stage, F. K. (2013), Minority-serving institutions and the education of U.S. underrepresented students. In F. K. Stage & R. S. Wells (Eds.), *New scholarship in critical quantitative research–Part 1, Studying institutions and people in context.* New Directions for Institutional Research, no. 158, pp. 65–76. San Francisco: Jossey-Bass.

Johnson, A. G. (2006). *Privilege, Power, and Difference* (2nd ed.). Boston: McGraw-Hill.

Johnston, M. P. (2014). The concept of race on campus: Exploring the nature of college students' racial conceptions. *Journal of College Student Development, 55*(3), 225–242.

Johnstone, C. (2004). Disability and identity: Personal constructions and formalized supports. *Disability Studies Quarterly, 24*(4). Retrieved from http://dsq-sds.org/article/view/880/1055

Jones, C. E., & Watt, J. D. (1999). Psychosocial development and moral orientation among traditional-aged college students. *Journal of College Student Development, 40,* 125–131.

Jones, C. E., & Watt, J. D. (2001). Moral orientation and psychosocial development: Gender and class standing differences. *NASPA Journal, 39,* 1–13.

Jones, H. J., & Newman, I. (1993, April). *A mosaic of diversity: Vocationally undecided students and the Perry scheme of intellectual and ethical development.* Paper presented at the annual meeting of the American Educational Research Association, Atlanta. (ERIC Document Reproduction Service No. ED 360 488)

Jones, K. C. (2013). Understanding student veterans in transition. *The Qualitative Report, 18*(74), 1–14.

Jones, N. A., & Smith, A. S. (2003). A statistical portrait of children of two or more races in Census 2000. In M.P.P. Root & M. Kelley (Eds.), *Multiracial child resource book: Living complex identities* (pp. 3–10). Seattle: MAVIN Foundation.

Jones, R. M., Vaterlaus, J. M., Jackson, M. A., & Morrill, T. B. (2014). Friendship characteristics, psychosocial development, and adolescent identity formation. *Personal Relationships, 21*(1), 51–67.

Jones, S. R. (1995). *Voices of identity and difference: A qualitative exploration of the multiple dimensions of identity development in women college students.* Unpublished doctoral dissertation, University of Maryland.

Jones, S. R. (1996). Toward inclusive theory: Disability as social construction. *NASPA Journal, 33*, 347–354.

Jones, S. R. (1997). Voices of identity and difference: A qualitative exploration of the multiple dimensions of identity development in women college students. *Journal of College Student Development, 38*, 376–386.

Jones, S. R. (2008). Student resistance to cross-cultural engagement: Annoying distraction or site for transformative learning? In S. R. Harper (Ed.), *Creating inclusive campus environments for cross-cultural learning and student engagement* (pp. 67–85). Washington, DC: NASPA.

Jones, S. R. (2009). Constructing identities at the intersections: An autoethnographic exploration of multiple dimensions of identity. *Journal of College Student Development, 50*, 287–304.

Jones, S. R., & Abes, E. S. (2011). The nature and uses of theory. In J. H. Schuh, S. R. Jones, & S. R. Harper (Eds.), Student services: A handbook for the profession (5th ed., pp. 149–167). San Francisco: Jossey-Bass.

Jones, S. R., & Abes, E. S. (2013). *Identity development of college students: Advancing multiple frameworks for multiple dimensions of identity*. San Francisco: Jossey-Bass.

Jones, S. R., & Abes, E. S. (with Quaye, S. J.). (2013). Critical race theory. In S. R. Jones & E. S. Abes (Eds.), *Identity development of college students: Advancing frameworks for multiple dimensions of identity* (pp. 160–190). San Francisco: Jossey-Bass.

Jones, S. R., Kim, Y. C., & Skendall, K. C. (2012). (Re-)Framing authenticity: Considering multiple social identities using autoethnographic and intersectional approaches. *The Journal of Higher Education, 83*, 698–724.

Jones, S. R., & McEwen, M. K. (2000). A conceptual model of multiple dimensions of identity. *Journal of College Student Development, 41*, 405–413.

Jones, S. R., Rowan-Kenyon, H. T., Ireland, S. M. Y., Niehaus, E., & Skendall, K. C. (2012). The meaning students make as participants in short-term immersion programs. *Journal of College Student Development, 53*, 201–220.

Jones, S. R., Torres, V., & Arminio, J. (2006). *Negotiating the complexities of qualitative research in higher education: Fundamental elements and issues*. New York: Routledge.

Jones, S. R., Torres, V., & Arminio, J. (2014). *Negotiating the complexities of qualitative research in higher education: Fundamental elements and issues, 2nd. ed*. New York: Routledge.

Jones, V. A. (2014). Centrality and circumstance: Influences of multidimensional racial identity on African American student organization involvement. *Journal of Critical Thought and Praxis, 3*(2), article 2. Available at: http://lib.dr.iastate.edu/jctp/vol3/iss2/2

Joppke, C. (1986). The cultural dimensions of class formation and class struggle: ON the social theory of Pierre Bourdieu. *Berkeley Journal of Sociology, 31*, 53–78.

Josselson, R. E. (1973). Psychodynamic aspects of identity formation in college women. *Journal of Youth and Adolescence, 2*(1), 3–52.

Josselson, R. E. (1982). Personality structure and identity status in women as viewed through early memories. *Journal of Youth and Adolescence, 11*, 293–299.

Josselson, R. E. (1987a). *Finding herself: Pathways to identity development in women*. San Francisco: Jossey-Bass.

Josselson, R. E. (1987b). Identity diffusion: A long term follow-up. *Adolescent Psychology, 14*, 230–258.

Josselson, R. E. (1991). *Finding herself: Pathways to identity development in women*. San Francisco: Jossey-Bass. (Original work published 1978)

Josselson, R. (1996). *Revising herself: The story of women's identity from college to midlife*. New York: Oxford University Press.

Jung, C. G. (1971). *Psychological types* (R. F. C. Hull, Ed.; H. G. Baynes, Trans.). Volume 6 of *The collected works of C. G. Jung.* Princeton, NJ: Princeton University Press. (Original work published 1923)

Kahn, R. L., & Antonucci, T. C. (1980). Convoys over the life course: Attachment, roles, and social support. In P. B. Baltes & C. O. Brim (Eds.), *Life-span development and behavior* (pp. 383–405). New York: Academic Press.

Kana'iaupuni, S. M., & Malone, N. (2006). This land is my land: The role of place in Native Hawaiian identity. In J. W. Frazier & E. Tettey-Fio (Eds.), *Race, ethnicity and place in a changing America* (pp. 291–305). Binghamton, NY: Global Academic Publishing.

Kandal, T. R. (1996). Gender, race, & ethnicity: Let's not forget about class. *Race, Gender, Class, 4*, 143–165.

Kaplan, K. (2005). *The definition of disability.* The Center for an Accessible Society. Retrieved from http://www.accessiblesociety.org/topics/demographics-identity/d kaplanpaper.htm.

Kaufman, P., & Feldman, K. A. (2004). Forming identities in college: A sociological approach. *Research in Higher Education, 45*, 463–496.

Kawaguchi, S. (2003). Ethnic identity development and collegiate experience of Asian Pacific American students: Implications for practice. *NASPA Journal, 40*(3), 13–29.

Keefe, S. E., & Padilla, A. M. (1987). *Chicano ethnicity.* Albuquerque: University of New Mexico Press.

Keeling, R. P. (Ed.). (2004). *Learning reconsidered: A campus-wide focus on the student experience.* Washington, DC: American College Personnel Association and National Association of Student Personnel Administrators.

Kegan, R. (1982). *The evolving self.* Cambridge, MA: Harvard University Press.

Kegan, R. (1994). *In over our heads: The mental demands of modern life.* Cambridge, MA: Harvard University Press.

Kegan, R. (2000). What "form" transforms? A constructive-developmental approach to transformative learning. In J. Mezirow (Ed.), *Learning as transformation* (pp. 35–69). San Francisco: Jossey-Bass.

Kegan, R., Broderick, M., Drago-Severson, E., Helsing, D., Popp, N., & Portnow, K. (2001). *Toward a new pluralism in ABE/ESOL classrooms: Teaching to multiple "cultures of mind."* Cambridge, MA: Harvard Center for the Study of Adult Learning and Literacy, Harvard University Graduate School of Education.

Kerlinger, F. (1964). *Foundations of behavioral research.* New York: Holt.

Kernberg, O. (1966). Structural derivatives of object relationships. *International Journal of Psychoanalysis, 47*, 236–253.

Kerwin, C., & Ponterotto, J. G. (1995). Biracial identity development: Theory and research. In J. G. Ponterotto, J. M. Casas, L. A. Suzuki, & C. M. Alexander (Eds.), *Handbook of multicultural counseling* (pp. 199–217). Thousand Oaks, CA: Sage.

Kerwin, C., Ponterotto, J. G., Jackson, B. L., & Harris, A. (1993). Racial identity in biracial children: A qualitative investigation. *Journal of Counseling Psychology, 40*, 221–231.

Kich, G. K. (1992). The developmental process of asserting a biracial, bicultural identity. In M.P.P. Root (Ed.), *Racially mixed people in America* (pp. 304–317). Newbury Park, CA: Sage.

Kilgannon, S. M., & Irwin, T. D. (1992). A longitudinal study about the identity and moral development of Greek students. *Journal of College Student Development, 33*, 253–259.

Kilson, M. (2001). *Claiming place: Biracial young adults of the post-civil rights era.* Westport, CT: Bergin & Garvey.

Kim, J. (1981). *The process of Asian-American identity development: A study of Japanese American women's perceptions of their struggle to achieve positive identities*. Unpublished doctoral dissertation, University of Massachusetts, Amherst.

Kim, J. (2001). Asian American identity development theory. In C. L. Wijeyesinghe & B. W. Jackson, III (Eds.), *New perspectives on racial identity development: A theoretical and practical anthology* (pp. 67–90). New York: New York University Press.

Kim, J. (2012). Asian American racial identity development theory. In C. L. Wijeyesignhe & B. W. Jackson, III (Eds.), *New perspectives on racial identity development: Integrating emerging frameworks* (2nd ed., pp. 138–160). New York: New York University Press.

Kimball, E. M., Mannes, M., & Hackel, A. (2009). Voices of global youth on spirituality and spiritual development: Preliminary findings from a grounded theory study. In M. de Souza, L. J. Francis, J. O'Higgins- Norman, & D. Scott (Eds.), *International handbook of education for spirituality, care, and wellbeing* (pp. 329–348). Dordrecht: Springer.

Kimmel, M. (1994). Masculinity as homophobia: Fear, shame and silence in the construction of gender identity. In H. Brod & M. Kaufman (Eds.), *Theorizing masculinities* (pp. 119–141). Newbury Park, CA: Sage.

Kimmel, M. S. (2003). Introduction: Toward pedagogy of the oppressor. In M. S. Kimmel & A. L Ferber (Eds.), *Privilege: A reader* (pp. 1–10). Cambridge, MA: Westview Press.

Kimmel, M. (2008). *Guyland: The perilous world where boys become men*. New York: Harper Collins.

Kimmel, M. (2010). Guyland: Gendering the transition to adulthood. *Men's Lives, 119–31*.

Kimmel, M., & Davis, T. (2011). Mapping Guyland in college. In J. A. Laker & T. Davis (Eds.), *Masculinities in higher education: Theoretical and practical considerations* (pp. 3–15). New York: Routledge.

Kincheloe, J. L., & McLaren, P. (2005). Rethinking critical theory and qualitative research. In N. K. Denzin & Y. S. Lincoln (Eds.), *The Sage handbook of qualitative research* (pp. 303–342). Thousand Oaks, CA: Sage.

King, A. R. (2008a). Student perspectives on multiracial identity. In K. A. Renn & P. Shang (Eds.), *Biracial and multiracial students*. New Directions for Student Services, no. 123, pp. 33–41. San Francisco: Jossey-Bass.

King, A. R. (2008b). *Uncertainty and evolution: Contributions to identity development for female college students who identify as multiracial/biracial-bisexual/pansexual*. Unpublished doctoral dissertation, Iowa State University.

King, P. M. (1978). William Perry's theory of intellectual and ethical development. In L. L. Knefelkamp, C. Widick, & C. A. Parker (Eds.), *Applying new developmental findings*. New Directions for Student Services, no. 4, pp. 35–51. San Francisco: Jossey-Bass.

King, P. M. (1990). Assessing development from a cognitive developmental perspective. In D. G. Creamer (Ed.), *College student development: Theory and practice for the 1990s* (pp. 81–98). Alexandria, VA: American College Personnel Association.

King, P. M. (2009). Principles of development and developmental change underlying theories of cognitive and moral development. *Journal of College Student Development, 50*, 597–620.

King, P. M., & Baxter Magolda, M. B. (2004). Creating learning partnerships in higher education. In M. Baxter Magolda & P. M. King (Eds.), *Learning partnerships: Theory and modes of practice to educate for self-authorship* (pp. 303–332). Sterling, VA: Stylus.

King, P. M., & Baxter Magolda, M. B. (2005). A developmental model of intercultural maturity. *Journal of College Student Development, 46*, 571–592.

King, P. M., Baxter Magolda, M. B., Barber, J. P., Brown, M. K., & Lindsay, N. K. (2009). Developmentally effective experiences for promoting self-authorship. *Mind, Brain, and Education, 3*(2), 108–118.

King, P. M., & Kitchener, K. S. (1994). *Developing reflective judgment: Understanding and promoting intellectual growth and critical thinking in adolescents and adults.* San Francisco: Jossey-Bass.

King, P. M., & Kitchener, K. S. (2002). The reflective judgment model: Twenty years of research on epistemic cognition. In B. K Hofer & P. R. Pintrich (Eds.), *Personal epistemology: The psychology of beliefs about knowledge and knowing* (pp. 37–61). Mahwah, NJ: Erlbaum.

King, P. M., & Mayhew, M. J. (2002). Moral judgment development in higher education: Insights from the defining issues test. *Journal of Moral Education, 31,* 247–270.

King, P. M., & Mayhew, M. J. (2005). Theory and research on the development of moral reasoning among college students. In J. C. Smart (Ed.), *Higher education: Handbook of theory and research, Vol. XIX* (pp. 375–440). Netherlands: Springer.

King, P. M., Perez, R. J., & Shim, W. J. (2013). How college students experience intercultural learning: Key features and approaches. *Journal of Diversity in Higher Education, 6*(2), 69–83.

King, P. M., & Shuford, B. C. (1996). A multicultural view is a more cognitively complex view: Cognitive development and multicultural education. *American Behavioral Scientist, 40,* 153–164.

Kitchener, K. S., & King, P. M. (1981). Reflective judgment: Concepts of justification and their relationship to age and education. *Journal of Applied Developmental Psychology, 2,* 89–116.

Kitchener, K. S., & King, P. M. (1990). The reflective judgment model: Ten years of research. In M. L. Commons et al. (Eds.), *Adult development: Vol. II. Models and methods in the study of adolescent and adult thought* (pp. 63–78). New York: Praeger.

Knefelkamp, L. L. (1974). *Developmental instruction: Fostering intellectual and personal growth in college students.* Unpublished doctoral dissertation, University of Minnesota, Minneapolis.

Knefelkamp, L. L. (1978). *A reader's guide to student development theory: A framework for understanding, a framework for design.* Unpublished manuscript.

Knefelkamp, L. L. (1999). Introduction. In W. G. Perry, Jr., *Forms of ethical and intellectual development in the college years: A scheme* (pp. xi–xxxvii). San Francisco: Jossey-Bass.

Knefelkamp, L. L., & Cornfeld, J. L. (1979, March). *Combining student stage and style in the design of learning environments.* Paper presented at the annual meeting of the American College Personnel Association, Los Angeles.

Knefelkamp, L. L., Widick, C., & Parker, C. A. (1978). Editors' notes: Why bother with theory? In L. L. Knefelkamp, C. Widick, & C. A. Parker (Eds.), *Applying new developmental findings.* New Directions for Student Services, no. 4, pp. vii–xvi. San Francisco: Jossey-Bass.

Knefelkamp, L. L., Widick, C., & Stroad, B. (1976). Cognitive-developmental theory: A guide to counseling women. *Counseling Psychologist, 6*(2), 15–19.

Knight, M. (2002). The intersections of race, class and gender in the teacher preparation of an African American social justice educator. *Equity and Excellence in Education, 35,* 212–224.

Kodama, C. M., McEwen, M. K., Liang, C., & Lee, S. (2001). A theoretical examination of psychosocial issues for Asian Pacific American students. *NASPA Journal, 38,* 411–437.

Kodama, C. M., McEwen, M. K., Liang, C.T.H., & Lee, S. (2002). An Asian American perspective on psychosocial student development theory. In M. K. McEwen, C. M. Kodama, A. Alvarez, S. Lee, & C.T.H. Liang (Eds.), *Working with Asian American college students.* New Directions for Student Services, no. 97, pp. 45–59. San Francisco, Jossey-Bass.

Koenig, H. G., McCullough, M. E., & Larson, D. B. (2001). *Handbook of religion and health.* New York: Oxford University Press.

Kohlberg, L. (1958). *The development of modes of moral thinking and choice in the years ten to sixteen.* Unpublished doctoral dissertation, University of Chicago.

Kohlberg, L. (1966). A cognitive-developmental analysis of children's sex-role concepts and attitudes. In E. E. Maccoby (Ed.), *The development of sex differences* (pp. 82–173). Stanford, CA: Stanford University Press.

Kohlberg, L. (1969). Stage and sequence: The cognitive developmental approach to socialization. In D. A. Goslin (Ed.), *Handbook of socialization theory and research* (pp. 347–480). Chicago: Rand McNally.

Kohlberg, L. (1975). The cognitive-developmental approach to moral education. *Phi Delta Kappan, 56,* 670–677.

Kohlberg, L. (1976). Moral stages and moralization: The cognitive-developmental approach. In T. Lickona (Ed.), *Moral development and behavior: Theory, research, and social issues* (pp. 31–53). New York: Holt, Rinehart, & Winston.

Kohlberg, L. (1979). Foreword. In J. R. Rest, *Development in judging moral issues* (pp. vii–xvi). Minneapolis: University of Minnesota Press.

Kohlberg, L. (1981). *Essays on moral development: Vol. I. The philosophy of moral development.* San Francisco: Harper & Row.

Kohlberg, L. (1984). *Essays on moral development: Vol. II. Psychology of moral development.* San Francisco: Harper & Row.

Kohlberg, L., & Hersh, R. H. (1977). Moral development: A review of the theory. *Theory into Practice, 16,* 53–59.

Kohlberg, L., Levine, C., & Hewer, A. (1984). The current formulation of the theory. In L. Kohlberg (Ed.), *Essays on moral development: Vol. II. Psychology of moral development* (pp. 212–319). San Francisco: Harper and Row.

Konik, J., & Stewart, A. (2004). Sexual identity development in the context of compulsory heterosexuality. *Journal of Personality, 72,* 815–844.

Korgen, K. O. (1998). *From black to biracial: Transforming racial identity among Americans.* Westport, CT: Praeger.

Kosciw, J. G., Greytak, E. A., Palmer, N. A., & Boesen, M. J. (2014). *The 2013 National School Climate Survey: The experiences of lesbian, gay, bisexual and transgender youth in our nation's schools.* New York: GLSEN.

Krivoski, J. F., & Nicholson, R. M. (1989). An interview with Arthur Chickering. *Journal of College and University Student Housing, 19*(2), 6–11.

Kroger, J. (1985). Separation-individuation and ego identity status in New Zealand university students. *Journal of Youth and Adolescence, 14,* 133–147.

Kroger, J., & Marcia, J. E. (2011). The identity statuses: Origins, meanings, and interpretations. In S. J. Schwartz, K. Luyckx, & V. L Vignoles (Eds.). *Handbook of identity theory and research* (pp. 31–54). New York: Springer.

Krolokke, C., & Sorensen, A. S. (2005). *Gender communication theories and analysis: From silence to performance.* Thousand Oaks, CA: Sage.

Kübler-Ross, E., & Kessler, D. (2005). *On grief and grieving: Finding the meaning of grief through the five stages of grief.* New York: Simon & Schuster.

Kuh, G. D. (1995). Cultivating "high-stakes" student culture research. *Research in Higher Education, 36,* 563–576.

Kuh, G. D., & Gonyea, R. M. (2005, July 11). *Exploring the relationships between spirituality, liberal learning, and college student engagement.* A special report for the Teagle Foundation. Retrieved January 12, 2007 from http://www.teaglefoundations.org/learning/pdf/20050711_kuh_gonyea.pdf

Kuh, G. D., Whitt, E. J., & Shedd, J. D. (1987). *Student affairs work, 2001: A paradigmatic odyssey.* Alexandria, VA: American College Personnel Association.

Kupo, V. L. (2010). *What is Hawaiian?: Explorations and understandings of native Hawaiian college women's identities.* Unpublished doctoral dissertation, Bowling Green State University.

Ladson-Billings, G. (1998). Just what is critical race theory and what's it doing in a *nice* field like education? *Qualitative Studies in Education, 11*(1), 7–24.

Ladson-Billings, G., & Donnor, J. (2005). Waiting for the call: The moral activist role of critical race theory scholarship. In N. K. Denzin & Y. S. Lincoln (Eds.), *Handbook of qualitative research* (3rd ed., pp. 279–301). Thousand Oaks, CA: Sage.

Lahey, L., Souvaine, E., Kegan, R., Goodman, R., & Felix, S. (1988). *A guide to the Subject-Object Interview: Its administration and interpretation.* Cambridge, MA: The Subject-Object Workshop.

Lally, P. S., & Kerr, G. A. (2005). The career planning, athletic identity, and student role identity of intercollegiate student athletes. *Research Quarterly for Exercise and Sport, 76,* 275–285.

Lamont, M., & Lareau, A. (1988). Cultural capital: Allusions, gaps and glissandos in recent theoretical developments. *Sociological Theory, 6,* 153–168.

Langhout, R. D., Drake, P., & Rosselli, F. (2009). Classism in the university setting: Examining student antecedents and outcomes. *Journal of Diversity in Higher Education, 2*(3), 166–181.

Langhout, R. D., Rosselli, F., & Feinstein, J. (2007). Assessing classism in academic settings. *The Review of Higher Education, 30,* 145–184.

Lareau, A., & Weininger, E. B. (2003). Cultural capital in educational research: A critical assessment. *Theory and Society, 32,* 567–606.

Lather, P. (2006). Paradigm proliferation as a good thing to think with: Teaching research in education as a wild profusion. *International Journal of Qualitative Studies in Education, 19,* 35–57.

Lather, P. (2007). *Getting lost: Feminist efforts toward a double(d) science.* Albany, NY: State University of New York Press.

Laughlin, A., & Creamer, E. G. (2007). Engaging differences: Self-authorship and the decision-making process. In P. S. Meszaros (Ed.), *Self-authorship: Advancing students' intellectual growth.* New Directions for Teaching and Learning, no. 109, pp. 43–51. San Francisco: Jossey-Bass.

Leak, G. K. (2003). Validation of the Faith Development Scale using longitudinal and cross-sectional designs. *Social Behavior and Personality, 31,* 637–641.

Leak, G. K. (2009). An assessment of the relationship between identity development, faith development, and religious commitment. *Identity: An International Journal of Theory and Research, 9,* 201–218.

Leak, G. K., Loucks, A. A., & Bowlin, P. (1999). Development and initial validation of a global measure of faith development. *International Journal for the Psychology of Religion, 9,* 105–124.

Ledesma, M. C., & Calderón, D. (2015). Critical race theory in education: A review of past literature and a look to the future. *Qualitative Inquiry, 21,* 206–222.

Lee, C. C. (2012). *Multicultural issues in counseling: New approaches to diversity* (4th ed.). Alexandria, VA: American Counseling Association.

Lee, E. B. (2012). Young, Black, and connected: Facebook usage among African American college students. *Journal of Black Studies, 43,* 336–354.

Lee, E. B. (2014). Facebook use and texting among African American and Hispanic teenagers: An implication for academic performance. *Journal of Black Studies, 45*(2), 83–101.

Lee, E. B. (2015). Too much information: Heavy smartphone and Facebook utilization by African American young adults. *Journal of Black Studies, 46*(1), 44–61.

Lee, E. M., & Kramer, R. (2013). Out with the old, in with the new? Habitus and social mobility at selective colleges. *Sociology of Education, 86*(1), 18–35.

Lee, J., Sleeter, C., & Kumashiro, K. (2015). Interrogating identity and social contexts through "Critical Family History." *Multicultural Perspectives, 17*(1), 28–32.

Lee, J. A. (1977). Going public: A study in the sociology of homosexual liberation. *Journal of Homosexuality, 3*, 49–78.

Lee, J. J. (2002). Changing worlds, changing selves: The experience of the religious self among Catholic collegians. *Journal of College Student Development, 43*, 341–356.

Lee, Y. J., & Won, D. (2014). Trailblazing women in academia: Representation of women in senior faculty and the gender gap in junior faculty's salaries in higher educational institutions. *The Social Science Journal, 51*, 331–340.

Lehmann, W. (2014). Habitus transformation and hidden injuries: Successful working-class university students. *Sociology of Education, 87*, 1–13.

Leonardo, Z. (2004). The color of supremacy: Beyond the discourse of "white" privilege. *Educational Philosophy and Theory, 36*(2), 137–152.

Lev, A. I. (2004). *Transgender emergence: Therapeutic guidelines for working with gender-variant people and their families.* New York: Haworth Clinical Practice Press.

Levine, H., & Evans, N. J. (1991). The development of gay, lesbian, and bisexual identities. In N. J. Evans & V. A. Wall (Eds.), *Beyond tolerance: Gays, lesbians and bisexuals on campus* (pp. 1–24). Alexandria, VA: American College Personnel Association.

Levinson, D. J. (1996). *The seasons of a woman's life.* New York: Ballantine.

Levinson, D. J. (with Darrow, C. N., Klein, E. B., Levinson, M. G., & McKee, B.). (1978). *The seasons of a man's life.* New York: Ballantine.

Lewin, K. (1936). *Principles of topological psychology.* New York: McGraw-Hill.

Lewis, P., Forsythe, G. B., Sweeney, P., Bartone, P., Bullis, C., & Snook, S. (2005). Identity development during the college years: Findings from the West Point longitudinal study. *Journal of College Student Development, 46*, 357–373.

Li, M., Olson, J. E., & Frieze, I. H. (2013). Students' study abroad plans: the influence of motivational and personality factors. Frontiers: *The Interdisciplinary Journal of Study Abroad, 22.*

Li, X., & Lal, S. (2005). Critical reflective thinking through service learning in multicultural teacher education. *Intercultural Education, 16*, 217–234.

Liddell, D. (1995). [Review of *Developing reflective judgment: Understanding and promoting intellectual growth and critical thinking in adolescents and adults*]. *Journal of College Student Development, 36*, 94–96.

Liddell, D. L., & Cooper, D. L. (2012). Moral development in higher education. In D. L. Liddell & D. L. Cooper (Eds.), *Facilitating the moral growth of college students.* New Directions for Student Services, no. 139, pp. 5–15. San Francisco: Jossey-Bass.

Lies, J. M., Bock, T., Brandenberger, J., & Trozzolo, T. A. (2012). The effects of off-campus service learning on the moral reasoning of college students. *Journal of Moral Education, 41*, 189–199.

Lightner, K. L., Kipps-Vaughan, D., Schulte, T., & Trice, A. D. (2012). Reasons university students with a learning disability wait to seek disability services. *Journal of Postsecondary Education and Disability, 25*, 145–159.

Linares, L.I.R., & Muñoz, S. M. (2011). Revisiting validation theory: Theoretical foundations, applications, and extensions. *Enrollment Management Journal, 2*, 12–33.

Lincoln, Y. S., & Guba, E. G. (1985). *Naturalistic inquiry.* Thousand Oaks, CA: Sage.

Lincoln, Y. S., & Guba, E. G. (2003). Ethics: The failure of positivist science. In Y. S. Lincoln & N. K. Denzin (Eds.), *Turning points in qualitative research: Tying knots in a handkerchief* (pp. 219–238). Walnut Creek, CA: AltaMira Press.

Lincoln, Y. S., & Guba, E. G. (2013). *The constructivist credo.* Walnut Creek, CA: West Coast Press.

Lind, G. (1986). Cultural differences in moral judgment competence? A study of West and East European university students. *Cross-Cultural Research, 20*(1–4), 208–225.

Linder, C. (2015). Navigating guilt, shame, and fear of appearing racist: A conceptual model of anti-racist white feminist identity development. *Journal of College Student Development, 56,* 535–549.

Linn, R. (2001). The heart has its reason and the reason has its heart: The insight of Kohlberg and Gilligan in moral development and counseling. *Social Behavior and Personality, 29,* 593–600.

Linton, S. (1998). *Claiming disability: Knowledge and identity.* New York: New York University Press.

Linvill, D. L. (2011). The relationship between student identity development and the perception of political bias in the college classroom. *College Teaching, 59*(2), 49–55.

Liou, D. D., Antrop-Gonzalez, R., & Cooper, R. (2009). Unveiling the promise of community cultural wealth to sustaining Latina/o students' college-going information networks. *Educational Studies, 45,* 534–555.

Liss, M., & Erchull, M. J. (2010). Everyone feels empowered: Understanding feminist self labeling. *Psychology of Women Quarterly, 34,* 85–96.

Liss, M., O'Connor, C., Morosky, E., & Crawford, M. (2001). What makes a feminist? Predictors and correlates of feminist social identity in college women. *Psychology of Women Quarterly, 25,* 125–133.

Livingston, W. G., Havice, P. A., Cawthon, T. W., & Fleming, D. S. (2012). Social camouflage: Interpreting male student veterans' behavior for residence life professionals. *The Journal of College and University Student Housing, 19*(1),176–184.

Lockett, C. T., & Harrell, J. P. (2003). Racial identity, self-esteem, and academic achievement: Too much interpretation, too little supporting data. *Journal of Black Psychology, 29,* 325–336.

Loevinger, J. (1976). *Ego development: Conceptions and theories.* San Francisco: Jossey-Bass.

Logan, R., Snarey, J., & Schrader, D. (1990). Autonomous versus heteronomous moral judgment types. *Journal of Cross-Cultural Psychology, 21,* 71–89.

Lombardi, A. R., Murray, C., & Gerdes, H. (2012). Academic performance of first-generation college students with disabilities. *Journal of College Student Development, 53,* 811–826.

Long, B. E., Sowa, C. J., & Niles, S. G. (1995). Differences in student development reflected by the career decisions of college seniors. *Journal of College Student Development, 36,* 47–52.

Lott, B. (2012). The social psychology of class and classism. *American Psychologist, 67,* 650–658.

Love, P. G. (2001). Spirituality and student development: Theoretical connections. In M. A. Jablonski (Ed.), *The implications of student spirituality for student affairs practice.* New Directions for Student Services, no. 95, pp. 7–16. San Francisco: Jossey-Bass.

Love, P. G. (2002). Comparing spiritual development and cognitive development. *Journal of College Student Development, 43,* 357–373.

Love, P. G., Bock, M., Jannarone, A., & Richardson, P. (2005). Identity interaction: Exploring the spiritual experiences of lesbian and gay college students. *Journal of College Student Development, 46,* 193–209.

Love, P. G., & Guthrie, V. L. (Eds.). (1999). *Understanding and applying cognitive development theory.* New Directions for Student Services, no. 88. San Francisco: Jossey-Bass.

Lownsdale, S. (1997). Faith development across the life span: Fowler's integrative work. *Journal of Psychology and Theology, 25,* 49–63.

Ludeman, R. B. (2011). Successful judicial interventions with college men. In J. A. Laker & T. Davis (Eds.), *Masculinities in higher education: Theoretical and practical considerations* (pp. 193–209). New York: Taylor & Francis.

Luna, V., & Prieto, L. (2009). Mentoring affirmation and interventions: A bridge to graduate school for Latina/o students. *Journal of Hispanic Higher Education, 8,* 213–224.

Lund, C. L., & Colin, S. A. J., III (Eds.). (2010). *White privilege and racism: Perceptions and actions. New Directions for Adult and Continuing Education,* no. 125. San Francisco, Jossey-Bass.

Lundberg, C. A. (2007). Student involvement and institutional commitment to diversity as predictors of Native American student learning. *Journal of College Student Development, 48,* 405–417.

Luyckx, K., Goossens, L., Soenens, B., & Beyers, W. (2006). Unpacking commitment and exploration: Preliminary validation of an integrative model of late adolescent identity formation. *Journal of Adolescence, 29,* 361–378.

Luyckx, K., Goossens, L., Soenens, B., Beyers, W., & Vansteenkiste, M. (2005). Identity statuses based on 4 rather than 2 identity dimensions: Extending and refining Marcia's paradigm. *Journal of Youth and Adolescence, 34,* 605–618.

Luyckx, K., Klimstra, T. A., Schwartz, S. J., & Duriez, B. (2013). Personal identity in college and the work context: Developmental trajectories and psychosocial functioning. *European Journal of Personality, 27,* 222–237.

Luyckx, K., Schwartz, S. J., Berzonsky, M. D., Soenens, B., Vansteenkiste, M., Smits, I., & Goossens, L. (2008a). Capturing ruminative exploration: Extending the four-dimensional model of identity formation in late adolescence. *Journal of Research in Personality, 42,* 58–82.

Luyckx, K., Schwartz, S. J., Goosens, L., Soenens, B., & Beyers, W. (2008b). Developmental typologies of identity formation and adjustment in female emerging adults: A latent class growth analysis approach. *Journal of Research on Adolescence, 18,* 595–619.

Luyckx, K., Schwartz, S. J., Soenens, B., Vansteenkiste, M., & Goossens, L. (2010). The path from identity commitments to adjustment: Motivational underpinnings and mediating mechanisms. *Journal of Counseling & Development, 88,* 52–60.

Lynn, M., & Dixson, A. D. (Eds.). (2013). *Handbook of critical race theory in education.* New York: Taylor & Frances/Routledge.

Lyotard, J.-F. (1984). *The postmodern condition: A report on knowledge* (G. Bennington & B. Massumi, Trans., Theory and History of Literature, Vol. 10). Manchester, England: Manchester University Press.

Ma, H. K. (1989). Moral orientation and moral judgment in adolescents in Hong Kong, mainland China, and England. *Journal of Cross-Cultural Psychology, 20,* 152–177.

Macari, D. P., Maples, M. F., & D'Andrea, L. (2005–2006). A comparative study of psychological development in non-traditional and traditional college students. *Journal of College Student Retention: Research, Theory, and Practice, 7,* 283–302.

Madaus, J., Miller, W., & Vance, M. L. (2009). Veterans with disabilities in postsecondary education. *Journal of Postsecondary Education and Disability, 22*(1), 10–17.

Magnusson, D. (1995). Individual development: A holistic, integrated model. In P. Moen, G. H. Elder, & K. Lüsher (Eds.), *Examining lives in context: Perspectives on the ecology of human development* (pp. 19–60). Washington, DC: American Psychological Association.

Magolda, P. M. (2007). Students serving Christ: Understanding the role of student subcultures on a college campus. *Anthropology & Education Quarterly, 38*(2), 138–158.

Magolda, P. M., & Ebben, K. (2006). College student involvement and mobilization: An ethnographic study of a Christian student organization. *Journal of College Student Development, 47,* 281–298.

Maguen, S., Floyd, F. J., Bakeman, R., & Armistead, L. (2002). Developmental milestones and disclosure of sexual orientation among gay, lesbian, and bisexual youths. *Applied Developmental Psychology, 23,* 219–233.

Malewski, E., & Phillion, J. (2009). International field experiences: The impact of class, gender, and race on the perceptions and experiences of preservice teachers. *Teaching and Teacher Education, 25,* 52–60.

Mangan, K. (2010, October 18). Colleges help veterans advance from combat to classroom. Chronicle of Higher Education. Retrieved from http://chronicle.com/article/Colleges-Help-Veterans-Adva/48846/

Manning, K., Kinzie, J., & Schuh, J. H. (2013). *One size does not fit all: Traditional and innovative models of student affairs practice.* New York: Routledge.

Maramba, D. C., & Palmer, R. T. (2014). The impact of cultural validation on the college experiences of Southeast Asian American students. *Journal of College Student Development, 55,* 515–530.

Marcia, J. E. (1966). Development and validation of ego-identity status. *Journal of Personality and Social Psychology, 3,* 551–558.

Marcia, J. E. (1975). Identity six years after: A follow-up study. *Journal of Youth and Adolescence, 5,* 145–160.

Marcia, J. E. (1980). Identity in adolescence. In J. Adelson (Ed.), *Handbook of adolescent psychology* (pp. 159–187). New York: Wiley.

Marcia, J. E. (1989a). Identity and intervention. *Journal of Adolescence, 12,* 401–410.

Marcia, J. E. (1989b). Identity diffusion differentiated. In M. A. Luszcz & T. Nettelbeck (Eds.), *Psychological development: Perspectives across the life-span* (pp. 289–295). North-Holland: Elsevier Science Publishers B.V.

Marcia, J. E. (1993a). The ego identity status approach to ego identity. In J. E. Marcia, A. S. Waterman, D. R. Matteson, & S. L. Archer (Eds.), *Ego Identity: A handbook for psychosocial research* (pp. 2–21). New York: Springer-Verlag.

Marcia, J. E. (1993b). The relational roots of identity. In J. Kroger (Ed.), *Discussions on ego identity* (pp. 101–120). Hillsdale, NJ: Erlbaum.

Marcia, J. E. (1993c). The status of the statuses: Research review. In J. E. Marcia, A. S. Waterman, D. R. Matteson, & S. L. Archer (Eds.), *Ego identity: A handbook for psychosocial research* (pp. 22–41). New York: Springer-Verlag.

Marcia, J. E. (1994). The empirical study of ego-identity. In H. A. Bosma, T.L.G. Graafsma, H. D. Grotevant, & D. J. de Levita (Eds.), *Identity and development: An interdisciplinary approach* (pp. 67–80). Thousand Oaks, CA: Sage.

Marcia, J. E. (1999). Representational thought in ego identity, psychotherapy, and psychosocial developmental theory. In I. E. Siegel (Ed.), *Development of mental representation: Theories and applications* (pp. 391–414). Mahwah, NJ: Erlbaum.

Marcia, J. E. (2002). Identity and psychosocial development in adulthood. *Identity: An International Journal of Theory and Research, 2*(1), 7–28.

Marin, G., Sabogal, F., Marin, B. V., Otero-Sabogal, R., & Perez-Stable, E. J. (1987). Development of a short acculturation scale for Hispanics. *Hispanic Journal of Behavioral Sciences, 9,* 183–205.

Marine, S. B. (2011a). "Our college is changing": Women's college student affairs administrators and transgender students. *Journal of Homosexuality, 58,* 1165–1186.

Marine, S. B. (2011b). Special issue: Stonewall's legacy—bisexual, gay, lesbian, and transgender students in higher education. *ASHE Higher Education Report, 37*(4), 1–145.

Marine, S. B., & Nicolazzo, Z. (2014). Names that matter: Exploring the tensions of campus LGBTQ centers and trans* inclusion. *Journal of Diversity in Higher Education, 7,* 265–281.

Marks, D. (1999). *Disability: Controversial debates and psychosocial perspectives*. London: Routledge.

Marrs, H., & Benton, S. L. (2009). Relationships between separate and connected knowing and approaches to learning. *Sex Roles, 60*, 57–66.

Marshak, L., Van Wieren, T., Ferrell, D. R., Swiss, L., & Dugan, C. (2010). Exploring barriers to college student use of disability services and accommodations. *Journal of Postsecondary Education and Disability, 22*(3), 151–165.

Martin, N. D. (2012). The privilege of ease: Social class and campus life at highly selective, private universities. *Research in Higher Education, 53*, 426–452.

Martinez, S., Torres, V., White, L. W., Medrano, C. I., Robledo, A. L., & Hernandez, E. (2012). The influence of family dynamics on ethnic identity among adult Latinas. *Journal of Adult Development, 19*, 190–200.

Martínez-Alemán, A. M., & Wartman, K. L. (2008). *Online social networking on campus: Understanding what matters in student culture*. New York: Routledge.

Mass, A. I. (1992). Interracial Japanese Americans: The best of both worlds or the end of the Japanese American community? In M.P.P. Root (Ed.), *Racially mixed people in America* (pp. 265–279). Newbury Park, CA: Sage.

Matteson, D. R. (1975). *Adolescence today: Sex roles and the search for identity*. Homewood, IL: Dorsey.

Mattis, J. S., Ahluwalia, M. K., Cowie, S. E., & Kirkland-Harris, A. M. (2006). Ethnicity, culture, and spiritual development. In E. C. Roehlkepartain, P. E. King, L. Wagener, & P. L. Benson (Eds.), *The handbook of spiritual development in childhood and adolescence* (pp. 83–296). Thousand Oaks, CA: Sage Publications, Inc.

Matusov, E., & Smith, M. P. (2012). The middle-class nature of identity and its implications for education: A genealogical analysis and reevaluation of a culturally and historically bounded concept. *Integrated Psychological Behavior, 46*, 274–295.

Mayhew, M. J. (2004). Exploring the essence of spirituality: A phenomenological study of eight students with eight different worldviews. *NASPA Journal, 41*, 647–674.

Mayhew, M. J. (2012). The multilevel examination of the influence of institutional type on the moral reasoning development of first year students. *The Journal of Higher Education, 83*, 367–388.

Mayhew, M. J., Bowman, N. A., & Bryant Rockenbach, A. (2014). Silencing whom? Linking campus climates for religious, spiritual, and worldview diversity to student worldviews. *Journal of Higher Education, 85*, 219–245.

Mayhew, M. J., & Bryant, A. N. (2013). Achievement or arrest? The influence of the collegiate religious and spiritual climate on students' worldview commitment. *Research in Higher Education, 54*, 63–84.

Mayhew, M. J., & Engberg, M. E. (2010). Diversity and moral reasoning: How negative diverse peer interactions affect the development of moral reasoning in undergraduate students. *The Journal of Higher Education, 81*, 459–488.

Mayhew, M. J., & King, P. M. (2008). How curricular content and pedagogical strategies affect moral reasoning development in college students. *Journal of Moral Education, 37*, 17–40.

Mayhew, M. J., Seifert, T. A., & Pascarella, E. T. (2012). How the first year of college influences moral reasoning development for students in moral consolidation and moral

Maylor, U. (2009). Is it because I'm black? A black female research experience. *Race Ethnicity and Education, 12*, 53–64.

McAleavey, A. A., Castonguay, L. G., & Locke, B. D. (2011). Sexual orientation minorities in college counseling: Prevalence, distress, and symptom profiles. *Journal of College Counseling, 14*, 127–142.

McAllister, L., Whiteford, G., Hill, B., Thomas, N., & Fitzgerald, M. (2006). Reflection in intercultural learning: Examining the international experience through a critical incident approach. *Reflective Practice: International and Multidisciplinary Perspectives, 7*(3), 367–381.

McCall, L. (2005). The complexity of intersectionality. *Signs: Journal of Women in Culture and Society, 30*, 1171–1800.

McCarn, S. R. (1991). *Validation of a model of sexual minority (lesbian) identity development.* Unpublished master's thesis. University of Maryland at College Park.

McCarn, S. R., & Fassinger, R. E. (1996). Revisioning sexual minority identity formation: A new model of lesbian identity and its implications for counseling and research. *Counseling Psychologist, 24*, 508–534.

McCubbin, L. D., & Dang, T. A. (2011). Native Hawaiian identity and measurement: An ecological perspective of indigenous identity development. In J. G. Ponterotto, J. M. Casas, L. A. Suzuki, & C. M. Alexander (Eds.), *Handbook of multicultural counseling* (3rd ed., pp. 269–282). Los Angeles: Sage.

McDermott, M. (2015). Color-blind and color-visible identity among American whites. *American Behavioral Scientist, 1–22.*

McDermott, M., & Samson, F. L. (2005). White racial and ethnic identity in the United States. *Annual Review of Sociology, 31*, 245–261.

McEwen, M. K. (2003a). The nature and uses of theory. In S. K. Komives, D. B. Woodard, Jr., & *Associates, Student services: A handbook for the profession* (4th ed., pp. 1153–178). San Francisco: Jossey-Bass.

McEwen, M. K. (2003b). New perspectives on identity development. In S. R. Komives & D. B. Woodard, Jr., & *Associates, Student services: A handbook for the profession* (4th ed., pp. 203–233). San Francisco: Jossey-Bass.

McEwen, M. K., Roper, L., Bryant, D., & Langa, M. (1990). Incorporating the development of African American students into psychosocial theories of student development. *Journal of College Student Development, 31*, 429–436.

McGill, D. W., & Pearce, J. K. (2005). American families with English ancestors from the colonial era: Anglo Americans. In M. McGoldrick, J. Giordano, & N. Garcia-Preto (Eds.), *Ethnicity and family therapy* (3rd ed., pp. 52–533). New York: Guilford.

McGuire, K. M., Berhanu, J., Davis, C. H., & Harper, S. R. (2014). In search of progressive black masculinities: Critical self-reflections on gender identity development among black undergraduate men. *Men and Masculinities, 17*, 253–277.

McIntosh, P. (1989, July/August). White privilege: Unpacking the invisible knapsack. *Peace and Freedom, 10–12.*

McIntosh, P. (2003). White privilege, male privilege: A personal account of coming to see correspondences through work in women's studies. In M. S. Kimmel & A. L Ferber (Eds.), *Privilege: A reader* (pp. 147–160). Cambridge, MA: Westview Press.

McIntosh, P. (2012). Reflections and future directions for privilege studies. *Journal of Social Issues, 68*, 194–206.

McIntosh, P. (2013). Teaching about privilege: Transforming learned ignorance into usable knowledge. Foreword. In K. A. Case (Ed.), *Deconstructing privilege: teaching and learning as allies in the classroom* (pp. xi–xvi). New York: Routledge.

McKinney, J. S. (2005). On the margins: A study of the experience of transgender college students. *Journal of Gay and Lesbian Issues in Education, 3*, 63–76.

McMahon, H. G., Paisley, P. O., & Skudrzyk, B. (2014). Individuals and families of European descent. In D. G. Hays & B. T. Erford (Eds.), *Developing multicultural counseling competence: A systems approach* (pp. 382–418). Upper Saddle River, NJ: Pearson.

McMahon, M., Watson, M., & Bimrose, J. (2014). 21 Implications for career practice. In J. Bimrose, M. McMahon, & M. Watson (Eds.), *Women's career development throughout the lifespan: An international exploration* (pp. 253–262). New York: Routledge.

McMahon, S. (2010). Rape myth beliefs and bystander attitudes among incoming college students. *Journal of American College Health, 59*(1), 3–11.

McNeil, D. W., Kee, M., & Zvolensky, M. J. (1999). Culturally related anxiety and ethnic identity in Navajo college students. *Cultural Diversity and Ethnic Minority Psychology, 5*, 56–64.

Meade, T., & Serlin, D. (2006). Disability and history. *Radical History Review, 94*, 1–8.

Means, D. R., & Jaeger, A. J. (2013). Black in the rainbow: "Quaring" the Black gay male student experience at historically Black universities. *Journal of African American Males in Education, 4*(2), 124–140.

Meeus, W., Iedema, J., Helsen, M., & Vollebergh, W. (1999). Patterns of adolescent identity development: Review of literature and longitudinal analysis. *Developmental Review, 19*, 419–461.

Means, D. R., & Jaeger, A. J. (2015). Spiritual borderlands: A Black gay male college student's spiritual journey. *Journal of Student Affairs Research and Practice, 52*, 11–23.

Mena, F. J., Padilla, A. M., & Maldonado, M. (1987). Acculturative stress and specific coping strategies among immigrant and later generation college students. *Hispanic Journal of Behavioral Sciences, 9*, 207–225.

Mentkowski, M., Moeser, M., & Strait, M. J. (1983). *Using the Perry scheme of intellectual and ethical development as a college outcomes measure: A process and criteria for judging student performance* (Vols. 1–2). Milwaukee, WI: Alverno College Productions.

Merriam, S. B. (Ed.). (2008). *Third update on adult learning theory.* New Directions for Adult and Continuing Education, no. 119. San Francisco: Jossey-Bass.

Merriam, S. B., & Bierema, L. L. (2014). *Adult learning: Linking theory and practice.* San Francisco, CA: Jossey-Bass.

Merriam, S. B., Caffarella, R. S., & Baumgartner, L. M. (2007). *Learning in adulthood: A comprehensive guide* (3rd ed.). San Francisco: Jossey-Bass.

Meszaros, P. S. (Ed.). (2007). *Self-authorship: Advancing students' intellectual growth. New Directions for Teaching and Learning,* no. 109. San Francisco: Jossey-Bass.

Meyer, I. H. (2003). Prejudice, social stress, and mental health in lesbian, gay, and bisexual populations: Conceptual issues and research evidence. *Psychological Bulletin, 129*, 674–697.

Meyer, P. (1977). Intellectual development: Analysis of religious content. *Counseling Psychologist, 6*(4), 47–50.

Mezirow, J. (Ed.). (2000). *Learning as transformation.* San Francisco: Jossey-Bass.

Mignano, A. C., Brewer, B. W., Winter, C. R., & Van Raalte, J. L. (2006). Athletic identity and student involvement of female athletes at NCAA Division III women's and coeducational colleges. *Journal of College Student Development, 47*, 457–464.

Mihesuah, D. A., & Wilson, A. C. (Eds.). (2004). *Indigenizing the academy: Transforming scholarship and empowering communities.* Lincoln: University of Nebraska Press.

Mihesuah, J. K. (2004). Graduating indigenous students by confronting the academic environment. In D. A. Mihesuah & A. C. Wilson (Eds.), *Indigenizing the academy: Transforming scholarship and empowering communities* (pp. 191–199). Lincoln: University of Nebraska Press.

Miller, J. G. (2006). Cultural psychology of moral development. In S. Kitayama & D. Cohen (Eds.), *Handbook of Cultural Psychology* (pp. 477–499). New York: Guilford Press.

Miller, J. G., & Bersoff, D. M. (1992). Culture and moral judgment: How are conflicts between justice and interpersonal responsibilities resolved? *Journal of Personality and Social Psychology*, *62*, 544–554.

Miller, T. K., & Prince, J. S. (1976). *The future of student affairs: A guide to student development for tomorrow's higher education*. San Francisco: Jossey-Bass.

Miller, V. W., & Ryan, M. M. (2001). *Transforming campus life: Reflections on spirituality and religious pluralism*. New York: Peter Lang.

Mills, R., & Strong, K. L. (2004). Organizing for learning in a division of student affairs. In M. Baxter Magolda & P. M. King (Eds.), *Learning partnerships: Theory and modes of practice to educate for self-authorship* (pp. 269–302). Sterling, VA: Stylus.

Mindrup, R. M., Spray, B. J., & Lamberghini-West, A. (2011). White privilege and multicultural counseling competence: The influence of field of study, sex, and racial/ethnic exposure. *Journal of Ethnic & Cultural Diversity in Social Work*, *20*(1), 20–38.

Mitchell, D., Jr., & Means, D. R. (2014). "Quadruple consciousness": A literature review and new theoretical consideration for understanding the experiences of Black gay and bisexual college men at predominantly white institutions. *Journal of African American Males in Education*, *5*(1), 23–35.

Mitchell, S. L., & Dell, D. M. (1992). The relationship between Black students' racial identity attitude and participation in campus organizations. *Journal of College Student Development*, *33*, 39–43.

Miville, M. L. (2005). Psychological functioning and identity development of biracial people: A review of current theory and research. In R. T. Carter (Ed.), *Handbook of racial-cultural psychology and counseling* (Vol. 1: Theory and Research, pp. 295–319). Hoboken, NJ: Wiley.

Miville, M. L. (2010). Latina/o identity development: Updates on theory, measurement, and counseling implications. In J. G. Ponterotto, J. M. Casas, L. A. Suzuki, & C. M. Alexander (Eds.), *Handbook of multicultural counseling* (3rd ed., pp. 241–282). Los Angeles: Sage.

Miville, M. L., Constantine, M. G., Baysden, M. F., & So-Lloyd, G. (2005). Chameleon changes: An exploration of racial identity themes of multiracial people. *Journal of Counseling Psychology*, *52*, 507–516.

Miville, M. L., Darlington, P., Whitlock, B., & Mulligan, T. (2005). Integrating identities: The relationships of racial, gender, and ego identities among white college students. *Journal of College Student Development*, *46*(2), 157–175.

Mohr, J. J. (2002). Heterosexual identity and the heterosexual therapist: An identity perspective on sexual orientation dynamics in psychotherapy. *Counseling Psychologist*, *30*, 532–566.

Mohr, J., & Fassinger, R. (2000). Measuring dimensions of lesbian and gay male experience. *Measurement and Evaluation in Counseling and Development*, *33*, 66–90.

Moi, T. (1991). Appropriating Bourdieu: Feminist theory and Pierre Bourdieu's sociology of culture. *New Literary History*, *22*, 1017–1049.

Moore, L. V., & Upcraft, M. L. (1990). Theory in student affairs: Emerging perspectives. In L. V. Moore (Ed.), *Evolving theoretical perspectives on students*. New Directions for Student Services, no. 51, pp. 3–23. San Francisco: Jossey-Bass.

Moore, W. S. (1989). The Learning Environment Preferences: Exploring the construct validity of an objective measure of the Perry scheme of intellectual development. *Journal of College Student Development*, *30*, 504–514.

Moore, W. S. (1994). Student and faculty epistemology in the college classroom: The Perry scheme of intellectual and ethical development. In K. W. Prichard & R. M. Sawyer (Eds.), *Handbook of college teaching: Theory and application* (pp. 43–67). Westport, CT: Greenwood Press.

Moore, W. S. (2002). Understanding learning in a postmodern world: Reconsidering the Perry scheme of intellectual and ethical development. In B. K. Hofer & P. R. Pintrich (Eds.), *Personal epistemology: The psychology of beliefs about knowledge and knowing* (pp. 17–36). Mahwah, NJ: Erlbaum.

Moradi, B., Mohr, J. J., Worthington, R. L., & Fassinger, R. E. (2009). Counseling psychology research on sexual (orientation) minority issues: Conceptual and methodological challenges and opportunities. *Journal of Counseling Psychology, 56*, 5–22.

Moradi, B., van den Berg, J., & Epting, F. (2009). Internalized lesbian and gay threat and guilt: Links with intrapersonal and interpersonal identity stressors. *Journal of Counseling Psychology, 56*, 119–131.

Moran, C. D. (2001). Purpose in life, student development, and well-being: Recommendations for student affairs practitioners. *NASPA Journal, 38*, 269–279.

Moran, G. (1983). *Religious education development: Images for the future*. Minneapolis: Winston.

Moreland, C., & Leach, M. M. (2001). The relationship between black racial identity and moral development. *Journal of Black Psychology, 27*, 255–271.

Morgan, E. M., Steiner, M. G., & Thompson, E. M. (2010). Processes of sexual orientation questioning among heterosexual men. *Men and Masculinities, 12*(4), 425–443.

Morgan, E. M., & Thompson, E. M. (2011). Processes of sexual orientation questioning among heterosexual women. *Journal of Sex Research, 48*, 16–28.

Mueller, J. A. (2012). Understanding the atheist college student: A qualitative examination. *Journal of Student Affairs Research and Practice, 49*, 249–266.

Mueller, J. A., & Cole, J. C. (2009). A qualitative examination of heterosexual consciousness among college students. *Journal of College Student Development, 50*(3), 320–336.

Muir, D. E. (1993). Race: The mythic root of racism. *Sociological Inquiry, 63*(3), 339–350.

Museus, S. D., & Neville, K. M. (2012). Delineating the ways that key institutional agents provide racial minority students with access to social capital in college. *Journal of College Student Development, 53*, 436–452.

Mussi, J. M. (2001, March 2). [Review of the book *Big questions, worthy dreams*]. Retrieved December 22, 2006 from http://www.collegevalues.org/spirit.cfm?id=448&a=1

Myers, I. B. (1980). *Gifts differing*. Palo Alto, CA: Consulting Psychologists Press.

Myers, S. A. (2010). Using the Perry scheme to explore college student classroom participation. *Communication Research Reports, 27*(2), 123–130.

Nagda, B. A., & Maxwell, K. A. (2011). Deepening the layers of understanding and connection: A critical-dialogic approach to facilitating intergroup dialogues. In K. E. Maxwell, B. A. Nagda, & M. C. Thompson (Eds.), *Facilitating intergroup dialogues: Bridging differences, catalyzing change* (pp. 1–22). Sterling, VA: Stylus.

Nagel, B., Matsuo, H., McIntyre, K. P., & Morrison, N. (2005). Attitudes toward victims of rape: Effects of gender, race, religion, and social class. *Journal of Interpersonal Violence, 20*, 725–737.

Narui, M. (2011). Understanding Asian/American gay, lesbian, and bisexual experiences from a poststructural perspective. *Journal of Homosexuality, 58*, 1211–1234.

Narvaez, D. (2005). The Neo-Kohlbergian tradition and beyond: Schemas, expertise and character. *Nebraska Symposium on Motivation, 51*, 119–163.

Nash, R. J. (2002). *Spirituality, ethics, religion, and teaching*. New York: Lang.

Nash, R. J. (2003). Inviting atheists to the table: A modest proposal for higher education. *Religion & Education, 30*(1), 1–23.

Nash, R. J., & Scott, L. (2008). Spirituality, religious pluralism, and higher education leadership development. Rethinking Leadership Practices in a Complex, Multicultural, and Global Environment: New Concepts and Models for Higher Education, Stylus Publishing, Sterling, VA, 131–150.

Nassar-McMillan, S. C. (2003). Counseling Arab Americans: Counselors' call for advocacy and social justice. *Counseling and Human Development, 35*(5), 2–12.

Nassar-McMillan, S. C., Gonzalez, L. M., & Mohamed, R. H. (2014). Individuals and families of Arab descent. In D. G. Hays & B. T. Erford (Eds.), *Developing multicultural counseling competence: A systems approach* (2nd ed., pp. 245–277). Boston: Pearson.

National Center for Education Statistics (NCES). (2014). *Digest of education statistics, 2013.* Washington, DC: U.S. Department of Education. Retrieved from http://www.mces.ed.gov/programs/digest/d13/

National Congress of American Indians (NCAI). (n.d.). Tribal nations and the United States: An introduction. Washington, DC: NCAI. Retrieved from http://www.ncai.org/about-tribes

Native American Journalists Association. (2014). *100 questions, 500 nations: A guide to Native America.* Canton, MI: David Crumm Media, LLC.

Navarro, K. M. (2014). A conceptual model of Division I student-athletes' career construction processes. *College Student Affairs Journal, 32*(1), 219–235.

Negy, C., Shreve, T. L., Jensen, B. J., & Uddin, N. (2003). Ethnic identity, self-esteem, and ethnocentrism: A student of social identity vs. multicultural theory of development. *Cultural Diversity and Ethnic Minority Psychology, 9,* 333–334.

Nelson, C. E., & Aleshire, D. (1986). Research in faith development. In C. Dykstra & S. Parks (Eds.), *Faith development and Fowler* (pp. 180–201). Birmingham, AL: Religious Education Press.

Nesbit, T. (2004). Class and teaching. In R. St. Clair & J. A. Sandlin (Eds.), *Promoting critical practice in adult education.* New Directions for Adult and Continuing Education, no. 102, pp. 15–24. San Francisco: Jossey-Bass.

Neugarten, B. L. (1979). Time, age, and the life cycle. *American Journal of Psychiatry, 136,* 887–894.

Neville, H. A., & Hamer, J. (2001). "We Make Freedom": An Exploration of Revolutionary Black Feminism. *Journal of Black Studies, 31,* 437–462.

Neville, H. A., Heppner, P. P., & Wang, L. (1997). Relations among racial identity attitudes, perceived stressors, and coping styles in African American college students. *Journal of Counseling and Development, 75,* 303–311.

Newman,L., Wagner, M., Cameto, R., Knokey, A. M., & Shaver, D. (2010). *Comparisons across time of the outcomes of youth with disabilities up to 4 years after high school: A report of findings from the National Longitudinal Transition Study-2 (NLTS2).* Menlo Park, CA: SRI International. (NCSER Report No. 2010–3008).

Nguyen, A.M.D., & Benet-Martínez, V. (2012). Biculturalism and adjustment: A meta-analysis. *Journal of Cross-Cultural Psychology, 44*(1), 122–159.

Nguyen, D. J., & Larson, J. B. (2015). Don't forget about the body: Exploring the curricular possibilities of embodied pedagogy. *Innovative Higher Education, 40*(4).

Nicholson, S. E., & Pasque, P. A. (2011). An introduction to feminism and feminist perspectives in higher education and student affairs. In P. A. Pasque & S. E. Nicholson (Eds.), *Empowering women in higher education and student affairs: Theory, research, narratives, and practice from feminist perspectives* (pp. 3–14). Sterling, VA: Stylus & ACPA.

Nicolazzo, Z. D. (2015). "Just go in looking good": The resilience, resistance, and kinship building of trans* college students. *Doctoral dissertation.* Oxford, OH: Miami University.

Nicolazzo, Z., & Marine, S. B. (2015). "It will change if people keep talking": Trans* students in college and university housing. *Journal of College and University Housing*.

Norris, T., Vines, P. L., & Hoeffel, E. M. (2012). The American Indian and Alaska Native Population: 2010. *2010 Census Briefs*. Washington, DC: U.S. Department of Commerce, Economics and Statistics Administration, U.S. Census Bureau.

Nuss, E. M. (2003). The development of student affairs. In S. K. Komives, D. B. Woodard, Jr., & *Associates, Student services: A handbook for the profession* (4th ed., pp. 65–88). San Francisco: Jossey-Bass.

Obear, K. (2007). Navigating triggering events: Critical skills for facilitating difficult dialogues. *Generational Diversity*, *15*(3). Retrieved from http://www.mauracullen.com/wp-content/uploads/2009/11/Navigating‐Triggers.pdf

Okagaki, L., Helling, M. K., & Bingham, G. E. (2009). American Indian college students' ethnic identity and beliefs about education. *Journal of College Student Development*, *50*, 157–176.

Olesen, V. L. (2000). Feminisms and qualitative research at and into the millennium. In N. K. Denzin & Y. S Lincoln (Eds.), *The handbook of qualitative research* (2nd ed., pp. 215–235). Thousand Oaks, CA: Sage.

Olkin R. (1999). *What psychotherapists should know about disability*. New York: Guilford Press.

Olson, J. K., & Finson, K. D. (2009). Developmental perspectives on reflective practices of elementary science education students. *Journal of Elementary Science Education*, *21*(4), 43–52.

Omi, M., & Winant, H. (2004). Racial formation. In Heldke, L & O'Connor, P. (Eds.), *Oppression, privilege, & resistance: Theoretical perspectives on racism, sexism, and heterosexism* (pp. 115–142). New York: McGraw-Hill.

Ong, A. D., Phinney, J. S., & Dennis, J. (2006). Competence under challenge: Exploring the protective influence of parental support and ethnic identity in Latino college students. *Journal of Adolescence*, *29*, 961–979.

Onorato, S., & Musoba, G. D. (2015). La Líder: Developing a leadership identity as a Hispanic woman at a Hispanic-serving institution. *Journal of College Student Development*, *56*, 15–31.

Orbe, M. P. (2008). Theorizing multidimensional identity negotiation: Reflections on the lived experiences of first-generation college students. In M. Azmitia, M. Syed, and K. Radmacher (Eds.), *The intersections of personal and social identities* (pp. 81–95). New Directions for Child and Adolescent Development, no. 120. San Francisco: Jossey-Bass.

Ortiz, A., & Rhoads, R. A. (2000). Deconstructing whiteness as part of a multicultural educational framework: From theory to practice. *Journal of College Student Development*, *41*, 81–93.

Ortiz, A. M., & Santos, S. J. (2009). *Ethnicity in college: Advancing theory and improving diversity practices on campus*. Sterling, VA: Stylus.

Ortman, P. E. (1993). A feminist approach to teaching learning theory with educational applications. *Teaching of Psychology*, *20*, 38–40.

Ortner, S. B. (1998). Identities: The hidden life of class. *Journal of Anthropological Research*, *54*(1), 1–17.

Ostrander, S. A. (1984). *Women of the upper class*. Philadelphia, PA: Temple University Press.

Ostrove, J. M. (1993). Belonging and wanting: Meanings of social class background from women's constructions of their college experiences. *Journal of Social Issues*, *59*, 771–784.

Ostrove, J. M. (2003). Privileging class: Toward a critical psychology of social class in the context of education. *Journal of Social Issues*, *59*, 677–692.

Ostrove, J. M., & Cole, E. R. (2003). Privileging class: Toward a critical psychology of social class in the context of education. *Journal of Social Issues*, *59*, 677–692.

Ostrove, J. M., & Long, S. M. (2007). Social class and belonging: Implications for college adjustment. *The Review of Higher Education, 30,* 363–389.

Ostrove, J. M., & Stewart, A. J. (1998). Representing Radcliffe: Perceptions and consequences of social class. *Journal of Adult Development, 5*(3), 183–193.

Owen, J. J., Rhoades, G. K., Stanley, S. M., & Fincham, F. D. (2010). "Hooking up" among college students: Demographic and psychosocial correlates. *Archives of Sexual Behavior, 39,* 653–663.

Ozer, S. (2015). Acculturation, adaptation, and mental health among Ladakhi college students: A mixed methods study of an indigenous population. *Journal of Cross-Cultural Psychology, 46,* 435–453.

Pace, C. R. (1984). *Measuring the quality of college student experience: An account of the development and use of the College Student Experiences Questionnaire.* Los Angeles: University of California, Higher Education Research Institute.

Painter, N. I. (2010). *The history of white people.* New York: WW Norton & Company.

Paredes-Collins, K., & Collins, C. S. (2011). The intersection of race and spirituality: Underrepresented students' spiritual development at predominantly white evangelical colleges. *Journal of Research on Christian Education, 20,* 73–100.

Parham, T. A. (1989). Cycles of psychological nigrescence. *Counseling Psychologist, 17,* 187–226.

Parham, T. A., & Helms, J. E. (1981). The influence of Black students' racial identity attitudes on preference for counselor's race. *Journal of Counseling Psychology, 28,* 250–257.

Parham, T. A., & Helms, J. E. (1985). Attitudes of racial identity and self esteem of black students: An exploratory investigation. *Journal of College Student Personnel, 26,* 143–147.

Park, J. J. (2011). "I needed to get out of my Korean bubble": An ethnographic account of Korean American collegians juggling diversity in a religious context. *Anthropology & Education Quarterly, 42*(3), 193–212.

Park, J. J. (2012a). "Man, this is hard": A case study of how race and religion affect cross-racial interaction for Black students. *The Review of Higher Education, 35*(4), 567–593.

Park, J. J. (2012b). When race and religion collide: The effect of religion on interracial friendship during college. *Journal of Diversity in Higher Education, 5*(1), 8–21.

Park, J. J. (2012c). It takes a village (or an ethnic economy): The varying roles of socioeconomic status, religion, and social capital in SAT preparation for Chinese and Korean American students. *American Educational Research Journal, 49*(4), 624–650.

Park, J. J. (2013). *When diversity drops: Race, religion, and affirmative action in higher education.* New Brunswick: Rutgers University Press.

Park, J. J., & Bowman, N. A. (2015). Religion as bridging or bonding social capital: Race, religion, and cross-racial interaction for college students. *Sociology of Education, 88*(1), 20–37.

Park, J.J., & Denson, N. (2013). When race and class both matter: The relationship between socioeconomic diversity, racial diversity, and student reports of cross-class interaction. *Research in Higher Education, 54*(7), 725–45.

Park, J.J., & Kim, Y. K. (2013). Interracial friendship, structural diversity, and peer groups: Patterns in Greek, religious, and ethnic student organizations. *The Review of Higher Education, 37*(1), 1–24.

Park, J. J., & Millora, M. (2010). Psychological well-being for White, Black, Latino/a, and Asian American students: Considering spirituality and religion. *Journal of Student Affairs Research and Practice, 47*(4), 445–461.

Parker, C. A. (1974). Student development: What does it mean? *Journal of College Student Personnel, 15,* 248–256.

Parker, C. A. (1977). On modeling reality. *Journal of College Student Personnel, 18,* 419–425.

Parker, S. (2011). Spirituality in counseling: A faith development perspective. *Journal of Counseling & Development, 89,* 112–119.

Parks, C., Hughes, T. L., & Matthews, A. K. (2004). Race/ethnicity and sexual orientation: Intersecting identities. *Cultural Diversity and Ethnic Minority Psychology, 10,* 241–254.

Parks, S. D. (1986a). *The critical years: Young adults and the search for meaning, faith, and commitment.* New York: HarperCollins.

Parks, S. D. (1986b). Imagination and spirit in faith development: A way past the structure-content dichotomy. In C. Dykstra & S. Parks (Eds.), *Faith development and Fowler* (pp. 137–156). Birmingham, AL: Religious Education Press.

Parks, S. D. (2000). *Big questions, worthy dreams: Mentoring young adults in their search for meaning, purpose, and faith.* San Francisco: Jossey-Bass.

Parks-Yancy, R. (2012). Interactions into opportunities: Career management for low-income, first-generation African American college students. *Journal of College Development, 53,* 510–523.

Parsons, F. (1909). *Choosing a vocation.* Boston: Houghton-Mifflin.

Pascarella, E. T., Pierson, C. T., Wolniak, G. C., & Terenzini, P. T. (2004). First-generation college students: Additional evidence on college experiences and outcomes. *The Journal of Higher Education, 75,* 249–284.

Pascarella, E. T., & Terenzini, P. T. (1991). *How college affects students.* San Francisco: Jossey-Bass.

Pascarella, E. T., & Terenzini, P. T. (2005). *How college affects students: A third decade of research* (2nd ed.). San Francisco: Jossey-Bass.

Patel, E. (2007), *Acts of faith: The story of an American Muslim, in the struggle for the soul of a generation.* New York: Beacon Press.

Patton, L. D. (2009). My sister's keeper: A qualitative examination of significant mentoring relationships among African American women in graduate and professional schools. *Journal of Higher Education, 80,* 510–537.

Patton, L. D. (Ed.)(2010). Culture centers in higher education: Perspectives on identity, theory and practice. Sterling, VA: Stylus Publishing.

Patton, L. D. (2011). Perspectives on identity, disclosure, and the campus environment among African American gay and bisexual men at one historically Black college. *Journal of College Student Development, 52,* 77–100.

Patton, L. D., & Catching, C. (2009). Teaching while black: Narratives of African American student affairs faculty. *International Journal of Qualitative Studies in Education, 22*(6), 713–728.

Patton, L. D., & Chang, S. (2011). Crossroads and intersections: Exploring LGBTQ identity development among millennial college students. In F. A. Bonner, A. Marbley, & M. F. Howard-Hamilton (Eds.), *Diverse millennial students in college* (pp. 193–212). Sterling, VA: Stylus Publishing.

Patton, L. D., & Harper, S. R. (2009). Using reflection to reframe theory-to-practice in student affairs. In G. McClellan & J. Stringer (Eds.), *The handbook for student affairs administration* (3rd ed., pp. 147–165). San Francisco-Jossey-Bass.

Patton, L. D., Harper, S. R., & Harris, J. C. (2015). Using critical race theory to (re)interpret widely-studied topics in U.S. higher education. In A. M. Martínez-Alemán, E. M. Bensimon, & B. Pusser (Eds.), *Critical approaches to the study of higher education* (pp. 193–219). Baltimore: Johns Hopkins University Press.

Patton, L. D., Kortegast, C., & Barela, G. (2011). Policies, practices, and current perspectives on working with LGBTQ millennial college students. In F. A. Bonner, A. Marbley, & M. F. Howard-Hamilton (Eds.), *Diverse millennial students in college* (175–192). Sterling, VA: Stylus Publishing.

Patton, L. D., & McClure, M. (2009). Strength in the spirit: African American college women and spiritual coping mechanisms. *Journal of Negro Education, 78,* 42–54.

Patton, L. D., McEwen, M., Rendón, L., & Howard-Hamilton, M. (Eds.). (2007). Critical race perspectives on theory in student affairs. *New Directions for Student Services,* no. 120, pp. 39–53. San Francisco: Jossey-Bass.

Patton, L. D., Njoku, N., & Rogers, J. (2015). Black feminist thought and examining the experiences of Black graduate women in the academy. In V. A. Anfara, Jr., & N. T. Mertz (Eds.), *Theoretical frameworks in qualitative research* (2nd ed., pp. 62–79). Thousand Oaks, CA: Sage.

Patton, L. D. & Simmons, S. (2008). Exploring complexities of multiple identities of lesbians in a black college environment. *Negro Educational Review, 59*(3-4), 197–215.

Paulsen, M. B., & St. John, E. P. (2002). Social class and college costs: Examining the financial nexus between college choice and persistence. *Journal of Higher Education, 73,* 189–236.

Pearce, J., Down, B., & Moore, E. (2008). Social class, identity and the "good" student: Negotiating university culture. *Australian Journal of Education, 52,* 257–271.

Pearlin, L. I., & Schooler, C. (1978). The structure of coping. *Journal of Health and Social Behavior, 19,* 2–21.

Peek, L. (2005). Becoming Muslim: The development of a religious identity. *Sociology of Religion, 66*(3), 215–242.

Peña-Talamantes, A. E. (2013). Empowering the self, creating worlds: Lesbian and gay Latina/o college students' identity negotiation in figured worlds. *Journal of College Student Development, 54,* 267–282.

Pérez, D. (2014). Exploring the nexus between community cultural wealth and the academic and social experiences of Latino male achievers at two predominantly White research universities. *International Journal of Qualitative Studies in Education, 27,* 747–767.

Pérez Huber, L. (2009). Challenging racist nativist framing: Acknowledging the community cultural wealth of undocumented Chicana college students to reframe the immigration debate. *Harvard Educational Review, 79*(4), 704–729.

Pérez Huber, L. (2010). Using Latina/o critical race theory (LatCrit) and racist nativism to explore intersectionality in the educational experiences of undocumented Chicana college students. *Educational Foundations, 24,* 77–96.

Perry, W. G., Jr. (1968). *Forms of intellectual and ethical development in the college years: A scheme.* New York: Holt, Rinehart, & Winston.

Perry, W. G., Jr. (1981). Cognitive and ethical growth: The making of meaning. In A. W. Chickering (Ed.), *The modern American college* (pp. 76–116). San Francisco: Jossey-Bass.

Peterson, R. D. (2014). Examining the intersection of race, gender, and environment using Bronfenbrenner's bioecological systems theory of human development. In V. A. Anfara, Jr., & N. T. Mertz (Eds.), *Theoretical frameworks in qualitative research* (2nd ed., pp. 198–215). Thousand Oaks, CA: Sage.

Pew Forum on Religion & Public Life. (2008). *U.S Religious Landscape Survey. Religious affiliation: Diverse and dynamic.* Washington, DC: Pew Research Center.

Pewardy, C., & Frey, B. (2004). American Indian students' perceptions of racial climate, multicultural support services, and ethnic fraud at a predominately White university. *Journal of American Indian Education, 43*(1), 32–60.

Phelps, R. E., Taylor, J. D., & Gerard, P. A. (2001). Cultural mistrust, ethnic identity, racial identity, and self-esteem among ethnically diverse Black university students. *Journal of Counseling and Development, 79,* 209–216.

Phelps, R. E., Tranakos-Howe, S., Dagley, J. C., & Lyn, M. K. (2001). Encouragement and ethnicity in African American college students. *Journal of Counseling and Development, 79,* 90–97.

Phillips, D. A., & Phillips, J. R. (2009). Privilege, male. In J. O'Brien (Ed.), *Encyclopedia of gender and society* (pp. 683–685). Thousand Oaks, CA: Sage.

Phillips, S. D., & Imhoff, A. R. (1997). Women and career development: A decade of research. *Annual Review of Psychology, 48,* 31–59.

Phinney, J. S. (1989). Stages in ethnic identity development in minority group children. *Journal of Early Adolescence, 9*(1–2), 34–49.

Phinney, J. S. (1990). Ethnic identity in adolescents and adults: Review of research. *Psychological Bulletin, 108,* 499–514.

Phinney, J. S. (1992). The multigroup ethnic identity measure. *Journal of Adolescent Research, 7,* 156–176.

Phinney, J. S. (1993). A three-stage model of ethnic identity development in adolescence. In M. E. Bernal & G. P. Knight (Eds.), *Ethnic identity: Formation and transmission among Hispanics and other minorities* (pp. 61–79). Albany, NY: State University of New York Press.

Phinney, J. S. (1995). Ethnic identity and self-esteem: A review and integration. In A. M. Padilla (Ed.), *Hispanic psychology: Critical issues in theory and research* (pp. 57–70). Thousand Oaks, CA: Sage.

Phinney, J. S. (2007). Conceptualization and measurement of ethnic identity: Current status and future directions. *Journal of Counseling Psychology, 54,* 271–281.

Phinney, J. S. (2010). Understanding development in cultural contexts: How do we deal with the complexity? *Human Development, 53,* 33–38.

Phinney, J. S., & Alipuria, L. L. (1996). At the interface of cultures: Multiethnic/multiracial high school and college students. *Journal of Social Psychology, 136,* 139–158.

Phinney, J. S., & Baldelomar, O. A. (2011). Identity development in multiple cultural contexts. In L. A. Jensen (Ed.), *Bridging cultural and developmental approaches to psychology: New syntheses in theory, research, and policy* (pp. 161–186). Oxford and New York: Oxford University Press.

Phinney, J. S., Chavira, V., & Williamson, L. (1992). Acculturation attitudes and self-esteem among high school and college students. *Youth & Society, 23,* 299–312.

Phinney, J. S., Dennis, J., & Osorio, S. (2006). Reasons to attend college among ethnically diverse college students. *Cultural Diversity and Ethnic Minority Psychology, 12,* 347–366.

Phinney, J. S., Jacoby, B., & Silva, C. (2007). Positive intergroup attitudes: The role of ethnic identity. *International Journal of Behavioral Development, 31,* 478–490.

Phinney, J. S., & Ong, A. D. (2007). Conceptualization and measurement of ethnic identity: Current status and future directions. *Journal of Counseling Psychology, 54,* 271–281.

Phinney, J. S., Torres Campos, C. M., Padilla Kallemeyn, D. M., & Kim, C. (2011). Processes and outcomes of a mentoring program for Latino college freshmen. *Journal of Social Issues, 67,* 599–621.

Piaget, J. (1950). *The psychology of intelligence.* San Diego, CA: Harcourt Brace Jovanovich.

Piaget, J. (1952). *The origins of intelligence in children.* New York: International Universities Press.

Piaget, J. (1973). *The child and reality* (A. Rosin, Trans.). New York: Viking. (Original work published 1956)

Piaget, J. (1977). *The moral judgment of the child* (M. Gabain, Trans.). Harmondsworth, England: Penguin. (Original work published 1932)

Pike, G. R., Smart, J. C., & Ethington, C. A. (2012). The mediating effects of student engagement on the relationships between academic disciplines and learning outcomes: An extension of Holland's theory. *Research in Higher Education, 53,* 550–575.

Pillay, Y. (2005). Racial identity as a predictor of the psychological health of African American students at a predominantly White University. *Journal of Black Psychology, 31*(1), 46–66.

Pinderhughes, E. (1995). Biracial identity—asset or handicap? In H. W. Harris, H. C. Blue, & E. E. H. Griffith (Eds.), *Racial and ethnic identity: Psychological development and creative expression* (pp. 73–93). New York: Routledge.

Piper, T. D. (1997). Empowering students to create community standards. *About Campus, 2*(3), 22–24.

Piper, T. D., & Buckley, J. A. (2004). Community Standards Model: Developing learning partnerships in campus housing. In M. Baxter Magolda & P. M. King (Eds.), *Learning partnerships: Theory and modes of practice to educate for self-authorship* (pp. 185–212). Sterling, VA: Stylus.

Pizzolato, J. E. (2003). Developing self-authorship: Exploring the experiences of high-risk college students. *Journal of College Student Development, 44*, 797–811.

Pizzolato, J. E. (2004). Coping with conflict: Self-authorship, coping, and adaptation to college in first-year high-risk students. *Journal of College Student Development, 45*, 425–442.

Pizzolato, J. E. (2005). Creating crossroads for self-authorship: Investigating the provocative moment. *Journal of College Student Development, 46*, 624–641.

Pizzolato, J. E. (2006). Complex partnerships: Self-authorship and provocative academic-advising practices. *NACADA Journal, 26*(1), 32–45.

Pizzolato, J. E. (2007). Assessing self-authorship. In P. S. Meszaros (Ed.), *Self-authorship: Advancing students' intellectual growth.* New Directions for Teaching and Learning, no. 109, pp. 31–42. San Francisco: Jossey-Bass.

Pizzolato, J. E. (2008). Advisor, teacher, partner: Using the learning partnerships model to reshape academic advising. *About Campus, 13*(1), 18–25.

Pizzolato, J. E., Chaudhari, P., Murrell, E. D., Podobnik, S., & Schaeffer, Z. (2008). Ethnic identity, epistemological development, and academic achievement in underrepresented students. *Journal of College Student Development, 49*, 301–318.

Pizzolato, J., Nguyen, T., Johnston, M., & Wang, S. (2012). Understanding context: Cultural, relational, & psychological interaction in self-authorship development. *Journal of College Student Development, 53*, 656–679.

Pizzolato, J. E., & Ozaki, C. C. (2007). Moving toward self-authorship: investigating outcomes of learning partnerships. *Journal of College Student Development, 48*, 196–214.

Plummer, K. (1975). *Sexual stigma: An interactionist account.* London: Routledge & Kegan Paul.

Pollock, D. C., & Van Reken, R. E. (1999) *The third culture kid experience: Growing up among worlds.* Yarmouth, ME: Intercultural Press.

Pope, R. L. (1998). The relationship between psychosocial development and racial identity of Black college students. *Journal of College Student Development, 39*, 273–282.

Pope, R. L. (2000). The relationship between psychosocial development and racial identity of college students of color. *Journal of College Student Development, 41*, 302–312.

Pope, R. L., Reynolds, A. L., & Mueller, J. A. (2004). *Multicultural competence in student affairs.* San Francisco: Jossey-Bass.

Pope-Davis, D. B., Liu, W. M., Ledesma-Jones, S., & Nevitt, J. (2000). African American acculturation and Black racial identity: A preliminary investigation. *Journal of Multicultural Counseling & Development, 28*(2), 98–112.

Porter, C. J. (2013). *Identity development in Black undergraduate women: A grounded theory study.* Unpublished doctoral dissertation, University of Georgia.

Portes, A. (1998). Social capital: Its origins and applications in modern sociology. *Annual Review of Sociology, 24*, 1–24.

Poston, W.S.C. (1990). The biracial identity development model: A needed addition. *Journal of Counseling and Development, 69*, 152–155.

Power, R. C. (2005). Motivation and moral development: A trifocal perspective. *Nebraska Symposium on Motivation, 51*, 197–249.

Poynter, K. J., & Tubbs, N. J. (2008). Safe zones: Creating LGBT safe space ally programs. *Journal of LGBT Youth, 5*(1), 121–132.

Pozzebon, J. A., Ashton, M. C., & Visser, B. A. (2014). Major changes personality, ability, and congruence in the prediction of academic outcomes. *Journal of Career Assessment, 22*(1), 75–88.

Prenksy, M. (2001a). Digital Natives, Digital Immigrants. *On the Horizon, 9*(5), 1–6.

Prenksy, M. (2001b). Digital Natives, Digital Immigrants, Part II. Do they really think differently? *On the Horizon, 9*(6), 1–6.

Prensky, M. (2009). H. sapiens digital: From digital immigrants and digital natives to digital wisdom. *Innovate: Journal of Online Education, 5*(3). From http://www.wisdompage.com/Prensky01.html

Pusch, R. S. (2005). Objects of curiosity: Transgender college students' perception of the reactions of others. *Journal of Gay and Lesbian Issues in Education, 3*(1), 45–61.

Quaye, S. J. (2012). Think before you teach: Preparing for dialogues about racial realities. *Journal of College Student Development, 53*, 542–562.

Quaye, S. J. (2014). Facilitating dialogues about racial realities. *Teachers College Record, 116*(8), 1–42.

Quinn J., & Radtke, L. (2006). Dilemmatic negotiations: the (un)tenability of feminist identity. *Psychology of Women Quarterly, 30*, 187–198.

Quintana, S. M. (2007). Racial and ethnic identity: Developmental perspectives and research. *Journal of Counseling Psychology, 54*, 259–270.

Radecke, M. W. (2007). Service-learning and faith formation. *Journal of College and Character, 8*(5), 1–28.

Radmacher, K., & Azmitia, M. (2013). Unmasking class: How upwardly mobile poor and working-class emerging adults negotiate an "invisible" identity. *Emerging Adulthood, 1*(4), 314–329.

Ramazanoğ lu, C. (with Holland, J.). (2002). *Feminist methodology: Challenges and choices.* Thousand Oaks, CA: Sage.

Ramirez, M., III. (1983). *Psychology of the Americas: Mestizo perspective on personality and mental health.* New York: Pergamon Press.

Rankin, S., Blumenfeld, W. J., Weber, G. N., & Frazer, S. (2010). *State of higher education for LGBT people.* Charlotte, NC: Campus Pride.

Raue, K., Lewis, L., & Coopersmith, J. (2011). *Students with disabilities at degree-granting postsecondary institutions: First look. NCES 2011-018.* Washington, DC: U.S. Department of Education.

Rauscher, L., & McClintock, M. (1997). Ableism curricular design. In M. Adams, L. A. Bell, & P. Griffin (Eds.), *Teaching for diversity and social justice* (p. 198–229). New York: Routledge.

Reason, R. D., & Kimball, E. W. (2012). A new theory-to-practice model for student affairs: Integrating scholarship, context, and reflection. *Journal of Student Affairs Research & Practice, 49*, 359–376.

Reisser, L. (1995). Revisiting the seven vectors. *Journal of College Student Development, 36*, 505–511.

Rendón, L. I. (1994). Validating culturally diverse students: Toward a new model of learning and student development. *Innovative Higher Education, 19*, 33–51.

Renn, K. A. (2000). Patterns of situational identity among biracial and multiracial college students. *Review of Higher Education, 23*(4), 399–420.

Renn, K. A. (2003). Understanding the identities of mixed race college students through a developmental ecology lens. *Journal of College Student Development, 44,* 383–403.

Renn, K. A. (2004). *Mixed race students in college: The ecology of race, identity, and community on campus.* Albany: State University of New York Press.

Renn, K. A. (2010). LGBT and queer research in higher education: The state and status of the field. *Educational Researcher, 39,* 132–141.

Renn, K. A. (2012). Creating and re-creating race: The emergence of racial identity as a critical element in psychological, sociological, and ecological perspectives on human development. In C. L. Wijeysinghe & B. W. Jackson, III (Eds.), *New perspectives on racial identity development: A theoretical and practical anthology* (2nd ed., pp. 11–22). New York: NYU Press.

Renn, K. A., & Arnold, K. D. (2003). Reconceptualizing research on peer culture. *Journal of Higher Education, 74,* 261–291.

Renn, K. A., Brazelton, G. B., & Holmes, J. M. (2014). At the margins of internationalization: Trends in publishing on international issues related to college student experiences, development, and learning, 1998–2011. *Journal of College Student Development, 55*(3), 278–294.

Renn, K. A., & Jessup-Anger, E. R. (2008). Preparing new professionals: Lessons for graduate preparation programs from the national study of new professionals in student affairs. *Journal of College Student Development, 49,* 319–335.

Renn, K. A., & Lunceford, C. J. (2002, November 23). *Because the numbers matter: Transforming racial/ethnic reporting data to account for mixed race students in postsecondary education. Paper presented at the annual meeting of the Association for the Study of Higher Education,* Sacramento, CA.

Renn, K. A., Nicolazzo, Z., Brazelton, G. B., Nguyen, D. J., & Woodford, M. (2014). The role of personal resilience and environmental buffers in LGBTQ college student success. *Paper presented at the American Educational Research Association Annual Meeting,* Philadelphia, PA

Renn, K. A., & Reason, R. D. (2013). *College students in the United States: Characteristics, experiences, and outcomes.* San Francisco: Jossey-Bass.

Rest, J. R. (1969). *Hierarchies of comprehension and preference in a developmental stage model of moral thinking.* Unpublished doctoral dissertation, University of Chicago.

Rest, J. R. (1979a). *Development in judging moral issues.* Minneapolis: University of Minnesota Press.

Rest, J. R. (1979b). *Revised manual for the Defining Issues Test.* Unpublished manuscript. MMRP Technical Report. Minneapolis: University of Minnesota Press.

Rest, J. R. (1986a). *The Defining Issues Test* (3rd ed.). Minneapolis: University of Minnesota, Center for the Study of Ethical Development.

Rest, J. R. (1986b). *Moral development: Advances in research and theory.* New York: Praeger.

Rest, J., & Narvaez, D. (1991). The college experience and moral development. *Handbook of Moral Behavior and Development, 2,* 229–245.

Rest, J. R., & Narvaez, D. (1998). *Defining Issues Test-2.* Minneapolis, MN: University of Minnesota.

Rest, J. R., Narvaez, D., Bebeau, M. J., & Thoma, S. J. (1999). *Postconventional moral thinking: A neo-Kohlbergian approach.* Mahwah, NJ: Erlbaum.

Rest, J., Narvaez, D., Thoma, S. J., & Bebeau, M. J. (2000). A neo-Kohlbergian approach to morality research. *Journal of Moral Education, 29,* 381–395.

Reynolds, A. L., & Hanjorgiris, W. F. (2000). Coming out: Lesbian, gay, and bisexual identity development. In R. P. Perez, K. A. DeBord, & K. Bieschke (Eds.), *Handbook of counseling and psychotherapy with lesbian, gay, and bisexual clients* (pp. 35–55). Washington, DC: American Psychological Association.

Reynolds, A. L., & Pope, R. L. (1991). The complexities of diversity: Exploring multiple oppressions. *Journal of Counseling and Development, 70,* 174–180.

Reynolds, A. L., Sodano, S. M., Ecklund, T. R., & Guyker, W. (2012). Dimensions of acculturation in Native American college students. *Measurement and Evaluation in Counseling and Development, 45,* 101–112.

Rezentes III, W. C. (1993). Na mea Hawai'i: A Hawaiian acculturation scale. *Psychological Reports, 73*(2), 383–393.

Rhatigan, J. J. (2000). The history and philosophy of student affairs. In M. J. Barr, M. K. Dresler, & Associates, *The handbook of student affairs administration* (pp. 3–24). San Francisco: Jossey-Bass.

Rhoads, R. A., & Black, M. A. (1995). Student affairs practitioners as transformative educators: Advancing a critical cultural perspective. *Journal of College Student Development, 36,* 413–421.

Rhoads, R. A., Lee, J. J., & Yamada, M. (2002). Panethnicity and collective action among Asian American students: A qualitative case study. *Journal of College Student Development, 43,* 876–891.

Rhoads, R. A., Saenz, V., & Carducci, R. (2005). Higher education reform as a social movement: The case of affirmative action. *The Review of Higher Education, 28,* 191–220.

Ribeiro, M. D., & Saleem, S. (2010). Providing outreach services to Muslim college women. *Journal of Muslim Mental Health, 5,* 233–244.

Rich, A. (1980). Compulsory heterosexuality and lesbian existence. *Journal of Women in Culture and Society, 5,* 631–660.

Richardson, T. Q., Bethea, A. R., Hayling, C. C., & Williamson-Taylor, C. (2010). African and Afro-Caribbean American identity development: Theory and practice implications. In J. G. Ponterotto, J. M. Casas, L. A. Suzuki, & C. M. Alexander (Eds.), *Handbook of multicultural counseling* (3rd ed., pp. 227–239). Los Angeles: Sage.

Risco, C. M. (2008). *Evaluation of a culturally inclusive model of sexual minority identity formation. Unpublished master's thesis.* College Park: University of Maryland.

Roberts, K. A. (2011). Imagine deep learning. *Michigan Sociological Review, 25,* 1–18.

Robinson, S. J. (2013). Spoketokenism: Black women talking back about graduate school experiences. *Race Ethnicity and Education, 16,* 155–158.

Robinson, S. (2013). Using technology and digital narratives to engage doctoral students in self-authorship and learning partnerships. *Cutting-Edge Technologies in Higher Education, 6,* 41–65.

Robinson, T. L., & Howard-Hamilton, M. (2000). *The convergence of race, ethnicity and gender: Multiple identities in counseling.* Upper Saddle River, NJ: Merrill.

Rocca, K. A. (2010). Student participation in the college classroom: An extended multidisciplinary literature review. *Communication Education, 59,* 185–213.

Rocco, T. S., & West, W. G. (1998). Deconstructing privilege: An examination of privilege in adult education. *Adult Education Quarterly, 48,* 171–184.

Rocconi, L. M., Ribera, A. K., & Laird, T. F. N. (2014). College seniors' plans for graduate school: Do deep approaches learning and Holland academic environments matter?. *Research in Higher Education, 1–24.*

Rockenbach, A. N., Mayhew, M. J., & Bowman, N. A. (in press). Perceptions of the campus climate for non-religious students. *Journal of College Student Development.*

Rockenbach, A. N., Mayhew, M. J., Davidson, J., Ofstein, J., & Clark Bush, R., (2015). Complicating universal definitions: How students of diverse worldviews make meaning of spirituality. *Journal of Student Affairs Research and Practice, 52,* 1–10.

Rockenbach, A. N., & Park, J. J. (in press). Religion, spirituality, and U.S. college students. In M. D. Waggoner & N. C. Walker (Eds.), *The Oxford Handbook of Religion and American Education.* New York: Oxford University Press.

Rockquemore, K. A. (2002). Negotiating the color line: The gendered process of racial identity construction among Black/White biracial women. *Gender & Society, 16*, 485–503.

Rockquemore, K. A., & Brunsma, D. L. (2002). *Beyond black: Biracial identity in America.* Thousand Oaks, CA: Sage.

Rodgers, R. F. (1980). Theories underlying student development. In D. G. Creamer (Ed.), *Student development in higher education* (pp. 10–95). Cincinnati, OH: American College Personnel Association.

Rodgers, R. F. (1990). Recent theories and research underlying student development. In D. Creamer & *Associates, College student development: Theory and practice for the 1990s* (pp. 27–79). Alexandria, VA: American College Personnel Association.

Rodriguez, E. M. (2009). At the intersection of church and gay: A review of the psychological research on gay and lesbian Christians. *Journal of Homosexuality, 57*(1), 5–38.

Rodriguez, E. M., & Ouellette, S. C. (2000). Gay and Lesbian Christians: Homosexual and Religious Identity Integration in the Members and Participants of a Gay-Positive Church. *Journal for the Scientific Study of Religion, 39*(3), 333–347.

Rodriguez, A. L., Guido-DiBrito, R., Torres, V., & Talbot, D. (2000). Latina college students: Issues and challenges for the 21st century. *NASPA Journal, 37*, 511–527.

Roehlkepartain, E. C., Benson, P. L., & Scales, P. C. (2011). Spiritual identity: Contextual perspectives. In S. J. Schwartz, K. Luyckx, & V. L. Vignoles (Eds.), *Handbook of identity theory and research* (pp. 545–562). Springer New York.

Rogers, J. L., & Dantley, M. E. (2001). Invoking the spiritual in campus life and leadership. *Journal of College Student Development, 42*, 589–603.

Rogers, J. L., Magolda, P. M., Baxter Magolda, M. B., & Knight Abowitz, K. (2004). A community of scholars: Enacting the learning partnerships model in graduate education. In M. Baxter Magolda & P. M. King (Eds.), *Learning partnerships: Theory and modes of practice to educate for self-authorship* (pp. 213–244). Sterling, VA: Stylus.

Rogers, M. S. (2004). An exploration of psychosocial development in community college students. *Dissertation Abstracts International, A65/06*, p. 2070.

Romer, N. (1991). A feminist view of moral development: Criticisms and applications. *Initiatives, 54*(3), 19–32.

Root, M.P.P. (1990). Resolving "other" status: Identity development of biracial individuals. In L. S. Brown & M.P.P. Root (Eds.), *Complexity and diversity in feminist theory and therapy* (pp. 185–205). New York: Haworth.

Root, M.P.P. (1995). The multiracial contribution to the psychological browning of America. In N. Zack (Ed.), *American mixed race: The culture of microdiversity* (pp. 231–236). Lanham, MD: Rowman & Littlefield.

Root, M.P.P. (1996). The multiracial experience: Racial borders as a significant frontier in race relations. In M.P.P. Root (Ed.), *The multiracial experience: Racial borders as the new frontier* (pp. xiii–xxviii). Thousand Oaks, CA: Sage.

Root, M.P.P. (1997). Mixed-race women. In N. Zack (Ed.), *Race/sex: Their sameness, difference, and interplay* (pp. 157–172). New York: Routledge.

Root, M.P.P. (2001). Factors influencing the variation in racial and ethnic identity of mixed-heritage persons of Asian ancestry. In T. Williams-León & C. L. Nakashima (Eds.), *The sum of our parts: Mixed-heritage Asian Americans* (pp. 61–70). Philadelphia: Temple University Press.

Root, M.P.P. (2003a). Five mixed-race identities. In L. I. Winter & H. L. DeBose (Eds.), *New faces in a changing America: Multiracial identity in the 21st century* (pp. 3–20). Thousand Oaks, CA: Sage.

Root, M.P.P. (2003b). Racial identity development and persons of mixed race heritage. In M.P.P. Root & M. Kelley (Eds.), *Multiracial child resource book: Living complex identities* (pp. 34–41). Seattle: MAVIN Foundation.

Rosario, M., Schrimshaw, E. W., & Hunter, J. (2004). Ethnic/racial differences in the coming-out process of lesbian, gay, and bisexual youths: A comparison of sexual identity development over time. *Cultural Diversity and Ethnic Minority Psychology, 10*(3), 215–228.

Rosenthal, D. A., & Feldman, S. S. (1992). The nature and stability of ethnic identity in Chinese youth: Effects of length of residence in two cultural contexts. *Journal of Cross-Cultural Psychology, 23*, 214–227.

Roth, B. (2004). *Separate roads to feminism: Black, Chicana, and white feminist movements in America's second wave.* Cambridge, England: Oxford University Press.

Rowe, W., Bennett, S. K., & Atkinson, D. R. (1994). White racial identity models: A critique and alternative proposal. *Counseling Psychologist, 22*, 129–146.

Rubin, M., Denson, N., Kilpatrick, S., Matthews, K. E., Stehlik, T., & Zyngier, D. (2014). "I am working-class": Subjective self-definition as a missing measure of social class and socioeconomic status in higher education research. *Educational Researcher, 43*, 196–200.

Rumann, C. B., & Hamrick, F. A. (2010). Student veterans in transition: Re-enrolling after war zone deployments. *The Journal of Higher Education, 81*, 431–458.

Rumann, C., Rivera, M., & Hernandez, I. (Eds.). (2011). *Student veterans and community colleges. New Directions for Community Colleges*, no. 155, pp. 51–58. San Francisco: Jossey-Bass.

Sabik, N. J., & Tylka, T. L. (2006). Do feminist identity styles moderate the relation between perceived sexist events and disordered eating? *Psychology of Women Quarterly, 30*, 77–84.

Sáenz, V. B., Bukoski, B. E., Lu, C., & Rodriguez, S. (2013). Latino males in Texas community colleges: A phenomenological study of masculinity constructs and their effect on college experiences. *Journal of African American Males in Education, 4*(2), 5–24.

Sáenz, V. B., Hurtado, S., Barrera, D., Wolf, D., & Yeung, F. (2007). *First in my family: A profile of first-generation college students at four-year institutions since 1971.* Los Angeles, CA: Higher Education Research Institute.

Salameh, F. (2011). Towards a new ecology of Middle East identities. *Middle Eastern Studies, 47*, 237–253.

Salisbury, M. H., Paulsen, M. B., & Pascarella, E. T. (2010). To see the world or stay at home: Applying an integrated student choice model to explore the gender gap in the intent to study abroad. *Research in Higher Education, 51*, 615–640.

Salter, D. W., & Persaud, A. (2003). Women's views of the factors that encourage and discourage classroom participation. *Journal of College Student Development, 44*, 831–844.

Saltzburg, S., & Davis, T. S. (2010). Co-authoring gender-queer youth identities: Discursive tellings and retellings. *Journal of Ethnic & Cultural Diversity in Social Work, 19*(2), 87–108.

Sanchez, D. (2013). Racial identity attitudes and ego identity statuses in Dominican and Puerto Rican college students. *Journal of College Student Development, 54*, 497–510.

Sanchez, D., & Carter, R. T. (2005). Exploring the relationship between racial identity and religious orientation among African American college students. *Journal of College Student Development, 46*, 280–295.

Sanders, J. L. (1998). Religious ego identity and its relationship to faith maturity. *Journal of Psychology, 132*, 653–658.

Sanders, M. R., & Mahalingam, R. (2012). Under the radar: The role of invisible discourse in understanding class-based privilege. *Journal of Social Issues, 68*, 112–127.

Sandoval, C. (2000). *Methodology of the oppressed: Theory out of bounds*. Minneapolis: University of Minnesota Press.

Sanford, N. (1962). Developmental status of the entering freshmen. In N. Sanford (Ed.), *The American college student* (pp. 253–282). New York: Wiley.

Sanford, N. (1966). *Self and society*. New York: Atherton Press.

Sanford, N. (1967). *Where colleges fail: The study of the student as a person*. San Francisco: Jossey-Bass.

Savin-Williams, R. C. (1995). Lesbian, gay male, and bisexual adolescents. In A. R. D'Augelli & C. J. Patterson (Eds.), *Lesbian, gay, and bisexual identities over the lifespan: Psychological perspectives* (pp. 165–189). New York: Oxford University Press.

Savin-Williams, R. C. (2011). Identity development among sexual-minority youth. In S. J. Schwartz, K. Luyckx, & V. L. Vignoles (Eds.), *Handbook of identity theory and research* (pp. 671–689). New York: Springer.

Sax, L. J. (2008). *The gender gap in college: Maximizing the potential of women and men*. San Francisco: Jossey-Bass.

Sax, L. J., Bryant, A. N., & Harper, C. E. (2005). The differential effects of student-faculty interaction on college outcomes for women and men. *Journal of College Student Development*, *46*, 642–657.

Scharmer, C. O. (2000, March 23). Grabbing the tail: Conversation with Robert Kegan. *Dialog on Leadership. Retrieved May 22, 2008 from* http://www.dialogonleadership.org/Kegan-1999.html

Schenkel, S., & Marcia, J. E. (1972). Attitudes toward premarital intercourse in determining ego identity status in college women. *Journal of Personality*, *40*, 472–482.

Schlossberg, N. K. (1989a). Marginality and mattering: Key issues in building community. In D. C. Roberts (Ed.), *Designing campus activities to foster a sense of community*. New Directions for Student Services, no. 48, pp. 5–15. San Francisco: Jossey-Bass.

Schlossberg, N. K. (1989b). *Overwhelmed: Coping with life's ups and downs*. Lexington, MA: Lexington Books.

Schlossberg, N. K., Lynch, A. Q., & Chickering, A. W. (1989). *Improving higher education environments for adults: Responsive programs and services from entry to departure*. San Francisco: Jossey-Bass.

Schlossberg, N. K., & Robinson, S. P. (1996). *Going to plan B*. New York: Simon & Schuster.

Schlossberg, N. K., Waters, E. B., & Goodman, J. (1995). *Counseling adults in transition* (2nd ed.). New York: Springer.

Schlosser, L. Z. (2003). Christian privilege: Breaking a sacred taboo. *Journal of Multicultural Counseling and Development*, *31*, 44–51.

Schommer-Aikins, M., & Easter, M. (2006). Ways of knowing and epistemological beliefs: Combined effect on academic performance. *Educational Psychology: An International Journal of Experimental Educational Psychology*, *26*, 411–423.

Schuh, J. H. (1994). [Review of *Education and identity* (2nd ed.)]. *Journal of College Student Development*, *35*, 310–312.

Schwandt, T. A. (2007). *Dictionary of qualitative research* (3rd ed.). Thousand Oaks, CA: Sage.

Schwartz, J. L., Donovan, J., & Guido-DiBrito, F. (2009). Stories of social class: Self-identified male Mexican students crack the silence. *Journal of College Student Development*, *50*, 50–66.

Schwartz, S. J., Zamboanga, B. L., Luyckx, K., Meca, A., & Ritchie, R. A. (2013). Identity in emerging adulthood: Reviewing the field and looking forward. *Emerging Adulthood*, *1*, 96–113.

Schwartz, S. J., Zamboanga, B. L., Mecca, A., & Ritchie, R. A. (2012). Identity around the world: An overview. In S. J. Shwartz (Ed.), *Identity around the world*. New Directions for Child and Adolescent Development, no. 138, pp. 1–18. San Francisco: Jossey-Bass.

Schwartz, S. J., Zamboanga, B. L., Wang, W., & Olthuis, J. V. (2009). Measuring identity from an Eriksonian perspective: Two sides of the same coin? *Journal of Personality Assessment, 91,* 143–154.

Seggie, F. N., & Sanford, G. (2010). Perceptions of female Muslim students who veil: Campus religious climate. *Race, Ethnicity, & Education, 13*(1), 59–82.

Seider, M. (2008). The dynamics of social reproduction: How class works at a state college and elite private college. *Equity & Excellence in Education, 41,* 45–61.

Seifert, T. (2007). Understanding Christian privilege: Managing the tensions of spiritual plurality. *About Campus, 12*(2), 10–17.

Seifert, T. A., & Holman-Harmon, N. (2009). Practical implications for student affairs professionals' work in facilitating students' inner development. In S. K. Watt, E. E. Fairchild, and K. Goodman (Eds), *Intersections of religious privilege: Difficult dialogues and student affairs practice.* New Directions for Student Services, no. 125, pp. 13–21. San Francisco: Jossey-Bass.

Sellers, R. M., Smith, M., Shelton, N. J., Rowley, S. J., & Chavous, T. M. (1998). Multidimensional model of racial identity: A reconceptualization of African American racial identity. *Personality and Social Psychology Review, 2,* 18–39.

Selman, R. (1980). *Growth of interpersonal understanding: Developmental and clinical analysis.* New York: Academic Press.

Sensoy, Ö., & DiAngelo, R. (2012). *Is everyone really equal?: An introduction to key concepts in social justice education.* New York: Teachers College Press.

Serpe, R. T., & Stryker, S. (2011). The symbolic interactionist perspective and identity theory. In S. J. Schwartz, K. Luyckx, & V. L. Vignoles (Eds.), *Handbook of identity theory and research* (pp. 225–248). Springer New York.

Shackleford, A. L. (2009). Documenting the needs of student veterans with disabilities: Intersection roadblocks, solutions, and legal realities. *Journal of Postsecondary Education and Disability, 22*(1), 36–42.

Shahjahan, R. A., & Kezar, A. J. (2013). Beyond the "national container": Addressing methodological nationalism in higher education research. *Educational Researcher, 42*(1), 20–29.

Shammas, D. S. (2009). Post 9/11 Arab and Muslim American community college students: Ethno-religious enclaves and perceived discrimination. *Community College Journal of Research and Practice, 33,* 283–308.

Shapiro, C. A., & Sax, L. J. (Eds.). (2011). *Major selection and persistence for women in STEM.* New Directions for Institutional Research, no. 152, pp. 5–18. San Francisco: Jossey-Bass.

Shattuck, P. T., Steinberg, J., Yu, J., Wei, X., Cooper, B. P., Newman, L., & Roux, A. M. (2014). Disability identification and self-efficacy among college students on the autism spectrum. *Autism research and treatment, 2014,* article ID 924182. Retrieved from http://www.hindawi.com/journals/aurt/2014/924182/abs. doi:10.1155/2014/924182

Sheehan, O.T.O., & Pearson, F. (1995). Asian international and American students' psychosocial development. *Journal of College Student Development, 36,* 523–530.

Shih, M., Bonam, C., Sanchez, D. T., & Peck, C. (2007). The social construction of race: Biracial identity and vulnerability to stereotypes. *Cultural Diversity and Ethnic Minority Psychology, 13,* 125–133.

Simola, S. (2014). Understanding moral courage through a feminist and developmental ethic of care. *Journal of Business Ethics.*

Simola, S. K., Barling, J., & Turner, N. (2010). Transformational leadership and leader moral orientation: Contrasting an ethic of justice and an ethic of care. *The Leadership Quarterly, 21*(1), 179–188.

Simon, J. A. (2011). Legal issues in serving students with disabilities in postsecondary education. In M. S. Belch (Ed.), *Fostering the increased integration of students with disabilities*. New Directions for Student Services, no. 134, pp. 95–107. San Francisco: Jossey-Bass.

Singh, A. A. (2013). Transgender youth of color and resilience: Negotiating oppression and finding support. *Sex Roles, 68,* 690–702.

Skoe, E.E.A. (1998). The ethic of care: Issues in moral development. In E.E.A. Skoe & A. L. von der Lippe (Eds.), *Personality development in adolescence: A cross national and life span perspective* (pp. 143–171). London: Routledge.

Skoe, E.E.A. (2008). Care, inventory of (ethic of care interview). In F. Clark Power, R. J. Nuzzi, D. Narvaez, D. Lapsley, & T. C. Hunt (Eds.), *Moral education: A handbook.* Vol. *1:* A – L (pp. 57–58.) Westport, CT: Praeger.

Small, J. L., & Bowman, N. A. (2011). Religious commitment, skepticism, and struggle among college students: The impact of majority/minority religious affiliation and institutional type. *Journal for the Scientific Study of Religion, 50,* 154–174.

Small, J. L., & Bowman, N. A. (2012). Religious affiliation and college student development: A literature review and synthesis. *Religion & Education, 39,* 64–75.

Smith, B. (2007). Accessing social capital through the academic mentoring process. *Equity & Excellence in Education, 40*(1), 36–46.

Smith, J. M. (2011). Becoming an atheist in America: Constructing identity and meaning from the rejection of theism. *Sociology of Religion, 72,* 215–237.

Smith, L. T. (1999). *Decolonizing methodologies: Research and indigenous peoples.* London: Zed Books.

Smith, N. (2014). More than white, heterosexual men: Intersectionality as a framework for understanding the identity of student veterans. *Journal of Progressive Policy & Practice, 2*(3), 231–238.

Smith, R. A., & Khawaja, N. G. (2011). A review of the acculturation experiences of international students. *International Journal of Intercultural Relations, 35,* 699–713.

Snarey, J. R. (1985). Cross-cultural universality of social-moral development: A critical review of Kohlbergian research. *Psychological Bulletin, 97,* 202–232.

Snyder, R., & Hasbrouck, L. (1996). Feminist identity, gender traits, and symptoms of disturbed eating among college women. *Psychology of Women Quarterly, 20,* 593–598.

Snyder, T. D., & Dillow, S. A. (2012). Digest of Education Statistics 2011. (NCES 2012-001). Washington, DC: National Center for Education Statistics, Institute of Education Sciences, U.S. Department of Education.

Sobel, J. (2002). Can we trust social capital? *Journal of Economic Literature, 40,* 139–154.

Sodowsky, G. R., & Carey, J. C. (1988). Relationships between acculturation-related demographics and cultural attitudes of an Asian-Indian immigrant group. *Journal of Multicultural Counseling and Development, 16,* 117–133.

Sodowsky, G. R., Kwan, K. K., & Pannu, R. (1995). Ethnic identity of Asians in the United States. In J. G. Ponterotto, J. M. Casas, L. A. Suzuki, & C. M. Alexander (Eds.), *Handbook of multicultural counseling* (pp. 123–154). Thousand Oaks, CA: Sage.

Solórzano, D. G. (1998). Critical race theory, race and gender microaggressions, and the experience of Chicana and Chicano studies. *International Journal of Qualitative Studies in Education, 11*(1), 121–136.

Solórzano, D., Ceja, M., & Yosso, T. (2000). Critical race theory, racial microaggressions, and campus racial climate: The experiences of African American college students. *Journal of Negro Education, 68*(1/2), 60–73.

Song, M. (2003). *Choosing ethnic identity.* Malden, MA: Blackwell.

Sonn, C. C., & Fisher, A. T. (2003). Identity and oppression: Differential responses to an in-between status. *American Journal of Community Psychology, 31*, 117–128.

Sowa, C. J., & Gressard, C. F. (1983). Athletic participation: Its relationship to student development. *Journal of College Student Development, 24*, 236–239.

Spaulding, E., & Wilson, A. (2002). Demystifying reflection: A study of pedagogical strategies that encourage reflective journal writing. *Teachers College Record, 104*, 1393–1421.

Speck, B. W. (2005). What is spirituality? In S. L. Hoppe & B. W. Speck (Eds.), *Spirituality in higher education*. New Directions for Teaching and Learning, no. 104, pp. 3–13. San Francisco: Jossey-Bass.

Spencer, M. B., & Markstrom-Adams, C. (1990). Identity processes among racial and ethnic minority children in America. *Child Development, 61*, 290–310.

Spencer, R. (2006). *Challenging multiracial identity*. Boulder, CO: Lynne Rienner.

Spencer, S. (2014). *Race and ethnicity: Culture, identity and representation* (2nd ed.). New York: Routledge.

Spurgeon, S. L., & Myers, J. E. (2010). African American males: Relationships among racial identity, college type, and wellness. *Journal of Black Studies, 40*, 527–543.

Squire, D. D., & Mobley, S. D., Jr. (2014, October 15). Negotiating race and sexual orientation in the college choice process of Black gay males. *The Urban Review, 1–26*. doi: 10.1007/s11256-014-0316-3

Stake, J. E., Roades, L., Rose, S., Ellis, L., & West, C. (1994). The women's studies experience: Impetus for feminist activism. *Psychology of Women Quarterly, 18*, 17–24.

Stamm, L. (2006). The dynamics of spirituality and the religious experience. In A. W. Chickering, J. C. Dalton, & L. Stamm (Eds.), *Encouraging authenticity and spirituality in higher education* (pp. 37–65). San Francisco: Jossey-Bass.

Standen, B.C.S. (1996). Without a template: The biracial Korean/white experience. In M.P.P. Root (Ed.), *The multiracial experience: Racial borders as the new frontier* (pp. 245–259). Thousand Oaks, CA: Sage.

Stanley, J. (2004). Biracial lesbian and bisexual women: Understanding the unique aspects and interactional processes of multiple minority identities. *Women and Therapy, 27*, 159–171.

Stanton, A. (1996). Reconfiguring teaching and knowing in the college classroom. In N. Goldberger, J. Tarule, B. Clinchy, & M. Belenky (Eds.), *Knowledge, difference, and power* (pp. 25–56). New York: Basic Books.

Staples, B. (2007, February 5). On race and the census: Struggling with categories that no longer apply. *New York Times*. Retrieved February 5, 2007, from http://www.nytimes.com/2007/02/05/opinion/05mon4.html?th=&emc=th&pagewanted=print

Stebleton, M. J. (2011). Understanding immigrant college students: Applying a developmental ecology framework to the practice of academic advising. *NACADA Journal, 31*(1), 42–54.

Steele, C. M., & Aronson J. (1995). Stereotype threat and the intellectual test performance of African Americans. *Journal of Personality and Social Psychology, 69*, 797–811.

Steinfeldt, J. A., Reed, C., & Steinfeldt, M. C. (2010). Racial and athletic identity of African American football players at historically Black colleges and universities and predominantly White institutions. *Journal of Black Psychology, 36*, 3–24.

Steinfeldt, J. A., Steinfeldt, M. C., England, B., & Speight, Q. L. (2009). Gender role conflict and stigma toward help-seeking among college football players. *Psychology of Men & Masculinity, 10*, 261–272.

Steinfeldt, M., & Steinfeldt, J. A. (2012). Athletic identity and conformity to masculine norms among college football players. *Journal of Applied Sport Psychology, 24*, 115–128.

Stephan, C. W. (1992). Mixed-heritage individuals: Ethnic identity and trait characteristics. In M.P.P. Root (Ed.), *Racially mixed people in America* (pp. 50–63). Newbury Park, CA: Sage.

Stephens, N. M., Fryberg, S. A., Markus, H. R., Johnson, C., & Covarrubias, R. (2012). Unseen disadvantage: How American universities' focus on independence undermines the academic performance of first-generation college students. *Journal of Personality and Social Psychology, 102*, 1178–1197.

Stephens, N. M., Townsend, S. S. M., Markus, H. R., & Phillips, T. (2012). A cultural mismatch: Independent cultural norms produce greater increases in cortisol and more negative emotions among first-generation college students. *Journal of Experimental Social Psychology, 48*, 1389–1393.

Stevens, R. A. (2004). Understanding gay identity development within the college environment. *Journal of College Student Development, 45*, 185–206.

Stevenson, J., & Clegg, S. (2012). Who cares? Gender dynamics in the valuing of extra-curricular activities in higher education. *Gender and Education, 24*, 41–55.

Stewart, A. J., & Ostrove, J. M. (1993). Social class, social change, and gender. *Psychology of Women Quarterly, 17*, 475–497.

Stewart, D. L. (2008). Being all of me: Black students negotiating multiple identities. *The Journal of Higher Education, 79*, 183–207.

Stewart, D. L. (2009). Perceptions of multiple identities among Black college students. *Journal of College Student Development, 50*, 253–270.

Stewart, D. L. (Ed.), *Building bridges, re-visioning community: Multicultural student services on campus.* Sterling, VA: Stylus Publishing.

Stewart, D. L. (2012). Promoting moral growth through pluralism and social justice education. In D. L. Liddell & D. L. Cooper (Eds.), *Facilitating the moral growth of college students.* New Directions for Student Services, no. 139, pp. 63–72. San Francisco: Jossey-Bass.

Stewart, D., & Kocet, M. M. (2011). The role of student affairs in promoting religious and secular pluralism and interfaith cooperation. *Journal of College & Character, 12*(1), 1–10.

Stimpson, D., Jensen, L., & Neff, W. (1992). Cross cultural gender differences in preference for a caring morality. *Journal of Social Psychology, 132*, 317–322.

Stiver, I. P. (1991). Beyond the Oedipus complex: mothers and daughters. In J. V. Jordan, A. G. Kaplan, J. B. Miller, I. P. Stiver, & J. L. Surrey (Eds.), *Women's growth in connection: Writings from the Stone Center* (pp. 97–121). New York: The Guilford Press.

St. John, E. P., Paulsen, M. B., & Carter, D. F. (2005). Diversity, college costs, and postsecondary opportunity: An examination of the financial nexus between college choice and persistence for African Americans and Whites. *The Journal of Higher Education, 76*, 545–569.

St. Louis, G. R., & Liem, J. H. (2005). Ego identity ethnic identity, and the social well-being of ethnic minority and majority college students. *Identity: An International Journal of Theory and Research, 5*(3), 227–246.

Stonequist, E. V. (1937). *The marginal man: A study in personality and culture conflict.* New York: Russell & Russell.

St. Pierre, E. A. (2000). Poststructural feminism in education: An overview. *Qualitative Studies in Education, 13*(5), 477–515.

Strange, C. C. (1994). Student development: The evolution and status of an essential idea. *Journal of College Student Development, 35*, 399–412.

Strange, C. C. (2001). Spiritual dimensions of graduate preparation in student affairs. In M. A. Jablonski (Ed.), *The implications of student spirituality for student affairs practice.* New Directions for Student Services, no. 95, pp. 57–67. San Francisco: Jossey-Bass.

Strauss, L. C., & Cross, W. E., Jr. (2005). Transacting black identity: A two-week daily diary study. In G. Downey, J. S. Eccles, & C. M. Chatman (Eds.), *Navigating the future: Social identity, coping, and life tasks* (67–95). New York: Russell Sage Foundation.

Strayhorn, T. L. (2014a). Beyond the model minority myth: Interrogating the lived experiences of Korean American gay men in college. *Journal of College Student Development, 55,* 586–594.

Strayhorn, T. L. (2014b). Making a way to success: Self-authorship and academic achievement of first-year African American students at historically Black colleges. *Journal of College Student Development, 55,* 151–167.

Strayhorn, T. L., & Mullins, T. G. (2012). Investigating Black gay male undergraduates' experiences in campus residence halls. *Journal of College and University Student Housing, 39,* 140–161.

Strayhorn, T. L., & Saddler, T. N. (2009). Gender differences in the influence of faculty-student mentoring relationships on satisfaction with college among African Americans. *Journal of African American Studies, 13,* 476–493.

Stubbs, B. B., & Sallee, M. W. (2013). Muslim, too: Navigating multiple identities at an American university. *Equity & Excellence in Education, 46*(4), 451–467.

Stuber, J. M. (2009). Class, culture, and participation in the collegiate extra-curriculum. *Sociological Forum, 24,* 877–900.

Subbiondo, J. L. (2006). Integrating religion and spirituality in higher education: meeting the global challenges of the 21st century. *Religion and Education, 33*(2), 20–38.

Sue, D. W. (2010). *Microaggressions in everyday life: Race, gender, and sexual orientation.* San Francisco: Jossey-Bass.

Sue, D. W. (2013). Race talk: The psychology of racial dialogues. *American Psychologist, 68,* 663–672.

Sue, D. W., & Sue, D. (1990). *Counseling the culturally different: Theory and practice.* New York: Wiley.

Sue, D. W., & Sue, D. (2003). *Counseling the culturally diverse: Theory and practice* (4th ed.). New York: Wiley.

Sue, D. W., & Sue, D. (2008). *Counseling the culturally diverse: Theory and practice* (5th ed.). New York: Wiley.

Sullivan, L., Meschede, T., Dietrich, L., Shapiro, T., Traub, A., Ruetschlin, C, & Draut, T. (2015). *The racial wealth gap: Why policy matters.* A policy report from the Institute for Assets & Social Policy, Brandeis University and DEMOS. Retrieved from: http://www.demos.org/sites/default/files/publications/RacialWealthGap_1.pdf

Summerlot, J., Green, S. M., & Parker, D. (2009). Student veterans organizations. In R. Ackerman & D. DiRamio (Eds.) *Creating a veteran-friendly campus: Strategies for transition and success. New Directions for Student Services,* no. 126, pp. 71–79. San Francisco: Jossey-Bass.

Swain, J. & French, S. (2000). Towards an affirmative model of disability. *Disability & Society, 15*(4), 569–582.

Swartz, D. (1977). Pierre Bourdieu: The cultural transmission of social inequality. *Harvard Educational Review, 47,* 545–555.

Swick, H. M. (1991, April). Fostering the professional development of medical students. *Paper presented at the annual meeting of the American Educational Research Association,* Chicago. (ERIC Document Reproduction Service No. ED 330 283)

Szymanski, D. M., Kashubeck-West, S., & Meyer, J. (2008). Internalized heterosexism: A historical and theoretical overview. *The Counseling Psychologist, 36,* 525–574.

Tajfel, H. (1981). *Human group and social categories.* Cambridge, UK: Cambridge University Press.

Talbot, D. M. (2008). Exploring the experiences and self-labeling of mixed-race individuals with two minority parents. In K. A. Renn & P. Shang (Eds.), *Biracial and multiracial students. New Directions for Student Services,* no. 123, pp. 23–31. San Francisco: Jossey-Bass.

Talburt, S. (2010). Developing students. In E. J. Allen, S.V.D. Iverson, & R. Ropers-Huilman (Eds.), *Restructuring policy in higher education: Feminist poststructural perspectives* (pp. 111–128). New York: Routledge.

Tang, J., Kim, S., & Haviland, D. (2015). Role of family, culture, and peers in the success of first-generation Cambodian American college students. *Journal of Southeast Asian American Education and Advancement, 8*(1), Article 2. Retrieved from 10.7771/2153-8999.1057

Tarrow, N., & Raby, R. L. (Eds.). (2014). *Dimensions of the community college: International, intercultural, and multicultural perspectives.* New York: Routledge.

Tatum, B. D. (1992). Talking about race, learning about racism: The application of racial identity development theory in the classroom. *Harvard Educational Review, 62*(l), 1–24.

Tatum, B. D. (2000). The complexity of identity: "Who am I?" In M. Adams, W. J. Blumenfeld, R. Castañeda, H. W. Hackman, M. L. Peters, & X. Zuñiga (Eds.), *Readings for diversity and social justice: An anthology on racism, anti-Semitism, sexism, heterosexism, ableism, and classism* (pp. 9–14). New York: Routledge.

Tatum, H. E., Schwartz, B. M., Schimmoeller, P. A., & Perry, N. (2013). Classroom participation and student-faculty interactions: Does gender matter? *The Journal of Higher Education, 84*, 745–768.

Tatum, J. L., Foubert, J. D., Fuqua, D. R., & Ray, C. M. (2013). The relationship between first year college men's religious affiliation and their moral development. *College Student Affairs Journal, 31*(2), 101–110.

Taub, D. J. (1995). Relationship of selected factors to traditional-age undergraduate women's development of autonomy. *Journal of College Student Development, 36*, 141–151.

Taub, D. J. (1997). Autonomy and parental attachment in traditional-age undergraduate women. *Journal of College Student Development, 38*, 645–654.

Taub, D. J., & McEwen, M. K. (1991). Patterns of development of autonomy and mature interpersonal relationships in Black and White undergraduate women. *Journal of College Student Development, 32*, 502–508.

Taub, D. J., & McEwen, M. K. (1992). The relationship of racial identity attitudes to autonomy and mature interpersonal relationships in Black and White undergraduate women. *Journal of College Student Development, 33*, 439–446.

Taylor, C. M., & Howard-Hamilton, M. F. (1995). Student involvement and racial identity attitudes among African American males. *Journal of College Student Development, 36*, 330–336.

Taylor, E. (2010). Cisgender privilege: on the privileges of performing normative gender. In K. Bornstein & S. B. Bergman (Eds.), *Gender outlaws: The next generation* (pp. 268–272). Berkeley, CA: Seal Press.

Taylor, J. M., Gilligan, C., & Sullivan, A. M. (1995). *Between voice and silence: Women and girls, race and relationship.* Cambridge, MA: Harvard University Press.

Taylor, L. (2005). Review of the book Mixed race students in college: The ecology of race, identity and community on campus. *Teachers College Record, 107*(7), 1467–1474.

Taylor, U. (1998). The historical evolution of black feminist theory and praxis. *Journal of Black Studies, 29*, 234–253.

Templeton, J. L., & Eccles, J. S. (2006). The relation between spiritual development and identity processes. In E. C. Roehlkepartain, P. E. King, L. Wagener, & P. L. Benson (Eds.), *The handbook of spiritual development in childhood and adolescence* (pp. 252–265). Thousand Oaks, CA: Sage Publications, Inc.

Tewari, N., Inman, A. G., & Sandhu, D. S. (2003). South Asian Americans: Culture, concerns and therapeutic strategies. In J. Mio & G. Iwamasa (Eds.), *Culturally diverse mental health: The challenges of research and resistance* (pp. 191–209). New York: Brunner Routledge.

Thelin, J. R. (2011). *A history of American higher education.* Baltimore, MD: Johns Hopkins University Press.

Thoma, S. J., & Rest, J. R. (1999). The relationship between moral decision making patterns of consolidation and transition in moral judgment development. *Developmental Psychology, 35,* 323–334.

Thomas, R., & Chickering, A. W. (1984). *Education and identity revisited. Journal of College Student Personnel, 25,* 392–399.

Thompson, C. P., Anderson, L. P., & Bakeman, R. A. (2000). Effects of racial socialization and racial identity on acculturative stress in African American college students. *Cultural Diversity and Ethnic Minority Psychology, 6,* 196–210.

Thompson, E. M., & Morgan, E. M. (2008). "Mostly straight" young women: Variations in sexual behavior and identity development. *Developmental Psychology, 44,* 15–21.

Tierney, W. G. (1992). An anthropological analysis of student participation in college. *Journal of Higher Education, 63,* 603–618.

Tillapaugh, D. (2013). Breaking down the "walls of a façade": The influence of compartmentalization on gay college males' meaning-making. *Culture, Society and Masculinities, 5*(2), 127–146.

Tillapaugh, D. (2015). Critical influences on sexual minority college males' meaning-making of their multiple identities. *Journal of Student Affairs Research & Practice, 52,* 64–75.

Tillapaugh, D. W. (2012). *Toward an integrated self: Making meaning of the multiple identities of gay men in college.* Unpublished doctoral dissertation, University of San Diego.

Tinto, V. (1993). *Leaving college: Rethinking the causes and cures of student attrition.* Chicago: University of Chicago Press. (Original work published 1987).

Tisdell, E. J. (2003). *Exploring spirituality and culture in adult and higher education.* San Francisco: Jossey-Bass.

Tomlinson, M. J., & Fassinger, R. E. (2003). Career development, lesbian identity development, and campus climate among lesbian college students. *Journal of College Student Development, 44,* 845–860.

Tompkins, A. (2014). Asterisk. *TSQ: Transgender Studies Quarterly, 1*(1-2), 26–27.

Torres, R. M., & Wicks-Asbun, M. (2014). Undocumented students' narratives of liminal citizenship: High aspirations, exclusion, and "in-between" identities. *The Professional Geographer, 66,* 195–204.

Torres, V. (1999). Validation of a bicultural orientation model for Hispanic college students. *Journal of College Student Development, 40,* 285–298.

Torres, V. (2003). Influences on ethnic identity development of Latino college students in the first two years of college. *Journal of College Student Development, 44,* 532–547.

Torres, V. (2004). The diversity among us: Puerto Ricans, Cuban Americans, Caribbean Americans, and Central and South Americans. In A. Ortiz (Ed.), *Addressing the unique needs of Latino American students.* New Directions for Student Services, no. 105, pp. 5–16. San Francisco: Jossey-Bass.

Torres, V., & Baxter Magolda, M. B. (2004). Reconstructing Latino identity: The influence of cognitive development on the ethnic identity process of Latino students. *Journal of College Student Development, 45,* 333–347.

Torres, V., & Hernandez, E. (2007). The influence of ethnic identity on self-authorship: A longitudinal study of Latino/a college students. *Journal of College Student Development, 48,* 558–573.

Torres, V., Howard-Hamilton, M. F., & Cooper, D. L. (2003). Identity development of diverse populations: Implications for teaching and administration in higher education. *ASHE-ERIC Higher Education Report, 29*(6). San Francisco: Jossey-Bass.

Torres, V., Jones, S. R., & Renn, K. A. (2009). Identity development theories in student affairs: Origins, current status, and new approaches. *Journal of College Student Development, 50,* 577–596.

Torres, V., Martinez, S., Wallace, L. D., Medrano, C. I., Robledo, A. L., & Hernandez, E. (2012). The connections between Latino ethnic identity and adult experiences. *Adult Education Quarterly, 62*(1), 3–18.

Tracey, T. J., Wille, B., Durr, M. R., & De Fruyt, F. (2014). An enhanced examination of Holland's consistency and differentiation hypotheses. *Journal of Vocational Behavior, 84,* 237–247.

Troiden, R. R. (1989). The formation of homosexual identities. *Journal of Homosexuality, 17,* 43–74.

Twine, F. W. (1996). Brown skinned white girls: Class, culture and the construction of white identity in suburban communities. *Gender, Place and Culture, 3,* 205–224.

Umaña-Taylor, A. J. (2001). *Ethnic identity development among Mexican-origin Latino adolescents living in the US.* Unpublished doctoral dissertation, University of Missouri-Columbia.

Umaña-Taylor, A. J. (2004). Ethnic identity and self-esteem: Examining the role of social context. *Journal of Adolescence, 27,* 139–146.

Umaña-Taylor, A. J. (2011). Ethnic identity. In S. J. Schwartz, K. Luyckx, & V. L. Vignoles (Eds.), *Handbook of identity theory and research* (pp. 791–810). New York: Springer.

Umaña-Taylor, A. J., Bhanot, R., & Shin, N. (2006). Ethnic identity formation during adolescence: The critical role of families. *Journal of Family Issues, 27,* 390–414.

Umaña-Taylor, A. J., & Fine, M. A. (2004). Examining ethnic identity among Mexican-origin adolescents living in the U.S. *Hispanic Journal of Behavioral Sciences, 23,* 347–362.

Umaña-Taylor, A. J., & Shin, N. (2007). An examination of ethnic identity and self-esteem with diverse populations. *Cultural Diversity and Ethnic Minority Psychology, 13,* 178–186.

Umaña-Taylor, A. J., Vargas-Chanes, D., Garcia, C. D., & Gonzales-Backen, M. (2008). A longitudinal examination of Latino adolescents' ethnic identity, coping with discrimination, and self-esteem. *Journal of Early Adolescence, 28,* 16–50.

Upcraft, M. L., & Moore, L. V. (1990).Evolving theoretical perspectives of student development. In M. J. Barr & M. L. Upcraft & *Associates, New Futures fro student affairs: Building a vision for professional leadership and practice* (pp. 41-68). SanFrancisco: Jossey-Bass.

Upcraft, M. L., & Schuh, J. H. (1996). *Assessment in student affairs: A guide for practitioners.* San Francisco: Jossey-Bass.

Utterback, J. W., Spooner, S. E., Barbieri, J. A., & Fox, S. N. (1995). Gender and ethnic issues in the development of intimacy among college students. *NASPA Journal, 32,* 82–89.

Vaccaro, A., & Mena, J. A. (2011). It's not burnout, it's more: Queer college activists of color and mental health. *Journal of Gay & Lesbian Mental Health, 15,* 339–367.

Vacchi, D. T. (2012). Considering student veterans on the twenty-first-century college campus. *About Campus, 15–21.*

Valentine, J. J., & Taub, D. J. (1999). Responding to the developmental needs of student athletes. *Journal of College Counseling, 2,* 164–179.

Valeras, A. (2010). "We don't have a box": Understanding hidden disability identity utilizing narrative research methodology. *Disability Studies Quarterly, 30*(3/4). Retrieved from http://dsq-sds.org/article/view/1267/1297

Vance, M. L., & Miller, W, K. II. (2009). Serving wounded warriors: Current practices in postsecondary education. *Journal of Postsecondary Education and Disability, 22*(1), 18–35.

Vandiver, B. J. (2001). Psychological nigrescence revisited: Introduction and overview. *Journal of Multicultural Counseling and Development, 29*(3), 165–173.

Veblen, T. B. (1946). *The higher learning in America: A memorandum on the conduct of universities by business men.* New York: Hill & Wang. (Original work published 1918)

Vignoles, V. L., Schwartz, S. J., & Luyckx, K. (2011). Introduction: Toward an integrative view of identity. In S. J. Schwartz, K. Luyckx, & V. L. Vignoles (Eds.), *Handbook of identity theory and research* (pp. 1–30). New York: Springer.

Vikan, A., Camino, C., & Biaggio, A. (2005). Note on a cross-cultural test of Gilligan's ethic of care 1. *Journal of Moral Education, 34,* 107–111.

Villalpando, O. (2003). Self-segregation or self-preservation? A critical race theory and Latina/o critical theory analysis of a study of Chicana/o college students. *Qualitative Studies in Education, 16,* 619–646.

Visek, A. J., Hurst, J. R., Maxwell, J. P., & Watson, J. C., II. (2008). A cross-cultural psychometric evaluation of the athletic identity measurement scale. *Journal of Applied Sport Psychology, 20,* 473–480.

Vrangalova, Z., & Savin-Williams, R. C. (2010). Correlates of same-sex sexuality in heterosexually identified young adults. *Journal of Sex Research, 47,* 92–102.

Vrangalova, Z., & Savin-Williams, R. C. (2012). Mostly heterosexual and mostly gay/lesbian: Evidence for new sexual orientation identities. *Archives of Sexual Behavior, 41,* 85–101.

Wadsworth, B. J. (1979). *Piaget's theory of cognitive development* (2nd ed.). New York: Longman.

Wagoner, K. G., Blocker, J., McCoy, T. P., Sutfin, E. L., Champion, H., & Wolfson, M. (2012). Free alcohol use and consequences: Gender differences among undergraduates. *American Journal of Health Behavior, 36,* 446–458.

Walker, A. (1983). *In search of our mothers' gardens: Womanist prose.* New York: Harcourt.

Walker, J.N.J., & Longmire-Avital, B. (2013). The impact of religious faith and internalized homonegativity on resiliency for black lesbian, gay, and bisexual emerging adults. *Developmental Psychology, 49,* 1723.

Walker, L. J. (1983). Sources of cognitive conflict for stage transition in moral development. *Developmental Psychology, 19,* 103–110.

Walker, L. J. (1988). The development of moral reasoning. *Annals of Child Development, 5,* 33–78.

Walker, L. J. (2006). Gender and morality. In M. Killen & J. Smetana (Eds.), *Handbook of moral development* (pp. 93–115). Mahwah, NJ: Erlbaum.

Walker, L. J., & Taylor, J. H. (1991). Stage transitions in moral reasoning: A longitudinal study of developmental processes. *Developmental Psychology, 27,* 330–337.

Wallace, K. R. (2001). *Relative/outsider: The art and politics of identity among mixed heritage students.* Westport, CT: Ablex.

Wallace, K. R. (2003). Contextual factors affecting identity among mixed heritage college students. In M.P.P. Root & M. Kelley (Eds.), *Multiracial child resource book: Living complex identities* (pp. 87–93). Seattle: MAVIN Foundation.

Walls, N. E., Griffin, R., Arnold-Renicker, H., Burson, M., Johnston, C., Moorman, N., Nelson, J., & Schutte, E. C. (2009). Mapping graduate social work student learning journeys about heterosexual privilege. *Journal of Social Work Education, 45*(2), 289–307.

Walpole, M. (2003). Socioeconomic status and college: How SES affects college experiences and outcomes. *The Review of Higher Education, 27*(1), 45–73.

Walpole, M. (2008). Emerging from the pipeline: African American students, socioeconomic status, and college experiences and outcomes. *Research in Higher Education, 49,* 237–255.

Walsh, W. B. (1973). *Theories of person-environment interaction: Implications for the college student.* Iowa City, IA: American College Testing Program.

Walters, L. M., Garii, B., & Walters, T. (2009). Learning globally, teaching locally: Incorporating international exchange and intercultural learning into pre-service teacher training. *Intercultural Education, 20*(sup1), S151–S158.

Wane, N. N. (2009). Black Canadian feminist thought: Perspectives on equity and diversity in the academy. *Race Ethnicity and Education, 12,* 65–77.

Wang, Y., & Rodgers, R. (2006). Impact of service-learning and social justice education on college students' cognitive development. *NASPA Journal, 43,* 316–337.

Warr, D. J. (2006). Gender, class, and the art and craft of social capital. *The Sociological Quarterly, 47,* 497–520.

Waterman, A. S. (1982). Identity development from adolescence to adulthood: An extension of theory and a review of research. *Developmental Psychology, 18,* 341–358.

Waterman, A. S., & Archer, S. L. (1990). A life-span perspective on identity formation: Developments in form, function, and process. In P. B. Baltes, D. L. Featherman, & R. M. Lerner (Eds.), *Life-span development and behavior* (pp. 29–57). Hillsdale, NJ: Erlbaum.

Waterman, S. J. (2012). Home-going as a strategy for success among Haudenosaunee college and university students. *Journal of Student Affairs Research and Practice, 49,* 193–209.

Waterman, S. J., & Lindley, L. S. (2013). Cultural strengths to persevere: Native American women in higher education. *NASPA Journal About Women in Higher Education, 6,* 139–165.

Waters, M. C. (2000). Multiple ethnicities and identity in the United States. In P. Spickard & W. J. Burroughs (Eds.), *We are a people: Narrative and multiplicity in constructing ethnic identity* (pp. 23–40). Philadelphia: Temple University.

Watt, S. K. (2003). Come to the river: Using spirituality to cope, resist, and develop identity. In M. F. Howard-Hamilton (Ed.), *Meeting the needs of African American women.* New Directions for Student Services, no. 104, pp. 29–40. San Francisco: Jossey-Bass.

Wawrzynski, K. S., & Jessup-Anger, J. E. (2014). Building bridges: Using the office consultation project to connect students to theory and practice. *Journal of Student Affairs Research and Practice, 51,* 85–97.

Wawrzynski, M., & Pizzolato, J. E. (2006). Predicting needs: A longitudinal investigation of the relation between student characteristics, academic paths, and self-authorship. *Journal of College Student Development, 47,* 677–691.

Waziyatawin, A. W., & Yellow Bird, M. (2005). *For indigenous eyes only: A decolonization handbook.* Santa Fe, NM: School of American Research Press.

Weber, L. (1998). A conceptual framework for understanding race, class, gender and sexuality. *Psychology of Women Quarterly, 22,* 13–32.

Weight, E., Navarro, K., Huffman, L., & Smith-Ryan, A. (2014). Quantifying the psychological benefits of intercollegiate athletics participation. *Journal of Issues in Intercollegiate Athletics, 7,* 390–409.

Weinstock, J. S., & Bond, L. A. (2000). Conceptions of conflict in close friendships and ways of knowing among young college women: A developmental framework. *Journal of Social and Personal Relationships, 17,* 687–696.

Weisskirch, R. S. (2005). Ethnicity and perceptions of being a "typical American" in relationship to ethnic identity development. *International Journal of Intercultural Relations, 29,* 355–366.

Welch, M., & Koth, K. (2013). A metatheory of spiritual formation through service-learning in higher education. *Journal of College Student Development, 54*(6), 612–627.

Welkener, M. M., & Baxter Magolda, M. B. (2014). Better understanding students' self-authorship via self-portraits. *Journal of College Student Development, 55,* 580–585.

Wells, R. S., & Lynch, C. M. (2012). Delayed college entry and the socioeconomic gap: Examining the roles of student plans, family income, parental education, and parental occupation. *The Journal of Higher Education, 83,* 671–697.

Wheeler, E. (2002). Black feminism and womanism. In A. M. Martinez Aleman, & K. A. Renn (Eds.) *Women in higher education: An encyclopedia* (p. 118–120). Santa Barbara, CA: ABC Clio.

Whiteman, S. D., Barry, A. E., Mroczek, D. K., & Wadsworth, S. M. (2013). The development and implications of peer emotional support for student service members/veterans and civilian college students. *Journal of Counseling Psychology, 60,* 265–278.

Whittaker, V. A., & Neville, H. A. (2010). Examining the relation between racial identity attitude clusters and psychological health outcomes in African American college students. *Journal of Black Psychology, 36,* 383–409.

Widick, C. (1975). *An evaluation of developmental instruction in a university setting.* Unpublished doctoral dissertation, University of Minnesota, Minneapolis.

Widick, C., Parker, C. A., & Knefelkamp, L. (1978). Erik Erikson and psychosocial development. In L. Knefelkamp, C. Widick, & C. A. Parker (Eds.), *Applying new developmental findings. New Directions for Student Services,* no. 4, pp. 1–17. San Francisco: Jossey-Bass.

Wijeyesinghe, C. L. (1995). Multiracial identity in a monoracial world. *Hispanic Outlook in Higher Education, 6*(8), 16.

Wijeyesinghe, C. L. (2001). Racial identity in multiracial people: An alternative paradigm. In C. L. Wijeyesinghe & B. W. Jackson III (Eds.), *New perspectives on racial identity development* (pp. 129–152). New York: New York University Press.

Wijeyesinghe, C. L. (2012). The intersectional model of multiracial identity. In C. L. Wijeyesinghe & B. W. Jackson, III (Eds.), *New perspectives on racial identity development: Integrating emerging frameworks* (pp. 81–107). New York: New York University Press.

Wilchins, R. A. (2002). Queerer bodies. In J. Nestle, C. Howell, & R. A. Wilchins (Eds.), *Genderqueer: Voices from beyond the sexual binary* (pp. 33–46). Los Angeles: Alyson.

Wildman, T. M. (2004). Framing faculty and institutional development. In M. Baxter Magolda & P. M. King (Eds.), *Learning partnerships: Theory and modes of practice to educate for self-authorship* (pp. 245–268). Sterling, VA: Stylus.

Wildman, T. M. (2007). Taking seriously the intellectual growth of students: Accommodations for self-authorship. In P. S. Meszaros (Ed.), *Self-authorship: Advancing students' intellectual growth.* New Directions for Teaching and Learning, no. 109, pp. 15–30. San Francisco: Jossey-Bass.

Williams, C. B. (2005). Counseling African American women: Multiple identities—multiple constraints. *Journal of Counseling and Development, 83,* 278–283.

Williams, L. B. (1997). Behind every face is a story. *About Campus, 3*(1), 16–21.

Williams, T. K. (1996). Race as process: Reassessing the "What are you?" encounters of biracial individuals. In M.P.P. Root (Ed.), *The multiracial experience: Racial borders as the new frontier* (pp. 191–210). Thousand Oaks, CA: Sage.

Williams, T. K., Nakashima, C. L., Kich, G. K., & Daniel, G. R. (1996). Being different together in the university classroom: Multiracial identity as transgressive education. In M.P.P. Root (Ed.), *The multiracial experience: Racial borders as the new frontier* (pp. 359–379). Thousand Oaks, CA: Sage.

Wilson, F. L. (2000). Measuring morality of justice and care among associate, baccalaureate and second career female nursing students. *Journal of Social Behavior and Personality, 14,* 597–606.

Windley, P. J. (2005). *Digital identity.* Sebastopol, CA: O'Reilly.

Winnicott, D. W. (1965). *The maturational processes and the facilitating environment.* New York: International Universities Press.

Winston, R. B., Jr., Miller, T. K., & Prince, J. S. (1979). *Student developmental task inventory* (Rev. 2nd ed.). Athens, GA: Student Development Associates.

Wise, T. (2011). *White like me: Reflections on race from a privileged son.* Berkeley, CA: Soft Skull Press.

Wise, T. (2014). F.A.Q.s: Frequently asked questions and their answers (Updated December 2014). Retrieved from http://www.timwise.org/f-a-q-s/

Wolbring, G. (2014). Ability privilege: A needed addition to privilege studies. *Journal for Critical Animal Studies, 12*(2), 118–141.

Wolfe, B. L., & Dilworth, P. P. (2015). Transitioning normalcy: Organizational culture, African American administrators, and diversity leadership in higher education. *Review of Educational Research.* Published online before print January 22, 2015, doi: 10.3102/0034654314565667.

Wong, M. P. A., & Buckner, J. (2008). Multiracial student services come of age: The state of multiracial student services in higher education in the United States. In K. A. Renn & P. Shang (Eds.), *Biracial and multiracial college students.* New Directions for Student Services, no. 123, pp. 43–51. San Francisco: Jossey-Bass.

Wood, J. L. (2014). Apprehension to engagement in the classroom: perceptions of Black males in the community college. *International Journal of Qualitative Studies in Education, 27*(6), 785–800.

Woodford, M. R., Chonody, J., Kulick, A., Brennan, D. J., & Renn, K. A. (in press). Assessing sexual orientation microaggressions on college campuses: An instrument development and validation study. *Accepted for publication in Journal of Homosexuality.*

Woodford, M. R., Kolb, C. L., Durocher-Radeka, G., & Javier, G. (2014). Lesbian, gay, bisexual, and transgender ally training programs on campus: Current variations and future directions. *Journal of College Student Development, 55,* 317–322.

World Health Organization. (2014). *What do we mean by "sex" and "gender"?* Retrieved from http://www.who.int/gender/whatisgender/en/

Worthington, R. L., Dillon, F. R., & Becker-Schutte, A. M. (2005). Development, reliability, and validity of the Lesbian, Gay, and Bisexual Knowledge and Attitudes Scale for Heterosexuals (LGB-KASH). *Journal of Counseling Psychology, 52*(1), 104–118.

Worthington, R. L., Navarro, R. L., Savoy, H. B., & Hampton, D. (2008). Development, reliability, and validity of the Measure of Sexual Identity Exploration and Commitment (MoSIEC). *Developmental Psychology, 44*(1), 22–33.

Worthington, R. L., & Reynolds, A. L. (2009). Within-group differences in sexual orientation and identity. *Journal of Counseling Psychology, 56,* 44–55.

Worthington, R. L., Savoy, H. B., Dillon, F. R., & Vernaglia, E. R. (2002). Heterosexual identity development: A multidimensional model of individuals and social identity. *Counseling Psychologist, 30,* 496–531.

Wright, B. (1988). "For the children of the Infidels"?: American Indian education in the colonial colleges. *American Indian Culture and Research Journal 12*(3), 1–14.

Wu, F. H. (2006). The multiracial classification can be detrimental. In E. Stanford (Ed.), *Interracial America: Opposing viewpoints* (pp. 37–43). Farmington Hills, MI: Greenhaven.

Xie, Y., Ke, F., & Sharma, P. (2008). The effect of peer feedback for blogging on college students' reflective learning processes. *The Internet and Higher Education, 11,* 18–25.

Yeager, D. S., & Walton, G. M. (2011). Social-psychological interventions in education: They're not magic. *Review of Educational Research, 81,* 267–301.

Yee, J. A. (2009). Ways of knowing, feeling, being, and doing: Toward an Asian American and Pacific Islander feminist epistemology. *Amerasia Journal, 35*(2), 49–64.

Yeh, C. J., & Huang, K. (1996). The collectivist nature of ethnic identity development among Asian American college students. *Adolescence, 31,* 645–661.

Yeskel, F. (2008). Coming to class: Looking at education through the lens of class; Introduction to the Class and Education special issue. *Equity & Excellence in Education, 41*(1), 1–11.

Yin, R. K., Hackett, E. J., & Chubin, D. E. (2008). Discovering "What's innovative": The challenge of evaluating education research and development efforts. *Peabody Journal of Education, 83,* 674–690.

Yip, T., Seaton, E. K., & Sellers, R. M. (2006). African American racial identity across the lifespan: Identity status, identity content, and depressive symptoms. *Child Development, 77,* 1504–1517.

Yoder, A. E. (2000). Barriers to ego identity status formation: A contextual qualification of Marcia's identity status paradigm. *Journal of Adolescence, 23,* 95–106.

Yoder, J. D., Fischer, A. R., Kahn, A. S., & Groden, J. (2007). Changes in students' explanations for gender differences after taking a psychology of women class: More constructionist and less essentialist. *Psychology of Women Quarterly, 31,* 415–425.

Yonkers-Talz, K. (2004). A learning partnership: U.S. college students and the poor in El Salvador. In M. Baxter Magolda & P. M. King (Eds.), *Learning partnerships: Theory and modes of practice to educate for self-authorship* (pp. 151–184). Sterling, VA: Stylus.

Yoon, E. (2011). Measuring ethnic identity in the ethnic identity scale and the multigroup ethnic identity measure-revised. *Cultural Diversity and Ethnic Minority Psychology, 17*(2), 144–155.

Yosso, T. J. (2005). Whose culture has capital? A critical race theory discussion of community cultural wealth. *Race, Ethnicity and Education, 8*(1), 69–91.

Young, I. M. (2000). Five faces of oppression. In M. Adams, W. J. Blumenfeld, R. Castañeda, H. W. Hackman, M. L. Peters, & X. Zuñiga (Eds.), *Readings for diversity and social justice: An anthology on racism, anti-Semitism, sexism, heterosexism, ableism, and classism* (pp. 35–49). New York: Routledge.

Zack, N. (1995). Life after race. In N. Zack (Ed.), *American mixed race: The culture of microdiversity* (pp. 297–307). Lanham, MD: Rowman & Littlefield.

Zajonc, A. (2003). Spirituality in higher education: Overcoming the divide. *Liberal Education, 89*(1), 50–58.

Zandy, J. (1996). Decloaking class: Why class identity and consciousness count. *Race, Gender, Class, 4*(1), 7–23.

Zaytoun, K. (2006). Theorizing at the borders: Considering social location in rethinking self and psychological development. *NWSA Journal, 18*(2), 52–72.

Zinger, L., & Cohen, A. (2010). Veterans returning from war into the classroom: How can colleges be better prepared to meet their needs. *Contemporary Issues in Education Research, 3*(1), 39–52.

Zosuls, K. M., Miller, C. F., Ruble, D. N., Martin, C. L., & Fabes, R. A. (2011). Gender development research in *Sex Roles*: Historical trends and future directions. *Sex Roles, 64,* 826–842.

Zúñiga, X. (2003). Bridging differences through dialogue. *About Campus, 7*(6), 8–16.

Zúñiga, X., Nagda, B.R.A., Chesler, M., & Cytron-Walker, A. (2011). *Intergroup dialogue in higher education: Meaningful learning about social justice.* ASHE Higher Education Report, Volume *32,* Number 4 (Vol. 115). San Francisco: Jossey-Bass.

INDEX

Page followed by *fig* indicate an illustrated figure.